The Bloomsbury Handbook of Global Education and Learning

ALSO AVAILABLE FROM BLOOMSBURY

The Bloomsbury Handbook of Religious Education in the Global South,
Edited by Yonah H. Matemba and Bruce Collet
The Bloomsbury Handbook of Theory in Comparative and International Education,
Edited by Tavis D. Jules, Robin Shields and Matthew A. M. Thomas

The Bloomsbury Handbook of Global Education and Learning

EDITED BY
Douglas Bourn

BLOOMSBURY ACADEMIC
LONDON • NEW YORK • OXFORD • NEW DELHI • SYDNEY

Bloomsbury Academic
An imprint of Bloomsbury Publishing Plc
50 Bedford Square, London, WC1B 3DP, UK
1385 Broadway, New York, NY 10018, USA

www.bloomsbury.com
BLOOMSBURY and the Diana logo are trademarks of Bloomsbury Publishing Plc

First published 2020

Cover Design: Tjaša Krivec
Cover image © designtools/Shutterstock

British Library Cataloguing-in-Publication Data

A catalogue record for this book is available from the British Library.

ISBN: HB: 978-1-3501-0873-8
ePDF: 978-1-3501-0874-5
ePub: 978-1-3501-0875-2

Library of Congress Cataloging-in-Publication Data

A catalog record for this book is available from the Library of Congress.

Typeset by Deanta Global Publishing Services, Chennai, India
Printed and bound in India

Contents

Illustrations

Figures

Tables

Acknowledgements

The idea for this handbook came from discussions with colleagues within the Academic Network of Global Education Learners (ANGEL) and with Global Education Network Europe (GENE), the network of European policy-makers on global education.

Within these networks, I would like to particularly thank my colleagues at the Development Education Research Centre who have not only contributed to this volume but helped me identify and comment on the drafts of chapters. I would also like to thank the Director of GENE, Liam Wegimont, for his support and comments on the development of this handbook.

I would also like to thank Eleni Belogianni for her support as editorial assistant for this volume and Elspeth Cardy for her help with copy editing.

I would also like to thank Bloomsbury Publishing for their support in bringing this volume to publication and seeing this as the prequel to a major new series on global education and learning.

Finally I would like to thank all of the contributors from all over the world for not only their chapters but their commitment and support to this volume, which I hope will make an important contribution to raising the profile of global education and learning and demonstrate its value to work towards a more just and sustainable world.

Douglas Bourn
(Editor)

Acronyms

ANGEL	Academic Network on Global Education & Learning
CARICOM	Caribbean Community
CCGL	Connecting Classrooms through Global Learning
CoE	Council of Europe
CPD	Continuing Professional Development
CSO	Civil Society Organizations
DE	Development Education
DEEEP	Development Education Exchange in Europe Programme
DERC	Development Education Research Centre
DESD	Decade of Education for Sustainable Development
DFID	Department for International Development
ESD	Education for Sustainable Development
GAP	Global Action Program
GCE	Global Citizenship Education
GE	Global Education
GENE	Global Education Network Europe
GLP	Global Learning Programme
HE	Higher Education
HEI	Higher Education Institute
MDGs	Millennium Development Goals
NGO	Non-Governmental Organization
OECD	Organisation for Economic Cooperation and Development
P4C	Philosophy for Children
PISA	Programme of International Student Assessment
SDGs	Sustainable Development Goals
SIDS	Small Island Developing States
UCL	University College of London
UNESCO	United Nations Educational, Scientific and Cultural Organization
UNESCO-IBE	United Nations Educational, Scientific and Cultural Organization–International Bureau of Education

Contributors

Yvette Allen has been an educator for almost thirty years, working across secondary, further and higher education. Her career has primarily focused on raising achievement and inclusivity, particularly for Black and minority ethnic pupils and those with Special Educational Needs (SEMH). Currently, Yvette spends her time between the UK and Tobago. She has recently secured a part-time position with the Tobago Institute of Literacy, where she is keen to support the development of adult literacy in Tobago.

Vanessa Andreotti is a full professor at the Educational Studies Department at the University of British Columbia. She is also a Canada Research Chair in Race, Inequality and Global Change. Her research explores questions of global justice that address our complicities and systemic violence.

Simon Eten Angyagre is a doctoral candidate at UCL Institute of Education and is undertaking research on global citizenship, global skills and internationalization of the curriculum in higher education in Ghana. He has experience teaching in secondary education level in Ghana and has worked in the civil society sector on education project implementation and management. His research interest spans global citizenship education, internationalization in higher education and the development of students' global skills in the context of African higher education.

Olutosin Awolalu is Lead Director of The Publishing Open Institute and has forty years of professional experience in book publishing, training, university teaching and administration, including nine years as Director of Instructional Resources at the National Open University of Nigeria. He holds a PhD in communication arts and a PGD in theology. As a first-generation Nigerian indigenous book editor, he has blended a successful publishing career with university-level teaching, training and research as well as local and international consultancy experience in African education textbooks provision.

Philip Bamber is Associate Professor and Head of the School of Education at Liverpool Hope University. His research is concerned with transformative education, service-learning, education for citizenship and values in education. It has been published in the *British Journal of Educational Studies*, *Journal of Beliefs and Values*, *Journal of Transformative Education* and *International Journal of Development Education and Global Learning*. Philip is Associate Director of TEESNet, the UK Teacher Education for Equity and Sustainability Network and was awarded the International Association of University Presidents International Education Faculty Achievement Award in 2013 for leadership in research and teaching in global citizenship.

Clare Bentall is a lecturer in education at UCL IOE. Her professional and research interests include the professional development of educators in formal education, generally and for development education. She is editor of the *International Journal of Development Education and Global Learning*.

Nicole Blum is a senior lecturer in the Development Education Research Centre at UCL Institute of Education. Her research interests include pedagogy and global learning, internationalization, study abroad, global perspectives in higher education and education for sustainable development. She has worked and conducted research in Costa Rica, Guatemala, India, the United States and the United Kingdom.

Emiliano Bosio is a PhD candidate at University College London, Institute of Education, UK. His work is centred on developing and integrating innovative, ethical and critical approaches to global learning and global citizenship education into university curriculum across East Asia, Europe and North America. He currently lectures at Yokohama City University, Japan, and is contributor to the Academic Network on Global Education and Learning (ANGEL), UK. He serves as a research committee member at the Center for Global Nonkilling (CGNK) in the United States.

Douglas Bourn is Professor of Development Education at University College London – Institute of Education and the author of *Theory and Practice of Development Education* (2015) and *Understanding Global Skills for 21st Century Professions* (2018**).**

Adelina Calvo has a PhD in pedagogy. She works as a senior lecturer at the University of Cantabria (Spain). Among her research interests are social inclusion and exclusion, student voice and school improvement in a qualitative paradigm. Her most recent research interests and publications are related to development education for global citizenship.

Pei-I Chou is a professor at National Sun Yat-Sen University, Taiwan. She was the former associate dean of the College of Social Sciences and the head of the Institute of Education. Her research interests include the areas of sociology of education and curriculum development, particularly global education and textbook analysis.

Ludmila de Almeida Freire is Professor at the University the State of Minas Gerais, Brazil. Her research interests are in the areas of Curriculum, Teaching and Policy Training Educational, and she is a member of the Nucleus of Studies, Researches and Policies Public Education (NEPPPE)/FAE/UEMG/Belo Horizonte.

Helmuth Hartmeyer worked for many years as a teacher – in schools and also in adult education – before he moved into development education, running two NGOs in this field, and into international work – he's worked for the Council of Europe and more recently GENE (Global Education Network Europe). During the last eleven years of his professional life, he worked for the Austrian Development Agency, being responsible for cooperation with civil society organizations and for funding development education. He wrote his PhD on the history of global learning in Austria and has been teaching global education at the Institute for International Development at Vienna University since 2008.

Nicholas Hoad is Sazani Associates Education Officer, a qualified teacher and community educator with a masters in environmental dynamics and climate change. He supports education and training projects, together with their monitoring evaluation and learning in Zanzibar, Tanzania, and Wales, UK. In this role he works with trainers, teachers, youth workers and young people to develop climate change awareness and broader learning for sustainable living.

Frances Hunt is Senior Research Officer in the Development Education Research Centre, UCL Institute of Education. Fran lead the research and evaluation for the 'Global Learning Programme' in England. She is currently involved in a range of research, evaluation and teaching activities related to development education and global learning.

Magdalena Kuleta-Hulboj holds a PhD and is assistant professor in the Faculty of Education, University of Warsaw, Poland. Her research interests focus on global and intercultural education. She teaches courses on social pedagogy, global education and Janusz Korczak's pedagogy. She has co-edited and contributed to *Edukacja globalna. Polskie konteksty i inspiracje* ('Global Education: Polish Contexts and Inspirations', 2015) and *Teoretyczne i praktyczne konteksty edukacji globalnej* ('Theoretical and Practical Context of Global Education', 2016). She is a member of the Polish Educational Research Association.

Madeleine Le Bourdon is a lecturer at Queen Mary's University in London and has been a researcher at Northumbria University, specializing in international education. Her research focuses on global civil society organization delivering global citizenship education and the micro-level practices of global citizenship. She has also worked with several INGOs, where she has trained educators and designed content for global learning.

Elina Lehtomäki has a PhD in education sciences and is Professor of Global Education at the University of Oulu, Finland; she leads the research team 'Education, Diversity, Globalization and Ethics'. Her research interests include global education and learning, social meaning of education, equity and inclusion in and through education, cross-cultural collaboration, and internationalization in higher education.

Mags Liddy is Senior Tutor for the MA in international development at Maynooth University. She was recently awarded the Nano Nagle Newman Fellowship in University College Dublin to work with female teachers working in educational leadership roles in India and Pakistan.

Cathryn MacCallum has been involved in development education and global learning since 1997, as a founding member of a development education centre in West Wales and then as co-founder and director of Sazani Associates, an NGO that focuses on sustainable livelihoods through education and training. With a PhD in sustainable livelihoods and global learning, from the UCL Institute of Education, she also lectured on DERC's MA in development education before joining an international consultancy. A specialist in participatory pedagogies, she has been active in enabling and supporting school links as a global learning process, and her chapter in this volume is an extension of this work.

Nicolle Chido Manjeya is a postdoctoral research fellow in the Faculty of Management Sciences at the Durban University of Technology in South Africa. She holds a PhD in management sciences, and her research interests are in academic literacy and development in higher education (operational and administrative frameworks of academic literacy in higher education). Nicolle Manjeya is an active researcher on the nature of the South African higher educational landscape. Her PhD focused on pedagogical growth and development of curriculum through writing centres.

Josephine Moate is a British educational researcher and teacher educator based at the University of Jyväskylä, Finland. Her research interests include teacher and student development, the role of language and culture in education and the contribution of dialogic theory to the development of pedagogical action and understanding across educational contexts.

Silvia Elisabeth Moraes is Teacher and Supervisor at the education postgraduate programme, Federal University of Ceará. Her postdoctorate research was on Habermas's theory of communicative action at the University of São Paulo. She held a Senior Internship at DERC, University of London. Silvia's main interests are curriculum theory, citizenship, theory of communicative action and post-colonialism.

Alison Morrison (Leonard) lectures at Canterbury Christ Church University; she has tutored teacher trainees in schools. She also taught geography in several government and independent secondary schools. Her particular interests are development education and global learning, geography education, school linking, special educational needs and disabilities (SEND), particularly visual impairment, and academic writing.

Eloísa Nos Aldás is Professor in the Department of Communication Sciences at UJI (Castellón, Spain), Researcher at the Interuniversity Institute for Social Development and Peace (IUDESP), Coordinator of the interdisciplinary 'Permanent Seminar of Educative Innovation' on *Media Literacy and Critical and Participatory Learning for Social Justice*. She has numerous international teaching and research stays on communication, civil society, peace cultures and social change.

Roy Tokunbo Olowu is the principal consultant for global learning at Soft Contents based in London, UK. Roy has almost two decades of project management experience in the IT industry. In an effort to contribute to the improvement of teacher training education in Nigeria, Roy attained an MA in development education from the Institute of Education, University College London. In the past three years Roy has organized global learning workshops for educators in Ondo, Lagos and Abuja in Nigeria, West Africa.

Opeyemi Aderonke Oyekan is a training and research fellow working with National Institute for Educational Planning and Administration (NIEPA), Ondo, Nigeria. Opeyemi is currently Acting Head of Research and Development Department of the Institute and former Head of Empirical Studies/Project Development Unit of the Research and Development Department. She studied educational management (Economics), educational management (Institutional

Administration) and educational evaluation and measurement and educational Management (Systems Administration) for her bachelors, masters and PhD respectively from University of Ibadan, Nigeria.

Karen Pashby is Reader of Education Studies at Manchester Metropolitan University. An experienced secondary school educator and teacher educator, her research draws on post-colonial and decolonial theoretical resources. She examines productive pedagogical tensions that promote critically reflexive classroom practices in education for global citizenship in Global North contexts.

Malgorzata Anielka Pieniazek is a PhD researcher at UCL Institute of Education in London and Scholarships and Bursaries Manager at the University Campus of Football and Business. Her doctoral journey was inspired through the experience she has made working with Kenyan partners during an international, educational project 'Makutano Junction: A multimedia approach to effective Development Education'. Anielka's research interests are focused around global issues, global citizenship and global education. She is examining the educational perspectives and concepts from the Global South in relation to the international debates around SDGs.

Hanna Posti-Ahokas PhD, Adjunct Professor is a senior researcher at the University of Jyväskylä, Finland. Her current research focuses on global education pedagogy in higher education and on internationalization of higher education through North–South collaboration.

Mark Proctor is Sazani Associates Executive Director and a co-founder of the NGO. An international expert in community engagement and conflict resolution, Mark has worked extensively in post-conflict and fragile states across Africa and Europe specializing in youth engagement. In addition to managing Sazani Associates projects, he is currently undertaking doctoral studies in social barriers to acceptance in the energy sector.

Antti Rajala has PhD and is a postdoctoral researcher at the Faculty of Educational Sciences, University of Helsinki. Currently, he is working for the project 'Constituting Cultures of Compassion in Early Childhood Education'. Rajala is one of the coordinators of the Finnish network of global education research. He is also co-editor of *Outlines: Critical Practice Studies*.

Tania Ramalho emigrated from Brazil to the United States, where she is a professor of social foundations of education at the State University of New York (SUNY) at Oswego. She teaches critical literacy and pedagogy in social justice-oriented graduate teacher education programs in the School of Education's Curriculum & Instruction Department. She addresses school and classroom issues of power concerning the intersections of race, sex/gender/sexuality, social class/poverty, age and ability.

Annette Scheunpflug holds a chair on 'Foundation in Education' at Otto-Friedrich-University of Bamberg in Germany. Her research focuses on global learning, quality of education and different aspects of anthropology in education. She is editor of *ZEP*, the journal of global learning research for German-speaking contexts.

Namrata Sharma is an adjunct professor at the State University of New York and an academic advisor with AlphaPlus consultancy, UK. Her research areas include global citizenship, international and comparative education. She is the author of *Value-Creating Global Citizenship Education: Engaging Gandhi, Makiguchi, and Ikeda as Examples* (2018).

Sharon Stein is an assistant professor in the Department of Educational Studies at the University of British Columbia. Her work draws on critical and decolonial perspectives to address issues of social and ecological accountability in higher education, especially as this relates to decolonization, internationalization and climate change.

Louise Sund is an experienced secondary school teacher, a teacher educator at Mälardalen University and a researcher in education at Örebro University. Louise has an interest in environmental and sustainability education and citizenship education. Her research interests include philosophical and post-colonial perspectives and approaches to education and sustainable development.

Rene Suša is a postdoctoral fellow at the Educational Studies Department at the University of British Columbia. His work explores the problematic and often unacknowledged ideas, ideals and desires that drive modern global imaginaries.

Ali Sutherland currently works at the intersection of global education and international development. She obtained her MA in educational studies at the University of British Columbia. Ali has particular research interests in systems change and development education.

Massimiliano Tarozzi is Co-Director of the Development Education Research Centre at UCL – Institute of Education. He also teaches global citizenship education at the University of Bologna. In the same university he is Founding Director of the International Research Centre on Global Citizenship Education. He has extensively published on the topics of global citizenship education, intercultural and social justice education; his works include *Global Citizenship Education and the Crises of Multiculturalism*, co-authored with C. A. Torres.

Liam Wegimont is the director of GENE. He was co-facilitator of the Maastricht Congress and co-founder of GENE, the *European Global Education Peer Review* and ANGEL. He has lectured, facilitated, networked and published widely on global education theory, practice, policy and research; and has been the Principal of Mount Temple Comprehensive school – a school increasingly devoted to global learning.

Chapter 1

Introduction

Douglas Bourn

Introduction

The contribution of education to understanding the forces of globalization and the impact of global issues on peoples' lives has become an increasingly important component of debates concerning policies and programmes for schools, colleges, universities and informal learning around the world. Terms such as 'learning to live and work in a global economy', 'being active global citizens', 'understanding issues such as climate change, human rights, gender equality and global poverty' can be seen in the curriculum of many countries and institutions around the world. International bodies such as the United Nations Educational, Scientific and Cultural Organization (UNESCO), the Organization for Economic Cooperation and Development (OECD), World Bank and the United Nations make reference to these themes in numerous policies that have been introduced since 2015. The launch of the Sustainable Development Goals (SDGs) in 2015 and their reference to these themes has given added impetus to these agendas.

However, to date there has been no major academic publication that has aimed to bring together current issues and debates concerning global education (GE). In 2017, Academic Network on Global Education and Learning (ANGEL), a new network of academics and researchers in the field of GE, was launched with the support of Global Education Network Europe (GENE) and administered by the Development Education Research Centre (DERC) at University College London in the UK. GENE is the network of national policy-makers across Europe who are supportive of GE. These are usually ministries covering aid and development budgets, education and in some cases environment.

ANGEL was formed in response to the need to establish and reinforce existing relationships among scholars and academic institutions working in GE and related areas. It aims

> to form a pool of experts which can become a resource for policymakers in search of strong research grounding for policy development, and to establish a network among early stage researchers, Doctoral students and Post-Doctoral researchers, who are currently engaged in research in fields related to Global Education.[1]

Most of the contributions in this volume have come from members of this network.

This handbook aims to demonstrate the differing ways GE is being interpreted and implemented around the world. GE and learning is here seen as relevant to all forms of education and in all

---

[1] https://angel-network.net/about

regions of the world. Wherever learning is taking place, there is a need for learners to make sense of and understand the wider world and their contribution to it.

Distinctiveness of this handbook

Themes related to the field of GE have been the subject of similar handbooks in recent years, including those on citizenship (Arthur, Davies and Hahn, 2008), sustainable development (Barth et al., 2016), global citizenship education (Davies et al., 2018) and critical education (Apple, Au and Gandin, 2009). Many of these handbooks aim to provide summaries of current policies, practices and research themes as a way of providing an introduction to the field. There is also *The Handbook of Global Education Policy* (Mundy et al., 2016), but this interprets the term as education around the world with a focus on education policies developed by international institutions.

What this handbook aims to do is to demonstrate the different ways themes such as learning about global issues, being a global citizen and bringing global perspectives into schools, communities and universities can contribute to a distinctive educational field of GE and learning. Many of the chapters are based on empirical research or posing new and innovatory ideas to GE and learning. They are therefore more substantial chapters than one might see in similar publications with the average word length being between 6,000 and 7,000 words.

A second distinctive feature of this volume is the space it has given to younger and newer researchers. Several of the chapters in this volume are related to recently completed or ongoing doctoral research. GE and learning is a growing field as the annual *Global Education Digest* produced since 2016 by DERC for ANGEL and GENE has shown. Over 400 articles, books or reports have been published in this field in the English language alone.[2]

A third distinctive feature of this handbook is to show the relevance and contribution of debates and research from all over the world. While it could be argued that twenty years ago, GE was seen predominantly as a field of education for and led by people from the Global North, this is clearly no longer the case. As can be seen from the contributions from the Caribbean, Latin America, Africa and Asia, the themes underpinning GE have relevance throughout the world.

Finally, this handbook does not aim through its chapters to follow similar structures or approaches. An important feature of GE and learning is its range of pedagogical approaches, voices and methodologies. As can be seen in this volume, there are a range of approaches, including a chapter on the work of Paulo Freire that uses a feature of his discourse in the form of letters. Another is the way in which several chapters consciously give space for the voices of people from the Global South through evidence from interviews. Several chapters also combine theoretical debates alongside empirical research and reviews of practice. This praxis-based approach is a key element of global education.

---

[2] https://angel-network.net/sites/default/files/Digest%202015%20-%2017%20online.pdf

Scope and terminology of global education and learning

As the chapters in this volume will demonstrate, GE as an educational field is open to different interpretations from education around the world to a specific pedagogical approach influenced by themes such as social justice.

For the purposes of this handbook, the dominant approach of the contributions locates their discussions on GE within a values base of social justice, equity and human rights. This means that while there are differing views expressed in this volume as to what are the key elements of GE, most of the chapters reflect a critical approach to the dominant neoliberal orthodoxies within much of education today.

The theme of learning for global citizenship is also present in many of the chapters, and this reflects one of the major changes taking place towards GE around the world and that is a closer relationship to the discourses around citizenship and active social engagement.

Another influential approach reflected in several chapters is that outlined by the Council of Europe and GENE who have seen GE as

> education that opens people's eyes and minds to the realities of the world, and awakens them to bring about a world of greater justice, equity and human rights for all. GE is understood to encompass Development Education, Human Rights Education, Education for Sustainability, Education for Peace and Conflict Prevention and Intercultural Education; being the global dimensions of Education for Citizenship.[3]

This usage of the term as encompassing a range of educational fields and traditions but with a central theme of social justice has enabled authors from their own perspectives to bring in specific issues and approaches that might be particularly dominant in certain countries.

In this handbook, different terms will be used that could be said to cover GE. The deliberate inclusion of 'learning' in the title of this handbook is one example of this. The term 'learning' implies a sense of process, of engagement in understanding issues. It also implies a focus on pedagogy. As I have written elsewhere,

> Global learning is a process of learning that recognises different approaches and different ways of understanding the world, and engages with them through different lenses. (Bourn, 2015:6)

Other terms such as 'global citizenship' and 'development education' are also referred to in this volume. They cover the same area of learning about global issues and themes, but there may be variations in their focus and emphasis depending on the theoretical positioning of the author or the specific national context. Chapters in this volume have retained the terminology used by the authors rather than having some common language and terms. This is deliberate because this handbook does not aim to present some uniform approach to GE but to reflect the differing ways in which terms and concepts are interpreted.

---

[3]   https://gene.eu/about-gene/global-education/

Contribution of practitioners

GE as an educational field has been part of the landscape of learning in Europe, North America and Australia for the past fifty years. Its main protagonists were, and in many countries remain, educational practitioners who are recognizing the need for learners to have the knowledge and skills to understand wider world issues. The results of this interest can be seen in the wealth of educational resources that have been produced covering themes such as 'In the Global Classroom', 'Thinking Globally' or 'The School as a Foundation for a Fair World'.

While this wealth of educational material has equipped many educationalists, particularly teachers, around the world, the field of global education has remained an area of interest primarily for enthusiastic teachers.

Influence of policy-makers

What has helped GE grow and remain a theme within educational provision has been the influence and support of policy-makers, particularly in Europe and to a lesser extent in Canada, Japan, Australia, New Zealand and some areas within the United States.

Ministries of foreign affairs and in some cases education have been champions of GE in many European countries for more than twenty years. While the terminology may vary in some countries from global learning to development education (DE) or global citizenship education (GCE), there is evidence from countries such as Norway, Portugal, Slovakia, Cyprus, Finland, Belgium and Ireland of strategies that aim to put GE as part of mainstream provision.

Elsewhere in the world while GE may not be so overt in policy statements, many of the themes that underpin this field can be seen in initiatives in countries such as Brazil, South Africa, Nigeria, Pakistan, India, China and Japan. The influences and drivers for the interest in GE may come from bodies concerned with citizenship, sustainable development or even more broadly political and moral education. But as will be shown in this volume, there is a richness today to the differing approaches and perspectives on GE that was perhaps not there a decade ago.

Need for research in global education

While there have been well-known academics involved in the field of GE for many years including in North America Robert Hanvey, Merry Merryfield, Toni Kirkwood-Tucker and Graham and in Europe David Selby and David Hicks, it is an area that has had few major empirically based research studies compared to say environmental education. The growth in interest in this field in Europe led particularly by Annette Scheunpflug in Germany, Rauni Räsänen in Finland and Manuela Mesa has over the past decade helped to change this culture (see Bourn, 2015). Vanessa Andreotti (2011) originally from Brazil, but now located in Canada, has also been a major influence through her work on GCE. In the UK, the work of the DERC has also helped to put research on the agenda of policy-makers and practitioners.

The field has also benefited from the emergence of numerous academic journals that focus exclusively on GE and related areas such as development and GCE.

As several of the chapters in this volume will demonstrate, the need for research and evidence to demonstrate its effectiveness, importance and impact remains central to progressing GE. It is an area, because of the themes it addresses, of being susceptible to changes in political priorities. GE, because it is an educational field that challenges many of the neoliberal priorities within education, can be open to ideological and political attacks. A consequence of this has been the constant changes in funding opportunities depending upon who was in political power at the time.

Main themes and structure

This handbook is divided into six themes with each theme having a number of chapters covering different approaches and evidence from a range of countries around the world.

The first theme is *Challenges for Today and Tomorrow*. This theme covers chapters by Douglas Bourn that outline the evolution of GE and suggest the need to move from consensus of approaches to dissensus. Liam Wegimont, the director of GENE, reviews the origins of the definition of 'global education' in Europe and suggests the need for a philosophical reflection as to the meaning of the term before outlining a suggested critical and transformative model for future policy and practice. Annette Scheunpflug outlines the importance of evidence and research to promote the value and importance of GE and learning to broader educational discourse and provision. Finally, Tania Ramalho in the form of an open letter to Paulo Freire outlines some of the challenges for GE today and the potential role that Freirean approaches can provide to addressing the theme of being a Global Citizen.

The second theme of the handbook looks at different *theoretical perspectives* and forms in which GE is interpreted across a range of educational areas. Sharon Stein reviews three different approaches to global learning within the context of higher education (HE), learning about difference, learning from difference and being taught by difference. Malgorzata Aniekla Pieniazek introduces the South African concept of Ubuntu to the discussions on theories of GE and its particular relevance to discussions on global citizenship and cosmopolitanism. Another different theoretical perspective is outlined by Namrata Sharma who looks at Asian perspectives on GCE particularly those of Mahatma Gandhi and Daisaku Ikeda.

The third theme is that of *Impact of Policies and Programmes*. This section begins with reviews of national strategies, policies and practices in Finland (Elina Lehtomäki and Antti Rajala) and Poland (Magdalena Kuleta-Hulboj). Massimiliano Tarozzi then reviews the specific contribution of non-governmental organizations (NGOs) to the development of policies across Europe. Pei-I-Chou provides a review of how GE has developed in Taiwan and its potential role within the school curriculum. Finally, in this section, Cathryn MacCallum, Nick Hoad and Mark Proctor review training and professional development of educators and community activists in Zanzibar. The evidence summarized in this chapter is based on a four-year funded programme which demonstrates the value of having resources and spaces to develop innovatory approaches towards learning.

The fourth theme of the handbook looks at *Global Perspectives in Higher Education*. Initiatives in HE that promote learning experiences around global themes have becoming increasingly popular in recent years. The first chapter in this theme is by Nicolle Manjeya, and through reviewing the ways in which GE has evolved in HE in South Africa, she suggests that this field needs to make closer connections to the areas of academic literacy and the effects of multiculturalism. This is followed by reviewing differing approaches to including global citizenship within specific degree courses in Japan, the United Kingdom and United States by Emiliano Bosio. Silvia Moraes and Ludmilla Freire follow this with a chapter that suggests the term 'planetary citizenship' rather than global citizenship is more appropriate because it brings in indigenous voices and the environmental dimension. It then outlines what this means in terms of research with student teachers at a university in Brazil. Hanna Posti-Ahokas, Josephine Moate and Elina Lehtomäki review an example of a master's degree programme through evidence from a specific seminar in Finland. Helmuth Hartmeyer follows this with a chapter that reviews the relationship of the global to the local in students learning in a masters' programme at the University of Vienna in Austria. Eloísa Nos Aldás reviews a course on communications at a university in Spain which brings in the importance of media literacy to discussions on GE. Finally, this section concludes with a chapter on global citizenship and GE with two case studies, one on initial teacher education and the other an online collaboration between students in UK and India by Phil Bamber.

The fifth theme looks specifically at research and evidence of the impact of *Global Education and Learning within Schools*. This theme is covered through a range of approaches to how global themes are reflected within schools. The first chapter in this section by Adelina Calvo looks at different approaches within Spain. This is followed by Alison Morrison's chapter on Global South–North Educational Partnerships and looks particularly at examples between the UK and Tanzania. Karen Pashby and Louise Sund then review research on sustainability education and global citizenship and the continued usage of 'us' meaning the Global North and 'them' the Global South. It then outlines evidence from research with teachers in three countries that poses a different way of looking at global issues. Simon Eten Angyagre's chapter looks at examples of ways in which the social studies curriculum in Ghana provides opportunities for GE. The section then has two chapters reviewing aspects of the impact of the Global Learning Programme (GLP) in England. The first by Frances Hunt looks at what a global learning school is seen to be by teachers and school leaders. This is followed by evidence on the importance of professional development opportunities for teachers in global learning within England by Clare Bentall. The final chapter in this section also looks at professional development for teachers based on evidence gathered from a course for teachers in Nigeria by Opeyemi Aderonke Oyekan, Roy Tokunbo Olowu and Olutosin Awolalu.

The final theme is on *Learning* and *Experience*, and *Being Global Citizens* shows through different examples of ways in which some forms of personal experience can relate to a sense of identity and views about the wider world. This theme is also deliberately included because a common feature of global education practice is to encourage learners to experience different social and cultural environments. Also as several of the chapters highlights, such approaches also pose questions as to what is meant by being a global citizen.

The first chapter in this section is on North–South community-engaged learning by Ali Sutherland, Rene Suša and Vanessa Andreottti. It includes discussion of a distinctive pedagogical framework, EarthCARE and illustrated examples from Canadian students visiting community projects in Brazil. The chapter by Madeleine Le Bourdon, based on her doctoral research, looks at how an international NGO works with young people in developing experiential learning practices. Mags Liddy, her chapter based on evidence from her doctorate, looks at the role and impact of oversees volunteering experience on a group of Irish teachers. Nicole Blum's chapter looks at the impact of students spending a year abroad from a UK university on developing their global outlook. Finally in this section, Yvette Allen's chapter, also based on her doctoral research on school linking, reviews the ways in which young people from Tobago in the Caribbean relate to the term 'global citizen'.

The volume concludes with some concluding comments from the editor, Douglas Bourn.

Bibliography

Andreotti, V. (2011) *Actionable Postcolonial Theory in Education*, London: Palgrave.

Apple, M., Au, W. and Gandin, L. A. (eds) (2009) *The Routledge International Handbook of Critical Education*, New York: Routledge.

Arthur, J., Davies, I. and Hahn, C. (eds) (2008) *The Sage Handbook of Education for Citizenship and Democracy*, London: SAGE.

Barth, M., Michelsen, G., Rieckmann, M. and Thomas, I. (eds) (2016) *Routledge Handbook of Higher Education for Sustainable Development*, Abingdon: Routledge.

Bourn, D. (2014) *The Theory and Practice of Global Learning*, DERC Research Paper no. 11, London, Development Education Research Centre, Institute of Education/Global Learning Programme.

Bourn, D. (2015) *The Theory and Practice of Development Education*, Abingdon: Routledge.

Davies, I., Ho, L.-I., Kiwan, D., Peck, C., Petersen, A., Sant, E. and Waghid, Y. (eds) (2018) *The Palgrave Handbook of Global Citizenship and Education*, London: Palgrave.

Mundy, K., Green, A., Lingard, B. and Verger, A. (eds) (2016) *The Handbook of Global Education Policy*, London: Wiley-Blackwell.

Part I

Challenges for Today and Tomorrow

Chapter 2

The Emergence of Global Education as a Distinctive Pedagogical Field

Douglas Bourn

Introduction

Over the past decade there has been a major expansion of literature in the field of global learning and education, development education (DE) and global citizenship. Most of this has been in response to greater promotion of these terms by international bodies such as United Nations Educational, Scientific and Cultural Organization (UNESCO), the continued practices by non-governmental organizations (NGOs) and the growth of academic research and journals covering this area. This chapter will address the different ways in which these terms have evolved and their status within education policies and programmes. It will suggest that an important feature of global education (GE) has been the continued evolution of a distinctive educational approach that is both an educational field and a pedagogy of global social justice.

Intellectual and policy routes

Interest in promoting learning about the wider world has its roots in geography and history education which for countries like the UK and France were closely linked to their role as colonial powers. However, between the wars, on the back of the formation of the League of Nations, there was interest in promoting initiatives that encouraged a sense of world citizenship particularly in Europe and North America. While the drivers for this in the 1930s came from policy-makers fearing the rise of fascism and the threats to democracy, there was a sense that there was a need to promote a more international outlook within education and society more widely.

Following the ending of the Second World War and the creation of various international institutions such as UN and UNESCO, there was a desire among policy-makers to promote a form of international education that encouraged mutual learning around the world. The promotion of the values of these international institutions was a major driver for a range of initiatives such as the establishment of UNESCO's Associated Schools Network and activities such as the UN Model School Assemblies.

While the Cold War provided obstacles to international education, themes such as intercultural understanding, peace education, human rights education and promoting learning about other countries gained support, particularly in Western Europe and North America. This led, in the 1970s in both the United Kingdom and United States for example, to the creation of what has today become known as GE.

Academics such as Kenneth Tye, James Becker, Robert Hanvey and later Jan Tucker and Merry Merryfield in the United States played a leading role internationally in promoting GE through their publications and activities. Their approach had a common theme of encouraging learning that broadens horizons and understanding of different perspectives (Hanvey, 1976). This approach had specific influence in the development of the social studies curriculum. However, this approach to education suffered attacks in the 1980s under the Reagan administration for being anti-American.

A similar history could be seen in the UK where, under the leadership of Robin Richardson and later Graham Pike and David Selby, a range of curriculum initiatives were developed that encouraged a sense of world-mindedness and a more learner-centred approach. What they identified was the need to see GE not as a subject but as the development of skills and values that had relevance across all subjects with the encouragement of learners to see themselves as active global citizens. But as in the United States, GE came under repeated ideological attack in the 1980s, and its influence became restricted to those who were already active enthusiasts for progressive approaches to education (Hicks, 2003).

These trends can also be seen in other European countries and in Japan, Canada and Australia during the 1970s and 1980s. Often these traditions were phrased under 'education for international understanding' 'or intercultural learning' and in the case of Japan, to make a clear break from its imperial past (Ishii, 2003).

What also became clear during this period is that learning about the wider world brought it into engagement with other emerging terms such as peace, intercultural, environmental and human rights education. These traditions, while having an identity and their own distinctive roots, shared with global educationalists a desire for a closer relationship between societal issues and what was taught in the classroom.

Development education

The other educational tradition that has had a major influence on shaping GE today has been that of DE. As far back as the 1950s, there were educational programmes in Norway related to fundraising and raising awareness of development assistance for India (O'Loughlin and Wegimont, 2009). In countries such as the UK, the emergence of DE needs to be seen as a response to the decolonization process of the 1960s and 1970s and the emergence of development and aid assistance programmes. DE came out of the desire by policy-makers and emerging international aid organizations to gain public support for development (Harrison, 2008; Bourn, 2015).

Where countries began to develop major aid programmes such as the UK, Norway, Canada, Sweden and the Netherlands, the call for projects that encouraged awareness and learning about aid and development resulted. While in some of these countries, such as Norway and Canada, there was a merging between a development and a broader internationalist outlook, it was clear that with the increasing interest, engagement and funding for this area coming from ministries and bodies responsible for aid, DE became the dominant focus of support for projects.

However, like GE, DE suffered from being closely aligned to progressive and radical social educational perspectives. For example, in the 1980s and again after 2010, in the UK with a conservative government, funding for DE was radically reduced. Similar stories can be found in Canada, Spain and most recently the Netherlands.

Influence of more critical approaches

Alongside the responses from policy-makers, the experiences of individuals involved in development work and the emerging area of international volunteering resulted in the creation of more critical discourses around what was the role and purpose of global and DE. Lissner (1977) had already started to pose the importance of including themes such as social justice, equity and solidarity. Experiences in Latin America particularly and the growing influence of the work of the Brazilian educator Paulo Freire led to the establishment of a body of educational practice, often led by civil society organizations, that started from a questioning of the dominant orthodoxies of education and encouraged an approach that was learner-centred and participatory, with an emphasis on social justice and combating inequality in the world.

By the 1990s, there was evidence in numerous countries in Europe particularly of programmes and projects that were grounded in a pedagogical approach that sought social change. This meant a move forward from promoting awareness of aid to equipping learners with the knowledge, skills and value base to secure social transformation. Part of this approach was also to recognize, encourage and promote the voices of the dispossessed, particularly from the Global South.

The changing nature of practice was influenced by governments who saw the priority being to fund and support civil society organizations. This can be seen particularly in Europe through the funding from the European Commission for major projects and initiatives that moved from merely giving information and raising awareness about development to encouraging a sense of international solidarity, engaging Southern partners and equipping educators with the skills to seek global social change. While most of these activities came under the umbrella of what was termed 'development education', it had a knock-on effect on the broader GE sector, as these themes now had funding and resources behind them.

Evolution of global education

Throughout the 1980s and 1990s, GE had developed as a distinctive pedagogical approach in the United States led by people such as Kenneth Tye and in the UK and later in North America by David Selby and Graham Pike. Pike and Selby (1988) saw GE as combining world-mindedness and child-centredness. Tye (1990), for example, referred to GE involving learning about those problems and issues that cut across national boundaries, about interconnectedness and recognizing the importance of looking at issues through the eyes and minds of others.

What was also significant about the approach of Selby and Pike was the ways in which they were bringing together distinctive pedagogical approaches with curricular content that brought together themes from peace, environmental, multicultural, human rights and DE movements (Mundy, 2007). While there were differences of emphasis among these figures, there was as Kirkwood-Tucker (2009) has noted, some commonality of approach that is closely aligned to Hanvey's five dimensions of a global awareness: multiple perspectives, state of the planet's awareness, comprehension and appreciation of other cultures, the world as an interrelated system and the significance of human choices (Landorf, 2009).

By the beginning of the twenty-first century, in North America, UK and Australia, themes such as open-mindedness, recognition of the importance of understanding different cultural approaches and an ability to take action to secure social change were becoming more noticeable (Petersen and Warwick, 2015: 18). Here one sees for the first time the use of the term 'global citizenship' as a way of recognizing the active element of GE.

What is also noticeable at the turn of the century is the conscious decision by leading figures in the field to move on from development to global forces as the dominant frame. This can be seen in discourses in Germany through the work of Klaus Seitz and Annette Schuenpflug. They both saw a response to the challenges of globalization as the basis of GE (see Hartmeyer, 2008).

Conceptual variations

This move towards the usage of the term 'global education' across many European countries, however, masks the increasing variation in conceptual thinking and approach. There were several reasons for this, including specific national policy agendas, the relative influence of NGOs and the growing body of academic debate in this field.

Alongside the umbrella term of 'global education', there was still in countries such as Ireland, Portugal and Spain continued use of the term 'development education'. In Ireland, there was an integration of intercultural and DE while in Sweden 'education for sustainable development (ESD)' was becoming the dominant term. Human rights was still a theme in a number of countries, but it did not become a dominant focus of policy debates within GE.

The biggest change in influence, directly due to changes in the agendas of civil society organizations, was the use of the term 'global citizenship education'. Oxfam in the UK had started to use the term in the late 1990s, and one can see its increasing usage by NGOs across Europe and also in North America as a way of identifying a distinctive break from development and GE. Behind this move towards the term 'global citizenship' was the encouragement of an active learning component framed within the context of globalization. There was also a desire from civil society organizations to make connections between the global agenda with the renewed interest in citizenship, and identity and a sense of place (see Tarozzi and Torres, 2016).

The increasing variety of terminology was also influenced by the differing ways in which national policy-makers were framing GE. Some still emphasized the link to the aid and development agenda, others tried to link it more to international debates such as ESD, while there were still distinctive national approaches that reflected the extent to which societies were becoming more culturally diverse.

The variations in terminology also reflected specific national histories of involvement in the field and the maturity of engagement in the field of GE. Manuela Mesa, although referring primarily to DE, has talked about this maturity in terms of five generations from a charitable and assistance-based approach through to a more solidarity-based approach to human and sustainable development, and finally to global citizenship education (GCE) (Mesa, 2011).

Increased engagement of policy-makers and emergence of a network in Europe

At a broader European level, a starting point for GE could be said to have come from the North–South Centre of the Council of Europe through its Global Education Charter published in 1997. This led to the establishment of the Global Education Network Europe (GENE) in 2001 and the Maastricht Declaration of 2002 which states:

> Global Education is education that opens people's eyes and minds to the realities of the world, and awakens them to bring about a world of greater justice, equity and human rights for all. GE is understood to encompass Development Education, Human Rights Education, Education for Sustainability, Education for Peace and Conflict Prevention and Intercultural Education; being the global dimensions of Education for Citizenship. (Hartmeyer and Wegimont, 2016: 10)

This interpretation of GE as bringing together of adjectival educations although framed in a new way built on interpretations and approaches that could be seen in the work of Selby and Pike during the previous decade. The influences of this interpretation can also be seen in the curriculum guidance publication for schools in England on the 'Global Dimension', first published in 2000 and revised in 2005, which included themes of human rights, citizenship, sustainable development, conflict resolution and social justice (DFES, 2000, 2005).

In 2001, a new Global Education network of policy-makers and coordinating bodies was founded: GENE.[1] This network has increasingly played an influential role across Europe in moving GE from the margins of education and international development policies to becoming much more centre stage through the development of strategies that bring policy-makers together.

The Maastricht Declaration of 2002 has become the basis for many national strategies in Europe on GE. This can be seen particularly in the series of peer reviews of different countries policies and practices undertaken by GENE (see, for example, McAuley and Wegimont, 2018)[2] and their overview reports (see McAuley, 2018). This evidence demonstrates that while there is considerable variation in terms of national government policies, there is a degree of commonality. This includes the importance of themes such as social justice, concern for human rights and sustainable development, and because of the leadership for these policies comes, from ministries

---

[1]   https://gene.eu

[2]   For details about all of these peer reviews go to: https://gene.eu/publications/national-reports/

with a stake in aid and development, a strong DE influence. GENE itself recognizes this in its definition of GE where it states on its website:

> GENE pays particular attention to development education. While using the term Global Education, GENE also welcomes the use of specific national terms.[3]

The broad nature of the GE definition as outlined at Maastricht and since promoted by GENE has enabled some degree of commonality and adaptability to specific national contexts and priorities.

In more recent years, the field of GE has also been greatly assisted by increased engagement of international bodies such as UN, UNESCO and OECD (Organization for Economic Cooperation and Development). Themes such as global citizenship have been promoted at a UN level, and there is today a distinctive educational programme on global citizenship within UNESCO.

This UNESCO programme sits alongside its more established work on ESD which culminated in the UN Decade from 2005 to 2014. OECD has also shown interest in this area most notably through its promotion of the Programme of International Student Assessment (PISA) test on global competencies in 2018.

Finally and perhaps most significant of all has been the role that global and sustainability themes now play within the UN Sustainable Development Goals (SDGs) most notably 4.7 which states:

> By 2030, ensure that all learners acquire the knowledge and skills needed to promote sustainable development, including, among others, through education for sustainable development and sustainable lifestyles, human rights, gender equality, promotion of a culture of peace and non-violence, global citizenship and appreciation of cultural diversity and of culture's contribution to sustainable development.[4]

Moving from consensus to divergent discourse and dissensus

Wegimont (2016) in reviewing the growth of GE in Europe identifies a key challenge in GE as the tension between encouraging consensus and letting a 'thousand flowers bloom'. For example, at European and many national policy levels, there has been pressure from strategic bodies to encourage a common vision and strategy. This has been influenced by pressures on ministries to demonstrate effectiveness, impact and value for money.

The tensions between consensus and dissensus can be seen in the European consensus document on DE first published in 2005. The strength of this document was that it emphasized the importance of giving space to the voices of the Global South and the importance of the link between globalization and development. This document also emphasized the importance of a distinctive pedagogical approach and the central role of education rather than awareness-raising

---

[3] https://gene.eu/about-gene/global-education/
[4] https://sustainabledevelopment.un.org/sdg4

and public communications. On the other hand, the consensus document could be said to have been rather cautious in its approach in not addressing the linkages to broader societal issues and concerns.

The debates around consensus versus dissensus are often played out at a national level in terms of funding strategies. For example, in most European countries, GE is resourced by a grants programme where civil society organizations and educational institutions can apply for funding for specific projects. This approach has enabled creative and innovatory projects to emerge. Its weaknesses have been the dangers of grants becoming forms of self-serving for civil society organizations, and the difficulties of identifying the impact of initiatives.

A consequence of this funding approach could be seen in the UK where governments who had some question marks about DE were able to use the lack of evidence of impact to justify reductions in funding (Bourn, 2015).

Although reductions in funding led to resources for DE being focused around a small number of strategic programmes, it did result in a more coherent approach. The Global Learning Programme (GLP) in the UK was one example of the success of this strategic approach that ensured greater coherence and wider impact within education.[5] But what it also resulted in was a decline in civil society organizations' engagement because of a lack of funding. What was also missing, and linked to lack of funding for NGOs, were the resources for innovatory approaches and risk-taking.

Another consequence of consensus has been that due to the influence and funding power of policy-makers, it is usually their perspective that tends to dominate, with a consequential emphasis on themes such as sense of common humanity, support for development and emphasis on economic growth. An example of the dangers of the influence of this approach can be seen in Andreotti's critique of the English curriculum document on the global dimension referred to earlier. Andreotti suggests that this publication emphasizes themes such as poverty rather than injustice, interconnectedness rather than power imbalances and sense of universalism rather than reflexivity and dialogue (Andreotti, 2008).

An example that reflects some of these debates and challenges is South Korea which is relatively new to the field of GE. This country has become one of the leading promoters of global citizenship and GE within the formal education system in the world led by its ministries of education and foreign affairs. But as Noh (2018: 8) has identified, this government drive to 'foster global citizenship education implies that the state enacts the cultivation of global citizens' and a neglect of critical and reflective approaches to learning. Instead, Koh suggests that if more resources were given to NGOs, it would encourage different perspectives. But Koh does note that NGOs have tended, however, to follow methodologies and pedagogical approaches from other international NGOs and not giving sufficient consideration to the specific national context of Korea.

GE and its related areas of DE and GCE have grown out of distinctive pedagogical approaches that could be said to have been counter-hegemonic, challenging dominant orthodoxies about global issues, posing participatory forms of learning and opening up spaces for the voices of the dispossessed to be heard. But as policy-makers, and particularly education ministries, become

---

[5] See chapters by Hunt and Bentall in this volume.

more actively involved in this field, there is always the danger of a weakening of this distinctive approach. Clearly there is a need for endorsement and recognition of the field of GE, but it also needs the creative spaces in which it can innovate and provide differing viewpoints. This is why the involvement and engagement of civil society organizations have historically been so important because they have provided, in many cases, perspectives and approaches that have challenged dominant educational and ideological orthodoxies.

What GE, however, for too long suffered from was a lack of a clear and distinctive intellectual tradition that had a life of its own. While strategic initiatives can help to maximize impact they can all too often result in the domination of one viewpoint. NGO initiatives on the other hand, while encouraging differing voices, can result in the domination of agendas of the organization rather than educational priorities. What is noticeable today are the ways in which GE has moved beyond this policy-makers versus NGO agendas in many countries to include the voices of academics and researchers.

In some countries, this engagement of academics and researchers has in some form always been present, particularly in North America. The decline in funding for civil society organizations in some European countries has resulted in the need for leadership to come from somewhere else. There has always been a need for an independent research focus for GE, but only in the last ten to fifteen years has a distinctive intellectual GE field emerged as can be seen through the growth of academic journals.

While a number of journals had been in existence in Germany,[6] United States, Ireland and the UK, they tended to be focused on professional practice rather than academic research. Only with the establishment of the *International Journal for Development Education and Global Learning* in 2008 and more recently similar journals in United States,[7] Portugal[8] and Spain[9] can a distinctive body of academic research be identified. There is clearly today a distinctive GE field with an international network, Academic Network on Global Education and Learning (ANGEL),[10] and an emerging body of evidence alongside a growing theoretical debate around what is meant by global citizenship, the extent to which social justice should be framing practice and the continuing influence of post-colonialism. For example, the Digest of recently published academic books and articles in 2018 identifies over 400 documents published in the previous 2 years with a GE theme. Key themes within those publications were references to the importance and influence of the SDGs, the growth in conceptual debate around the term 'global citizenship', empirical research on global learning within school and ways in which global social justice themes are becoming part of the discourses around internationalization in higher education (HE).[11]

---

[6]   https://www.waxmann.com/waxmann-zeitschriftendetails/?tx_p2waxmann_pi2[zeitschrift]=ZEI1009&tx_p2waxmann_pi2[action]=show

[7]   https://scholarcommons.usf.edu/jger/

[8]   http://www.sinergiased.org

[9]   http://educacionglobalresearch.net/en/

[10]   https://angel-network.net/about

[11]   https://angel-network.net/publications/global-education-digest

Global education as an educational field

The emergence of GE as a distinctive educational field was identified by Scheunpflug and Asbrand in 2006, although they stated then that it faced conceptual challenges, lack of evidence and distinctive forms of implementation.[12] Marshall (2005: 78) had the previous year stated GE 'has consisted of a variety of different traditions each with their own distinct histories, pedagogic approaches and objectives – I call the movement a 'field' because it most effectively caters for this heterogeneity'. Landorf in the United States has said that from the literature and various initiatives it could be seen as a field of study, a movement, a curriculum, an approach to learning or as components and objectives (Landorf, 2009: 54).

This usage of the term 'educational field' to describe GE is helpful in that it moves it to beyond being seen as a distinctive academic discipline or even a community of practice. An academic discipline could mean a subject of study which is something most proponents of GE have tried to avoid. From Hanvey to Richardson, to Selby and Pike and more recently Scheunpflug, the emphasis has been on its interdisciplinary focus, applicability across subjects and bodies of learning (see Scheunpflug, 2012). The limitations of seeing GE as a community of practice could mean perceiving GE as some form of distinct body of activity, self-contained with its own internal logic. Such an approach could lead to a rather elitist approach with GE being only open to a small body of experts.

If an educational field is seen as an approach to learning which has some distinctive characteristics in the same way that a field such as citizenship or health education is, then GE can be seen to have developed over the past decade as a distinctive body of thinking, research, ways of working and practices. The most obvious manifestation of this has been the academic journals already mentioned. This emerging field has also been helped by the launch in 2017 of the international network of academics and researchers in GE with the support of GENE. This network aims to form a pool of experts which can become a resource for policy-makers in search of strong research grounding for policy development, and to establish a network among early stage researchers, doctoral students and postdoctoral researchers, who are currently engaged in research in fields related to GE.[13]

While seeing GE as an educational field has enabled the area to have a higher profile and to encourage and support research in the area, there is also the danger of the area remaining a rather loose term and open to wide variations in interpretation.

What is suggested here is for GE to be seen as something more and as a pedagogical approach.

Global education as a distinctive pedagogical approach – A pedagogy for global social justice

Implicit in much of the literature around GE since the 1970s and 1980s has been the assumption that the field has a distinctive approach to learning. However, this has rarely been articulated in

---

[12] This theme of global education as an educational field and also as a distinctive pedagogical approach is further discussed by Pieniazek in her chapter in this volume on the concept of Ubuntu.

[13] https://angel-network.net/about

relation to discussions of pedagogy. Elsewhere I have written about a pedagogy of global learning as a process of learning 'within which learners interpret and engage in debates on development and include reference to their personal experiences, wider social and cultural influences, and their viewpoints on the wider world' (Bourn, 2015: 20). I went further and suggested that this pedagogy should

- 'deepen an understanding of different worldviews and perspectives on development and global poverty;
- encourage a critical reflection of teachers' and pupils own perceptions of development, aid and poverty;
- promote an emphasis on contextualising learning that places development and poverty themes within historical, cultural and social traditions and frameworks of social justice'. (Ibid: 21)

While this approach was framed within a narrower development than global lens, similar themes could be used for a pedagogy for GE that could perhaps emphasize perspectives on globalization and the wider world, reflections on pupils' own perceptions of global issues and that contextualizes learning with the influence of global forces and power relations in the world. What such a pedagogy could also suggest is a specific focus on social justice, for this could be at the heart of any form of distinctive GE approach.

By emphasizing power relations and social justice, GE goes beyond mere interconnectedness and broadening of horizons, important as they are, to locate the discourse in the context of globalization.

There is evidence from a range of doctoral level research, articles in the journals already referred to and in the expansion of literature on GCE that a distinctive pedagogical approach based on social justice is gaining increased influence and recognition. Since 2015, for example, over twenty PhDs in Europe alone have been completed that could be said to come within the GE field. As the other chapters in this volume demonstrate, GE is becoming a feature of both theoretically and empirically driven research in many countries around the world.

Conclusion

This chapter has reviewed the ways in which GE and its related fields have evolved. It has identified the historical contribution of civil society organizations and the increasing interest of policy-makers at both national and international level. It has further suggested that as GE has become mainstream, there have been dangers of appealing too much to policy-makers in order to achieve a consensus, resulting in some weakening of its distinctiveness.

The chapter then identified that an important influence in this emerging educational field has been a growing number of academics and researchers. Thus, it has also resulted in GE becoming more than just an area of education. It is becoming a distinctive pedagogical approach that in many ways is counter-hegemonic and that challenges the dominant orthodoxies and ideologies that have historically influenced educational theory and practice.

Bibliography

Andreotti, V. (2008) Development versus Poverty: Notions of Cultural Supremacy in Development Education Policy. In: Bourn, D. (ed.) *Development Education: Debates and Dialogues*. London: Bedford Way Papers, 45–63.

Asbrand, B. and Scheunpflug, A. (2006) Global Education and Education for Sustainability. *Environmental Education Research*, 12 (1), pp. 33–46.

Bourn, D. (2015) *The Theory and Practice of Development Education*. Abingdon: Routledge.

DFES (2000, 2005–2nd edn) *Developing a Global Dimension to the School Curriculum*. London: DFES.

Hanvey, R. (1976) *An Attainable Global Perspective*. Denver: Center for Teaching International Relations.

Harrison, D. (2008) Oxfam and the Rise of Development Education in England from 1959 to 1979. Unpublished PhD. London: Institute of Education.

Hartmeyer, H. (2008) *Experiencing the World Global Learning in Austria: Developing, Reaching Out, Crossing Borders*. Münster: Waxmann.

Hartmeyer, H. and Wegimont, L. (eds) (2016) *Global Education in Europe Revisited- Straties and Structures, Policy, Practice and Challenges*. Münster: Waxmann.

Hicks, D. (2003) Thirty Years of Global Education, *Education Review*, 55 (3), pp. 265–75.

Ishii, Y. (2003) *Development Education in Japan: A Comparative Analysis of the Contexts for Its Emergence, and Its Introduction into the Japanese School System*. London: RoutledgeFalmer.

Kirkwood-Tucker, T. F. (ed.) (2009) *Visions in Global Education*. New York: Peter Lang.

Landorf, H. (2009) Toward a Philosophy of Global Education. In: Kirkwood-Tucker, T. F. (ed.) *Visions in Global Education: The Globalization of Curriculum and Pedagogy in Teacher Education and Schools – Perspectives from Canada, Russia, and the United States*. New York: Peter Lang, 47–67.

Lissner, J. (1977) *Politics of Altruism, Study of the Political Behaviour of Voluntary Development Agencies*. Geneva: Lutheran World Federation.

Marshall, H. (2007) Global Education in Perspective: Fostering a Global Dimension in an English Secondary School. *Cambridge Journal of Education*, 37 (3), pp. 355–74.

McAuley, J. (ed.) (2018) *The State of Global Education*. Dublin: GENE.

McAuley, J. and Wegimont, L. (eds) (2018) *Global Education in Cyprus- The European Peer Review Process*. Dublin: GENE.

Merryfield, M. (2009) Moving the Center of Global Education: From Imperial Worldviews that Divide the World to Double Consciousness, Contrapuntal Pedagogy, Hybridity, and Cross-Cultural Competence. In: Kirkwood-Tucker, T. F. (ed.) *Visions in Global Education*. New York: Peter Lang, 215–39.

Mesa, M. (2011) Evolution and Future Challenges of Development Education. *Education Research Global*, 0, pp. 141–60.

Multi-Stakeholder Forum (2005) *The European Consensus on Development: The Contribution of Development Education and Awareness Raising*. Brussels: DEEEP.

Mundy, K. (2007) *Charting Global Education in Canada's Elementary Schools: Provincial, District and School Level Perspectives*. Toronto: OISEUT/UNICEF.

Noh, J.-E. (2018) Global Citizenship Education in South Korea: The Roles of NGOs in Cultivating Global Citizens. In: Petersen, A., Stahl, G. and Soong, H. (eds) *The Palgrave Handbook of Citizenship and Education*. London: Palgrave, 1–17.

O'Loughlin, E. and Wegimont, L. (2009) *Global Education in Norway-GENE Peer Review*. Amsterdam: GENE.

Petersen, A. and Warwick, P. (2015) *Global Learning and Education*. Abingdon: Routledge.

Pike, G. and Selby, D. (1988) *Global Teacher, Global Learner*. Sevenoaks: Hodder & Stoughton.

Scheunpflug, A. (2012) Identity and Ethics in Global Education, Becoming a Global Citizen. In: Jasskelained, L., Kaivola, T., O'Loughlin, E., Wegimont, L. (eds) *Proceedings of the International Symposium on Competencies of Global Citizens*. Amsterdam: GENE, 31–9.

Tarozzi, M. and Torres, C. (2016) *Global Citizenship Education and the Crises of Multiculturalism*. London: Bloomsbury.

Tye, K. (ed.) (1990) *Global Education: From Thought to Action Alexandria*. Virginia: ASCD.

Wegimont, L. (2016) Global Education: Paradigm Shifts, Policy Contexts, Conceptual Challenges and a new Model for Global Education. In: Hartmeyer, H. and Wegimont, L. (ed.) *Global Education in Europe Revisited*. Münster: Waxmann, 225–42.

Chapter 3

Global Education in Europe: From Genesis to Theory and a New Model for Critical Transformation

Liam Wegimont

Introduction

Global education (GE) in Europe has come a long way in the almost two decades since the Maastricht Congress in 2001. It has grown in scope and reach, in practice, policy and in research. Then it was led by tiny minorities within development non-governmental organizations (NGDOs), environmental NGOs or human rights organizations, along with a handful of teachers and other educators and a few policy-makers. Since then, it has moved from the margins to the mainstream in international relations, development discourse and increasingly in educational policy and research (Bourn, 2015). There is also a growing research base, as can be seen in this volume and in the work of ANGEL – the Academic Network on Global Education and Learning.[1]

Nevertheless, the concept of GE has been critiqued, while in recent years other, competing umbrella terms have emerged such as education for sustainable development (ESD) or global citizenship education (GCE). The activist, engaged, advocating work of GE – both in its initiation with NGOs and civil society and in its emergence within the work of international organizations and institutions – has been its strength, but may also lead to structural weakness. The same may be equally true of other umbrella concepts currently in vogue. The way in which policy, practice and research have been and are being developed may contain some unquestioned assumptions and unseen anomalies that could prove to be fatal flaws, if not addressed. Whichever term is preferred, there is the need to ask deep and fundamental questions about the nature of GE, and about the inherent contradictions in the way in which it is conceptualized. This chapter seeks to address some of these issues, in order to propose a model for developing theory from policy and practice in GE.

---

[1] See https://angel-network.net/ (last accessed 1 April 2019).

Global Education and the Maastricht definition – Genesis and genealogy

The Maastricht definition of GE states,

> Global education is education that opens people's eyes to the realities of the world, and awakens them to bring about a world of greater justice, equity and human rights for all.

> Global Education is understood to encompass Development Education, Human Rights Education, Education for Sustainability; Environmental Education; Peace Education; Intercultural Education; and the global dimensions of Education for Citizenship.[2] (see Wegimont (2002) and O'Loughlin and Wegimont (2003))

Let's begin with the genesis of the construct of GE – where it came from. Following an initial brief and provisional outline of the construct of GE, this section describes these fields, in a narrative, genealogical, paradigmatic fashion,[3] based on the authors' experience over three decades of GE practice, advocacy and engagement in policy processes at a national (Irish), European and global level. I will explore the advent, genesis and history of the field, before moving to identify some structural issues and challenges.

This methodology is informed by the hermeneutics of the imagination as described by the Irish philosopher Richard Kearney, building on the work of the French philosopher of critical hermeneutics, Paul Ricoeur. Kearney, in his monumental work on the history of Western conceptions of creativity (1988: 16–17), outlines his own method thus: 'The hermeneutic method used in this study ... we would call this method genealogical. Every concept tells a story. ... We should also add that this genealogical reading is paradigmatic. This means that our analysis proceeds less in terms of a singular linear history than in terms of a number of "paradigm shifts" which signal decisive mutations in the human understanding' of the phenomenon under consideration. I return to questions of methodology in a later section.

The global education construct – An initial outline

GE as a construct per se emerged in a definite way in Europe in preparation for and follow up to the United Nations Conference on Environment and Development, which took place in Rio de Janeiro in 1992. Here, through a parallel NGO Global Forum which brought together development and environment NGOs from around the world, it became clear that the concerns of sustainable

---

[2] This definition was first proposed by the current author in 2000, by the Global Education Week network Council of Europe, in 2001, and was subsequently adopted, the GENE network, and adapted and adopted as the basis for the Maastricht Declaration on Global Education in November 2002.

[3] See also Ricoeur (2004), particularly 'Interpretation in History', pp. 333–42, and in particular Ricoeur's notion of 'good subjectivity'. See also the debate between Kearney and Ricoeur in Kearney (2004: 48), where Ricoeur suggests that 'there is more in the past than what happened. And so we have to find *the future of the past,* the unfulfilled potential of the past' (emphasis in original).

environmental education and the concerns of development education (DE) overlapped; that there were common concerns, common local and global agendas, and common (as well as diverse) methodologies; but that there were uncommon constituencies, national and international forums, sources of funding and areas of power and influence.

Those involved in bringing together the concerns of environmental education and DE began to recognize the duplication of effort. Strategies for integration into curricula had been developed independently, sometimes with environmental and development educators competing for curricular space in already packed curricula; competing for funding, policy support and official recognition; or independently learning lessons and devising strategies which might, perhaps, more readily have been achieved together. In each case these 'educational' interests within the 'larger movements' of environmentalism and global development were a minority interest, and also might be considered to be on the most critical edge of their respective movements.

It also became clear that similar incongruities existed, not only between DE and environmental education but also between a number of interrelated fields of educational advocacy for social change, local and global: human rights education, development education, environmental education, intercultural education, peace education, education for sustainability and the global dimensions of education for citizenship.

Each of these areas had much in common. Each was focused on education for social change in favour of greater justice, local and global. Each had grown a committed, highly skilled and strategic advocacy base among educators internationally. Many were networked effectively at national, regional and even global level. Some had effectively lobbied for structures of support and funding from within particular line ministries devoted to international development (from Ministries of Foreign Affairs), to human rights (from Ministries of Justice or the Interior), to environment (from Environment Ministries) and so on – or within development NGOs or broader civil society movements. Some had even achieved limited support from ministries of education or educational NGOs.

Yet there was little communication and networking across the boundaries between these different arenas. With some notable exceptions development education, human rights education and so on worked as subsets of the particular social change movements from whence they had been born, with a paucity of reference to one another as educational movements or areas of educational advocacy.

Growing recognition of the incongruity of this situation, captured well in Robin Richardson's parable of Elephant Education (Richardson, 1990), led to strengthening commitment to drawing together the strategies and skills of these competing areas of common educational concern, led, by the mid-1990s, in Europe at least,[4] to the development of the GE construct.

In the mid- to late-1990s a number of European practitioners, policy-makers and engaged theorists, sharing this concern, came together. Facilitated by the North–South Centre of the Council of Europe, they engaged in a process to develop a Global Education Charter.[5] The purpose of this

---

[4] The history of the similarly named concept in North America is very different.

[5] The author was involved in the formulation of the Global Education Charter as part of the Global Education Advisory Committee of the North–South Centre of the Council of Europe in the late 1990s. I was also involved in a critical analysis of the Charter as part of an external evaluation. See 'Evaluation of the Global Education and Youth programme of the North South Centre'. Wegimont, L. 1997, NSC, Lisbon. This document concluded that the

initiative was to define GE in a way that was both politically and practically fruitful. This Charter was strong on process but ultimately was limited in product (Wegimont, 1997). There was also deep and detailed criticism from both the DE and the human rights education (HRE) communities. Nevertheless, through this and other processes initiated in the mid-1990s, the construct of GE began to achieve wider parlance in some countries in Europe. The definition, informed by the work of the Global Education Advisory Committee of the Council of Europe's North–South Centre, was proposed by the current author, to the Global Education Week network in 2001 (Wegimont, 2002). It was adapted and adopted by that network, which involved national activists leading Global Education Week in a growing number of European countries. It was then further adapted and used as the basis for discussion for the preparatory Working Group of the Maastricht Congress, and adopted by the Congress, which comprised governments, parliamentarians, civil society organizations and local authorities form over 40 European countries, in November 2002, as the definition of the Maastricht Declaration (O'Loughlin and Wegimont, 2003). This definition has been used by both GENE and the North–South Centre of the Council of Europe in the intervening period.

Since then, GE has come increasingly to be understood as an umbrella term for the varieties of education for social change towards greater justice, local and global. I use the definition of GE contained in the Maastricht Declaration on GE (2002). I use this construct as my initial provisional understanding of GE for a number of reasons – biographical, conceptual and strategic.

Global education – Considerations biographical, conceptual and strategic

I use the construct because it was born, in conversation with others, out of my own policy engagement, practice and theoretical reflection. Along with others, we developed this definition, based on the experience of doing DE, HRE and environmental education with children, young people, adult learners, and their organizations, in a number of European countries, in Europe and globally, and also informed by the experience of developing or seeking to influence policy at national, European and UN levels in related areas.

It should be recalled that the definition was embedded in a political declaration that had been agreed, in the political context of the Council of Europe, by ministries and agencies, civil society structures, local and regional authorities, and parliamentarians, and with strong engagement by leading academics in the field and with other international organizations. It was based on developing political consensus for growth in the field, and led to the development of a number of

process of formulation of the GE charter was highly constructive for the conceptualization of Global Education in Europe, but the Charter itself was of limited political or policy-making use. Learning from this process informed the development of the Maastricht Declaration and of the GENE network. The journey of developing this concept was always a communal one, informed by colleagues such as Helmuth Hartmeyer, Luisa Teotonia Pereira, Arnfinn Nygaard, Doug Bourn, Annette Scheunpflug, Susanne Hoeck, Claudia Bergmüller, Gregor Lang-Wojtasik, Julia Franz, Louise Hauxthausen, Henny Helmich, Norbert, Noisser, Eddie O'Loughlin, Elisabeth Van Der Steenhoven, Anita Reddy, Christian Sundgren, Alessio Surian, Antonio Torres, Christian Wilmsen, Liisa Jaaskalinen and many other colleagues from GENE.

national strategic initiatives engaging a variety of stakeholders. It was also adopted by the GENE – Global Education Network Europe – network and by the North–South Centre of the Council of Europe; in their work of policy networking between ministries and agencies and national activists, respectively. So, as one of the initial authors/propagators of the definition, informed by many others, I have a *biographical* stake in its development.

I also choose what has become known as the Maastricht definition of GE for *conceptual* reasons. It contains within it a balance. This balance captures, on the one hand, a focus on the core meaning of the concept – the critical educational process, the core content, the justice-focused values base and the clear political commitment of GE. On the other hand, the concept carries within it a strategic, synthetic, 'gathering forces' intent – to bring together what had been previously developed, and considered, separately. This conceptual balancing act of the definition is, for me, part of the allure of the tension and the depth of the Maastricht definition of GE.

Finally, I chose, and have chosen, this definition for *strategic* reasons. The Maastricht definition should be read, in my view, according to the hermeneutical understanding of Paul Ricoeur, in regard to not only the 'meaning behind the text' but also the 'meaning in front of the text' (Ricoeur, 1981). A text, political or otherwise, may have authorial intention behind it, and may carry political weight; we tend to ask – 'what did the authors mean?' But, according to Ricoeur, what is also as instructive is the way in which a text functions as it goes out into the world, beyond the intentions of the authors, to the interpretation and action of the reader. How has this text, this concept, gathered meaning in the world? What are, and have been, the implications of this definition for national policy and strategy, for the practice and for theory? What is the effect on the world of this text? From my perspective, the definition has worked well in strengthening the policy networking, the practice, the theory and the research of GE (Bourn, 2015; Scheunpflug and Rainer 2017; Hartmeyer and Wegimont, 2016; Hartmeyer and McAuley, 2017; McAuley, 2018).

So, I choose the Maastricht Declaration as my starting point, conscious of my own biographical engagement in its development (and therefore possible short-sightedness regarding some dimensions), and also that it is a definition in progress.

Global Education – Initial analysis and meaning in front of the text

Now back to the definition itself:

> Global education is education that opens people's eyes to the realities of the world, and awakens them to bring about a world of greater justice, equity and human rights for all.

> Global Education is understood to encompass Development Education, Human Rights Education, Education for Sustainability; Environmental Education; Peace Education; Intercultural Education; and the global dimensions of Education for Citizenship.[6]

---

[6] As mentioned above, this definition was first proposed by the current author in 2000, was adopted by the Global Education Advisory Committee North–South Centre, Council of Europe, in 2001, and subsequently adopted by the

So, key dimensions of the content/process element of the definition include understandings of the world, of education and of the relationships between the two.

Its dimensions include

- The real world
- Realities of the world
- Education as an eye-opening process
- Education as awakening
- Education as commitment, not only to learning about the world as it is but also to learning about how to change the world, and in particular directions
- Education has effects in the real world
- Justice, equity, human rights are not just concepts to be learnt about but possibilities to be brought about, in the face of injustice and inequality and lack of and denial of human rights
- 'For all people …' – this definition involves a universal pledge

Meanwhile, the synthetic/bringing together dimension of the definition is clear: understanding GE as an umbrella term for all the other varieties of education for social change, local and global, mentioned. This is also clearly with intent – as silo-ization of differing types of GE persist.

GE, like many umbrella terms, suffers from a certain vacuous ambiguity. While this emptiness has proved useful politically and strategically, in bringing together other, at times competing definitions, herein lies both its strength and its weakness. The definition relies on the varieties of educational practice – DE, HRE and so on that it brings together, to provide detailed content. As Argentinean educationalist Dr Alicia Cabezudo points out, it can also be accused of lacking what she describes as a clear outline of the 'non-negotiables' – that is, what is it that, without which, makes an educational practice not GE (Wegimont, 2002). Bourn, on the other hand, suggests that this understanding of GE is a 'different approach' to that of Pike and Selby, who emphasize systemic thinking and interdependence (Bourn, 2008). This umbrella term may be accused of being more synthetic.

Nevertheless, in spite of the limitations the idea developed, and the GE construct has led to the development of a number of structures, programmes and processes, at both European and national level, devoted to broadening the learning between the varieties of education for social change, local and global, that GE encompasses. It has proven useful in the promotion of structures of support, policy learning frameworks, and increased political support and funding in Europe in the past decade. It has been used as the overarching concept by the GENE network[7] for promoting policy learning across borders in Europe, between ministries and agencies with national responsibility for this and related fields. It has been the umbrella term which has enabled the European GE Peer Review process to both affirm and seek to improve national policy, coordination, support, funding and provision in this and related fields in many European

---

Global Education Week network, by the GENE network, and adapted and adopted as the basis for the Maastricht Declaration on Global Education in November 2002.

[7] www.gene.eu (last accessed 24 February 2019).

countries as diverse as Cyprus and Finland, Austria and Portugal, Ireland and Slovakia, Belgium and the Czech Republic, Poland and Norway. It has also been used to ensure that national policy learning could be shared across borders, and across differing though related terminologies that are nationally favoured and linguistically flavoured. This has been possible without in any way undermining the diversity of usage, as, in some countries in Europe, the terms 'development education', 'education for development' or 'global development education' continue to be the national terminology of choice.

The language of the Maastricht definition was complimented by what I have described elsewhere as the 'ultimate horizon of the work' – 'Working towards the day when all people in Europe, in solidarity with peoples globally, will have access to quality global education'. It has provided a common language for the development of national strategies in a growing number of European countries that focus on quality and reach, but that have what I have described elsewhere as a 'universalist, rights-based approach'. This language was developed consciously at the time of the Maastricht Declaration, based on related international processes, including the Aarhus Convention of the Right of Access to Information, Public Participation in decision-making and access to justice in environmental issues, and the work of the United Nations Educational, Scientific and Cultural Organization (UNESCO) on the right to human rights education; both of which were effecting policy-making in related fields at the time, and provided strong policy-effect models.

The definition has also proved useful at the national level and not only at the level of policy learning across borders. It is my contention that the Maastricht definition has proved useful for:

- The strengthening or emergence of combining practice in countries as diverse as Austria, Cyprus, the Czech Republic, Finland, Poland, Portugal, and Slovakia;
- The development of national strategies, and the inclusion of benchmarking at national and sectoral level in a number of countries;
- Development of the European Peer Review process – allowing for the specificity of national situations, the identification of good practice and policy learning at national level across boundaries and sectors and at international level across borders;
- The sharing of research across disciplines and interdisciplinary fields and languages;
- The possibility of developing pan-European policy learning initiatives, respecting national particularities and differing educational systems, while enabling a common policy language to emerge;
- The possibility of gathering data and evidence regarding the state of policy and practice in the field (e.g. through the now annual State of Global Education in Europe reports) (Hartmeyer and Wegimont) (2016); Hartmeyer and McAuley ((2017) and McAuley (2018)).

So I suggest that the concept has proved useful in practice, policy development, policy learning and research. Nevertheless, given what has been written above, particularly about the biographical, there is a need to consider this concept more critically, and before any further critical analysis, to turn to methodological concerns. In the next section we move from this consideration of GE as a concept to consider a methodology for approaching the challenge of developing theory from policy and practice in the field.

Methodological considerations – Proposing a hermeneutical methodology for developing theory from practice and policy in global education, drawing on the work of Paul Ricoeur

For thirty years I have been involved in the practice of GE. I have also been involved in policy-making, development of the field, reflection on practice, evaluation and the creation of policy frameworks, policy learning and policy networking in the field. I have been professionally responsible – for better or worse, in failure and mistake and sometimes success – for some of the national and international initiatives that may have contributed to where the field finds itself today. I have also, throughout, been involved in theoretical and academic debates in the field. Since 1995 I have been critiquing the lack of theory, the sometime anti-theoretical bias of the field (Wegimont, 1995). At the same time, I have continued to lobby for more, while seeking for better. I have been involved and continue to be involved (see Wegimont, 2007).

How, then, to create a model of GE that reflects on practice, is accurate to the history of the conceptual development of the field, is adequate and appropriate, and has a sound theoretical basis? And how can a critical model be proposed by one who is so involved? A plethora of recent philosophical considerations and ideas, from Antonio Gramsci's notion of the organic intellectual (Gramsci, 1971) to Michel Foucault's analysis of the relationship of knowledge and power – along with contemporary philosophy of science, contemporary education theory, action research, participatory appraisal, etc. – have in various ways discredited the notion that there is a necessary dichotomy between the engaged activist and the neutral, objective, scientific observer. This false opposition is one of those that Paul Ricoeur also seeks to counter.[8] Nevertheless,

the question of engaged theory raises further methodological issues and requires a turn to the question of methodology. The methodology I propose for developing theory from policy and practice draws heavily on the philosophical anthropology and hermeneutical work of the French post-structuralist philosopher Paul Ricoeur, and is also influenced by readings of Ricoeur in conversation with others in contemporary European continental philosophy, and by readings of Ricoeur by others, most notably the Irish philosopher Richard Kearney (Kearney, 1986, 1989, 1991, 2004).

We have begun in the last section to look at the concept of GE. Our work starts with histories, or traditions, of varieties of GE. According to Ricoeur,

A tradition remains living … only if it continues to be held in an unbroken process of reinterpretation … only if it continues to form a partnership with innovation. … With regard to innovation, an important aspect of the rereading and reappraisal of transmitted traditions … consists in discerning past promises which have not been kept. Indeed, the past is not only what is bygone – that which has taken place and can no longer be changed – it also lives in the memory thanks to the arrows of futurity which have not been fired or whose trajectory

---

[8] 'Ricoeur does not oppose the stereotype of a neutral social science with the opposite stereotype of a partisan science, but rather with an original hermeneutic theory of personal engagement.' Jervelino (1996: 75).

has been interrupted. The unfulfilled future of the past forms perhaps the richest part of our tradition. (Ricoeur, 1996: 8)

It should be pointed out that the methodology is also heavily influenced by Richard Kearney's methodological journey, in his monumental opus *The Wake of Imagination: Ideas of Creativity in Western Culture* (1988). In particular, his emphasis on moving through deconstruction to reconstruction, from a hermeneutics of suspicion to a hermeneutics of affirmation, and from a praxis of engagement through a theoria of genealogical paradigms to a poetics of the possible, all have been influential on the current proposal regarding how we might move to a deeper theory and praxis of GE.

The methodology I propose, drawing also heavily on Ricoeur, is one which moves from initial interpretation, an outlining of the genealogy and the species or genus of things (first section, Global Education and the Maastricht Definition – Genesis and Genealogy). Starting with the phenomenological, we must move from a recollection of the genesis or genealogy of the concept, through a hermeneutics of suspicion – examining the depth structures, hidden meanings, internal contradictions and aporias inherent in the order of things or in the way in which we order things.[9]

Here, taking Ricoeur's analysis of 'meaningful action considered as a text', we consider the underlying meaning of some of the issues emerging, not only in terms of the 'meaning behind' the initiatives and issues. (We can be fairly assured that those involved in GE are not in it for the fame or fortune, but have good and trustworthy intentions.) However, the intention, the meaning behind the text, is, as mentioned above, only half the story. What is perhaps even more interesting, and more fruitful in terms of textual interpretation, and, by extension, the interpretation of meaningful action, is that which Ricoeur describes as the 'meaning in front of the text'. Meaningful action, like written texts, carries in front of it a meaning beyond the intention of the author/actor; the effects of the action, as it goes out into the world, how the action is read by and responded to by others, this is where we may find both the hidden contradictions that enable more in-depth analysis and insight and the germs of reinterpretation, regeneration.

In order to arrive at more in-depth meanings, we must take detours. A full-frontal approach is not always the way to achieve understanding. We are, were, have been and will be engaged in this field. There is nothing wrong with this, indeed, there is no other place to start but from human engagement in a field. The problem this throws up, however, is, put simply: How do we know what we own as our own to be true, and how do we achieve enough critical distance to gain a deeper truth?

Here it is also instructive to draw on Ricoeur, and in particular the concepts of *appropriation* and *distanciation*.

We are considering in this work the texts and the meaningful actions of GE– in terms of practice, reflection on practice, policy initiatives and frameworks – in an effort to gain deeper and more meaningful understanding. The first moments in this movement have the characteristic of readings of the foundational texts of the area. This history is our own, we have already been engaged with it, but we reread it again, creating anew the tradition, refreshing it, making the (recent, yet nonetheless historical) tradition once again contemporary. This moment in the

---

[9] 'In the social sciences we proceed from naive interpretations to critical interpretations, from surface interpretations to depth interpretations through structural analysis' Ricoeur (1981: 220).

movement towards understanding is usefully adumbrated by the hermeneutical concept of appropriation. It is worth citing Ricoeur at length:

> 'Appropriation' is my translation of the German term Aneignung. Aneignung means 'to make one's own what was initially "alien". ... According to the intention of the word, the aim of all hermeneutics is to struggle against cultural distance and historical alienation. Interpretation brings together, equalises, renders contemporary and similar.'(Ricoeur, 1981: 185)

So appropriation is about owning the past; but if appropriation is about elaborating things past and making them present, it is also about playing with the surface meaning in order to find a deeper meaning. If appropriation is about owning the meaning, it is 'also and primarily about letting go' (Ricoeur, 1981: 193). The moment of appropriation renders unhidden the hidden and also acknowledges the possibility of the 'conflict of interpretations' (Ricoeur, 1981) and at the same time the impossibility of absolute knowledge.

So if we belong to the tradition of GE, we must, however, also move away from it, gain perspective, enlarge our frame of reference, if we are to be anything other than ideological, and if we are to move from explanation to critical understanding. According to Ricoeur, critique requires a movement from proximity to distance. I am and have been deeply involved in this field; I must draw back, in order to gain deeper insight and understanding. 'Critique rests on the moment of distanciation. ... The concept of distanciation is the dialectical counterpart of the notion of belonging, in the sense that we belong to a historical tradition through a relation of distance which oscillates between remoteness and proximity' (Ricoeur, 1991b: 25). Distanciation, following appropriation, is what we are at here.

Thus, the interplay of appropriation and distanciation leads us, on the one hand, to the recognition of both the anomalies and inherent contradictions in the field, and the deep weaknesses inherent in what passes for theorizing in the field, and on the other hand, to the question of the need for theory, and the sources of deeper theory and a more adequate model.

The questions raised lead to the articulation of foundational questions, which require deeper exploration. If the first section, Global Education and the Maastricht Definition – Genesis and Genealogy, is *genealogical*, we need to move to the *archaeological* – uncovering sources for an adequate and appropriate foundation for an emerging critical theory of GE. But if this is, in hermeneutical terms, an archaeological moment, it is also teleological moment, as we move from a hermeneutics of suspicion to a teleology of affirmation. For Ricoeur, unlike some others, the moment of deconstruction must be followed by a moment of reconstruction. If we need to be deconstructive, we also need to be reconstructive – to propose foundations for adequate and appropriate theories of GE, and propose sources for the construction of a more adequate model.

Ricoeur articulates the possibilities of such models. Drawing on a number of authors in the field of model theory, Ricoeur summarizes their work by saying that 'models are to certain forms of scientific discourse what fictions are to certain forms of poetic discourse. The trait common to models and to fictions is their heuristic force, that is to say, their capacity to open and unfold new dimensions of reality by means of our suspension of disbelief in an earlier description' (Ricoeur, 1991a: 168–87 and 175). A model allows us to see what is and what is not, enables us to determine the important dimensions of things in their manifold relations and the ways in which they interrelate. It enables practice to build theory, and theory to inform practice.

The next section provides a framework for integrating necessary philosophical and theoretical perspectives into a more appropriate and adequate model of GE – one which, I suggest, might enable the synthesis of a variety of schools of thought in the development of necessary dimensions of the model – alternate ontologies, epistemologies, philosophical sociologies; competing schools of thought on international relations; divergent ethics; disagreeing sociologies of education; and varying curricular and pedagogical perspectives. Such a model provides a space not for consensus – which has gained the field political credibility and integration, but at the expense of conceptual clarity and development – and instead provides a framework for what Lyotard terms 'paralogy'. It may be time to move from consensus to dissensus.

> Theories are no more than dissimulated narratives that should not be allowed to be omnitemporal. Therefore, to have constructed a narrative, at some point, which has come to assume the figure of a seamless system, in no way removes the task of starting all over here and now. (Lyotard, 1977: 29)

So we will now move from appropriation to distanciation, from an initial outline and ownership of the term 'Global Education' to a more critical analysis, particularly highlighting a number of contradictions, of aporias, of unquestioned assumptions that underlie the concept.

Global education and related constructs such as ESD and GCED – Some limitations, contradictions, anomalies, aporias

I should start by suggesting that while this summary outline of critical questions and the structural limitations arising from practice, from policy and from research is focused on GE, I would contend that some of the internal contradictions are equally evidenced in other tributary fields of GE (e.g. DE, HRE). Furthermore, as other umbrella terms such as ESD, GCE and so on, each with their own traditions and advocating international organizations, currently vie for our attention and policy commitment, I would respectfully suggest that the self-same internal contradictions and aporias, albeit in different forms and with different nuances, are present and need to be considered.

Looking critically at any of the tributary fields of GE – DE, HRE, intercultural education suggest a number of hidden assumptions, conceptual limitations, contradictions or aporias or structural limitations.

I would suggest the following limitations are among those prevalent in our work:

First Limitation: Concepts arrived at by consensus.

Second Limitation: Lack of critical thought regarding interdisciplinarity and the interdisciplinary nature of the field, leading to interdisciplinary balance.

Third Limitation: Assumed Educational Models.

Fourth Limitation: History of the Field – choosing shallow histories over deeper histories.

Fifth Limitation: Assumptions regarding the nature of the individual.

Sixth Limitation: Assumptions regarding the nature of human knowledge, understanding and interpretation.

Seventh Limitation: Assumptions regarding the nature of Social Change.

Eight Limitation: Assumptions regarding the relationship of the individual to society, and of individual action to social change and of action to learning and to identity.

Ninth Limitation: Assumptions regarding the nature of curriculum, of what learners need to know and of how we choose what we need to know.

Tenth Limitation: Assumptions regarding pedagogical choices, how we decide how learning should be structured, and how decisions are made regarding how educators structure learning.

While it is beyond the scope of this chapter to deal adequately with every one of these limitations, here I will deal with a small sample.

First Limitation: Definition and consensus

The fact that there is a diversity of traditions within GE is seen by many practitioners as strength to be built upon, and yet there is increasing overlap. The question of course is not 'which tradition?', but how do we mediate between differing traditions in GE. And with the recent growth in interest in a number of related umbrella terms, such as ESD, GCED and so on, the question also becomes how do we chose between competing umbrella terms.

Such a question cannot be adequately answered, beyond going around in circles or limiting oneself to pragmatic or political considerations, without some recourse to a theoretical framework. Theory is required. Furthermore, the history of defining and consensual processes for arriving at agreed useable definitions, while politically and strategically useful up until now, has led to a stultifying of debate, dissent, 'dissensus' and the development of differing schools of thought in GE. We require what Jean Francois Lyotard describes as 'paralogy'.[10] Not monologue but many, parallel, competing dialogues and trialogues.

Second Limitation: Lack of critical thought regarding interdisciplinarity and the interdisciplinary nature of the field, leading to interdisciplinary balance.

A detailed analysis of the genesis of GE and its varieties of forms suggests that it has suffered from an over-reliance on one parent discipline, and in each case, the discipline other than education. Check out the potted histories that are available, for example, in the histories that preface textbooks. DE histories start with 'development' in the 1960s or 1970s. HRE histories start with the Universal Declaration. It is somewhat remarkable to discover that one discipline in an interdisciplinary field – education – is neglected in favour of the more recent field. That education is discovered to be the neglected parent in each of these areas may come as news, but is not terribly surprising – particularly given that the genesis of these types of education in each case was based on the notion of education as some sort of harbinger, or, what I term 'education as messenger-boy'. Education started life in these areas as the conduit or 'popularizer' for the serious stuff of the other discipline or activities, and so it sometimes remains.

But if it is not surprising, it is a serious strategic mistake. The global resources – human, intellectual, theoretical, historical, even financial – of education are far greater than those of any of the other disciplines – development, human rights, environmental studies. But beyond this self-evident truth, in this issue we remain at the level of oversimplification. In any question regarding the appropriate balance between, or the proper relationship between, differing disciplines, in an interdisciplinary or transdisciplinary field, we must have recourse to a theoretical framework,

---

[10] Lyotard (1977).

and at the very least be informed by debates in regard to interdisciplinarity in other related fields. Theory is required.

Limitation Three: Assumed educational models

A third limitation that I mention is the fact that GE, variously understood, works on the basis of assumed, rather than chosen, debated or appropriate models of education. For many years, the assumption that the 'concepts, skills, attitudes' trichotomy is the only model available by which to order our understanding of learning is just one example of this. More recently, the enthusiasm for embracing a competency-based approaches, informed perhaps as much by public sector reform movements as from any solid educational model or philosophy, while framed at times as a response to the inadequacies of the 'concepts, skills, attitudes' model, is, from another vantage point, just more of the same: an unreflected model of education, transposed into the field of GE, without adequate reflection regarding the appropriateness or adequacy of such a model to the field. I believe that this widespread perspective, and the practice on which it is based, not only is mistaken – we're hitching our wagon to the wrong star (Wegimont, 2004) – but also more or less ensures that our practice is counterproductive. To overcome this, theory is required (educational theory!).

Limitation Four: History

The Irish playwright Brian Friel once commented that 'to remember everything is a form of madness', and histories are both constructed and chosen, be it wisely and sagaciously or in a totalizing or schizophrenic manner. It's the way that histories of DE, HRE and so on are constructed that concerns us here. It is surprising with the depth and richness of the human history of struggle for greater justice, freedom, and all human rights for all, and with the equally rich histories of education and learning that preceded, enabled, empowered, recorded, retold, re-embodied and reinvented anew such histories; that those creating the (albeit potted) histories of these fields should choose such arbitrary and recent phenomenon as the signing of the Universal Declaration or the 'birth of development'. While this of course could be interpreted as an example of the disciplinary imbalance mentioned above, it also makes no sense from a historiographical point of view. Why choose the lesser resources of the flimsy or quasi-disciplines that are decades young and, in the case of development, highly questionable, when we can tap into the intellectual resources of millennia? In each case, what has happened is that the brief history contains within it a null curriculum and a hidden curriculum – masking what is omitted. The only way to counter the predominance of forgetfulness and the refusal to consider deeper histories is by bringing these issues to light and turning them into a problematic; and the only way to address this problematic is with recourse to a theoretical framework and some understanding of the construction of history. Again, theory is required.

As can be seen from each of the very brief samples of the limitations outlined above, not only is GE plagued with some internal contradictions, but, in each case, the way forward requires theory.

We now come to the heart of the matter; theory is missing from GE, either through a commitment to the achievement of a consensus of understanding in the use of the terms 'development education', 'human rights education' or 'global education' and so on (leading to normative defining and the reification of agreed definitions, and thereby stultifying the possibility of the development of competing theories, dialectical exchange or the emergence of schools of thought in the field) or through an explicit anti-theoretical bias. To counter these directions theory is required. Of course, we need theory that is 'grounded' in the practice of past decades, but also in the theoretical traditions and reflections of practice of education for freedom and justice developed over centuries and millennia.

But what theory is required and where shall theory be found? In the next sections we turn to outline some proposal in regard to the dimensions of the theory needed, which are and make some tentative proposals for the dimensions of such a model and the research agenda that might follow.

Proposing the foundational philosophical questions for a more adequate model of global education

In this section we move beyond critique of prevailing conceptions in GE, to examine some philosophical foundations – foundations that are necessary for GE, if the field is to overcome the various anomalies outlined in previous chapters.[11]

Which philosophical foundations? While this question could be approached from a myriad of angles, what we require is philosophical foundations which are *adequate* to the scope of the field, *appropriate* for the nature of the field and which provide all necessary dimensions for a well-rounded model of GE. I suggest that there are *eight dimensions* or areas of necessary philosophical foundation, which the field requires.

A well-rounded model of GE must address the question of what it means to be human. GE makes assumptions about how we are as human beings, what it means to be human. A *philosophical anthropology* is required.

GE, as all education, makes assumptions regarding the nature of being and becoming, of existence and of change. A consideration of this field is required, and foundations questions need to be asked and addressed regarding the nature of being and becoming – an *ontology* is required.

All educational fields, and particularly one such as GE, must address the question of the nature of knowledge, of understanding, of interpretation. An adequate model of GE requires access, therefore, to an *epistemology*, some philosophical reflection regarding the nature of human knowledge, of understanding, of truth and of the related area of *hermeneutics*, of how we interpret meaning.

GE often addresses itself to issues that assume positions in regard to good and bad, right and wrong, truth and justice, but often with a basis in assumption rather than reflection. A fourth area of philosophical reflection – ethics – concerns questions of the right and the good, of right and wrong, of justice. An ethical reflection is required; a consideration of *ethics* is required.

GE is concerned with issues of globality, and of the relationships between the individual, the nation state and the global policy. *Geopolitical reflection* in a philosophical vein is required.

---

[11] An earlier version of this proposal appeared in Wegimont, Hartmeyer and Wegimont (2017).

GE also concerns social change – both in regard to the relationship between the individual and society and as regards the individual, education and society. A philosophical *sociology of social change* is required.

As an educational field, philosophical reflection underpinning decisions regarding what is to be learnt, and how we chose what is to be learnt, is required. Again GE and related fields tend to make assumptions regarding the nature of the curriculum, what needs to be kept and what needs to change, without much in the way of deep or deepening the reflection on the nature of how we chose what should be remembered and what should be forgotten, what should be passed on and what should be passed over – a *philosophy of Curriculum*, or at least a foray into the field of philosophical reflection in *Curriculum Studies*, is required.

Finally, all education, and all dimensions of GE, require an adequate understanding of how we choose how to lead and organize learning and how to teach. While GE practitioners and policy-makers may make a clear statement regarding the choice of participative methodologies, the need for pedagogical practices that are democratic and involving and engaging and coherent with the focus and content of GE, and may rely on deeply philosophical approaches to pedagogy, such as the work of Paulo Freire and more recent critical theorists, nevertheless, much decision-making regarding pedagogical principles in GE could be critiqued for being ideological rather than educational – pragmatic rather than based on a well-thought-out philosophy of pedagogical principles. A deeper philosophy of *pedagogical principles*, a 'philosophical pedagogy' for GE is required.

The following table is an overview of the areas of philosophical reflection required:

Table 3.1 Areas of Philosophical Reflection for Global Education

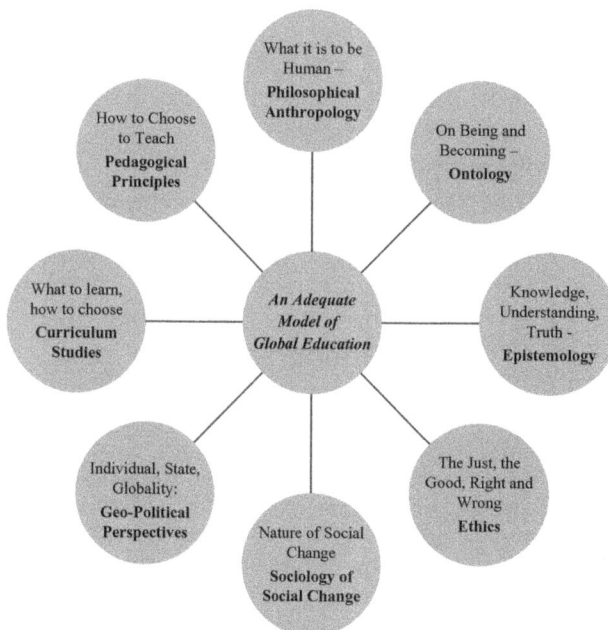

Why are they required? Because, as we have seen above, the field has a number of fault lines or fissures that require response; and unless there is a firm philosophical foundation underpinning each of these areas, a set of assumptions, assumed positions or, in the worst cases, ideologies take the place of philosophical foundations. Not only is it highly questionable (and indeed slightly ironic) that, in a field such as GE, some assumptions or agreed positions take on the character of absolute truths or unquestionable assertions; it is also a prescription for narrow focus, for lack of sustainability, and possibly for counterproductive policy, strategy and educational practice.

Are there only eight areas or foundations required? I chose to focus on eight; I believe this to provide a well-rounded model, which explores all necessary dimensions. And in regard to each while I might argue for a particular thinker, debate, focus or school of thought within the philosophical field to be particularly apt for GE, the point is not to choose one but instead to give access within each of the eight spheres of necessary reflection to possibilities for deepening the reflection and basis through research, dialogue and recourse to theoretical reflection.

This being said, there are, however, certain dimensions which do not fit precisely into such a structure. For example, one area of philosophical concern which cuts across some of the above areas of philosophical reflection, and which is also crucial to a model of GE, involves our understandings of *action, human agency,* and *the relationship between action, education and learning.*

In suggesting such a model, no answers are given. There are manifold ways of addressing each of the domains above, and in some cases competing schools of thought in regard to the way in which the philosophical base should be conceived and how it relates to the person, to education, to social change. Nevertheless, I would respectfully suggest that such a model, or a version thereof, might provide for both a means of addressing the anomalies outlined above and the basis for developing stronger theory from practice, a model of GE more appropriate to the ultimate aims of the field, more adequate policy coherence and a more critical and self-reflective interdisciplinary field.

In conclusion, in this chapter I have outlined the genesis of the concept of GE in Europe, have proposed a methodology for developing theory from practice and policy and have attempted to begin to use that methodology to unearth a number of anomalies inherent in the field. These anomalies have led to a clear need for theory and philosophical reflection. I have proposed a model for developing philosophical foundations in eight dimensions – while hinting at, but without outlining in detail, the research agenda that would emerge – for a more adequate, more reflective and ultimately more transformative model of critical GE.

Bibliography

Bourn, D. (2008) 'Development Education: Towards a Re-conceptualisation', *International Journal of Development Education and Global Learning*, vol. 1, no. 1 (2008), pp. 5–22.

Bourn, D. (2015) *The Theory and Practice of Development Education*. Oxford/New York: Routledge.

Gramsci, A. (1971) 'The Intellectuals', in *Selections from the Prison Notebooks*. Translated and edited by Hoare, Q. and Smith, G. N. New York: International Publishers, pp. 3–23.

Hartmeyer, H. and McAuley, J. (eds) (2017) *The State of Global Education in Europe 2017*. Dublin: GENE.

Hartmeyer, H. and Wegimont, L. (eds) (2016) *The State of Global Education in Europe 2015*. Dublin: GENE.

Hartmeyer, H. and Wegimont, L. (eds) (2017) *Global Education in Europe Revisited: Policy, Practice and Theoretical Challenges*. Münster/New York: Waxmann, 2017.

Jervelino, D. (1996) 'Gadamer and Ricoeur on the Hermeneutics of Praxis', in Kearney, R. (ed.) *Paul Ricoeur: The Hermeneutics of Action*. London: SAGE, p. 75.

Kearney, R. (1986) *Modern Movements in European Philosophy*. Manchester: University Press.

Kearney, R. (1988) *The Wake of Imagination: Ideas of Creativity in Western Culture*. London: Hutchinson.

Kearney, R. (1989) 'Paul Ricoeur and the Hermeneutic Imagination', in Kemp, T. P. and Rasmussen, D. (eds) *The Narrative Path: The Later Works of Paul Ricoeur*. Cambridge: MIT Press, 1–31.

Kearney, R. (1991) *Poetics of Imagining: From Husserl to Lyotard*. London: HarperCollinsAcademic.

Kearney, R. (1996) 'Introduction', in Kearney, R. (ed.) *Paul Ricoeur: The Hermeneutics of Action*. London: SAGE, p. 1.

Kearney, R. (2004) *Debates in Continental Philosophy: Conversations with Contemporary Thinkers*. New York: Fordham.

Lyotard, J. F. (1977) *Instructions Païennes*. Paris: Galilée, 29. Translated by and cited in Kearney, R. (1991) *Poetics of Imagining: From Husserl to Lyotard*. London: HarperCollinsAcademic, pp. 197–8.

McAuley, J. (ed.) (2018) *The State of Global Education in* Europe, *2018*. Dublin: GENE.

O'Loughlin, E. and Wegimont, L. (eds) (2003) *Global Education in Europe to 2015: Strategy, Policies and Perspectives*. Lisbon: North-South Centre.

Richardson, R. (1990) 'Elephant Education', in *Daring to be a Teacher*. Stoke-on-Trent, Trentham Books, pp. 91–2.

Ricoeur, P. (1981) 'The Model of the Text: Meaningful Action Considered as a Text', in Ricoeur, P. (ed.) *Hermeneutics and the Human Sciences*. Cambridge/Paris: Cambridge University Press/Maisons des Sciences de l'Homme, pp. 197–222.

Ricoeur, P. (1991a) 'Imagination in Discourse and Action', in *From Text to Action: Essays in Hermeneutics II*. Translated by Blamey, K. and Thompson, J. B. London: Northwestern University Press; Chicago: Athlone Press, pp. 168–87.

Ricoeur, P. (1991b) 'Phenomenology and Hermeneutics', in *From Text to Action: Essays in Hermeneutics* II. Translated by Blamey, K. and Thompson, J. B. London: Northwestern University Press; Chicago: Athlone Press.

Ricoeur, P. (1996) 'Reflections on a New Ethos for Europe', in Kearney, R. (ed.) *Paul Ricoeur: The Hermeneutics of Action*. Sage: London.

Ricoeur, P. (2004) *Memory, History and Forgetting*. Chicago: University of Chicago Press.

Scheunpflug, A. and Rainer, U. (2017) 'What Do We Know about Global Learning and What Do We Need to Find Out? A Summary of Empirical Evidence', in Hartmeyer, H. and Wegimont, L. (eds) *Global Education in Europe Revisited: Policy, Practice and Theoretical Challenges*. Münster/New York: Waxmann.

Wegimont, L. (1995) 'The Challenge to Develop Theory from Practice in Development Education'. *Address to the NODE (Network of Development Educators) Annual Conference*, Dublin. Dublin: NODE.

Wegimont, L. (1997) *Evaluation of the Global Education and Youth Work Programme of the North South Centre of the Council of Europe*. Lisbon: North-South Centre.

Wegimont, L. (ed.) (2002) *One Sustainable World: Strategies for Increasing and Improving Global Education*. Lisbon: North-South Centre.

Wegimont, L. (2002) 'What is Global Education', in O'Loughlin, E. and Wegimont, L. (eds), *Strategies for Increasing and Improving Global Education*. Lisbon: North-South Centre, pp. 35–42.

Wegimont, L. (2004) 'Hitching Our Wagon to the Wrong Star: Beyond the "Attitudes, Concepts and Skills" Trichotomy and Towards a More Adequate Educational Foundation for Development and Global Education', *The Development Education Journal*, vol. 11, no. 1 (2004). Available at https://think-global.org.uk/wp-content/uploads/dea/documents/dej_11_1_wegimont.pdf, last accessed 11 February 2019.

Wegimont, L. (2007) 'Global Education: Questioning Practice, Turning to Theory, Building Philosophical Foundations', Paper given to the Nurnberg Conference 'Global Education: Practice, Theory and Research'. Fredrich Alexander University, Erlangen-Nurnberg, October 2007.

Wegimont, L. (2017) 'Global Education: Paradigm Shifts, Policy Contexts, Conceptual Challenges and a New Model of Global Education', in Hartmeyer, H. and Wegimont, L. (eds) *Global Education in Europe Revisited: Policy, Practice and Theoretical Challenges*. Münster/New York: Waxmann.

Chapter 4

Evidence and Efficacy: A Compulsion for Global Education?

Annette Scheunpflug

Global education (GE) or global learning deals with sustainability and social equity. In the Maastricht Declaration from 2002, GE is conceptualized as 'education that opens people's eyes and minds to the realities of the world, and awakens them to bring about a world of greater justice, equity and human rights for all' (GENE 2002). This chapter reflects the challenges concerning evidence-based global learning, following the understanding of the Maastricht Declaration. The argumentation calls for evidence and reflects the problems of achieving evidence at the same time. A strategy for this is conceptualized.

The more and more global learning is established in the formal education system and the more and more governments and civil societies invest in GE, the more often the effectiveness and efficiency of these contributions come into consideration. Hence the need to bring evaluation into the discussions. Policy-makers around the world who are supportive of promoting GE seek and need evidence to demonstrate its impact on individuals and communities. By asking 'what works' people reflect educational processes and resources and search for rational governance and intelligent financial decisions for proving its efficacy, in order to enhance quality and give legitimization to this work.

However, besides the need for rationality in a new and prospering field, there is the danger of shortcuts and the problem of what we mean by 'efficient global learning'. An under-complex understanding of global learning might lead to an under-complex understanding of its efficiency. As concepts of global learning reach for a complex understanding of the globalizing world, measuring the evidence and efficacy of global learning might be understood as a compulsion in relation to the objectives linked with this concept. On the one hand, knowing what works would help the field to grow and to enhance a global understanding of the world. On the other hand, awareness of the validity of this knowledge might be appropriate.

This chapter seeks to enlighten the spectrum of options and pitfalls of evidence in global learning. It will first explain what the term 'evidence' means. Second, it will describe why and in which ways global learning is challenged – from the perspective of education and development cooperation – in providing evidence. The main part of this contribution describes the underlying conditions by searching for evidence and related challenges. A reflection of how to be liberated from the assumed compulsion between evidence and global learning summarizes the chapter.

Evidence in global learning: How to make the invisible visible?

How to understand evidence in the field of global learning? Evidence means the reason to believe that something works. It is linked to the understanding that something can be visible even if it is not easy to see, related to the complexity of the situation. The intelligence-service of the Austro-Hungarian dual monarchy was called the 'office of evidence' (Moll 2005; Muigg 2007), and until today the documentation centres of the supreme courts in Austria are called 'offices of evidence'.[1] To look for evidence aims to uncover connections and facts, which are not easily visible in daily life. The understanding of an evidence-based practice was first used in medicine to underline causality between treatment and the recovery process, by providing statistical data. In this way, knowledge about the effects and non-effects of therapies was provided. The concept of evidence expresses the empirical proof of a relationship.

Talking about evidence in global learning therefore seeks the empirical proven relation of a learning input and a learning outcome or – in other words – the impact of activities of global learning. Talking about efficacy then means the use of evidence-proofed forms of learning arrangements. Through evidence, educational practice and educational policies should achieve a solid foundation for decision-making and planning as well as transfer from theory into practice (Davies 1999; Davies, Nutley and Smith, 2004; Schrader 2014). The discourse differs between different levels of evidence: level 1 (as the best grade of evidence) means finding by meta-studies. Meta-studies are summarizing a variety of different studies related to one field. By the systematic compilation of these studies, the findings acquire a high certainty. Level 2 is given by randomized field research. This type of research is characterized as research in real conditions. Some subjects would receive a treatment and others – randomly chosen – not. In order to avoid disturbance through other aspects as given by the treatment (i.e. an intervention of global learning inputs), the number of persons involved and the background variables to be controlled should be taken into consideration. Level 3 of evidence is provided by quasi-experimental studies, for example in a pre-post-design. Comparative and correlative studies show level 4 evidence and the weakest level 5 is shown by single studies (Schrader 2014: 203).

Searching for evidence may strengthen an educational field. It helps to identify relevant knowledge for the implementation of concepts. It supports the professionalization of people working in the field of global learning. It enhances educational practice. It supports decision-making concerning the implementation of innovations and the efficient use of financial and human resources.

Background of the discourse: Why the call for evidence in global learning?

Global learning is expected – more than other forms of learning developed from social movements such as environmental education or human rights education (HRE) – to show evidence and

---

[1] http://www.ogh.gv.at/de/evidenzbuero

efficiency in the sense of a measurable impact in shaping societies. This is linked to the fact that in the discourse of GE, two discourses merge which both have national and international traditions of evaluation and assessments.

One of these sources derives from development cooperation. Since the 1990s, it is standard among donors to reflect on their own work by evaluation and assessment. This standard is internationally ensured, that is, in the so-called Paris Declaration concerning the impact of development cooperation (OECD 2005). These days donor organizations engage evaluation departments, and it was only a question of time before these desks started to spread to development education (DE) in the North and pledged to deliver evaluation and evidence in global learning.

The other strand comes from the international discourse on competence measurement in schools, including large-scale assessments of school performance by competence testing. Although national structures may differ, the common focus is on students' performance as a governance tool enhanced by the commitment of the Organization for Economic Cooperation and Development (OECD) in this area, which proactively offers tools and structures for evidence-based studies in the education sector.

Both strands come together in offerings for global learning. Therefore, it is no coincidence that there has been an intensive debate about quality measurement for more than twenty years. This debate sometimes refers to 'evaluation', sometimes to 'competence measurement' and 'evidence', whereby 'evaluation' tends to subsume praxeological approaches to quality measurement and 'evidence' to science-based approaches, albeit with fluid transitions without a sharp boundary (OECD 2008; Scheunpflug, Bergmüller and Schröck 2010; Bergmüller and Scheunpflug 2017).

Searching for evidence: Operationalizing global learning

When evidence means looking for invisible relationships in order to make them visible, it is very important to know what to look for. What are the elements between invisible relationships which should be made visible? Therefore, the operationalization of fuzzy terms and concepts – global learning is one – is crucial. In the following, the question of how to operationalize global learning in order to seek evidence is dealt with: What should be learned? What should be offered as the learning arrangement? What is the relationship between the learning outcome and the learning arrangement? Evidence-creating research forces the observed complex realities to be transformed into a sharp operationalization, which already by itself enhances discussions. In this way, the spotlight of this approach sheds light on the complexity of holistic practical experiences, with its claim to analytic reflections and its empirical confirmation, thus enabling – in addition to the actual search for evidence – a rich development of pedagogical concepts and perceptions of experiences.

What should people learn by global education? Outcome of learning processes

As an outcome of global learning, a bundle of different behavioural changes is expected. Not only do these differ, but also how they should be operationalized differs – as distinct fields of knowledge or beliefs, as broader competencies and thus as an execution of actions, or as 'Bildung' in the understanding of a free-acting person. The three concepts are described in the following.

Knowledge, beliefs and skills

Global learning should lead to knowledge about social justice in the face of globalization and about sustainability and climate change; it should also lead to appropriate knowledge about interventions. In addition, it deals with attitudes and dispositions, such as interest in life in the South, willingness to change perspective or a critical view on each other's paternalism. Various studies have worked on the structure of this knowledge including the related beliefs and skills (Beneker, van Stalborch and van der Vaart 2009; Bourn 2018). Bourn (2018) has recently published a systematic review and a conceptual framework of skills for global learning related to different professions such as teaching, engineering or health professionals. An empirically founded consensus on which knowledge formations to build on and how they relate to each other is not yet available. It is also unclear how certain areas of knowledge are associated with which dispositions.

Competencies

Another prominent position reflecting the outcome of global learning refers to competencies linked with this approach. As a general concept, competencies are understood as cognitive, motivational and action-related dispositions: 'Competencies are understood as a disposition which enables individuals to solve defined forms of problems' (Artelt and Riecke-Baulecke 2004: 27). Competencies do link accumulated knowledge with individual skills to be used in different situations (Klieme 2004: 13). Competencies are about the 'ability to successfully meet complex demands in a particular context' (Rychen and Salganik 2003: 2). Weinert in his definition on competencies pointed out: 'The concept of competence refers to an individually or interindividually available collection of prerequisites for successful action in meaningful task domains.' (Weinert 1999: 6) According to him, cognitive skills and knowledge related to attitudes and values (as motivation and volitional and social readiness) will lead to successful action.

Important aspects of patterns of competencies are their structure in components, reflecting different subjects, its domain specificity and structure in different levels of competencies (Klieme et al. 2003: 61 et seq.). Important for such an approach is the understanding that empirical research is not focusing on *the subjective* learning progress (in the sense that people tell you what they think they have learnt), but measuring *the objective* progress (in the sense that by looking at the learning process and asking people to do something, they thereby prove their own learning), using special methods as reconstructive research or task formats (see, for example, Asbrand 2008; Rost 2005; Scheunpflug, Franz and Krogull 2016).

Until now, there is no clear consensus on the competencies linked to global learning. Wiek, Withycombe and Redman (2011) sorted out a systematic review as a kind of meta-analysis of forty-three concepts of competencies in education for sustainability and described systems-thinking competence, anticipatory competence, normative competence, strategic competence and interpersonal and intercultural competence as core competencies in education for sustainability. The UNESCO-Framework on Global Citizenship Education (UNESCO 2015) describes competencies and operationalization over different ages. This framework has been internationally agreed to however, from a scientific standpoint these competencies are not clearly enough developed to allow differentiating each competency at various levels.

Bildung

In addition, global learning is conceptualized especially in the German discourse, as Global Bildung, taking its meaning from humanism and neo-humanism. With the understanding of Bildung the perspective of the subject shaping his or her learning process is emphasized, and through this the individual striving for individual freedom, emancipation and freedom in a global world society context (Meyer, Scheunpflug and Helleskamp 2018; Roselius and Meyer 2018). The understanding of global learning as Bildung focuses on individual reflexivity, individuality and long-term processes in building a global identity as cosmopolitism or world citizenship. It emphasizes readiness for self-reflection and thus minimizing the negative consequences of individual behaviour. Bildung reflects learning as an open process to an open future. This concept is important to global learning as globalization is not just a blueprint to follow, but needs critical thinking, new ideas and open questions. Global Bildung includes competencies but enlarges the concept by focusing on the way individuals reflect themselves in a world society and world culture (Klieme, Hartig and Rauch 2008: 6). Bildung underlines the free character of learning from economic or ecological necessities but concentrates on the liberation of humans from immaturity in the understanding of Kant, where the needs of others limit individual free evolvement (Scheunpflug 2008).

Global learning outcome

Considering these debates, it becomes obvious that the explanation of the outcome of global learning has to be reflected on when aiming for evidence on global learning.

What should global learning look like? Input quality criteria for global learning

Another approach to the quality of global learning is to reflect on the input quality of the learning arrangement. Here there is more or less consensus, as there have been intensive debates since the year 2000. For example, the German association VENRO (Verband Entwicklungspolitik und Humanitäre Hilfe deutscher Nichtregierungsorganisationen e.V. – Association of German NGO's for development and humanitarian aid, an umbrella organization with 140 single organizations) launched quality criteria for global learning in 2012 (VENRO 2012a; Richter 2015). Following this consensus, the process of planning, the quality of the provided content and the didactical quality of the learning process itself are the main components of the quality of global learning. For the process of planning, it should include an analysis of the target group, clear objectives, a reflection of one's own position, a coherent planning and a preparation of the (self-) evaluation of the learning outcome (VENRO 2012a: 5–6). The quality of the content is described by (1) relationship to globalization and its local meaning, (2) illustration of social complexity and avoidance of simplifying presentation, (3) multi-perspectivity and transparency of own point of view, (4) teaching of interdisciplinary knowledge, (5) addressing uncertainty and non-knowledge and (6) providing thinking in alternatives (VENRO 2012a: 7–8). Taking into account the needs of the participants, a variety of learning methods, gender equality, competence orientation and participation lead to didactical quality of the learning process itself (VENRO 2012a: 9–10). In cooperation between ministries, non-governmental organizations (NGOs) and research in the Netherlands, a shared canonical overview on topics related to global learning has been developed, considered as the basics in global learning (Beneker, van Stalborch and van der Vaart 2009).

Another important input into the learning process is learning materials or toolkits. The following quality criteria for toolkits and materials on global learning may be seen as consensus (VENRO 2012a: 10): (1) the toolkit or the learning material is related to a target group, (2) it allows a variety of learning methods and approaches, (3) all that is needed to use the material is accessible, (4) the topics are presented in a 'glocal' way (which means that they address global issues and relate them to the local world), (5) values as human rights, gender equality and antiracism are taken into account, (6) the learning materials offer possibilities to act and (7) all statements of the material are linked to references.

Especially for work in schools, the free opinion-forming process of the students themselves is an important contribution to the quality of global learning. Students should find their own political position based on the free democratic constitution. This so-called ban of overpowering students is sometimes a challenge for development NGOs working in schools, as they stand for specific political statements which they want to advocate.

These input criteria are relatively easy to control and therefore are often used as indicators for evaluation. However, up till now their evidence is not really given in a rigorous way. Of course, these quality standards have their dignity in themselves, as they describe what global learning means in a reflective way. The problem is that the minimum-standard is not clear. There is no research on showing, for example, the impact of a 'glocal' arrangement for the learning process. There is a high probability (e.g. as shown by Wagener 2018) that, for example, paternalism is imposed in the micro-didactics in the classroom, which is not covered by those standards. Despite these aspects, standards on global learning are an important step towards quality.

What are causes? Relationships between learning arrangements and outcome of global learning

As mentioned above, it is crucial for the understanding of evidence to relate learning arrangements and outcomes. Research looking for evidence seeks to identify conditions of causal effects.

In contrast to causality in a deterministic legality, this causality is understood as a statistical likelihood, which expresses an expectation of a relation based on probabilities. Therefore, only a regular sequence may be measured, but not its causal relation. By this, causality changes into a theory-assumed relationship, which is not possible to observe. The observing person constructs causality, and therefore this causality is not an observation but an insight, which is as much valid as it can be falsified. How to understand this causality is an important foundation in proving evidence.

In 2012–13 in Germany an intensive debate on evidence in global learning took place, in which VENRO claimed a 'chain of effects' on global learning and asked for 'impact orientation in Global Learning' (VENRO 2012b). An intensive debate thus started about the challenges and conditions in finding the relationship between input and outcome in global learning. Critical researchers (Bergmüller et al. 2013) raised four arguments against a simple understanding of impact and a technological view of a chain of effects. The first argument raised recalled the constructive character of learning. Global learning does not mean copying blueprints but is a constructive process of reorganizing world views. Especially as global learning relates to values and judgements, the relationship between a learning process and an observable behaviour is not linear and needs sound reflection. For example, somebody not buying fair trade tea in a supermarket may either not have learnt about fair trade or may have decided that the fair trade seal in the supermarket is not good enough as salaries but not climate change are taken into account. So connecting 'learning about fair trade' with the behaviour 'buying fair trade in the supermarket' may be a shortcut. The second argument reflects the relationship between a learning outcome and the input in a way that the outcome relates to the input. However, there might be a so-called attribution gap. Does a lesson in a school class really enhance the understanding of global poverty or might a related movie on television at the same time not provoke a certain step of learning? In mathematics, the relationship between teaching and outcome is much closer as the school is nearly the only agent working on the understanding of mathematics. However, in global learning, society itself shapes the understanding of global issues in manifold ways. How then to relate the learning input to the learning outcome? The third argument points out the problem of systematic learning. Until now, the development of competencies towards global social justice is unclear. What comes first – the knowledge or the empathy? How to balance experiences which might lead to paternalism? As in mathematics, it is clear that multiplication first needs knowledge in addition. This logic needs to be understood better for global learning. This hinders strong evidence so far. Furthermore, to ask persons about their subjective learning and beliefs will not be sufficient, as competencies are not easily estimated by the individuals themselves. The fourth argument recalls that the expected support for planning and decision-making by evidence may be overestimated, as the research needed is long-term and resources require endeavour, especially if one reflects on the open future and the related open learning process.

The discussion shows that a learning field such as global learning, which on the one hand is related to formal learning in institutions, but on the other hand takes place in informal and non-formal situations, needs deeper reflection on evidence than learning which only takes place in formal situations. There is an ongoing debate about evidence in such cases, and with more research knowledge (see the next paragraph), a deeper understanding might become possible of the relationship between learning arrangement and learning outcome. However, as racism, paternalism or open-minded world views are constructs in constant development over the lifespan, ambitious research designs might be expected. Unplanned encounters and irritations might play a more important role than are visible at the moment.

Liberation of compulsion

These reflections on evidence-based global learning lead to the following consequences:

> Increasing meaning of empirical research in Global Learning and the need for a committed research agenda.

Global learning needs an underlying basic structure through empirical research. In recent years, increasing relevance and activity concerning empirical research has become obvious. In any claim of completeness, the following spotlights give a short overview:

- Research on the importance of individual beliefs shows the contribution of opinion polls and individual epistemological beliefs (Scheunpflug and Mehren 2016). There is a need to avoid socially desirable answers and to find appropriate methodological approaches (see the proposition of Scheunpflug, Franz and Krogull 2016).
- There is more and more research on the impact of subject-related concepts, as in geography, history or others (Kultusministerkonferenz 2017).
- There are first approaches of large-scale competencies, carried out by the Programme of International Student Assessment (PISA)-consortium on 'global competencies' (OECD 2016). This approach is at the moment still problematic as the operationalization of the measurement relates to a very under-complex understanding of global learning, focusing only and in a very limited way on intercultural interest (see the critique by Sälzer and Rochen 2018; Conolly, Lehtomäki and Scheunpflug 2019). Therefore, the existing data do not give any evidence about factual global learning. However, the approach itself may be promising, given further development to enlighten the debate about competencies of global learning.
- Research on non-formal and informal global learning, as studies on child-sponsorship and its consequences for the understanding of globalization (Wagener 2018), on the impact of North–South and South–North encounters (Krogull 2018) or on voluntary work (Richter 2018) show, confirms how easily learning arrangements with good intentions may lead to paternalistic world views. Following this research, approaches to overcome paternalism and neocolonial attitudes seem to be underestimated (Scheunpflug 2014).
- Research on policy implementation in different European countries (Hartmeyer 2017) and on funding resources and its outcome (Bergmüller et al. 2019) could contribute to systematic funding decisions and a stronger structure of the field.

Of course, this list is only a very small extract from what is presently carried out in research. It shows, however, that most of the studies are single case studies, and therefore related to the lowest level of evidence. Besides a strong research agenda, searching for evidence in global learning needs more studies on higher levels of evidence. Meta-studies on global learning as the foundation of evidence are still a desideratum and therefore a strong need (see, as an exception, Goren and Yemini 2017).

Evidence and innovation

Searching for evidence is per se an ambivalent endeavour. On the one hand, evidence gives power and certainty to the field and leads to visibility and professionalism. With this form of perfectibility, it is an important contribution to strengthening global learning. On the other hand, evidence is promising that it is possible to give certainty to a field which is dealing with big transformation processes of societies, the need for sustainability and the uncertainty of the future. Learning in this field might be related to failure, limitations, human failure and guilt. These challenges need ethical, psychological and maybe even theological and philosophical reflections, which are not related to perfectibility linked to evidence.

Global learning therefore needs evidence for a rigorous search for quality and empirical foundations. As its objectives are related to very important issues such as climate change and global social justice, the maximum evidence should be achieved. At the same time, global learning needs enough space to search for innovations, which sometimes leads to inefficient loops. Innovations are not always efficient, as they require the courage for overcoming at the start not well worked-out attempts.

Conclusion: What to do and what not to do?

By careful consideration of the arguments in this chapter, a strategy towards evidence in global learning becomes obvious.

First, it can be stated that evidence in global learning is very important in order to reach a necessary quality and impact. In order to achieve this, more, better and systematically related research is mandatory. Cumulative knowledge on global learning is needed. Research on global learning needs to reach a high level of evidence. Single studies are a good starting point, but do not yet provide strong evidence. Research cooperation, strategic projects and systematic research reviews, combining single studies with bigger picture studies are the way to go. Causality should be interpreted with caution. Existing research should be well understood regarding its limitations concerning validity and framing conditions. Therefore, the pressure of delivering evidence in a field which is under pressure should be resisted, as long as the research base is not as it should be.

On the other hand, a simple sequence from one single study to another single study will not give the necessary strength to the field of global learning or to national related discourses. The generalization of findings needs to be explicit and well reflected. There is a global demand for complex forms of learning in order to achieve global competencies enhancing global social justice and sustainability. Gradually, reflected evidence may become reality.

The utopian surplus of global learning

Global learning is dealing with survival topics for humankind. The question 'where should education lead to?' (Adorno 1970: S.110) has an urgency, which calls for efficient approaches concerning the needs of social justice and sustainable development on a global planet. This question may not be answered merely by empirical observations and evidence-based practice on global learning. This question needs a surplus of utopic thinking, hope and imagination.

Bibliography

Adorno, W. T. (1970), *Erziehung zur Mündigkeit, Vorträge und Gespräche mit Hellmut Becker* [Education for Emancipation: Speeches and Talks with Hellmut Becker]. 1959–1969, Frankfurt: Suhrkamp.

Artelt, C. and Riecke-Baulecke, T. (2004), *Bildungsstandards. Fakten, Hintergründe, Praxistipps* [Standards on Education], München.

Asbrand, B. (2008), 'How Adolescents Learn about Globalisation and Development', in Bourn, D. (ed.), *Development Education: Debates and Dialogues*, 28–44, London: Institute of Education, University of London.

Beneker, T., van Stalborch, M. and van der Vaart, R. (2009), *Windows on the World: Report of the Canon for Global Citizenship Committee*, Amsterdam, Utrecht: NCDO and Utrecht University's Faculty of Geosciences.

Bergmüller, C., Causemann, B., Höck, S., Krier, J. M. and Quring, E. (2019), *Wirkungsorientierung in der entwicklungspolitischen Inlandsarbeit.* [Impact Orientation in Development Education], Münster: Waxmann.

Bergmüller, C. and Scheunpflug, A. (2017), 'Evaluation entwicklungsbezogener Bildungsarbeit' [Evaluation of Development Education], in Lang-Wojtasik, G. and Klemm, U. (eds), *Handlexikon Globales Lernen*, 76–80, Ulm: Klemm & Oelschläger.

Bergmüller, C., Scheunpflug, A., Franz, J. and Krogull, S. (2013), 'Zur Überprüfungen entwicklungsbezogenen Lernens. Anmerkungen zum VENRO-Diskussionspapier "Wirkungsorientierung in der entwicklungspolitischen Inlandsarbeit"' [Discussion on the paper of VENRO in regard to orientations towards outcome], *Zeitschrift für Evaluation* [Journal for Evaluation] 12(1): 151–60.

Bourn, D. (2018), *Understanding Global Skills for the 21st Century*, London: Palgrave Macmillan.

Conolly, J., Lehtomäki, E. and Scheunpflug, A. (2019) (in press), *Measuring Global Competencies, GENE Policy Brief*, Dublin.

Davies, P. (1999), 'What Is Evidence-based Education?' *British Journal of Educational Studies* 47(2): 108–21.

Davies, H. T. O., Nutley, S. M. and Smith, P. C. (eds) (2004), *What Works? Evidence-based-Policy in Public and Practice Services*, Bristol: Policy Press.

GENE [Global Education Network Europe] (2002), *Maastricht Global Education Declaration – A European Strategy Framework For Improving and Increasing Global Education in Europe to the Year 2015,* Dublin

Goren, H. and Yemini, M. (2017), 'Global Citizenship Education Redefined – A Systematic Review of Empirical Studies on Global Citizenship Education', *International Journal of Educational Research* 82: 170–83.

Hartmeyer, H. (2017), 'Europa als bildungspolitischer Akteur in der Entwicklungszusammenarbeit' [Europe as policy stakeholder in Development], *Zeitschrift für Internationale Bildungsforschung und Entwicklungspädagogik - ZEP* 40(4): 25–8.

Klieme, E. (2004), 'Kompetenzen' [Competencies], *Pädagogik* 7(8): 10–13.

Klieme, E., Avenarius, H., Blum, W., Döbrich, P., Gruber, H., Prenzel, M. and Vollmer, H. J. (2003), *Expertise zur Entwicklung nationaler Bildungsstandards*. [Expertise on Development of national educational standards], Bonn: Federal Ministry of Education and Research.

Klieme, E., Hartig, J. and Rauch, D. (2008), 'The Concept of Competence in Educational Contexts', in Hartig, J., Klieme, E. and Leutner, D. (eds), *Assessment of Competencies in Educational Contexts*, 3–22, Göttingen: Hogrefe.

Krogull, S. (2018), *Weltgesellschaft verstehen* [Understanding World Society], Wiesbaden: Springer.

Kultusministerkonferenz (2017), *Curriculum Framework Education for Sustainable Development*, Berlin: Cornelsen.

Meyer, M. A., Scheunpflug, A. and Hellekamps, S. (2018), 'Allgemeinbildung in Zeiten der Globalisierung'. Editorial. [Bildung in Times of Globalization], *Zeitschrift für Erziehungswissenschaft* 21(2): 211–15. DOI: 10.1007/s11618-018-0822-2

Moll, M. (2005), 'Austro-Hungarian Counter-intelligence Activities Prior to World War I: The Local Level', *Journal of Intelligence History* 5(1): 1–14. DOI: 10.1080/16161262.2005.10555105

Muigg, M. (2007), 'Geheim- und Nachrichtendienste in und aus Österreich. 1918–1938' [Intelligence services in and from Austria 1919-1938], *SIAK-Journal – Zeitschrift für Polizeiwissenschaft und polizeiliche Praxis* 3: 64–72. DOI: 10.7396/2007_3_G

OECD (2005), *Paris Declaration on Aid Effectiveness*, Paris: OECD.

OECD (2008), *Building Public Awareness of Development: Communicators, Educators and Evaluation*. OECD Development Center, Policy Brief No 35, Paris: OECD.

OECD (2016), *Global Competences for an Inclusive World*, Paris: OECD.

Richter, S. (2015), 'Qualität im Globalen Lernen in der Schule' [Quality in Global Learning in Schools], in GLIS - *Globales Lernen in der Schule*, vol. 1, Münster: Comenius-Institut.

Richter, S. (2018), 'Lernen zwischen Selbst und Fremd. Zur Qualität von Lernprozessen in Freiwilligendiensten im Globalen Süden' [Learning between Self and Others – The Quality of Learning Processes in Voluntary Services in the Global South], *Zeitschrift für Internationale Bildungsforschung und Entwicklungspädagogik – ZEP* 41(1): 17–22.

Roselius, K. and Meyer, M. A. (2018), 'Bildung in Globalizing Times', *Zeitschrift für Erziehungswissenschaft* 21(2): 217–40. DOI: 10.1007/s11618-018-0821-3

Rost, J. (2005), 'Messung von Kompetenzen Globalen Lernens' [Measuring Competencies in Global Learning], *Zeitschrift für internationale Bildungsforschung und Entwicklungspädagogik (ZEP)* 28(2): 14–18.

Rychen, D. S. and Salganik, L. H. (eds) (2003), *Key Competencies for a Successful Life in a Well-Functioning Society*, Göttingen: Hogrebe.

Sälzer, C. and Roczen, N. (2018), 'Assessing Global Competence in PISA 2018: Challenges and Approaches to Capturing a Complex Construct', *International Journal of Development Education and Global Learning* 10(1): 5–20.

Scheunpflug, A. (2008), 'Why Global Learning and Global Education? An Educational Approach Influenced by the Perspectives of Immanuel Kant', in Bourn, B. (ed.), *Development Education. Debates and Dialogue*, 18–27, London: Institute of Education.

Scheunpflug, A. (2014), 'Globales Lernen und die Debatte um Postkolonialität – die Komplexität der Stärkung mündiger Subjekte'. [Global Learning and the Debate on Postcolonialism – the Complexity of Enhancing Emancipation], *Zeitschrift für Internationale Bildungsforschung und Entwicklungspädagogik* 4: 31–4.

Scheunpflug, A., Bergmüller, C. and Schröck, N. (2010), *Evaluation entwicklungsbezogener Bildungsarbeit* [Evaluation of Development Education], Münster: Waxmann.

Scheunpflug, A., Franz, J. and Krogull, S. (2016), 'Understanding Learning in the World Society – Qualitative Re-constructive Research in Global Learning and Learning for Sustainability', *International Journal for Global Learning and Development Education* 7(3): 6–23.

Scheunpflug, A. and Mehren, R. (2016), 'What Do We Know about Global Learning and What Do We Need to Find Out?' in Hartmeyer, H. and Wegimont, L. (ed.), *Global Education in Europe Revisited*, 205–25, Münster: Waxmann.

Schrader, J. (2014), 'Analyse und Förderung effektiver Lehr-Lernprozesse unter dem Anspruch evidenzbasierter Bildungsreform' [Analysis and Promotion of Effective Teaching and Learning Processes in Light of Evidence-based Education Reforms], *Zeitschrift für Erziehungswissenschaft* 17(2): 193–223. DOI: 10.1007/s11618-014-0540-3

UNESCO (ed.) (2015), *Global Citizenship Education, Topics and Learning Objectives*, Paris: OECD.

VENRO (2012a), 'Qualitätskriterien für die entwicklungspolitische Bildungsarbeit' [Quality Criteria for Development Education], *VENRO Discussionpaper 1/2012*, Bonn: VENRO.

VENRO (2012b), 'Wirkungsorientierung in der entwicklungspolitischen Inlandsarbeit' [Impact Orientation in Development Education]. *VENRO Discussionspaper 2/2012*, Bonn: VENRO.

Wagener, M. (2018), 'What Do Young People Learn When Sponsoring a Child in the Global South? Empirical Findings on Learning Experiences of Young Sponsors in Germany', *International Journal of Development Education and Global Learning* 10(1): 90–102.

Weinert, F. E. (1999), *Konzepte der Kompetenz*, Paris: OECD [published in English: Weinert, F. E. (2001). 'Concept of Competence: A Conceptual Clarification', in D. S. Rychen and L. H. Salganik (eds), *Defining and Selecting Key Competencies*, 45–65, Paris: OECD].

Wiek, A., Withycombe, L. and Redman, C. L. (2011) 'Key Competencies in Sustainability: A Reference Framework for Academic Program Development', *Sustainability Science* 6(2): 203–18.

Chapter 5
Paulo Freire: Accidental Global Citizen, Global Educator

Tania Ramalho

Never did a happening, a fact, a feat, a gesture of anger or of love, a poem, a painting, a song, a book have only one reason behind them. A happening, a fact, a feat, a song, a gesture, a poem, a book are always involved in dense plots, touched by multiple reasons for being in which some are closer to the occurrence or to the creation, and others are more visible while reasons-to-be. That is why I have been more interested in comprehending the process in which things happen and how, than in the outcome itself

(Freire, 1992: 18)

In this passage, Paulo Freire was revisiting his experience of writing *Pedagogy of the Oppressed* (1970/1978), the book that led the way for his voice to be heard in the global context. He was clear about life's complex, enmeshed plots. When I had the insight about Freire becoming an 'accidental' global citizen, I wanted to trace the general outlines of the 'dense plot' that led him into this path. I also chose to write in his most preferred genre, epistolary.

Until the advent of the World Wide Web in 1991 and email becoming an efficient mode of communication, 'snail mail' – letters – were the principal means of communication. Letters narrated events and conveyed feelings, engaged business transactions and provided means of exchange of theoretical discussions between scholars. Freire lived in the time of letters, and they disclose his background, personality and thoughts.

Freire wrote personal letters, especially to his mother during the painful years of exile separation. He would not see her alive again, as he was not allowed to return to Brazil. His works, *Pedagogy in Process: The letters to Guinea-Bissau* (1978); *Letters to Cristina: Reflections on My Life and Work* (1996) and *Teachers as Cultural Workers: Letters to Those Who Dare Teach* (1998), reflect the comfort he felt communicating through letters, always in dialogical mode. He was, by all accounts, a gentle man, curious, present and engaged with others in the process of understanding, re-envisioning and reconstructing the world. He wrote to his niece Cristina,

My experience in exile was enriched by the letters I wrote to friends. My correspondence with students and teachers was far more intense, however. When they came through Santiago, or when they heard about the literacy work I had done in Brazil and Chile, students and teachers would write to me, either to continue a dialogue or to begin one; in some cases, these conversations continue even today. This process was part of my ten years in exile in Chile, the United States, and Switzerland. (Freire, 1996: 5)

My letter to Freire, below, entertains two ideas. We can regard him as an 'accidental' global citizen resulting from an unplanned and fortuitous life path that led him to the global stage. This plot involved militarism and entrenched conservative forces against social justice in unholy alliances between national and international elites. Second, I engage in an initial exploration of a proposed pedagogy of global citizenship education (GCE) that reflects Freirean concepts.

My dear Paulo,

Twenty years and counting since you left us on 2 May 1996. You looked forward to the twenty-first century with a heart full of hope. It has been a rough start, as the world still seems to be on the brink of chaos. Many cling to political right-wing views, now fed systematically to people through spurious news channels in the Americas. People also hold disbelief towards issues of climate change and global warming that threaten life on Earth.

At the same time, we also have – almost – a critical mass worldwide ready to do something about this mess, from waging peace in war-torn areas and providing safer homes to refugees all over the world, too numerous to count, to finding sustainable solutions for the many problems that plague the globe. Many public and private organizations such as NGOs lead the way, including the UN system, clarifying goals, amassing knowledge and acting on diverse projects to better the quality of life globally, despite contradictions and setbacks.

Who will prevail? I can only support what you posed at the start of the *Pedagogy of the Oppressed*: humanisation is our only vocation (Freire, 1970: 30).

I am the granddaughter of a family, like you, from the Northeast of Brazil. Now I am a critical pedagogy teacher educator based in the United States. Reading your texts, I 'hear' your tender voice and the marked accent so familiar from my youth. I have followed your well-documented life (Ramalho, 2018), from childhood to adolescence and young adulthood in Recife and Jaboatão, Pernambuco state.

As a young man, you married Elza, an educator, your collaborator, supporter, companion and mother of your five children. She was present to share your growth as educator, your love of language, linguistics and of teaching our language, Portuguese. She was not surprised at your disappointing entry into and quick exit from the barrister profession. Soon you would assume the education and culture directorship at the newly created SESI (Social Service for Industry) where you could observe and experiment on educational issues relevant to workers and their families.

At the university in Recife, you participated in the progressive Popular Culture Movement (MCP), with its community-building model that resulted in the Angicos literacy initiative. 'Circles of culture' were formed with local illiterate participants, who soon learnt to read words and were conscious of themselves as political beings. The results so impressed the new Brazilian president João Goulart (1961–4) that he extended an invitation for you to move to the newly built capital, Brasília, for the nationwide implementation of the already famous Freire 'method' of literacy teaching/learning through dialogic processes. You were meant to solve the problem of critical adult literacy in Brazil once and for all, an important phase of national development. That plot, however, was never actualized.

April's fool day, 1964, struck: the take-over by the military dictatorship that ruled Brazil for the next twenty years (the coup was part of an inter-American military strategy to stop the spread of Cuban-like socialist ideas and revolutionary practices). With the Goulart administration deposed for its progressive politics, along with many others you were jailed (riding on public transportation, Elza and the children brought pots of beans to prison so you could break bread with other imprisoned 'subversives' of the established order). You were among the lucky ones who was not physically tortured or assassinated. Eventually you were let go with the veiled recommendation that, not being welcomed under the military regime, it was for the best that you left the country – a new plot.

The moment of your transition to exile marks an identity shift from the local scholar-activist from Recife, a *pernambucano*, a *nordestino* (from the Northeast of Brazil), to a man who had just lost his country but was fortunate to be welcomed elsewhere as a political refugee. With openings that the dictatorship-enforced diaspora provided, Freire, the national citizen, would become Freire, the global citizen, whose work would soon impact education worldwide. From geographical displacement a new amalgam of a man emerged, one who had been forced to face different cultures, work settings and life challenges. This banished man acknowledged bringing former experiences to his new trails:

> No one gets anywhere alone, even less to exile. Even those who arrive without the company of their family, wife, children, parents, siblings. No one leaves their world, penetrated by its roots, with an empty or dry body. We carry the memory of many plots, the body wet with our history and culture. (Freire, 1992: 33)

You first stopped for a month in La Paz (October to November 1964), where a coup took place shortly after. It was fortunate. The altitude of Bolivia's capital had been so difficult for you that when arriving at Arica, Chile, you praised oxygen (Freire, 1992: 35). For four and half years Chile provided you with more than air – you were employed quickly, and your family was able to join you in 1965. Foremost, Chile could at the time still offer a global political environment infused with the utopian hope of the Cuban revolution. Revolutionaries, their progressive ideas, practices and their sentiments of love for humanity nurtured you (Freire, 1992: 44–5).

Pedagogy of the oppressed was created in this passionate environment. You brought to it knowledge learnt from lifelong habits of reading expansively; from the work done in Brazil, especially in the Northeast; along with the Chilean experiences and a seminal first trip to the United States in 1967, when you conferred with Civil Rights leaders. With the *Pedagogy of the Oppressed*, Paulo, came unbound opportunities for the exercise of global citizenship. You had a brief stay at Harvard where you forged lifelong personal and professional friendships. You also made a final informed choice to accept a position at the World Council of Churches in Geneva, Switzerland, where paths for action in many countries and all continents opened for you – except in your country of birth, still occupied by its own military. From your life and work you learnt what is termed a common understanding of GCE: 'A sense of belonging to a broader community and common humanity, promoting a 'global gaze' that links the local to the global and the national to the international' (UNESCO, 2014: 14).

This concept, global citizenship, and its correlate, GCE, is not without controversy, as you could well have expected, Paulo. These ideas exploded during the first two decades of the twenty-first century as the phenomenon of globalization, in its interconnected social, economic, political and cultural aspects, took centre stage in the global imagination. Related questions about the possibility of global citizenship asked: How can a global *citizen* even exist without reference to a state? (Noddings, 2004; UNESCO, 2014). Surrounded by increasingly stronger and convincing theoretical contexts of post-colonialism and coloniality, concerns about global citizenship being yet another colonial subterfuge, an imposition of the Global North over the Global South were and continued to be raised (Andreotti, 2006, 2008; Biccum, 2010; Shultz, 2007).

Along with the ongoing academic polemics, some consensus has also been achieved, particularly in what it refers to as the practice of GCE. While the Council of Europe and other public and private organizations in Europe and in the UK have been addressing issues of national and global citizenship and citizenship education, the United Nations Educational, Scientific and Cultural Organisation (UNESCO) has become a leader in the field, impacting their worldwide constituency of 193 member states in 2019. In 2012, the UN secretary general, South Korean Ban Ki-moon, launched the Global Education First Initiative (GEFI), with GCE as one of three important educational issues for the organization, which also included providing every child access to quality of education. Through this initiative, UNESCO (2014, 2015, and 2018) has prepared texts about global citizenship and education, available online for education administrators, teachers and scholars.

Paulo, if we examine the statement on pedagogical principles of GCE according to UNESCO (2014: 21–2), you would be happy to identify familiar ideas found throughout your work. The described role of the educator is that of 'enabler' or 'facilitator', not of a 'banking educator' transmitter of knowledge (Freire, 1970, Chapter 2). The 'transformative' pedagogy suggested, aligned with critical education as practice of freedom, is learner-centred and dialogical; you wrote that 'dialogue is an existential exigency' where reflection and action become solidary in addressing the world to be transformed (Freire, 1970: 93). Furthermore, GCE aims at promoting critical thinking and creativity as it raises consciousness about the formation of values within cultural norms and prevailing policies, which participants are to examine together.

Most importantly, GCE must foster action and competence. It is not supposed to be 'all talk' but about real engagement in local projects with a global dimension – it is glocalized. Each one of these directives, Paulo, is also part of your proposed theory where transformative education is envisioned as dialogical cultural action (Freire, 1970, Chapter 4) inspired in problem-oriented themes which participants generate from the contexts of their lives:

> The investigation of the 'generative themes' or the people's meaningful themes, with the fundamental objective of capturing the basic themes from which knowledge makes possible the organisation of a programmatic content for any action; instates itself as the point of departure of the action process, a cultural synthesis. (Freire, 1970: 214)

Meaningful generative themes codify what you called 'limiting situations' [my translation] – oppressive states and conditions in human life that need to be overcome through action. You called such acts that push through limitations, 'limit acts' (Freire, 1970, Chapter 3). The critical pedagogy of GCE calls for the young to participate in 'limit acts' as they work to address 'limiting situations' in their immediate communities.

Here, the UN suggests general global themes (and their local expressions) to be entertained and acted upon in the curriculum of GCE. These are compiled in seventeen Sustainable Development Goals (SDGs), 'limiting situations' in need of repair: poverty; food insecurity, nutrition and sustainable agriculture; health conditions; quality education; gender inequality; water supply and sanitation; sustainable energy; access to productive work; infrastructure needs;

inequality within and among countries; cities; production and consumption; climate change; oceans and waterways; land resources; peace; and cooperation among stakeholders to address these goals. Such an ambitious agenda provides a map for critical global citizenship educators to address.

Paulo, in UNESCO Bangkok (2018: 7–11) you will find a description of historical initiatives concerning education about global 'limiting situations' that have led to today's central focus on GCE: Education for International Understanding, Disarmament Education, Human Rights Education (HRE), Intercultural and Multicultural Education, Peace Education or Education for a Culture of Peace, Values Education, Education for the Four Pillars of Learning (learning to know, to do, to be and to live together), Citizenship Education, Education for Gender Equality, Global Education (GE), Education for Sustainable Development (ESD), Education for 21st Century Skills and Competences, Education for Preventing Violent Extremism and the recent Education for Digital Citizenship. These diverse initiatives comprise a rich history of knowledge and action, still primarily from Western perspectives. For clarity's sake, I highlight four main branches of such initiatives in a simplified chart. This image is not a perfect codification of the many fields, but it provides a centre, four directions and interconnections (Figure 5.1).

In essence, *GE* subsumes the traditions in Education for International Understanding, Development Education (DE) and Global Learning initiatives (Boulding, 1988; Bourn, 2015; UNESCO, 2018). *Intercultural Communication* has amassed a strong body of knowledge on the barriers and pathways to communicating across cultures, particularly facilitating but not limited to business transactions globally (Asante, Miike and Yin, 2013; , 2003; Lustig and Koester, 2010). It has also been linked to multicultural education identified as a North American, Anglo-Saxon and northern European educational tradition (Tarozzi and Torres, 2016).

Peace and Conflict Mediation Education have a long tradition from an early start at the turn of the twentieth century (Bajaj and Hantzopoulos, 2016; Boulding, 2000). The more

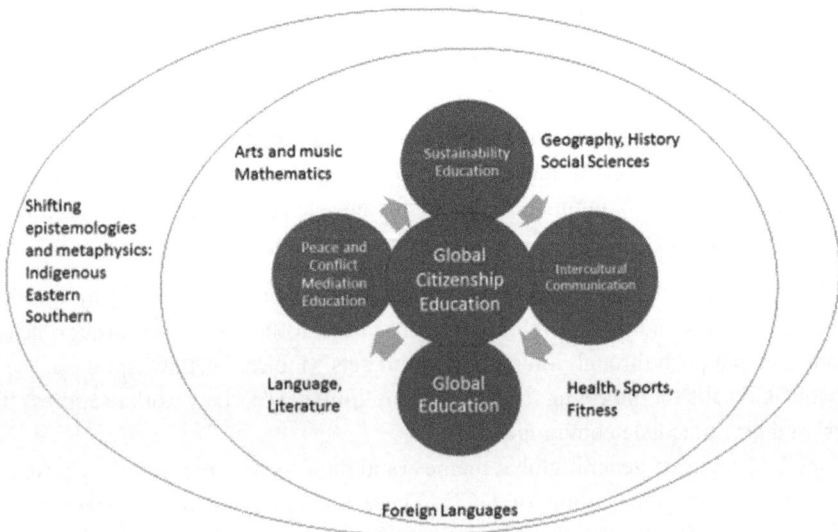

Figure 5.1 Representation of global citizenship education. Four contributing fields in shifting disciplinary fields.

recent *Sustainability Education* initiatives relate to teaching and learning about the concept of sustainability itself and the SDGs, following the United Nations Decade of Education for Sustainable Development (DESD, 2005–14).

These four interdisciplinary fields, 'ladies-in-waiting' of GCE, are supported by scholarly disciplines, such as history, geography, mathematics, the sciences, language and literature and the like. As studied by scholars and taught in school curricula worldwide, disciplines have compiled comprehensive background knowledge from which to draw understanding of glocal issues. Notwithstanding, such disciplines are not static. Their theories and methods continue to be challenged by critics. Consequently, paradigm shifts are in process as new epistemologies and metaphysics gain visibility and acceptance. New ways of seeing, feeling and behaving are being incorporated as repressed and neglected indigenous, Southern and Eastern knowledges gain traction (e.g. the work of Andreotti and associates; Santos; and Smith, Tuck and Yang). Truly inclusive and global knowledges are growing.

From such evolving and interconnected fields learners are to acquire the core cognitive, social-emotional and behavioural dimensions of GCE (UNESCO, 2015: 15). These are, respectively, understanding the interconnectedness and interdependency of cultural and natural local, national and global issues; developing a sense of being human and a human among others, with equal and mutual rights and responsibilities towards each other and the natural environment; and acting towards the actualization of a more just and peaceful life in a respected and cared-for natural environment.

Paulo, your work and life are documented as impacting the GCE agenda. Sharma, in her study of the contribution of Gandhi, Makiguchi and Ikeda to GCE, writes, 'Paulo Freire and other critical pedagogues who have emphasised the need for dialogue in education also deserve to be recognised' (p. 63). Bourn, of the Development Education Centre of the Institute of Education, University of London, in reviewing the history of DE writes about the emergence, within DE, of more critical, social justice-oriented educational approaches:

A more political agenda emerged, influenced in part by continued struggles against Portuguese continued colonisation in Africa but also by hearing about radical educational approaches, notably the work of Paulo Freire (1972). ... Osler (1994) in her study on development education noted during the 1980's the increasingly radical tone of much of the practice, influenced particularly by Freire. (Bourn, 2015: 15)

Your educational, political and philosophical contributions here and elsewhere acknowledged (see, for example, Tarozzi and Torres, 2016) were forged on the global stage where you operated after being forced to leave Brazil, Paulo. Further recognition came when you received the 1986 UNESCO Peace Education Prize. During the awards ceremony, you addressed the assembly in typical Freire fashion, connecting to the people of all walks of life who helped you think and act for a more just world, pushing limiting situations with your many 'limit acts' as educator and writer. Your pronouncement at the Paris ceremony refers to the impact of your work as a global citizen, even if an accidental one. Acknowledging that you were in debt to many different people from all continents who were peasants, workers and students, you said:

Together with many of these men, women and young people, I have learnt a fundamental lesson, and their doubts and ingeniousness have often taught me a great deal. ... A less naive view of the world does not necessarily result in a commitment to the struggle to transform the world, much less in that transformation itself, as some idealists believe. From the nameless, unfortunate and exploited people of the world I have learnt, above all, that peace is fundamental, indispensable, but that it must be fought for. Peace is something which is created, built up, transcending reality, the perverse facts of social life. Peace is created and developed in the never-ending construction of social justice. (UNESCO, 1986: 27)

Citizens everywhere still have doubts and ingeniousness, and the struggles for social justice and the fight for peace are far from over. Supporting the creation of peace, GCE backs the search for answers through engagements with practice in the never-ending mission of fostering social – and environmental – justice.

Thank you, Paulo, for reminding us of the work that needs to be done. The world continues to learn from your legacy.

Tania Ramalho
Oswego, New York
Valentine's Day, 2019

Bibliography

Andreotti, V. (2006). Soft versus critical global citizenship education. *Development Education Policy and Practice* 3, autumn: 83–98.

Andreotti, V. and Souza, L. (2008). Translating theory into practice and walking minefields: Lessons from the project 'Through Other Eyes'. *International Journal of Development Education and Global Learning* 1, no. 1: 23–36.

Andreotti, V. and Souza, L. (eds) (2012). *Postcolonial Perspectives on Global Citizenship Education*. New York: Routledge.

Asante, M. K., Miike, Y. and Yin, J. (eds) (2013). *The Global Intercultural Communication Reader*. 2nd edn. London: Routledge.

Bajaj, M. and Hantzopoulos, M. (2016). *Peace Education: International Perspectives*. London: Bloomsbury.

Biccum, A. (2010). *Global Citizenship and the Legacy of Empire*. Abington: Routledge.

Boulding, E. (1988). *Building a Global Civic Culture: Education for an Interdependent World*. New York: Teachers College Press.

Boulding, E. (2000). *Cultures of Peace: The Hidden Side of History*. Syracuse: Syracuse University Press.

Bourn, D. (2015). *The Theory and Practice of Development Education: A Pedagogy for Global Social Justice*. Abingdon: Routledge.

Freire, P. (1970/1978). *Pedagogia do oprimido* [Pedagogy of the oppressed]. Rio de Janeiro: Editora Paz e Terra.

Freire, P. (1992). *Pedagogia da esperança. Um reencontro com a Pedagogia do oprimido.* [Pedagogy of hope. A re-encounter with the Pedagogy of the oppressed]. São Paulo: Editora Paz e Terra.

Freire, P. (1996). *Letters to Cristina: Reflections on My Life and Work*. New York: Routledge.

Gudykunst, W. B. (ed.) (2003). *Cross-Cultural and Intercultural Communication*. Thousand Oaks: Sage.

Lustig, M. W. and Koester, J. (2010). *Intercultural Competence: Interpersonal Communication across Cultures*. New York: Pearson/Allyn & Bacon.

Noddings, N. (ed.) (2004). *Educating Citizens for Global Awareness*. New York: Teachers College Press.

Ramalho, T. (2018). Paulo Freire. *Oxford Research Encyclopedias: Communications*. Retrieved from http://oxfordre.com/communication/view/10.1093/acrefore/ 9780190228613.001.0001/acrefore-978 0190228613-e-608

Santos, B. de S. (2014). *Epistemologies of the South: Justice against Epistemicide*. New York: Routledge.

Sharma, N. (2018). *Value-creating Global Citizenship Education: Engaging Gandhi, Makiguchi, and Ikeda as Examples*. Cham: Palgrave Macmillan.

Shultz, L. (2007). Educating for global citizenship: Conflicting agendas and understandings. *Alberta Journal of Educational Research* 53, no. 3: 248–58.

Tarozzi, M. and Torres, C. A. (2016). *Global Citizenship Education and the Crises of Multiculturalism. Comparative Perspectives*. London: Bloomsbury.

UNESCO (n.d.). UNESCO Prize 1986 and 1987 for Peace Education. Retrieved from https://unesdoc. unesco.org/in/rest/annotationSVC/DownloadWatermarkedAttachment/attach_import_13c615a2-4e0e-46ed-b774-cf966f4220e7?_=122930engo.pdf

UNESCO (2014). Global citizenship education. Preparing learners for the challenges of the 21st century. Retrieved from http://www.unesco.org/new/en/gefi/resources/gced/

UNESCO (2015). Global citizenship education. Topics and learning objectives. Retrieved from http://www.unesco.org/new/en/gefi/resources/gced/

UNESCO (2017). Education for sustainable development goals: Learning objectives. Retrieved from http://www.unesco2030.it/uploads/1/2/0/9/12092833/learning_objectives.pdf

UNESCO Bangkok (2018). Preparing teachers for global citizenship education. A template. Retrieved from https://bangkok.unesco.org/content/preparing-teachers-global-citizenship-education-template

United Nations (n.d.). Sustainable development goals. Home Page. Retrieved from https://www.un.org/sustainabledevelopment/

Part II

Theoretical Perspectives

Chapter 6

Pluralizing Possibilities for Global Learning in Western Higher Education

Sharon Stein

There is a growing consensus among educators that the contemporary era is, and will be for the foreseeable future, characterized by significant global challenges related to political, economic and ecological uncertainty and instability. In Western higher education institutions (HEIs), there is also recognition that the scope and scale of contemporary challenges require a more globalized approach to learning than has been traditionally pursued, so as to prepare students for the increasingly complex, diverse, interconnected and multi-polar world they will inherit. In this chapter I affirm the importance of infusing global learning into HE settings, yet I also emphasize that there is more than one possible approach to doing so. If we conflate these different possibilities under a single heading of 'global learning', then there is a risk that institutional commitments to addressing global challenges will circularly reproduce a colonial politics of knowledge that re-centres the West and presumes the universality of colonial modernity's onto-epistemological frames. This is particularly troublesome when we consider the possibility that those frames are themselves at the root of many of our contemporary challenges; if this is the case, then the solutions that are found within those frames will likely reproduce more of the same. Thus, inspired by the work of Biesta (2013) and Bruce (2013), in this chapter I denaturalize those frames and consider their relation to three possible approaches to global learning in HE: *learning about difference*; *learning from difference* and *being taught by difference*. Each approach diagnoses and describes contemporary global problems differently, and in turn, proposes different responses.

I begin by briefly addressing the contemporary context of global challenges, and how global learning is framed as important for addressing those challenges. Then I identify and historicize some primary elements of the onto-epistemological frames that dominate in Western universities, and are often adopted elsewhere, drawing on decolonial and post-colonial critiques.[1] From there, I outline the three different approaches to global learning and how each approach might conceptualize ideas of global citizenship, internationalizing the curriculum and global social

---

[1] 'The West' is not limited to an ontologically fixed geographical location, but rather captures a socially and historically constituted, onto-epistemological category, generally understood in contrast to various iterations of the 'non-West'. These categorizations have both material and conceptual dimensions. Nonetheless, when I refer to 'Western higher education', I generally refer to institutions within the specific geographies of Europe, the United States, Canada, New Zealand and Australia, even as some institutions outside of these geographies have taken on a Westernized approach to higher education (Grosfoguel, 2013).

change. I conclude the chapter by addressing how educators might create spaces in which the gifts and limitations of these different possible approaches to global learning can be considered, and new ones can be imagined – that is, how we might foster an education that enables not any particular possibility, but rather, the 'possibility of possibilities' (Barnett, 2014).

Global learning as a response to global challenges

There is no single definition of what constitutes a 'global challenge' in HE discourse, but the broad idea of unprecedented existing and impending global challenges has often been used to justify the need to internationalize Western HEIs and scholarly associations so that they can become more responsive to these challenges (Stein, 2017). Different framings of this term emphasize different dimensions but are not necessarily mutually exclusive. Below I review some of the more common discourses about 'global challenges', which are sometimes discussed interchangeably as 'global crises', and their relationship to HE contexts.

One genre of global challenge/crisis discourse specifically emphasizes those challenges related to international development in the Global South.[2] For instance, the Association of Commonwealth Universities (ACU) launched a campaign, 'Beyond 2015', to coincide with the announcement of the United Nations (UN) Sustainable Development Goals (SDGs) in 2015, in which they frame global challenges in HE as those related to 'government support for university-community engagement and knowledge exchange, encouragement of developmental research, and strengthening of universities' efforts across developing and developed countries to share expertise in directing knowledge to the benefit of society' (p. 2). In these discourses, the Global South is generally framed as lacking adequate resources to address these challenges on their own, yet the historical and ongoing reasons for these unequal resources are not addressed. There is also presumed to be a central role for HEIs in the Global North in addressing these challenges, suggesting that the knowledge they produce is universally applicable, and that they are benevolent, neutral and disinterested parties (Stein, Andreotti, & Suša, 2019). This supposedly universal knowledge is then understood in contrast to the knowledge that is held and produced by communities in the Global South, whose ways of knowing are presumed to be anachronistic, and whose theories of change are minimized or ignored.

---

[2]   As is the case regarding the Western/non-Western distinction, I recognize that the usage of the binary divides of Global North/South may paradoxically reify them, and obscure the heterogeneity within the groups that these terms are problematically meant to describe. However, I make use of these terms in this chapter in order to indicate and emphasize enduring uneven social, political and economic relationships. As Mohanty (2003) notes, 'North/South is used to distinguish between affluent, privileged nations and communities and economically and politically marginalised nations and communities, as is Western/non-Western. While these terms are meant to loosely distinguish the northern and southern hemispheres, affluent and marginal nations and communities obviously do not line up neatly within this geographical frame. And yet, as a political designation that attempts to distinguish between the "haves" and "have-nots", it does have a certain political value. An example of this is Arif Dirlik's formulation of North/South as a metaphorical rather than geographical distinction, where North refers to the pathways of transnational capital and South to the marginalised poor of the world regardless of geographical distinction' (p. 505).

Another way of framing HE's response to global challenges is as an effort to extend the modern tradition of HE's public service to national societies to a more global scale. For instance, in her contribution to a collection entitled *Taking Responsibility: A Call for Higher Education's Engagement in a Society of Complex Challenges*, Morse (2006) writes, 'We've got global warming, we've got poverty, and we've got limited access to educational opportunity – you fill in the blank. The bottom line of this particular statement is that none of these problems will be solved without higher education' (p. 27). Similarly, in a UNESCO (2009) report, it is argued,

> Faced with the complexity of current and future global challenges, higher education has the social responsibility to advance our understanding of multifaceted issues, which involve social, economic, scientific, and cultural dimensions and our ability to respond to them. It should lead society in generating global knowledge to address global challenges, inter alia food security, climate change, water management, intercultural dialogue, renewable energy and public health. (p. 2)

Within this effort to globalize the 'public good' role of HE, the possible conflicts and complexities that might arise in seeking to define a universally relevant set of goods and values for the entire planet are rarely addressed, because global challenges themselves are presented in a de-politicized manner. Thus, for example, the disproportionate contribution of Western nations to total global carbon emissions and the role of economic growth in contributing to climate change are not addressed.

Yet another framing of global challenges emphasizes that the speed of change and the growth of competition threatens national competitiveness, which means that HEIs need to better prepare students with marketable global skills and competencies, and produce more globally significant research (Tannock, 2007). Compared to the other two, this framing is the most clearly centred around preserving the power and resources of Western institutions and nations; however, I will argue that in fact all three framings tend to emphasize the perpetuation of Western epistemological and ontological authority, even when they do so under the guise of benevolence.

Despite the differences in how global challenges and crises are themselves conceived, these approaches tend to position HE as indispensable in responding to these challenges. Furthermore, HE is situated as having a unique responsibility to respond. Global learning, which falls under the larger heading of HE internationalization, encompasses one set of possible responses to global challenges. In this chapter I specifically use 'global learning' to describe activities and changes related to global citizenship education (GCE), internationalizing the curriculum, and conceptualizing the role of HE in global social change. What often goes unsaid in conversations about these activities is nonetheless implied: that it is specifically *Western* HEIs and associations that will lead in responding to these global challenges. It is these organizations that are thought to have the most knowledge and resources to do so, as well as the most responsibility. Further, it is these organizations that are most understood to be 'global', offering solutions and knowledge that are relevant beyond their immediate context. In the section that follows, I draw on decolonial and post-colonial critiques to argue that the presumptive universalism of Western institutions is naturalized though the onto-epistemological frames of colonial modernity, which masks their actual provincialism, and invalidates the potential importance of other onto-epistemologies (whether institutionalized or not) in offering practical strategies and inherited wisdom to face today's global challenges/crises.

Colonial continuities, decolonial possibilities

As Lowe (2015) suggests, colonial modernity is not a single event or even a historical era, but rather an enduring set of contested categorical divisions, social relations and extractive processes, which 'governs and calibrates being and society in an ongoing way, through spatial and temporal operations of inclusivity and exclusivity, and through both geographical and historical differentiation and connection' (pp. 92–3). In their critiques of colonial modernity, decolonial and post-colonial critiques point to enduring divisions that have political but also economic, cognitive, ecological, relational and affective dimensions (Ahenakew et al., 2014; Andreotti et al., 2015; Grande, 2004). Although the exact formations of these divisions vary across context, and have shifted somewhat over the past several centuries, they generally remain united by a single story that designates different populations as being more or less developed on a supposedly universal path of human progress. Specifically, white/Euro-descended peoples are narrated within colonial modernity's onto-epistemological frames as the most intellectually and morally advanced iteration of humanity. This claim of superiority has served as an alibi for the direct and indirect subjugation of indigenous and racialized peoples by way of the forcible global spread of capitalist social relations, the universalization of Western rationality, the naturalization of the nation state as the primary mode of political governance and the objectification/commodification of 'nature' as a resource that is separate from humans and meant to be exploited. According to decolonial and post-colonial critiques, the self-proclaimed 'leaders of humanity' have only been able to accumulate wealth, claim authority and assert epistemic universality by enacting violence against other humans, as well as other-than-human beings.

Grosfoguel (2013) outlines the power of this single story of human progress and development in shaping and limiting the available possibilities for Western HE. He does so by tracing the historical processes through which ideologies of Western supremacy and universality were normalized at the onset of colonial modernity. He argues that through four genocides enacted by European powers in the sixteenth century (of indigenous peoples in the Americas, enslaved African peoples, Jews and Muslims in Spain, and women accused of being witches in Europe), material violence paved the way for the enduring epistemic violence of HEIs in which Western knowledge is understood as universal, despite its actual provincialism. Thus,

> In Westernized universities, the knowledge produced by other epistemologies, cosmologies, and world views arising from other world-regions with diverse time/space dimensions and characterized by different geopolitics and body-politics of knowledge are considered 'inferior' in relation to the 'superior' knowledge produced by the few Western men of five countries. ... The knowledge produced from the social/historical experiences and world views of the Global South, also known as 'non-Western', are considered inferior and not part of the canon of thought. Moreover, knowledge produced by women (Western or non-Western) are also regarded as inferior and outcast from the canon of thought. The foundational structures of knowledge of the Westernized university are simultaneously epistemically racist and sexist. (Grosfoguel, 2013, p. 75)

The effect of colonial modernity's onto-epistemological frames in HE is that they naturalize and valourize certain possibilities, and invisibilize and invalidate others. As a result, the Western model of HE not only reproduces notions of Western supremacy and universality internally but also has often been framed as the model to which all countries should aspire (Nandy, 2000; Rhoades, 2011).

One of the many insights that can be garnered from decolonial and post-colonial critiques in relation to the question of global challenges is that often what appears as unprecedented for those in the Global North is in fact an old, recurrent pattern for those in the Global South (as well as for marginalized, especially indigenous and racialized, populations within the Global North itself). The 'forgetting' of these precedents is not incidental, as in many ways centuries of relative stability among the advantaged populations of the Global North have been subsidized by the political, economic and ecological destabilization and subjugation of other populations. Often, the latter populations not only have experienced some version of contemporary crises previously but also are the most severely affected by new iterations of old patterns (Menzel, 2010). As Chakravartty and Silva (2012) note regarding the sub-prime mortgage crisis in the United States, '"new territories" of consumption and investment have been mapped on to previous racial and colonial (imperial) discourses and practices' (p. 368). Similarly, Whyte (2017) notes, 'indigenous scholars discuss climate vulnerability as an intensification or intensified episode of colonialism' (p. 155). Yet, many mainstream accounts of contemporary crises exceptionalize the present and leave out these histories because of the benefits that are guaranteed by continued forgetting, and because of the fact that the populations that have been most affected historically are deemed expendable within the colonial calculus of mattering. That is, violence and harm only becomes perceived as a political and ethical crisis once it starts affecting humanity's 'leaders'; up until then, it simply appears as the necessary cost of human progress.

Menzel (2010) suggests the possibility that 'the term 'crisis' ... can itself participate in the maintenance of epistemological ignorance, and thus ironically prevent the enlarged narration that genuine solutions to crises both entail and require'. I suggest a similar dynamic is often at work in discussions of contemporary 'global challenges' in HE. That is, despite a stated commitment and interest in expanding (globalizing) frames of reference, there is a risk of colonial continuities. According to Menzel, these colonial continuities operate through the reproduction of epistemologies of ignorance about colonialism and white supremacy, which refer to not simply a lack of knowledge or information but rather a wilful forgetting or refusal to acknowledge one's structural complicity in racialized harm (Mills, 2007), and how one benefits from the uneven distribution of vulnerabilities and life chances (Spade, 2011).

To face the truth about individual and institutional colonial complicity challenges Western moral authority and intellectual mastery, and the social and material entitlements that are believed to follow from these supposed supremacies. This, in turn, threatens to interrupt the ontological securities and enjoyments that the supposed 'leaders of humanity' derive from their presumed cultural superiority, epistemological certainty and financial stability. Thus, even as moments of acute crisis can unsettle the universality of colonial modernity's onto-epistemological frames and create openings for addressing the partiality of those frames, the reaction among those who are most invested in those frames is often one of resistance and denial (Stein, Hunt, Suša & Andreotti, 2017).

Many contemporary crises have their roots in colonial modernity's onto-epistemological frames and thus potentially call into question the universality of those frames – including capitalist social relations, Western rationality, the nation state and humanity's separation from nature.

However, rather than address those challenges by rethinking the frames themselves, the solutions to contemporary crises are often sought within those frames, reasserting their universality and reinvesting in their promised securities. In particular, Menzel (2010) argues that it is often the case that Western institutions and intellectuals position themselves as objective authorities (leaders of humanity) who are best suited to address global crises, in which they are the 'subjects of solution to crisis' whereas those most affected by crises are framed as 'objects undergoing crisis'. This also means that alternative responses to global crises that are formulated from outside of these frames, often by those who have been most harmed by colonial modernity, are deemed unintelligible or otherwise delegitimized. When this happens, the gifts of other ways of knowing and being are denied (Ahenakew, 2016), and proposed solutions remain ethnocentric and paternalistic.

Thus, although current global challenges and crises can be understood as a precarious opportunity to interrupt colonial patterns and gesture towards alternative futures by way of global learning, this is by no means the only possible or even the most likely outcome. In the next section, I consider three possible approaches to global learning and how each relates to the onto-epistemological frames of colonial modernity that I have outlined in this section. In addition to outlining each approach, I consider how each might envision and implement programmes related to global citizenship, internationalizing the curriculum and global social change in Western universities.

Learning about difference

An approach to global learning organized by the notion of *learning about difference* is firmly rooted within the onto-epistemological frames of colonial modernity. Within this framing, global challenges are largely understood as the result of a lack or absence of sufficient knowledge, information or technology. Thus, the solution is to accumulate more knowledge about difference so that the 'leaders of humanity' might be better prepared to address the risks and avoid future uncertainties that threaten the rest of the planet and the continuation of existing political economic systems. In turn, these leaders can then share their purportedly universal knowledge and technology with those who are perceived to lack it. Knowledge is therefore understood as a means to the ends of mastery and authority: by naming the world, it is presumed that Western knowledge producers can control it and put it within a universal logic and order, thereby managing existing challenges in an orderly way, and avoiding further impending crises.

As Pashby, da Costa, Stein and Andreotti (forthcoming) note,

> Global Citizenship Education (GCE) is an increasingly important area of research and practice in education. Its inclusion in the United Nations Sustainable Development Goals (Target 4.7) reflects its standing as an international discourse. Since the turn of the twenty-first century, there has been increasing attention to both its usefulness as an agenda for education and to its inherently contested nature.

Approaches to global citizenship informed by learning about difference would seek to develop global citizens who will assume a position of leadership for the rest of the world, dispensing knowledge and values to those who are presumed to trail behind in the path of universal progress and are thus presumed to be ill-equipped to conceptualize their own approaches to addressing global challenges. While this can be understood as a kind of affirmation of responsibility that extends outward beyond the self and beyond one's immediate or national contexts, it is also an extension of the historical colonial idea of the 'white man's burden', that is, his presumed benevolence and authority to lead. These presumptions are summarized by Spivak (2004): 'I am necessarily better, I am necessarily indispensable, I am necessarily the one to right wrongs, I am necessarily the end product for which history happened, and that New York is necessarily the capital of the world' (p. 532). In this approach, not only is global citizenship reserved for select individuals, but the position of the global citizen helps to affirm their subjectivities as morally and intellectually superior.

A 'learning about difference' approach to global learning tends to presume that true (universal) knowledge moves in one direction: from the Global North to the Global South. There is little suggestion that different knowledge systems might view and engage the world in substantively different ways, or that those knowledge systems might have something to teach students and faculty in Western institutions about global challenges. Internationalizing the curriculum from this perspective might entail including information about different populations and their cultures, which are framed as objects to be mastered and accumulated by the knowing subjects of Western HEIs. Thus, in the curriculum of an 'internationalized' history class organized by an approach to learning about difference, one might learn about the history of Africa as written from a Eurocentric perspective. The emphasis would be on diversifying course content, rather than on rethinking dominant conditions of knowledge production, transmission and valuation. Thus, the 'global' or' international' content is still produced and transmitted within Western history's disciplinary frames, and Western modes of knowledge production and transmission.

With regard to questions of global social change, learning about difference within Western HEIs is driven by the imperative to discern what will be the most efficient and utility-maximizing means of engaging with different populations, and ensuring their participation in and support for predetermined universal solutions to global challenges. Engaging and accounting for difference therefore becomes a means to arrive at an end that has already been determined by those with the most power. This approach to social change is clearly evident in the enduring presumption that material poverty is best addressed through economic growth. This vision of change ignores that poverty results from racialized global capitalist relations (rather than from a 'lack' of wealth), unfettered growth has devastating environmental consequences, and alternative visions for organizing labour and conceptualizing equitable and sustainable resource use already exist (such as *bien vivir*, or degrowth) (Escobar, 2016; Restrepo, 2014).

Learning from difference

An approach to global learning that is organized by the notion of *learning from difference* starts to challenge the single story of human progress and development that is naturalized by the onto-epistemological frames of colonial modernity. Global challenges are understood as the result of excluding certain people from efforts to move forward and make positive change, and thus the remedy for this is to include their perspectives. There is a commitment to incorporate multiple ways of knowing into mainstream HEIs to supplement existing practices and pedagogies. In particular, this means adding more diverse people to the student body and professoriate, and more diverse voices to research and curriculum. Exposure to different kinds of people and knowledges is understood to generate tolerance and empathy, to in turn enable students to work together in more efficient and harmonious ways towards shared goals.

Global citizenship education oriented by the imperative to learn from difference would emphasize intercultural understanding as a means to both affirm human equality (Killick, 2012) and appreciate different cultures and perspectives. However, because this approach to global learning emphasizes engagements that will develop positive individual attributes and interpersonal relations, it tends to avoid addressing the structural relations that are shaped by global patterns of unequal power. There is a desire to challenge dominant worldviews, but also an intention to ultimately return to social and political equilibrium premised on certainty, stability and consensus. Thus, although the intention of 'learning from difference' is to expand one's frames of reference, this is done selectively, and in ways that avoid social conflict or individual discomfort.

This selective engagement also translates to internationalizing the curriculum. Learning from difference emphasizes scholarship and theories written by non-dominant communities about their own experiences and perspectives. However, there is little reflexivity about the epistemological infrastructures that make it difficult for those in dominant positions to actually hear radically different perspectives without distorting them in ways that affirm the listener's benevolence and epistemic authority (Spivak, 1988). Thus, knowledge systems that are potentially disruptive are avoided, or selectively engaged (Ahenakew, 2016). For instance, Simpson (2005) notes, when indigenous knowledges (IK) are understood to complement the Western scientific method, they are seen as 'holding answers to the environmental problems afflicting modern colonising societies, while the spiritual foundations of IK and the indigenous values and worldviews that support it are of less interest often because they exist in opposition to the world view and values of the dominating societies' (pp. 373–4). Conversely, the spiritual dimensions of IK may be extracted for use by non-indigenous people without addressing indigenous political theory and its critical challenges to ongoing colonialism (Deloria, 1998).

Learning from difference in relation to global social change emphasizes the need to revise dominant visions of change in ways that incorporate more diverse perspectives so that we can move forward together, in a more inclusive direction of transformation that recognizes both our differences and our interconnections. It is understood that different communities will have their own unique interpretation of and approach to this transformation, but the basic orienting vision is ultimately meant to be shared. To use the example of the ACU's 'Beyond 2015' campaign, although the campaign solicited diverse perspectives about the role of HE in supporting change via the UN SDGs, its orienting questions were framed in such a way that precluded consideration of how some universities might be complicit in creating the problems the goals sought to address. Further, there was little critique of the goals themselves, despite various concerns that they centred Western powers, marginalized or tokenized dissenting (particularly, non-Western) voices, and failed to substantively challenge dominant geopolitical and economic relations (Stein, Andreotti, & Suša, 2019). Thus, although the campaign nominally invited 'a wide range of voices' to share their visions for global social change, given this framing, the scope of what would be perceived as viable perspectives was highly circumscribed from the outset.

Being taught by difference

Being taught by difference is an approach to global learning that is articulated and practised from the edge of the onto-epistemological frames of colonial modernity, looking outward towards other possibilities, but committed to learning from the mistakes of those frames, and cautious of how to engage ethically beyond them. From this approach, global challenges are understood not as the result of a lack of knowledge, information or consensus, but rather the result of the imposition of a single imaginary that is premised on a set of supposedly universal knowledges and visions for the future; in turn, structures of political and economic domination are required in order to assert that universality. Thus, the proposition in response to this diagnosis is to face the limits and harms of the promises of colonial modernity (including security, certainty, supremacy, autonomy and universality), and the colonial habits of knowing and being that they foster, and to encounter radically other ways of knowing, being and relating without trying to control the outcome of that encounter – that is, without projecting one's understandings, hopes and desires on to others and the world. The idea is that through this mode of engagement, other modes of knowing, being and relating that are currently invisibilized and unimaginable might come to be seen as viable.

Within the context of global citizenship, an approach to global learning oriented around being taught by difference can be understood in contrast to learning from difference. Drawing on Biesta (2013), Bruce (2013) offers this distinction: while *learning from* implies learning something that is expected, intelligible and then assimilated into existing frames of knowledge and worldviews, *being taught by* entails de-centring and suspending preconceptions about the 'other' in order to open up to being taught by difference and thus, to unexpected and potential disruptive rearrangements of knowing, being and desiring (Spivak, 2004). Describing how this might work in the context of service-learning, Bruce (2013) suggests that the possibility of being taught by requires that one at least temporarily bracket the modern onto-epistemological imperative to predetermine and control the directionality and outcomes of engaging with and across difference. This intention is, of course, easier said than done, as it requires engaging not only the cognitive but also the affective and relational dimensions of learning (and unlearning), which are rarely given adequate attention in the practice of global learning. In particular, cognitively it requires disarming the colonial imperative of consuming and defining difference into predetermined categories; affectively it requires the courage and stamina to face the full range of emotional responses that arise when those socialized within colonial modernity's frames are faced with epistemic uncertainty; and relationally it requires cracking inherited patterns of relationship premised on authority and extraction so that new, non-paternalistic forms of responsibility can be practised.

In the context of internationalizing curricula, being taught by difference would entail not simply adding more marginalized knowledges into existing coursework, but also considering the difficulties of ensuring that these knowledges are engaged in ways that open up truly different horizons of possibility, honouring and revering their gifts without romanticizing them (Ahenakew, 2016). This would require respecting the intrinsic integrity of marginalized knowledges and knowledge producers, beyond any imperative of translation into pre-existing categories or experiences. Only if this respect is in place will students and scholars be open to the possibility of being taught by these knowledges on their own terms. In turn, encountering other knowledges from this approach can help learners to identify the internal limits, partialities and blind spots of Western onto-epistemological frames. Indeed, in this approach to global learning it would be imperative that all knowledge systems are reframed as partial and contextually relevant interventions that both enable and foreclose different possibilities (Santos, 2007).

An approach to global social change oriented by the imperative to be taught by difference asserts that because the onto-epistemological frames of colonial modernity are at the root of contemporary global challenges, solutions to these challenges are not likely to be found (solely) within them (Stein, 2017). In order to approach global social change without reproducing these frames would require that those within Western universities: unlearn investments in epistemic universality; process affective resistances to 'giving up' perceived entitlements to economic advantage, political authority and moral superiority; engage responsibly with different knowledge systems without seeking to master them; and learn to relate to one another and the world in ways that are not determined by sameness or universal values, but rather humility, compassion and affirmation of our responsibilities to each other as part of interconnected metabolism. In this approach to global social change, although the general direction of change might be imagined, its precise character and outcomes cannot be predetermined in advance of its doing; rather, transformation must be iteratively co-created by walking together into the unknown, learning from our mistakes and our successes as we go (Table 6.1).

Table 6.1 Different Approaches to Global Learning in Western Higher Education

	Learning about difference	*Learning from* difference	*Being taught by* difference
Diagnosis of the cause of global challenges	Lack of knowledge, information, consensus	Lack of diversity and inclusion in shared vision of progress, change	Single story of progress premised on certainty, domination and sameness
Proposition in response to global challenges	Accumulate and disseminate more universal knowledge within dominant frames and institutions	Revise dominant frames and institutions to make them more inclusive of local knowledges	Denaturalize the presumption of shared frames and institutions as a prerequisite for living together
Global citizenship	Assume a position of benevolent leadership for the world; achieve/ acquire cultural competency	Appreciate shared qualities and differences to deepen understanding and improve relations, respect	Bracket desires for control and certainty, open up to the possibility of being unsettled and transformed by difference
Internationalization of the curriculum	Learn/accumulate knowledge about the non-West	Provincialize the West to revise universal truths	Provincialize all knowledges to pluralize possibilities
Global social change	Apply universal solutions to particular contexts for predetermined futures	Adjust universal solutions to particular contexts for predetermined futures	Unlearn the desire for universality, experiment with other possibilities to create as-yet-unknown and emergent futures

Education for pluralizing global learning

In this chapter, I have sought to open up a conversation through which we might pluralize the available frameworks for global learning that have been articulated in response to global challenges within the context of Western universities. Each of the three approaches to global learning that I have identified – learning about difference, learning from difference and being taught by difference – has a contrasting orientation to colonial modernity's onto-epistemological frames. As a result, each has a different diagnosis of contemporary global challenges, and a different proposition about how we might respond to these challenges in general, and particularly in the context of global citizenship, curriculum internationalization and conceptualizing global social change.

Rather than conclude by advocating for one particular approach to global learning, which either maintains or revises the dominant frames, or replaces them with something different, I instead propose an overarching educational orientation that creates spaces for students to critically and self-reflexively assess the gifts and limitations of existing approaches to global learning (which exceed the three that I have mapped here), and to imagine and experiment responsibly with new ones. What might an approach to global learning in HE look like that enabled not any particular possible future, but rather nurtured the 'possibility of possibilities' (Barnett, 2014)?

This would require that we prepare students with the critical literacies, sensibilities and sensitivities that would equip them to identify and analyse where each of the different approaches to global learning come from, where they lead, what they assume, what they enable and what they foreclose – as well as to consider what other approaches might be viable but remain absent and invisible for those still embedded and invested in the frames of colonial modernity. Sensitizing students to uneven power relations and historical patterns of global engagement can prompt them to consider why certain approaches to global learning tend to dominate over others. This would also need to be accompanied by ongoing conversations that attune students to enduring political, epistemological and affective barriers to enacting change, and the resulting risks of colonial continuities in efforts to enact 'global learning'. Rather than try and prepare students for potential futures that we cannot foresee, I suggest the need to prepare them with the courage and the stamina to make, and take responsibility for, their own decisions in the face of complexity, uncertainty, plurality, contingency and complicity.

Bibliography

Ahenakew, C. (2016). Grafting Indigenous ways of knowing onto non-Indigenous ways of being: The (underestimated) challenges of a decolonial imagination. *International Review of Qualitative Research*, *9*(3), 323–40.

Ahenakew, C., Andreotti, V. D. O., Cooper, G. and Hireme, H. (2014). Beyond epistemic provincialism: De-provincializing Indigenous resistance. *AlterNative: An International Journal of Indigenous Peoples*, *10*(3), 216–31.

Andreotti, V. D. O., Stein, S., Ahenakew, C. and Hunt, D. (2015). Mapping interpretations of decolonization in the context of higher education. *Decolonization: Indigeneity. Education & Society*, *4*(1), 21–40.

Barnett, R. (2014). Thinking about higher education. In P. Gibb and R. Barnett. (ed.), *Thinking about Higher Education* (pp. 9–22). Springer International Publishing.

Biesta, G. (2013). Receiving the gift of teaching: From 'learning from' to 'being taught by'. *Studies in Philosophy and Education*, *32*(5), 449–61.

Bruce, J. (2013). Service learning as a pedagogy of interruption. *International Journal of Development Education and Global Learning*, *5*(1), 33–47.

Chakravartty, P. and Silva, D. F. D. (2012). Accumulation, dispossession, and debt: The racial logic of global capitalism – an introduction. *American Quarterly*, *64*(3), 361–85.

Dean, S. (2011). *Normal Life: Administrative Violence, Critical Trans Politics, and the Limits of Law*. Brooklyn: South End Press.

Deloria, P. J. (1998). *Playing Indian*. New Haven, CT: Yale University Press.

Escobar, A. (2016). Thinking-feeling with the Earth: Territorial struggles and the ontological dimension of the epistemologies of the South. *AIBR. Revista de Antropología Iberoamericana*, *11*(1), 11–32.

Grande, S. (2004). *Red Pedagogy: Native American Social and Political Thought*. Lanham, MD: Rowman & Littlefield.

Grosfoguel, R. (2013). The structure of knowledge in westernized universities: Epistemic racism/sexism and the four genocides/epistemicides of the long 16th century. *Human Architecture*, *11*(1), 73.

Killick, D. (2012). Seeing-ourselves-in-the-world: Developing global citizenship through international mobility and campus community. *Journal of Studies in International Education*, *16*(4), 372–89.

Lowe, L. (2015). History hesitant. *Social Text*, *33*(4 (125)), 85–107.

Menzel, A. (2010). Crisis and epistemologies of ignorance. Paper presented at the APSA Annual Meeting. Retrieved from: https://papers.ssrn.com/sol3/papers.cfm?abstract_id=1644543

Mills, C. (2007). White ignorance. In S. Sullivan and N. Tuana (eds), *Race and epistemologies of ignorance*. Albany, NY: State University of New York Press.

Mohanty, C. T. (2003). 'Under western eyes' revisited: Feminist solidarity through anticapitalist struggles. *Signs: Journal of Women in Culture and Society*, *28*(2), 499–535.

Morse, S. (2006). 'Regrouping, rethinking, and redirecting energies around higher education for the public good: A keynote address'. In P. A. Pasque, L. A. Hendricks and N. A. Bowman (eds), *Taking Responsibility: A Call for Higher Education's Engagement in a Society of Complex Challenges* (pp. 26–46). Ann Arbor, MI: National Forum on Higher Education and the Public Good.

Nandy, A. (2000). Recovery of indigenous knowledge and dissenting futures of the university, In S. Inayatullah and J. Gidley (eds), *The University in Transformation: Global Perspectives and the Future of the University* (pp. 115–23). Westport, CT: Bergin & Garvey.

Pashby, K., da Costa, M., Stein, S. and Andreotti (forthcoming). Mapping typologies of global citizenship education: From description to critique.

Pasque, P. A., Hendricks, L. A. and Bowman, N. A. (eds) (2006). *Taking Responsibility: A Call for Higher Education's Engagement in a Society of Complex Global Challenges*. Ann Arbor: National Forum on Higher Education for the Public Good.

Restrepo, P. (2014). Legitimation of knowledge, epistemic justice and the intercultural university: Towards an epistemology of 'living well'. *Postcolonial Studies*, *17*(2), 140–54.

Rhoades, R. (2011). The U.S. research university as a global model: Some fundamental problems to consider. *Interactions: UCLA Journal of Education and Information Studies*, *7*(2), 1–27.

Santos, B. S. (2007). Beyond abyssal thinking: From global lines to ecologies of knowledges. *Review (Fernand Braudel Center)*, *30*(1), 45–89.

Simpson, L. R. (2005). Anticolonial strategies for the recovery and maintenance of Indigenous knowledge. *The American Indian Quarterly*, *28*(3), 373–84.

Spade, D. (2011). *Normal Life: Administrative Violence, Critical Trans Politics, and the Limits of Law*. Brooklyn, NY: South End Press.

Spivak, G. C. (1988). Can the subaltern speak? In C. Nelson and L. Grossberg (eds), *Marxism and the Interpretation of Culture* (pp. 271–313). Chicago: University of Illinois Press.

Spivak, G. C. (2004). Righting wrongs. *South Atlantic Quarterly*, *103*(2–3), 523–81.

Stein, S. (2017). Internationalization for an uncertain future: Tensions, paradoxes, and possibilities. *The Review of Higher Education*, *41*(1), 3–32.

Stein, S., Andreotti, V. D. O. and Suša, R. (2019). 'Beyond 2015', within the modern/colonial global imaginary? Global development and higher education. *Critical Studies in Education*, *60*(3), 281–301.

Stein, S., Hunt, D., Suša, R. and de Oliveira Andreotti, V. (2017). The educational challenge of unraveling the fantasies of ontological security. *Diaspora, Indigenous, and Minority Education*, *11*(2), 69–79.

Tannock, S. (2007). To keep America number 1: Confronting the deep nationalism of US higher education. *Globalisation, Societies and Education*, *5*(2), 257–72.

UNESCO (2009). Communiqué: World conference on higher education: The new dynamics of higher education and research for societal change and development. Retrieved from: http://unesdoc.unesc o.org/images/0018/001832/183277e.pdf

Whyte, K. (2017). Indigenous climate change studies: Indigenizing futures, decolonizing the Anthropocene. *English Language Notes*, *55*(1–2), 153–62.

Chapter 7

Ubuntu: Constructing Spaces of Dialogue in the Theory and Practice of Global Education

Malgorzata Anielka Pieniazek

Introduction

Global education (GE) is a terrain of not only academic research but also a complex and contested concept, manifested in policy and civil society contexts and shaped by diverse philosophical and ideological perspectives. While the concept has been a subject of ongoing interest among scholars, educators, global institutions and governmental actors for over a few decades, it can be argued that much of the work concerning GE to date has focused on evidence, theories and research emanating from the Global North[1] (Bhattacharya and Ordonez Llanos, 2017). The perspectives from the Global South have often been underrepresented, mediated by non-governmental organization (NGOs) or excluded from the international debates (Jooste and Heleta, 2017). This has been the case despite there being a variety of activities going on in Africa, Asia, and Latin America ... that resonate with various types of global education (Gaudelli and Wyllie, 2012).

Drawing on a literature review of a Sub-Saharan African concept of *Ubuntu*, this chapter poses questions on how indigenous philosophies from the Global South contribute to the international debates around GE. It can thus be seen as situated within the critical strand of the discourses around GE and global citizenship that recognize the significance of addressing unequal power relations and the importance of engagement with voices who have been historically disadvantaged (see Andreotti, 2016; Swanson and Pashby, 2016). It offers a self-reflective approach of learning from *Ubuntu* and examining the ways in which the concept poses complex and fundamental questions of global social justice, including cognitive justice in the academia as well how the theoretical underpinnings, values and practice embedded in the concept can enrich GE.

---

[1] The terms 'Global South' and 'Global North' are used strategically to describe certain regions in the world and power relations that operate between them. The usage of this terminology is an attempt to refrain from using the expressions that dominate the economic discourses, such as 'developed' and 'developing' countries or 'first world' and 'third world', as they are value laden and position some regions as better off than others, without considering the complexities of these regions. At the same time, the author acknowledges limitations, complexities and divisions that are charged in the Global North–Global South binary framework.

Conceptual framework of global education

To begin a discussion of GE and its relationship to Global South, an examination of the contexts and disciplines within which the notion 'GE' operates is required. Based on a review of available literature on the subject in English between years 2000–18 I suggest five interpretations of GE: (1) an international policy framework; (2) an overarching umbrella term incorporating related educational traditions; (3) an educational field of theory and practice; (4) a body of knowledge on global issues and (5) a pedagogical framework to teaching and learning about local and global problems (see Hartmeyer and Wegimont, 2016a; Bourn, 2015a; Peterson and Warwick, 2015; Shultz, 2015; Standish, 2014; Andreotti, 2010b; Tye, 2009; Hicks, 2008; Merryfield, 2001).

Global education as an international policy framework

In some contexts, the term 'global education' has been used to refer to international policy frameworks, defined as multi-level strategies, guidelines and action plans agreed by public and private actors to tackle common issues (see United Nations Committee for Development Policy, 2012). International policy frameworks that are linked to GE address ongoing or emerging global challenges. In the literature on the topic, the Decade of Education for Sustainable Development (DESD) and the two major international development agendas, the UN Millennium Development Goals (MDGs) and the UN Sustainable Development Goals (SDGs) have been mentioned as the most recent globally recognized international policy frameworks linked to GE (see Skinner et al., 2013). Equally important in shaping GE were the international policy frameworks on GE itself, such as the Global Education First Initiative (GEFI), the work of United Nations Educational, Scientific and Cultural Organization (UNESCO) on Global Citizenship Education (GCE) and Education for Sustainable Development (ESD). On a European level, a key international policy framework regarding global and development education (DE) was agreed at the Maastricht Congress in 2002 (see Hartmeyer and Wegimont, 2016b).

Global education as an overarching umbrella term incorporating related educational traditions

Numerous articles offer an understanding of GE as an umbrella term that incorporates related educational traditions, such as DE, Human Rights Education (HRE), Education for Sustainability, Education for Peace and Conflict Prevention, Intercultural and Interfaith Education, GCE and so on, under a broader social field (see Cabezudo, et al., 2008). In this interpretation GE is seen as a unifying concept, encompassing the common grounds of the 'adjectival movements' to integrate a variety of educational traditions under one term and increase the understanding of global issues from different angles (see Bourn, 2015a: 12).

Global education as an educational field of theory and practice

'Global education' is a term mentioned in various educational contexts around the world. In a range of discussions in the literature, it is referred to as an educational field, a socially constituted space of dialogue among theorists and practitioners, that encompasses the work of academics, educators and NGO practitioners concerned with generating knowledge about global issues (see Hicks, 2007: 27; Scheunpflug and Asbrand, 2006). In this interpretation GE is similar to other fields, such as Health Education or Physics Education; however, the uniqueness comes from the multidimensional and multidisciplinary character of the field of study and the fact that it brings together ideas and approaches of diverse groups, similarly to, for example, the field of comparative education. A recent example of a European community of practice enabling cooperation and sharing of work on the topic of GE between researchers in the field and policy-makers can be seen in the 2017 launch of the Academic Network on Global Education & Learning (ANGEL) (see DERC, 2018). International academic journals that publish research findings and theoretical studies on the concepts of DE, global learning, global citizenship and GE can be seen as another example of a source of knowledge on GE and the broader field.[2]

Global education as a body of knowledge on global issues

GE can be seen as a body of knowledge, a set of topics that relate to global issues. These are reflected within national curricula, resources created by NGOs and UN agencies as well as the international policy frameworks such as SDGs. There is no exhaustive list of global challenges, but they are generally linked to the process of globalization and described as increasingly complex social, economic, political and environmental problems that transcend national borders and jurisdictions and can affect communities on both a local and global scale (see Osler and Vincent, 2002; Stromquist, 2002). In his definition of GE, Standish (2014: 183) presented a list of global issues that are frequently taught as a part of the knowledge on the topic. These included 'poverty and malnutrition, environmental and ecological problems, equity, peace and conflict resolution, health, human rights, social justice, population growth, trade and technological change'. Global knowledge builds a foundation of GE and is needed to understand the contemporary events affecting the people and the world. However, how this content is delivered to the general public

---

[2] *ZEP* – Journal for International Educational Research and Development Education in Germany, available at: https://www.uni-bamberg.de/?id=79740; Policy & Practice (Ireland), available at: http://www.developmentreview.com; *International Journal of Development Education and Global Learning* (UK), available at: http://ioepress.co.uk/journals/international-journal-of-development-education-and-global-learning/; Sinergias: diálogos educativos para a transformação Synergies – Educational dialogues for social change (Portugal), available at: http://www.sinergiased.org/; Critical Literacy: Theories and Practices (Canada), available at: http://www.criticalliteracyjournal.org/; Journal of Global Citizenship & Equity Education (Canada), available at: http://journals.sfu.ca/jgcee/index.php/jgcee; Journal of Global Education and Research (Association of North America Higher International), available at: https://jger.anahei.org/

through media or through teaching to students becomes equally critical, as it influences the understanding of this knowledge and shapes the attitudes.

Global education as a pedagogical framework to teaching and learning about interdependent local and global problems

The concept of GE is often proposed as a multidimensional pedagogical framework that aims at raising learners' awareness of the complex and interdependent local and global problems which societies currently face (Andreotti, 2010b). The pedagogical framework refers to a process of transforming the body of knowledge around global issues into teaching practice. In many cases this approach has a normative character; it is underpinned by a value system around the ideals of global social justice that promotes social change through active global citizenship (see Bourn, 2015b, Bourn chapter in this volume). Equally important in GE as a model of learning are skills and competencies required to tackle global issues. These include among others, critical and reflective thinking, ability to communicate effectively and approach problems from different angles and deal with complexity, capability to work cooperatively, make connections between own life and the lives of others and readiness to engage with difference (see Bourn, 2014; Cabezudo, et al., 2008). According to Robin Richardson, an awareness of a global problem is not enough, the background to its occurrence and the causes to its existence need to be explored first, along with values that people hold, in order for an appropriate action to be taken to resolve it (see Hicks, 2007: 15).

Applying the framework

The outlined typology provides a brief overview of the five possible interpretations of GE, and it can be used to develop an understanding of the concept. Depending on a lens through which the framework is examined, it can serve as a starting point in discussions on what kind of perspectives are dominant within each of the interpretations and which ones are being marginalized and missing in the mainstream debates. As mentioned earlier, with the understanding of the world being much broader than the Western perspectives, knowledge construction about global themes should take place in diverse settings and be reported from diverse perspectives (Odora Hoppers, 2015). This was the leading motivation that has led me to search for alternative approaches to studying GE.

Learning to understand *Ubuntu*

While looking for the non-Northern interpretations of GE, a continued reference to the concept of *Ubuntu* has been revealed in the literature (see Waghid, 2018; Assié-Lumumba, 2017; Eze, 2017;

Torres, 2017). *Ubuntu* has been understood as an ethic, philosophy or characterized in terms of a set of norms and values in a number of Sub-Saharan African societies (Eze, 2008; Letseka, 2013; Ramose 1999).

Ubuntu is a word from the Nguni language family, a group of Bantu languages spoken in southern Africa encompassing among others Zulu, Xhosa, Swati and Ndebele (van Binsbergen, 2001). It originates from the proverbial expressions: '*Motho ke motho ka batho babang*' in Sotho languages or '*Umuntu ngumuntu ngabantu*' in Nguni languages (Letseka, 2013; Le Grange, 2012) and is often summarized as 'a person is a person through their relationship to others' (Swanson, 2015: 34), 'a person is a person through other persons' or 'I am because we are' (Mboti, 2015: 127; Metz and Gaie, 2010: 275). *Ubuntu* can thus be understood as trying to capture the essence of what it is to be human, highlighting the interconnectedness and unity between human beings and linking the individual to the collective (Swanson, 2015; Kayira, 2015; Ngcoya, 2009). While the meaning of *Ubuntu* cannot be condensed into one word as this would reduce its semantic richness, it has often been translated as 'humanness' (Broodryk 2002: 13; Le Grange, 2012: 61; Metz, 2007: 323; Ramose, 1999: 105), 'humanity' (Nussbaum, 2003: 21; Shutte 2001: 2) or 'human interconnectedness' (Waghid and Smeyers, 2012: 6). It should, however, never be considered as an -ism, as in the word 'humanism' (Ramose, 1999: 51; Kimmerle, 2000: 191), because the -ism suffix would imply that *Ubuntu* may be understood as an ideology, something fixed and absolute (Ramose, 1999: 51; van Norren, 2014). According to Bewaji and Ramose (2003: 382) *Ubuntu* tries to capture qualities and characteristics of personhood. In this sense, *Ubuntu*, the essence of being human, the complexity of human existence, the personhood, is expressed through qualities like acceptance, respect, compassion, empathy, generosity, hospitality (Eze, 2017: 99; Stuit, 2016: 2; Tutu, 2011: 22).

The literature suggests that the notion of *Ubuntu* has been theorized in a wide range of academic contexts (Letseka, 2013; Gade, 2012; Metz, 2007; Broodryk, 2002; Shutte, 2001; Mbiti, 1969) by both African philosophers and non-African scholars. These academic discussions provide diverse, non-uniform interpretations and ways of understanding the idea. *Ubuntu* has been viewed as a moral principle, an ancient world view, a value system, an African philosophy, an ethic and a moral theory (Biney, 2014: 29).

International symbolic expressions of *Ubuntu*

The growing interest in the notion of *Ubuntu* outside of the African continent is often linked to two key South African Nobel Peace Prize laureates, Archbishop Desmond Tutu and President Nelson Mandela, who through their political involvement and advocacy raised the profile of the concept internationally (Ngcoya, 2009). Some of the usage of the word *Ubuntu* in the international contexts can be found through the following examples: Ubuntu Linux (free operating system) is a globally known open-source software platform which runs on personal computers, servers and smartphones and so on (Canonical)[3] and is inspired by the philosophy of *Ubuntu*, Ubuntu Education Fund is a non-profit organization that provides health, housing and educational support to orphaned and vulnerable children in Port Elizabeth in South Africa

---

[3]   https://www.canonical.com/

(Ubuntu Education Fund, 2016), the Ubuntu Network is an Irish organization based in the Department of Education and Professional Studies at University of Limerick which has been established to support the integration of DE into initial teacher education (Ubuntu Network).[4]

These examples demonstrate that there is a presence of the ideas of *Ubuntu* within the international domain. However, the term has often been used as a brand name, dissociated from its roots and indigenous heritage and applied in tokenistic and decontextualized ways. Jefferess (2016: 91) criticizes the usage of *Ubuntu* in the discourse of international development claiming that it's often used to reaffirm voluntarism, charitable actions and humanitarianism where organizations and institutions use indigenous words and concepts as a way of legitimizing their empathy and solidarity with the people from the Global South, but do not internalize or engage with the conceptual debates behind these concepts nor take into account their historical and cultural anchoring.

This appropriation of indigenous knowledges contradicts the goals and principles of GE. In response, the sections below will propose a self-reflective approach of learning from *Ubuntu* that challenges paternalism and instead promotes a respectful engagement with the concept to advance an argument for its relevance to the international debates on GE.

Global education shaped and informed by *Ubuntu*

In this section, I will then attempt to make a connection between *Ubuntu* and different interpretations of GE and discuss what role *Ubuntu* can play in the GE theory and practice. I will be only covering some examples of the relationship of *Ubuntu* to interpretations of GE by applying three understandings of GE from the conceptual framework introduced earlier. I will consider the resonance of *Ubuntu* with the human rights discourses and how both frameworks can influence, complete and complement one another (within the interpretation of GE understood as an overarching umbrella term incorporating related educational traditions). After this, I will move on to the analysis of the SDGs agenda and explore how it can be linked with the concept of *Ubuntu* to make the SDGs more inclusive and relevant on the African continent (within the interpretation of GE understood as an international policy framework). Finally, I will discuss *Ubuntu* as a pedagogical tool for raising awareness about global issues and promoting global solidarity (within the interpretation of GE understood as a model of learning and raising awareness about global issues).

Application of *Ubuntu* in the context of global education: *Ubuntu* and human rights education

The white tribes have taken inventions and gone far up-river with them. We can learn a great deal from them. But we have taken humanity and gone far up-river with it, and we can teach them a lot about humanity.

(African-Surinamese leader, interviewed by Alan Counter and James Earl Jones, Counter, et al. 1978, cited in Assié-Lumumba, 2017: 11)

---

[4] http://www.ubuntu.ie/about.html

One of the interpretations of GE refers to it as an umbrella term that incorporates related educational traditions such as HRE. HRE advocates for engagement with the human rights principles and gives particular emphasis to the dignity and humanity of all people which stems from the fact that they have been born as human beings (see Gaudelli, 2016: 61). Conceptualized as a part of the GE discourse, HRE examines economic, political, environmental and social circumstances that lead to injustices. It raises awareness of global human rights concerns and promotes the ideals of global social justice, empathy and solidarity with people around the world to tackle these inequalities and violations (see Bourn, 2015a).

From the perspective of the post-colonial theory, HRE is a contested site. Post-colonial critique of the human rights discourse draws attention to the problematic claims to universality of human rights, pointing that their conceptualization as a set of norms, remains tied to European modernity, Eurocentric understandings and legal traditions (see Zembylas, 2017b: 488). This critique also illustrates that the framework in which prevailing understandings of human rights are discussed is embedded in the Western epistemological, cultural and political contexts that have historically silenced different, non-Western moral traditions and approaches. It does not reject the framework itself but urges HRE to become critically engaged with these aspects to be able to 'provide a useful approach to moral education that addresses issues of injustice, inequality and wrong-doing' (Zembylas, 2014: 1150).

In accord with this, I argue that an engagement with the concept of *Ubuntu* addresses the need for re-examination of the human rights discourse by offering a different angle to the mainstream conceptualizations of human rights. A common thread running through the analyses of the concept of *Ubuntu* across the literature depicts it as an interplay between 'humanness' and 'community'. According to Tim Murithi (2006: 25), *Ubuntu* may be achieved through the principles of empathy, sharing, cooperation and responsibility towards others. The author observes elsewhere that the importance of *Ubuntu* lies in 'the recognition that it is not possible to build a healthy community at peace with itself unless the human dignity of all members of the community is safeguarded'. (Murithi, 2007: 282). What follows from this is that practice of *Ubuntu* is a part of life in a community, where interconnectedness between human beings results in the interconnectedness of obligations as well as rights of individual members of the community (Assié-Lumumba, 2017: 12).

However, it must be noted that over glorification of the communal aspect of *Ubuntu* can be problematic and has sparked serious debates among the critics of the concept. The main reservations relate to the issues of inclusion and exclusion, the positioning and role of an individual in the society and whose interests matter more, the individuals' or the community's (see Matolino and Kwindingwi, 2013; Enslin and Horsthemke, 2004). This dichotomy is addressed by Yusef Waghid who argues that highlighting the communal orientation towards life in the notion of *Ubuntu* should not automatically be equated as being at the expense of the individual. Instead, it should be understood in the context of 'an individual's aspirations and actions as constitutive, as an extension of the community' (Waghid, 2014b: 5). In this interpretation, *Ubuntu* relies on the principles of respect for others, solidarity and cooperation in order to advance human well-being.

Linking the above with the human rights discourse, the contribution of *Ubuntu* stems from the fact that apart from recognizing the significance of the individual self and the individual other, as it is in the classic formulations of human rights discourses, *Ubuntu* places an emphasis on collective commitments and efforts to safeguard this collective welfare (Swanson, 2015: 36).

At the same time, as aptly recognized by Praeg (2014), the meanings of *Ubuntu* have undergone some transformations as well, as it has been influenced by the global discourses such as the human rights framework and Christianity, which made it become a 'glocal phenomenon'. Praeg argues that this has allowed 'Ubuntu to feed back into the global discourse as a locally based critique and expansion of those very discourses' (Praeg, 2014: 37).

Application of *Ubuntu* in the context of global education: *Ubuntu* and international policy framework

The shortcomings of the former global development and educational agendas, the UN MDGs and the GE for All, to achieve many of its aims and objectives (Schultz, 2015) provides ground for claims that the transfer of global policies and practices from Global North to Global South in its current forms requires questioning. The interconnectedness of global challenges, such as unequal access to natural resources, poverty, environmental degradation and climate change, on the one hand and their specificity and locality on the other, calls for international development policies to be guided by strategies that will include transformative dimensions of planning and decision-making.

The absence of intercultural and interreligious exchange of ideas raises questions to whether the current conceptualizations of SDGs are inclusive and meaningful enough to transcend cultural horizons and ensure their implementation on the regional and local levels by communities and individuals. As Biney (2014: 48) argues abstract ideas 'are likely to make little sense to the consciousness of the woman or man in the Kenyan slums of Kibera or to the young men scraping a living in the toxic dump site of Agbogbloshie on the outskirts of Ghana's capital, Accra'. This perhaps radical observation may in a way oversimplify the problem; however, it draws attention to the need of relevance in proposing solutions to tackle global inequalities, especially for the programmes to be negotiated with different stakeholders and underpinned by knowledges and value systems of different civilizations as well rooted in people's everyday experiences (Shultz, 2015; van Norren, 2014). *Ubuntu* forms an important part of cultural heritage of African societies (Ramose, 1999) and can thus serve as a basis to make SDGs more relevant to the Sub-Saharan African context. The application of SDGs through *Ubuntu* can open dialogue and bring a sense of ownership and encouragement to use local expertise and generate solutions that address local concerns and needs and at the same time are aligned with a broader global agenda.

On a macro policy level, embracing *Ubuntu*, as concept that emphasizes the aspects of shared humanity and the responsibilities towards another human being (Eze, 2017), can serve as a stimulus to promote attitudes of collective obligation and cooperation to resolve the global challenges, key in the formulation of the SDG17 and by extension the realization of all SDGs. In her discussion of *Ubuntu*'s potential contribution to the global development agenda, van Norren (2014: 264) draws attention to the concept's emphasis on forgiveness and restorative justice and its application within the work of the Truth and Reconciliation Commission in South Africa. She thus makes a direct link to its beneficence to the area of peace and security. From this perspective, there may be scope for *Ubuntu* to inspire and play a supporting role in the SDG 16. The philosophy of *Ubuntu* stresses the interconnectedness of humans and the importance of fostering relations between people based on the notion of solidarity (Stuit, 2016). Reducing inequalities (SDG 10), tackling poverty (SDG1) and achieving food security in all regions of the world (SDG2) requires engagement with the questions of global social justice and reformulation of ideas of solidarity when addressing the global inequalities, therefore drawing from the philosophy of *Ubuntu* may aid this process. According to Assié-Lumumba (2017: 16), through the foundation and values that are encompassed in *Ubuntu*, it 'may or ought to be used to conceptualize, design, and implement policies factoring in new social and unfolding realities'.

It's important to mention, however, that outlining of the potential of *Ubuntu* philosophy is not intended to act as a formula to be uncritically adopted in global development policy, instead it points to the need of discussions about (re)designing global policies to draw from locally relevant values and knowledge systems. As Lewis Gordon (2014: 22) attentively suggests, 'It means admitting that purported universal normative language is limited and that each generation of humanity has the task of raising the standards of what we claim to be the best in all of us.'

Application of Ubuntu in the context of global education: *Ubuntu* pedagogical framework to teaching and learning

In his vision of GCE, Carlos Torres (2017: 84) provides an inspiration to think differently about GE in the twenty-first century. He calls for GCE that considers multiple perspectives from different knowledge systems and is 'grounded and contextualized in localities but combines multiple knowledges and multi-civic virtues that transcend borders for actions that endeavour to defend humanity and global commons'. Torres outlines a direction to be taken in redefining the field that means searching and reaching to the repertoire of the ideas from the Global South. He suggests that 'Ubuntu is an African collective ethos of the universal bond between people based upon the sharing and collectivity of all humanity, which can be the foundation for GCE programs not only in relevant communities but might have the possibility of resonating with others around the world' (Torres, 2017: 84). By pointing to the GCE programmes, the author also opens a dialogue about the contribution of non-Western concepts to the learning framework of GE, an argument that will be further discussed in this section.

GE can be characterized 'by pedagogical approaches based on human rights and a concern for social justice which encourage critical thinking and responsible participation' (Osler and Vincent, 2002: 2). In his book, *African Philosophy of Education Reconsidered: On Being Human* (2014), Yusef Waghid reflects on this process and outlines an innovative use of African philosophy of education founded on *Ubuntu* to challenge inequalities and provide solutions to social challenges. Drawing attention to the fact that *Ubuntu* brings together elements of human rights, peace and conflict resolution and social justice, Waghid argues how *Ubuntu*, through the characteristics it encompasses such as 'acknowledgement of humanity', 'cooperation and sharing', can guide the pedagogical actions to harness these elements and enable students' growth and development (Waghid, 2014b: 13). He suggests that *Ubuntu* can stimulate students to learn to recognize humanity in themselves and others and lead 'towards imaginative action and a renewed consciousness of possibility' (Waghid, 2014a: 270–1). Waghid's argument considers an encounter with *Ubuntu* in terms of its role in opening possibilities for the learners to become independent-minded and take collaborative actions against social inequalities.

When deployed in the educational contexts, *Ubuntu* may be beneficial for both learners from the Global North and the Global South. In the Global North settings, GE inspired by and enriched by the philosophy of *Ubuntu* may support learners to develop an understanding that the world is much broader than the Western conceptualizations of thereof and may be used as a pedagogical tool for discussions about unequal economic and power relations and cultural diversity. It may be used to encourage learners to critically reflect on their own role in the world and their position within the matrix of power relations. Furthermore, the inclusion of the philosophy of *Ubuntu* as a part of the GE curricula initiates engagement with overlooked concepts and authors from the Global South and may help to foster an understanding among the Northern learners that their experiences, history and perspectives are one of many available forms of knowing the world. This approach is anchored on the idea of Boaventura de Sousa Santos's concept of 'ecology of knowledges' (Santos, 2014: 239) that acknowledges the existence of multiple sources of knowledge and at the same time highlights that what counts as knowledge can also be measured differently. He states that 'there are not only very diverse forms of knowledge of matter, society, life, and spirit but also many and very diverse concepts of what counts as knowledge and the criteria that may be used to validate it' (Santos, 2014: 245, cited in Zembylas, 2017a: 403). For ecology of knowledges to be recognized, there is a need for intercultural dialogue, where Northern and Southern, local and indigenous knowledges are treated equally and are given an equal, legitimate status (see Zembylas, 2017a: 403). This renewed approach towards epistemologies of the Global South creates spaces of mutual understanding of different knowledge systems and cultures that enables, 'a more democratic, egalitarian and ethical engagement of human beings in relationship with each other' (Swanson, 2015: 36).

Ubuntu inspired GE can also play a very important role in the context of educational outcomes in the Global South. Takyi-Amoako suggests that the principles of *Ubuntu* should be discussed among African policy-makers and that adoption of programmes based on this philosophy 'will help address the power inequalities, and result in indigenously led and relevant educational policy, practice and outcomes for sustainable development in Africa' (Takyi-Amoako, 218: 212–13). Other scholars also argue that the ethic can provide a framework for African philosophy of education, citizenship and democratic education (Waghid, 2014b). N'dri Assié-Lumumba brings to the fore the fact that contemporary education in various African countries is constructed on a juxtaposition of European and African systems of learning and examines how education informed by *Ubuntu* can offer a constructive dialogue between the two (Assié-Lumumba, 2017: 16). In her conceptualization of African education, Assié-Lumumba advocates for an educational framework that considers African wisdoms, traditions and knowledge systems when addressing the needs of modern-day societies, enables the integration of the past and the present and most importantly is able to elevate Africans to 'new positions of strength based on a collective ethos, they will be able to address, apart from their own problems, those of the global community' (Assié-Lumumba, 2017: 16). Yusef Waghid's articulation of education founded on *Ubuntu* seems to provide this kind of vision. Waghid (2014b: 8) attentively suggests that the objective of philosophy of education informed by *Ubuntu* is to empower communities through learning possibilities that will at the outset allow for educational development and then as a consequence release a potential for solving inequalities on the African continent by these empowered communities. In this sense *Ubuntu* inspired education can result in increasing of motivation for people to become active as responsible global citizens for a sustainable future.

Conclusion

The intention of this chapter was to build on the discussions about countering epistemological hegemony and allowing diverse forms of understanding the world to be a part of the GE discourse. In this sense, an engagement with the Sub-Saharan African concept of *Ubuntu* gives an opportunity for non-Western and indigenous epistemologies to come into dialogue in the discussions about GE. There always exists a danger of interpretation that *Ubuntu* is an answer and a solution to the direction in which GE research should move towards. However, the aim of this chapter was to pose questions and open discussions. As Stuit (2016: 18) reminds us concepts are never constant; rather, they are continually developed through 'movement through time and across various disciplines, where they encounter new contexts, new objects, and also other concepts'. As a result, the encounter of *Ubuntu* with the field of GE has the potential to create possibilities and open new spaces for formulating more inclusive understandings. Moreover, the embeddedness of *Ubuntu* within the Global South domains of knowledge production addresses in practice the call for decolonization of knowledge and consideration of multiple perspectives, generating knowledge from diverse spaces. It is about achieving theoretically informed GE that upholds cognitive justice and epistemological pluralism in non-tokenistic ways (see Bourn, 2015a; Andreotti, Ahenakew and Cooper, 2011).

Bibliography

Andreotti, V. (2010) Global Education in the 21st Century: Two Different Perspectives on the Post of Postmodernism, *International Journal of Development Education and Global Learning*, 2(2): 5–22.

Andreotti, V. (2016) Global Education and Social Change: The Imperative to Engage with Different Discourses. In Hartmeyer, H. and Wegimont, L. (eds) *Global Education in Europe Revisited: Strategies and Structures Policy and Practice Challenges*, Muenster: Waxmann, 199–203.

Andreotti, V., Ahenakew, C. and Cooper, G. (2011) Epistemological Pluralism: Ethical and Pedagogical Challenges in Higher Education, *AlterNative: An International Journal of Indigenous Peoples*, 7(1): 40–50.

Assié-Lumumba, N.' D. T. (2017) The Ubuntu Paradigm and Comparative and International Education: Epistemological Challenges and Opportunities in Our Field, *Comparative Education Review*, 61(1): 1–22.

Bewaji, J. A. I. and Ramose, M. B. (2003) The Bewaji, Van Binsbergen and Ramose debate on Ubuntu, *South African Journal of Philosophy*, 22(4): 378–415.

Bhattacharya, D. and Ordonez Llanos, A. (eds) (2017) *Southern Perspectives on the Post-2015 International Development Agenda*, New York: Routledge.

Biney, A. (2014) The Historical Discourse on African Humanism: Interrogating the Paradoxes, In Van Binsbergen, W. (2001), Ubuntu and the Globalization of Southern African Thought and Society, *Quest: An African Journal of Philosophy*, XV(1–2): 53–89.

Bourn, D. (2014) The Theory and Practice of Global Learning, Research Paper No.11 for the Global Learning Programme, London: Development Education Research Centre, Institute of Education.

Bourn, D. (2015a) *The Theory and Practice of Global Learning*, London: Development Education Research Centre, Institute of Education.

Bourn, D. (2015b) A Pedagogy of Development Education. In Maguth, B. and Hilburn, J. (eds), *The State of Global Education: Learning with the World and Its People*, London: Routledge, 13–26.

Broodryk, J. (2002) *Ubuntu: Life lessons from Africa*, Pretoria: Ubuntu School of Philosophy.

Cabezudo, A., Christidis C., da Silva, M., Demetriadou-Saltet, V., Halbartschlager, F. and Mihai, G.-P. (2008) *Global Education Guidelines: A Handbook for Educators to Understand and Implement Global Education*, Lisbon: North-South Centre of the Council of Europe.

DERC (2018) *IOE Centre Launches New Network for Global Education Researchers*, available at: http://www.ucl.ac.uk/ioe/news-events/news-pub/feb-2018/network-global-education-research (last accessed 28 April 2018).

Enslin, P. and Horsthemke, K. (2004) Can Ubuntu Provide a Model for Citizenship Education in African Democracies? *Comparative Education*, 40(4): 545–58.

Eze, M. O. (2008) What is African Communitarianism? Against Consensus as a Regulative Ideal, *South African Journal of Philosophy*, 27(4): 386–99.

Eze, M. O. (2017) I Am Because You Are: Cosmopolitanism in the Age of Xenophobia, *Philosophical Papers*, 46(1): 85–109.

Gade, C. B. N. (2012) What is Ubuntu? Different Interpretations among South Africans of African Descent, *South African Journal of Philosophy*, 31(3): 484–503.

Gaudelli, W. (2016) *Global Citizenship Education: Everyday Transcendence*, New York: Routledge.

Gaudelli, W. and Wylie, S. (2012) Global Education and Issues-Centered Education. In Totten, S. and Pedersen, J. (eds) *Educating about Social Issues in the 20th and 21st Centuries: A Critical Annotated Bibliography*, Charlotte: Information Age, 293–320.

Gordon, L. (2014) Justice Otherwise: Thoughts on Ubuntu. In Praeg, L. and Magdala, S. (eds) *Ubuntu: Curating the Archive*, Pietermaritzburg: University of KwaZulu-Natal Press, 10–26.

Hartmeyer, H. and Wegimont, L. (eds) (2016a) Crosscutting Issues in Global Education 2015: An Analytical Framework For Policy Learning, GENE Policy Paper, GENE Secretariat, available at http://gene.eu/wp-content/uploads/GENE-Policy-paper-2016-Cross-Cutting-Issues-and-Policy-Learning.pdf (last accessed 3 April 2018).

Hartmeyer, H. and Wegimont, L. (eds) (2016b) *Global Education in Europe Revisited: Strategies and Structures Policy and Practice Challenges*, Muenster: Waxmann.

Hicks, D. (2007) Principles and Precedents. In Hicks, D. and Holden, C. (eds) *Teaching the Global Dimension: Key Principles and Effective Practice*, London: Routledge, 14–30.

Hicks, D. (2008) Ways of Seeing: The Origins of Global Education in the UK, Background Paper for: UK ITE Network Inaugural Conference on Education for Sustainable Development/Global Citizenship.

Jefferess, D. (2016) Cosmopolitan Appropriation or Learning? Relation and Action in Global Citizenship Education. In Langram, I. and Birk, T. (eds) *Globalization and Global Citizenship: Interdisciplinary Approaches*, New York: Routledge, 87–97.

Jooste, N. and Heleta, S. (2017) Global Citizenship Versus Globally Competent Graduates: A Critical View From the South, *Journal of Studies in International Education*, 21(1): 39–51.

Kayira, J. (2015) (Re)creating Spaces for uMunthu: Postcolonial Theory and Environmental Education in Southern Africa, *Environmental Education Research*, 21(1): 106–28.

Kimmerle, H. (2000) Review of Mogobe B. Ramose: African Philosophy Through Ubuntu, *African Philosophy*, 13(2):189–97.

Le Grange, L. (2012) *Ubuntu, Ukama* and the Healing of Nature, Self and Society, *Educational Philosophy and Theory*, 44(S2): 56–67.

Letseka, M. (2013) Educating for Ubuntu: Lessons from Basotho Indigenous Education, *Open Journal of Philosophy*, 3(2): 337.

Matolino, B. and Kwindingwi, W. (2013) The End of Ubuntu, *South African Journal of Philosophy*, 32(2): 197–205.

Mbiti, J. S. (1969) *African Religions and Philosophy*, London: Heinemann.

Mboti, N. (2015) May the Real Ubuntu Please Stand Up? *Journal of Media Ethics*, 30(2): 125–47.

Merryfield, M. (2001) Moving the Centre of Global Education: From Imperial Worldviews that Divide the World to Double Consciousness, Contrapuntal Pedagogy, Hybridist, and Cross-cultural Competence. In Stanley, B. W. (ed.) *Critical Issues in Social Studies for the 21st Century*, Greenwich: Information Age Publishing, 179–208.

Metz, T. (2007) Ubuntu as a Moral Theory: Reply to Four Critics, *South African Journal of Philosophy*, 26(4): 369–87.

Metz, T. and Gaie, J. B. R. (2010) The African Ethic of Ubuntu/Botho: Implications for Research on Morality, *Journal of Moral Education*, 39(3): 273–90.

Murithi, T. (2006) Practical Peacemaking Wisdom from Africa: Reflections on Ubuntu, *The Journal of Pan African Studies*, 1(4): 25–34.

Murithi, T. (2007) A Local Response to the Global Human Rights Standard: The Ubuntu Perspective on Human Dignity, *Globalisation, Societies and Education*, 5(3): 277–86.

Ngcoya, M. (2009) *Ubuntu: Globalization, Accommodation, and Contestation in South Africa*. PhD Thesis, Faculty of the School of International Service, American University, Washington DC.

Van Norren, D. E. (2014) The Nexus between Ubuntu and Global Public Goods: Its Relevance for the Post 2015 Development Agenda, *Development Studies Research*, 1(1): 255–66.

Nussbaum, B. (2003). *Ubuntu*: Reflections of a South African on Our Common Humanity, *Reflections*, 4: 21–6.

Odora Hoppers, C. (2002) Indigenous Knowledge Systems, Sustainable Livelihoods and the Intellectual Property System: A Peace Action Perspective, *Journal of Peacebuilding & Development*, 1(1): 106–12.

Odora Hoppers, C. (2015) Cognitive Justice and Integration without Duress The Future of Development Education: Perspectives from the South, *International Journal of Development Education and Global Learning*, 7(2): 89–106.

Osler, A. and Vincent, K. (2002) *Citizenship and the Challenge of Global Education*. Stoke-on-Trent: Trentham Books.

Peterson, A. and Warwick, P. (2015) *Global Learning and Education: An Introduction*, New York: Routledge.

Praeg, L. (2014) *A Report on Ubuntu*, Pietermaritzburg: University of KwaZulu-Natal Press.

Praeg, L. and Magdala, S. (eds) (2014) *Ubuntu: Curating the Archive*, Pietermaritzburg: University of KwaZulu-Natal Press.

Ramose, M. B. (1999) *African Philosophy Through Ubuntu*, Harare: Mount Pub.

Santos, B. S. (2014) *Epistemologies of the South: Justice Against Epistemicide*, Boulder: Paradigm.

Scheunpflug, A. and Asbrand, B. (2006) Global Education and Education for Sustainability, *Environmental Education Research*, 12(1): 33–46.

Shultz, L. (2015) Decolonizing UNESCO's Post-2015 Education Agenda: Global Social Justice and a View from UNDRIP, *Postcolonial Directions in Education*, 4(2): 96–115.

Shutte, A. (2001) *Ubuntu: An Ethic for the New South Africa*, Pietermaritzburg: Cluster Publications.

Skinner, A., Blum, N. and Bourn, D. (2013) Development education and education in international Development policy: Raising Quality through critical pedagogy and global skills, *International Development Policy*, 5(2): 89–103.

Standish, A. (2014) What Is Global Education and Where Is It Taking Us? *The Curriculum Journal*, 25(2): 166–86.

Stromquist, N. (2002) *Education in a Globalized World: The Connectivity of Economic Power, Technology, and Knowledge*, Boulder: Rowman and Littlefield.

Stuit, H. (2016) *Ubuntu Strategies: Constructing Spaces of Belonging in Contemporary South African Culture*, New York: Palgrave Macmillan.

Swanson, D. M. (2015) Ubuntu, Indigeneity, and an Ethic for Decolonizing Global Citizenship. In Abdi, A. A., Shultz, L. and Pillay, T. (eds) *Decolonizing Global Citizenship Education*, Rotterdam: Sense Publishers, 27–38.

Swanson, D. M. and Pashby, K. (2016) Towards a Critical Global Citizenship? A Comparative Analysis of GC Education Discourses in Scotland and Alberta, *Journal of Research in Curriculum & Instruction*, 20(3): 184–95.

Takyi-Amoako, E. J. (2018) Towards an Alternative Approach to Education Partnerships in Africa: Ubuntu, the Confluence, and the Post- 2015 Agenda. In Takyi-Amoako, E. J. and N'Dri Thérèse Assié-Lumumba, N. T. (eds) *Re-Visioning Education In Africa: Ubuntu Inspired Education for Humanity*, New York: Palgrave Macmillan, 205–28.

Torres, C. (2017) *Theoretical and Empirical Foundations of Critical Global Citizenship Education*, London: Routledge.

Tutu, D. M. (1999) *No Future without Forgiveness*, New York: Doubleday.

Tutu, D. M. (2011) *God Is Not a Christian: And Other Provocations*, New York: HarperOne.

Tye, K. (2009) A History of the Global Education Movement in the United States. In Tucker, K. (ed.) *Visions in Global Education: The Globalization of Curriculum and Pedagogy in Teacher Education and Schools*, New York: Peter Lang Publishing, 3–24.

Ubuntu Education Fund (2016) *Annual Report*, available at https://issuu.com/ubuntueducationfund/do cs/2016_annual_report (last accessed 10 September 2017).

United Nations Committee for Development Policy (2012) *The United Nations Development Strategy Beyond 2015*, New York: United Nations Publications, available at http://www.un.org/en/development/ desa/policy/cdp/cdp_publications/2012cdppolicynote.pdf (last accessed 3 April 2018).

Waghid, Y. (2014a) African Philosophy of Education as a Response to Human Rights Violations: Cultivating *Ubuntu* as a Virtue in Religious Education, *Journal for the Study of Religion* 27(1): 267–82.

Waghid, Y. (2014b) *African Philosophy of Education Reconsidered: On Being Human*, Abington: Routledge.

Waghid, Y. (2018) Global Citizenship Education: A Southern African Perspective. In Davies, I., Ho, L.-C., Kiwan, D., Peck, C. L., Peterson, A., Sant, E. and Waghid, Y. (eds) *The Palgrave Handbook of Global Citizenship and Education*, London: Palgrave Macmillan, 97–109.

Waghid, Y. and Smeyers, P. (2012) Reconsidering Ubuntu: On the educational potential of a particular ethic of care, *Educational Philosophy and Theory*, 44(2): 6–20.

Zembylas, M. (2014) The Teaching of Patriotism and Human Rights: An Uneasy Entanglement and the Contribution of Critical Pedagogy, *Educational Philosophy and Theory*, 46(10): 1143–59.

Zembylas, M. (2017a) The Quest for Cognitive Justice: Towards a Pluriversal Human Rights Education, *Globalisation, Societies and Education*, 15(4): 397–409.

Zembylas, M. (2017b) Re-contextualising Human Rights Education: Some Decolonial Strategies and Pedagogical/Curricular Possibilities, *Pedagogy, Culture & Society*, 25(4): 487–99.

Chapter 8

Integrating Asian Perspectives within the UNESCO-led Discourse and Practice of Global Citizenship Education: Taking Gandhi and Ikeda as Examples

Namrata Sharma

Introduction

This chapter expands on the arguments made within my recently published book, *Value-Creating Global Citizenship Education: Engaging Gandhi, Makiguchi and Ikeda as Examples* (Sharma 2018), and attempts to fill an existing gap within the practice of global citizenship education (GCE) by offering selected values-based perspectives of three thinkers. Their perspectives, although situated in Asian historical contexts, are also rooted in an existential dialogue with other non-Western as well as Western perspectives. In this book, Soka or value-creating education developed by the Japanese educators Tsunesaburo Makiguchi (1871–1944) and Daisaku Ikeda (b. 1928) is compared to the ideas of the Indian political leader Mahatma Gandhi (1869–1948). My previous study of their respective thoughts and movements makes suggestions for the practice of the three domains of learning within the GCE conceptual dimensions of the United Nations Educational, Scientific and Cultural Organization (UNESCO 2015) – the cognitive, socio-emotional and behavioural.

The focus of this chapter is to outline the theoretical discussions in my earlier work and develop one of the six themes proposed for the practice of *value-creating GCE*. The theme from my previous work discussed in this chapter is concerned with broadening awareness of climate change. It mandates an urgent action and concern for the planet as citizens of the earth. Further, as this chapter argues, such action must draw from the vast repository of human wisdom, from different cultures and traditions, as considered during the drafting process of the Earth Charter (see Vilela and Corcoran 2005).

The Earth Charter, as the name indicates, is an ethical and values-based framework for building a just, sustainable and peaceful global society in the twenty-first century. This 'people's charter' was launched in 2000 and since then has been endorsed by over 6,000 organizations, including many governments and international organizations. It is considered to be a 'soft law document', as outlined by the Earth Charter Initiative website, 'Soft law documents like the Universal Declaration of Human Rights are considered to be morally, but not legally, binding on state governments that agree to endorse and adopt them, and they often form the basis for the development of hard law.'[1] The importance of paying attention to different philosophical understandings and values-based perspectives is that it can bring forth diverse and creative solutions to global issues such as environmental degradation and climate change. Further, it can propel people and communities to take part in local, national, regional and global solutions as engaged citizenry whose values inform their action for positive personal, social and environmental transformation. Examples include the Green Belt Movement in Kenya pioneered by Wangari Maathai (1940–2011) and inspired by African tradition, such as the mythology surrounding the Sycamore Fig Tree (Wilde 2012; also see SGI 2014). Similarly, the success of Gandhi and Ikeda as leaders of the largest mass movements of their respective countries in recent history has been in their ability to enthuse ordinary people to act based on their values and beliefs. In the realm of education, one of the core challenges of fostering youth as future world citizens needs to be a focus on the values, beliefs and interests of the individual learner. This chapter argues that a broader engagement with the human/personal dimension is necessary for the success of education for global citizenship which is part of the UN's 2030 Agenda and its 17 Sustainable Development Goals (SDGs) which 'seek to eradicate extreme poverty and strengthen universal peace by integrating and balancing the three dimensions of sustainable development – economic, social and environmental' (UNESCO 2018: 3).

Education has been a priority for UNESCO both as an SDG and as the means for attaining all the other SDGs. While maintaining its focus on and giving agency to the individual human being, education for global citizenship must also not get trapped in promoting individualism, which as has been pointed out through recent scholarly work is the hallmark of GCE informed by a neoliberal paradigm (Andreotti n.d., 2006; Bourn 2018; Dill 2013; Merryfield 2009; Tarozzi and Torres 2016). In this context, a value-creating paradigm can have a substantive role in nurturing individuals who can lead contributive lives through education for global citizenship.

Value-creating global citizenship education: A pedagogical approach

Value-creating education

Soka or value-creating education has been developed by the Japanese educators Makiguchi, Josei Toda (1900–58) and Ikeda. Makiguchi's educational pedagogy published in 1930 is titled *Soka kyoikugaku taikei* or The System of Value-Creating Pedagogy. The key term in Makiguchi's pedagogy is *soka* (創価) or value creation, a neology formed from the two words, *so* from *sozo* (創造) or creation and *ka* from *kachi* (価値) or value. One of the core ideas of this work, as Bethel explains, is that 'creation of value is part and parcel of what it means to be a human being. Human beings do not have the ability to create material; but they can create value, and it is in the creation of value that the unique meaning of human life lies' (Bethel 1973: 49).

---

[1]   Retrieved from http://earthcharter.org/discover/what-is-the-earth-charter/

Further, according to Makiguchi, the aim of human life and education should be the happiness of the individual human being and one's ability to live contributively, that is, by creating meaning and value that is of benefit to the individual self, as well as contributing to the well-being of others. Ikeda has emphasized key aspects of Makiguchi's value-creating pedagogy in his extensive lectures and educational proposals on 'Soka Education' and *ningen kyoiku* (humanistic education) (see Ikeda 2010). It should be mentioned here that although there have been several studies on Makiguchi and Ikeda's ideas, it is only more recently that significant research is being conducted on Toda's educational work (see Sharma 2018: 6).

Ikeda is the leader of the lay Buddhist organization, the Soka Gakkai. He is also a prolific writer, poet and founder of several institutions promoting peace, culture and education across 192 countries and territories. This includes fifteen Soka kindergartens, primary and secondary schools, women's colleges and universities in seven countries across Asia and the Americas. His educational ideas also inform several other schools and universities, as well as thousands of educators and school leaders worldwide. His annual peace proposal and several initiatives launched by the Soka Gakkai International (SGI) Office for UN Affairs are among many ongoing efforts to support the UN's efforts to build a peaceful and sustainable world.

In my previous comparative studies on Makiguchi, Ikeda and Gandhi, I found several commonalities between their views on education and religion, as well as their intercultural experiences and their ability to enthuse large numbers of people to work for social justice (Sharma 1999, 2008, 2018). The key common focus in all their endeavours was the human being and human development. Their respective religious beliefs were rooted in non-dualistic philosophies that perceive an inextricable link between the lives of oneself and others (see Sharma 2018: 62). For Makiguchi and Ikeda it was their practice of Buddhism, and for Gandhi it was Jainism and Hinduism. Ikeda explicitly draws a link between the Buddhist view of interdependence and his proposals on education for global citizenship. In a lecture entitled 'Thoughts on Education for Global Citizenship' delivered at the Teachers College, Columbia University in 1996 he states,

> The following scene from the Buddhist canon provides a beautiful visual metaphor for the interdependence and interpenetration of all phenomena. Suspended above the palace of Indra, the Buddhist god who symbolizes the natural forces that protect and nurture life, is an enormous net. A brilliant jewel is attached to each of the knots of the net. Each jewel contains and reflects the image of all the other jewels in the net, which sparkles in the magnificence of its totality. (Ikeda 2008: 444–5)

Here Ikeda is alluding to the Buddhist concept of 'dependent origination', which he explains elsewhere as the view that 'all beings and phenomena exist or occur in relation to other beings or phenomena. Everything is linked to an intricate web of causation and connection – and nothing – whether in the realm of human affairs or of natural phenomena – can exist or occur solely of its own accord' (Ikeda 1991: 4).

Gandhi had a similar understanding of the interdependence of life that stemmed from his religious belief (see Gandhi 1991: 174). As Parekh notes about Gandhi,

> In Gandhi's favourite metaphor, the cosmos was not a pyramid of which the material world was the base and human beings the apex, but a series of ever-widening circles encompassing human kind, the sentient world, the material world, and the all-including cosmos. Since the

cosmic spirit pervaded or infused the universe and was not outside it, the so-called natural world was not natural or material, terms he generally avoided, but spiritual or divine in nature. (Parekh 1997: 38)

Gandhi's values and beliefs propelled him to act for the sake of social justice, galvanizing millions of people to be involved in the non-violent *satyagraha* (lit. 'truth-force') movement for India's independence from the British regime. As discussed previously in a comparative study on my above-selected thinkers, 'Their notion of interdependency was embedded in their political and educational activism. However, they were not just activists but also thinkers who used their creative imagination to build an intimate connection between the autonomous, morally self-sustained and self-governed citizen and a fully-fledged, self-reflective and self-correcting socio-political and educational community' (Sharma 2008: 153).

Global citizenship education

Before moving on with the arguments of this chapter, this section briefly introduces Global Citizenship Education (GCED, referred to henceforth as GCE), which is one of the strategic areas of UNESCO's education sector programme for the period 2014–21. UNESCO's work in this field is guided by the Education 2030 Agenda and Framework for Action, notably Target 4.7 of the SDGs 4 (on education), which calls on countries to ensure that all learners are provided with the knowledge and skills to promote sustainable development, including, among others, through education for sustainable development (ESD) and sustainable lifestyles, human rights, gender equality, promotion of a culture of peace and non-violence, global citizenship and appreciation of cultural diversity and of culture's contribution to sustainable development.[2]

Several recent scholarly works have challenged the Western-dominated agendas and the underlying Western world view in GCE (see Sharma 2018: 46–7). This includes the heavy influence of Enlightenment liberalism. Dill's work (2011, 2012, 2013), for instance, expounds the dominant epistemological and ontological assumptions of Western liberal capitalism, and its ties to GCE, focusing on the tension that exists within education to respond to the contending interests of the individual and society, self and the other, local and global. Further discussions must therefore be centred on integrating non-Western perspectives so that the practice of global citizenship has a more intercultural focus. As recent studies suggest, intercultural sensitivity is a key skill desired by students and employers but needs 'the engagement and support of educational policymakers and bodies responsible for professional development and training' (Bourn 2018: 97, see Bourn and Sharma 2008). As argued through my long-term study, the above Asian examples can make important contributions to the discourse and practice of GCE. For example, these leaders have shown that there is a variety of ways of thinking, acting, being and living that inform people and communities to create positive individual and social change.

---

[2]   Retrieved from https://en.unesco.org/themes/gced/definition

Value-creating global citizenship education

The term 'value-creating global citizenship education' is a phrase based on my two decades of study on the educational ideas of Makiguchi, Ikeda and Gandhi.[3] In contrast to a Western liberal-individualistic framework for GCE, a value-creating education framework at the most basic level subscribes to a non-dualistic view of life aimed at enhancing relationships in education (see Goulah and Ito 2012; Ikegami and Rivalland 2016; Nagashima 2016; Takazawa 2016). Its central concern is to perceive, acknowledge and remove 'the arrow of a discriminatory consciousness, an unreasoning emphasis on difference ... piercing the hearts of the people' (Ikeda 1993: 2).

A shift in paradigm and perspectives can have a significant bearing on the praxis and the three domains of learning within the GCE conceptual dimensions of UNESCO – the cognitive, socio-emotional and behavioural (UNESCO 2015: 14–15). These correspond to the four pillars of learning described in the UNESCO (2001) report *Learning: The Treasure Within*: learning to know, to do, to be and to live together. For example, an acknowledgement of one's common humanity would give emphasis to perceiving the divisiveness and alienation that is present within modern societies. That is, it would place a strong emphasis within the curriculum to tackle stereotyping and foster the socio-emotional capacity of compassion towards all inhabitants of the earth while also recognizing the nature and forms of power structures in an increasingly globalized world and the unseen perpetuation of colonial perspectives. The behavioural response to solve global issues would be rooted in a non-dualistic belief system that through an intuitive examination of the depth of human life subscribes to the view that an attitudinal change within each person can impact upon their environment (see Ikeda 2003b: 106). The educational environment will be developed to foster meaningful life-to-life connections among people – between students and teachers, schools and communities and so on.

In my previous work I developed themes and approaches for the practice of value-creating GCE. As mentioned, these pedagogical approaches can be incorporated within formal, non-formal and informal education settings across a variety of different subjects and disciplines (Sharma 2018: 90). These themes can be used to develop age-specific learning objectives. The proposed framework covers six themes within the practice of value-creating GCE that aim to promote the necessary knowledge, skills, values and attitudes to enable learners to develop:

- A Sense of Interdependence, Common Humanity and a Global Outlook.
- An Awareness of Climate Change as Planetary Citizens.
- A Commitment to Reflective, Dialogic and Transformative Learning.
- A Commitment to Sustainable Development through Intercultural Perspectives.
- A Belief in the Value-Creating Capacity for Social-Self Actualization.
- An Understanding of Peace and Non-Violence as being Central to the Human Rights Agenda (Figure 8.1).

---

[3] Extracts and arguments made in this section appear in Sharma 2018: 92–3.

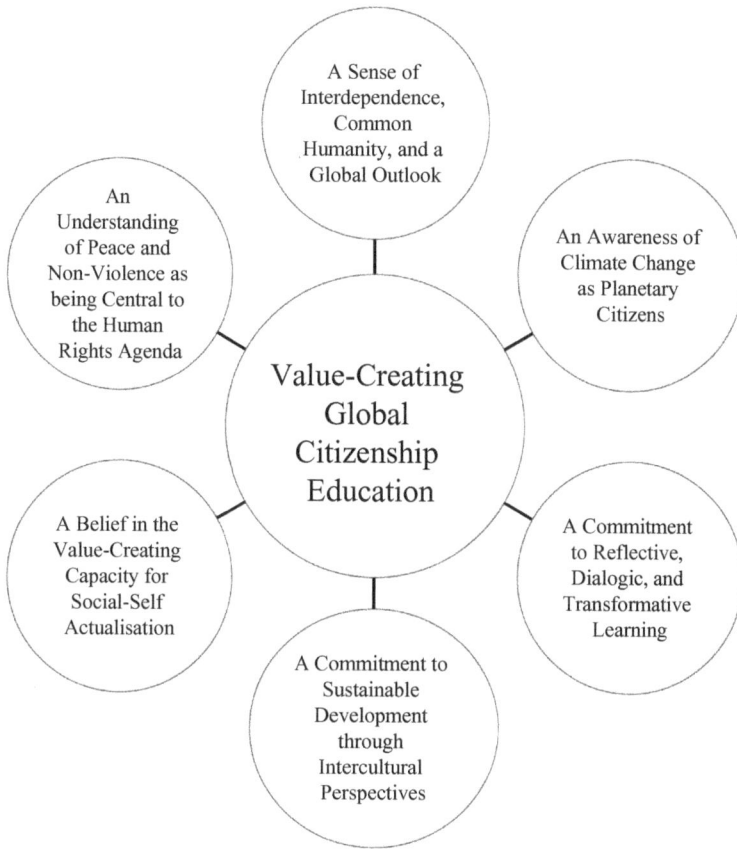

Figure 8.1 Framework for value-creating global citizenship education (Sharma 2018: 94).

An awareness of climate change as planetary citizens: Challenging assumptions, offering suggestions for practice

One of the influences of the scientific-industrial revolution originating from the West is a mechanistic and reductionist view of life.[4] On the other hand, a non-dualistic view perceives the dynamic relationship between the self and the natural/social environment as being fluid and in a constant state of creative engagement and coexistence.[5] While the wisdom and energy to take action in tackling climate change are perceived here as being important, it should also be with an attitude of reverence for life as suggested in the Earth Charter that resonates with Makiguchi's sentiments described in his work *Jinsei chirigaku* or the *Geography of Human Life* (Makiguchi 1983).

It is worth noting that the success of the Earth Charter and its adoption by several schools is not only that it offers a comprehensive overview as an invaluable educational resource but that, as

---

[4] Extracts and arguments made in this section appear in Sharma 2018: 97–8.

[5] See Sharma 2018, Chapter 4 for further details.

mentioned earlier and as Ikeda points out, 'the manner in which this 'people's charter' was drafted is significant ... in the drafting process, efforts were made to incorporate the essential wisdom of cultures and traditions from all regions of Earth' (Ikeda 2002). In his Columbia Speech referred to earlier, Ikeda proposes as an essential element of a global citizen 'the wisdom to perceive the interconnectedness of all life and living' (Ikeda 2008: 444). This wisdom, Ikeda notes, is a 'living wisdom' that can be learnt from various cultural traditions that appreciate the unity and connectedness of life, such as the Desana people of the Amazon and the Iroquois people of North America (Ikeda 2002). One of the consequences of similar worldviews has led some nation states, including Ireland and India, to give constitutional rights to trees and rivers as being sacred.

This section further develops the suggestions for practice made in my previous work (Sharma 2018: 98). As mentioned, climate change is a reality that still does not have universal consensus. (The United States withdrawing from the Paris Agreement on climate change in 2017 is a startling example.) Since the publication of my earlier work, the Intergovernmental Panel on Climate Change (IPCC 2018) special report on the impacts of global warming and related global greenhouse gas emissions, and the 2018 *Lancet* Countdown by a British medical journal in its annual account of how climate change affects public health, among others, have strengthened the urgency for a climate policy, as well as the need to develop a commitment towards tackling climate change as outlined by UNESCO's ESD programme and the follow-up GAP launched by UNESCO in 2014.

Moving beyond a cognitive approach, education for climate change should create a learning environment that can cause a socio-emotional response in students to develop a reverence for nature, and care and responsibility as citizens of this planet. Further, a critical understanding is required of the causal relationship between human strife and suffering, and the destruction of natural and other forms of life (the Syrian crises and conflicts in the Middle East are among such examples). As a starting point the following references can be used to approach these issues from a value-creating perspective: Henderson and Ikeda's (2004) dialogue *Planetary Citizens*; Makiguchi's (1983) book, *The Geography of Human Life* (Bethel 2002 for an edited English translation; also see Bethel 2000; Takeuchi 2004), the *Earth Charter Initiative*[6] (also see Rockefeller 2015) and UNESCO's climate change education and awareness initiatives.[7]

The UNESCO Climate Change Initiative was launched in 2009, and in recent years teaching about climate change has been given a thrust across school curricula in various nation states. UNESCO,[8] organizations like the Center for Global Education (CGE) at Asia Society in the United States and Oxfam in UK have been taking the lead in providing guidelines for teachers, including through engaging with the challenge of teaching climate change as a controversial issue (Oxfam 2018). Further, the Asia Society has taken bold and active steps to compensate for the deletion of entire datasets and websites documenting climate change by the Trump administration.[9] While various important developments are being made by non-governmental organizations (NGOs) as well as through policy initiatives, as Bourn (2018) points out based on the findings of a co-authored report for UNESCO, 'all too often the dominant mode of teaching

---

[6]   http://earthcharter.org/discover/the-earth-charter/

[7]   https://en.unesco.org/themes/addressing-climate-change/climate-change-education-and-awareness

[8]   See resources available via this link https://en.unesco.org/themes/addressing-climate-change/climate-change-education-and-awareness

[9]   https://asiasociety.org/education/climate-change-and-environment

is a whole class approach with an emphasis on the use of textbooks' (ibid. 175), and argues the need for skills to teach themes such as global poverty, sustainable development, climate change and human rights so that learners can be exposed to a variety of perspectives.

Although emerging scholarly work suggests different approaches to the practice of UNESCO's GCE initiative, there is a dearth of literature that draws meaningful linkages between teaching GCE and ESD. One of the UNESCO guidelines on global citizenship clarifies that GCE and ESD are not to be treated as independent areas of work, 'both are concerned with global challenges and actions that are needed to tackle them, while the thematic topics associated with them tend to be specific – GCE is more associated with global challenges related to peace and conflict, and ESD with global challenges related to environmental warnings and natural resources' (UNESCO 2016b: 3). In this context further research is required that can bring together the discourse on GCE (SDG 4.7) and how this could impact ESD, for example, teaching SDG 13 on 'Climate Action' to combat climate change and its impacts[10] (UNESCO 2015, 2016a, 2017). Clarification of the terms 'global citizenship', 'education for sustainable development' and their respective learning objectives outlined by UNESCO (2017) needs to expand on what is currently being offered as suggestions, perspectives and approaches to teaching ESD.

For example, drawing upon various ongoing studies Yemini (2017) notes that, depending on the definition of global citizenship and the various dispositions and agendas it embodies, the definitions and models of GCE and its focus on its goals in terms of student outcomes changes. Let me illustrate this further through the argument that Yemini makes by using Andreotti's (2006) differentiation between 'soft' and 'critical' global citizenship. Yemini shows that teaching GCE would depend on how GE itself is conceptualized.

> While soft GCE could be equated with education that provides students with an understanding of the world and encourages cultural tolerance (as per Marshall 2011), critical GCE requires deeper engagement. Critical GCE, which Andreotti (2010) later developed into post-critical and post-colonial GCE, requires students and teachers to 'unlearn' their previous assumptions regarding the supremacy of Western culture and the distribution of power and replace them with a completely novel understanding of the world. This type of GCE provides students with the skills to reflect upon and engage with global issues involving conflict, power and opposing views; to understand the nature of assumptions; and to strive for change. (Yemini 2017: 61)

Aligning the emerging and ongoing discourse on different approaches to GCE with ESD would mean, for example, in consideration of Andreotti's above conceptualization on global citizenship, that the curriculum for each of the 17 SDGs should be framed with the aim to develop a deeper critical engagement through the process of learning.

UNESCO currently offers three key pedagogical approaches in ESD, which are, 'a learner-centered approach', 'action-oriented learning' and 'transformative learning' (UNESCO 2017: 55). It is argued here the need for integrating a 'value-creating approach' that places an emphasis on building relationships between the learner and his or her natural and social environment. To elaborate on this approach using Ikeda's words, value-creating education advocates an 'ethic of coexistence ... a spirit that seeks to encourage mutual flourishing and mutually supportive

---

[10]   http://unesdoc.unesco.org/images/0024/002474/247444e.pdf

relationships among humans and between humans and nature' (Ikeda 2003a: 9). As I argued earlier based on my study of Gandhi, Makiguchi and Ikeda, the central question is to rethink education that can develop the capacity within the learner to facilitate the development of what Ikeda refers to as a 'creative coexistence' (Ikeda 2010: 89). On a similar note, several scholarly works suggest that there seems to be an emphasis within Soka Education on building relationships through the curriculum – between the individual and other people, with nature and the community (see Goulah 2010: 264–9; Nagashima 2016; Obelleiro 2012: 44; Sharma 2008: 111–16, 145–7). As I argued earlier, this has important lessons for the current UNESCO-led practice of GCE that can expand beyond the current focus on individual empowerment (see UNESCO 2015: 16) to develop the learner's value-creating skills through the process of building relationships. This shift in emphasis can enhance the aim of education for global citizenship to foster capable citizens who contribute to the development of their own lives and that of others (see Sharma 2018: 50).

The disposition and agenda that value-creating GCE promotes are criticality for social justice and value creation for social-self-actualization. It places an emphasis on taking collective action along with individual responsibility, as is suggested within one of the UNESCO (2017) guidelines for teaching climate change and the increased greenhouse gas emissions as an anthropogenic phenomenon. Further discussions in teaching SDG 13 must also be centred on the learners' perspectives about human life and the natural environment that they bring into the classroom. It is also important that students engage with class materials that view the creativity and coexistence of all forms of life, as well as life's capacity to create value under the most challenging circumstances. These different perspectives can widen the scope of inquiry within the topics and objectives suggested by UNESCO, for example, by providing students with the opportunity to discuss issues around existential questions, such as are asked within the core curriculum at Soka University of America (Ikeda 2010: 103–4, see Sharma 2018: 50–1):

- What is an individual human life?
- What is the relationship between the individual and the physical environment in which we live?
- What is the relationship between the individual and the human environment in which we live?
- What are the global issues in peace, culture and education?

Exploring these questions from a range of perspectives is at the core of a value-creating paradigm that aims to foster critical global citizens who can challenge their own assumptions while developing an awareness of the sanctity, dignity and creative potential within human and other forms of life. It is also argued here that while discussions on the anthropocentric cause of climate change are pertinent and can give agency to students, efforts to solve global issues can also easily become individualistic (see Dill 2013), and can lead to students perceiving themselves as 'rescuers of the planet',[11] an image that might inadvertently be promoted through recent video games designed to inform learners about the SDGs.

---

[11] http://mgiep.unesco.org/games-for-learning

Conclusion

This chapter has argued the case for teaching about the ecosystem and climate change in a non-anthropocentric way and from a value-creating perspective that situates the individual human being at the centre of the action for creating positive change.[12] *Value-creating GCE* is suggested as a pedagogical approach to GCE and ESD in addition to and complementing other approaches mentioned within the recent UNESCO guidelines (especially 2015 and 2017). This chapter argues that there are several lessons to be learnt from a study of alternative ways of thinking about ourselves, society, nature and the universe that can add to the intercultural dimension of GCE and ESD. Whereas sustainable development has often been associated with environmental concerns (Morris 2008), an approach to issues of sustainability from an intercultural perspective can draw from diverse wisdom and understandings that is in line with UNESCO's aims for ESD (see Gundara and Sharma 2010).

Some efforts are being made to bring the wisdom of thinkers like Ikeda, Gandhi and the Earth Charter to re-engage with the discourse on climate change from Western and non-Western perspectives, that focus on exploring the interdependence and creative coexistence of all forms of life (see BRC 1997a and b; and Sarabhai, Raghunathan and Modi 2010). These efforts need to be combined with more serious scholarly engagement that can draw the attention of policy-makers and practitioners to explore the relevance of diverse perspectives to sustain human and universal life that exists on our planet.

The theme developed in this chapter on creating an awareness of climate change as planetary citizens can be infused within teaching for global citizenship. This would fill the present gap within UNESCO's proposals for sustainable development (including SDG 13) by adding the personal dimension to the currently proposed economic, social and environmental dimensions. For example, it has been argued that while it is urgent to equip the learner with accurate facts and information related to climate change, education for climate change should also engage with the values, interests and perceptions that students bring into the classroom to create a learning environment that reflects different perspectives. Katherine Hayhoe, who is an expert on global warming, is also an Evangelical Christian. A recent report suggests that she 'has emerged in recent years as a leading voice sharing the science of climate change to skeptics – many of whom are fellow evangelical churchgoers', and 'Hayhoe said it is that same Christianity that fuels her dedication to climate science' (Hayhoe 2018). This is a pertinent example that makes the case for a values-based approach to GCE so that the individual learner can articulate how one's own personal values align with their action to combat climate change and achieve other SDGs.

These suggestions need to be part of the discussion across different subject areas that have the aim to foster capable citizens of the twenty-first century. Similar efforts can be made to better understand the place and context within which GCE and ESD are being carried out, for example drawing on the values and perceptions of teachers, needs of the community and wisdom of the lives of those who are engaged with the task of education for global citizenship and climate change. The proposals made in this chapter can be integrated within UNESCO's (2016a) guidelines on a whole-institution approach to ESD and climate change. The thematic approaches offered within

---

[12]   For further thoughts on this topic see https://vcgce.wordpress.com/

value-creating GCE widen the discussions from a non-anthropocentric perspective and engage the human dimension of learning.

Bibliography

Andreotti, V. (n.d.). *Engaging the (Geo)political Economy of Knowledge Construction: Towards Decoloniality and Diversality in Global Citizenship Education.* Retrieved from https://www.ucalgary .ca/peacestudies/files/peacestudies/Engaging%20the%20(geo)political%20economy%20of%20knowl edge%20construction.pdf

Andreotti, V. (2006). Soft versus critical global citizenship education. *Development Education: Policy and Practice, 3*(Autumn), 83–98.

Andreotti, V. (2010). Global education in the 21st century: Two different perspectives on the post of postmodernism. *International Journal of Development Education and Global Learning, 2*(2), 5–22.

Bethel, D. M. (1973). *Makiguchi the Value Creator: Revolutionary Japanese Educator and Founder of Soka Gakkai.* Tokyo: Weatherhill.

Bethel, D. M. (2000). The legacy of Tsunesaburo Makiguchi: Value creating education and global citizenship. In D. Machacek and B. Wilson (eds), *Global Citizens: The Soka Gakkai Buddhist Movement in the World* (pp. 42–66). Oxford: Oxford University Press.

Bethel, D. M. (ed.) (2002). *The Geography of Human Life.* San Francisco: Caddo Gap Press.

Bourn, D. (2018). *Understanding Global Skills for 21st Century Professions.* Cham: Palgrave Macmillan.

Bourn, D. and Sharma, N. (2008). Global and sustainability issues for engineering graduates. *Proceedings of the Institution of Civil Engineers – Municipal Engineer, 161*(3), 199–206.

BRC (Boston Research Center for the 21st Century) (1997a). *Buddhist Perspectives on the Earth Charter.* Cambridge: Boston Research Center for the 21st Century.

BRC (Boston Research Center for the 21st Century) (1997b). *Women's Views on the Earth Charter.* Cambridge: Boston Research Center for the 21st Century.

Dill, J. S. (2011). *Schooling Global Citizens: The Moral Pedagogy of Twenty-first Century Education.* Unpublished doctoral dissertation, Department of Sociology, University of Virginia, Charlottesville, VA.

Dill, J. S. (2012). The moral education of global citizens. *Society, 49*, 541–6.

Dill, J. S. (2013). *The Longings and Limits of Global Citizenship Education: The Modern Pedagogy of Schooling in a Cosmopolitan Age.* New York: Routledge.

Gandhi, M. K. (1991). Letter to P.G. Mathew, Yeravda Mandir, September 8, 1930. In R. Iyer (ed.), *The Essential Writings of Mahatma Gandhi* (223–6). New Delhi: Oxford University Press.

Goulah, J. (2010). From (harmonious) community life to (creative) coexistence considering Daisaku Ikeda's educational philosophy in the Parker, Dewey, Makiguchi, and Ikeda 'reunion'. *Schools: Studies in Education, 7*(2), 253–75. http://www.jstor.org/stable/10.1086/656075

Goulah, J. and Ito, T. (2012). Daisaku Ikeda's curriculum of Soka education: Creating value through dialogue, global citizenship, and "human education" in the mentor–disciple relationship. *Curriculum Inquiry, 42*(1), 56–79.

Gundara, J. S. and Sharma, N. (2010). Interculturalism, sustainable development and higher education institutions. *International Journal of Development Education and Global Learning, 2*(2), 23–34.

Hayhoe, K. (2018, March 6). At U.N. summit, an evangelical Christian makes the case for climate change [blog]. Retrieved from http://katharinehayhoe.com/wp2016/2018/03/06/at-u-n-summit-an-evangelical-c hristian-makes-the-case-for-climate-change/

Henderson, H. and Ikeda, D. (2004). *Planetary Citizenship: Your Values, Beliefs and Actions Can Shape a Sustainable World.* Santa Monica: Middleway Press.

Ikeda, D. (1991). *The Age of 'Soft Power' and Inner-motivated Philosophy.* Lecture delivered at Harvard University, Cambridge, MA, USA on 26 September. Retrieved from https://www.daisakuikeda.org/sub/ resources/works/lect/lect-01.html

Ikeda, D. (1993). *Mahayana Buddhism and Twenty-First Century Civilization*. Lecture delivered at Harvard University on 24 September 1993. Retrieved from http://www.daisakuikeda.org/sub/resources/works/lect/lect-04.html

Ikeda, D. (2002). *The Challenge of Global Empowerment: Education for a Sustainable Future*. Retrieved from https://www.sgi.org/about-us/president-ikedas-proposals/environmental-proposal-2002.html

Ikeda, D. (2003a). *A Global Ethic of Coexistence: Toward a 'Life-Sized' Paradigm for Our Age*. Tokyo: Soka Gakkai International.

Ikeda, D. (2003b). *Unlocking the Mysteries of Birth and Death … and Everything in between: A Buddhist View of Life* (2nd edn). Santa Monica: Middleway Press.

Ikeda, D. (2008). Thoughts on education for global citizenship. In D. Ikeda (ed.), *My Dear Friends in America: Collected U.S. Addresses 1990–1996* (2nd edn, pp. 441–51). Santa Monica: World Tribune Press.

Ikeda, D. (2010). *Soka Education: For the Happiness of the Individual* (Rev. edn). Santa Monica: Middleway Press.

Ikegami, K. and Rivalland, C. (2016). Exploring the quality of teacher–child interactions: The Soka discourse in practice. *European Early Childhood Education Research Journal*, 24(4), 1–15.

IPCC (Intergovernmental Panel on Climate Change) (2018). *Global Warming of 1.5°C*. Retrieved from https://www.ipcc.ch/sr15/

Makiguchi, T. (1983). *Jinsei Chirigaku* [The geography of human life]. *Makiguchi Tsunesaburo zenshu* [Complete works of Tsunesaburo Makiguchi] (Vols. 1–2). Tokyo: Daisan Bunmeisha.

Marshall, H. (2011). Instrumentalism, ideals and imaginaries: Theorising the contested space of global citizenship education in schools. *Globalisation, Societies and Education*, 9(3–4), 411–26.

Merryfield, M. (2009). Moving the center of global education: From imperial worldviews that divide the world to double consciousness, contrapuntal pedagogy, hybridity, and cross-cultural competence. In T. F. Kirkwood-Tucker (ed.), *Visions in Global Education* (pp. 215–39). New York: Peter Lang.

Morris, L. V. (2008). Higher education and sustainability. *Innovative Higher Education*, 32(179), 180.

Nagashima, J. T. (2016). *The Meaning of Relationships for Student Agency in Soka Education: Exploring the Lived Experiences and Application of Daisaku Ikeda's Value–Creating Philosophy through narrative Inquiry*. Unpublished doctoral dissertation, University of Pittsburgh, Pittsburgh, PA.

Obelleiro, G. (2012). A moral cosmopolitan perspective on language education. *Critical Inquiry in Language Studies*, 9(1–2), 33–59. https://doi.org/10.1080/15427587.2012.648064

Oxfam (2018). *Teaching Controversial Issues: A Guide for Teachers*. Oxford: Oxfam. Accessed from https://www.oxfam.org.uk/education/resources/teaching-controversial-issues

Parekh, B. (1997). *Gandhi*. Oxford: Oxford University Press.

Rockefeller, S. C. (2015). *Democratic Equality, Economic Inequality, and the Earth Charter*. San Jose, Costa Rica: Earth Charter International.

Sarabhai, K., Raghunathan M. and Modi, A. (2010). *Earth Charter and Gandhi: Towards a Sustainable World*. Ahmedabad: Center for Environment Education.

SGI (Soka Gakkai International) (2014). *A Quiet Revolution* [video file]. Retrieved from https://www.youtube.com/watch?v=ytSHqNw7UM8

Sharma, N. (1999). *Value Creators in Education: Japanese Educator Makiguchi & Mahatma Gandhi and their Relevance for the Indian Education* (2nd edn). New Delhi: Regency Publications.

Sharma, N. (2008). *Makiguchi and Gandhi: Their Educational Relevance for the 21st Century*. Lanham, MD: University Press of America and Rowman & Littlefield.

Sharma, N. (2018). *Value-Creating Global Citizenship Education: Engaging Gandhi, Makiguchi, and Ikeda as Examples*. Cham, Switzerland: Palgrave Macmillan.

Takazawa, M. (2016). *Exploration of Soka Education Principles on Global Citizenship: A Qualitative Study of U.S. K-3 Soka Educators*. Unpublished doctoral dissertation. The University of San Francisco, San Francisco. Retrieved from https://repository.usfca.edu/diss/324/

Takeuchi, K. (2004). The significance of Makiguchi Tsunesaburo's Jinsei Chirigaku (Geography of Human Life) in the intellectual history of geography in Japan: Commemorating the centenary of its publication. *The Journal of Oriental Studies*, 14, 112–32.

Tarozzi, M. and Torres, C. A. (2016). *Global Citizenship Education and the Crises of Multiculturalism: Comparative Perspectives*. London: Bloomsbury Academic.

UNESCO (International Bureau of Education) (2001). Learning to live together: Have we failed? In *Forty-Sixth Session of UNESCO'S International Conference on Education*. Geneva: UNESCO, International Bureau of Education.

UNESCO (2015). *Global Citizenship Education: Topics and Learning Objectives*. Paris: UNESCO.

UNESCO (2016a). *Getting Climate-Ready – A Guide for Schools on Climate Action*. Paris: UNESCO.

UNESCO (2016b). *The ABCs of Global Citizenship Education*. Paris: UNESCO.

UNESCO (2017). *Education for Sustainable Development Goals: Learning Objectives*. Paris: UNESCO.

UNESCO (2018). *Preparing Teachers for Global Citizenship Education: A Template*. Paris: UNESCO.

Vilela, M. and Corcoran, P. B. (2005). Building consensus on shared values. In P. B. Corcoran, M. Vilela and A. Roerink (eds), *The Earth Charter in Action: Toward a Sustainable World* (pp. 17–22). Amsterdam: KIT Publishers.

Wilde, S. (2012, August 16). Queen of Africa's trees: The sacred fig tree [blog]. Retrieved from https://www.greenbeltmovement.org/node/374

Yemini, M. (2017). *Internationalization and Global Citizenship: Policy and Practice in Education*. Cham, Switzerland: Palgrave Macmillan.

Part III

Impact of Policies and Programmes

Chapter 9

Global Education Research in Finland

Elina Lehtomäki and Antti Rajala[1]

Introduction

This chapter offers a review of global education (GE) research in Finland for over ten years, starting from 2007. The discussions on GE have involved a broad range of partners from the government, non-governmental organizations (NGOs) and academia. In this review we aim to identify the contributions of the research on these discussions as well as what gaps in knowledge have been identified. The main question addressed in this chapter is this: What key themes and findings characterize Finnish research in GE?

The roots of GE in Finland can be traced back to the 1970s, when internationalization was introduced in the nine-year comprehensive school curriculum. Over decades there has been evident public support to international cooperation and interest in global issues, yet in formal education the responsibility for implementing internationalization activities has been left to individual teachers. In 2004 the Global Education Network Europe's peer review on GE in Finland observed that some good initiatives that have succeeded, for instance, in increasing awareness about development cooperation could be scaled up only by longer strategic funding and clearer inter-ministerial commitment to GE (North–South Center of the Council of Europe 2004). Furthermore, the report recommended development of a strategy for GE that would include a strong Southern perspective and representatives of migrants in Finland as an important resource. As a response to the peer review report, the Finnish Ministry of Education launched a national action programme on international education (Jääskeläinen 2016: Ministry of Education 2006).

Jääskeläinen (2016), a member of the National Board of Education who was responsible for coordinating the working group set to design the project for 2007 to 2009, emphasized how it introduced a *change in perspective*, evident in the concepts used for defining future goals, as the proposal introduced the term 'global education' in the country:

> The debate over the concept had been going on for some time. The change of concept from international to global education points to the key issue: It is not enough anymore that we focus in education (international education) on communication or cooperation between different peoples. Each individual needs to be able to cooperate and communicate with people coming from different backgrounds. International cooperation is not enough; we need to learn to understand globalisation and its consequences, even on the scale of the entire planet.

[1] Rajala wishes to thank the Academy of Finland project no. 299191 for the financial support for preparing this chapter.

> The economy is globalising, cultures are merging and becoming more uniform, mobility and communication are on the increase, and the changes in the condition of the environment concern us all. We must learn to understand these phenomena. (p. 107)

The project (2007–9) covered the five dimensions of GE (development, peace, human rights, intercultural and sustainability) as defined in the Maastricht Declaration and aimed to create a common understanding of GE and its value basis. The final project report emphasized GE as a key to 'individual's growth into *global responsibility* with the purpose of finding solutions to the challenges and problems facing humanity collectively – in other words, educating the individual to take responsibility for promoting good living and a sustainable future on a global scale' (Lampinen and Melén-Paaso 2009, pp. 7–8, 187). The project succeeded in engaging education experts from different fields and their reports showed ways of integrating global responsibility in a wide array of activities in both informal learning and formal education, from early childhood education to physical education and sports, and youth work. The government commitment and its collaboration with NGOs and academia have contributed to the inclusion of GE in curriculum development. Through a national project *As a global citizen in Finland*, the National Agency for Education in collaboration with its partners applied the Organization of Economic Cooperation and Development (OECD) twenty-first century skills framework to the Finnish context and defined seven transversal competences for learning: learning to learn, global citizen's ethics, sustainable lifestyle, intercultural competence, civic competence, responsibility and partnerships, and economic competence (Jääskeläinen 2016).

The 2014 national core curriculum for basic education defined GE as a cross-cutting theme (Finnish National Agency for Education 2014) which has led to discussions on including GE in early childhood education as well as upper secondary education. The core curriculum states that changes in the world affect pupils' development and well-being as well as schools' functioning. Therefore, education is required to encounter the changes openly yet critically assessing them and bearing responsibility for choices that contribute to future. GE aims to create conditions for social justice and sustainable development in line with the UN Sustainable Development Goals (SDGs). The expectation is that basic education positively contributes in society both locally and globally.

Finland has been the only European country with GE as a clearly mentioned cross-cutting issue in the national basic education core curriculum, integrated across the subjects and school activities (Hartmeyer and Wegimont 2016). In addition to curriculum design, the Finnish Ministry of Education and the National Agency for Education have actively promoted GE by funding projects and producing guidelines and publications (e.g. Jääskeläinen 2011; Kaivola 2008; Kaivola and Melén-Paaso 2007; Lampinen and Melén-Paaso 2009). For example, as part of its project Education for Global Responsibility (2007–9), Ministry of Education published the edited collection *Education for Global Responsibility – Finnish Perspectives* (Kaivola and Melén-Paaso 2007). The collection included chapters from academics of different disciplines (e.g. social sciences, education and law) who reflected on their understanding of GE and gave their suggestions for the further development of the field.

Teacher educators have developed guidelines and materials to assist teachers in integrating GE dimensions across school subjects for phenomenon-based learning which refers to a multidisciplinary approach that encompasses various dimensions and methods to understand a complex phenomenon such as climate change (e.g. Cantell 2015). NGOs have also been active in coordinating projects and publishing reports, and more recently, provided web-based learning forums and materials (especially the Finnish Development NGOs, KEPA (today FINGO), the Peace Education Institute, UNICEF). GE activities have continued to be mainly project-based and short term. In schools as well as in teacher education it still depends on teachers' interest to what extent and how they implement GE. There can be observed, however, a growing interest in GE both in research and collaboration initiatives between schools, NGOs and the research community. Considering that in Finland the governments, regardless of their political differences, have given quality of education a high priority, and that teacher education and professional development aim to be research-based, it is important to know what research informs us about GE.

In this review, we focus on research publications. In the following, we first describe the material and methods of our thematic review study. Then we present the findings organized by the five dimensions of GE as defined in the Maastricht Declaration (O'Loughlin and Wegimont 2003). The chapter concludes with a discussion of the findings in light of international research in GE.

Thematic review

Our review of GE research in Finland follows United Nations Educational, Scientific and Cultural Organization (UNESCO)'s (2015) and Marginson's (2016) conceptualization of education as a global common good comprising four dimensions: individual, collective, national and global. The literature reviewed has been selected on the basis of their global dimension though not always directly using 'global education', 'global learning' or 'global citizenship education' as key words. The selected material was organized on the basis of the five main dimensions of GE as defined in the 2002 Maastricht Declaration by the Council of Europe: *Development Education (DE), Human Rights Education (HRE), Education for Sustainability, Education for Peace and Conflict Prevention* and *Intercultural Education* (O'Loughlin and Wegimont 2003). The material includes published research reports, books and journal articles and doctoral dissertations that focus on GE in Finland. Finnish university library and internet-based academic databases have been used in the literature search. We complemented these searches by using our research networks in the field of GE and related fields as well as by scrutinizing the reference lists of the identified publications. The material covers literature published in English and Finnish.

The search is to be considered only as indicative as some publications, such as book chapters, related to the five dimensions yet not clearly stating that in their contents or using key words marking the scope may have been left out. Other authors who have conducted reviews of global citizenship education (GCE) also mention this kind of limitation and the difficulty in using a sufficiently wide range of search terms (Goren and Yemini 2017; Oxley and Morris 2013). In this literature search we tried, however, to find and read research reports widely and discussed our views on the materials' relevance in terms of GE research. Therefore, research on citizenship and democracy without a global connection were, for instance, not included in the review.

The focus of this review is on exploring the issues raised by the GE research in Finland. To respond to the research question we organized the material first by the five dimensions of GE, followed by the main themes and key findings of the research. The material covers issues related to different actors, phases and forms of the Finnish education system. Thus, this review differs from previous research reviews on GE or GCE that tend to have focused on curriculum, schools, teachers and students in basic education or on different levels of education. In this review the wider variety of topics may reflect the Finnish approach to GE as a more holistic perspective, aiming to transform the entire education system, from early childhood education and care to higher education (HE) and lifelong learning.

Findings

We have organized the identified key themes and findings by the five dimensions of GE as defined in the Maastricht Declaration (DE, HRE, Education for Sustainability, Education for Peace and Conflict Prevention and Intercultural Education). Intercultural education seems to be a leading theme, while other dimensions have been studied much less. We then present an additional theme specific to the Finnish context: *research in GE as a cross-cutting issue.*

Development education

In the Ministry of Education 2007–9 project, DE was perceived not only as increasing knowledge about global development goals and challenges but also, moreover, as aiming to create a sense of global responsibility (Kaivola 2008; Kaivola and Melén-Paaso 2007; Lampinen and Melén-Paaso 2009). In practice, development NGOs, in particular KEPA (nowadays FINGO), have had a leading role in providing DE both for schools and the general public (Anttalainen and Lampinen 2009). Their work and also school-level DE projects have been supported by the Ministry for Foreign Affairs. In addition, some universities have introduced study programmes and courses in development. From 2009, the Finnish University Partnership for International Development (UniPID), a network of fourteen universities established in 2002, has offered an optional twenty-five ECTS credits minor in development studies to students of member universities. It is notable that NGOs and bachelor's or master's students have produced a number of reports on DE, but in research this dimension of GE has received little attention. At the interface of educational research and development studies the focus has been on education development in the so-called low-income or development countries. However, the need for improving the *understanding of development issues as globally connected phenomena* and for responding to the public interest in development cooperation has been recognized especially by the NGOs providing GE.

Directly addressing DE as a part of GE can be seen in Alasuutari's (2011; 2015) research. She examined the ethical commitments in development cooperation partnerships from the perspectives of participants in the North and South. Her conclusion is that some of the challenges in partnerships can be traced to the ethnocentric and uncritical approaches in global and DE, as previously noted by Andreotti (2006) and Bourn (2008; 2015). The national core curriculum guides teaching, but teachers enjoy autonomy in choosing their approaches and implementing

development and GE. Alasuutari (2015: 108–9) identified a risk and responsibility related to this autonomy:

> The responsibility for what global issues to address and how to address them remains with the teacher. Teachers might discuss global issues and development in their classrooms, for example, within the rhetoric of development aid, without challenging the asymmetry, superiority, or ethnocentrism that are part of the development aid discourse. This kind of approach could end up in outcomes that are contradictory to those of development and global education policies that seem to promote mutuality and reciprocity in the area of global and development education.

Janhonen-Abruquah, Lehtomäki and Kahangwa (2017) with their colleagues explored DE as a mutual learning task between African and Finnish university students and teachers. The results suggest that long-term collaboration and dialogue are conditions for joint goal setting, increased understanding and co-creation of knowledge.

Intercultural education

The notions of multicultural education and intercultural education have been used interchangeably in Finnish research (Dervin 2015). While 'intercultural education' emerges from the European context and is a preferred term of the European Union and the Council of Europe, 'multicultural education' has been used more commonly in the United States, where it originates from the civil rights movement (Tarozzi 2012). In Europe, multicultural education has often been associated with static description of a society comprised of a diversity of cultures, whereas intercultural education often refers to interactions of and relationships between cultural groups in culturally diverse settings (Holm and Zilliacus 2009; Jokikokko 2010). In this section, we use both terms interchangeably to refer to a wide variety of different approaches for dealing with cultural diversity in education. We will also discuss research that critically discusses the established approaches and terminology.

Research in intercultural education has addressed different levels of education. Themes include teachers' and students' competencies, schools and subjects as learning contexts, curriculum and textbooks, diversity, racism and institutional or structural enabling versus constraining factors in education systems. While multicultural education has been perceived as a response to the challenges of immigration and the gradually increasing diversity in education and society with the emphasis on how to encounter the 'other', in research there is an evident attempt to critically review underlying assumptions and worldviews in education.

The first Finnish professor of GE (then named as 'international education') Rauni Räsänen (2007a,b) emphasized international and intercultural education as *ethical commitments*. Instead of discussing diversity and searching for efficient ways in which education may respond to the increasing diversity, she analysed how ethics in teaching and learning contributes to mutual respect, understanding and thus guides interaction. Thereby she has pioneered in promoting at the same time a deeper as well as wider perspective to intercultural education. The ultimate goal of global and intercultural education to her is becoming a *globally responsible citizen* (Räsänen 2007c).

In kindergarten teacher education students' discussions on *intercultural critical incidents* Layne and Lipponen (2016) identified three approaches: categorizing, anti-categorizing and affective. Layne (2016) emphasizes that knowledge alone is insufficient in teacher education and teaching, to her ethical intercultural teaching is 'to recognize unjust structures and to connect with those who are affected by them' (p. 68).

Research in teachers' *cultural competences* has examined teachers' own perceptions and reports, and also peer evaluations. Critical pedagogy guided Jokikokko's (2010) phenomenography and narrative research on teachers' intercultural learning and competence. The main finding was that teachers perceive their intercultural competence as a holistic approach to issues and an ethical orientation to people, life and diversity. Learning processes involve both formal and informal learning. Furthermore, strong emotional experiences related to work experiences in diverse contexts contribute to the development of intercultural competences when teachers have opportunities to reflect and share their experiences (Jokikokko and Uitto 2017). Laitinen's (2014) research on teachers' intercultural sensitivity, effectiveness and cultural intelligence using internet-based instruments showed that applied science university teachers perceived their intercultural competence at a relatively high level and were motivated for intercultural communication but assessed their intercultural performance being weaker. Results of the peer evaluation by educational leadership and students were consistent with the teachers' self-assessment.

Acquah (2015) investigated the cultural competence of international pre-service teacher education students from over twenty-five different countries, and pre-service and practising Finnish teachers. The main finding was that a course fostering identity development positively influenced the participants' knowledge and attitudes towards diversity. While knowledge was a central part of cultural competence, equally important aspects were abilities to use students' language and culture, work effectively with multilingual learners' parents/guardians, link the students' cultural backgrounds, prior knowledge and experience to instruction and modify classroom instruction. He pointed out, however, that self-reported data may represent biases and suggested classroom observations to reveal teachers' action and competences in real school life.

Dervin and Layne (2013) noted how internationalization in higher education institutions (HEIs) is characterized as hospitality towards international students, how cultures are used as excuses and how internationalization is perceived as making foreign students Finnish. Lanas (2014) questioned whether intercultural education has failed to increase the understanding of diversity due to students' experiences of inequity. Benjamin and Alemanji (2017) analysed the meaning of 'international' in two international schools situated in Finland and France. Their discourse analysis focused on interviews of staff members who were responsible for the management, branding or marketing of the schools. They argued that the notion of international education is used to signify privilege as contrasted to multicultural education, in a similar way as underprivileged 'immigrants' are contrasted to more privileged 'expatriates'. They also critiqued the implicit Anglo-centric approach in the primarily native English speaking staff of the international schools and the implied cultural and linguistic imperialism. Their findings suggest that the dominance of Western educator perspectives may have negative implications for recognition of otherness and diverse worldviews. Poulter, Riitaoja and Kuusisto (2016) challenge the liberal secularist world view that they claim underlines the dominant approach of multicultural education. They argue that the deconstruction of the binary categories of 'religious' and 'non-religious' could advance understanding of the complexity of worldviews as well as foreground and problematize epistemic, social and political hegemonies.

Recently, the critical debates on the conceptual underpinnings of the intercultural and multicultural education have culminated into suggestions to revise the terminology in use. Dervin (2015) suggested replacing the commonly practised intercultural education and related approached by a post-intercultural approach in which critical attention is paid to expressions, negotiation and co-construction of cultures and identities in social interactions. In this perspective students' identities should be seen as intersectional, that is, as being composed of multiple potentially conflicting identities in interplay. Alemanji (2016) critiques both multicultural and intercultural education and proposes 'antiracist education' in their stead. From the perspective of antiracist education, race is not a biological category describing individuals but rather an artificial construct that is implicitly and explicitly used to classify people into differently privileged groups based on skin colour and ancestry. In his study, Alemanji examined racism in Finland from the perspectives of Finnish exceptionalism, coloniality of power, whiteness theory and denial of racism. The study illuminates structural hierarchies related to the construct of race implicit in the Finnish society and education system. Youth research has also paid attention to racism as experienced by young people in society (Souto 2011).

Research in intercultural education can be characterized as having a critical approach. The conceptual and socio-historical underpinnings of the concepts of multicultural education, intercultural education, international education and culturally responsive teaching have been questioned. Also, the need to study teaching and learning practices has been recognized.

Human rights education

HRE was included in the Finnish national core curricula for basic and upper secondary education in 2004 (Finnish National Agency for Education 2014). In the national curriculum guidelines, human rights is mentioned as a fundamental value, and it is included in the mandated teaching contents of various subjects. In 2011 the National Agency made an amendment that the Holocaust should be studied as an example of human rights violation in the curricula of lower and upper secondary school regarding the teaching of history, secular ethics and philosophy (Salmenkivi 2011).

Between 2007 and 2017 there had not been much research on HRE. Toivanen (2007) argues that one obstacle for the investment in HRE is a tendency to think that it is mainly something that other, non-Finnish people in distant countries need (see also Matilainen 2011). Yet, Toivanen adds that human rights problems (such as high domestic violence rate, child abuse or racism) are also characteristic of Finland, which, she argues, is seldom addressed in the human rights courses or course materials. A recent report based on interviews and document analysis showed that although human rights are considered a fundamental value by teacher educators and student teachers and they are included as mandatory contents in the curriculum documents, there is hardly explicit teaching of HRE in Finnish teacher education programmes (Rautiainen, Vanhanen-Nuutinen and Virta 2014). This lack of attention to HRE is noteworthy because all teachers might not have an adequate understanding and expertise on the topic, and the teaching practice can in the worst case even run contrary to human rights ethos (Toivanen 2007).

Matilainen (2011) studied how teachers and students understood human rights and HRE in an upper secondary school, by means of thematic content analysis. The findings of the study indicated that the HRE goals as specified by UN were not fully reached in the school under study. The students and the teachers had only partial understanding of the notion of human rights. Human rights were both taken for granted and perceived as a strange and difficult topic that was not relevant in the local setting. Some of the student responses could even be read as xenophobic or even racist. Although the teachers reported that they considered human rights important, they did not consider themselves as human rights educators. Accordingly they addressed human rights in their teaching either very little or not at all. Both the teachers and the students associated human rights mostly with one or more of the following school subjects: religious studies, history or social studies.

Apart from Matilainen's study research on HRE has been quite strongly connected with Christian religious education (Matilainen and Kallioniemi 2011; Poulter et al. 2017). Matikainen (2017) examined the philosophical basis of human rights and the educational implications in the work of theist philosopher Nicholas Wolterstorff. An additional, more practically oriented research strand on HRE emerges from the NGO sector. NGOs such as Amnesty, UNICEF and The Finnish League for Human Rights have been important promoters of HRE. For example, in an action research study the Finnish National Committee for UNICEF developed and examined a participatory and holistic model of HRE based on drama education (Hassi et al. 2015).

Overall, the studies that were reviewed for this chapter were mainly uncritical of the notion of human rights. Yet, some voices took a critical lens on human rights and HRE. Halme (2008) questioned the dominant position and unreflective adoption of human rights discourse in the Finnish educational policy and curricula. She pointed to the need to critically scrutinize the liberal sociopolitical and historical grounding of human rights discourse and the position of human rights as a universal symbol of good will and promise of a brighter future. In her empirical study of a HRE programme for university faculty and students, she showed how the practical activity of HRE can give rise to hierarchical positions between experts who are educating and laymen who are educated in human rights. These positions, furthermore, had a tendency to reproduce privileged positions for some people (mainly for whites and men) and underprivileged positions for others (mainly for non-whites and women). Thus, Halme's study underlines that while it is important to advance human rights in education, it is equally important to recognize their liberal Western ideological roots and what are the implicit positions for diverse people that are produced when HRE is practised.

Education for peace and conflict prevention

Although there is a strong tradition of peace work and peace education in Finland, in the last decade research explicitly addressing the topic has been scarce. Löfström and Ahonen (2014) confirm this observation; they conducted a literature search to find Finnish texts about peace education. Out of the 183 papers they found, a great majority were published before the 1990s. For this review, we were able to locate only two research papers fitting the scope of our study. Both of them addressed history teaching and focused on historical conflicts and their reconciliation. Ahonen (2014) discusses the role of history teaching in the reconciliation process of three countries that have gone through a major armed conflict. She defines history teaching as conciliatory and resonant with peace education when it fosters the dialogic encounters between varied antagonist versions of the conflicts. Regarding Finland, Ahonen analyses how the 1917 civil war stemming from a communist revolution was reflected in history textbooks and history teaching in the various sociopolitically distinct stages of Finnish history. Löfström (2014) examined thematic focus group interviews of upper secondary school students regarding their views of institutional symbolic and material compensations of historical wrongdoings. He showed that analysing historical moral problems in teaching can develop youths' empathy and capacity for peaceful conflict resolution and ethical reflection.

Education for sustainability

The UNESCO policy and Decade for Education for Sustainability (ESD) and related research networks have offered important reference frames for researchers in the fields of education and sustainability in Finland. Both the 2007–9 project plan on Global Responsibility of the Finnish Ministry of Education and its final report defined education for sustainable development (ESD) important especially in terms of sustainable futures that require not only ecological sustainability but also ethical, social and cultural commitments. Their view has been further supported in research. For instance, the guest editors of a recent special issue on ESD have underlined ESD as an alternative to the dominant trend of economic growth leading globalization (Salonen, Palmberg and Aarnio-Linnavuori 2017). Developing a sense of satisfaction or being content with life and a commitment to sustainable futures characterize their alternative approach which seems evident also in recent research on ESD. In this review, we highlight only some examples that show the line of research in ESD.

Siirilä (2016) studied how the concept of sustainable development has been interpreted in the Finnish school curricula. The main finding was the prediction of *social change* that requires developmental sustainability and a sustainable way of life. This implied that the education system was expected to contribute to the society's commitment to sustainable development, to prepare citizens who understand the meaning of sustainable development in their lives and participate to achieve a sustainable society and future.

Uitto and Saloranta (2017) used a nationally representative sample ($n = 2,361$) ninth grade basic education pupils from forty-nine schools, subjects teachers ($n = 442$) and headmasters ($n = 49$) in their surveys on ESD in schools. Individual-level values, knowledge and experiences explained most of the variation in students' self-efficacy, yet factors related to the school culture were associated with the students' self-efficacy in terms of ESD. The indicators for school culture were practical implementation of sustainable development, collaboration within school and cooperation with external stakeholders. Furthermore, a significant finding was that teachers directly increase their students' self-efficacy by using inquiry-based and interactive teaching methods. School leadership plays a central role in creating a school culture that promotes sustainable development. Both Uitto and Saloranta have several publications on ESD in Finnish schools.

In 2017, the leading educational research publication venue in Finland, the Finnish Journal of Education published a special issue on education for sustainability. The guest editors Salonen, Palmberg and Aarnio-Linnavuori (2017) highlight the importance of positive experiences in learning and satisfaction in the advancement of sustainable development. They conclude that more research is needed to show how human behaviour can be transformed towards common good by focusing on satisfaction, instead of negative or forbidding approaches. Furthermore, they propose research of the co-variation of life satisfaction and action in support of sustainable development to produce a more holistic view for further development of learning and ESD both in Finland and internationally (Salonen, Palmberg and Aarnio-Linnavuori 2017). The special issue offers cutting-edge knowledge on the status of ESD in the country. Eco-social development characterizes the articles, thus representing the attempt in Finnish education and curriculum (National Agency for Education 2014) as well as in research to go beyond the dichotomy between 'ecological' and 'social' and to promote an overall holistic and systemic approach in ESD and GE. Most of the papers concentrate on environmental dimensions of sustainability yet clearly place environmental education within a broader eco-social perspective.

Global education as a cross-cutting issue in education

The implementation of the first phase of mainstreaming GE in basic education from 2007 faced challenges in practice. When the government introduced a GE 2010 programme with the aim to reach all schools, teachers and principals found GE as an additional task and reported on lack of sufficient time, knowledge, skills and materials (Pudas 2015). According to Pudas (2015: 137),

> Even though almost 60 per cent of the principal respondents (N=87) were aware of the GE 2010 programme, it was not systematically implemented in any of the schools. Moreover, none of the respondent schools had a GE action plan or were planning to draft one in the near future.

Pudas (2015) suggested that in addition to including GE in teacher education, school leadership also needs knowledge about GE. Her data, however, came from the time before the 2014 national core curriculum entered into use. In the new core curriculum GE is defined as a cross-cutting theme. Whether the curriculum and implementation guidelines offer sufficient information about the goals and criteria requires follow-up.

GE as a part of learning in education sciences in terms of understanding GE development, global connectedness and shared responsibility have been themes of Lehtomäki, Moate and Posti-Ahokas (2015; 2016). They have explored university students' significant learning experiences related to designed learning events that have combined knowledge, critical reflections, cross-cultural dialogues and participation in learning community activities. Their main finding is that transformative learning requires multidimensional approaches that challenge students and support them to identify themselves as future education professionals, who have experienced collaboration and are making a difference.

Henriksson's study (2017) gives additional insight on the foundational role of the 2014 national core curriculum as well as the UN Agenda 2030 SDGs as sources of epistemic capital in the implementation of GE in Finnish schools. She analysed observation and interview data from twenty-one NGOs involved in GE. Her findings also point to the importance of NGOs when supporting schools in addressing the GE goals of the 2014 curriculum and the AGENDA 2030 goals. Henriksson found that the NGOs have strong expertise also in participatory methods for supporting students' agency and societal participation as part of school teaching. Moreover, NGOs consider involvement in curriculum development important. An emerging topic is cultural sustainability in education. Laine's (2017) findings show that education for cultural sustainability requires attention on young children's human potential, and need for recognition and cultural inclusion, from early childhood education and care.

For GE research and development curriculum design is central. Finnish curriculum discourse shows a clear effort to support students' multi-layered and multicultural identities (Zilliacus, Paulsrud and Holm 2017). Teaching and learning seem to succeed in supporting students' identity development, as Finnish teenagers report being open and international, and as having multidimensional, that is national, European and global, identities. They experience group pressure that may contribute to discrimination and contradictions in identification between global and national identities. The teenagers expect school to provide diverse perspectives on societal issues (Lestinen, Autio-Hiltunen and Kiviniemi 2017).

Discussion

There is a growing interest in research on GE both in Finland and internationally (DERC 2018; Goren and Yemeni 2017). This review shows that of the five areas or dimensions of GE as defined by the Maastricht Declaration, there has been more research in intercultural education (and related approaches) and ESD than in DE, HRE and education for peace and conflict prevention. In addition, we found research that approaches GE holistically as a cross-cutting theme. This holistic approach to GE is not unique to Finland (see for example, Hicks 2003), but it is explicitly supported by the Finnish national core curriculum for basic education (Finnish National Agency for Education 2014) as well as GE NGOs and the national network of GE researchers. The variety of research themes related to the five dimensions may represent the researchers' interests as well as the pragmatic need for knowledge to guide practice. International cooperation and the continuous dialogue between the government, NGOs and academia have contributed to choices of research themes.

Our study of the Finnish context adds to the understanding of regional emphases on GE. Goren and Yemeni (2017) review study exemplifies the existing research on how GE is approached in research in different parts of the world. While not focusing specifically on Finland, their study suggests that in Europe the GE curricula have emphasized immigration, war and adjustment to multiculturalism. The ethos of GE, according to Goren and Yemeni, relied mainly on moral and cultural cosmopolitanism (see also Oxley and Morris 2013; Schattle 2008). Citing a single study (Andreotti, Biesta and Ahenakew 2015), Goren and Yemeni maintain that Finnish GE is conceived mostly in terms of learning about the other, without much critical perspective. Our review includes Finnish studies more broadly and shows a different and more varied picture of the Finnish GE research.

Whereas the cosmopolitan ethos is to some extent evident also in our sample of studies, especially regarding HRE, the Finnish research includes also more critical and advocacy perspectives (Andreotti 2006; Oxley and Morris 2013). In fact, our review shows a development trend in Finnish GE research towards more critical perspectives. Maintaining a balance and dialogue between soft (i.e. mainly introducing knowledge and fostering empathy) and critical approaches (requiring involvement and enactment; Andreotti 2006) appears to be characteristic to many of the Finnish studies. Researchers have, for instance, recognized the importance of questioning assumptions and perceptions in intercultural education, combined different types of methods, including critical self-reflection and peer reviews, and suggested more research to be carried out in real interaction situations from multiple perspectives. Our study confirms that similar to the other European countries multiculturalism and immigration have also been major research themes in Finland.

Our review shows that there is an ongoing debate about the terminology and concepts used to characterize the field in Finland, in a similar manner as in the European and international discussions (Bourn 2018; DERC 2018; Goren and Yemeni 2017; UNESCO 2018). This is evident, especially in the attempts to redefine intercultural education and multicultural education and replace them with concepts that involve more critical perspectives, such as antiracist education. Similar developments have also taken place internationally (see for example, Seriki and Brown 2017; Cole 2017). The terminological debate reflects profound differences and controversies in the theoretical and ethical foundations of research on GE and related research fields.

The debates on concepts and terminology are consequential because the terminology in use influences how funding is channelled for research and practical development. For example, the radically decreased number of studies in peace education likely reflects the way it is defined and conceptualized. Indeed, the meaning of peace education has changed from a broad umbrella concept – more or less synonymous to GE – into a narrower concept that posits peace education as just one component of GE. Similarly, the changes in the concepts and terminology can also help us understand why *DE* is neglected in recent Finnish research. Bourn (2014) states that the notions of GE and global learning can provide a wider frame to interpret DE, yet the shift of focus may also limit the issues addressed. He suggests ensuring an integrated approach to global *learning*, thus emphasizing also the expected results of GE.

During the last decade, GE has been used as the overarching concept in Finland, for example, in the national core curriculum and the guidelines for government funding of projects. In this respect critics maintain that compared to earlier dominant concepts, such as international education and peace education, the notion of GE may shift the focus to individual competences and instrumental economic concerns away from discussions of *international solidarity* and *structural injustices* that are more politically contested (Järvelä 2002). Furthermore, research related to GE as an *ethical commitment* (Räsänen 2007b) seems lacking. Also, translations of concepts usually pose a challenge.

Overall, our review shows how research in Finland follows European and international trends yet maintains a critical stance to identify issues related to its specific sociopolitical contexts and aims to have a holistic view of education development. Recently in Europe, global learning has gained research attention with a focus on learning understood widely (Bourn 2018; Scheunpflug and Mehren 2016), while several organizations (including Brookings Institute and UNESCO; OECD) have attempted to develop instruments to measure global competencies and global citizenship skills as universal. In Finland, assessment of the global competencies is an emerging topic though there seems to be more emphasis on the holistic eco-social approach aiming to the system-level development of the whole school community. This holistic approach offers a frame for integrating the five dimensions in education which can be interpreted as an attempt to continue the Finnish (and Nordic) tradition to value education as the collective, social and global common good.

Bibliography

Acquah, E. O. (2015), *Responding to Changing Student Demographics in Finland: A Study of Teachers' Developing Cultural Competence*. Turku: University of Turku.

Ahonen, S. (2014), Historia: konfliktintekijä vai sovittaja? *Kosmopolis*, 44: 1 [History: Conflict contributor or resolver?].

Alasuutari, H. (2011), Conditions for mutuality and reciprocity in development education policy and pedagogy. *International Journal of Development Education and Global Learning*, 3 (3): 65–78.

Alasuutari, H. (2015), *Towards More Ethical Engagements in North–South Education Sector Partnerships*. Oulu: University of Oulu.

Alemanji, A. A. (2016), *Is there Such a Thing …? A Study of Antiracism Education in Finland*. Helsinki: University of Helsinki.

Andreotti, V. (2006), Soft versus critical global citizenship education. *Policy and Practice – A Development Education Review*, 3: 40–51.

Andreotti, V. de Oliveira, Biesta, G. and Ahenakew, C. (2015), Between the nation and the globe: Education for global mindedness in Finland. *Globalisation, Societies and Education*, 13 (2): 246–59.

Anttalainen, K. and Lampinen, J. (2009), Tietoa, taitoa ja asenteita - esimerkkejä hyvistä käytänteistä. In Lampinen, J. and Melen-Paaso, M. (eds), *Tulevaisuus meissä: Kasvaminen maailmanlaajuiseen vastuuseen*, 139–49. Helsinki: Opetusministeriön julkaisuja 40. [Knowledge, skills and attitudes – examples of good practices. Future in us: Growing into global responsibility.]

Benjamin, S. and Alemanji, A. (2017), 'That makes us very unique'. A closer look at the institutional habitus of two international schools in Finland and France. In Itkonen, T. and Dervin, F. (eds), *Silent Partners in Education*, 93–116. Charlotte: Information Age.

Bourn, D. (2008), Towards a re-conceptualisation of development education. *International Journal of Development Education and Global Learning*, 1 (1): 5–22.

Bourn, D. (2014), The Theory and Practice of Global Learning. Research Paper No.11. London: Development Education Research Centre, Institute of Education in partnership with the Global Learning Programme. Available online: http://discovery.ucl.ac.uk/1492723/1/DERC_ResearchPaper11-TheTheoryAndPracticeOfGlobalLearning%5B2%5D.pdf (accessed 18 December 2018).

Bourn, D. (2015), From development education to global learning: Changing agendas and priorities. *Policy & Practice: A Development Education Review*, 20 (Spring): 18–36.

Bourn, D. (2018), A conceptual framework for global skills. In Bourn, D. (ed.), *Understanding Global Skills for 21st Century Professions*, 111–32. Cham: Palgrave Macmillan.

Cantell, H. (ed.) (2015), *Näin rakennat monialaisia oppimiskokonaisuuksia*. [Guide for designing multidisciplinary learning modules.] Jyväskylä: PS-kustannus.

Cole, M. (2017), Multicultural and Antiracist Education in the US and the UK. In Cole, M. (ed.), *Critical Race Theory and Education: A Marxist Response*, 105–24. New York: Palgrave Macmillan.

DERC (Development Education Research Centre) (2018), Global Education Digest 2015–2017, Compiled by the Development Education Research Centre. Available online: http://discovery.ucl.ac.uk/10044872/1/Digest%202015%20-%2017.pdf (accessed 5 January 2019).

Dervin, F. (2015), Towards post-intercultural teacher education: Analysing 'extreme' intercultural dialogue to reconstruct interculturality? *European Journal of Teacher Education*, 38 (1): 71–86.

Dervin, F. and Layne, H. (2013), A guide to interculturality for international and exchange students: An example of Hostipitality? *Journal of Multicultural Discourses*, 8 (1): 1–19.

Finnish National Agency for Education (2014), *National Core Curriculum for Basic Education 2014*.

Goren, H. and Yemini, M. (2017), Global citizenship education redefined – A systematic review of empirical studies on global citizenship education. *International Journal of Educational Research*, 82: 170–83.

Hague Appeal for Peace (1999), Available online: http://www.haguepeace.org (accessed 5 January 2019).

Halme, M. (2008), *Human Rights in Action*. Helsinki: University of Helsinki.

Hartmeyer, H. and Wegimont, L. (2016), Global education in Europe: European policy development. Growing access in Europe for global education. In Hartmeyer, H. and Wegimont, L. (eds), *Global Education in Europe Revisited: Strategies and Structures, Policy, Practice and Challenges*, 13–24. Münster: Waxmann.

Hartung, C. (2017), Global citizenship incorporated: Competing responsibilities in the education of global citizens. *Discourse: Studies in the Cultural Politics of Education*, 38 (1): 16–29.

Hassi, M. L., Niemelä, H., Paloniemi, A., Piekkari, J. and Wolde, K. (2015), Drama in child rights education; developing a pedagogical model. *The European Journal of Social & Behavioural Sciences*, 14 (3): 1902–14.

Henriksson, H. (2017), Kansalaisjärjestöt ja valtavirtaistuvan globaalikasvatuksen episteeminen hallinta. *Kasvatus*, 48 (5): 429–40. [NGOs and epistemic governance in the process of mainstreaming global education. The Finnish Journal of Education.]

Hicks, D. (2003), Thirty years of global education: A reminder of key principles and precedents. *Educational Review*, 55 (3): 265–75.

Holm, G. and Zilliacus, H. (2009), Multicultural education and intercultural education: Is there a difference? In Talib, M., Loima, J., Paavola, H. and Patrikainen, S. (eds), *Dialogs on Diversity and Global Education*, 11–28. New York: Peter Lang.

Jääskeläinen, L. (2011), Mitä maailmankansalaisen kompetenssit voisivat olla. In Jääskeläinen, L. and Repo, T. (eds), *Koulu kohtaa maailman. Mitä osaamista maailmankansalainen tarvitsee?* Opetushallitus. Oppaat ja käsikirjat 16. [What could be the competences of global citizens?]

Jääskeläinen, L. (2016), Short history of global education in Finland: From the perspective of a curriculum developer. In Hartmeyer, H. and Wegimont, L. (eds), *Global Education in Europe Revisited: Strategies and Structures, Policy, Practice and Challenges*, 97–114. Münster: Waxmann.

Janhonen-Abruquah, H., Lehtomäki, E. and Kahangwa, G. (2017), Culturally responsive education: From vision to practice. In Lehtomäki, E., Janhonen-Abruquah, H. and Kahangwa, G. (eds), *Culturally Responsive Education: Reflections from the Global South and North. Routledge Studies in Culture and Sustainable Development*, 3–13. London: Routledge.

Järvelä, M. L. (2002), Tavoitteena interkulttuurinen opettajankoulutus. Orientaatioperusta ja epistemologia. In Räsänen, R., Jokikokko, K., Järvelä, M. L. and Lamminmäki-Kärkkäinen, T. (eds), *Interkulttuurinen opettajankoulutus. Utopiasta todellisuudeksi toimintatutkimuksen avulla*, 31–47. Oulu: Oulun yliopisto. [Intercultural teacher education as a goal.]

Jokikokko, K. (2010), *Teacher's Intercultural Learning and Competence*. Oulu: University of Oulu.

Jokikokko, K. and Uitto, M. (2017), The significance of emotions in Finnish teachers' stories about their intercultural learning. *Pedagogy, Culture & Society*, 25 (1): 15–29.

Kaivola, T. (ed.) (2008), Puheenvuoroja maailmanlaajuiseen vastuuseen kasvamisesta. Opetusministeriön julkaisuja 13. [Viewpoints on Education for Global Responsibility.]

Kaivola, T. and Melén-Paaso, M. (eds) (2007), *Education for Global Responsibility – Finnish Perspectives*. Ministry of Education, Publications 31.

Laine, M. (2017), Kulttuurisesti kestävän kasvatuksen koulutus- ja kehitystarpeet. *Kasvatus*, 48 (5): 441–55. [Educational and developmental needs of culturally sustainable education.]

Laitinen, E. (2014), *Ammattikorkeakoulujen opettajien kulttuurienvälinen kompetenssi ja sen mittaaminen*. Tampere: Tampere University. [Intercultural competencies of teachers in universities of applied sciences and assessment of the competencies.]

Lampinen, J. and Melen-Paaso, M. (eds) (2009), *Tulevaisuus meissä: Kasvaminen maailmanlaajuiseen vastuuseen*. Helsinki: Opetusministeriön julkaisuja 40. [Future in us: Growing into global responsibility.]

Lanas, M. (2014), Failing intercultural education? 'Thoughtfulness' in intercultural education for student teachers. *European Journal of Teacher Education*, 37 (2): 171–82.

Layne, H. (2016), *'Contact Zones' in Finnish (Intercultural) Education*. Helsinki: University of Helsinki.

Layne, H. and Lipponen, L. (2016), Student teachers in the contact zone: Developing critical intercultural 'teacherhood' in kindergarten teacher education. *Globalisation, Societies and Education Globalisation, Societies and Education*, 14 (1): 110–26.

Lehtomäki, E., Moate, J. and Posti-Ahokas, H. (2016), Global Connectedness in Higher Education: Student voices on the value of cross-cultural learning dialogue. *Studies in Higher Education*, 41 (11): 2011–27.

Lehtomäki, E., Posti-Ahokas, H. and Moate, J. (2015), Meaningful internationalisation at home: Education students' voices on the value of cross-cultural learning dialogue. In Kricke, M., Kurten, L. and Amrhein, B. (eds), *Internationalisierung der LehrerInnenbildung*, 99–109. Münster: Waxmann.

Lestinen, L., Autio-Hiltunen, M. and Kiviniemi, U. (2017), Suomen nuorten käsityksiä kansallisesta identiteetistään ja eurooppalaisuudestaan. *Kasvatus*, 48 (2): 96–109. [Finnish teenagers' perceptions of their national cultural identity and being European.]

Löfström, J. (2014), Edistävätkö historialliset anteeksipyynnöt rauhaa ja sovintoa: suomalaislukiolaisten ajattelun analyysiä. *Kosmopolis*, 44: 1.

Löfström, J. and Ahonen, S. (2014), Pääkirjoitus: rauha, konfliktit ja kasvatus. *Kosmopolis*, 44: 1. [Editorial: Peace, conflicts and education.]

Marginson, S. (2016), *Higher Education and the Common Good*. Carlton: Melbourne University.

Matilainen, M. (2011), *Ihmisoikeuskasvatus lukiossa – outoa ja itsestään selvää*. Helsinki: University of Helsinki. [Human rights education in upper secondary schools: Alien yet obvious.]

Matilainen, M. and Kallioniemi, A. (2011), Headmasters' conceptions of the Finnish religious education – solution from the perspective of human rights. *Nordidactica: Journal of Humanities and Social Science Education*, 2: 1–14.

Matikainen, P. (2017), *Oikeudenmukaisuus sisäsyntyisinä oikeuksina ja kasvatus oikeudenmukaisuuteen dialogisen pluralismin kontekstissa: näkökulmia ja tulkintoja Nicholas Wolterstorffin kokonaisfilosofiasta*. Jyväskylä: University of Jyväskylä. [Justice as inherent rights and education for justice within the framework of dialogical pluralism. Perspectives and interpretations of Nicholas Wolterstorff's philosophical thinking.]

Ministry of Education, Finland (2006), *Kansainvälisyyskasvatus 2010. Ehdotus kansalliseksi kansainvälisyyskasvatuksen toimenpideohjelmaksi*. Helsinki: Ministry of Education. [International Education 2010. A proposal of Finland's national strategy on international education.]

North-South Centre of the Council of Europe (2004), *Global Education in Finland. The European Global Education Peer Review Process, National Report on Finland*. https://gene.eu/wp-content/uploads/Gene_NationalReport-Finland.pdf

O'Loughlin, E. and Wegimont, L. (eds) (2003), *Global Education in Europe to 2015: Strategy, Policies, and Perspectives*. Maastricht Global Education Congress 15–17 November 2002. Lisbon: North-South Centre of the Council of Europe.

Oxley, L. and Morris, P. (2013), Global citizenship: A typology for distinguishing its multiple conceptions. *British Journal of Educational Studies*, 61 (3): 301–25.

Poulter, S., Kuusisto, A., Malama, M. and Kallioniemi, A. (2017), Examining religious education in Finland from a human rights perspective. In Sjöborg, A. and Ziebertz, H.-G. (eds), *Religion, Education and Human Rights*, 49–61. Cham: Springer.

Poulter, S., Riitaoja, A. L. and Kuusisto, A. (2016), Thinking multicultural education 'otherwise'–from a secularist construction towards a plurality of epistemologies and worldviews. *Globalisation, Societies and Education*, 14 (1): 68–86.

Pudas, A.-K. (2015), *A Moral Responsibility or An Extra Burden? A Study on Global Education as Part of Finnish Basic Education*. Oulu: University of Oulu.

Räsänen, R. (2007a), International education as an ethical issue. In: Hayden M., Levy J. and Thompson, J. (eds), *The SAGE Handbook of Research in International Education*, 57–69. Trowbridge: The Cromwell.

Räsänen, R. (2007b), Education for intercultural, multi-levelled citizenship in Europe: the case of Finland. In Kotthoff, H. G. and Moutsios, S. (eds), *Education Policies in Europe. Economy, Citizenship, Diversity*, 221–37. New York: Waxmann.

Räsänen, R. (2007c), Intercultural education as education for global responsibility. In Kaivola, T. and Melen-Paaso, M. (eds), *Education for Global Responsibility – Finnish Perspectives*, 17–30. Helsinki: Ministry of Education.

Räsänen, R. (2009), Transformative global education and learning in teacher education in Finland. *International Journal of Development Education and Global Learning*, 1 (2): 25–40.

Rautiainen, M., Vanhanen-Nuutinen, L. and Virta, A. (2014), *Demokratia ja ihmisoikeudet: Tavoitteet ja sisällöt opettajankoulutuksessa*. Helsinki: Ministry of Education and Culture. [Democracy and human rights: Goals and contents in teacher education.]

Salmenkivi, E. (2011), The Philosophical Basis of Teaching about the Holocaust in Human Rights Education. Paper presented at NERA-congress, 10–12 March 2011, Jyväskylä, Finland.

Salonen, A., Palmberg, I. and Aarnio-Linnavuori, E. (2017), Tyytyväisyyskasvatuksella kehitys kestäväksi? *Kasvatus*, 48 (5): 401–2. [Sustainable development through education for satisfaction?]

Schattle, H. (2008), Education for global citizenship: Illustrations of ideological pluralism and adaptation. *Journal of Political Ideologies*, 13 (1): 73–94.

Scheunpflug, A. and Mehren, R. (2016), What do we know about global learning and what do we need to find out? In Hartmeyer, H. and Wegimont, L. (eds), *Global Education in Europe Revisited*, 205–25. Waxmann: Münster.

Seriki, V. D. and Brown, C. T. (2017), A dream deferred: A retrospective view of culturally relevant pedagogy. *Teachers College Record*, 119 (1): 1–32.

Siirilä, J. (2016), *Tulkintoja kestävän kehityksen käsitteestä YK:n kestävää kehitystä edistävän kasvatuksen teemavuosikymmenen 2005–2014 yhteydessä*. Helsinki: University of Helsinki. [Construction of the concept of sustainable development under the United Nations Decade of Education for Sustainable Development 2005–2014.]

Souto, A. M. (2011), *Arkipäivän rasismi koulussa. Etnografinen tutkimus suomalais- ja maahanmuuttajanuorten ryhmäsuhteista*. Helsinki: Nuorisotutkimusseura, Julkaisuja 110. [Everyday racism in school. An ethnographic study of group relations between Finnish and immigrant youths.]

Tarozzi, M. (2012), Intercultural or multicultural education in Europe and the USA. In della Chiesa, B., Scott, J. and Hinton, C. (eds), *Languages in a Global World: Learning for Better Cultural Understanding*, 392–406. Paris: OECD.

Toivanen, R. (2007), Education on Human Rights – a method for inducing global critical thinking. In Kaivola, T. and Melén-Paaso, M. (eds), *Education for Global Responsibility – Finnish Perspectives*, 33–44. Helsinki: Ministry of Education.

Uitto, A. and Saloranta, S. (2017), Subject teachers as educators for sustainability: A survey study. *Education Sciences*, 7 (8): 1–19.

UNESCO (2015), Rethinking Education: Towards a Global Common Good? Paris: UNESCO. Available online http://unesdoc.unesco.org/images/0023/002325/232555e.pdf (accessed 5 January 2019).

UNESCO (2018), *Preparing Teachers for Global Citizenship Education: A Template*. Available online http://unesdoc.unesco.org/images/0026/002654/265452e.pdf (accessed 5 January 2019).

Vesa, U. (2007), On the importance of peace education. In Kaivola, T. and Melén-Paaso, M. (eds), *Education for Global Responsibility – Finnish Perspectives*, 47–56. Helsinki: Ministry of Education.

Zilliacus, H., Paulsrud, B. and Holm, G. (2017), Essentializing vs. non-essentializing students' cultural identities: Curricular discourses in Finland and Sweden. *Journal of Multicultural Discourses*, 12 (2): 166–80.

Chapter 10
Global Education in Poland

Magdalena Kuleta-Hulboj

Introduction

Along with the cosmopolitan trend in social sciences (Beck and Grande 2010), global education (GE) has sparked interest in many countries. Its popularity has increased also in Poland. The most engaged stakeholders here are the non-governmental development organizations (NGDOs). However, contrary to the common view (Jasikowska 2018; Witkowski 2012), the NGDOs were not the first to think about a global perspective in education. Such reflection began in the late 1940s but evolved neither into educational practice nor into a theory of GE.

The aim of this chapter is twofold: first, to provide an overview of the origins, development and current state of GE in Poland (as a pedagogical idea, research area and educational practice); second, to explore the sociopolitical context and important factors influencing GE.

The chapter begins with a glimpse into the beginnings of GE in Poland with a special focus on Bogdan Suchodolski, who pioneered a global dimension in education. It then overviews the important role of NGDOs in GE practice. Subsequently, the chapter analyses the Polish context and points out the country's semi-peripheral status; and provides a brief description of the state of GE in formal education and the academia. Finally, the chapter looks at important challenges GE faces nowadays in Poland.

I will begin with the definition of GE agreed upon by the NGDOs, the Ministry of Foreign Affairs and the Ministry of Education. It defines it as 'the part of civic education and upbringing, which broadens their scope through making a person aware of the existence of global phenomena and interdependencies. Its main objective is to prepare the recipients to face the challenges related to all humankind' (Grupa Zagranica 2011). Although this fails to meet the criteria of a scientific definition, I will refer to it as it is commonly used.

The beginnings of global education in Poland

Several authors argued that NGDOs paved the way for the rise of GE in Poland (Chimiak 2016; Jasikowska 2018; O'Loughlin and Wegimont 2009; Witkowski 2012). Regarding educational practice, this claim may be justified. However, considering a theoretical reflection on global perspective in education, it began much earlier and can be traced back to the beginning of the twentieth century, when the New Education Movement, known also as progressive education, was gaining widespread popularity. Like progressive educators in other European countries, several Polish intellectuals, interested in international understanding and building world peace through education, looked at ways to include these topics in education. As Poland had just regained its independence after 123 years of partitions, the interest in world issues was intertwined with the urge for strengthening national identity and patriotism.

After the Second World War, which changed the world order, Poland came into the Soviet sphere of influence. In the beginning, there was some intellectual freedom. Bogdan Suchodolski was the first Polish educationalist reflecting on education for world citizenship. Having noticed deep changes in the world, growing interdependence and interconnections, he called for educating citizens to be responsible both for the Polish state and the globalizing world (Suchodolski 1947).

These observations led him to formulate the need for new attitudes, knowledge and behaviour, and therefore a new approach in education that would overcome the limitations of traditionalism and progressivism, and prepare people for future challenges. He envisioned education cultivating a sense of world community, global responsibility and global ethics; education that develops the ability to think globally, not locally.

Although the communist times were far from being conducive to intellectual freedom, Suchodolski and Irena Wojnar, his disciple and collaborator, continued this reflection in various forums. They were active at the international level and extensively cooperated with international organizations, such as the UN, the Club of Rome and World Futures Studies Federation.

Their thoughts were convergent with UNESCO ideas on education for international understanding and peace. One may also find some similarities to the work of Pike and Selby (1988) or Hicks (2001), especially with regard to the futures dimension. However, searching for ways that would profoundly transform people's consciousness and thus their lives, Suchodolski and Wojnar focused on general and aesthetic education. The best way, as they saw it, was a humanistic revival of general education infused with a global perspective. It was a programme of 'humanisation of the world and the human being' in order to ensure a peaceful future, deeply rooted in humanistic ideals.

Neither Suchodolski nor his disciples developed these ideas into more comprehensive theory of GE. Similarly, they failed to translate their ideas into educational practice, which is why later on NGDOs felt they were starting from scratch.

The pivotal role of NGDOs

It was in the 1990s that non-governmental organizations (NGOs) entered the scene. Political, economic and social transformation, which began in 1989, enabled the self-organization of civil society and fostered a substantial growth of voluntary organizations in Poland. Their emergence was strongly supported by foreign aid – private and public donors providing financial resources, technical assistance and know-how.

Among burgeoning NGOs were internationally oriented organizations, active abroad and working within the framework of development cooperation – the non-governmental development organizations (NGDOs). It is hard to overestimate their role in the development of both GE and Polish development cooperation. In fact, they began development cooperation in Poland:

democratization projects implemented in post-communist European countries preceded the creation of Polish Aid, the official Polish development cooperation programme (Chimiak 2016). NGDOs were flexible, quickly responding to local needs and 'successful in putting foreign aid to good use' (Chimiak 2016: 56). It took them relatively little time to gain international experience, establish partnerships in the Global South and build development cooperation know-how. Soon, the NGDOs surpassed the Ministry of Foreign Affairs in this respect. They shaped Polish Aid and influenced establishing its priorities and aid modalities (Chimiak 2016).

While over recent years, in the area of development cooperation, the capacity of the Ministry of Foreign Affairs has exceeded that of NGDOs, which remains stagnant; this cannot be said in relation to GE. Although the Ministry of Foreign Affairs performs a leadership role in GE in Poland – it provides funding for GE activities – it is NGDOs that are the most engaged and active stakeholders in this area. Grupa Zagranica, the NGDO national platform, plays a seminal role here. NGDOs activities include not only education but also coordination, promotion, advocacy, campaigning and monitoring. Similarly, the Ministry of National Education, responsible for facilitating GE within the formal education sector, plays a peripheral role in comparison with the NGDOs. It provides the in-service training system (cascade training and a national GE trainers network) through its agency, the Centre for Education Development (Ośrodek Rozwoju Edukacji, ORE), a national teacher training institution, but in collaboration with the NGDOs.

In the beginning, the NGDOs emulated foreign examples and good practices, largely facilitated by participation in international GE networks and NGDO platforms (e.g. CONCORD). Although NGDOs themselves emphasized the importance of bottom-up solutions, this was, paradoxically, a kind of imitating modernization (Chimiak 2016: 170). Later, through debates within Grupa Zagranica's GE working group and thanks to increasing experience, they started to innovate and develop their own ideas, principles and content, more relevant to the Polish context.

NGDOs activity related to GE can be summarized by pointing to the following areas: development of educational resources (textbooks, teaching guides, online courses); in-service teacher training (commissioned by ORE) and collaboration with the formal education sector (Wieczorek 2016). The latter is the most popular and widespread form, from short-term workshops in schools, through courses lasting several weeks, to long-term cooperation.

Some of the NGDOs are very competent, and their expertise exceeds that of the Ministry of Foreign Affairs or the Ministry of Education, which lack specialists (Chimiak 2016). Grupa Zagranica's GE working group has also put much effort into improving the quality of NGDOs educational activities, to stimulate the organizations to look for innovative and high-quality projects and to ensure the sustainability and effectiveness of GE. This includes a joint peer review of activities and educational materials started in 2012, and a review of secondary school textbooks run since 2013. Worth mentioning is the work of two NGOs, the Centre for Citizenship Education (Centrum Edukacji Obywatelskiej) and the Institute of Global Responsibility (Instytut Globalnej Odpowiedzialności). The former initiated the analysis of the place of GE in the core curriculum (Centrum Edukacji Obywatelskiej 2010) and the research on GE in secondary schools teachers' practice (Ocetkiewicz and Pająk-Ważna 2013). The latter published a guide 'How to talk about the Majority world?' (Gontarska et al. 2015).

A milestone in the development of GE in Poland was an educational reform in 2008 that incorporated GE into the national curriculum. This was partly due to the lobbying efforts of Grupa Zagranica, and also the NGDOs which initiated the national multi-stakeholder process on

GE in Poland (2009–11). This chapter will not detail the whole process, as a range of publications have done so already (Jasikowska and Witkowski 2012; Witkowski 2012). Instead, it will focus on the consequences.

As a result of the process, the Ministry of Foreign Affairs, the Ministry of Education and Grupa Zagranica signed the official multi-stakeholder agreement on GE. It was the beginning of institutionalized cooperation between these parties. By signing the agreement, stakeholders committed to use a common definition of GE, to expand the activities undertaken so far and to promote and support the development of GE. However, a few years after the agreement (and the change of government in 2015), the state funds earmarked for GE are now decreasing. According to the Development Co-Operation Plans, in 2016–18, respectively, from 2.4 per cent to 1.5 per cent of the state budget target reserve was earmarked for GE projects, implemented by civil society organizations and the Centre for Education Development (Ministry of Foreign Affairs 2015a, 2016, 2017).

Despite insufficient funds, shortage of long-term financing and an unfavourable political climate (more on this later), Polish NGDOs continue their engagement in GE. In recent years, the number of organizations implementing GE projects has increased. Most of them are small, newly established and locally active entities. This was possible due to numerous training events for trainers and organizations, and thanks to the programme of micro-grants (granted by the Education for Democracy Foundation from MFA funds) (Wieczorek 2016).

Factors influencing global education in Poland

The role the NGDOs have been playing in developing GE in Poland is fundamental. However, there were also other influential factors. Among them was Poland's accession to the European Union in 2004. In the official narrative, this was a turning point, marking the country's transition from ODA beneficiary to donor. Poland became a part of EU development cooperation policy and was obliged to have its own development cooperation, resulting in the establishment of Polish Aid. The first official Polish Aid grant programme was announced in 2005. Chimiak notes that due to their previously gained know-how and experience 'Polish NGOs became natural partners for the MFA and started implementing projects financed by Polish Aid' (Chimiak 2016: 159). GE has been one of their areas of activity.

After the accession, Polish NGDOs gained access also to EU funds (like Development Education and Awareness Raising programme), which enabled them to launch wider-scale activities, in larger consortia. This, in turn, has contributed to a growth in experience, knowledge and skills. However, the requirements of applicants' financial contribution to European projects have been hard to meet for many NGDOs, given insufficient local funds (Chimiak 2016).

The growing importance of GE in EU development cooperation and educational policy, and the increasing financial support have stimulated the development of GE in Poland. The rapid changes taking place in the world and the growing awareness of global mega-crises (Jasikowska 2018) have also had an impact in this respect.

Apart from the EU-related factors, there have also been others. According to János Setényi cited in Witkowski (2012), the following features differentiate the Polish (and other Visegrad countries') context from the Western European context, and influence GE decreasing interest in global issues: relative ethnic, cultural and religious homogeneity of the society;[1] lack of colonial legacy; and memory of totalitarian oppression.

Having similar factors in mind, Chimiak writes about Poland as an 'in-between' country: 'In spite of the end of the Cold War and the end of the First, Second, and Third World divide, some of the divisions dating back to the Cold War times still hold true. The current bipolar divides ... have not obliterated the in-between status of some former communist states, including Poland' (Chimiak 2016: 138). However, in a broader context of development cooperation, she regards this status as Poland's comparative advantage. This is because many Poles still remember how life was in the communist era, and despite the economic growth and sociopolitical changes, they still have a lot in common with aid recipients. Due to this, Polish people may appear more eager to support and become engaged in development activities.

On the other hand, however (and Chimiak also does note this), to this day the prevalent belief is that Poland does not belong to the affluent part of the world. According to the 2015 public survey, there are eighty-one countries (on average) poorer and less developed than Poland (Ministry of Foreign Affairs 2015b). Therefore, despite being generally supportive of development cooperation, many Poles still tend to regard themselves as aid recipients rather than donors.

Although Poland has never had formal colonies, which sometimes results in a sense of moral superiority over former colonial empires, one needs to mention the Polish pre-war dreams of hegemony in the East, expansionism and paternalism towards its Eastern neighbours as well as the existence of certain organizations promoting the idea of Polish colonies (e.g. the Maritime and Colonial League) (Jasikowska 2018). These colonial intentions did not materialize, mainly because of the weakness of the state and partly for financial and political reasons.

Additionally, one should mention here the sense of cultural superiority towards other Eastern European nations, especially the Russians. In its auto-stereotype, Poland is a bulwark against the East, *antemurale christianitatis* (more in Marung 2012). Over recent years, this tradition has been reinterpreted so as to proclaim Poland as a bridge between the West and the East, but the belief about Poland's special historical role also resonates here.

All these factors constitute a complex baggage of various experiences influencing GE in Poland. It may be a valuable resource, but also a limitation; and it requires deep reflection on its shape, scope and content. As Starnawski (2015) argues (drawing on the works of Wallerstein), Poland could be seen as a semi-peripheral country, in terms of its economic, political and cultural status. And as such, it remains at the heart of the Global South–Global North relations. Starnawski calls for a GE that would problematize the global context in the perspective of a semi-peripheral country and deconstruct North–South and West–East binaries. This is what still remains to be done.

---

[1] According to the latest national census of Główny Urząd Statystyczny (2012), 96 per cent of Polish citizens have been of Polish nationality and 85 per cent – the followers of Roman Catholicism. Until the Second World War, two-thirds of Polish citizens were Roman Catholic and 69 per cent were of Polish ethnic-national identity.

Global education in schools

As already mentioned, GE has been a part of the national curriculum since 2008. Representatives of Grupa Zagranica took part in consultations on the core curriculum; this was an important stimulus for GE and contributed to numerous activities implemented in schools. As teachers were not sufficiently prepared to teach GE, the Centre for Education Development (ORE) started its first GE teacher training project. Since 2010, ORE has been conducting training courses for teachers, publishing educational materials and organizing school project competitions. It has also been developing a network of regional GE coordinators.

The majority of school-based GE activities take place during the annual Global Education Week in November. Many of them are delivered by NGDOs as short-term projects (i.e. workshops, games, school campaigns). There are also schools that have long-term cooperation with NGDOs which culminates in Global Education Week. Some enthusiastic teachers implement their own GE projects: as cross-curricular themes, discussion clubs or extra-curricular activities. However, the most common way of teaching GE in schools is to introduce single topics or activities during a subject lesson.

Although there is little research concerning GE in schools, several surveys were undertaken. According to Ocetkiewicz and Pająk-Ważna (2013), Czaplicka and Lisocka-Jaegermann (2014) and Świdrowska and Tragarz (2017), GE is to a greater or lesser extent present in Polish primary (grades 4–8) and secondary schools.

Czaplicka and Lisocka-Jaegermann comment, however, that it is significantly easier for teachers to introduce GE content to their lessons than to attempt to develop favourable attitudes and to change beliefs. This reflects a broader problem of education in the neoliberal era: prioritizing the acquisition of knowledge and skills over other functions of education: socialization, identity formation, subjectification (see also Biesta 2009 and the problem of 'learnification' of education).

What hinders the implementation of GE in schools? Participants in three surveys pointed to similar factors: lack of time and overloaded subject curriculum; focus on assessment and testing and shortage of educational resources. While the first two issues are well known, the latter appears somewhat surprising, as there are a lot of materials prepared by the NGDOs and easily available. Apparently, teachers have little knowledge of them or do not know how to access them. This prompted the authors to recommend a broad promotion of not only GE itself but also the support the teachers can receive from NGDOs and ORE. Czaplicka and Lisocka-Jaegermann (2014) suggested also that there was an urgency to create a hub storing a wealth of GE resources. Since 2014, this role has been played by the web portal http://e-globalna.edu.pl/, run by the Education for Democracy Foundation.

The teachers reported a demand for gaining deeper knowledge in GE as well as for the distribution of educational materials in accordance with the core curriculum, and tailored to the specific needs and requirements of different groups of teachers. Because the teachers feel overloaded with work, they also need resources that are ready to use and which do not require additional effort or time. Tips on how to incorporate GE topics in the teaching of particular subjects would also be useful. There is also a need for training in how to discuss and teach controversial issues in the classroom (Świdrowska and Tragarz 2017).

After the parliamentary elections in 2015 won by the Law and Justice party (PiS), the new conservative government launched a controversial and rapid reform of the education system. Despite widespread protests, it phased out lower secondary schools and restored an eight-year primary school and a four-year high school (as prior to the major educational reform in 1999). This brought a lot of confusion among teachers, students and parents. It resulted, among other things, in two different core curricula being compulsory in different classes at the same level: 'the old' and 'the new'.

Having been prepared in a hurry, the new core curriculum was criticized by numerous experts (academics, teachers and civil society organizations), who considered it as inconsistent, anachronistic and overloaded. They also pointed out some factual and methodological errors. Criticism also focused on the marginalization of citizenship education, polono- and euro-centrism and the reinforcement of nationalistic sentiments. Numerous critical voices raised the issue of not including the development of critical thinking.

One of these bodies was Grupa Zagranica, who in 2017 evaluated the core curriculum draft in terms of the presence and principles of GE. Grupa Zagranica emphasized that it could reinforce stereotypes and prejudices about the Global South (through generalizations, non-inclusive and biased language, or euro-centric readings). It also criticized the absence of Global South perspectives as well as the significant prevalence of Poland-related content over that of others. Grupa Zagranica offered several recommendations, such as incorporating content related to non-European regions and cultures, presenting them in a non-stereotypical manner or emphasizing the development of a sense of connection and solidarity with others. It suggested also framing GE topics as cross-cutting issues, discussed during various school classes (Grupa Zagranica 2017). Some of these recommendations were recognized and introduced into the final version of the core curriculum, but it certainly cannot be called a curriculum with a global dimension.

In conclusion, despite integrating GE into the national curriculum in 2008 and its presence in schools' educational practice, there still remains a lot to be done. Permanent reform of the educational system – curricular and structural – is not conducive to establishing GE in schools. Overloaded curricula and the focus on assessment do not leave space for topics that reach beyond the basics. Surveys show also that although GE is present in the curriculum, many teachers are not conscious of that. Last but not least, recent neo-conservative and nationalistic trends also pose challenges for GE.

Academic interest in global education in Poland

In the 1990s, when NGDOs began developing GE practice, academic reflection and research in this area were neglected. Until now, GE has been a niche in academia. It lacks a high academic profile. There is relatively little literature on GE and only a few scholars deal mainly with this phenomenon. Although several authors have undertaken topics related to global perspectives in education (Lewowicki, Nikitorowicz, Pilch 2002; Theiss 2012), none of them developed any theory of GE. They have focused on globalization processes, their challenges and the pedagogical responses needed in a new era, but GE per se has never attracted their attention.

However, there were some exceptions in this respect. Zbyszko Melosik (1989) familiarized Polish readers with the American approach to GE. A few years later, drawing on postmodern studies, he provided a critical analysis of this approach and claimed it was 'an arrogant pedagogical project of the modernist era' (Melosik 2007: 181).

Only recently has GE gained greater popularity and emerged as an area of educational and sociological scholarship. There is slow but steady growth in empirical and theoretical studies. Several authors continue the general reflection on GE, its necessity as well as its theoretical and axiological foundations (Ciążela and Tyburski 2012; Kuleta-Hulboj 2015; Theiss 2012).

Jasikowska, Pająk-Ważna and Klarenbach (2015), adopting a mixed-method research design, analysed the state of GE in schools in the Lesser Poland province. Despite the study's limitations (focusing only on teachers' perspectives and the limited geographical coverage of the research), it is a valuable source of information on how teachers understand and implement GE at all levels of education.

The studies cited in the previous part of this chapter are also worth mentioning (Czaplicka and Lisocka-Jaegermann 2014; Ocetkiewicz and Pająk-Ważna 2013; Świdrowska and Tragarz 2017). Although they do not go beyond simple surveys and in most cases the samples were not representative, they offer some insight into teachers' practice and the state of GE in Polish schools.

The teachers and their preparedness for GE are also of interest to other researchers. Markowska-Manista and Dąbrowa (2012) analysed an initial and in-service teacher training in GE in Poland, while Gmerek (2015) pointed to teachers' competences and attitudes needed in GE.

The NGDOs perspectives have also been explored. From the (engaged) sociological perspective, Jasikowska (2018) investigated the development of GE in Poland, focusing on the role of the Third Sector. Drawing on critical and post-colonial theories and being both a researcher and an activist, she calls for critical GE that goes beyond the neoliberal frameworks and seeks alternatives.

Kuleta-Hulboj (2016) adopted a similar (although pedagogical) theoretical perspective while exploring how employees of Polish NGDOs conceptualized the notions of the global citizen and global citizenship. She identified critical and non-critical patterns of conceptualization of the global citizen and provided a complex picture of NGDOs' global citizen ideals.

To complete the picture, one should also add poor collaboration between the NGDOs and academia. In general, academics do not seek cooperation or partnership with NGDOs in delivering educational activities in schools or non-formal settings; equally, NGDOs' educational practice is not firmly rooted in theoretical thought. While academia tends to disregard the NGDOs as serious partners contributing to the development of theory, the NGDOs think that the academics have nothing interesting to offer. If there is any collaboration at all, it is usually founded on personal ties.

However, examples of effective collaboration can still be found, such as joint publications (Jasikowska et al. 2015; Kuleta-Hulboj and Gontarska 2015), or postgraduate studies in humanitarian aid (a joint initiative of the University of Warsaw and the Polish Humanitarian Action). They do not, however, exhaust the range of possibilities of a fruitful cooperation: from examining the effectiveness of NGDOs' educational interventions through to enriching their practice with theoretical background and to implementing joint projects.

Conclusions: The challenges of global education in Poland

Initial thoughts about the global dimension in education began in Poland shortly after the Second World War, related to the work of Suchodolski. However, neither he nor his disciples have developed their ideas into a theory of GE or into educational practice. For the NGDOs that started educational activities in the 1990s, it was like building from scratch.

Lack of collaboration between the Third Sector and academia and the scholars' belated interest in GE resulted in relative isolation, little knowledge about their respective work and non-harmonious development of GE. The most important role in this process was played by the NGDOs. This exerted an impact on GE, which is an under-researched and under-theorized area. This has started to change, but there are still many gaps that need to be bridged.

Closer collaboration might be beneficial to both parties, resulting in theoretical enrichment of educational practice as well as provision of empirical data about the processes of global learning. These may include examining results of educational interventions, researching the effectiveness of particular methodologies and instructional approaches, or exploring the actual learning process taking place during the workshops.

There is a need for more theorization of GE in Poland, especially given the semi-peripheral status of the country. In what ways do the factors highlighted in this chapter influence GE? How to conceptualize GE in a semi-peripheral or 'in-between' country, to make it relevant and significant in people's lives?

Among all the factors explored above, there is a neo-conservative trend ongoing in Poland, which is similar to what is happening in other countries, also outside Europe. This has been particularly noticeable since the parliamentary elections in 2015. Orientation towards national values in public life, increasing xenophobia and playing on nationalistic sentiments by the ruling party create serious challenges for GE. Surveys show that liking for other nations has recently been decreasing in Poland (CBOS 2018) and at the same time the number of instances of hate crimes and incidents of hate speech has increased (Winiewski et al. 2017). Although the numbers are still quite low in comparison to other countries, it is most disturbing and requires appropriate action.

As Winiewski et al. (2017) comment, more frequent contact with hate speech leads to desensitization and correlates with the acceptation of hate speech and violence. This raises an important question as to how GE may respond to growing xenophobia and nationalism. How should it address people's identity needs, and compete with the essentialist and exclusion-based identities that seem to prevail nowadays?

In terms of the formal education sector, there is a demand for more initial and in-service teacher training, tailored to the specific needs and requirements of different groups of teachers. The teachers also need more thorough information on the NGDOs' educational resources available in print and online, and inspiration on how to integrate GE into overloaded subject curricula. As many teachers admit, in the era of assessment and measurement, most teachers will spend only a few minutes during their lessons on GE topics (Świdrowska and Tragarz 2017).

With regard to the non-governmental sector, apart from the previously signalled funding limitations, there emerge difficulties that relate to a shortage of long-term financing, which results in lack of organizational stability, emergence of *projectariat* (the precariat class of project workers in insecure employment in the public or non-governmental sector) and reduced possibilities of building organizational capacity.

I will finish by expressing my personal belief, hopefully shared by many people: in this world of rapidly changing geopolitical and socio-economic conditions, we more than ever need thoughtful and locally relevant GE. This is a joint task for all stakeholders.

Bibliography

Beck, U. and E. Grande (2010), 'Varieties of second modernity: The cosmopolitan turn in social and political theory and research', *The British Journal of Sociology*, 61 (3): 409–43.

Biesta, G. (2009), 'Good education in an age of measurement: On the need to reconnect with the question of purpose in education', *Educational Assessment, Evaluation and Accountability*, 21 (1): 33–46.

CBOS (2018), *Stosunek do innych narodów* (Attitudes Towards Other Nations), Warszawa. Available online: https://www.cbos.pl/SPISKOM.POL/2018/K_037_18.PDF (accessed 30 October 2018).

Centrum Edukacji Obywatelskiej (2010), *Treści edukacji globalnej w podstawie programowej kształcenia ogólnego* (Global Education Content in the National Curriculum), Warszawa.

Chimiak, G. (2016), *The Growth of Non-governmental Development Organizations in Poland and their Cooperation with Polish Aid*, Warsaw: Wydawnictwo IFiS PAN.

Ciążela, H. and W. Tyburski, eds (2012), *Odpowiedzialność globalna i edukacja globalna: Wymiary teorii i praktyki* (Global Responsibility and Global Education: Dimensions of Theory and Practice), Warszawa: Wydawnictwo Akademii Pedagogiki Specjalnej.

Czaplicka, K. and B. Lisocka-Jaegermann (2014), *Edukacja globalna w szkołach gimnazjalnych i ponadgimnazjalnych w Polsce. Raport z badania* (Global Education in Lower and Higher Secondary Schools. Research Report), Warszawa. Available online: http://www.edukacjaglobalna.ore.edu.pl/pl/d/1092f386c02620ce37c1f5f07a01de3e (accessed 30 October 2018).

Główny Urząd Statystyczny (2012), *Raport z wyników. Narodowy Spis Powszechny Ludności i Mieszkań 2011* (Results report. National Census of Population and Housing 2011), Warszawa. Available online: https://stat.gov.pl/cps/rde/xbcr/gus/lud_raport_z_wynikow:NSP2011.pdf (accessed 30 October 2018).

Gmerek, T. (2015), 'Nauczyciel edukacji globalnej (kilka uwag teoretycznych)' (Global education teacher (a few theoretical notes)), in J. Ł. Pyżalski (ed.), *Nauczyciel w ponowoczesnym świecie: Od założeń teoretycznych do rozwoju kompetencji* (Teacher in Post-Modern World: From the Theoretical Assumptions to the Skills Development): 22–38, Łódź: the Q studio.

Gontarska, M., E. Kielak, A. Huminiak, A. Kucińska and M. Qandil (2015), *Jak mówić o większości świata?: Jak rzetelnie informować o krajach globalnego Południa?* (How to Talk about the Majority World? How to Pass Accurate Information on the Global South?), 4th edn, Warszawa: Instytut Globalnej Odpowiedzialności.

Grupa Zagranica (2011), *Report on the Multi-Stakeholder Process on Global Education*, Warsaw. Available online: http://zagranica.org.pl/sites/zagranica.org.pl/files/attachments/Dokumenty/Ministerialne/report_on_multistakeholder_process_ge.pdf (accessed 30 October 2018).

Grupa Zagranica (2017), *Komentarz grupy roboczej ds. edukacji globalnej do projektu rozporządzenia Ministra Edukacji Narodowej w sprawie projektu podstawy programowej poszczególnych przedmiotów przewidzianych w ramowych planach nauczania dla publicznych szkół ponadpodstawowych* (The Notes of the Global Education Working Group to the draft regulation of the Ministry of National Education concerning the project of the national curriculum for specific subjects in public lower and higher secondary schools). Available online: http://zagranica.org.pl/sites/zagranica.org.pl/files/attachments/Rzecznictwo/Konsultacje/konsultacje_men_grupa_zagranica_26052017.pdf (accessed 25 October 2018).

Hicks, D. W. (2001), 'Re-examining the Future: The challenge for citizenship education', *Educational Review*, 53 (3): 229–40.

Jasikowska, K. (2018), *Zmieniając świat!: Edukacja globalna między zyskiem a zbawieniem* (Changing the World!: Global Education between the Profit and Salvation), Kraków: Oficyna Wydawnicza 'Impuls'.

Jasikowska, K. and J. Witkowski (2012), 'Global Education in statu nascendi: Some reflections on Poland', *The International Journal of Development Education and Global Learning*, 4 (3): 5–25.

Jasikowska, K., M. Klarenbach, G. Lipska-Badoti and R. Łuczak (2015), *Edukacja globalna: Poradnik metodyczny dla nauczycieli II, III i IV etapu edukacyjnego* (Global Education: Methodological Guidebook for the Teachers of the 2nd, 3rd and 4th Stage in Education), Warszawa: Ośrodek Rozwoju Edukacji.

Jasikowska, K., E. Pająk-Ważna and M. Klarenbach (2015), *Edukacja globalna w Małopolsce: Podmioty, praktyki, konteksty* (Global Education in the Lesser Poland Province: Actors, Practices, Contexts), Kraków: Oficyna Wydawnicza 'Impuls'.

Kuleta-Hulboj, M. (2015), 'Kilka uwag o heterogeniczności edukacji globalnej' (A few remarks on heterogeneity of global education'), *Teraźniejszość – Człowiek – Edukacja*, 69 (1): 67–80.

Kuleta-Hulboj, M. (2016), 'The global citizen as an agent of change: Ideals of the global citizen in the narratives of Polish NGO employees', *The Journal of Critical Education Policy Studies*, 14 (3): 220–50.

Kuleta-Hulboj, M. and M. Gontarska, eds (2015), *Edukacja globalna: Polskie konteksty i inspiracje* (Global Education: Polish Contexts and Inspirations), Wrocław: Wydawnictwo Naukowe Dolnośląskiej Szkoły Wyższej.

Lewowicki T., J. Nikitorowicz and T. Pilch, eds (2002), *Edukacja wobec ładu globalnego* (Education vs Global Order), Warszawa: 'Żak'.

Markowska-Manista, U. and E. Dąbrowa (2012), 'Wdrażanie założeń edukacji globalnej w systemie edukacji formalnej w Polsce. Przygotowanie nauczycieli' (Implementation of the global education into the national curriculum in Poland. Training of teachers), in H. Ciążela and W. Tyburski (eds), *Odpowiedzialność globalna i edukacja globalna: Wymiary teorii i praktyki*: 144–58, Warszawa: Wydawnictwo Akademii Pedagogiki Specjalnej.

Marung, S. (2012), 'Moving borders and competing civilizing missions: Germany, Poland, and Ukraine in the context of the EU's eastern enlargement', in M. Silberman (ed.), *Walls, Borders, Boundaries: Spatial and Cultural Practices in Europe*: 131–52, New York: Berghahn Books.

Melosik, Z. (1989), '"Edukacja skierowana na świat" – ideał wychowawczy XXI wieku' („World-centred education" – pedagogical ideal in the 21st century), *Kwartalnik Pedagogiczny*, 3 (133): 159–73.

Melosik, Z. (2007), *Teoria i praktyka edukacji wielokulturowej* (Theory and Practice of Multicultural Education), Kraków: Oficyna Wydawnicza 'Impuls'.

Ministry of Foreign Affairs (2015a), *2016 Development Cooperation Plan*, Warsaw. Available online: https://www.polskapomoc.gov.pl/download/files/Dokumenty_i_Publikacje/Plan_wspolpracy_2016/Development_Cooperation_Plan_2016.pdf (accessed 30 October 2018).

Ministry of Foreign Affairs (2015b), *Poles on Development Assistance: Findings from a TNS Polska Study for the Ministry of Foreign Affairs*, Warsaw. Available online: https://www.polskapomoc.gov.pl/download/files/Aktualnosci2015/Badanie_opini_2015/Wyniki_badania_2015_en.pdf (accessed 30 October 2018).

Ministry of Foreign Affairs (2016), *2017 Development Cooperation Plan*, Warsaw. Available online: https://www.polskapomoc.gov.pl/download/files/Dokumenty_i_Publikacje/Plan_wspolpracy_2017/Development_Cooperation_Plan_2017.pdf (accessed 30 October 2018).

Ministry of Foreign Affairs (2017), *2018 Development Cooperation Plan*, Warsaw. Available online: https://www.polskapomoc.gov.pl/download/files/Development_Cooperation_Plan_2018.pdf (accessed 30 October 2013).

Ocetkiewicz, I. and E. Pająk-Ważna (2013), *Edukacja globalna w polskiej szkole. Raport z badań wśród nauczycielek i nauczycieli III etapu edukacyjnego* (Global Education in the Polish School: Report on the Research Conducted among the Teachers of the 3rd Stage of Education), Warszawa. Available online: https://globalna.ceo.org.pl/sites/globalna.ceo.org.pl/files/raport_edukacja_w:polskiej_szkole.pdf (accessed 25 October 2018).

O'Loughlin, E. and L. Wegimont (2009), *Global Education in Poland: The European Global Education Peer Review Process: National Report on Global Education in Poland*, Amsterdam: Global Education Network Europe.

Pike, G. and D. Selby (1988), *Global Teacher, Global Learner*, London: Hodder and Stoughton.

Starnawski, M. (2015), 'Edukacja globalna – perspektywa Polski jako europejskiego kraju półperyferyjnego' (Global education – Poland's perspective as a European semi-peripheral country), in M. Kuleta-Hulboj and M. Gontarska (eds), *Edukacja globalna: Polskie konteksty i inspiracje*: 39–59, Wrocław: Wydawnictwo Naukowe Dolnośląskiej Szkoły Wyższej.

Suchodolski, B. (1947), *Wychowanie dla przyszłości* (Education for the Future), Warszawa: Książnica Polska.

Świdrowska, E. and M. Tragarz (2017), *Edukacja globalna w szkole podstawowej: Perspektywa przedmiotowa: język polski, matematyka, geografia, religia i etyka. Raport z badan* (Global Education in a Primary School; Subject-related Perspective: Polish, Mathematics, Geography, Religious Education and Ethics. Research Report), Warszawa. Available online: https://globalna.ceo.org.pl/sites/globalna.ceo.org.pl/files/raport.pdf (accessed 20 October 2018).

Theiss, W. (2012), 'Pamięć Hiroszimy i edukacja globalna' (Hiroshima memory and global education), in I. Kubiaczyk (ed.), *Wartości, symbole i znaki dobra w pedagogice społecznej* (Values, Symbols and Signs of Good in Social Pedagogy): 157–62, Poznań–Środa Wlkp.

Wieczorek, A. (2016), 'Współpraca organizacji pozarządowych z sektorem oświaty i szkolnictwa wyższego w dziedzinie edukacji globalnej w Polsce' (Co-operation of the NGOs with the Ministry of Education and the higher education sector in the area of global education in Poland), in Z. Babicki and M. Kuleta-Hulboj (eds), *Teoretyczne i praktyczne konteksty edukacji globalnej* (Theoretical and Practical Contexts of Global Education): 197–224, Warszawa: Wydawnictwo Uniwersytetu Kardynała Stefana Wyszyńskiego.

Winiewski, M., K. Hansen, M. Bilewicz, W. Soral, A. Świderska and D. Bulska (2017), *Mowa nienawiści, mowa pogardy: Raport z badania przemocy werbalnej wobec grup mniejszościowych* (Speech of Hatred and Contempt: Report on the Research on Verbal Violence against the Minority Groups), Warszawa: Fundacja im. Stefana Batorego. Available online: http://www.batory.org.pl/upload/files/pdf/MOWA_NIENAWISCI_MOWA_POGARDY_INTERNET.pdf (accessed 25 November 2013).

Witkowski, J. (2012), 'Strengthened co-operation for improving quality', *ZEP: Zeitschrift für internationale Bildungsforschung und Entwicklungspädagogik*, 4: 21–6.

Chapter 11

Role of NGOs in Global Citizenship Education

Massimiliano Tarozzi

Introduction

As many chapters in this handbook show, Global Citizenship Education (GCE) has currently become prominent in the discourse of governments, educational institutions and scholars worldwide, as well as within civil society. It has been argued that a new paradigm is currently influencing education policy discourse towards a 'curricular global turn' (Mannion et al., 2011). This chapter explores the role of civil society organizations (CSOs) and non-governmental organizations (NGOs) in promoting, disseminating and implementing GCE practice and policy in school curricula. Based on a comparative policy analysis carried out in the European context, the political role of NGOs is explored, stressing their main areas of engagement and achievement, and their weaknesses, especially the cultural conflict between them and other political agents. Results show that NGOs, civil society and grass-roots social movements play a crucial political role in widening the decision-making basis and bringing critical voices from below into the global political arena. Unlike institutional bodies, NGOs are more flexible and open to change, they can reconcile the agenda of different governmental bodies and on different topics, and they have the potential to create links between different actors. In addition, civil society's political participation in decision-making processes in education is important not only because bottom-up approaches are more equitable and promote democratic engagement, but also as they are more effective in grounding policies in educational practice.

Therefore, my argument is that NGOs and CSOs can play a major role in promoting GCE policy and practice, especially in a post-national global context, but they cannot operate in isolation. They are expected to work in close cooperation with academia, to deepen the conceptualization of terms and issues, and with school staff, to overcome contrasting cultures and to reconcile tensions and conflicts between diverse theories, visions and methods.

This chapter is structured as follows. After an introduction on the design and method of the Global school research carried out in ten European countries, some results are presented, especially focusing on those related to the NGOs' role. Then three domains of NGOs commitments and achievements, theory, practice and policy are highlighted. Finally, after having stressed some critical issues and tensions with other critical agents, the chapter concludes with some remarks summarizing the role that NGOs can play in a multi-layered political sphere in promoting GCE in formal education and school reform.

The emergence of a new global civic society and the GCE promotion

In the last decade, the political role NGOs, in particular International ones (INGO), has been widely debated. As well as many other civil society organizations, they can play a major role in bringing civil society's voice into the educational policy debate and global decision-making processes (Fogarty, 2011; Kamat, 2004; Martens, 2006). Indeed, the process of globalization has shifted the debate from the national domain to the global one, prompting the emergence of a global civil society and of ad hoc forms of global governance (Castells, 2008).

According to Mary Kaldor (2003), and Manuel Castells (2008), the global dimension of economics, politics and information has expanded the public sphere – as the space of debate on public affairs – from the national to the global domain, and has prompted the emergence of a new political actor, the 'global civil society', acting in what has been defined a 'cosmopolitan democracy' (Archibugi and Held, 1995; Archibugi, 2008).

Although their political responsibility as the 'new global civil society' generated by globalization processes is growing in the international public sphere, and their innovative educational value-based approach is increasingly recognized, NGOs' role in (transnational) educational policy-making is also controversial (Witteborn, 2010) for many reasons that will be better outlined later in the text.

For better or for worse, NGOs are closely related to education policy and practice aiming a promoting GCE and related issues in formal and non-formal education, thanks to their well-established tradition of dealing with issues such as global citizenship, development and sustainability, from a sound and original educational perspective.

Not surprisingly, NGOs emerge from the present analysis as well as from other research (GENE, 2017) as key actors in the early attempts of implementing GCE policies in the majority of EU countries.

Besides, due to their attention to reducing global poverty and supporting Global South communities, international NGOs, as well as many other grass-roots organizations, bring into school practice an unprecedented far-reaching global outlook and a new commitment for fighting economic inequalities. In education, moreover, INGOs, which have been producing development education (DE) programming since the late 1950s (Weber, 2014), introduce into formal education untraditional learning approaches that are more transformative, participatory and critical. While the lack of attention for cognitive skills and knowledge has been criticized (Scheunpflug and Asbrand, 2006; Marshall, 2005), NGOs promote value-based pedagogies aimed at securing global social change through empowerment, democratic engagement and a strong values base around equity, human rights and social justice (Bourn, 2015).

Although their political responsibility as the 'new global civil society' generated by globalization processes is growing in the international public sphere, and their innovative educational value-based approach is increasingly recognized, nevertheless NGOs' social role and active commitment to search and rescue migrants in the Mediterranean Sea or to support their integration has been very recently menaced by growing nationalism and anti-immigrant policies across Europe (see, for example, the cases of Hungary or Italy: *The Guardian*, 2018). NGOs are frequently accused (without any evidence) to represent a *pull factor* for illegal immigration and even criminalised for being colluded with 'migrant smugglers' (*Financial Times*, 2016).

Yet this chapter is focusing on their role in educational policy-making which is also controversial (Bourn and Kybird, 2012; Tota, 2014) but for opposite reasons. The inclusion of international NGOs in the transnational political sphere is seen as a source of legitimacy for global governance institutions in the dimensions of morality, legality, technical competence, democracy and charismatic leadership (Jaeger, 2007; Tota, 2014). For others, NGOs' value-based education is criticized for imposing a non-neutral perspective (Standish, 2012) or is confused with fundraising activity and campaigning (Bourn and Kybird, 2012).

This discussion has become particularly relevant after the so-called global turn in education (Mannion et al., 2011) when after the public commitment of UN and UNESCO in particular, several European bodies have widely promoted a global perspective in education providing greater space for NGO activities.

In Europe, which is at the core of this chapter, a global perspective in education can be tracked even earlier. After the seminal work of the Global Education Charter, adopted by the Council of Europe (CoE) in 1997, the Maastricht Declaration embraced in 2002 by the CoE represents a framework for a European strategy on global education (GE) (Forghani-Arani et al., 2013). The CoE – in its three bodies as Education Committee, Ministries of Foreign Affairs and the North–South Centre – has been the most influential political actor at European level. In 2002 the Global Education Network Europe (GENE) was established by CoE to facilitate the sharing of policy across EU member states. This network of ministries and agencies with national responsibility for GE in European countries has supported national EU governments through round tables, reports and peer reviews, and has facilitated the inclusion of NGOs among political stakeholders.

In addition, the European Commission's Directorate-General for International Cooperation and Development has supported projects addressed to civil society's actors that seek to inform EU citizens about the interconnectedness of the world and to empower them to become critically engaged on global development issues, especially in education. In particular, the EU DEAR (Development Education Awareness Raising) Programme, aimed at CSGs, from 2004 to 2012 provided approximately 256 million euro, with 77,000,000 expected for 2018–20. This debate demonstrates the need for further research exploring the political and education contribution of NGOs in particular to GE, which is now emerging as an education policy priority.

GCE educational policies and teacher education practices in ten EU countries

I will draw my analysis mostly from a comparative study on GCE implementation in ten EU countries, co-funded within the DEAR programme,[1] in the framework of a mixed-methods inquiry on GCE implementation in primary schools across Europe.

---

[1] The project, called *Global Schools,* was a three-year-long European project carried out in ten EU countries by seventeen partners, led by the Autonomous Province of Trento, Italy. It was co-funded by the DEAR Programme of

In particular, the first research phase (2015–16) consisted of a comparative policy analysis in ten European countries highlighting the role of political actors in enhancing GCE policies.

Through the political comparative analysis, the research team I coordinated[2] aimed at analysing existing educational policies, strategies and school curricula in some EU countries. We were also interested in exploring and comparing the 'implementation' process of GCE education policies. Following Ball (2012), I prefer not to use the word 'implementation' in the proper use of the term, since it refers to always complex interactive and multi-layered processes, where several political actors intertwine their visions, ideologies and agencies. Instead, the word 'enactment' better denotes the complexity of the process and multiplicity of actors involved.

Not surprisingly, there are very few comparative policy analyses at European level on the enactment of GCE polices (Goren and Yemini, 2017). Exceptions are few and these mostly relate to national case studies (Hartmeyer and Wegimont, 2016; Concorde, 2018).[3] Yet comparative research on complex processes of policy agenda setting, formulation and implementation of public educational policies (Gunter, Hall and Mills, 2014) is difficult but necessary for at least two reasons: first of all, a comparative dimension is required to understand a global concept in an abstract and decontextualized way; and, second, in a globalized world, which has seriously challenged the way to compare education policies (Lingard and Rawolle, 2011), national public policies do not exist in isolation and cannot be disjointed from the global dimension.

Given the multi-level nature of these processes another dimension we aimed at exploring was related to who are the main actors that promote (or hamper) the implementation of GCE. The plurality of powerful political agents – supra-national, national, local governments, different ministries, role of NGOs and school authorities – demands a rethink of classical implementation studies (Hill and Hupe, 2002), overcoming the study of pure legal transposition of (non-binding) European directives (Löfgren, 2015). Therefore, empirical evidence to reconstruct the interactive and multi-layered (Rizvi and Lingard, 2010) discourse surrounding such a polity process is needed to also highlight the NGOs bargaining role.

The second phase of the research (2016–17) was aimed at investigating the emerging processes of GCE teacher education in four European cases (Austria, Czech Republic, Ireland and Italy).[4] The broad purpose of the qualitative inquiry was to analyse pioneering GCE teacher education

---

the European Commission. Within this project a study focused on ten European countries (Austria, Bulgaria, Czech Republic, France, Ireland, Italy, Latvia, Spain, Portugal, UK), was conducted.

2   The research team was coordinated by Massimiliano Tarozzi supported by the research assistant Carla Inguaggiato; data have been collected in each country by Helmuth Hartmeyer (AT), Zlatina Siderova (BG), Martina Novotná (CR), Luís García Arrazola and María Álvarez Roy (ES), Clémence Héaulme (FR), Sive O' Connor (IE), Carla Inguaggiato and Debora Antonucci (IT), Inga Belousa (LV), La Salete Coelho (PT), Helen Lawson (UK).

3   Twelve national reports on Global Education policy have been undertaken by the GENE as a result of their peer review processes, and they represent a valuable source of research information for the study of global education policy in a number of EU countries. http://gene.eu/publications/national-reports/ (retrieved 25 February 2019).

4   The research team for this second part was coordinated by Massimiliano Tarozzi, supported by research assistant Carla Inguaggiato; data was collected in each country by Martina Novotná (CR), Benjamin Mallon (IE), Carla Inguaggiato and Debora Antonucci (IT), and Sandra Altenberger AU). Both reports are available here: http://www.globalschools.education/Activities/Research

programmes in order to identify success factors, conditions for failure, promising and innovative practices (Tarozzi and Mallon, 2019).

In-service teacher education practices were ethnographically explored to investigate who, where and how they provide teachers with the required skills, knowledge and competences to effectively embed GCE in their curriculum and teaching practice.

The overall research design is extremely broad and encompasses a number of research questions following several research directions. Elsewhere I have explored the role of ministries in the political process of policy formulation and implementation (Tarozzi and Inguaggiato, 2018). Here I narrow my presentation to non-institutional actors, namely focusing on the role that NGOs play in the promotion of GCE, especially in embedding it in school curricula. This topic is meaningful for many reasons. Not only because NGOs bring critical voices from below into the global political arena but also because their involvement in the GCE national policy-making process is a clear sign of the adoption of a multi-stakeholder approach widely promoted by UNESCO for the governance of GE policies at the national level. Moreover, providing in-service teacher education and stimulating initiatives for pre-service training is considered a key enabling factor of a successful policy-making process (UNESCO, 2015).

Research methods

The policy analysis part of the research is grounded in three main sources of data:

1. Relevant policy documents, both recommendatory and normative, for a total of 186 documents in 10 partners countries, plus 6 from Finland, Germany and Greece, and 10 from supra-national bodies such as the European Union or international institutions (UNESCO, OECD (Organization for Economic Cooperation and Development)).
2. Descriptive fiches of policy documents – 'Policy Document Synopsis' – (in English) following a shared classification scheme by national researchers, based on national legislative documents.
3. In-depth interviews with key informants. Twenty-four policy-makers (authors of documents, political executors of the education policy device), experts (university consultants) and practitioners (teachers, educators, principals) were interviewed.

Five types of data for the ethnographic part were systematically collected, observing nine pioneering in-service teacher education courses in GCE (or related themes) in four countries, namely

- 246 hours of observation in the field,
- 45 interviews (formal and informal),
- document collection (n.120),
- 200 pre- and post-programme questionnaires and
- 29 analytical memos.

Both parts of the research used diverse but complementary analytical approaches. For the first comparative part, data were analysed by two independent coders, using some coding procedures of constructivist grounded theory approach. Three macro themes emerged: (a) levels and modes of implementation of GCE in primary school; (b) political actors, conceptualizing roles, functions and relationships; (c) conceptual definition, prevailing use of national terms and related various adjectival educations in several countries. In this chapter I focus on the second (b), and in particular on NGOs.

The second part adopted a multiple-site case study design, using ethnography as an overall methodological approach for data collection and analysis. Data were analysed using two main strategies: (1) a thick description of national settings following a shared schema of relevant domains and peoples; and (2) an inductive collaborative analysis to identify relevant codes and themes. Through this inductive analysis a common codebook was developed. The codebook, tested by independent coders to ensure reliability and credibility, was both a result as such, providing a definition of every category and subcategory, and a coding schema for inspecting all data. Through a systematic and collaborative coding of all the data collected in each country, nine themes and thirty-two sub-themes were identified, but only three of these emerged as the most meaningful, based on the frequency of occurrences and on their conceptual density: '*Teaching approaches*' '*Contrasting cultures*' and '*GCE conception*'. In this chapter I will focus on the role of the NGOs as it emerges transversely from these three themes.

NGO as a political and pedagogical actor in promoting GCE

There is a multiplicity of actors involved both at the political level and in teacher education practice. This section provides an outline of the main actors involved in both processes, their functions and their relationships.

To enact education policy is a complex and multifaceted endeavour, involving several actors, different time phases and several political levels. The comparative analysis shows that the Ministries of Education and Foreign Affairs are the main political governmental actors for GCE implementation. But their effectiveness largely depends on their willingness and ability to work together and with other key stakeholders, including local authorities, higher education institutions (HEIs) and, above all, NGOs.

Three-fourth out of the sixty-two most influential policy documents are issued by Ministries of Education or Foreign Affairs and include greater regulatory activities, but there are other actors producing normative or recommendatory documents such as general policy recommendations and guidelines or temporary funding programmes. Since we considered a policy in a broad way as a wide-ranging process of implementation of ideas into practices, a policy encompasses also plans, programmes and guidelines. Accordingly, 10 per cent of the political documents examined in 2015 were issued by NGOs. Moreover, interviews indicated that NGOs stand out as the fundamental political actors in all countries examined, in particular in Portugal, Spain, England and Latvia.

Similarly, there are a number of different actors involved in the process of teacher education for GCE, with similarities in the four countries, which sometimes overlap with policy actors. Research provides clear evidence that in every analysed country, NGOs play a structural role in funding, delivering or supporting teacher education practices.

Teaching unions, as CSO, are also involved in teacher education practice at least in one place (Figure 11.1).

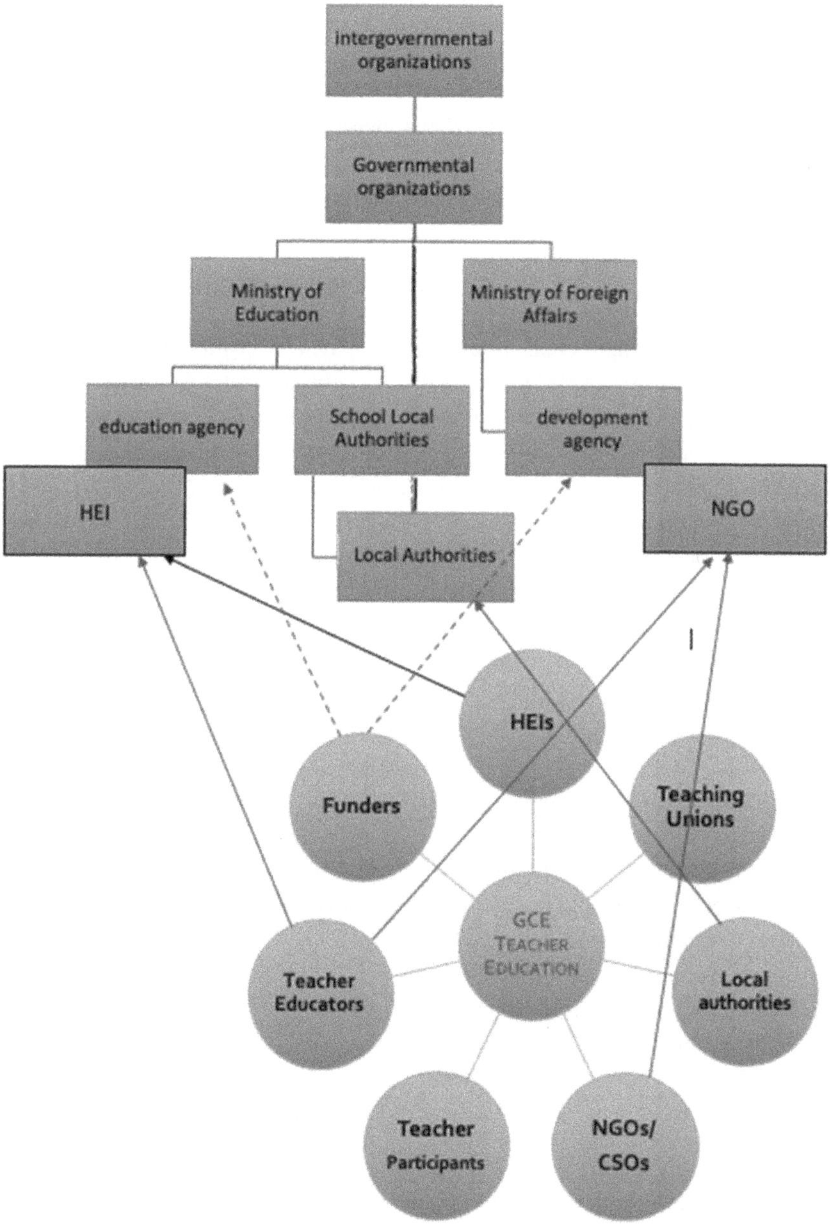

Figure 11.1 Overlapping actors involved in policy enactment and in teacher education.

NGOs' main areas of engagement and achievement

To summarize what emerges from both parts of the research and what has been discussed in the current literature, NGOs play a pivotal role in the following three main areas of engagement and achievement:

1. *Theory*. They contribute to spreading sensitivity to the GCE concept.
2. *Practice*. They promote innovative educational practices, even in teacher education.
3. *Policy*. They play a key role in policy-making processes.

In the following section I will address these domains with reference to the results emerging from the European research.

Theory

In general, NGOs have brought GCE, or even development education, from the margins to the mainstream of education discourse. In particular in some countries (Austria, Czech Republic, Italy, Portugal), they endorsed the term 'GCE' in contributing to its dissemination.

They have enhanced discussion about terms and promoted a new sensitivity especially in formal education. They are reputed by school teachers as experts of the contents, and therefore they are expected to handle concepts such as global citizenship, DE and sustainability in a professional and competent way. This is perhaps not surprising, as the term is traditionally owned by NGOs and spreading it can also be seen as a way of raising their profile, communicating their message and consolidating their ability in fundraising and advocacy.

But beyond the widespread and growing use of the term, there is a general theoretical poverty in the way in which NGOs deal with GCE. GCE conceptualization remains disputed and non-univocal and many people, including CSO activists, claim that they lack clear understanding and research. According to recent research carried out by Concorde Europe,[5] frequent conceptual and/or nominal changes are perceived by practitioners and in particular by NGOs, as particularly disturbing (Concorde, 2018).

More research is needed and here universities and research centres are asked to carry out an important job for both policy-makers and NGO activists to conceptualize these notions. While the quest for an objectively defined common term is an illusory misplaced expectation, a better understanding of the theoretical implications behind the nominal use of conceptual labels is important. Due to the multiple stances in which GCE can be rooted, a clear understanding of different ideologies behind the general call for GCE is critical. Moreover, while theoretical studies on GCE conceptualization are recently proliferating (Camicia and Franklin, 2011; Andreotti, 2011; Andreotti, Biesta, and Ahenakew, 2015; Enns, 2015; Gardner-McTaggart, 2016;

---

[5] Concorde (CONfederation for COoperation of Relief and DEvelopment) is a confederation of NGOs made up of member organizations, national platforms and international networks representing more than 2,600 NGOs and acting as interlocutor with the EU institutions on development policy. https://concordeurope.org

Mannion et al., 2011; Parmenter, 2011; Pashby, 2011; Salter and Halbert, 2017; Veugelers, 2011), NGO activists are not fully aware of this scholarly debate and its implication in national educational agendas and complex policy-making processes.

Practice

The innovative role of the NGO for the dissemination of GCE is particularly evident at the practical level. There are several evidences from the above-mentioned research demonstrating this claim. NGOs directly carry out innovative school activities with children, usually involving teachers and students together in a range of projects and activities (Bulgaria, Czech Republic, Ireland, Portugal); they provide values-based pedagogical approaches to education that are active, transformative, experiential, learner-centred and socially relevant (England). They elaborate and circulate guidelines, lesson plans, activity descriptions, support materials (Latvia, Portugal); they also run award programmes (England), participate in the preparation of many official materials (Czech Republic), translate and implement educational materials and resources (Bulgaria, Czech Republic, France, Ireland, Italy), for formal and informal education (Latvia). According to the Portuguese Policy Document Synopsis, 'NGOs are the main actors in the field of DE in Portugal. ... The main role of NGOs in the introduction of GCE in the formal education is due to their projects within schools, giving classes to the students but also doing teacher training and developing materials. ... There is also an advocacy work that needs to be highlighted' (Portugal, PDS).

Among educational practice, teacher education stands out for its crucial role as an enabling factor for GCE implementation in school curricula. As a major driver of GCE implementation in education policy, teacher education is regarded as the first indicator to assess the achievement of the SDG 4.7.

Almost everywhere, NGOs provide in-service teacher education (especially in Austria, Italy, Ireland, Portugal, Spain, England) and push initiatives for pre-service teacher education (Austria, Bulgaria) and teachers' support (Ireland, Italy, Portugal), or teacher Freireian 'concienciación' (Spain).

In particular, NGOs promote an innovative approach, and especially a value-based approach, which is in essence transformational, aimed at changing teacher attitude and not only to equip teachers with the knowledge, skills and abilities required to educate pupils to GCE. It is aimed at engaging teachers to embrace values or to activate them to promote school change.

Our research shows that NGOs are recognized by school staff as providers of knowledge and expertise. Teachers recognize, sometimes not without tension, that values, beliefs or an ethos are important to be developed throughout teacher education programmes.

In general, it has been observed that a value-based pedagogical approach is a major driver in the observed programmes run by NGOs, aimed at empowering teachers as agents of change (Bourn, 2016). Following Biesta and collaborators, values and beliefs have a huge impact on developing teacher agency (Biesta, Priestley and Robinson, 2017) which is crucial for promoting a real and durable school change. Therefore, value-based teacher education can be regarded as a political apparatus to school reform, and this brings us to the third domain: policy-making.

Policy

Comparative analysis shows that the Ministry of Education and Ministry of Foreign Affairs are the fundamental political governmental actors for GCE implementation. However, they do not always cooperate significantly with each other or with other key stakeholders, including local authorities, HEIs, educational bodies, media and, above all, NGOs. Therefore, the bargaining process between governmental and non-governmental organizations in enacting a global policy is one of the key issues for effective integration of a policy agenda in schools. Unlike institutional bodies, flexibility and adaptability allow NGOs to bridge the gap between diverse actors, and in particular to disseminate the concept and practices of GCE among them.

In the national contexts examined, NGOs carry out constant advocacy and lobbying activities. To this purpose, they build national and regional platforms to disseminate information, practices, knowledge and resources, such as in the Czech Republic (Global Development Education and Awareness Work Group of the Czech Forum for Development Cooperation: https://www.devex.com/organizations/czech-forum-for-development-cooperation-fors-54000), France (Educasol: http://www.educasol.org), Latvia (LAPAS: http://lapas.lv/en/about-us/about-lapas/), Portugal (Platform of Development NGOs: http://en.plataformaongd.pt/platform/who-are-we/), Spain (CONGDE: https://coordinadoraongd.org) and the European umbrella networks Concord or Bridge 47[6] (https://www.bridge47.org).

In many European countries NGOs play a role in the early attempts of GCE policy-making, especially in bottom-up national strategies.

In combining the agendas of different governmental bodies, NGOs have been strategic in promoting and encouraging the creation of national strategies linking multiple stakeholders. This function is recognized, for example, by an Austrian policy-maker, involved in the national Strategic Group:

> NGOs are an important bridge to the practice. They support teachers; their materials and experience are widely used. It is positive that they are well represented in the Strategy Group. They are partners on the same level. (Austria – policy-maker 1)

National strategies are frameworks for a long-term vision of GCE and are expected to ensure structural support, constant funding, coordination and policy coherence. In the last decade, such a political device has been strongly encouraged by UNESCO internationally and at the European level by supra-national bodies such as GENE.

Thanks to their aptitude for networking between different actors, in four of the analysed countries NGOs have played a crucial role in promoting GCE national strategies and bridging the gap between the conflicting roles of governmental organizations.

Currently among the countries studied, some forms of strategies exist in Austria, Czech Republic, Portugal, Ireland, Latvia and Spain, but there are also strategies in Finland, Germany, Poland and Slovakia and, recently, Italy.

---

[6] Bridge 47 is a project consortium, co-created by fifteen European and global organizations, aimed at mobilizing civil society all around the world to do their part for global justice and eradication of poverty with the help of Global Citizenship Education in the framework of Agenda 2030, target 4.7.

Of course, there are different forms of national strategy, depending on the 'ownership' (Hartmeyer and Wegimont, 2016) and on the political scale direction (bottom-up or top-down). Consequently, our analysis shows that national strategies can be placed along a continuum of stakeholder engagement, from an extreme bottom-up approach, highly participative and promoted by civil society, to another extreme, governed from above more or less participative but with a clear ministerial or multi-ministerial ownership. Therefore, depending on the type of strategy, the contribution of NGOs is diverse.

A bottom-up multi-stakeholder national strategy enhances a fruitful cooperation between diverse actors, not only governmental ones (such as ministries or national agencies) but also civil society representatives, local authorities, expert groups and educational institutions such as universities and pedagogical colleges. In our research, examples of these multi-stakeholders' highly collaborative national strategies can be found only in Austria and in Portugal. The latter is an emblematical example:

> At the beginning of the history of development education in Portugal, the main actor was civil society, 'bottom-up', and it was civil society to contaminate state actors, who came later but took the task responsibly. (Portugal, PDS)

In Portugal the National Strategy for Development Education 2010–15 has been enhanced by the National Strategy of Education for Development Strategic Group, formed by Camões, the former Portuguese Institute for Development Assistance (IPAD), Ministry of Education, represented by the Directorate-General for Education (DGE), the Portuguese NGDO Platform and CIDAC (a Portuguese NGO, member of GENE). The main actor was civil society, through the platform of NGOs and that it was the civil society to contaminate state actors, who came later but took the task responsibly. This strategy has been renewed and relaunched with a new action plan in 2018.

NGO real and potential challenges

In summary, NGOs' role is significantly relevant for a number of reasons. First, NGOs are able to bring critical voices from below into the global political arena, where they also promote new ideas and approaches. In particular, since they are committed to supporting Global South communities in reducing global poverty, they can bring a large-scale outlook to the national policy arena (Bourn, 2015). Second, unlike institutional bodies, NGOs' bureaucracies and procedures are more flexible and open to change. Third, they can merge the agenda of different political actors and various topics, and consequently they have the potential to create or strengthen links between them. Fourth, on a practical level, they bring an innovative, values-based, transformative approach into school practice and teacher education programmes. Finally, their involvement in the GCE national policy-making process can be regarded as a sign of the political inclination to adopt a multi-stakeholder approach for the governance of GE policies at national level.

However, apart from these potential achievements there are also a few critical issues regarding NGO active involvement in the GCE enactment.

First of all, sometimes NGOs, due to their tendency towards self-reference, are likely to be too isolated, not dialoguing with other political and educational actors. They have their own ethical and values mission, sometimes blurred with a fundraising and campaigning agenda (Bourn, 2015), and this vision it is not negotiable. Thus, the above-mentioned ability to build a meaningful dialogue with different subjects requires the ability to overcome – and willingness to negotiate – values, approaches and styles that each NGO has over time developed around their own identity.

Second, and related to the previous point, NGOs constantly need visibility, because visibility brings more funds, which are essential in the current so-called global 'edu-business' (Ball, 2012). This exigency sometimes directs the choice of projects which allow more visibility than others, and longer-term educational projects are often not suitable for the purpose (Weber, 2014). As one NGO activist claimed in an interview:

> I think it just would come down to the sort of very boring practical element of time and everyone is so busy chasing funding to be in existence in six months' time, that I think the things that do go fairly quickly are presence on big platforms, especially if you've got to fund yourself to get there or to start having more advocacy roles that doesn't maybe set outcomes that you could then report back on. (UK, NGO activist)

Third, another element related to fundraising is the NGO lack of independence due to the constant need for public funds. Since they typically depend on Ministry of Foreign Affairs funds they are sometimes not independent, and tend towards an acceptance rather than a questioning of governmental development policy (Bourn and Kybird, 2012). In general they are 'trapped in the aid industry', because of their financial dependence on the development sector and Official Development Assistance (Krause, 2016).

An English social activist from an NGO admitted: 'So I think in a freer funding environment, many more interesting projects come out and people are less driven to just look after their own; but of course they do because they need to pay the building rent and everything and make sure they've got full costs recovery on all the projects they undertake' and 'Somebody I heard called it "mission drift". Wherever the funding is, we do that, and then suddenly now actually we do this and I think it means that it's destabilising' (UK, NGO activist).

International NGOs have complained about being 'used' by governmental institutions (particularly internationally) and being incorporated by them into their political agendas and procedures as a source of legitimacy. Moreover, NGOs are criticized for 'softening' their critical voices (Tota, 2014) and for depoliticizing the global governance (Jaeger, 2007), fostering social reproduction or even for becoming accomplices of a hegemonic desire to 'civilize' less developed countries (Berry and Gabay, 2009) or to impose a vertical form of global citizenship (Shukla, 2009).

These last criticisms should be seriously taken into consideration, but they mostly refer to international NGOs, and are less evident for national ones, which are the focus of this chapter. At national level, community-based NGOs or national branches of international NGOs are more rooted in the local community and are authoritative and trusted partners in the public political sphere, as demonstrated by their role in national strategic groups or national conferences, as examples of a bottom-up participatory approach. Moreover, our research showed their contribution to introducing a global outlook and a sensitivity for the Global South in national policy debate, by enhancing new sensitivity, a renovated dictionary, as well as innovative practice in school settings.

Fourth, on a more national scale NGOs are likely to be too isolated and self-referencing. Some criticize NGOs' value-based education for promoting their own agenda, perspective and world view (Standish, 2012) or regard it as a mechanism for securing additional income, for communicating information and key messages about their activities (Bourn and Kybird, 2012).

Fifth, our data indicates some tensions between NGOs and the formal education systems, which sometimes result in forms of conflict between NGOs and school staff. In carrying out school activities research shows that between teachers and NGOs activists, quite often different perspectives, worldviews, beliefs or even what we coded as 'contrasting cultures' appear (Mallon, 2019). These conflicting theoretical frameworks, aims, pedagogies, approaches, methods often create potential or actual inter-groups conflicts and tensions, as an Italian teacher observed: 'NGO educators have not a real experience in school activities and an adequate preparation in teaching methods.' Another remarks that NGOs 'should not substitute teachers in class'. Sometimes there is a clear negative perception of some of the motivations for NGO involvement in teacher education, as a Czech teacher brutally exemplifies: 'I feel like they often want to get money.'

Likewise, some scholars outlined a potential conflict between NGOs' and schools' educational culture, where the former risk overemphasizing the affective and ethical dimensions and paying less attention to the cognitive dimensions (Marshall, 2005), knowledge and skills (Scheunpflug and Asbrand, 2006).

Concluding remarks

In this chapter, in contrast with the growing wave accusing NGOs to be a pull factor for illegal immigration, I have argued that NGOs currently play a key political role as global civil society, in a post-national global context, in promoting GCE policy and practice. While they are not the only ones, they promote democratic engagement, by widening the decision-making basis and bringing grass-roots voices from below into the political debate. Comparative research across European countries shows that NGOs tend to be more flexible and open to change, and therefore they are in the best position to create connections between different actors. There are, however, a number of challenges that NGOs should be able to face in order to preserve their independence, strengthen their critical voices and not get trapped in self-referencing isolation.

They should not operate in isolation, but they are asked to work in close cooperation with academia, to deepen the conceptualization of terms and issues, and with school staff to overcome the potential clash of contrasting pedagogical cultures. In particular, research clearly shows that one of the top priorities is to keep open the dialogue with schools. Both NGOs and school staff should make every possible effort to reconcile tensions and conflicts between diverse theories, visions and methods.

NGOs engage more traditional schools and traditionally politically neutral teachers in raising value-based committed voices. Without NGOs in some of the analysed countries, such awareness may never have emerged. On the other hand, NGOs should be open to understanding the school learning environment and its unique features and constraints.

Another crucial gap to be closed is the one between HEI and NGOs. As mentioned, more research is needed to provide a better theoretical understanding of key concepts and the ideologies behind them. But also research as well as professional expertise is necessary to improve teacher education, by studying practices, assessing and comparing GCE teacher education programmes, currently in their early and pioneering stages.

But NGOs' role is also critical in education policy agenda setting, policy formulation and implementation, where they can promote a collaborative agenda and close the gap between traditionally separate political actors.

Ultimately, the very concept of GCE as a 'framing paradigm', especially against the Agenda 2030 background, promotes an educative holistic approach that has more to do with joining than separating. NGOs and more broadly civic society, social movements, universities and also teachers as agents of change might play an important role in this process, by connecting conflicting visions and contrasting cultures, aims, approaches, pedagogies and bureaucracies.

Bibliography

Archibugi, D. (2008). *The Global Commonwealth of Citizens: Toward Cosmopolitan Democracy.* Princeton: Princeton University Press.

Archibugi, D., and Held, D. (1995). *Cosmopolitan Democracy: An Agenda for a New World Order.* Oxford: Polity Press.

Ball, S. J. (2012). *Global Education Inc: New Policy Networks and the Neo-liberal Imaginary.* London: Routledge.

Ball, S., Maguire, M., and Braun, A. (2012). *How Schools Do Policy: Policy Enactments in Secondary Schools.* New York: Routledge.

Berry, C., and Gabay, C. (2009). Transnational political action and 'global civil society' in practice: The case of Oxfam. *Global Networks, 9*(3), 339–58. http://doi.org/10.1111/j.1471-0374.2009.00257.x

Biesta, G., Priestley, M., and Robinson, S. (2017). The role of beliefs in teacher agency. *Teachers and Teaching. Theory and Practice, 21*(6), 624–40. http://doi.org/10.1080/13540602.2015.1044325

Bourn, D. (2015). *The Theory and Practice of Development Education: A Pedagogy for Global Social Justice.* London and New York: Routledge.

Bourn, D. (2016). Teachers as agents of social change. *International Journal of Development Education and Global Learning, 7*(3), 63–77. http://doi.org/10.18546/IJDEGL.07.3.05

Bourn, D., and Kybird, M. (2012). Plan UK and Development Education – the contribution of an international development organisation to learning and understanding about global and development issues. *International Journal of Development Education and Global Learning, 4*(2), 45–63.

Camicia, S. P., and Franklin, B. M. (2011). What type of global community and citizenship? tangled discourses of neoliberalism and critical democracy in curriculum and its reform. *Globalisation, Societies and Education, 9*(3–4), 311–22. http://doi.org/10.1080/14767724.2011.605303

Castells, M. (2008). The new public sphere: Global civil society, communication networks, and global governance. *The ANNALS of the American Academy of Political and Social Science, 616*(1), 78–93. http://doi.org/10.1177/0002716207311877

Concorde (2018). *Global Citizenship Education in Europe. How Much Do We Care?* Brussels: Concord Europe. Retrieved from https://concordeurope.org/wp-content/uploads/2018/03/CONCORD_GCE_FundingReport_2018_online.pdf?56c6d0&56c6d0

de Oliveira Andreotti, V. (2011). (Towards) decoloniality and diversality in global citizenship education. *Globalisation, Societies and Education, 9*(3–4), 381–97. http://doi.org/10.1080/1476772 4.2011.605323

de Oliveira Andreotti, V., Biesta, G., and Ahenakew, C. (2015). Between the nation and the globe: education for global mindedness in Finland. *Globalisation, Societies and Education, 13*(2), 246–59. http://doi.org/10.1080/14767724.2014.934073

Enns, C. (2015). Transformation or continuation? A critical analysis of the making of the post-2015 education agenda. *Globalisation, Societies and Education, 13*(3), 369–87. http://doi.org/10.1080/14767724.2014.959894

Financial Times (2016). 15 December. https://www.ft.com/content/3e6b6450-c1f7-11e6-9bca-2b93a6856354

Fogarty, E. A. (2011). Nothing succeeds like access? NGO strategies towards multilateral institutions. *Journal of Civil Society, 7*(2), 207–27. http://doi.org/10.1080/17448689.2011.573670

Forghani-Arani, N., Hartmeyer, H., O'Loughlin, E., and Wegimont, L. (2013). *Global Education in Europe: Policy, Practice and Theoretical Challenges*. Münster: Waxmann Verlag.

Gardner-McTaggart, A. (2016). International elite, or global citizens? Equity, distinction and power: The International Baccalaureate and the rise of the South. *Globalisation, Societies and Education, 14*(1), 1–29. http://doi.org/10.1080/14767724.2014.959475

GENE (2017). *The State of Global Education in Europe 2017: Global Education Network Europe.* Retrieved (28 August 2018) from https://gene.eu/wp-content/uploads/State-of-Global-Education-2017-low-res.pdf

Goren, H., and Yemini, M. (2017). Global Citizenship Education Redefined. A Systematic Review of Empirical Studies on Global Citizenship Education. *International Journal of Educational Research, 82*, 170–83.

Gunter, H. M., Hall, D., and Mills, C. (eds) (2014). Edu*cation Policy Research: Design and Practice at a Time of Rapid Reform*. London: Bloomsbury Academic.

Hartmeyer, H., and Wegimont, L. (2016). *Global Education in Europe Revisited*. Münster: Waxmann.

Hill, M., and Hupe, P. (2002). *Implementing Public Policy*. Los Angeles: Sage Publications.

Jaeger, H. M. (2007). 'Global Civil Society' and the Political Depoliticization of Global Governance. *International Political Sociology, 1*(3), 257–77.

Kaldor, M. (2003). *Global Civil Society: An Answer to War*. Cambridge: Polity Press.

Kamat, S. (2004). The privatization of public interest: theorizing NGO discourse in a neoliberal era. *Review of International Political Economy, 11*(1), 155–76. http://doi.org/10.1080/0969229042000179794

Krause, J. (2016). From promoting aid towards Global citizenship empowerment for change. In Hartmeyer, H. and Wegimont, L. (2016) *Global Education in Europe Revisited*. Münster: Waxmann, 149–69.

Lingard, B., and Rawolle, S. (2011) New scalar politics: implications for education policy. *Comparative Education, 47*(4), 489–502.

Löfgren, K. (2015). Implementation studies: Beyond a legalistic approach. In Lynggaard, K., Manners, I. and Löfgren, K. (eds) *Research methods in EU studies*. Basingstoke: Palgrave, pp. 154–67.

Mallon, B. (2019). Contrasting cultures. In Tarozzi, M. and Inguaggiato, C. (eds) (2018) 'Teachers' Education in GCE: Emerging Issues from a Comparative Perspective'. Research deliverable published within the European project 'Global Schools'. Bologna: University of Bologna Repository, pp. 135–43. DOI: http:/doi.org/10.6092/unibo/amsacta/6070

Mannion, G., Biesta, G., Priestley, M., and Ross, H. (2011). The global dimension in education and education for global citizenship: Genealogy and critique. *Globalisation, Societies and Education, 9*(3–4), 443–56. http://doi.org/10.1080/14767724.2011.605327

Marshall, H. (2005). Developing the global gaze in Citizenship Education : Exploring The Perspectives Of Global Education NGO Workers In England. *International Journal of Citizenship and Teacher Education, 1*(2), 76–92. Retrieved from http://www.citized.info

Martens, K. (2006). Policy arena: NGOs in the United Nations system: Evaluating theoretical approaches. *Journal of International Development, 18*(5), 691–700. http://doi.org/10.1002/jid.1303

Parmenter, L. (2011). Power and place in the discourse of global citizenship education. *Globalisation, Societies and Education, 9*(3–4), 367–80. http://doi.org/10.1080/14767724.2011.605322

Pashby, K. (2011). Cultivating global citizens: Planting new seeds or pruning the perennials? looking for the citizen-subject in global citizenship education theory. *Globalisation, Societies and Education, 9*(3–4), 427–42. http://doi.org/10.1080/14767724.2011.605326

Rizvi, F., and Lingard, B. (2010). *Globalizing Education Policy*. London: Routledge.

Salter, P., and Halbert, K. (2017). Constructing the [parochial] global citizen. *Globalisation, Societies and Education, 15*(5), 694–705. http://doi.org/10.1080/14767724.2016.1264290

Scheunpflug, A. and Asbrand, B. (2006). Global education and education for sustainability. *Environmental Education Research, 12*(1), 33–46.

Shukla, N. (2009). Power, discourse, and learning global citizenship. *Education, Citizenship and Social Justice, 4*(2), 133–47. http://doi.org/10.1177/1746197909103933

Standish, A. (2012). *The False Promise of Global Learning: Why Education Needs Boundaries*. London: Bloomsbury.

Tarozzi, M., and Inguaggiato, C. (2018). Implementing GCED in EU primary schools: the role of ministries between coordinate and parallel action. *International Journal of Development Education and Global Learning, 10*(1), 21–38.

Tarozzi, M., and Mallon, B. (2019). Educating teachers towards global citizenship: A comparative study in four European countries. *London Review of Education, 17*(2), 112–25.

The Guardian (2018). https://www.theguardian.com/world/2018/jun/19/hungary-anti-immigration-plans-ngo-tax-orban-bill-criminalise-aid

Tota, P. M. (2014). Filling the gaps: The role and impact of international non-governmental organisations in 'Education for All'. *Globalisation, Societies and Education, 12*(1), 92–109. http://doi.org/10.1080/14767724.2013.858988

UNESCO (2015). *Rethinking Education: Toward a Global Common Good?* Paris: UNESCO.

Veugelers, W. (2011). The moral and the political in global citizenship: Appreciating differences in education. *Globalisation, Societies and Education, 9*(3–4), 473–85. http://doi.org/10.1080/14767724.2011.605329

Weber, N. (2014). Didactic or dialogical ? The shifting nature of INGO development education programming in England and Canada. *International Journal of Development Education and Global Learning, 6*(1), 27–51.

Witteborn, S. (2010). The role of transnational NGOs in promoting global citizenship and globalizing communication practices. *Language and Intercultural Communication, 10*(4), 358–72. http://doi.org/10.1080/14708477.2010.497556

Chapter 12

The Development of Global Education in Taiwan's Curriculum

Pei-I Chou

Introduction

Many East Asian educational systems are well-positioned at the dawn of the twenty-first century (Jackson 2014). For example, Taiwan has been one of the top ranked countries in Programme of International Student Assessment (PISA) (Yang and Lin 2015). However, facing unprecedented challenges and opportunities related to increased globalization, no society is free from the constant need for reform and improvement of its education. *The Maastricht Global Education Declaration* promotes global education (GE), which can open people's eyes and minds to the realities of the globalized world and awaken them to bring about a world of greater justice, equity and human rights for all (Europe-Wide Global Education Congress 2002). Organization for Economic Cooperation and Development (OECD 2016, 2018) advocates educating for global competence for an inclusive and sustainable world, whereby individuals can examine local, global and intercultural issues, understand and appreciate different perspectives and world views, interact successfully and respectfully with others, and take responsible action towards sustainability and collective well-being.

According to OECD (2018), global competence is a multidimensional capacity that is supported by knowledge of global issues, which can affect lives locally and around the globe, and intercultural knowledge. Several attempts have recently been made to systematically incorporate global issues into a coherent sequence of lessons and learning materials at all curriculum levels (IBO 2012; OECD 2018; Oxfam 2015; Reimers 2017). OECD (2018) asserts that a curriculum for global competence should pay attention to the following four knowledge domains: (a) culture and intercultural relations, (b) socio-economic development and interdependence, (c) environmental sustainability and (d) global institutions, conflicts and human rights. Oxfam's curriculum for global citizenship knowledge and understanding includes social justice and equity, identity and diversity, globalization and interdependence, sustainable development, peace and conflict, human rights and power and governance (Oxfam 2015). *The Maastricht Global Education Declaration* claims that GE encompasses development, human rights, sustainability, peace, conflict prevention and intercultural education (Europe-Wide Global Education Congress 2002).

Global competence is a combination of knowledge, skills, attitudes and values for dealing with a variety of global issues (OECD 2018). A comprehensive discussion on global competence is beyond the scope of this chapter; therefore, this chapter will focus on five knowledge domains of global issues to analyse Taiwan's curriculum, namely global system, multiculturalism, social justice and human rights, world peace and ecological sustainability. In addition, the analysis of a country's curriculum development from a perspective of GE cannot be detached from its social context. Since the order of martial law was lifted in 1987, Taiwan's society has gone through radical movements of political democratization and education reform, which increased social awareness of local and global issues. Grade 1–9 Curriculum (MOE 2011b) and Grade 1–12 Curriculum (MOE 2014) have been two major curriculum reforms in the past two decades in Taiwan (Chen and Huang 2017). It has been declared that both of these reforms, aimed at developing students' core competences, can improve Taiwan's global competitiveness in the new century. In 2011, the MOE published the *White Paper on International Education for Primary and Secondary Schools* with a view to developing our next generation's global competences. On the surface, the rhetoric in these policy documents seems to echo international trends in educational reforms for cultivating our next generation's global competences. In practice, the manner in which GE in Taiwan's curriculum can be contextualized has posed a challenge, since the concept of global competence and related curriculum knowledge are primarily developed from Western countries' practice, and their development in Taiwan is still in its early stages. In recent decades, the clash of Chinese cultural tradition and Taiwanese localization movement has often manifested itself in the education reforms in Taiwan. This has sparked off heated policy debates, which have sometimes distracted policy-makers and/or educators from the concerns of GE. To explore how the elements of GE have been evolving in the short period since they were introduced into Taiwanese curriculum, we need to trace Taiwan's historical background to understand the competing priorities for cultivating Taiwanese subjectivity, Chinese cultural literacy and global competence, even though they should be interconnected and interdependent.

This chapter therefore intends to explore the past, present and future trends of GE in Taiwan's curriculum. First, the development of GE in Taiwan's historical and cultural context will be reviewed. Second, the current state of GE in the curriculum will be analysed. Finally, the prospect of promoting GE in the new curriculum will be examined.

The historical background of Taiwan's education

The largest ethnic group in Taiwan is the *Han*, whose traditional heritage can be traced to China; the amalgam of this heritage alongside its language, religion and culture (Jennings 2017) is famously known as Confucianism. Confucianism emphasizes the value of education and respect for the authority of teachers (Chen et al. 2017; den Brok et al. 2002; Fwu and Wang 2002). In imperial China, the Confucian Classics were the subjects in the Imperial Examination, which was used to select the top talent to serve the empire. Confucian teachings have deeply influenced Taiwanese teachers' instruction and students' learning until now (Chen et al. 2017; Ho 1998; Hwang 2005; Kung 2017). In Taiwanese classrooms, for example, teacher-centred instruction, focused on transmitting knowledge rather than interactive activities, is favoured. Most Taiwanese students spend their formative years in preparing for tests to enter their ideal advanced schools. A passive learning mode such as memorizing textbook contents and practising tests repeatedly are common scenes in Taiwanese classrooms (Chou, Su and Wang 2018; Kung 2017). Taiwanese students work diligently towards high academic achievement, which is regarded as a passport to the social upper class. They also demonstrate excellent performance in various international competitions and assessments (e.g. PISA) (Yang and Lin 2015). Following a Confucian tradition, Taiwanese people tend to attach greater value to the learning of theory than that of practice. In other words, the pursuit of theory has been the focus of upper-class people, whereas the learning of practical skills has been associated with lower-class individuals (Tu 2007). However, pursuing theory or knowledge accumulation is insufficient for global competency. The manner in which Taiwanese students can be motivated to develop their skills, attitudes, values and actions for dealing with a variety of global issues (OECD 2018) has been found to pose a challenge.

From 1895 to 1945, Taiwan was a colony of Japan. After the end of the Japanese colonial period, Taiwan's new government from China took over the regime and soon imposed martial law on Taiwan. Taiwanese people could not freely interact with the international community or access global information. In order to forge Chinese national identity, the government proposed all-out Sinonisation educational policies and a nationalistic curriculum based on assimilationism. Under the strict control of the government, the content of all subjects was China-centred, while the content related to Taiwan was very limited. Confucian Classics were given a superior position in the national curriculum to declare Taiwan as the legitimate representative of Chinese culture and to clear the remains of Japanese colonialism from education. Mandarin Chinese replaced Japanese as the official language, and Taiwanese dialects were officially banned (Chou, Su and Wang 2018; Kung 2017; Tu 2007).

In the 1970s, Taiwan's economy witnessed a rapid expansion, helping it to transform from an agricultural society into an industrial and commercial one. Even though it lacked natural resources and official diplomatic relations, Taiwan, as one of 'Asia's four little tigers', managed to develop a vibrant economy, fed by globalized economic networks based on its strong international trade and industry clout (Morris 1996; Thomas and Yang 2013; Tu 2007). Taiwan's education system greatly contributed to the development of quality human resources to support economic growth.

In 1987, the order of martial law was lifted. Afterwards, Taiwan's society went through the political democratization movements, helping it to transform from a totalitarian regime into a free and democratic country. Various social movements emerged to pursue transitional justice, personal dignity, human rights, political democracy and Taiwanese identity and cultures. These movements promoted public participation in social affairs and led to the establishment of many non-governmental organizations (NGOs), which facilitated grass-roots activities and informal educational programmes on local and/or global issues (Huang 2006; McBeath and McBeath 2011; Tu 2007). On the other hand, Taiwanese government announced several acts and laws to address these issues. In a constitutional amendment in 1997, the government recognized multiculturalism, in an effort to promote the diverse cultural development and empowerment of minority groups (Jackson 2014). In 2004, Gender Equity Education Act was announced to promote substantive gender equality, eliminate gender discrimination, uphold human dignity and improve and establish education resources and environment of gender equality. It requires that staff members in each school engage in a four-hour gender equity education programme per year.

In 2010, the government adopted the Environmental Education Law to assist citizens to understand the interrelationship between individuals and society on the one hand and the environment on the other, with a view to enhancing their environmental awareness, ethics and responsibility. This requires that staff members in public offices, business firms and universities engage in a four-hour environmental education programme on a yearly basis (McBeath and McBeath 2011). These acts and laws represent a significant expansion of multicultural education, human rights education (HRE) and environmental education (aka education for sustainable development in Taiwan).

During the 1990s, Taiwan underwent dramatic reforms of liberalization and diversification in education. On 10 April 1994, a mass demonstration was staged to demand education reforms, which subsequently became known as '410 Demonstration for Education Reform'. The demonstrators' main appeal was to remove the unreasonable restraints that the authoritarian government had imposed on education and to focus on student-centred education instead (Tu 2007). In order to put the appeal into effect, the Basic Law on Education was enacted in 1999 to assure people's right to education and equality of educational opportunity (Huang 2006). After a short while, the government promoted curriculum reforms, which systematically decreased Chinese nationalistic elements and increased the diversity of the curriculum; the reform also included abundant curriculum content focused on Taiwan (Jackson 2014). As Taiwan's former minister of education indicated, one of the most important educational changes after the 410 Demonstration concerned the textbook policies (Tu 2007). In the past, the compilation and publication of school textbooks were regulated by the central government. Today, private publishers are allowed to compile and publish textbooks after the approval of professional reviews. The decision on adopting textbooks now falls within the purview of school curriculum committees. Teachers can also develop their own teaching materials to meet individual instructional needs.

It is worth noting that in the 1990s, educational reform policies emphasized that the localization of Taiwan's internal affairs should not be aligned with mainland China and its assimilationist rhetoric and policies (Wang 2002, 2004; Damm 2012). In the meantime, Taiwanese people gradually felt the growing impact of globalization and its competitive pressures. For example, Taiwan joined the World Trade Organization (WTO) in 2001, which inevitably affected domestic finances and society (Chen 2007; Thomas and Yang 2013). Higher education (HE) rapidly expanded following the 410 Demonstration appeal for the liberalization of education. However, it seems that it mainly expanded in quantity rather than quality and was not very successful in enhancing young people's global competitiveness for highly competitive global markets. The public has blamed HE policies for inappropriate distribution or waste of educational funds, and for the introduction into society of highly educated but unemployed or low-paid young people (Tomas and Yang 2013). In addition, Taiwan is currently suffering from depopulation or a rather marked decline in birth rate, while the number of new immigrants from Southeast Asia has increased in the past two to three decades (NIA 2012). Despite the growth in the immigrant population, Taiwan's curriculum has not paid sufficient attention to the emerging minority cultures and identities of these newcomers (Wu 2012). In short, Taiwan's curriculum has been criticized for being confined to Taiwan's internal affairs rather than looking to global affairs (Chen 1996; Jackson 2014; Wu 2012). Understanding the manner in which the education system can and should be adjusted to meet the challenge of globalization has become imperative for the Taiwanese government and people.

The current state of global education in Taiwan's curriculum

Grade 1–9 Curriculum and Grade 1–12 Curriculum have been two major curriculum reforms in the past two decades in Taiwan (Chen and Huang 2017). Grade 1–9 Curriculum Guidelines were adopted in 2001 and were subsequently revised several times (MOE 2011b). In place of the previous curriculum that emphasized a standardized curriculum and rigid requirements and was focused on knowledge accumulation, Grade 1–9 Curriculum aimed to cultivate students' core competences with a view to improving their global competitiveness in the twenty-first century. This curriculum streamlines and integrates courses to stress interdisciplinary teaching and learning; it also strengthens the link between knowledge and experience in real life. With the flexibility for adjustment, the curriculum delegates more curriculum decision-making power to schools, and encourages professional autonomy for teachers to develop a school-based curriculum (Chen and Huang 2017; Huang 2006; MOE 2011b).

Grade 1–9 Curriculum divides the national curriculum into seven learning areas: language arts, mathematics, health and physical education, integrative activities, social studies, science and technology, and arts and humanities. In Grades 1 and 2, the final three learning areas are integrated into one area called the life curriculum. In addition, six major issues have been included in the curriculum: HRE, gender equality education, environment education, information technologies education, home economics education and career planning (MOE 2011b). In 2012, a major new issue – marine education – was added. However, international/global education has not been included among the major issues in the guidelines, despite its close link to human rights, gender equality and environmental education.

The guidelines aim to develop students' ten core competences. One core competence – cultural learning and international understanding – is directly related to international/global education (MOE 2011b). A system of detailed competence indicators has been formulated for each learning area and major issue, aimed at cultivating these core competences. The curriculum and instruction on these major issues are required to be integrated into those of the learning areas. In order to preserve native languages, local cultures and to enhance international understanding, for the first time the primary curriculum teaches both native languages and the English language. Both of these subjects share teaching hours with Mandarin Chinese in the language arts area, forcing them to compete with one another for teaching hours. To complicate matters further, native language subjects suffer from a shortage of teachers and materials (Chen and Huang 2017). To comply with the guidelines on the learning areas, textbooks have been developed by private publishers, reviewed by professionals and subsequently approved by the government.

In 2011, the MOE (2011a) published the *White Paper on International Education for Primary and Secondary Schools*, which emphasized the necessity for educational reform, mainly because the highly competitive global markets demand quality human resources. The White Paper aimed to pave the way for the development of the next generation's global competences and to prepare them for life in the twenty-first century, which is very similar to the aim of Grade 1–9 Curriculum Guidelines. The White Paper recommends some strategies to schools for the implementation of international education, including adopting a school-based approach, integrating international education into the current curriculum and encouraging cooperation among MOE, local governments and schools.

The White Paper intends to cultivate students' four global competencies: national identity, international awareness, global competitiveness and global responsibility. Based on these four global competencies, a system of competence indicators for international education has been developed. Schools can refer to these indicators to develop school-based international education programmes and apply for grants from the MOE (MOE 2012). In Taipei, Taichung and Kaohsiung, the local educational authorities cooperate with the British Council in promoting the International Education Award Granting Programme to Grade 1–12. However, international/ global education is not included in the major issues in the guidelines, nor is it mandatory for curriculum developers, schools and teachers. Even though an increasing number of schools have participated in school-based international education projects and continue to make progress in implementing international/global education, most of these school-based projects are short term and only intended for special events, such as the international student exchange programme or visiting foreign students; ideally, these school-based projects would have been long-term and sustainable by, for example, systematically integrating international education into regular curricula.

On the surface, Grade 1–9 Curriculum Guidelines seem to pay attention to international trends for educational reforms, aimed at improving Taiwanese global competitiveness in the twenty-first century; the guidelines also provide comprehensive coverage of several international components (MOE 2011b). However, some studies have been probing deeply to understand the extent to which global issues are presented in Taiwan's curriculum, and whether some global issues are neglected or inadequately addressed. Chou et al. (2015) conducted content analysis on Grade 1–9 Curriculum Guidelines, and a year later, Chou and Ting (2016) analysed the primary school textbooks. Both studies focused on five of the most common global issues: global system, multiculturalism, social justice and human rights, world peace and ecological sustainability. The authors of these two studies found that, in general, about 10 per cent of the content was related to global issues, in both the guidelines and textbooks. This implies that the national curriculum has begun to recognize the importance of global issues and to integrate some of them into the existing learning areas, although there is still considerable room for improvement.

Among the global issues, both the guidelines and textbooks pay limited attention to the issues relating to human rights and social justice. There are still difficulties in tackling such controversial issues in the Taiwanese curriculum, even though HRE has been included as a major issue in the guidelines and is required to be integrated into every learning area. On the other hand, multicultural issues have drawn the greatest attention in Taiwan's curriculum guidelines, whereas textbooks place considerable emphasis on the issues of ecological sustainability. The reason for this gap might be because the ideas of multiculturalism in the guidelines are more radical, ideal, abstract and theoretical and thus difficult to incorporate into the content of textbooks for each learning area; in contrast, the ideas and activities relating to ecological sustainability are easily seen and done on campus, in the surrounding community and in the media; they are also more common in textbooks and tangible for primary students (Chou et al. 2015; Chou and Ting 2016).

Learning areas vary considerably in terms of their inclusion of global issues in the guidelines and textbooks, which largely depend on the relevance of the global issues to the subject knowledge of the learning areas. The highest proportion of global issues is found in two learning areas: social studies and integrative activities. The latter is a special learning area in which teachers design the learning activities to facilitate students' integration of knowledge and skills across the areas. These two learning areas are given greater prominence compared to the other areas, with about 30–40 per cent of the content in the guidelines and textbooks being related to global issues. A notable outcome is that only social studies have been consistently offered across all the global issues; unlike other learning areas, only the social studies guidelines have indicators that are related to social justice and human rights, except for some sparse information in the integrative activities and health and physical education textbooks. The other areas focus only on one or two global issues or just neglect them altogether. For example, science and technology has a major focus on ecological sustainability and a minor focus on global system; around 10 per cent of the competency indicators in the English guidelines are related to multicultural issues, while scant attention has been paid to the other global issues. The English textbooks are less concerned about global issues than the guidelines are; they are even less concerned about multicultural issues. There seems to be a gap between the practical curriculum content and the expectations of the White Paper (MOE 2011a), which emphasizes foreign language learning and proficiency as a means to increasing students' global competitiveness. The mathematics area is simply unrelated to any global issues (Chou et al. 2015; Chou and Ting 2016).

In 2014, to improve the articulation of Grade 1–9 and Grade 10–12 Curriculum Guidelines, new Grade 1–12 Curriculum General Guidelines were published by the MOE (2014). Recently, many political controversies and debates concerning Taiwanese national identity and Chinese cultural tradition have been raised over the new curriculum and have delayed its progress. The development of Grade 1–12 Curriculum falls within the remit of the Kuomintang (KMT) government. In 2016, the Democratic Progressive Party (DPP) defeated the KMT and gained the presidential seat and a majority of the Legislative Yuan. The DPP government put more emphasis on Taiwan-centric identity and Taiwan's domestic affairs than the KMT – which used to closely identify with the Chinese tradition – leading to a limited focus on China-related content. Due to the political debates between KMT and DPP and the procedural problems of reviewing curriculum guidelines, the implementation of the new curriculum has been postponed until 2019.

The introduction of Grade 1–12 Curriculum General Guidelines stresses the need for curriculum reform to respond to the radical social changes, including diminishing birth rates and a growing elderly population, frequent interaction among diverse groups, expansion of the internet and information, increasing opportunities for new jobs, growing awareness of democracy and social justice, sustainable development of ecology and globalization and internationalization (MOE 2014). It appears that more global issues have come to the attention of the public during the transition to the new curriculum.

In general, the structure of the Grade 1–12 Curriculum is similar to that of Grade 1–9 Curriculum, except for the learning area of science and technology, which is divided into two learning areas, and the new immigrants' languages, which are included in the guidelines (MOE 2014). One of the nine core competences in the new guidelines is multicultural and international understanding, which is similar to the core competence of cultural learning and international understanding in the Grade 1–9 Curriculum Guidelines. International education is now one of the nineteen major issues to be integrated into the learning areas. At present, the substantial influence of GE on the new curriculum is still far from being completely felt. For the further development of the new curriculum, it is crucial to strike a balance between the impact of globalization and localization. The analysis of the current curriculum (Chou et al. 2015; Chou and Ting 2016) can serve as a basis for assessing and incorporating elements of GE into the subject knowledge of textbooks and/or school-based teaching materials, encouraging curriculum developers and teachers to rethink the value of these underrepresented issues and contribute to a fairer and more balanced representation of global issues, for students' global learning in learning areas and cross curricula activities.

Conclusion

A broader social intention and concern is essential for the elements of GE to be effectively incorporated into the curriculum and implemented in school teaching. Unlike Western societies that have a long history of developing a variety of cross-curricular programmes linked to GE (Hicks 2008), the development of GE in Taiwan is still in its early stages. It needs to compete with the traditional Chinese method and Taiwan-centred approach for a limited space in a packed curriculum. Today, the Chinese-based curriculum approach is weakening and being supplanted by a curriculum that gives priority to Taiwanese localized affairs. A curriculum approach for global competency is emerging. It is urgent for Taiwan's policy-makers and educators to go beyond the distinctions between localization and globalization and promote a more globally oriented curriculum that is able to integrate local and national levels with global levels.

Following the Confucian tradition, Taiwanese people think highly of education; Taiwanese students study hard to gain knowledge and perform well in academic fields. It benefits Taiwanese students to learn about global issues. However, cultivating students' competency in global issues goes beyond acquiring the knowledge of global issues. Teachers need to go further and help students play more active roles as responsible members of the local and global society (OECD 2018). Hence, the didactic method of teaching and the passive mode of learning in Taiwanese classrooms must be transformed.

Since the economic growth in the 1970s, the movements for political democratization in the 1980s, the deregulation of the educational system and the localized and internally oriented educational reforms in the 1990s, and the introduction of the Grade 1–9/1–12 Curricula of the new millennium, the potential for Taiwan's curricula to accommodate global issues has been increasing. Taiwan's education reforms have now reached critical milestones to include key issues which were once banned from the school curriculum during the martial law period. Issues such as multiculturalism, social justice, human rights and ecological sustainability have become a part of official knowledge, although they have not yet form a substantial part in the curriculum, and some learning areas continue to pay limited attention to these issues.

During transition to the Grade 1–12 Curriculum, it is important for educational leaders and policy-makers in Taiwan to think globally and act locally; they need to bridge the GE gap between rhetoric and reality. For GE to move from abstraction to action, it has been recommended that global issues and topics should be integrated into existing subjects, and that the local and global connections of these issues should be established (Klein 2013; OECD 2018; UNESCO 2014). Teaching controversial issues, such as human rights and social justice, may be difficult for Taiwanese teachers who are accustomed to the didactic method of teaching rather than debating issues. It is therefore vital to develop new teacher training programmes to equip teachers from different learning areas and levels of education with the requisite knowledge and capability to integrate global issues into curriculum content; they also need to hone their skills in transformative pedagogies, so as to promote students' global competences to improve people's lives, locally and around the globe.

Bibliography

Chen, G. X. (1996), 'The Cultural Studies of Decolonialism', *Taiwan: A Radical Quarterly in Social Studies*, 21: 73–139.

Chen, H. C., I. Chen, S. Y. Lin and Y. Chen (2017), 'Cultural Influences in Acquiescent Response: A Study of Trainer Evaluation Biases', *International Journal of Selection and Assessment*, 25 (1): 1–10.

Chen, H. L. S. and H. Y. Huang (2017), *Advancing 21st Century Competencies in Taiwan*. Taipei: The Center for Global Education at Asia Society.

Chen, T. J. (2007), 'WTO Commitments by Taiwan and China and the Domestic Consequences', in J. Chang and S. M. Goldstein (eds), *Economic Reform and Cross-Strait Relations: Taiwan and China in the WTO*, 43–72, Boston: World Scientific.

Chou, P. I. and H. J. Ting (2016), 'How Closely Are the National Curriculum and the Global Dimension Related? A Content Analysis of the Global Dimension in Elementary School Textbooks in Taiwan', *Asia Pacific Education Review*, 17 (3): 533–43.

Chou, P. I., M. C. Cheng, Y. L. Lin and Y. T. Wang (2015), 'Establishing the Core Concepts and Competence Indicators of Global/International Education for Taiwan's Grade 1–9 Curriculum Guidelines', *Asia-Pacific Education Researcher*, 24 (4): 669–78.

Chou, P. I., M. H. Su and Y. T. Wang (2018), 'Transforming Teacher Preparation for Culturally Responsive Teaching in Taiwan', *Teaching and Teacher Education*, 75: 116–27.

Damm, J. (2012), 'Multiculturalism in Taiwan and the Influence of Europe', in J. Damm and P. Lim (eds), *European Perspectives on Taiwan*, 84–105, New York: Springer.

den Brok, P. J., J. Levy, R. Rodriguez and T. Wubbels (2002), 'Perceptions of Asian-American and Hispanic-American Teachers and their Students on Teacher Interpersonal Communication Style', *Teaching and Teacher Education*, 18 (4): 447–67.

Europe-Wide Global Education Congress (2002), *European Strategy Framework for Improving and Increasing Global Education in Europe to the Year 2015*. Maastricht: Europe-Wide Global Education Congress.

Fwu, B. J. and H. H. Wang (2002), 'The Social Status of Teachers in Taiwan', *Comparative Education*, 38 (2): 211–24.

Hicks, D. (2008), 'Ways of Seeing: The Origins of Global Education in the UK', *Paper Presented at the Conference of UK Initial Teacher Education Network for Education for Sustainable Development and Global Citizenship*. London, UK.

Ho, M. C. (1998), 'Culture Studies and Motivation in Foreign and Second Language Learning in Taiwan', *Language Culture and Curriculum*, 11 (2): 165–82.

Huang, M. (2006), 'Human Rights Education in Taiwan: Current Situation and Future Challenges', *Human Rights Education in Asian Schools*, 9: 73–81.

Hwang, C. C. (2005), 'Effective EFL Education through Popular Authentic Materials', *Asian EFL Journal*, 7 (1): 90–101.

IBO (2012), *What Is an IB Education?* Cardiff: International Baccalaureate Organisation.

Jackson, L. (2014), 'Under Construction: The Development of Multicultural Curriculum in Hong Kong and Taiwan', *The Asia-Pacific Education Researcher*, 23 (4): 885–93.

Jennings, R. (2017), 'Taiwan Finds a lot to Like about its Former Colonizer, Japan', *Los Angeles Times*, 6 November. Available online: http://www.latimes.com/world/asia/la-fg-taiwan-japan-20171106-story.html (accessed 24 January 2019).

Klein, J. D. (2013), 'Making Meaning in a Standards-based World: Negotiating Tensions in Global Education', *Educational Forum*, 77 (4): 481–90.

Kung, F. W. (2017), 'Teaching and Learning English as a Foreign Language in Taiwan: A Socio-cultural Analysis', *TESL-EJ*, 21 (2). Available online: http://www.tesl-ej.org/wordpress/issues/volume21/ej82/ej82a4/ (accessed 24 January 2019).

McBeath, J. and J. H. McBeath (2011), 'Environmental Education in Taiwan, with Comparisons to China', *Paper Presented at the 53rd Annual Conference of the American Association for Chinese Studies*. Philadelphia, PA.

MOE (2011a), *A White Paper on International Education for Primary and Secondary Schools*. Taipei: Ministry of Education.

MOE (2011b), *Grade 1–9 Curriculum Guidelines*. Taipei: Ministry of Education.

MOE (2012), *General Statistics of the New Immigrants' Children Population in Elementary and Junior High Schools*. Taipei: Ministry of Education.

MOE (2014), *The General Curriculum Guidelines of 12-year Basic Education*. Taipei: Ministry of Education.

Morris, P. (1996), 'Asia's Four Little Tigers: A Comparison of the Role of Education in their Development', *Comparative Education*, 32 (1): 95–109.

NIA (2012), *Year 2011, December, Statistics Bulletin of Internal Affairs (Marriage Registration Profile in Year 2011)*. Taipei: National Immigration Agency. Available online: https://www.immigration.gov.tw/public/Attachment/212016212134.xls (accessed 24 January 2019).

OECD (2016), *Global Competency for an Inclusive World*. Paris: Organization for Economic Co-operation and Development.

OECD (2018), *Preparing our Youth for an Inclusive and Sustainable World*. Paris: Organization for Economic Co-operation and Development.

Oxfam (2015), *Education for Global Citizenship, a Guide for Schools*. Oxford: Oxfam GB.

Reimers, F. (2017), *Empowering Students to Improve the World in Sixty Lessons. Version 1.0*. North Charleston: CreateSpace Independent Publishing Platform.

Thomas, M. K. and W. L. Yang (2013), 'Neoliberalism, Globalization, and Creative Educational Destruction in Taiwan', *Educational Technology Research and Development*, 61 (1): 107–29.

Tu, C. S. (2007), 'Taiwan's Educational Reform and the Future of Taiwan', *Paper Presented at London School of Economics and Political Science*. London, UK.

UNESCO (2014), *Global Citizenship Education: Preparing Learners for the Challenges of the 21st Century*. Paris: United Nations Educational, Scientific and Cultural Organization.

Wang, L. J. (2004), 'Multiculturalism in Taiwan: Contradictions and Challenges in Cultural Policy', *International Journal of Cultural Policy*, 10 (3): 301–18.

Wang, Y. H. (2002), *Limits of Ethnic Recognition: A Preliminary Analysis of Multicultural Competence of Aboriginal Teachers on Curriculum Philosophy*. Exeter: Annual Conference of the British Educational Research Association.

Wu, Y. L. (2012), *Sociocultural Contexts and Learning: Vietnamese Immigrant Women in Taiwanese Vocational Training Programs*. Chiayi: Philosophy of Education Society of Australasia Annual Conference.

Yang, K. L. and F. L. Lin (2015), 'The Effects of PISA in Taiwan: Contemporary Assessment Reform', in K. Stacey and R. Turner (eds), *Assessing Mathematical Literacy*, 261–73. New York: Springer.

Chapter 13

Global Learning: Addressing Attitudes, Behaviours and Competencies (ABC) in Teaching and Learning in Zanzibar

Cathryn MacCallum, Mark Proctor and Nicholas Hoad

Introduction

The ability of teachers to build the skills and competencies of their students to live in an increasingly globalized world has been widely acknowledged as important (Bourn, 2011; UNESCO, 2013). This means more than simply passing on additional knowledge of a global nature and involves the fostering of skills and competencies required as global citizens. This chapter gives the overview of a project run by Sazani Associates (Sazani), a UK-based non-governmental organization (NGO), that has been delivering education and livelihood programmes in Zanzibar for fifteen years. It reflects on the recent project period and assesses the integration of global learning into the curriculum and the building of critical-thinking skills in the context of wider pupil performance.

Zanzibar is a semi-autonomous small island state in the Indian Ocean, part of the United Republic of Tanzania. The islands of Zanzibar exist in a global context framed by a series of complex political, economic, social and environmental pressures and forces, common to many Small Island Developing States (SIDS).

Sazani, through its Attitudes, Behaviour and Competences for Quality Education Project (ABC Project) in Zanzibar, is currently supporting teachers, learners and communities to negotiate the global forces and pressures described above. The project utilizes a combined approach of lesson study and cascade training to embed global learning across a school curriculum, as a model to improve the quality of teaching and learning in Zanzibar. It draws on participatory pedagogies and contextualized curricula delivered through a continually evolving professional global learning community (PGLC) initiated through a British Council school linking initiative that started eighteen years ago, in 2000.

The ABC Project, funded by Comic Relief UK, UKAID and an American foundation, is working with fifty-one lower secondary schools on the islands of Unguja and Pemba, Zanzibar. The project is currently in its third year of an initial four-year implementation programme, scheduled to run until April 2020.

The longitudinal nature of the relationship with the education system in Zanzibar is a key contributor to the success of Sazani's work, especially considering the transferability of knowledge and learning approaches, as teachers get regularly moved between schools.

This reflection on the effectiveness of the ABC Project and the global learning journey of the last eighteen years focuses on the achievements, challenges and opportunities presented by the combined approach. The impact of the model on both the direct and indirect beneficiaries, measured through a monitoring, evaluation and learning (MEL) framework, is assessed, and provides a practical case study in the application of global learning to the challenges posed to education in a country with extensive development challenges.

Through this, the importance of critical thinking to the development of citizens equipped with the skills to address the challenges faced in an increasingly globalized world is set out in the context of this SIDS.

Zanzibar: A microcosm of global development challenges

Situated in the Indian Ocean, about thirty-five miles off the coast of mainland Tanzania, lies the Zanzibar archipelago. It is a semi-autonomous, small island state, with a combination of both rural and urban poverty within a relatively small geographical area (Belghith and De Boisseson, 2017). Zanzibar presents a microcosm of many of the major challenges facing the world today, especially within the Global South. This is further demonstrated by the contrasting complexities of urban and rural existence, of uplands and lowlands, of coastal and inland areas and their respective vulnerability to local and global threats and the rapid degradation and destruction of fragile ecosystems.

What sets Zanzibar apart from other SIDS is its sociopolitical history: its demise from being an independent, prosperous small island state to becoming a protectorate under the British, later regaining independence and ending up as a semi-autonomous appendix to a poor African nation allied to the Soviet Bloc. Following that, there was the collapse of the Soviet Bloc and subsequent African and European responses to neoliberalism. Zanzibar emerged from a 'single-party democracy' into a multiparty democracy with two political parties. There have been contested elections, coalition government and, most recently, the annulling of the election result by the ruling party and their subsequent uncontested election back into power. Contrasting with the colonial history of many other SIDS, pre-independence Zanzibar is widely regarded, by Zanzibaris at least, as the 'Golden Age' (MacCallum, 2014). The result of twentieth-century geopolitics was that a once-thriving, outward-looking island state was reframed as a poor semi-autonomous developmental state, oppressed by mainland Tanzania (Middleton, 1994).

During the 1990s the onset of tourism as a global force raised expectations among the political, mercantile and rural people as an alternative source of financial capital. In practice, those driving tourism have engaged in an overexploitation of natural capital assets such as water, land, forests and marine resources while simultaneously under-exploiting human capital, with less than 20 per cent of all employment going to Zanzibar nationals (ZRG, 2010). Tourism draws primarily on the assets of the poor, such as knowledge, natural resources and rural space, thereby impacting negatively upon local people's livelihoods and resilience in this vulnerable small island state. The wide range of negative effects on culture and the traditional way of life is, as Peak (1989, p. 124) suggests, 'a final form of oppression is the modern tourist trade, in which once again outsiders exploit the Swahili' (as cited in Middleton, 1994). Tourism Concern (2012) identified Zanzibar as the most socially unjust location on the planet regarding access to drinking water.

Successive Zanzibar government policy has acknowledged the need to understand and respect rural coastal community views, for integrative thinking and to involve them in decision-making processes. In their 2010 coastal strategy document, it stated that 'Communities, especially those living in coastal areas, need to be made aware of the importance of coastal resources to their livelihood and thus, their wise use of the resources is so crucial' (ZRG, 2010, p. 33).

With close historical, social and trade links to the Arabian Gulf States and Somalia, Zanzibar has seen an emergence of Salafist fundamentalist Islam. In rural areas, this is moving cultural attitudes from one espousing plural traditions to one of a singular social religious perspective articulated by well-resourced, foreign-educated Islamic scholars. The impact on rural gender equality and women's voices of the proliferation of this form of Islam is not difficult to deduce. As such, Zanzibar provides a 'development interface' where the traditional endogenous knowledge of rural, community actors contrasts, often conflicts, with the external scientific and 'expert' knowledge of development professionals, educators and government representatives. As a small island state, its vulnerability to these global pressures and forces necessitates the population to be able to conceptualize, adapt to and/or militate against change. To engage in either of these without an understanding of the drivers of these global pressures and forces is at best reactionary and ineffective.

Education in Zanzibar

Education in Zanzibar is compulsory and free until the age of sixteen. The current education system involves staying at school until an individual has completed at least seven years of primary and four years of secondary education. There have been significant changes in the last few years in terms of the use of English in schools. Maalim (2017) states, 'Kiswahili was used as a language of instruction in primary schools in Zanzibar for more than four decades and English as a language of instruction in secondary schools. The increasing hegemony of English has led to the introduction, from 2014, of the use of English as medium of instruction from Grade 5 onwards in primary schools.' It is hard to deny Maalim's argument where he goes on to assert that learners are disadvantaged having to study in a language they have not used outside school. Similarly, his views on the impacts of this approach on marginalizing African languages are clear and well supported. Those critiques aside, in practical terms English is critical in Zanzibar for anyone engaging in livelihood activities linked to the main economic driver, tourism or wanting to advance within the education system. Teaching through English does provide significant challenges to teachers as well as learners and teacher proficiency in English compounds the challenges facing learners.

In Zanzibar, gross enrolment rates and attendance figures vary according to the season. There are certain times of the year when there is a noticeably higher number of girls than boys in school, despite the under-twenty population being 49 per cent male and 51 per cent female (Ministry of Education, ZRG, 2009). This relates to relative freedoms given to boys and girls and alternative opportunities linked to livelihoods that may out-compete an education that does not stimulate or engage. Teacher retention is poor, especially in rural areas, and the quality of provision largely depends on teachers with few formal qualifications and inadequate training, as across most of Africa (UNESCO 2017). Teacher salaries are low with very few incentives being offered and many of the well-qualified teachers migrate either to private schools or to the mainland. In common with many cultures, education is still seen as necessary to gain choices, but not to increase knowledge regarding traditional activities. This is not unique in African countries and is a recognized development challenge (Maalim 2017).

Educational statistics are increasingly difficult to access in Zanzibar. The 2014 UNESCO Education for All (EFA) report illustrated that primary school completion rate had been hugely variable over time with 2012 showing an improvement of less than 1 per cent (from 77.2 per cent to 78.4 per cent) as compared to 2003 in Zanzibar, although other years had showed much better results (UNESCO, 2014). Teacher motivation, or lack of it, is a contributing issue to poor school attainment (UNESCO, 2017). This report also identified that the relative size of the pool of educated people as prospective teachers compared to the massive requirement to meet the growing number of learners is shrinking. There has been no correlation between increased enrolment and completion with attainment, suggesting that despite increasing access to education, as an institution, the quality of provision has not improved.

It is within this context that Sazani has been working to introduce and foster critical-thinking skills through global learning, driven by the belief that poor quality education provision contributes to the marginalization of young people disenfranchized by sociopolitical instability.

Why global learning?

Global learning is a process of realized critical thinking, a reflective consideration of social, cultural, economic, political and environmental issues from a variety of perspectives and contexts (MacCallum, 2014). It sits alongside and overlaps with what Bourn and Brown (2011, p. 257) refer to as the 'adjectival educations' and 'just pedagogies'. These include development education, peace education, rights-based education, education for sustainable development, global citizenship education and global education. As a construct, it has evolved from and is increasingly associated with an interchangeable concept with many of these pedagogies. It challenges parochial and provincial, single-order attitudes and encourages exploring issues from a range of perspectives to support informed decision-making (Scheunpflug, Gogolin and Baumert, 2011; Bourn, 2008; Bourn and Issler, 2010).

Global learning, as a pedagogy, seeks to 'provide learners with the knowledge and skills needed to live in a globalised world' (Scheunpflug, 2008, p. 18) and is 'about enabling people to understand the links between their lives and those of people throughout the world' (Bourn, 2008, p. 3). It seeks to develop learners' ability to enquire from a critical perspective, assisting them in 'learning to unlearn, learning to listen, learning to learn and learning to reach out' (Andreotti and De Souza, 2008, p. 29).

Sazani's work recognizes that educators of children and young people need to acknowledge the 'other' and the interactions between identity and difference. Educators need to understand the multiple ways in which they negotiate everyday lived realities and through which they experience their identity in order to understand and value the environment and their living heritage. This requires competences gained through confidence to explore and acquire language and concepts to unpack the challenges they and their students face before they can be in a position to lead educational discourse with students.

Understanding how one's own life is framed and interactions between self and other is important, as Spivak (2013) concurs, and so is understanding of how identities are constructed, not only within the communities to which they belong but also between different communities. The centrality and importance of identity in securing confidence to consider another's perspective or situation resonates with the global learning emphasis on the consideration of 'the other'. Andreotti and De Souza (2008), Bourn and Issler (2010) and Scheunpflug, Gogolin and Baumert (2011) all include local voices and perspectives in their writings, and concur that there are often multiple perspectives to consider. A global learning space can, as Bourn and Issler (2010, p. 255) suggest, provide 'opportunities for intercultural research and learning based on equality of partnership. ... [It] supports international understanding, but also investigation of indigenous cultures and provides a voice for minority and marginalised groups in any society.'

Global learning, in this guise, becomes a globally relevant construct and one with the potential to liberate education in Zanzibar from trying to pay lip service to the Programme for International Student Assessment (PISA) and other neoliberal ideals and can support it to become an effective mechanism to challenge the social exclusion of rural communities and young people. Learners who actively engage in education enter into a process of socialization that is influenced by larger economic, social and political forces. It has been widely accepted that those most likely to succeed are those who align themselves with, and participate in, other mainstream communities of practice that are congruent with the dominant culture and elites. Those least likely to succeed and most likely to experience difficulties are those who are different and socially excluded, people on the margins, women, ethnic minorities and those who are poor. Global learning provides a means to actively challenge these exclusions.

Through gaining a range of perspectives and engaging in a critical reflection in a classroom or social-learning setting this in turn provides opportunities to cross borders of dominance. Vibrant self-criticism should be coupled with social criticism in order to reject 'the seductive persuasions of certainty' (Hussein, 2002, p. 297) and to foster critical positions without becoming intractable or dominant: 'The role of engaged intellectuals was not to consolidate authority but to understand, interpret and question it' (Said, 1994, p. 9).

From contextualized resources to contextualized learning

Sazani Associates started working in Zanzibar in 2005, as an implementing partner to an UNESCO: FAO Flagship Project called Education for Rural People (ERP). The project was funded through the Europe Aid predecessor to DEAR funding. The project focused on how to improve access, capacity and quality of education provision in rural areas globally. Through this project Sazani highlighted that unless learning and education are made relevant to local realities and enable exposure to different perspectives, they achieve no more than what Freire would consider to be 'information banking'. Simply increasing basic literacy, as it is currently taught in Zanzibar and other countries will not advance a sustainable society. If communities and nations such as Zanzibar hope to identify sustainability goals and work towards them, they must focus on skills, values and perspectives that encourage and support public participation and community decision-making. To achieve this, basic education needs to be reoriented to address sustainability and expanded to include critical-thinking skills, skills to organize and interpret data and information, skills to formulate questions and the ability to analyse issues that confront communities (Al Kanaan, 2007, p. 12).

In response, Sazani combined the ERP project with a school linking initiative between Wales and Zanzibar, working with a team of educationalists (Welsh and Zanzibari teachers) to develop a series of global learning resources contextualized to Zanzibar and Wales, tailored to the national curriculum of both countries. Through this combined approach Sazani was able to put people at the centre of their learning and development, enabling them to critically assess their values to inform resultant choices and decisions in what Sen (1997) would regard as enhancing freedoms and capabilities.

The school links and partnerships evolved over the next ten years, culminating in the development of a Healthy and Sustainable Schools Programme (HSSP) in Zanzibar, as an adaptation of the Health Promoting Schools award piloted in Wales, to incorporate global learning and critical thinking. Relating learning to local realities focused on the learning process, supported critical thinking, self-reflection and the independent choices of the learner. It became evident that learning can lead to a profound change in individuals and communities; it can increase active citizenship and cultural awareness and expression, building upon knowledge, skills, values and attitudes that lead to effective personal and civil society relationships.

Across the islands, State Teachers Centres (TCs) exist to administer training for teachers. Sazani identified these TCs as the vehicle to provide support in an effective way targeting the main objective of up-skilling teachers in Zanzibar. The beneficiaries from each district/TC were identified through previous work as those who are dedicated and enthusiastic teachers but who lacked the knowledge or incentives to improve the quality of their teaching. This tactile, historically informed approach to targeting effort further enabled relationships to develop with schools, teachers and government and made the targeted approach more effective and embedded.

A critical evaluation of the progress and achievements of Sazani Associates work in Zanzibar, in 2015, suggested that while teacher and pupil motivation and engagement in participating schools had certainly improved and an understanding of humanity, global social justice and responsibility had been developed, there was no measure of improved school performance, without which it was difficult to justify continuation of funding.

ABC for quality teaching and learning

The evaluation coincided with Development Education Research Centre (DERC) research that focused on global learning and school performance (Alcock and Barker 2016), the publication of a colleague's PhD thesis on the value of cascade teaching in improving teacher and pupil performance (Lange 2016), and another colleague's experience of an action research approach to classroom development called 'Lesson Study'. The culmination of this inspired the 'ABC for Quality Teaching and Learning in Zanzibar' project (ABC Project). Four years funding was secured through Comic Relief (UK) and the American foundation that had commissioned the critical evaluation and was perceived to address their concerns.

ABC stands for *A*ttitude, *B*ehaviour and *C*ompetence, and the project aims to target these challenges in both learners and teachers. The project builds on the successes of the healthy and sustainable schools award programme. Teacher competence and motivation is being enabled through a lesson study (LS) combined with cascade learning.

The aim is to improve student results and the ability of students to progress educationally within the school system, through improving the quality of teaching and learning. The project, focusing on four core skill areas – numeracy, literacy, English and critical thinking and embedding change within existing institutions – is actively pursued through the delivery approach.

> This form of collaborative working, with its aims of 'promot[ing] and sustain[ing] the learning of all professionals in the school community with the collective purpose of enhancing pupil learning' (Stoll et al., 2005, p. 1), thereby raising standards, promoting pupil participation, and developing effective leadership and management, can be viewed as a vital tool in creating effective policy and shared practice for global learning. (MacCallum and Salam, 2014)

Sazani's experience indicated that the creation of a safe learning space for teachers to accept and act reflexively on their own learning needs was critical to better learning outcomes for learners. LS has more than 140 years of history in Japanese schools and has been shown to dramatically improve learning, teaching and practice in schools and suggested as a method of building pedagogical knowledge of teachers (Ono and Ferreira, 2010; Cerbin and Kopp, 2006). Its application was a natural extension of Sazani's participatory and critical approach to education through global learning in Zanzibar, building on trust and relationships forged for well over a decade. Combining cascade approaches with lesson study, through classroom-based action research cycles, frames the approach. Central to this is the notion of 'criticality' and the belief that content cannot be taught separately from thinking. Teaching knowledge requires not only the passing on of facts, but also teaching how to think and how to use knowledge.

Sazani is supporting continuing joint professional development (CJPD) over four years within fifty-one secondary schools, working with over 300 teachers in Zanzibar. Cascading lesson study through the Healthy and Sustainable Schools Award enables Sazani to continue to support motivated teachers incentivizing them to become cascade teachers and peer educators for their respective schools. Lesson study involves supporting curriculum linked triads (three teachers teaching similar subjects) to work together to plan and peer evaluate each other's lessons, through an action research cycle of plan, do and review. The Healthy and Sustainable School Award, with its focus on whole school development, contextualized curricula and student action, provides a series of cross-curricular topics relevant to the living reality of Zanzibar for the triads to use to support classroom delivery.

Two years in, we are in a position to reflect on the significant achievements and identify challenges of this programme.

Achievements and challenges

In most countries, institutional support is essential for an educational project to happen. Zanzibar, as a small state, is no exception. The Ministry of Education is staffed predominantly by ex-teachers and school heads, who understand the challenges their teachers face and often find it difficult to say no to educational initiatives. Participating schools in return, while grateful for additional resources provided by such initiatives, often find it difficult to combine classroom delivery with project demands. Understanding the limitations of the current education system in Zanzibar, Sazani has focused on the enablers, the deliverers, the teachers and the trainers of teachers. This was grounded in the acknowledgement of the restricted capacity of Sazani as an NGO, without the resources or the will to focus on equipping schools and ministerial offices with artefacts. Through our long association with Zanzibar, Sazani is regarded by the Ministry of Education as being small but very effective, building teacher competence rather than classrooms.

Further to the ministry's blessing and their input, we extended our work to both islands of Zanzibar, meaning that we would be working in Pemba as well as Unguja Island. This presented an initial challenge; as with our initial group of Cascade Teachers in Unguja, we selected teachers we had worked with on previous projects, who had been to Wales and had become global learning practitioners. However, after twenty-four months and provision of training and support to an initial cohort, Cohort A, of thirty-four cascade teachers from seventeen schools across both islands, our mid-term evaluation identified sustainable improvements to the quality of teaching and learning by the transfer of participatory teaching methods between teachers. The review identified that Cascade and Triad teachers alike were committed to the project and motivated by the positive response of pupils, in many cases, using these methods with all the classes they teach, not just the classes involved in the ABC Project.

The review detailed that teachers had a degree of ownership over the project. In the words of one Triad teacher from Pemba Island, 'they are ready to learn, ready to change, ready to teach' (2017 Review). Teacher motivation is critical to learning so has been targeted as a critical resource to develop. The approach has been well received – reportedly pupils are now 'braver', more readily asking for help and expressing their misunderstandings. This was noticed particularly in lower ability students who had previously been fairly disengaged in their learning. Through the Triads, the teachers have displayed a change in approach to problem-solving and discussions in the classroom. The peer reviews have demonstrated increased confidence to engage learners in discussions and to contextualize learning through adapting the healthy and sustainable topic guides for use with their students. Through lesson study the Triads, supported by their cascade teachers, have created safe spaces for teachers, as participants, to interrogate their social attitudes and the general cultural orientation, which underpins their livelihoods and approach to learning, opening 'people's minds to the realities of the world' (Bourn, 2008, p. 8). These collaborative interactions provided a starting point for a 'critical pluralism' (Said, 2003). They have extended the integration of different perspectives, initiated by our previous projects, resulting in an appreciation of vulnerability, interdependence and dissonance.

Teachers and students through active engagement in pupil-centred activities demonstrated enthusiasm to learn and participate. Relating learning to local realities has focused on the learning process, and supported critical thinking, self-reflection and the independent choices of the learner. From focus groups and informal discussion with teachers, it has been seen that while teachers notice the extra workload, the benefits of the action research approach to their practice and to the learning of the students outweighs this.

A profound change was noted in the Pemban Cascade Teachers as well as the Triad Teachers on both islands. Through peer support, peer pressure and collective thought were challenged both at a teacher and a classroom level. Observations have noted an increase in interactions and discussions on what it is to be Zanzibari, Tanzanian, African and an individual as well as discussing the notion of the other, focusing on tourism, and the influx of economic migrants from across East Africa looking for work as well as the tourists themselves. Working to encourage global learning on a small island in the Indian Ocean which has a unique cultural diversity but which has also seen a huge influx of tourists, it is important to promote cultural values and identity in schools.

These findings, while expected and not dissimilar from the outcomes of our previous projects, were welcomed, especially in Pemba. But what of pupil performance? Classroom motivation was indeed a successful outcome, measured through a range of qualitative methods including focus group discussions, classroom observations and learning walks. From focus groups and observations, it can be seen that students in lessons with an ABC teacher are showing more active engagement in their learning.

'Students are being given the opportunity to think and work out answers by themselves, very few teachers in our observations are attempting this unsuccessfully. From these observations we are also seeing that the majority of teachers are also planning participatory tasks which help students enjoy learning in a safe and unthreatening environment' Sazani MEL Report (2018).

The HSSP has been embraced by the vast majority of schools in the programme, demonstrating that teachers are enriching the curriculum through cross-curricular materials, activities and projects. The HSSP student action projects initiated by each school have been varied and demonstrate the diversity of thinking taking place in each school, demonstrating that both teachers and students are engaged and participating. Some projects have been particularly outstanding; examples include herb gardens, breakfast clubs and environmental groups.

Changes in knowledge, attitudes and practice (KAP) of participating teachers and pupils cognitive skills have been assessed through using digital testing with KioKits. KioKits comprise of a box of fifty digital tablets enabling whole classes and teachers groups to be to be assessed three times a year (Figure 13.1).

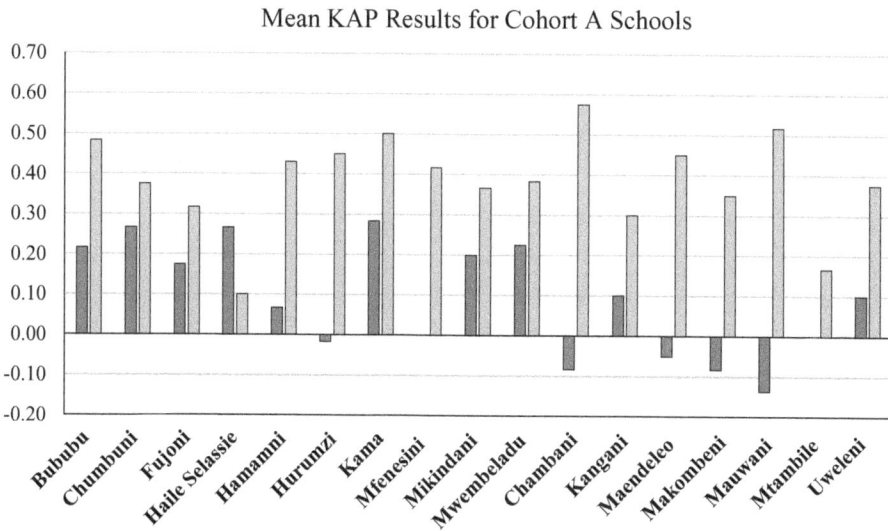

Figure 13.1 Teachers and pupils change in knowledge attitude and practice.

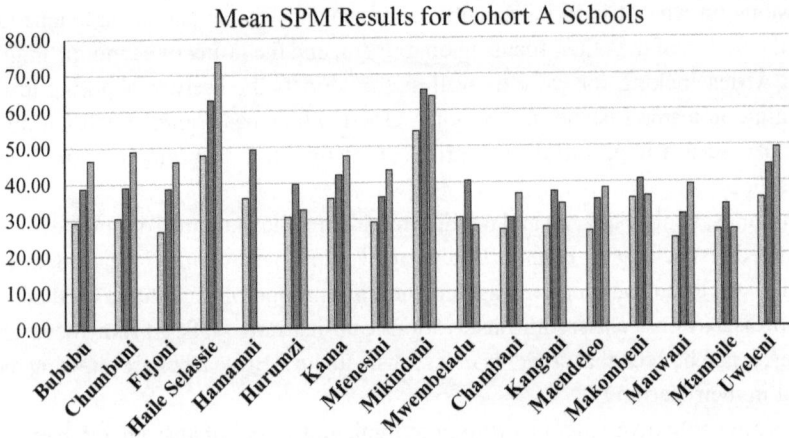

Mean SPM Results for Cohort A Schools

Figure 13.2 Teachers facilitating groupwork, Zanzibar.

From the cohort A data shown in Figure 13.1, the baseline results and the mid-term test results are shaded in two shades of grey. It can be seen that in all except one school, there has been an improvement in the average KAP index. Our lesson observations are highlighting how teachers are confident in using participatory and critical-thinking techniques in their lessons. In particular, group work is often used to stimulate discussion, ideas and learning through peer dialogue (Figure 13.2).

These School Performance Monitoring (SPM) tests were developed using Form 2 (year 2 secondary) past papers and additional questions developed by the Project team, all approved by the Zanzibar Ministry of Education, to assess numeracy, literacy, English language as well as critical thinking, through problem-solving.

From the Cohort A mean SPM results, we are seeing widespread improvements in many schools, From the baseline (light grey), through the midline (dark grey) to, where available the endline (mid grey). All fourteen schools show improvements between the baseline and the midline and ten continue this trend into the endline results.

Lessons learned

The CPD training delivered through the ABC Project has been underpinned by participation and participatory methods. It has drawn extensively on Freire's (1970) approach to generating reflection and critical thinking as a foundation for building and strengthening social change towards informed choice and change. Sazani's work in Zanzibar over the last thirteen years has shown that for participation to be meaningful and productive in transforming a situation, power should be expanded and this requires a combination of trust, reciprocity, reflexivity and self-scrutiny. Sazani's approach to participation continues to ensure that it is not just the 'users and choosers' who are involved. From the ERP Project through to ABC there have been opportunities to strengthen the critical understanding of power and its ability to influence change (MacCallum, 2014; Kabeer, 2005) to make sure that participation is not tokenistic or a way of maintaining power relations. Through the Cascade and Triad Teachers working together across disciplines and subject areas to develop cross-curricular whole school approaches, there was an expansion of understanding and choice and ultimately values, determined by critical scrutiny and reflection on the situation at hand from a range of perspectives. This is what Sen (1997) refers to as freedoms and choice to be and do what you value. This has implications for wider development practice, in terms of the power of identity, sense of place and belonging. All of this contributes to a global learning journey that is as Pettit (2012) suggests, empowering participatory practice that is power-conscious and involves engagement in reflective, experiential and embodied learning to complement analytical insights and processes.

Through the HSSP contextualized curriculum materials and topic guides, Sazani relates this back to Zanzibar's local realities and a critical understanding of global pressures such as tourism and Salafism. The ABC Project continues the global learning journey to develop capability to make informed social and political choices, and encourages development of cognitive skills and key competences, fostering the individual freedoms associated with participation and empowerment, to consider rather than to 'not question'.

8 Global learning for sustainable change

Education in the twenty-first century requires not just a few 'add on skills' but attention to the development of competencies, within which certain skills, values, attitudes, knowledge and understanding are required. The idea that learning can lead to profound change in individuals and communities is an important link between cognitive and basic skills competencies because both the notion of competence as we have described it and the notion of personal and social change are historical, contextualized and value dependent: they imply a sense of direction leading towards a 'desired end'.

Sazani's work in Zanzibar has adopted an approach that is learner-centred, and the ABC programme has shown that learner-centred guidance, group work and inquiry projects can result in better skills and competencies. The ABC Project has so far demonstrated that interactive forms of discussion and inquiry can lead to a more reflective, deeper and participative learning experience, as well as improving individual and whole school performance. Learning by doing, inquiry learning, problem-solving, creativity and so on all play a role as competencies for innovation, and can be enriched and improved. The project has nurtured new and innovative learning approaches, ensured educators are aware of their potential and has supported them in delivering learning.

Taking the Northern construct of global learning out of the Northern classroom and redefining it as a lesson study process in the Global South, it has contributed to the global challenges of plurality and sustainability, to stop making assumptions and to develop adaptive capabilities.

Bibliography

Adger, W. N. (2006). 'Vulnerability'. *Global Environmental Change*, 16 (3), 268–81.

Al Kanaan, C. S. (2007). *Education Assessment of Zanzibar ERP Flagship*. FAO: UNESCO Paris.

Al Kanaan, C. S. and Proctor, M. (2008). 'Sustainable Livelihoods Analysis of Youth in Zanzibar', Unpublished research report Sazani Associates, UK.

Alcock, H. L. and Ramirez Barker, L. (2016). 'Can Global Learning Raise Standards within Pupils' Writing in the Primary Phase?' DERC Research Paper no. 16 for the GLP. London: UCL Institute of Education.

Andreotti, V. and De Souza, L. M. (2008). 'Translating Theory into Practice and Walking Minefields'. *International Journal of Development Education and Global Learning*, 1 (1), 23–36. London: Trentham Books.

Belghith, N. B. H. and De Boisseson, P. M. A. (2017). *Zanzibar Poverty Assessment (English)*. Washington DC: World Bank Group.

Blum, N. (2012). *Education, Community Engagement and Sustainable Development: Negotiating Environmental Knowledge in Monteverde, Costa Rica*. Springer.

Bourn, D. (2008). 'Development Education: Towards a Re-conceptualisation'. *International Journal of Development Education and Global Learning*, 1 (1), 5–22. London: Trentham.

Bourn, D. (2011). 'Global Skills: From Economic Competitiveness to Cultural Understanding and Critical Pedagogy'. *Critical Literacy: Theories and Practices*, 6(1), 3–20.

Bourn, D. (2012). 'Global Learning and Subject Knowledge'. DERC Research Paper No.4, London: IOE.

Bourn, D. and Brown, K. (2011). 'Young People and International Development: Engagement and Learning'. DERC Research Paper No. 2, London: IOE.

Bourn, D. and Issler, S. (2010). 'Transformative Learning for a Global Society'. In G.Elliott, C. Fourali and S. Issler (eds), *Education and Social Change: Connecting Localand Global Perspectives*, 225–37. London: Bloomsbury Publishing.

Cerbin, W. and Kopp, B. (2006). 'Lesson Study as a Model for Building Pedagogical Knowledge and Improving Teaching'. *International Journal of Teaching and Learning in Higher Education*, 18 (3), 250–7.

Cornwall, A. and Brock, K. (2005). 'Beyond Buzzwords: "Poverty Reduction," "Participation" and "Empowerment" in Development Policy', *Overarching Concerns Programme Paper*. Geneva, UNRISD.

Crockett, L., Jukes, I. and Churches, A. (2011). *Literacy Is Not Enough: 21st Century Fluencies for the Digital Age*. Thousand Oaks: Corwin.

DFID (2012). 'Economics of Climate Change in Zanzibar'. DFID, UK.

Freire, P. (1970). *Pedagogy of the Oppressed*. New York: Seabury Press.

Gaventa, J. (2004). 'Participatory Development or Participatory Democracy? Linking Participatory Approaches to Policy and Governance'. *Participatory Learning and Action*, 50, 150–9.

Giroux, H. A. (2012). *B order Crossings: Cultural Workers and the Politics of Education*. New York: Routledge.

Hopkins, D. (2007). *Every School a Great School*. London: Open University Press.

Hussein, A. A. (2002). *Edward Said: Criticism and Society*. London: Verso.

Kabeer, N. (2005). *Inclusive Citizenship: Meaning and Expressions*. London: Zed Books.

Lange, S. (2016). *Achieving Teaching Quality in Sub-Saharan Africa*, VS Verlag für Sozialwissenschaften. DOI: 10.1007/978-3-658-14683-2

Maalim, H. A. (2017). 'Students' Underachievement in English-medium Subjects: The Case of Secondary School in Zanzibar', *Southern African Linguistics and Applied Language Studies*, 35(1), 53–62. DOI: 10.2989/16073614.2017.1284008

MacCallum, C. S. (2014). 'A Global Learning Journey from Sustainable Livelihoods to Adaptive Capabilities in a Small State, Zanzibar'. Ph.D. thesis, University of London.

MacCallum, C. S. (2017). *Zanzibar: A Small Island in a Global Arena in Education in South Asia and the Indian Ocean Islands,* by H. Letchamanan and D. Dhar. London: Bloomsbury Academic Press.

MacCallum, C. S. and Salam, I. (2014). 'Making a Meal out of Global Learning'. *International Journal of Development Education and Global Learning,* 6 (3), IOE Press, UK.

Middleton, J. (1994). *The World of the Swahili: An African Mercantile Civilization.* Yale University Press.

Ono, Y. and Ferreira, J. (2010). 'A Case Study of Continuing Teacher Professional Development Rough Lesson Study in South Africa'. *South African Journal of Education,* 30, 59–74.

Peak, R. (1989). 'Swahili Stratification and Tourism in Malindi Old Town, Kenya'. *Africa,* 59 (2), 209–20.

Pettit, J. G. (2012). 'Getting to Grips with Power: Action Learning for Social Change in the UK', *IDS Bulletin,* Brighton: IDS.

Said, E. (1983). *The World, the Text and the Critic.* Cambridge: Harvard University Press.

Said, E. (1993). *Culture and Imperialism.* New York: Knopf.

Said, E. (1994). *Representations of the Intellectual: The 1993 Reith Lectures.* New York: Vintage Books.

Said, E. (2003). ' At the Rendezvous of Victory'. In D. Barsamian (ed.), *Edward Said, Culture and Resistance.* Cambridge: South End Press.

Scheunpflug, A. (2008). 'Why Global Learning and Global Education? An Educational Approach Influenced by the Perspectives of Immanuel Kant'. In D. Bourn (ed.), *Development Education: Debates and Dialogue,* 18–27. London: Institute of Education.

Scheunpflug, A., Gogolin, I. and Baumert, J. (2011). 'Transforming Education. Largescale Reform Projects in Education Systems and their Effects Umbau des Bildungswesens: bildungspolitische Gro ß reformprojekte undihre Effekte. Wiesbaden: VS Verl'. für Sozialwiss (Sonderheft Zeitschrift für Erziehungswissenschaft, 13).

Sen, A. (1997). 'Editorial: Human Capital and Human Capability'. *World Development,* 25 (12). Ford Foundation.

Spivak, G. (2013). *The Spivak Reader: Selected Works of Gayatri Chakravorty Spivak.* London: Routledge.

Stoll, L., Bolam, R., McMahon, A., Thomas, S., Wallace, M., Greenwood, A. and Hawkey, K. (2005). *What Is a Professional Learning Community? A Summary.* London: DfES.

Tompkins, E. (2005). 'Planning for Climate Change in Small Islands: Insights from theCayman Islands Government', *Global Environmental Change Part A,* 15, 139–49. DOI: 10.1016/j. gloenvcha.2004.11.002

Tourism Concern (July 2012). *'Water Equity in Tourism – A Human Right', A Global Responsibility.* Tourism Concern, UK.

Turner, B. S. (2008). *The Body and Society: Explorations in Social Theory.* ThousandOaks: Sage.

UNESCO (2000). *Education for All, Country Assessment Report, Zanzibar.* Paris: UNESCO.

UNESCO (2013). Education for Sustainable Development (ESD) in the UK – Current status, best practice and opportunities for the future, Policy Brief 9. London: UK National Commission for UNESCO.

UNESCO (2014). 'Education for All 2015, National Review Report'. United Republic of Tanzania – Zanzibar.

UNESCO (2017). Accountability in education: meeting our commitments; Global education monitoring report, 2017/8. UNESCO, Paris.

VSO International (2011). *Leading Learning A Report on Effective School Leadership and Quality Education in Zanzibar.* VSO International, London.

Zanzibar Revolutionary Government (2009). *The Status of Zanzibar Coastal Resources:Towards the Development of Integrated Coastal Management Strategies and ActionPlan.* Zanzibar, Tanzania.

Zanzibar Revolutionary Government (2010). *National ICM Strategies and Action Planfor Zanzibar the National ICM Technical Committee.* Zanzibar, Tanzania.

Zhu, C. and Wang, D. (2014). *Asia Pacific Education Review,* 15 (2), 299–311.

Part IV

Global Perspectives in Higher Education

Chapter 14

Global Education and Integration: A Look into South African Higher Education

Nicolle Chido Manjeya

Introduction

Global education (GE) has remained a very important issue in education over the years. The reputation of education globally has often been around the issue of whether the curriculum being offered in certain countries is good enough to create marketable professionals internationally. A pivotal point of departure: is the given curriculum producing fit professionals for both the local and the international market? Williams (2008) explains that finding African solutions to African problems represents the best approach to keeping peace in Africa. However, in as much as this approach seems to be a solution to solving African problems, more centrally it stands the risk of isolating Africa in educational and developmental aspects. Williams (2008) goes on to explain that instead of searching for 'African solutions', policy-makers should focus on developing effective solutions for the complex challenges that Africa faces, not only in politics but also in education. This chapter seeks to explore how the South African higher educational landscape has approached the idea of global educational integration in the past two decades. The chapter explores salient aspects such as the themes *(actors, transactions, mechanisms, procedures and values)* seen in South African educational history, the link between these themes and social justice, and equity and curriculum content. The chapter also explores the three types of universities in South Africa and how their structures respond to social justice and GE integration. The discussion frame of this chapter looks at how the given policy for GE is designed to train and nurture professionals on theory and practice that is very close to home yet suitable for the global educational platform. This chapter will also give an in-depth definition of GE in the South African context.

Global education

The concept of GE can be looked at from many aspects. In one way, it can be referred to as education that transcends borders and is mainly catered to by distance learning in educational institutions. Alger and Harf (1985) define GE as education that enables people to make decisions while considering the ways in which they are affected by diversity in socio-economic realms of operation. This chapter, therefore, looks at the concept of global policies in education, and hence it is imperative to define what GE in this context is. *Collins Dictionary* (2016) explains that the term 'global' refers to something that happens in and affects all parts of the world. With reference to the above topic under discussion, GE is, therefore, the invisible policies, trends and curricula that set the pace for international standards in education. It is, however, imperative to note that the argument about the notion of GE is that although it is premised on trends that are set globally, in most cases, not all players including the South are involved in the creation of these policies (Bhattacharya and Llanos, 2016). As a result, the concept of GE itself remains a relative term.

In pursuit of understanding this notion Alger and Harf (1985) explain that an adequate understanding of GE can be obtained by focusing on five chosen themes which are the following:

- values
- transactions
- actors
- procedures
- mechanisms

This chapter will explore these themes in relation to the South African system of education to interrogate how the nation's higher education (HE) system is being integrated into the GE system. Alger and Harf (1985) go on to explain that these themes represent a coherent foundation for global understanding that can lead to thoughtful participation and integration.

South African educational background

The complexity of government educational systems in developing countries is such that with the attainment of independence came the adoption of the 'clean slate' rule (Schachter, 1992). This clean slate ensured the transition to a government without any debt or the problems of the previous administration. It is, however, imperative to note, in many states that have been colonized, that the new state government had no history or track record of governing educational systems, and, therefore, they adopted the existing educational scheme from the exiting government. This meant that the educational system established at independence was that of the colonial system. This set a precedent for the curriculum that most countries have today. However, this has not been updated to suit the post-independence development of the new state and educational system. As a result, although the various systems have positively worked to promote education in African models of academic literacy, some countries continue to lag behind in adopting updated policies and in catching up with GE developments. For instance, on the eve of independence in South Africa in 1994, the existing educational system was the Bantu educational system. This system allowed for the education of the larger populace but with specific benefits for the white minority; the majority black populace in South Africa were crippled by silence and forced to accept educational standards that neither developed nor grew beyond the South African borders. It was a system of education that did not value equality, equity and inclusivity (Govender and Rampersad, 2016) not only within South African borders but also internationally. This type of education represented what can be referred to as 'education in chains'. This term 'education in chains' depicts a situation where, although the new government adopted colonial educational systems, it only focused on improving access for the majority and removing access from the minority, as the Bantu system had established. The system, therefore, overlooked future development in education that would keep the profile of HE moving. Radebe (2017) in an article on colonial educational systems posits that 'the continent's colonial education system remains unchanged. It was meant to produce clerks and administrators with a handwriting so beautiful you'd be jealous, but it's totally irrelevant in the world that has moved into a high-tech environment.' This shows that the prospects of development for global integration have been delayed, as issues to do with social justice and equity in the educational system remain unchanged. Like other newly independent states the government had adopted a system of education founded on values non-reflective of what they had fought for, but which they could not change as knowledge of governing educational systems in line with equity and social justice was not available to the new administration. This required time, to learn how to break down the barriers that stigmatized the educational platforms, to see no colour or race in eligibility for education but rather to see the establishment of equity and social justice, and to grow the South African education platform to reach beyond its borders to the global community.

In the years that followed independence, the new administration realized this flaw, and the Department of Higher EducationTraining (2013) (South Africa Department of Education, 1997) established a White Paper in 1997. This White Paper focused on transforming the face of HE and responded to the inequalities in the education system at various levels to eradicate the fragmented and un-coordinated educational system that crippled South Africa.

As a result, the current generation of education has been marred by various attempts to continually adjust to the educational landscape, not only to educate the vast populace in local theories applicable to the South African context but also to fit into global educational trends and developments. In order to develop frameworks that support and encourage integration into the global atmosphere, there was and is a need to look into the educational policies and how they accommodate integration into global education. Before we look into the history of South African education and the main themes that define integration into global education, an overview is described in Figure 14.1.

The above cycle illustrates that South African educational policies revolve around the main core themes of mechanisms, transactions, values, procedures and actors. In drafting the South African policies, all themes have constantly and intricately been included to put together a curriculum suitable for regional, continental and global integration. Watson (2009) explains that the blueprint of these structures mimics not only global standards but also African regional standards to seamlessly merge curriculum policy into regional clusters of GE and to link it to global clusters of education. While this is a positive move in the right direction, it is imperative to note that HE analysis at the level of national policy is no longer adequate to account for the many changes in curriculum, as most educational policies and frameworks are simultaneously dealing with the challenges arising from integration in GE (Moja and Cloete, 2001; Enders, 2004; Watson, 2009). As a result, the cost of integration into GE holds strong implications for the identity of national and regional educational perspectives. However, in as much as integration comes at a cost, these moves are a significant blueprint in the development of policies that are suitable for global integration. Looking at the South African perspective it is important to understand the themes in Figure 14.1:

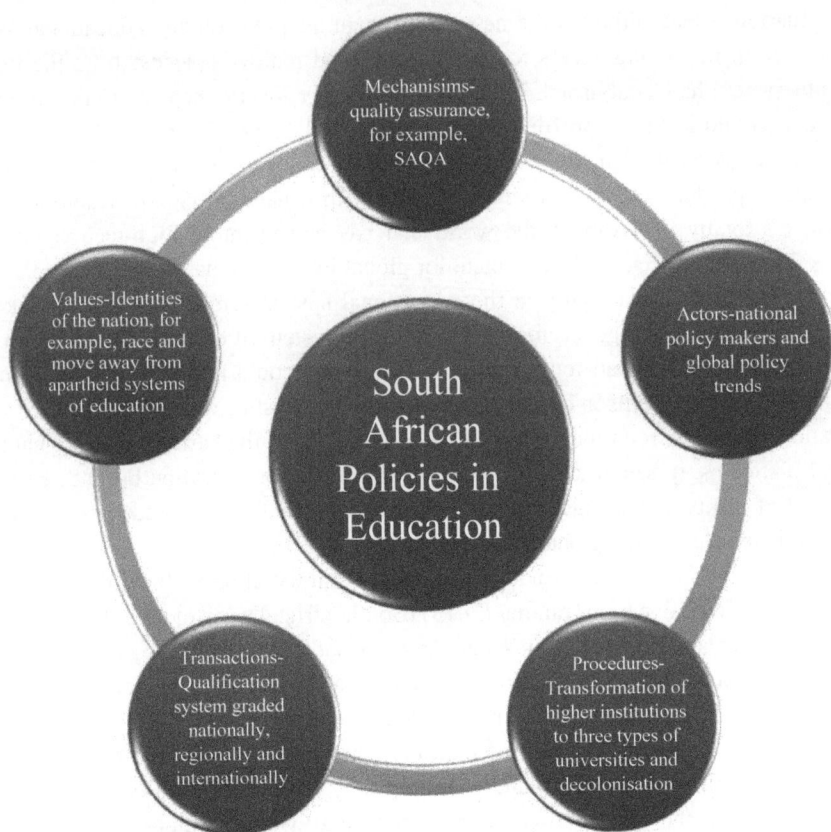

Figure 14.1 South African educational themes.

Mechanisms: These identify the processes in HE that promote the exchange and transfer of qualifications across borders. In the South African context an example can be the South African Qualification Authority (SAQA), which is a regional mechanism to qualify educational standards within the region. The operational framework of this body is structured to advance the objectives of the National Qualifications Framework (NQF) of South Africa both nationally and globally (South African Qualifications Authority, 2014) Therefore, as an instrument facilitating the integration of global education, SAQA has managed to gain support and recognition by similar qualification authorities globally (Van der Westhuizen and Van Vuuren, 2007).

Values: Aspects of the theme of values cover the identity of the nation and the region and embrace the specific struggles of that nation which are embedded in the policies that form the basis of all curriculum plans. In the case of South Africa, the values that include the creation of GE polices were guided by precepts of experiences from apartheid.

Transactions: These are the systems that govern the standards that integrate qualifications into national, regional, continental and global benchmarks. This theme is brought to life by qualification bodies that define the true position of a university or any institution offering professional education to be marketable not only nationally but beyond borders, defining GE integration.

Procedures: This theme is strongly linked to transactions and this is the stage in which the process that defines global integration is brought to life. This theme constitutes the transformation of universities and introduction of a new grading system that is marketable globally. The procedures are also linked to values as they have in place issues such as decolonization of the curriculum, a very salient issue in HE which identifies with the core national values of a state (decolonization is not explored in this chapter but used as an example).

Actors: These comprise of the national policy-makers and drafters of the curriculum and the global actors whose influence is of pivotal importance in drafting curricula for HE.

As a result, the above themes define the main aspects that govern integration into the GE platform. This chapter will slot the above themes into the educational histology of South African education and examine how these themes encouraged the introduction of universities of technology (UoTs), comprehensive universities and traditional universities in South African HE and how these important aspects identify with GE integration. It is safe to note that there are more clarifying issues that identify with South African integration into HE, but this chapter will focus solely on the transformation and history of South African education and how the above themes continue to impact on the development of South African HE into the global platform.

The history and evolution of South African education

The history of South African education falls under the themes of *values*, *actors* and *mechanisms*. This idea is premised on the fact that the build-up of the South African educational system was based on core values that emanated from the apartheid system of education. The values embraced adopting a system that advocated for equal education and access to all races regardless of colour. It is imperative to note that the histology of South African education is based on the 1990 turnaround, which marked an important turning point in South African curriculum debates. Until 1990 the educational platform was characterized by a uniform and predictable curriculum policy environment (Jansen and Christie, 1999). The main values that characterized the South African system of HE were derived from the need to impose a design that entrenched power and privilege to the white minority (Bunting, 2006). All HE systems that were established prior to 1994 were to serve the goals and strategies of successive apartheid governments. This aligned well with the core themes of values, actors and mechanism. The value system was based on the protection of the white minority in education, actors being the white minority themselves and the mechanisms had little or close to no endeavours towards global integration, relying purely on a privilege system of education.

There is much debate around the values and actors of this system and how it not only disadvantaged the black majority but also lacked global integration in its education mechanisms. Bunting (2006) explains that South Africa's first and second democratic governments sought to reshape the system to one that identified with the national values, procedures, transactions, mechanisms and actors of the new government, and to restructure in a way that fits the regional and global standards in education. This reshaping focused on moving away from the fragmented and un-coordinated educational system that had been established in the 1980s under the apartheid regime but did nothing to reshape the system for future technological advancements in education.

Cooperation and Development (2008) explains that

historically, education was central to successive Apartheid governments' efforts to segregate racial groups and maintain white minority rule, and featured prominently in the struggle that eventually brought about a negotiated settlement in 1994. The new democratic government was faced with the task of both rebuilding the system and redressing past inequalities. It has concentrated on creating a single unified national system, increasing access (especially to previously marginalised groups and the poor), decentralising school governance, revamping the curriculum, rationalising and reforming further and higher education and adopting pro-poor funding policies.

These reforms are focused not only on improving access to education within the local spheres of education but also on expanding the ambit of education beyond the South African borders.

The themes in education systems identified with the histology of the South African context are what created a strong foundation that builds on the integration of the nation's HE into global trends and curriculum structures.

Structure of higher education in South Africa

As we have already discussed the themes that define and shape South African educational policy and GE integration, this section looks at the structure of HE in South Africa. The structures of South African universities explain the theme *mechanisms* because the restructuring of HE marked a step forward in global integration and standards in education. *Procedures* as a theme indicated the expansion of HE to upgrade the South African standards to match global ideals. Finally, the *actors* who are the types of universities in South Africa identify with policy-makers who constantly work to make sure mechanisms and procedures are suitable to ensure smooth identification and integration into the global educational community.

Configuration of the South African HE landscape was initiated in 1995 (Du Pre, Reddy and Scott, 2004). This was a move that had been coupled by efforts to eradicate the Bantu educational system which created rifts and gaps in HE not only for the educators but also for the learners. As a result, in 2004, through a process of mergers and re-designation, South Africa's thirty-six HE institutions (twenty-one traditional universities and fifteen Technikons) were trimmed down to twenty-three, consisting of eleven traditional universities, six comprehensive universities (arising out of mergers between traditional universities and Technikons) and six universities of technology (created from eleven merged and unmerged Technikons) (CHE, 2010). The creation and re-designation of these universities were based on offering and providing career-oriented programmes and to further streamline and harmonize the activities of all tertiary institutions in South Africa in order to position them in line with global benchmarks to attract the finest students and staff. The South African government, therefore, introduced three main universities: first, the Traditional University that comprised of the universities already existent prior to the restructuring of the educational platform. These universities offer theoretically oriented degrees; the second type of university established was the Comprehensive University, arising from the merger of Technikons and universities. These universities offer a variety of theoretically oriented degrees and vocational diplomas and degrees; and finally, the UoTs that are research informed and not research driven, their primary focus being on strategic and applied research that can be transformed into professional practice. The UoT environment in South Africa is such that the institutions offer technical subjects with a strong connection to practice in industry and, as a result, are practice-oriented. UoTs, therefore, have skilled lecturers in not only theory but also the practical aspects of each subject area that the institution covers. Because these types of institution are only recently developing into research hubs and moving away from technical institutions, they are located in areas that are closely related to the main expertise of the particular region. For instance, Durban University of Technology is located in the KwaZulu-Natal province which has its main operations and expertise around maritime studies, operations management and engineering, all professions that support the economic growth of this region.

As a result, universities in South Africa have evolved and grown to suit the context in which they are based, and have harmonized their activities with the global community through integrating their specific curriculum to suit the current educational debate in Africanization and indigenization on the nature of the South African HE curriculum (Le Grange, 2016).

Table 14.1 An Illustration of the Structure of HE in South Africa

Universities of Technology	Comprehensive Universities	Traditional Universities
Cape Peninsula University (CPU)	The University of Johannesburg (UJ)	North West University (NWU)
The Central University of Technology (CUT)	Nelson Mandela Metropolitan University (NMMU)	Rhodes University (RU)
Durban University of Technology (DUT)	The University of South Africa (UNISA)	The University of Cape Town (UCT)
Mangosuthu University of Technology (MUT)	The University of Venda (UV)	The University of Free State (UFS)
The University of Mpumalanga	The University of Zululand (UNIZULU)	The University of KwaZulu-Natal (UKZN)
Sol Plaatje University	Walter Sisulu University (WSU)	The University of Limpopo (UL)
Tshwane University of Technology (TUT)	Sol Plaatje University (SPU)	The University of Pretoria (UP)
Vaal University of Technology (VUT)	Mpumalanga University (MP)	The University of Stellenbosch (US)
		The University of the Western Cape (UWC)
		The University of Witwatersrand (UW)
		University of Fort Hare (UFT)

The composition and structure of universities in South Africa show that in mechanisms there have been significant strides to integrate the HE system into the global community. The issue of international engagement in South African universities is, however, marred by various stumbling blocks. A specific example is the international office in UoT. In a meeting on decolonizing the curriculum, a staff member noted that international integration in education is only seen as engagement with the West instead of engagement with our SADC or African Union counterparts. As this was a view from a highly engaged staff member in the international office of UoT, the question now is the following: What are the engagement paradigms in a traditional or comprehensive university?

The notion of engagement with international platforms shows the level to which HE is developing. Through engagement there is a shared repertoire and exchange of knowledge which highlights the developments in global education, hence opening doors for development and change.

Therefore, our main focus goes back to how the design of these three institutions addresses the principal themes of global education. Muller (2010) explains the structure of all three universities as being characterized by three main pillars: research, teaching and community engagement. By design these three pillars are able to cater for all the themes in education required for integration regionally, continentally and internationally. This then seems to take the bottom-up approach to integration, beginning from what serves this region, then the continent and lastly the world. This structure of integration is explained by processes that define communities of practice, as explained by (Tight and Development, 2004) and (Wenger, 2010). It is only through social-learning systems and shared knowledge and understanding that policies which are favourable to and support equity and social justice are established. It is the establishment of such policies in all universities and their types that defines how South Africa has designed its integration into the global platform of education. This provides a re-designation and design that nurture a system of HE that is relevant in practice and theory. This relates to previous discussions on the values of the governing systems of the apartheid system of government, which identified regions as individual countries and grouped them thus (Bunting, 2006). These specific links were derived from the mechanisms and procedures of apartheid educational policies, whose ambit did not stretch into a global system of education but rather was centralized to address and cater for the values, transactions, procedures and mechanisms of the system.

Education, social justice and equity: The South African educational paradigm

The themes in education systems around the world have defined and set the pace for various nations' educational sectors and curriculum content. Because of the ubiquity of politics most of the content and set-up structures have been separated from the influence of politics nationally and globally. The South African educational paradigm has been shaped and marred by various influences, from the Bantu educational system to democratic structures with social justice and equity for all. Brennan and Naidoo (2008) explain that concepts such as equity and social justice

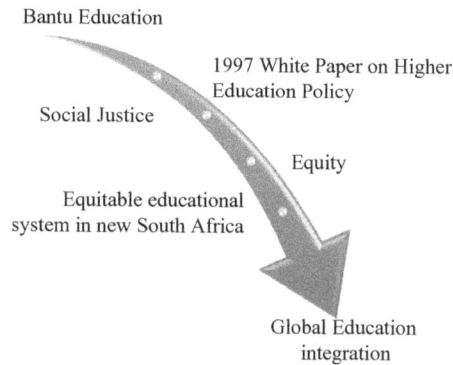

Figure 14.2 South African educational paradigm.

in education have received considerable attention, hence questioning whether the educational landscape in South Africa before it integrates into the GE community offers equitable and fair access to HE for all. With reference to this statement and having traced the evolution of South African education and the themes that influence interaction not only regionally but also connected with the GE community, Figure 14.2 illustrates the South African educational paradigm.

This illustration shows that prior to 1997 the system of education did not represent or embody social justice, equity or space for curriculum growth and development. This was so because the existing system did not cater for equitable engagements with the community to enhance the educational system and the community, nation and continent and so on. This idea is explicitly explained by Muller (2010) and Hall (2010) who, in their analysis of the various arguments made by various scholars on community engagement in South African HE, conclude that because community engagement in tertiary education at this point in South Africa could not be theorized and explained, the structure of universities supported research and teaching and learning activities and had little or no funding for engagement activities; hence social justice, equity and curriculum development were issues thrown around the surface of HE, significant only to the contexts in which they were raised.

With much dissatisfaction around the structure of Bantu education and the limitations it presented, not only locally but internationally, the government of South Africa decided to implement a White Paper on HE in 1997 (South Africa Department of Education, 1997). This White Paper marked the transformation of HE in South Africa. Policies became more intentional in embracing values, mechanisms, transactions and procedures that encouraged the curricula of tertiary education to grow, to embrace research, teaching and learning and the debatable issue of community engagement. It was under this huge umbrella that social justice was catered for, by allowing free access to education for the previously marginalized. Inclusion of social justice in HE as part of the procedures and mechanisms to improve education restructured operational and administrative frameworks of institutions to include engagement with the community. This change fitted the definition of social justice by Zajda, Majhanovich and Rust (2006) as embracing an equitable and just society of education for everyone. Hence, equity and growth of the curriculum followed, by considering that the exchange in teaching and research was open to the global educational platform. In as much as this was a move in the right direction it should not be discounted that the previous educational system had its advantages and served its purpose well for its time and era. However, moving forward, the new transformation and age represented by the White Paper in 1997 did have its challenges, with the very same purposes for which it was created. These challenges represented the main themes that shape education, but also questioned their existence with regard to structure, support and funding for engagement processes for social justice in education, which impacted on research and teaching and learning. From one's analysis the question then arises: If this new system continues to question social justice and equity without engaging locally, how will global educational integration then be incorporated?

Global education and social justice

The idea of social justice in HE continues to receive much attention with regard to how the concept itself engages with the main themes in HE in South Africa. This is because one cannot talk about transactions, values, mechanisms, procedures and actors without regarding the positive or negative connotations of social justice to these themes. Brennan and Naidoo (2008) question how social justice can be used to create more equitable and just educational spaces for all – nationally, regionally and globally. The problem that often happens with social justice research in HE is that instead of looking outside for the support structures of HE that promote social justice through engagement (Hall, 2010), universities often only look inward. A brief look into the operational policy framework of HE in South Africa reveals that core responsibilities of HE revolve around research, teaching and engagement. However, the arm that supports engagement is the arm which has unfortunately been neglected because of lack of resources, funding and motivation. Engagement in HE connects research and learning not only to the community but also to the global educational platform, as it encourages engagement that looks both inside and outside, to develop both communities and resemble social justice.

With regard to the core values of HE, Brennan and Naidoo (2008) discuss that the structure of HE imports equity and social justice from a wider society to integrate with the global community by starting locally. This is seen in how the pillars of HE were shifted in 1997 (Hall, 2010; Muller, 2010; Bender, 2008; South Africa Department of Education, 1997; Department of Higher Education Training, 2013). The landscape thus negotiated required the main pillars in education to include a community engagement clause. Thus, the original pillars were teaching and research, then the extension of community engagement was added. This extension ensured equity and social justice: by involving and promoting social and economic interaction with the community, the institutions came a step closer in improving social justice and equity, moving towards global integration through the operational frameworks of the institution. The intersection and infusion models of community engagement, as coined by Bender (2008), represent how the South African HE landscape is moving towards global integration. Both models advocate for service-learning, community-based research and learning, and simultaneous functioning of research, teaching and engagement. The notion of social justice argues that it is only promoted when there is social, economic and political access to learning and teaching for all. By integrating and promoting social interaction, HE in South Africa is rapidly moving towards global integration in education.

It is important to note that community engagement as a pillar supports the themes explained by Alger and Harf (1985). Only by making these dependant on each other, as when teaching, learning, research and community engagement are put together, do social justice and equity exist at the core of all active processes, values, mechanisms and transactions. These pillars are operated with the central focus of promoting social justice and eventually bear a strong influence on the curriculum. The impact of social justice is influenced by looking inside the institution on how to develop civic responsibility and extending engagement outside for structures that encourage curriculum development in support of the three pillars in education.

Conclusion

Global education like IT continues to change its profile, and procedures and mechanisms in which nations can keep abreast of each other are constantly being changed and tested through transaction, values and actors. The South African educational landscape has experienced many changes from a system of education that was dominated by a powerful minority to a more democratic and equitable system of education that embraces social justice and equity in education. This chapter has explored the main themes that built up the South African HE system, and has interrogated how the changes experienced in this evolution and transformation promoted global educational integration. The chapter has looked at the educational paradigm in South African HE and the journey it has taken from Bantu educational systems to equitable educational systems that are moving towards global education. The chapter, therefore, concludes that HE in South Africa continues to move towards more equitable policies and structures in order to promote global integration and interaction by focusing on models that cut across values, procedures, mechanisms, transactions and actors to encourage equitable and equal policies in education. Hence, it is safe to note that South African HE continues to work towards these structures and policies to provide education that is marketable nationally and internationally.

Bibliography

Council on Higher Education (CHE) (2010). *Universities of Technology: Deepening the Debate*. In CHE (ed.), Pretoria, South Africa: Council on Higher Education.

Alger, C. F. and Harf, J. E. (1985). *Global Education: Why? For Whom? About What?*. Washington: American Association for teacher Education.

Bender, G. J. P. I. E. (2008). Exploring conceptual models for community engagement at higher education institutions in South Africa: Conversation. *Perspectives in Education* 26, 81–95.

Bhattacharya, D. and Llanos, A. O. (2016). *Southern Perspectives on the Post-2015 International Development Agenda*, Taylor & Francis.

Brennan, J. and Naidoo, R. J. H. E. (2008). Higher education and the achievement (and/or prevention) of equity and social justice. *Higher Education* 56, 287–302.

Bunting, I. (2006). The higher education landscape under apartheid. In N. Cloete et al. (eds), *Transformation in Higher Education*, Dordrecht: Springer, 35–52.

Collins Dictionary (2016). *Collins English Dictionary – Complete & Unabridged 2012 Digital Edition*, William Collins Sons & Co. Ltd.

Department of Higher Education Training (2013). White Paper for Post-School Education and Training. Building an expanded, effective and integrated post-school system. Department of Higher Education and Training Pretoria.

Du Pre, R., Reddy, J. and Scott, G. (2004). The philosophy of a university of technology in South Africa: An introduction. *Sediba sa Thuto* 1, 19–37.

Enders, J. J. H. E. (2004). Higher education, internationalisation, and the nation-state: Recent developments and challenges to governance theory. *Higher Education* 47, 361–82.

Govender, V. and Rampersad, R. (2016). Change management in the higher education landscape: a case of the transition process at a South African University. *Risk governance & control: financial markets & institutions* 6 (1), 43–51.

Hall, M. (2010). Council of Higher Education. *Community engagement in South African higher education*. South Africa: Jacana Media.

Jansen, J. D. and Christie, P. (1999). *Changing Curriculum: Studies on Outcomes-based Education in South Africa*, Juta and Company Ltd.

Legrange, L. (2016). Decolonising the university curriculum: Leading article. *South African Journal of Higher Education*, 30, 1–12.

Moja, T. and Cloete, N. (2001). Vanishing borders and new boundaries. In: Castells, M., Muller, J., Cloete, N. and Badat, S. (eds) *Challenges of Globalisation: South African Debates with manuel Castells*. Cape Town: Maskew Miller Longman (pty) Ltd, 244–70.

Muller, J. J. C., (2010). *Community Engagement in South African Higher Education*, Johannesburg: Council of Higher Education. Engagements with Engagements.

Organisation of Economic Co-operation and Development (OECD) (2008). *Reviews of National Policies for Education*. South Africa: OECD publishing.

Radebe, H. (2017). Overhaul Colonial Education System. *News 24*, 28 May 2017.

Schachter, O. (1992). State Succession: The Once and Future Law. *Heinonline* 33, 253.

South Africa Department of Education (1997). Education White Paper 3: A programme for the transformation of higher education. In Department of Education (ed.), Department of Education Pretoria, South Africa.

South African Qualifications Authority (2014). South African Qualifications Authority [Online]. South Africa: South African Qualifications Authority. Available: http://www.saqa.org.za/show.php?id=5658 (Accessed 25 March 2019).

Tight, M. (2004). Research into higher education: An a-theoretical community of practice? *Higher Education Research and Development* 23, 395–411.

van der Westhuizen, P. and van Vuuren, H. (2007). Professionalising principalship in South Africa. *South African Journal of Education* 27, 431–46.

Watson, P. (2009). Regional themes and global means in supra-national higher education policy. *Higher Education* 58 (3), 419–38.

Wenger, E. (2010). Communities of practice and social learning systems: the career of a concept. In: Blackmore, C. (ed.). *Social learning systems and communities of practice*. United Kingdom: Springer, 179–98.

Williams, P. D. (2008). Keeping the peace in Africa: Why 'African' solutions are not enough. *Ethics & International Affairs*, 22, 309–29.

Zajda, J., Majhanovich, S. and Rust, V. (2006). Education and social justice: Issues of liberty and equality in the global culture. *Education and Social Justice*, Springer.

Chapter 15

Towards an Ethical Global Citizenship Education Curriculum Framework in the Modern University

Emiliano Bosio

Introduction

Global Citizenship Education (GCE) has been described by some scholars as crucial to humans flourishing in a context of global interdependence (Bosio and Gaudelli, 2018, February 7), as an educational process which fosters learners who may appreciate others more for their differences than for their similarities (Bosio and Torres, 2019) and as a combination of educational practices which aims at fostering 'contributive' students (Bosio and Joffee, 2018, November 18). On the other hand, given the circumstances of knowledge societies (Castells, 1997) and growing neoliberalism (Bourn, 2018; Held and McGrew, 2000), teachers are challenged to recognize the fluctuating profiles of learners' learning, knowledge and societies (Bosio and Schattle, 2017, November 6) and offer appropriate pedagogical responses that support students to develop ethics through facilitating the development of skills and knowledge that are thought necessary for students to be able to critically assess and evaluate inequitable educational and societal structures and practices (Giroux, 1988a), and inspire them to shape and exercise their agency in cognizant ways (Andreotti, 2011; Bosio and Torres, 2018, March 3).

Applying this principle to the definition of a GCE-curriculum requires an acknowledgement that as an ethical imperative it can be understood and consequently designed and implemented by teachers, in different ways, from diverse theoretical orientations; yet, while a growing number of universities positioned themselves as leading players in fostering 'global citizens' (Bourn, 2018/2011; Dorio, 2017; Bosio, 2017a; Bosio et al., 2018; Shultz, 2007), few studies (Rapoport, 2010; Moon and Koo, 2011; Dill, 2013; Schweisfurt, 2006; Goren and Yemini, 2016) have specifically examined teachers' perspectives on how they engage in implementing principles of global citizenship in a modern university curriculum.

This chapter examines GCE in relation to the higher education (HE) curriculum in the United States, the United Kingdom and Japan. Forty-four teachers teaching global citizenship graduate and undergraduate courses at public and private universities located in the United States, the United Kingdom and Japan responded to an open-ended questionnaire which asked them to describe the core elements of their GCE-curriculum design that best equip their graduates to be 'global citizens'. Through the teachers' responses, the author identifies three dimensions of a GCE-curriculum design: (1) inclusive self/identity, (2) critical cognizance and (3) ecotistical/ ecocritical view. This chapter concludes by suggesting that an ethical GCE-curriculum, designed around the development of these three dimensions, provides a potential framework to teaching and learning in HE that challenges dominant neoliberal notions of the linkages between globalization and education, and adequately equips educators to respond to the complex local and global challenges that they currently face in fostering learners to be global citizens.

GCE-curriculum: A multivocal 'symbol'

A possible understanding of a GCE-curriculum is that it is simply a list of topics to be taught in order to equip students to 'go-global' and be readily employable in a globalized job market. However, a more nuanced, and perhaps more rooted, conceptualization considers that a GCE-curriculum is based on ethics and that teachers' beliefs about the nature of knowledge, and the nature of teaching and learning about global citizenship, will all play an important role in GCE-curriculum decision-making. In other words, the kind of 'global learning' that teachers want students to engage in will frame many of the GCE-curriculum choices they make.

Nonetheless, GCE-curriculum as it applies in the modern university includes a variety of interpretations and ideologies which situate it as a multivocal symbol (Turner, 1975). Each actor brings their own interests and priorities when addressing this topic and in turn, these ideologies can come into conflict with each other as each party stakes its claim as the dominant interpretation. These ideological positions are reflected in the language and discourse that is used to describe GCE-curriculum. Whether these ideologies prioritize neoliberalism, humanitarianism or critical social justice, the choices of language, rhetoric and logic construct their own definition of GCE-curriculum.

'Ideologies are the frameworks of thinking and calculation about the world – the "ideas" that people use to figure out how the social world works, what their place is in it, and what they ought to do' (Hall, 1986, p. 97). Ideologies are constructed and circulated through discourse. For instance, a GCE-curriculum articulating a position regarding identity, values, participation and knowledge constitutes an expression of belief about citizenship. Such expressions, by the very language and ways of thinking they employ, construct meanings of citizenship, privileging some meanings over others by means of choices of language, logic or rhetoric.

Neoliberal as a 'dominant' expression of GCE-curriculum

The 'dominant' expression of a GCE-curriculum, the *Neoliberal* has been described by some researchers as 'the new imperialism' (Archibugi, 2008), 'corporate cosmopolitanism' (Rizvi, 2009) and as 'neoliberal cosmopolitanism' (Gowan, 2009). By others, this type of approach to a GCE-curriculum is characterized as the international elite intent upon colonizing an ever-expanding 'neoliberalizing space' of privatization and deregulation (Bosio, 2017a), competition and economic efficiency, and freedom of individual choice (Peck and Tickle, 2002). The idea of a GCE-curriculum based on these neoliberal and corporatist principles, as described by Rizvi (2009, p. 259), 'suggests that the market, as a single global sphere of free trade, has the potential to promote greater intercultural understanding and peace'. Or, as advocated by Gowan (2001, p. 79), it proposes 'a single human race peacefully united by free trade and common legal norms, led by states featuring civic liberties and representative institutions'. Calhoun (2002) and Ray (2007) are more 'extreme' and refer to neoliberal perspectives of a GCE-curriculum as tools to 'mask' the persistent and growing inequalities within and across societies. These inequalities, they believe, are both structural and systemic, but are also part of consciousness and everyday life. Indeed, it is precisely because inequalities are internalized in this way – as part of the taken-for-granted, 'given' and 'natural' order of life as we live it – that they become structurally and systemically embedded within the curriculum and classroom practices.

In explicit terms, a neoliberal curriculum is one that promotes competition and where the word 'global' suggests above all a focus on profitability. The Global Business Center (GBC) at the University of Washington Foster School of Business in Seattle embodies neoliberal discourse. With options fluctuating from study abroad to case competitions, the GBC mission states that they 'develop [students'] global business expertise by hosting and sponsoring outstanding international education initiatives', the conclusive goal being achieved in the aggressive job market. They operate on a number of MBA courses and certificates (e.g. the Global Business Certificate), and cyclical 'case competitions' that include explicit emphasis on preparing students for success in international markets. Examples include the *Global Business Case Competition* – 'an annual international case competition that brings together undergraduate university students from across the globe to compete in a fast-paced and challenging business case study'; the *Russell Investments International Case Competition* – 'an annual event in which teams of undergraduate business students apply their knowledge and skills to a real-life international business problem'; and the *Global Business Forum* – 'an engaging MBA class and discussion forum where professionals from around the world share their insights into the complexities of doing business globally – differences encountered, obstacles overcome, advantages discovered, and solutions developed' (Foster School of Business, n.a.).

Yet, the upfront emphasis of GBC on market-readiness through curriculum goals that are aimed at teaching students 'doing business' and 'to compete in a fast-paced and challenging business' would suggest a focus on fostering 'global workers' (Hammond and Keating, 2018) who are readily employable for the job market rather than 'global citizens' who should utilize knowledge, skills and values gained in the programme to shape more just and peaceful societies (Bosio et al., 2018).

Critical/post-colonial, transformative and value-creating as anti-hegemonic perspectives of GCE-curriculum

There are discursive perspectives that challenge narrow, competition-based and typically Western-centric neoliberal conceptions of GCE-curriculum to call for more critical, transformative and spiritual stances. For example, a 'critical post-colonial GCE-curriculum' addresses the origins of global poverty and inequality (de Oliveira Andreotti et al., 2016), contrasting 'ahistorical and depoliticized conceptualizations of poverty, presumption of a single, unilinear path of human progress, and of the universal value of Western knowledge, technology, mode of governance (i.e., liberal democracy), and capitalist economy', and as an attempt to subvert 'continuation of colonial logics' (Stein, Andreotti and Suša, 2016, pp. 5–6). It seeks to reveal how discourses of internationalization, globalization and neoliberalism perpetuate unequal relations of colonialism. Such a perspective draws attention to the false universalism of globalization and show how contemporary social, political, economic and cultural practices continue to be located within the processes of cultural domination through the imposition of imperial structures of power (Rizvi, 2007). It also attempts to redress the inequalities, exploitation and injustices that are imposed by (neo)colonization on former colonies and also to disrupt 'the persistent "neo-colonial" relations within the "new" world order' (Bhabha, 1994, p. 6).

An example of critical/post-colonial discourse is the master's degree (MA) in global and international citizenship education at the University of York in the UK where faculty members teach about global citizenry through courses such as citizenship education which examines 'ideas about citizenship as a formal legal and political status, as identity and as a set of practices'; gender, sexuality and education which examines 'ways in which gender influences children and young people's access to, participation in, and outcomes of education' and social justice and education which explores 'overarching conceptual considerations to do with social justice in educational contexts (e.g. achieved by exploring educational issues through the lens of inclusion, equality, diversity)' (University of York, n.a.). Through these and other similar courses the curriculum places major emphasis on identity, gender and social justice in a global context; in this perspective, teachers encourage their students to learn about globalization from a critical rather complimentary stance.

Approaches to a GCE-curriculum have also been defined by some as being 'transformative' (e.g. multicultural, rights-based, universal and collaborative) (UNESCO, 2014; Gaudelli, 2016; Tarozzi and Torres, 2017; Bosio, 2017b); this approach calls for a curriculum that aims to foster and promote not only skills but, most importantly, values such as empathy, solidarity and respect for differences and diversity, and actions to address human rights, poverty and environmental issues. A transformative approach to a GCE-curriculum acknowledges that there is a need to transform not only university practices and systems but also personal and cultural mindsets. It has a clear focus on self-reflection, awareness and action, which are all necessary for challenging global power structures. It is both a skill-set and a mindset. Mezirow (2003, p. 58) described transformative learning as leading to students becoming 'more inclusive, discriminating, open, reflective and emotionally able to change'. Elias (1997) suggested three dimensions of transformative learning: (1) an interpersonal setting that offers emotional support and guarantees that all participants have equivalent access to information and practices of information exchange; (2) personal capacities for self-awareness, discernment and inner dialogue, and critical reflection; and (3) the 'elasticity' within students and the group to approach the learning experience critically. An important part of transformative learning is then for learners to change their frames of reference by diagnostically reflecting on their assumptions and beliefs and consciously making and implementing plans that bring about new ways of defining their worlds (Clark and Wilson, 1991).

The MA in global citizenship, identities and human rights offered by the University of Nottingham in the UK offers an example of a transformative GCE-curriculum. This MA explores 'recent changes to the global cultural and political landscape, and what these mean for individuals and groups accessing their human rights'. Specifically, faculty members focus on teaching sensitive issues such as 'war, migration, climate change, credit crunch, nationalism, global media, sex tourism, modern slavery, gender and sexuality, and contemporary racism'. Two examples of modules within the MA include human rights and critical modern slavery module and globalization, citizenship and identity module. In the former, teachers focus on topics such as 'human trafficking, prostitution, domestic servitude, worst forms of child labour, forced labour and bonded labour in a number of sectors and regions' by offering to students 'an opportunity to critically deconstruct the theoretical and political assumptions that underpin this discourse'; through the latter module, which examines topics from 'imagined communities to the shock of denationalization', faculty members discuss in the classroom about 'ethnicity, globalisation and resistance identities, transnationalism and diasporas, and theories of contemporary racism' (University of Nottingham, n.a.). It is through this process of critical thinking, perceptiveness and metacognition (see Elias, 1997) that teachers support their MA students to acquire a renewed or 'transformed' perspective of societal relationships in relation to local and global: Global North and Global South.

In a view of global citizenship influenced by Buddhist ideals (Schattle, 2008), a group of scholars proposes a *value-creating* orientation to the GCE-curriculum (Bosio, 2017a; Sharma, 2018; Goulah and Ito, 2012) which emphasizes the need to address the persistent development of students' humanity through creative coexistence with others and the development of their capacity to find meaning, to enhance one's own existence and contribute to the well-being of others, under any circumstance. The value-creating dimension of GCE has its origins in the notion of Soka (hereafter value-creating), as it was articulated by the Japanese educator Tsunesaburo Makiguchi (1871–1944). In Makiguchi's view, value-creating education focuses on the development of fully engaged human beings and makes developing the three dimensions of wisdom (i.e. to recognize the interconnectedness of all human lives), courage (i.e. not to reject differences and to attempt to comprehend people from different walks of life) and compassion (i.e. that which is beyond one's immediate contexts and encompasses those suffering in distant places) the objective of each individual (Makiguchi, 2000). In his 1903 work on geography, Makiguchi proposed a three-tiered scheme of identity, urging that we be aware of ourselves as simultaneously citizens of a local community, of the national community and of the world. Thus, Makiguchi's positing of 'society' implicitly opens up the idea of intercultural negotiation towards the formation of a larger moral consensus, and ultimately the values of a value-creating GCE-curriculum (Gebert, 2009; Noddings, 2003). In this view, Makiguchi's vision for value-creating GCE, as outlined in his book *A Geography of Human Life* (Makiguchi, 2002) and subsequently in his pedagogical philosophy, could be translated into a core number of 'requirements' that learners might embrace in order not only to understand the notion of global citizenship but perhaps, most importantly, to act as 'global citizens'. As I illustrated in previous publications (Bosio, 2017b), these are (1) respect for the sanctity of life and acknowledgement of the dignity of every human being, (2) to strive to realize a mission for the betterment of society by living with great compassion and (3) a pledge to protect humanity and live their life to fulfil this vow.

The online Master of Education (MEd) in Value-Creating Education for Global Citizenship offered by DePaul University in Chicago embodies value-creating discourse. The programme 'engages students in understanding and applying value-creating education for global citizenship in theory, research, policy and practice in local and global contexts' and it is 'for those who wish to pursue professional preparation in the internationally growing discipline of value-creating education and strengthen their current position in schools, universities or community organizations'. Faculty members teach about value-creating global citizenship through courses such as Theoretical Foundations of Value-Creating Education which 'introduces [learners] to the Eastern and Western theoretical foundations undergirding the educational philosophies and practices of [Japanese educators and peace advocates] Tsunesaburo Makiguchi, Josei Toda, and Daisaku Ikeda'; and Dialogue and Education which 'explores dialogue relative to questions of justice, culture, and education'. Lastly, the course in Education for Global Citizenship which 'engages global citizenship from its historical development in the Western philosophical tradition, beginning in Ancient Greece, through the Enlightenment and into its most recent incarnation as a response to conditions of globalization' (DePaul University, n.a.). In this perspective, teachers in this MA course train their graduates with spiritual, interdisciplinary, Western and non-Western value-creating standpoints to help them shape the quality of education.

On a first-level analysis then, it is clear that the approaches examined here propose a variety of intentions, in some cases intersecting, in how a GCE-curriculum is understood and conceptualized. While GCE-curricula, to date, seem to be situated within predominantly neoliberal discourses, it should also be recognized that teachers, as 'emissaries' of social change (Bourn, 2016), have agency to ethically question, negotiate and modify these discursive influences (Baildon et al., 2013) and are in a distinctive position to impact students' values at critical stages in their lives in the classroom setting (Merryfield, 2002). In this context, the author questioned what method would be adequate for surfacing the meaning and practices of GCE-curricula across faculties that were positioned to teach global citizenship courses in a variety of university programmes on different continents.

Methods

This chapter is part of a larger study of the GCE-curriculum among universities in the United States, the United Kingdom and Japan, the aim of which was to examine the phenomenon from the perspectives of their teaching personnel. The study involved a qualitative approach and was constructed on an interest in exploring empirically and theoretically teachers' perspectives on how they engage in implementing principles of global citizenship into a modern university curriculum. Considering that 'the challenge for global citizenship is not to continue to speak to and for global elites' (Shultz, Abdi and Richardson, 2011, p. 14), this examination looked specifically into teachers' diversity of understanding and conceptualizations of the notion of a GCE-curriculum. In order to recognize the way a GCE-curriculum functions as a discursive and practical field across countries, the open-ended questionnaire asked the teachers to describe the core elements of their GCE-curriculum design that equip their graduates to be 'global citizens'. The data for this study were collected in twenty-one universities across the United States (seven), Japan (seven) and the United Kingdom (seven). Of the forty-four teachers involved with the teaching of global citizenship courses in the analysis, the largest number of respondents was from the United States (44 per cent), followed by Japan (37 per cent) and the UK (19 per cent). More than half of the faculties surveyed teach at private universities (twenty-three), while the rest teach at public HE institutions. The programmes taught by the participants varied significantly among the institutions selected as to where in the university these programmes were housed. However, half of all faculties (twenty-two) taught on programmes housed in a department specifically dedicated to global citizenship. Other faculties taught at programmes dispersed among the education colleges (eight), humanities (seven), global studies (eight) and political science (one). The open-ended questionnaire sought to allow for a wide array of responses without directing teachers towards a single definition. Types of questions included, for instance, 'Tell me about your GCE-curriculum design and introduce reasons why you endorse the teaching of global citizenship and how this connects to your academic journey?' or 'Are there any particular theoretical approaches that you try to address/endorse in your GCE-curriculum design?'

Data analysis was built on grounded theory methodology, first developed by Glaser and Strauss (1967). Grounded theory provides a key method for data analysis and theory construction in qualitative research. This method enables demonstration of the participants' points of view on the GCE-curriculum while simultaneously aiming towards an interpretive dimension, which comprises the core of content analysis. Through it, I attempted to uncover social mechanisms, power relations, cultures, ideologies and hidden agendas. I pinpointed segments of teachers' perspectives that addressed the research question and then arranged preliminary and overlapping categories using the constant comparison method (CCM) which 'combines systematic data collection, coding, and analysis with theoretical sampling in order to generate theory that is integrated, close to the data, and expressed in a form clear enough for further testing' (Conrad et al., 1993, p. 280). CCM incorporates four stages: '(1) comparing incidents applicable to each category, (2) integrating categories and their properties, (3) delimiting the theory, and (4) writing the theory' (Glaser, p. 439). This process revealed pertinent information and passages, which I organized, connecting data to themes or categories (Merriam and Grenier, 2019). The findings below are presented within themes that were coded from the data. To support and elucidate each theme, I used direct quotes from teachers that are blended with my interpretation and relevant literature.

I support each section by offering lesson-samples (Tables 15.1, 15.2 and 15.3) drawn from a range of modules within graduate and undergraduate courses focused on traditional GCE themes such as difference and similarity, prejudice and environmental impact. Example of lessons have been chosen because they describe, either explicitly or implicitly, the pedagogical strategies employed by a selected group of university teachers that foster learners' critical cognizance, ecotistical/ecocritical views and inclusive self/identity in the classroom setting. Lesson-samples draw on ethnographic fieldwork (Amit, 2003) and document analysis (Bowen, 2009) of primary materials (e.g. syllabi) from doctoral research in four university case studies located in the United States, the United Kingdom and Japan between September 2017 and May 2018. During this time, I interviewed twelve teachers (four for each university case study) multiple times and attended their lessons throughout the day and this enabled me to directly experience GCE from the teachers' perspectives. All teachers gave permission for me to observe their lessons.

Table 15.1 Global Citizenship Education, Poverty and Global Inequalities (Graduate Module, US University)

Curriculum dimension	Teacher's pedagogical approach	Example of dynamics and students' comments in the classroom
Crossing ideological boundaries and developing an appreciation for diversity	The teacher divided the class into groups and asked the groups to be formed in ways that students from different nationalities would work together (e.g. Americans, Chinese, Japanese, Mexicans, and Ghanaians); then introduced the first activity. The topic of poverty and global inequalities was discussed through central questions, for example why understanding ideological stances which create poverty is an integral part of GCE? How can the notion of 'global citizenship' help overcome dangerous ideologies (e.g. extreme nationalism and populism, racism, fascism, predatory capitalism/neoliberalism)? How can GCE encourage you to appreciate diversity?	Students discussed a variety of ideological approaches to Global Citizenship Education (GCE) (e.g. neoliberal, transformative, post-colonial, spiritual) as well as the contrast among the notions of nationalistic or patriotic, versus global citizenship. Students concluded their discussions by addressing how to best appreciate diversity in a world characterized by increasing racism and right-wing populism. An interesting note herewith: 'Pro-Trump' students were highly engaged in this discussion and by the end of it, they seemed much more critical towards the US president policy.
Perceiving connections between knowledge, language and power	The teacher wrote on the board a list of racist or highly charged statements made by current politicians; then, he added a few questions: Why do people in power, although they generally receive a high level of education from prestigious institutions, make racist statements? Why are some of them not able to appreciate diversity and seem to fuel hate? How can GCE foster a different type of leader?	Students chose one statement and discussed it with a specific focus on the questions proposed by the teacher. They commented in a variety of critical ways: 'Receiving good education does not make a politician a wise person, a sustainable vision is needed', 'Power and money are often more important than education according to some people in the government', 'How a politician speaks tells you a lot about his vision'.
Recognizing the violence of modernity	The teacher concluded the topic by asking the students to brainstorm a PowerPoint presentation in the classroom that would address the following question: Is the 'Trump administration family separation policy' a case of violence of modernity? If so, why? If not, why? The teacher concluded by assigning a ten-slide PowerPoint presentation take-home assignment for the next class.	Students worked on brainstorming the Power Point in a collaborative fashion, some focusing on the traumas caused to parents and child by the family separation policy, others highlighting the origins of immigration.

Table 15.2 Global Citizenship Education and the Environment (Undergraduate Module, Japanese University)

Curriculum dimension	Teacher's pedagogical approach	Example of dynamics and students' comments in the classroom
Encouraging a vision of oneness of life and its environment	The teacher divided the class period into three sections. In the first section, the teacher employed Smallman and Brown's (2011) university text *Introduction to International and Global Studies* which includes a wide variety of resources that place emphasis on environment, gender, race and colonialism in a global context. This work is employed by teachers around Japan as a resource, and, in some cases, as a unit guide for inquiring about globalization. The teacher began the lesson with a reading on the history of the environmental movement, its tenets and contributions, points and counterpoints in the general discourse between strong environmentalists and pragmatists such as Bjorn Lomborg, the Danish author of *The Skeptical Environmentalist* (2003) and examples from the Brazilian rain forest and northern Arctic were presented. Atmosphere and climate issues – in particular, climate change's effects – were explored. An underlying theme within the lesson was the notion that environmental issues reflect globalization. The teacher then asked the student to discuss a variety of topics related to environment versus globalization.	Students took notes of what the teacher said; then identified and discussed a variety of topics in their groups; for example pollution, water scarcity and nuclear waste; the discussion turned out to be engaging and lively with students sharing their thoughts with excitement. Here are some examples of students' reactions: 'We are heading towards a nuclear war, the only way to stop this is to develop awareness through quality education', 'I believe that, since in Japan we do not appreciate enough the fact that we have abundance of water, in the future serious problems will arise in relation to how to sustain disparities, for example, with countries such as Yemen. Something needs to be done, we should do it.'
'Switching ego-to eco-'	The teacher encouraged students to examine and question underlying assumptions about the possible causes and solutions to environmental problems, how people relate to other beings that share our environment and the contribution that GCE can make to understanding environmental relations. The question for discussion was the following: Can the notion of 'global citizenship' help humans become less ego-centric and more eco-centric?	Students discussed the questions proposed by the teacher in their groups; subsequently, they tried to identify how GCE can help humans become more eco-centric. Students asked a number of questions to the teacher on the notion of eco-centric, as it appeared that the concept was 'new' to them. The teacher encouraged them to search academic articles on 'Google Scholar' on the topic of eco-centredness and reference them in their next task (informative poster).

(Continued)

Table 15.2 (Continued)

Curriculum dimension	Teacher's pedagogical approach	Example of dynamics and students' comments in the classroom
Supporting sustainability through actions	The teacher asked the students to design a creative and informative poster with their group on a topic they selected. In choosing the topic students had to try to identify what are the effects of humans' actions on the environment and how GCE can encourage sustainable activities rather than 'predatory' ones. The teacher concluded the lesson by assigning a 600-word essay take-home assignment for the next class and asked the students to focus on the following theme: 'What is the connection between becoming a global citizen and caring about the environment?'	Students worked on the informative poster, sharing their thoughts on how to achieve sustainability through actions. Interesting thoughts emerged: 'We are devastating the environment and GCE can help us to develop a critical attitude towards predatory actions', 'GCE is an educational philosophy that can help us to put into practice our love for the planet Earth. We do not have an option B, we must act now'. 'A useful way to act for the environment is to act cautiously in our daily lives; this to me is global citizenship'.

Critical cognizance

A portion of responses suggests that university GCE-curricula should encourage a positive appreciation for cultural, religious and other forms of diversity through a GCE-curriculum rooted in critical pedagogy and crossing ideological boundaries as proposed by Giroux's (2006/2007) and Torres's (2017) theory of the global commons defined by three principles: our planet is our home, global peace is an intangible cultural good and a treasure of humanity with immaterial value and the need to find ways for people to live with a strong spirit of solidarity – these in turn build on the work of Paulo Freire (2018) and his 'critical consciousness' understanding of relationships through dialogue and reflection. Peter[1], a professor in the Faculty of Media and Society from a private university in California, said that in our diverse and increasingly globalized world, 'we should foster learners who critically analyze injustices and peaceably interact with persons from different backgrounds; in designing my GCE-curriculum I hope helping my students to comprehend the causes of immigration and refugee's crisis by engaging them in inter-civilization and inter-faith discussions'. Joseph, Associate Professor in the Faculty of Social Studies at a UK public university, adds,

> my GCE-curriculum offers a broad overview of human diversity including racial, cultural, ethnic, gender, gender identity, sexual orientation, national origin, immigrant status, religious, disability, age and generational differences. I tend to encourage my students to critically define various aspects of human diversity, understand nuances in terms like race, culture, ethnicity, gender, identity, sexual orientation, national origin, immigrant status, religious diversity, disability, and age/generational differences.

---

[1] Interviewees are quoted under a pseudonym.

Table 15.3 Migration, Identity and Global Citizenship (Graduate Module, UK University)

Curriculum Dimension	Teacher's pedagogical approach	Example of dynamics and students' comments in the classroom
Developing a sense of belonging	The teacher's focus in this class was on migration. Discussions in the classroom examined migration from a modern perspective and investigated how migration reshapes identity and citizenship. The teacher's introduction to the topic looked at the current refugee crisis in European countries and in relation to the global context. In the first activity, the teacher read with the students Gielis's (2009) article 'A global sense of migrant places: Towards a place perspective in the study of migrant transnationalism'. In relation to this article, the teacher asked the students to discuss a core question: Are we going towards a multicultural society? If so, how do notions of identity and global citizenship connect to this type of multicultural society?	The students discussed the question posed by the teacher and used their notes from Gielis (2009) to share concrete examples with their peers and/or support their viewpoints. Based on their comments this was a challenging task which required them to look at the bigger picture rather than what is happening in their country. Students comments were diverse: 'I can't really understand how a multicultural society looks like, because I grew up here in the UK and never felt the need to be a global citizen; however, through my studies I am developing a broader view of the world', 'It's difficult to define identity, for me we have multiple identities and this connects to global citizenship. To be a global citizen means to feel a sense of belonging towards all society; that's to me global citizenry'.
Fostering oneness with humanity and 'greater-self'	The second activity looked into the notions of identity and belonging in relation to cosmopolitanism, 'otherness' and diversity. The teacher read with the students selected passages from Delanty's (2006) article 'The cosmopolitan imagination: critical cosmopolitanism and social theory'. Then he asked the students to take turns and express their opinions on the paper.	Students took turns and shared their ideas on the notion of otherness. It was surprising to see that students shared deep thoughts on the meaning of 'cosmopolitan imagination' beyond Western views. For example, one student commented: 'We should stop thinking from a Western perspective only and start understanding more cultures different from our own. This is to me cosmopolitanism', 'In relation to this and to the previous article, I believe that we are not ready to welcome refugees because we are fundamentally 'ignorant'. We ignore their history, culture and reasons why they are escaping wars'.
Encouraging sense of engagement with the 'glo-cal'	The teacher concluded the class by reading short excerpts from Wodak's (2015) book *The Politics of Fear: What Right-Wing Discourses Mean.* Then he asked the students to brainstorm some ideas for a PowerPoint presentation for their next class. The topic assigned was: What actions can you take on a daily basis that would discourage you to feel fear about diversity?	Students took notes from the teacher's readings and started working on brainstorming ideas for their presentation. Students proposed several questions for analysis to their peers; for example, 'How can we put efforts into our daily life in order to feel that we are contributing to something?' 'How can we take actions that would discourage our fear if we do not know exactly what our mission in life is?' 'What kind of actions would help us not to fear diversity?' and 'Why are right-wing politicians promoting a culture of fear?'

In this perspective, a detailed example of how teachers might practically foster students' *critical cognizance* is offered in a lesson-sample (Table 1) from the graduate module in Global Citizenship Education, Poverty and Global Inequalities (USA, University). 'This is a type of GCE-module which helps student seeing the world through another person's perspective whose experiences and ideology may differ from their own', says Jacob, dean of a public university in New York City, suggesting that 'we do need to design an inclusive curriculum; in my classes, I include manifold activities where students participate in conversations about racism, poverty, and diversity.'

The teachers mentioned above also recognized the importance of integrating rooted post-colonialist perspectives, as proposed by Spivak (1990) on the complexity and non-homogeneity of indigenous and mainstream cultures and knowledge. In addition, they suggested that a GCE-curriculum should pay attention to the connections between knowledge, language and power which influence global processes. This is well outlined by Andreotti and De Souza's (2008) approach towards learning that identifies various perspectives and voices and promotes dialogue and enquiry.

A conclusive point was made by Distinguished Professor Roger, who teaches at a public university in Los Angeles. He described, 'The importance of developing in his learners a recognition of the violence of modernity' by referring to the work of Walter Mignolo (2000a,b; 2011; see also Andreotti, 2011), who explains that 'modernity's "shine" is articulated in ways that hide its shadow, or the fact that the very existence of the shiny side requires the imposition of systematic violence on others' (de Oliveira Andreotti et al., 2015, p. 23).

Ecotistical/ecocritical view

A second core dimension of a GCE-curriculum suggested by the participants is rooted in ecocritical pedagogical frameworks (Lupinacci and Happel-Parkins, 2015; Martusewicz, Edmundson and Lupinacci, 2015). Six teachers indicate that a GCE-curriculum may foster an ecotistical stance; the term 'ecotistical' draws on Weintraub's et al. (2006) definition of 'humans relating to the nonhuman environment in a harmonious, respectful, and pragmatic manner' (p. 55). Weintraub et al., 2006 suggested (as cited in Lupinacci 2017, p. 21) that by switching ego- to eco-, the 'focus [is directed] away from self and toward home or habitat' in response to 'the absence of any opposite terminology for anthropocentric – the privileging of humanity – and egocentric – the privileging of self'.

The module in Global Citizenship Education and the Environment within an undergraduate course (Japanese university) is an example of how teachers might foster students' ecotistical/ecocritical views (Table 2). In this module the teacher critically examines a wide variety of resources that place emphasis on environment, gender, race and colonialism in the global context. By doing so, the teacher aims to encourage learners' vision of unity of life and environment as well as sustainable actions based on ecocritical perspectives. In this perspective, Albert, Professor in the Faculty of Political Science at a private Japanese university, says: 'I put efforts in designing a GCE-curriculum that helps learners to identify and confront deep cultural assumptions informing world-views in efforts to support sustainability.' Haruto, Associate Professor at a Japanese public university, adds: 'The term eco-centric is an adjective for ecological consciousness; my GCE-curriculum seeks to develop learners' consciousness that we are not alone and human beings are not at the center – I always remind them in my courses to respect all living beings and act accordingly'; this quote finds a theoretical corroboration in Martusewicz and Edmundson (2005) proposal of an 'eco-ethical consciousness' (p. 73) that entertains the social and environmental impact of decision-making and accepts them as inextricably linked.

The primary emphasis of a growing body of educators identifying their GCE approaches as ecocritical is a recognition, as Lupinacci and Happel-Parkins (2016b) suggest (as cited in Lupinacci, 2017, p. 21), 'of the limitations of how we—as subjects of Western industrial culture—understand and situate ourselves—humans—as a species that exists separate from and superior to all other forms of living and non-living beings'. On a more spiritual level, this point is embodied in the Buddhist theory of 'Esho Funi' or 'oneness of life and its environment'. This theory maintains that though two separate entities in the phenomenal world, life and environment are essentially one (Toynbee and Ikeda, 2007). Classically, one's view of life and questions of existence are shaped by a consciousness of self, as echoed in Descartes's (1970) famous declaration, 'I think, therefore I am.' We hold the self to be the basis of reality, and everything else is seen in relation to it. This gives rise to a view of life structured in terms of dichotomies – self/other, internal/external, body/mind, spiritual/material and human/nature. From the standpoint of certain Buddhist traditions (e.g. the Mahayana Buddhist scriptures), however, the self is a temporary phenomenon, a nonpermanent combination of matter and mental/spiritual functions (i.e. body and mind).

Inclusive self/identity

This dimension is rooted in the social identity theory (SIT), which suggests that when individuals psychologically identify with a particular group – the global citizens, for instance – they are likely to view themselves as representatives of that shared category (Reysen and Katzarska-Miller, 2013). In this perspective, according to seven teachers, a curriculum for GCE should support students to understand that a 'globally inclusive' human identity does not deny the possibility of other 'nested' identities that derive from the rich diversity that characterizes humanity. Any given individual 'holds multiple, overlapping, non-exclusive, partial identities based on things like gender, age, family, ethnicity, nationality, religious beliefs, occupation, personal interest, socioeconomic status, and so forth; this is what I convey to my students', says Professor Christopher from the Faculty of Communication Studies at a public university in Michigan. The quote suggests that none of these 'partial' identities necessarily exclude a sense of oneness with humanity or a commitment to act as a responsible global citizen. In addition, according to the participants, learners should be helped in developing a 'global-self' which engages with several levels of community services – congruent with what some participants defined as a 'greater self', which should span different levels, from individual to regional to all of humanity. For instance, Stephanie, a lecturer in the Department of Education Studies in a private Japanese university, says 'My approach to the GCE-curriculum aims at developing learners' greater self. By taking actions to help others in the local community, students develop a sense of engagement that can then be extended to the global society; when my curriculum design helps them in this way, then that is a good achievement I believe.'

The quotes above echo ten additional teachers' voices who identify and describe two layers connected with the development of learners' inclusive identity:

- *Authentic self*: 'A curriculum for GCE in the modern university', says Professor Hinata, who teaches in the Faculty of Education at a private Japanese university, 'should help students living towards their authentic self; this means a complete balance and interaction of all multifaceted parts of the self that make up identity in the pursuit of answering the lifelong question of "who am I?" in the context of increasing global capitalism.' Dean Jennifer, who directs a Graduate School of Education at a public university in Japan, adds, 'The authentic identity, which my GCE-curriculum design seeks to promote is one who can identify the social impositions, which oppress or privilege oneself and recognize the balance of all social roles in relation to personal experience and formation. This is what I try to teach in my GCE courses.' Associate Professor Patricia and Programme Head Robert, both teaching in the Department of Education Studies at a private university in the UK, suggest that their approaches to a GCE-curriculum attempt to foster global citizens with an 'authentic self that is conscious of social barriers or privileges'.

- *Beyond Self-centred Attitude*: This means, according to eight participants, a way of living which is altruistic and which helps others while establishing a 'Global We', as stated by Julie, a lecturer in education at a private university in the UK. Julie explains that a 'self-actualised self can accommodate multiple secondary distinctions between "us" and "them" when those distinctions are not understood in a hostile or adversarial manner; fundamentally, when I think of my GCE-curriculum design, it means to me fostering students' Global We'. Teachers also identify the development of a 'beyond self-centred attitude' as the courage students should be supported to develop, through a GCE-curriculum, in order to understand the value of helping their comrades to overcome feelings of uncertainty about the world around them, which they seem unable to influence. In relation to this, John, Director of the Graduate School of Education at a private university in Chicago, suggests that 'when learners are encouraged to expand solidarity by going beyond their self-centered attitude, a paradigm shift from a conception of "society of egoism" to a "society of altruism" might get triggered, and ultimately this leads to learners potentially wanting to contribute to a more ethical society'. In other words, going beyond a self-centred attitude leads to what the Japanese educator Makiguchi calls a 'contributive life' (Noddings, 2005) which, according to Jean, a professor within the Faculty of Political Science in Japan, 'encourages individuals to develop an awareness of the complementing nature of our lives and the connections that link us to others and our environment; that's the link I think of when I design my GCE-curriculum'.

The graduate module in Migration, Identity and Global Citizenship (UK, University) offers a concrete example of how teachers might develop students' inclusive self/identity (Table 3). The teacher looks into the current dynamics in Europe through historical perspectives, referring to the current refugee crisis as a starting point, and placing it in a global context in an attempt to develop students' sense of belonging and possibly oneness with humanity complemented with a sense of engagement.

Towards an ethical GCE-curriculum

This chapter has reviewed the trends in how GCE-curricula in HE have been conceptualized in the context of globalization. As has been indicated, while these trends have tended to lead to a reinforcement of the dominant ideological views (e.g. neoliberal) regarding the purpose of HE GCE-curricula, they have also created spaces and openings for interpretations and debates that challenge these notions (e.g. transformative, post-colonial and value-creating). However, as Fujikane (2003) (as cited in Bourn, 2011) argues, there is still 'the need for a new curriculum, since the world is changing and previous world views are no longer appropriate. There is also the need for the creation of new world citizens with proper knowledge of, skills for, disposition applicable to, the globalized world' (p. 565). Findings from the teachers interviewed in this study suggested the emergence of three dimensions: (1) inclusive self/identity, (2) critical cognizance and (3) ecotistical/ecocritical view. This provides a potential framework to teaching and learning in HE that equips educators to respond to the complex local and global challenges that they currently face in fostering learners to be global citizens. In this perspective, I concur with Widdows (as cited in Sund and Pashby, 2018, p. 4) that 'a pedagogy of global ethics would explicitly consider how teachers and learners can engage with the plurality of contexts and ethical considerations that define today's pressing global issues'. Such a pedagogy has 'a fundamental commitment to including global concerns in all ethical reasoning and decision-making … what matters is not just the consideration of global issues, but how these issues are approached and the methodology, ethical framework and assumptions adopted'.

Based on the findings, I suggest here a move towards a 'yet-to-come' ethical GCE-curriculum framework (Figure 15.1) which challenges traditional views and assumptions, allows students to introduce and access non-dominant perspectives and encourages sustainable ways of thinking.

The graphic places an ethical GCE-curriculum at the centre of four interconnected circles (other GCE-curricular theories) and it connects it to the three ethical dimensions emerging in this study. The characteristics of each of the three dimensions within this framework are summarized in Figure 15.1. To foster 'ethical global citizens' teachers should engage with all seven of these areas: teachers shall first help students to gain critical consciousness through a particular issue or concern related to the graphic, to include, for example, acknowledging forms of neoliberal GCE in order to develop critical consciousness/awareness of the damage deriving from unethical capitalistic perspectives of societies. That is why the author felt the need to engage with the neoliberal GCE-curriculum in this framework. As this critical consciousness grows, teachers may move towards the next stage of the educational process: supporting learners in the development of an inclusive self/identity required to address the issue or concern of society. As inclusive self/identity is gained, students may then act and, ultimately, effect change in their local and/or global communities, while developing ecotistical/ecocritical views. Each learner will enter the process at a different phase. This process does not need to follow a set order; it can be understood by the teachers as circular. This means that developing learners' critical consciousness may lead to fostering an inclusive identity at a later stage and vice versa. This educational process, however, needs to be grounded in the notion of mutual respect and responsibility at all times. Teachers shall help students to learn to recognize both the positive and negative moral obligations of being human, for example, by acknowledging the role that developed nations play in creating systems

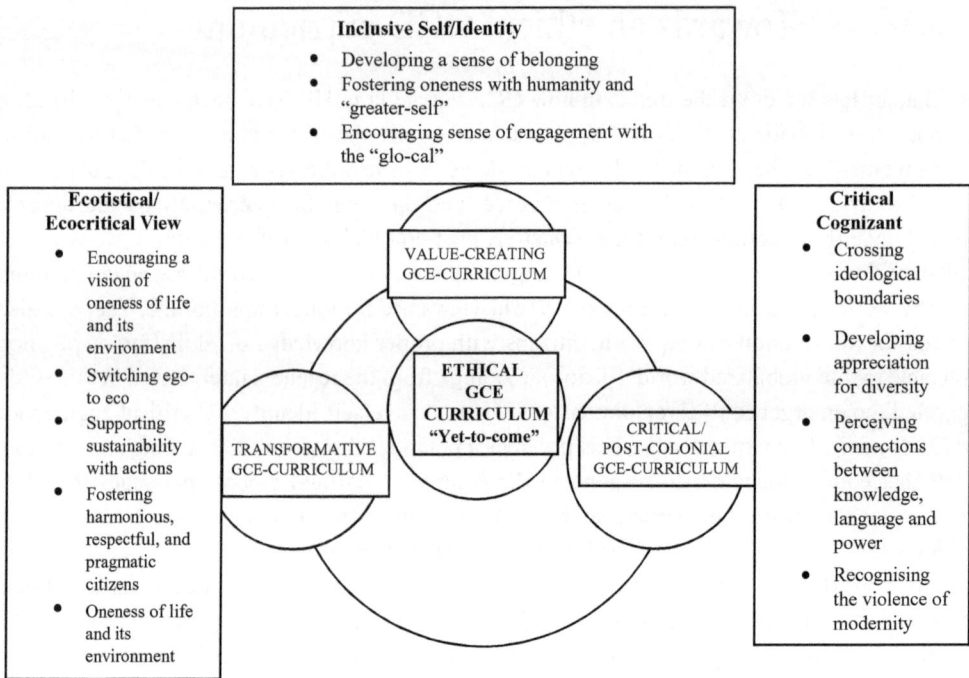

Figure 15.1 Ethical GCE-curriculum framework.

of inequality, injustice and oppression. Universities may adapt the above framework to their own specific context, purpose and needs.

Conclusion

What kind of society is a GCE-curriculum designed to promote? Said (2003) addressed this question impeccably; he stressed that it is crucial to be conscious that the way we obtain knowledge is the result of a process that exposes certain interests, that it is extremely motivated. The role that teachers play, through their expectations, their teaching strategies and particularly through their curricular emphases and pedagogical orientations, is crucial in endorsing the repertoire of cognitive and affective characteristics and skills that graduates 'need' to be global citizens and to move down the path from natal culture (the local) to college or university culture (the educational setting) to the culture of the larger society ('global' society). Yet, as Labaree (1999) points out in his book *How to Succeed in School Without Really Learning: The Credentials Race in American Education*, globally, social mobility (i.e. the preparation of individuals for competitive social positions) and social efficiency (i.e. the preparation of workers) have overtaken democratic equality (i.e. the preparation of citizens) as the primary goal of education. The result is a system of education geared to favour private gains over public interests; in other words, the pursuit of status outweighs the acquisition of values-based knowledge. In order to contrast market-driven only approaches to global citizenship we need to constantly redefine what the GCE-curriculum means in characterizing the kind of citizens needed to engage actively in the creation of world peace today and to achieve the transformations imperative for attaining more just societies. This vision needs to be transposed holistically as an ideal aim of university core curricula, not separately labelled as an 'international programme'. An ethical GCE-curriculum has therefore at its core a notion of knowledge as infinitely inter-connective and endlessly engaging, for, as Heisenberg (2000, p. 140) puts it, 'The existing scientific concepts cover always only a very limited part of reality, and the other part that has not yet been understood is infinite.'

Bibliography

Amit, V. (ed.) (2003). *Constructing the Field: Ethnographic Fieldwork in the Contemporary World.* Routledge.

Andreotti, V. (2011). *Actionable Postcolonial Theory in Education.* New York: Palgrave Macmillan.

Andreotti, V., and De Souza, L. M. (2008). Translating theory into practice and walking mine-fields. *International Journal of Development Education and Global Learning, 1*(1), 23–36.

Archibugi, D. (2008). *The Global Commonwealth of Citizens: Toward Cosmopolitan Democracy.* Princeton: Princeton University Press.

Baildon, M., Loh, K. S., Lim, I. M., İnanç, G., and Jaffar, J. (eds) (2013). *Controversial History Education in Asian Contexts.* Routledge.

Bhabha, H. K. (1994). *The Location of Culture.* New York: Routledge.

Bosio, E. (2017a). Educating for global citizenship and fostering a nonkilling Attitude, in J. Evans Pim and S. Herrero Rico (eds), *Nonkilling Education* (pp. 59–70). Honolulu: Center for Global Nonkilling.

Bosio, E. (2017b). How do we create transformative global citizens? University World News. Retrieved from http://www.universityworldnews.com/article.php?story=20171129082744388

Bosio, E., and Gaudelli, W. [Emiliano Bosio]. (2018, February 7). *Dr. William Gaudelli Global Citizenship Education – Interview Series Emiliano Bosio* [Video file]. Retrieved from https://youtu.be/CuiAEL45fDw

Bosio, E., Ibe A., Matsui B., and Rothman, J. R. (2018). GILE SIG Forum: Educating for global citizenship, in A. B. Gallagher (ed.), *The 2017 PanSIG Journal: Expand Your Interest* (pp. 222–31). Available at http://pansig.org/publications/2017/2017_PanSIG_Journal.pdf

Bosio, E., and Joffee, M. [Emiliano Bosio]. (2018, November 18). *Dr. Monte Joffee Global Citizenship Education – Interview Series Emiliano Bosio* [Video file]. Retrieved from https://youtu.be/-geu2cTJf9k

Bosio, E., and Schattle, H. [Emiliano Bosio]. (2017, October 12). *Dr. Hans Schattle Global Citizenship Education – Interview Series Emiliano Bosio* [Video file]. Retrieved from https://youtu.be/Wg3EWF88vi8

Bosio, E., and Torres, C. A. [Emiliano Bosio]. (2018, March 3). *Dr. Carlos Alberto Torres Global Citizenship Education – Interview Series with Emiliano Bosio* [Video file]. Retrieved from https://youtu.be/hNVZRIuBS-w

Bosio, E., and Torres, C. A. (2019). Global citizenship education: An educational theory of the common good? A conversation with Carlos Alberto Torres. *Policy Futures in Education, 17*(6), 745–60. https://doi.org/10.1177/1478210319825517

Bourn, D. (2011). From internationalisation to global perspectives. *Higher Education Research & Development, 30*(5), 559–71.

Bourn, D. (2016). Teachers as agents of social change. *International Journal of Development Education and Global Learning, 7*(3), 63–77.

Bourn, D. (2018). *Understanding Global Skills for 21st Century Professions.* Springer.

Bowen, G. A. (2009). Document analysis as a qualitative research method. *Qualitative Research Journal, 9*(2), 27–40.

Calhoun, C. (2002). The class consciousness of the frequent travellers: Towards a critique of actual existing cosmopolitanism, in S. Vertovec and R. Cohen (eds), *Conceiving Cosmopolitanism: Theory, Context and Practice* (pp. 86–109). Oxford: Oxford University Press.

Castells, M. (1997). *The Power of Identity: The Information Age: Economy, Society and Culture* (Vol. 2). Oxford: Blackwell.

Clark, M. C., and Wilson, A. L. (1991). Context and rationality in Mezirow's theory of transformational learning. *Adult Education Quarterly, 41*(2), 75–91.

Conrad, C., Neumann, A., Haworth, J. G., and Scott, P. (1993). *Qualitative Research in Higher Education: Experiencing Alternative Perspective and Approaches*. Needham Heights, MA: Ginn Press.

Delanty, G. (2006). The cosmopolitan imagination: Critical cosmopolitanism and social theory. *The British Journal of Sociology, 57*(1), 25–47.

de Oliveira Andreotti, V., Stein, S., Ahenakew, C., and Hunt, D. (2015). Mapping interpretations of decolonization in the context of higher education. *Decolonization: Indigeneity, Education & Society, 4*(1), 21–40.

de Oliveira Andreotti, V., Stein, S., Pashby, K., and Nicolson, M. (2016). Social cartographies as performative devices in research on higher education. *Higher Education Research & Development, 35*(1), 84–99.

DePaul University (n.d.). *Value-Creating Education for Global Citizenship (Med)*. Retrieved from https://education.depaul.edu/academics/leadership-language-curriculum/graduate/value-creating-eduction-global-citizenship-med/Pages/default.aspx

Descartes, R. (1970). I think, therefore I am. René Descartes, 1596–1650.

Dill, J. S. (2013). *The Longings and Limits of Global Citizenship Education: The Moral Pedagogy of Schooling in a Cosmopolitan Age*. New York: Routledge.

Dorio, J. N. (2017). Lessons from Los Angeles: Self-study on teaching university global citizenship education to challenge authoritarian education, neoliberal globalization and nationalist populism. *Journal of Global Citizenship & Equity Education, 6*(1), 1–30.

Elias, D. (1997). It's time to change our minds: An introduction to transformative learning. *ReVision, 20*(1), 2–6.

Freire, P. (2018). *Pedagogy of the Oppressed*. Bloomsbury Publishing USA.

Fujikane, H. (2003). Approaches to global education in the United States, the United Kingdom and Japan, *International Review of Educatio, 49*(1–2), 133–52.

Gaudelli, W. (2016). *Global Citizenship Education: Everyday Transcendence*. New York: Routledge.

Gebert, A. (2009). The role of community studies in the Makiguchian pedagogy. *Educational Studies, 45*(2), 146–64.

Gielis, R. (2009). A global sense of migrant places: Towards a place perspective in the study of migrant transnationalism. *Global Networks, 9*(2), 271–87.

Giroux, H. A. (1988a). *Schooling and the Struggle for Public Life: Critical Pedagogy in the Modern Age*. Minneapolis: University of Minnesota Press.

Giroux, H. (2006). *America on the Edge: Henry Giroux on Politics, Culture, and Education*. Springer.

Giroux, H. A. (2007). *Border Crossings: Cultural Workers and the Politics of Education*. Routledge.

Glaser, B. G. (1965). The constant comparative method of qualitative analysis. *Social Problems, 12*(4), 436–45.

Glaser, B., and Strauss A. (1967). *The Discovery of Grounded Theory: Strategies for Qualitative Research*. London: Wiedenfeld and Nicholson.

Goren, H., and Yemini, M. (2016). Global citizenship education in context: Teacher perceptions at an international school and a local Israeli school. *Compare: A Journal of Comparative and International Education, 46*(5), 832–53. http://dx.doi.org/10.1080/03057925.2015.1111752

Goulah, J., and Ito, T. (2012). Daisaku Ikeda's curriculum of Soka education: Creating value through dialogue, global citizenship, and 'human education' in the mentor–disciple relationship. *Curriculum Inquiry, 42*(1), 56–79.

Gowan, P. (2001). Neoliberal cosmopolitanism. *New Left Review, 11*, 79.

Gowan, P. (2009). The ways of the world (Interview with M. Newman and M. Bojcun). *New Left Review* (Second Series), *59*(September/October), 51–70.

Hall, S. (1986). Signification, representation, ideology: Althusser and the poststructuralist debates. *Critical Studies in Mass Communication*, *2*(2), 91–113.

Hammond, C. D., and Keating, A. (2018). Global citizens or global workers? Comparing university programmes for global citizenship education in Japan and the UK. *Compare: A Journal of Comparative and International Education*, *48*(6), 915–34.

Heisenberg, W. (2000). *Physics and Philosophy: The Revolution in Modern Science*. London: Penguin Books.

Held, D., and McGrew, A. (2000). *The Global Transformations Reader: An Introduction to the Globalization Debate*. Cambridge: Polity Press.

Labaree, D. F. (1999). *How to Succeed in School without Really Learning: The Credentials Race in American Education*. Yale University Press.

Lomborg, B. (2003). *The Skeptical Environmentalist: Measuring the Real State of the World* (Vol. 1). Cambridge: Cambridge University Press.

Lupinacci, J. J. (2017). Addressing 21st Century challenges in education: An ecocritical conceptual framework toward an ecotistical leadership in education. Impacting Education: *Journal on Transforming Professional Practice*, *2*(1), 20–7.

Lupinacci, J., and Happel-Parkins, A. (2015). Recognize, resist, and reconstitute: An ecocritical framework in Teacher Education. *The SoJo Journal: Educational Foundations and Social Justice Education*, *1*(1), 45–61.

Lupinacci, J., and Happel-Parkins, A. (2016). (Un)Learning anthropocentrism: An ecoJustice education framework for teaching to resist humansupremacy in schools, in S. Rice and A. Rud (eds), *The Educational Significance of Human and Non-Human Animal Interactions: Blurring the Species Line* (pp. 13–30). New York: Palgrave.

Makiguchi, T. (2000). *L'educazione creativa*. Firenze: La Nuova Italia.

Makiguchi, T. (2002). *A Geography of Human Life*. Caddo Gap Press.

Martusewicz, R., and Edmundson, J. (2005). Social foundations as pedagogies of responsibility and eco-ethical commitment, in D. W. Butin (ed.), *Teaching Social Foundations of Education: Contexts, Theories, and Issues* (pp. 71–92). Mahwah: Lawrence Erlbaum Associates, Publishers.

Martusewicz, R., Edmundson, J., and Lupinacci, J. (2015). *EcoJustice Education: Toward Diverse, Democratic, and Sustainable Communities* (2nd edn). New York: Routledge.

Merriam, S. B., and Grenier, R. S. (eds) (2019). *Qualitative Research in Practice: Examples for Discussion and Analysis*. Jossey-Bass.

Merryfield, M. M. (2002). The difference a global educator can make. *Educational Leadership*, *60*, 18–21.

Mezirow, J. (2003). Transformative learning as discourse. *Journal of Transformative Education*, *1*(1), 58–63.

Mignolo, W. (2000a). *Local Histories/Global Designs: Coloniality, Subaltern Knowledges, and Border Thinking*. Princeton: Princeton University Press.

Mignolo, W. (2000b). The many faces of cosmo-polis: Border thinking and critical cosmopolitanism. *Public Culture*, *12*(3), 721–48.

Mignolo, W. (2011). *The Darker Side of Western Modernity: Global Futures, Decolonial Options*. Durham: Duke University Press.

Moon, R. J., and Koo, J. W. (2011). Global citizenship and human rights: A longitudinal analysis of social studies and ethics textbooks in the Republic of Korea. *Comparative Education Review*, *55*, 574–99. http://dx.doi.org/10.1086/660796

Noddings, N. (2003). *Happiness and Education*. Cambridge University Press.

Noddings, N. (ed.) (2005). *Educating Citizens for Global Awareness*. Teachers College Press.

Peck, J., and Tickle, A. (2002). Neoliberalizing space. *Antipode*, *34*, 380–404.

Rapoport, A. (2010). We cannot teach what we don't know: Indiana teachers talk about global citizenship education. *Education, Citizenship and Social Justice*, *5*, 179–90. http://dx.doi.org/10.1177/174619791 0382256

Ray, L. (2007). *Globalization and Everyday Life*. London: Routledge.

Reysen, S., and Katzarska-Miller, I. (2013). A model of global citizenship: Antecedents and outcomes. *International Journal of Psychology*, *48*(5), 858–70.

Rizvi, F. (2007). Postcolonialism and globalisation in education. *Cultural Studies Critical Methodologies*. http://csc.sagepub.com

Rizvi, F. (2009). Towards cosmopolitan learning. *Discourse*: *Studies in Cultural Politics in Education*, *30*(3) (September), 253–68.

Said, E. W. (2003). *Orientalism*. London: Penguin. (Original work published 1978).

Schattle, H. (2008). *The Practices of Global Citizenship*. Rowman & Littlefield.

Schweisfurth, M. (2006). Education for global citizenship: Teacher agency and curricular structure in Ontario schools. *Educational Review*, *58*, 41–50. http:// dx.doi.org/10.1080/00131910500352648

Sharma, N. (2018). *Value-Creating Global Citizenship Education: Engaging Gandhi, Makiguchi, and Ikeda as Examples*. Springer.

Shultz, L. (2007). Educating for global citizenship: Conflicting agendas and understandings. *The Alberta Journal of Educational Research*, *53*(3), 248–58.

Shultz, L., Abdi, A. A., and Richardson, G. H. (eds) (2011). *Global Citizenship Education in Post-secondary Institutions: Theories, Practices, Policies*. New York: Peter Lang.

Smallman, S. C., and Brown, K. (2011). *Introduction to International and Global Studies*. Chapel Hill: University of North Carolina Press.

Spivak, G. (1990). *The Post-colonial Critic: Interviews, Strategies, Dialogues*. New York: Routledge.

Stein, S., Andreotti, V. D. O., and Suša, R. (2019). 'Beyond 2015', within the modern/colonial global imaginary? Global development and higher education. *Critical Studies in Education*, *60*(3), 281–301.

Sund, L., and Pashby, K. (2018). 'Is it that we do not want them to have washing machines?': Ethical global issues pedagogy in Swedish classrooms. *Sustainability*, *10*(10), 3552.

Tarozzi, M., and Torres, C. A. (2017). *Global Citizenship Education and the Crizes of Multiculturalism*. Comparative Perspectives. London: Bloomsbury.

Torres, C. A. (2017). *Theoretical and Empirical Foundations of Critical Global Citizenship Education*. New York: Routledge.

Toynbee, A., and Ikeda, D. (2007). *Choose Life: A Dialogue*. I.B. Tauris.

Turner, V. (1975). Symbolic studies. *Annual Review of Anthropology*, *4*(1), 145–61.

UNESCO (2014). Global citizenship education: Preparing learners for the challenges of the 21st century. Retrieved from http://unesdoc.unesco.org/images/0022/002277/227729E.pdf (accessed 21 August 2018).

University of Nottingham (n.d.). *MA in Global Citizenship, Identities and Human Rights*, Retrieved from https://www.nottingham.ac.uk/pgstudy/courses/sociology-and-social-policy/global-citizenship-identities-and-human-rights-ma.aspx

University of Washington. Foster School of Business (n.d.). *The Global Business Center (GBC)*, Retrieved from https://foster.uw.edu/centers/gbc/

University of York (n.d.). *MA Global and International Citizenship Education*, Retrieved from https://www.york.ac.uk/study/postgraduate-taught/courses/ma-global-international-citizenship-education/#course-content

Weintraub, L., Phillips, P. C., Smith, S., Godfrey, D., Vesna, V., Weintraub, L., Rosenthal, A., Haynes, D. J., Kochhar-Lindgren, K., Burns, D., Higgins, H., Bower S., and Weintraub, L. (2006). Forum: Eco-tistical art. *Art Journal*, *65*(1), 54–81.

Widdows, H. (2014). *Global Ethics: An Introduction*. Durham: Acumen.

Wodak, R. (2015). *The Politics of Fear: What Right-wing Discourses Mean*. London: Sage.

Chapter 16

Planetary Citizenship in Brazilian Universities

Silvia Elisabeth Moraes and Ludmila de Almeida Freire

Introduction

Speaking of citizenship in Brazil is never repetitious or dated. The large number of citizens who still suffer from not having their most basic needs met or rights respected demands that the subject never disappears, particularly from the context of educational institutions whose purpose and competence are to convert citizenship into a concrete practice inspired in the ideals of democracy. Society has attributed to these institutions the task of educating world citizens capable of finding the much-needed solutions for the complex issues we face, which nowadays range from local to planetary. Social justice, sustainability, peaceful coexistence, cultural respect and ethics in world relations require that, at the university, together with our students, we foster and coordinate studies on these matters.

In our field of action, which is the curriculum, we have been working on a project that aims to support the inclusion of planetary citizenship as a transdisciplinary theme in Brazilian universities. Our intention is to place the university in the prominent position of educating citizens with a planetary consciousness – that is to say, with an awareness that we, as people of all ethnic origins, cultures, colours and knowledges, share a home and a common future for which we are fully responsible.

Given the varied interpretations associated with the concept of planetary citizenship, it is here treated as a *floating signifier* (Laclau, 2007). As such, it will be articulated in concrete projects with groups from different areas and types of knowledge, working inter- and transdisciplinarily. We have found support for our argument in recent educational legislation, students' contributions during school and university teaching practice, discussions on postmodernism and post-colonial theory, Paulo Freire's dialogical education, Habermas's theory of communicative action and Boaventura Sousa Santos's ecology of knowledges. We end with examples of articulation of planetary citizenship at the Federal University of Ceará (UFC) and other institutions.

Citizenship in progress in educational documents

In the last four decades, we have observed a gradual but constant progress in the idea of citizenship in the educational sphere. The Federal Constitution of 1988, written after twenty-four years of military dictatorship, establishes as the aim of education: the full development of the student, his preparation for the exercise of citizenship and qualification for work. The National Educational Law (LDB, 1996) emphasizes the acquisition of skills to be a citizen, to be successful at work and in later studies.

The National Curricular Parameters (PCN – MEC, 1998), an important document in Brazilian school curriculum that deeply influenced higher education (HE), emphasizes the role of the school in constructing democracy, which necessarily concerns knowledge, understanding and practice of rights and responsibilities in relation to personal, collective and environmental life. The PCN suggests ethics, cultural pluralism, health, environment, sexual orientation, work and consumption and local themes to be approached interdisciplinarily and transversally (Moraes, 2003). According to this transversal vision of the curriculum, the knowledge transmitted through conventional areas is not enough to attain the goal of educating for citizenship. Transversality brings up a critical view on concepts and ways in which institutions, people and modes of production, distribution and consumption control and dominate cultural and collective life, distorting man's view of nature (Moraes, 2000, 2005). Transversality is the first step in the evolution of Brazilian curriculum. It started in the school and gradually influenced the university curriculum.

In the Basic Education Curriculum Guidelines (DCN, Brazil, MEC, 2013), we find that citizenship suggests a notion of 'access of individuals to goods and services of a modern society', a contemporary discourse of an era in which many Brazilian social movements fought essentially to obtain, from the state, more dignified living conditions, from a dominantly material point of view. This discourse has changed in favour of a citizenship now understood as the active participation of individuals in public decisions in order to ensure better conditions in a civilized life. In the school context, according to DCN, the main issue around which the curriculum should be constructed is what kind of education men and women need in the next twenty years in order to participate in such a diverse world.

Regarding graduation courses of all areas, citizenship has become a major theme in the last twenty years. In the *Licenciaturas*,[1] the guidelines establish that the course must provide the student with 'a solid general and humanistic education, with the ability to analyse and articulate concepts and arguments, interpretation and appreciation of legal and social phenomena, combined with a reflective posture and critical vision that fosters the ability to work in a team, aptitude for autonomous and dynamic learning, as well as qualifications for life, work and the development of citizenship'.

The inclusion of themes such as cultural pluralism, environment and citizenship, to be treated interdisciplinarily, transversally and transdisciplinarily, evidences an evolution in Brazilian curriculum design traditionally characterized by linearity, fragmentation and alienation. Interdisciplinarity, transdisciplinarity and transversality are at the same time epistemological and methodological approaches, since they not only challenge the disciplinary boundaries but also add new analyses of reality. They require discursive contexts with actors from different areas, different spaces, with different world visions, working cooperatively, reflecting on current issues.

---

[1]   Teacher degree courses where students of various areas of knowledge obtain pedagogical skills.

'It is praxis, which implies action and reflection upon the world in order to transform it' (Paulo Freire, 2005, p. 77).

In order to achieve such objectives, we have been using project pedagogy (PP) or project-based learning (PBL), based on Paulo Freire's and Habermas's ideas, at the *Licenciaturas*'s and Education postgraduate course at the Federal University of Ceará (UFC) since 2008, a didactic experience which we will report on in the next section.

The epochal unit of UFC students with their generative themes

Taking advantage of the student body from multiple areas of knowledge, at the *Licenciaturas* and Education postgraduate course, we develop thematic projects on themes chosen by the students themselves – renewable energy, Amazonia, global warming, consumerism, Evolution, hunger around the world, pollution, biodiesel, the Universe, ethanol, television, industrial waste, water, Res Publica and citizenship constitute the students' *thematic universe* – the complex of their *generative themes* (Freire 2005). They are the concrete representation of their *epochal unit* – 'ideas, conceptions, hopes, doubts, values, challenges, in dialectic interaction with their contraries, in search of plenitude' (ibidem, p. 107). Their scope naturally goes beyond geographical boundaries, prompting a reflection on what it is to be a citizen in Brazil and in the world today (Moraes and Freire, 2017).

The methodology of that investigation is dialogical, affording the opportunity both to discover and to stimulate people's awareness regarding these themes. Consistent with the liberating purpose of dialogical education, 'the object of the investigation is not persons, as if they were anatomical fragments, but rather their thought-language referred to reality, the levels at which they perceive that reality, their world view of the world, in which their generative themes are found' (ibidem p.101). Generative themes can be located in concentric circles, starting from the most general to the most particular, acquiring a universal character, contained in the broader epochal unit, covering a whole range of units, sub-units, continental, regional, national, global and we add, planetary.

In the thematic projects, we also get inspiration from Habermas's (1984) communicative action theory. Communicative action, derived from communicative rationality, seeks understanding and consensus among the several social actors. It is opposed to strategic action that results from cognitive–instrumental rationality and seeks domination. Rationality in Habermas refers to how the speaking and acting subjects acquire and use knowledge. The projects have the aim of reaching something near Habermas's ideal speech situation (ISS), when all speakers have equal chances of selecting and employing speech acts and when they can assume interchangeable dialogue roles. The speech acts are based on an underlying consensus which is formed in the reciprocal recognition of at least four claims to validity: the comprehensibility of an utterance, the truth of its propositional component, the correctness and appropriateness of its performatory component and the authenticity of the speaking subject. Reaching understanding, says Habermas, is a process of arriving at an agreement between subjects, on a rational basis, based on common convictions; it cannot be imposed by any of the parts involved.

Understanding both rationalities, cognitive–instrumental and communicative, is important for students to analyse what lies behind the production and distribution of knowledge. The investigation around generative themes is a path towards a critical and creative consciousness. As a student from a Physics *Licenciatura* confessed, a little dramatically, in front of the whole classroom: *I shall never look at the world the same way: these thematic projects opened my head like an axe.*

Postmodernism and post-colonialism and their influence in the curriculum

Introduced in Brazilian education after the military dictatorship (1964–85) postmodernism and post-colonialism theories have influenced the field of the curriculum from the 1990s onwards, permeating the debate with Marxist critical theories, especially with the thoughts of Paulo Freire and his critical pedagogy, causing students to establish connections between situations and their social and political contexts. Contributions related to the power relations that surround the curriculum had great impact, as expressed in the Curriculum Working Group (GT) of the National Association of Research and Postgraduate Studies in Education (ANPED). At the end of this decade, postmodern approaches began to coexist with the critical perspective of Foucault, Derrida, Deleuze, Guatari and Morin, as well as poststructuralist texts translated by a Brazilian curriculum specialist Tomaz Tadeu da Silva. These theories constituted real cultural hybrids (Lopes and Macedo, 2010), having enough expression in the National Education legislation in that period.

Responding to advances in curriculum theory, in December 1996, to celebrate the thirtieth anniversary of UNICAMP (University of Campinas, SP), the Faculty of Education research group on HE organized a seminar entitled 'Science, University and Post-modernity'. To keep a record of this event, Santos Filho and Moraes (2000) organized a book with contributions from five lecturers – Santos Filho, Featherstone, Goergen, Pereira and Moraes. They analysed modern and postmodern characteristics in curricular reforms, using as references the work of Apple (1979), Bobbio (1987, 1990), De Alba (1995), Doll (1989, 1997), Giroux (1986), Habermas (1984), Harvey (1989), Jameson (1996), Japiassu (1976), Lyotard (1986), Morin (1996), Touraine (1981, 1995), among others. *Grosso modo*, according to what was discussed in the seminar and registered in Santos Filho and Moraes (2000), postmodernism paradigmatic shift is evidenced by

- vision of a complex universe, not a simple, harmonious, stable, Newtonian one;
- disbelief in metanarratives like capitalism, socialism and Marxism;
- perception of a multiple, variable, temporal, unpredictable and complex reality, with multiple interacting forces;
- discredit of the concept of a pure and universal reason; affirmation of the local, microphysical, different;
- erosion in the idea of a state that administers social life efficiently; loss of credibility in the political class;
- suspicion of the non-neutrality of science; ethics should be side by side with science;
- discredit of human dominance over nature, ecology and environmental education;

- feeling of indeterminacy and uncertainty about the future;
- emergence of a world citizenship and solidarity;
- disregard of the idea that erudite culture is superior to popular culture, and cultural pluralism;
- problem-based learning and collective work, and teacher–student interaction;
- interdisciplinary and transdisciplinary together with disciplinary (specialist) knowledge.

In Doll's postmodern perspective on the curriculum (1997), the model is not linear, uniform, measured and determined, but is one of emergence and growth, made possible by interaction, transaction, disequilibrium and consequent equilibrium. Transformation should be the rule, and open-endedness is an essential feature of the postmodern framework. The teacher's role is not causal, but transformative. The curriculum is not the racecourse, but the journey itself; metaphors can be more useful than logic in generating dialogue in the community; and educative purpose, planning and evaluation are flexible and focused on process, not product.

In the scenario of the paradigmatic transition announced by postmodernity, post-colonial theory emerges as another theoretical basis for our proposal, especially in regard to the affirmation of the local and different, of a world citizenship, of popular culture and cultural pluralism.

Post-colonial theory aims to discuss the vast web of power relations interwoven among nations that share a heritage from the European colonization process. The theory emphasizes that it is only possible to understand the organization of the current globalized world if we consider the power relations between nations and the various implications of the European colonial adventure, especially for those people who were colonized (Silva, 1999).

Quijano (2000) points out that modern intellectual rationality is connected to the knowledge of colonial, capitalist, Eurocentric domination process, commonly referred to as Eurocentrism. This category does not involve all the cognitive history throughout Europe. In other words, it does not refer to all modes of knowledge of all Europeans and in all times, but to a specific rationality or perspective that became globally hegemonic, colonizing and overlapping all previous or different others, both in Europe and in the rest of the world. It also promotes a profound distortion of historical self-image developed by the colonized countries.

The most severe criticism post-colonial studies offer is vindication, recognition and inclusion of a range of knowledge, traditions, culture and world views that do not conform to the European canon and, therefore, are discarded as vulgar, irrelevant, superstitious and primitive from the Eurocentric model. This domination, still rooted and poignant on current relationships, penetrates various spheres of collective and subjective thinking (Silva, 2014). It also promotes a profound distortion of historical self-image developed by the colonized countries, as Quijano (2000) notes: 'The Eurocentric perspective of knowledge operates as a mirror that distorts what it reflects' (Quijano, 2005, p. 239).

Among the important notions that act as a delegitimization instrument of identity and culture of the subjugated nations is the concept of representation. Representation, according to this theory, refers to the forms of expression upon which the Other is represented, with the very illustrative example of the arts and literature, able to propagate an image aesthetically caricatured, derogatory and/or superficial of certain people and their culture. The relationship between culture and aesthetics is distorted. It is through representation that we build the identity of the Other and, at the same time, our own identity. It was by representing the West, along the path of its colonial expansion, that an 'other' was built, supposedly inferior and possessed of a wild and unbridled sexuality. Seen as a form of knowledge of the Other, the representation is at the heart of the connection of knowledge to power (Quijano, 2000).

Since the beginning of the colonization process, knowledge was deeply tied to power. The settler, at the heart of the connection from the beginning, made the colony and its natives the object of his research, perceiving them from their perspective of domination and exploitation, characterizing them as exotic, and picturesque regarding their own civility references, thus strengthening their self-perception of superiority.

Another interesting point to be considered in our analysis is that it was not enough to process the colonial exploitation and physical subjugation of people: it was also necessary, through education and religion, to assert the superiority of white culture – European, Christian, patriarchal – over every 'primitive and barbarian' world view of colonized peoples.

It is necessary, however, to ratify that this whole process of enculturation did not occur without resistance. The colonial and post-colonial process reveals the presence of miscegenation, syncretism, hybridity, 'Obviously, the result is favourable to power but never so crystal, never completely, never so definitely as desired. The hybrid bears the marks of power, but also the marks of resistance' (Quijano, 2000, p. 129).

Post-colonial theory proposes an analysis that can shed light on the knowledge and the rationality born and raised in the university. We seek to understand to what extent the present narratives in academic curricula continue to propagate the European imperial model at the expense of our own cultural constructions. We must investigate what new forms of cultural domination of the consumer society can nowadays influence academic projects, setting up a neocolonialism. The issues raised by post-colonial discussion should not imply that the academic or other educational institution curriculum can or should be impartial, free of bias, but rather to understand that the curriculum is a territory of dispute, to clarify the correlation of forces between knowledge, power, aesthetics and culture.

Post-colonial studies demystify the supposed neutrality that modern scientific knowledge has postulated and that the university, supported by its ethical commitment, needs to unveil, assuming the 'why' and 'who' of their educational project (Moraes and Freire, 2016). Its main contribution to social and educational thinking is that it creates the conditions for 'the possibility of theorizing a non-coercive relationship or dialogue with the excluded 'Other' of Western humanism' (Gandhi, 1998, p. 39, in Andreotti, 2011).

Our next section is about the excluded 'Others' in our case: the victims of discrimination in society and at the university, and their insertion in the context of our proposal.

Fighting discrimination within the university

Our proposal of such an inclusive theme as planetary citizenship would be incomplete if we did not mention social and colour discrimination, or simplifying it, *racism* – this remote effect of colonization that remains veiled in curricular and educational practices. Stuart Hall contributed to the discussion in a lecture 'Race: The floating signifier', given at Goldsmiths College, University of London. In our culture, he says, there is an urge to classify humans into different types according to their physical or intellectual characteristics. In a way, this is a positive cultural impulse, because we now understand the importance of all forms of classification to meanings. Once you are classified, a whole range of other things falls into place. Racism as a philosophy holds that there is a natural connection between the appearance (differences of colour, hair and bones) and what people think and do, how smart they are, whether they are good athletes, good dancers or even 'civilized'. Racists believe that these features are the result not of the environment but of our genetics. However, all attempts to substantiate the concept of race scientifically, in biological or genetic terms, have proven unsustainable.

According to Quijano (2000), in America the idea of race originated in reference to the phenotypic differences between conquerors and conquered. It was built by reference to supposed differential biological structures between those groups. The formation of social relations based on this idea produced historically new social identities, Indians, blacks and mestizos, and redefined others. Spanish and Portuguese terms, which until then indicated only geographic origin or country of origin, became references to new identities with a racial connotation, to the extent that social relations that were being configured were relations of domination. Such identities were associated with hierarchies, places and corresponding social roles, as constitutive of them and, therefore, the pattern of colonial domination was imposed. In other words, race and racial identity were established as instruments of basic social classification of the population.

Over time, the colonizers codified the phenotypic traits of the colonized such as colour, assumed as the emblematic characteristic of racial category. This coding was initially established, probably in the Anglo-American area. Blacks were there not only as the most important exploited, because the main part of the economy lay in their work. They were, above all, the most important colonized race, since Indians were not part of that colonial society.

Race was a way to give legitimacy to the relations of domination imposed by the conquest. The subsequent constitution of Europe as a new identity, after America and the expansion of European colonialism on the rest of the world, led to the development of the Eurocentric perspective of knowledge, and with it the theoretical elaboration of the idea of race as a naturalization of these colonial domination relations between Europeans and non-Europeans. Historically, this meant a new way of legitimizing the already old ideas and practices of relations of superiority/inferiority between dominant and dominated. Since then it has proved itself as the most effective and lasting instrument of universal social domination: the conquered and dominated were placed in a natural position of inferiority and consequently also their phenotypic traits as well as their mental and cultural discoveries. Thus, race became the first fundamental criterion for the distribution of the world population in the ranks, places and roles in the power structure of the new society.

In terms of what measures have been taken to eliminate social and colour discrimination from the university, we can mention the quotas, the improvement in the access and enrolment of less favoured classes in terms of grants, and the inclusion of projects and lines of research in the curriculum that introduce Indian and black culture. The latter will be discussed in the next section.

Regarding the quotas, Law no. 12.711/2012, sanctioned in August of this year, guarantees the reservation of 50 per cent of enrolments per course, in the fifty-nine federal universities and thirty-eight federal institutes of education, science and technology, to students from public schools, from families of income equal to or less than a minimum salary and for black, *pardo*[2] and

---

[2] *Pardo* is a census category to which many Brazilians of mixed ethnic heritage ascribe themselves.

indigenous people. The remaining 50 per cent of the vacancies remain for wide competition. The race criterion will be self-declaring, as occurs in the demographic census and in any affirmation policy in Brazil. The minimum percentage corresponding to the sum of blacks, *pardos* and indigenous people in the state will also be taken into account, according to the latest demographic census of the Brazilian Institute of Geography and Statistics (IBGE).

The federal programme that awards grants to *pardo*, black and indigenous students at universities has been a major step towards equity and it comes along with initiatives to introduce popular knowledge in the curriculum. No doubt this is a great measure to start solving the problem; however, we must be aware of the implementation of these *restorative multicultural* (Canen, 2010) policies. They can only guarantee the repair of historical social debts with these groups if, in addition to access, the university allows them to learn from a curriculum close to their cultural and economic realities.

The difficulty we face in educational terms is that, as Paulo Freire, Milton Santos and Darcy Ribeiro mention, we never think of Brazil for its people. Freire (1967) declared himself in action against an alienated elite, who sees people as 'things' (p.35), who imposes an 'education' for 'domestication', for alienation instead of an education for freedom. Milton Santos (2015) and Darcy Ribeiro (1995) were in line with this perspective of developing a new national praxis for the formation of a mestizo elite, from our roots, capable of understanding the dilemmas of Brazil, committed to autonomy and sovereignty of the country. More recently, the works of European scientists critical of cultural imperialism, such as Pierre Bourdieu, Homi Bhabha, Boaventura de Sousa Santos, help us to better understand how post-colonial domination operates and to reflect on how a Brazilian education could be, if the origins and identity of its people were taken into consideration.

Becoming planetary: Reaction of The Global South university

The Global South is not a geographical concept even though the great majority of its populations live in countries of the Southern hemisphere. The South is rather a metaphor for the human suffering that has been caused by capitalism and colonialism on the global level (Santos, 2016, p. 17).

The university lives in a main contradiction in its supposed universality: it has restricted itself to producing and propagating scientific/occidental knowledge, while on the other hand, it has excluded the knowledge accumulated for centuries by people who have long inhabited this land. The ecology of knowledges offers a path for overcoming such contradiction.

In the context of an alternative model of reason, that Santos (2002) calls 'cosmopolitan rationality', lies the proposal of the ecology of knowledges. Within this new rationality, Santos recommends the practice of a *sociology of absences* (Santos, 2007), the epistemological exercise of looking at the present in a more democratic and comprehensive way to identify and give visibility to a wide range of cultural, epistemological and experiential possibilities, made invisible by a hegemonic logic that disqualifies and delegitimizes these other forms of social action. The ecology of knowledge considers necessary a constant dialogue between traditional popular and scientific knowledges, an alternative way of dealing with the monoculture of closed scientific thinking. It is anchored in the belief that all inequality is also irremediably a cognitive inequality. 'Reality is inaccessible to any knowledge system', argues Sousa Santos. That is when the incompleteness of human beings becomes even more visible. However, any type of knowledge must pass through the filter of critical analyses to reveal its tacit and implicit meaning, its cosmovision, its contradictions, absences and exclusions. In principle, all visions of epistemic communities should be accepted but they should also be submitted to scrutiny from different angles. Especially in countries of strong immigration – nowadays practically all countries have multicultural populations – on both sides, of immigrants and natives, the selective incorporation of traditions is useful to make conviviality possible. The credibility that these other types of knowledge enjoy among its actors should be enough for the establishment of a dialogue with the scientific knowledge, without them being considered inferior or of a subordinate condition. This is a very compelling premise in Sousa Santos's works – that there is not an ignorance in general, but that all ignorance is ignorant of certain knowledge and all knowledge overcomes a particular ignorance.

A very hard choice had to be made in this phase of our text, among the examples of the articulation of planetary citizenship at UFC and other institutions that are taking initiatives in this direction.

- In the Education postgraduate programme of UFC (PPGE-UFC), we seek to understand the remote impact of colonization on Brazilian economy, society and culture through lines of research on rural education, environmental education, spirituality, culture of peace, art, Africanism and Afro-descendance, ethnicity, culture, subjectivity and gender, social movements and Paulo Freire's popular education.[3] The project also offers important insights for contemporary debates involving intercultural studies, coloniality/decoloniality, dialogues about the new epistemological paradigms and their influence on educational processes.

- Brazilian music is perhaps one of the best examples of multicultural synthesis. At UFC's Music course, we have groups that criticize the conservatorial model of teaching, with all that it brings of Eurocentrism, and propose alternative musical training that take into account the very rich local production, seeing it as it really is – a multi-secular social elaboration that involves African, American and European contributions, creating something new. In this sense, the emphasis is on collective teaching, learning and creation practices, based on local sound experiences and on the *Epistemologies of the South*[4] where Bach, Mozart and Beethoven, together with Pixinguinha, Luis Gonzaga and Chico Buarque,[5] establish a most fruitful dialogue.

---

[3] Popular education is an approach where participants engage each other and the educator as co-learners to critically reflect on the issues in their community and then take action to change them

[4] In Santos (2016), the epistemology of the south is 'an engagement with the ways of knowing from the perspectives of those who have systematically suffered the injustices, dominations and oppressions caused by colonialism, capitalism, and patriarchy' (p. 18).

[5] Popular Brazilian composers and singers.

- The School of Advanced Studies (Colégio de Estudos Avançados – CEA) has promoted interdisciplinary panels bringing to round-tables areas of knowledge that are rarely discussed like science and creativity, science and citizenship, and science and poetry. As part of the activities of CEA, in 5 December 2018, Prof Boaventura Sousa Santos gave a lecture on Epistemologies of the South and the Defence of the University arguing that the university is under threat due to the pressure of capitalist society and its market ideology.
- In the Paulo Freire Institute (IPF), the House of World Citizenship (CCP – Casa da Cidadania Planetária) aims to develop programmes, projects, discussion forums and social mobilization, contributing to the construction of a planetary citizenship, active and critical in different educational spaces, from the perspective of a culture of sustainability.
- The First International Meeting of Pachamama[6] at the UFC Law School, 21–23 November 2018, had students, activists, teachers, researchers and artists debating the rights of nature, uniting traditional and scientific knowledge.
- Theatre and lectures marked the Human Rights Week (10–14 December 2018), an event that included cultural presentations showing the daily life of exclusion and social prejudice experienced by young black people.
- Postgraduate students in Education developed the project *Sertão, Saberes e Vivências* (Hinterland, Knowledges and Experiences) meant to articulate the floating signifier planetary citizenship in schools and pedagogy courses. The proposed activities have a horizontal dimension, in the sense of the inter/transdisciplinary approach and at the same time a vertical dimension, that covers the curriculum from pre-school to high school The project dedicated a special section to one of the icons in the *sertão* Antônio Gonçalves da Silva, well known as Patativa[7] do Assaré, a popular/oral poet, improviser, composer, singer and guitar player born in 1909 in Serra de Santana, Assaré, a small town in Ceará. In his poetry, Patativa relates the *sertão* and its *sertanejo* to the universal, singing of beautiful nature, when the scarce rain turns the soil green, and of merciless nature, with the dryness of the earth and the blistering sun. Patativa is our favourite planetary citizen and the university has a lot to learn from him (Patativa do Assaré, 2005).
- Institutions, such as the Federal University of Outro Preto, University of Brasília, State University of Ceará and UNICAMP (State University of Campinas) are engaged in what they call an 'epistemic and pedagogical experimentation': the Encontro de Saberes (Encounter of Knowledges), an initiative of the National Institute of Science, Technology and Inclusion in Higher Education and Research (INCTI), based at the University of Brasília.
- In December 2018, UNICAMP applied its first indigenous entrance exam with indigenous students writing about themselves and their proposals. UNICAMP also created a Work Group on indigenous inclusion.

---

[6] 'Pachamama' is a goddess revered by the indigenous people of the Andes. She is also known as the earth/time mother. [1]In Inca mythology, Pachamama is a fertility goddess who presides over planting and harvesting, embodies the mountains and causes earthquakes. She is also an ever-present and independent deity who has her own self-sufficient and creative power to sustain life on this earth. Her shrines are hallowed rocks, and the boles of legendary trees, and her artists envision her as an adult female bearing harvests of potatoes and coca leaves. https://en.wikipedia.org/wiki/Pachamama

[7] Patativa is the name of a local little bird of plain appearance, but with a powerful song.

- With the creation of ethnic–racial quotas, the use of grades in the National High School Examination (ENEM) for the first time and the expansion of test sites, the university's main objective is to achieve a balance between students from private and public schools, with 50 per cent for each side, and reaching the target of 37.2 per cent of students declaring themselves black or *pardos*.

There are many other examples of inclusion in Brazilian universities nowadays. We can say that under the influence of universities, together with some cultural institutions, we are waking up to the diversity, the richness and the danger of losing forever such important knowledge that we are so lucky to be part of.

Conclusion

As stated in the beginning of this chapter, the theme of citizenship in Brazil can never disappear from our educational institutions. In fact, it has always been there. We have evidenced that it is fluctuating among institutions in need of some systematization and the right context for our proposal of a planetary citizenship as an inter/transdisciplinary theme is the Brazilian university curriculum.

Contextualizing it, we cited documents that have emphasized citizenship in the educational sphere since 1988. We showed our pedagogical experience in the *Licenciaturas* using Paulo Freire's generative themes in interdisciplinary projects, to increase students' levels of perception of reality and of the context around them. We were also inspired by Habermas's communicative action theory that makes us postulate another rationality, seeking to confront the supremacy of modern science – not to suppress it but to redirect it to the complexity of life and to a sense of social emancipation. We concluded that interdisciplinary and transdisciplinary proposals only have sense and coherence if based on issues that concern the real world of people, reinforcing interdisciplinarity and transdisciplinarity as categories of action.

We contextualized the use of planetary citizenship as a floating signifier in postmodern and post-colonial theories, which poses questions and issues that defy the university's conventional wisdom, its historically constructed identity and its place and function in a complex society. Approaching the theme as a floating signifier seems more appropriate to the context, the structure and the purpose of a postmodern, post-colonial university. The institutional initiatives cited have evidenced a different attitude of the university in relation to its social role.

The challenges this proposal faces lie in overcoming barriers originated from discipline-oriented courses, such as epistemological delimitations, specific vocabulary, research methodologies or even physical facilities in buildings that were created to keep areas apart from one another. However, the articulation of a planetary citizenship in the curriculum is encountering much acceptance from professors and students who are willing to face the challenges. They see that this epistemological experience tends to promote the re-elaboration and enrichment of methodologies, making them more appropriate to the complexity of the research contexts and more in tune with the planet.

We conclude that planetary citizenship as a transdisciplinary theme enables a curriculum as a negotiable contract between participants, with open ends that favour the unexpected and the creative and that questions the canons of Western culture. It is inclusive because participants can come from all social segments; it is receptive because it implies that popular knowledge must be accepted without prejudice; it is effective because it provides our society with answers that come on the wings of new technologies and in the voices of new participants; and it is democratic because it favours attitudes and values that transcend barriers of skin colour, class, religion, sex or politics.

Bibliography

Andreotti, V. (2011) *Actionable Postcolonial Theory in Education*. New York: Palgrave Macmillan, 268p.

Apple, M. (1979) *Ideologia e currículo*. São Paulo: Brasiliense, 288p.

Assaré, Patativa do (2005) *Inspiração Nordestina: Cantos de Patativa*. São Paulo: Hedra, 351p.

Bobbio, N. (1987) *Sociedade e Estado na filosofia política moderna*. São Paulo: Brasiliense, 180p.

Bobbio, N. (1990) *Estado, governo, sociedade*. São Paulo: Paz e Terra, 256p.

Brasil-MEC (1998) *Parâmetros Curriculares Nacionais*. Brasília: MEC/SEF.

Brasil-MEC (2012) *Diretrizes Curriculares Nacionais para a Educação Ambiental* (DCN/EA-2012).

Brasil-MEC (2013) *Diretrizes Curriculares Nacionais da Educação Básica* (DCN/EB).

Canen, A. (2010) Sentidos e dilemas do Multiculturalismo: Desafios Curriculares para o novo milênio, in Lopes, A. C. and Macedo, E., *Currículo: Debates Contemporâneos*, 3 edn. São Paulo: Cortez, 174–95.

De Alba, A. (org) (1995) *Postmodernidad y educación*. Mexico: SESU, 313p.

Doll, W. E. Jr (1989) Foundations for a post-modern curriculum. *Journal of Curiculum Studies*, 21(3), 243–53.

Doll, W. E. Jr (1997) *Currículo: uma perspectiva pós-moderna*. Porto Alegre: Artes Médicas, 224p.

Featherstone, M. (2000) Da universidade a pós-modernidade? Explorando as possibilidades de novas formas de comunicação, in Santos Filho, J. C. and Moraes, S. E. (orgs), *Escola e Universidade na Pós-modernidade*. Campinas, SP: Mercado de Letras, 61–99.

Freire, P. (1967) *Educação como prática de liberdade*. Rio de Janeiro: Paz e Terra, 158p.

Freire, P. (2005) *Pedagogia do Oprimido*, 46th edn. Rio de Janeiro: Paz e Terra, 213p.

Gandhi, L. (1998) *Postcolonial Theory: A Critical Introduction*. New York: Columbia University Press, 201p.

Giroux, H. A. (1986) *Teoria Crítica e resistência em educação – para além das teorias de reprodução*. Petrópolis: Vozes, 336p.

Goergen, P. (2000) A crise da universidade Moderna, in Santos Filho, J. C. and Moraes, S. E. (orgs), *Escola e Universidade na Pós-modernidade*. Campinas, SP: Mercado de Letras, 101–61.

Habermas, J. (1984) *The Theory of Communicative Action- Reason and the Rationalization of Society* Translated by Thomas McCarthy, vol. 1. Boston: Beacon Press, 465p.

Hall, S. (1997) 'Race: The floating signifier'. Northampton, MA: Media Education Foundation. Online: www.mediaed.org/assets/products/407/transcript_407.pdf (accessed 29 June 2014).

Harvey, D. (1989) *Condição pós-moderna*. São Paulo: Loyola.

Jameson, F. O. (1996) *Pós-modernismo*. São Paulo: Ática, 431p.

Japiassu, H. (1976) *Interdisciplinaridade e patologia do saber*. Rio de Janeiro: Imago, 111p.

Laclau, E. (2007) *Emancipation(s)*. London: Verso, 126p.

Lopes, A. C. and Macedo, E. (2010) O pensamento curricular no Brasil, in Lopes, A. C. and Macedo, E., *Currículo: Debates Contemporâneos*, 3 edn. São Paulo: Cortez, 13–53.

Lyotard, J. F. (1986) *O pós-moderno*. Rio de Janeiro: José Olimpio, 128p.

Moraes, S. E. (2000) Currículo, transversalidade e pós-modernidade, in Santos Filho, J. C. and Moraes, S. E. (orgs), *Escola e Universidade na pós-modernidade*. Campinas, SP: Mercado de Letras, 201–45.

Moraes, S. E. (2003) In search of a vision: How Brazil is struggling to envision citizenship for its public schools, in Pinar, W. (ed.), *International Handbook of Curriculum Research*. New Jersey: Lawrence Erlbaum Associates, 205–19.

Moraes, S. E. (2005) Interdisciplinaridade e transversalidade mediante projetos temáticos, in *Revista Brasileira de Estudos Pedagógicos (RBEP)*, Brasília, v. 86n. 213/214, pp. 38–54, maio/dez.

Moraes, S. E. (2014) Global citizenship as a floating signifier: Lessons from UK universities. *International Journal of Development Education and Global Learning*, 6(2), 27–42.

Moraes, S. E. and Freire, L. de A. (2016) The University Curriculum and the Ecology of Knowledges towards building a Planetary Citizenship. *Transnational Curriculum Inquiry*, 13(1), 36–55.

Moraes, S. E. and Freire, L. de A. (2017) Planetary citizenship and the ecology of knowledges in Brazilian universities. *International Journal of Development Education and Global Learning*, 8(3), 25–42.

Morin, E. (1996) Epistemologia da complexidade, in Schnittmann, D. F., *Novos paradigmas, cultura e subjetividade*. Porto Alegre: Artes Médicas, 294p.

Pereira, E. M. (2000) Pós-modernidade: desafios à universidade, in Santos Filho, J. C. and Moraes, S. E. (orgs), *Escola e Universidade na Pós-modernidade*. Campinas, SP: Mercado de Letras, 163–200.

Quijano, A. (2000) Colonialidad del poder, eurocentrismo y América Latina. *En libro: La colonialidad del saber: eurocentrismo y ciencias sociales. Perspectivas Latinoamericanas*. Edgardo Lander (comp.) CLACSO, Consejo Latinoamericano de Ciencias Sociales, Buenos Aires, Argentina. Julio. http://bib liotecavirtual.clacso.org.ar/ar/libros/lander/quijano.rtf (Accessed 23 August 2015).

Quijano, A. (2005) Colonialidade do poder, eurocentrismo e América Latina, in Lander, E. (org), *A colonialidade do saber: eurocentrismo e ciências sociais. Perspectivas latino-americanas*. Colección Sur Sur, CLACSO, Ciudad Autónoma de Buenos Aires, Argentina. September 2005, pp. 227–78. http://bibliotecavirtual.clacso.org.ar/ar/libros/lander/pt/Quijano.rtf (Acesso em 10 February 2015).

Ribeiro, D. (1995) *O povo brasileiro – a formação e o sentido do Brasil*. Rio de Janeiro: Companhia das Letras, 477p.

Santos, B. S. (2002) *Um discurso sobre as ciências*. Porto: Edições Afrontamento, 26p.

Santos, B. S. (2007) Beyond abyssal thinking: From global lines to ecologies of knowledges. *Review*, XXX(1), 45–89.

Santos, B. S. (2016) Epistemologies of the South and the future. *From the European South: A Transdisciplinary Journal of Postcolonial Humanities*, 1, 17–29.

Santos, M. (2010) *Por uma outra globalização (do pensamento único à consciência universal)*. http://www. educadores.diaadia.pr.gov.br/arquivos/File/2010/sugestao_leitura/sociologia/outra_globalizacao.pdf

Santos, M. (2015) *Por uma outra globalização: do pensamento único à consciência universal*. São Paulo: Record. 24ª edição, 88p.

Santos Filho, J. C. (2000) Universidade, modernidade e pós-modernidade, in Santos Filho, and Moraes, S. E. and Santos Filho, J. C. (orgs), *Escola e Universidade na Pós-modernidade*. Campinas, SP: Mercado de Letras, 15–60.

Silva, T. T. (1999) *Documentos de identidade*. Belo Horizonte: Autêntica, 157p.

Silva, T. T. (2014) *Teorias do Currículo*. Porto: Porto Editora, 157p.

Touraine, A. (1981) *O pós-socialismo*. Porto: Edições Afrontamento, 231p.

Touraine, A. (1995) *Crítica da Modernidade*. Petrópolis: Vozes, 431p.

Chapter 17

How Do Higher Education Students Negotiate Global Responsibility in Education?

Hanna Posti-Ahokas*[1], Josephine Moate[2] and Elina Lehtomäki[3]

Introduction

The notion of global responsibility is essential to understanding the complexities related to achieving global development targets, including the UN Sustainable Development Goals (SDGs). Higher education (HE) plays an important role in analysing and developing the understanding of the connections between the local and the global (Rumbley and Altbach, 2016; Lehtomäki, Moate and Posti-Ahokas, 2019) and in prompting critical and reflective questions about the development agenda itself (Odora Hoppers, 2015; Stein, Andreotti and Suša, 2016). In this chapter, we focus on discussing a pedagogical intervention in the context of Finnish HE aiming to go beyond the global education (GE) development rhetoric and supporting critical thinking within and around GE development through the notion of global responsibility. This approach acknowledges that the concept of development carries connotations requiring critical reflection and that HE students should critically engage with and challenge the common assumptions and dominant theoretical frameworks of mainstream development discourses (Bryan, 2008; Bourn, 2014a).

Development education (DE) promotes a global outlook on global development issues. Bourn's (2014b) depiction of DE as a *process of learning* is reflected both in the pedagogical intervention presented here and in our continued collaborative research on our students' learning and on our own pedagogical practice on themes related to international education development. Our previous studies have focused on identifying university students' meaningful learning experiences (Lehtomäki, Moate and Posti-Ahokas, 2016) and exploring how students assign global responsibility at different levels (Lehtomäki, Moate and Posti-Ahokas, 2019). In this chapter, complexity, critical thinking and commitment to social justice are emphasized as key characteristics and objectives of DE (e.g. Bourn, 2014a,b; Brown, 2014). We have found Brown's (2014) description of transformative pedagogies in DE particularly inspiring. To summarize Brown (2014: 9), the role of DE is to ensure that outdated or inequality-producing norms and stereotypes are not reinforced, yet assumptions and biases are challenged in a fair and meaningful

[1]   University of Jyväskylä, Finland (hanna.posti-ahokas@jyu.fi).
[2]   University of Jyväskylä, Finland.
[3]   University of Oulu, Finland.

way, learners are informed and free to act, and the values and objective of social justice are maintained.

This understanding of DE is particularly useful when working on the complex notion of global responsibility. It connects the importance of (historical) understanding of inequality and injustice with the commitment to and promotion of social justice and places the learners at the centre in making such connections, through a deeply engaging learning dialogue. According to Brown (2014), recognition of biases is allowed by exploring and challenging both personal and sociocultural assumptions in dialogue. A safe space for the dialogue is required for discovering and questioning deeply held assumptions and their influence on opinions (Bakhtin, 1986), recognizing that as human beings we are both the objects and the subjects as we make and are made by history (Freire, 1998). Critical thinking can be seen as a precondition for *critical engagement* in HE, which Pashby and Andreotti (2016) suggest as a strategy towards ethical internationalization. Through students' critical engagement, social justice may gain a normative and strategic role in HE discourses (Singh, 2011) with the political becoming more pedagogical as the languages of critique and possibility come together (Giroux, 1985) and as students of education seek to take up their places in the 'process of change' (Freire, 1985: 129).

The aim of this study is to better understand how university students respond to critical conceptualizations of global responsibility in education and develop their own understanding of global responsibility. The study was conducted in connection with a seminar on GE development and a course focusing on international policies and practices in education at the University of Jyväskylä, Finland, in autumn 2017. The students in an international master's programme in Educational Sciences represent diverse educational backgrounds, and they brought experiences from all parts of the world to the joint learning dialogues. Analysing how these future education professionals view and negotiate the stakeholders and conditions for realizing global responsibility in education development should contribute to understanding the complex notion of global responsibility in education development.

Approaches to global responsibility in education development

Critical research on the global SDGs has pointed to problems related to the continued north–south division of SDGs (Bexell and Jönsson, 2017), development vision being largely based on the transfer of Western knowledge (Stein, Andreotti and Suša, 2016) and a failure to recognize contextuality in target setting (Sayed and Ahmed, 2015). Bexell and Jönsson (2017) characterize the SDGs as products of international political and power relations reliant on moral commitments and political resolve in combination with financial and institutional capacities. From this perspective, the issue of global responsibility becomes central in work towards achieving the SDGs.

Global responsibility, however, can be conceptualized in different ways. In their analysis of SDG summit documents, Bexell and Jönsson (2017) identify three main forms of responsibility – cause, obligation and accountability – that build on each other. The authors explain that the historical causality of current problems influences the identification of obligations, whereas accountability demands that obligations be clearly defined beforehand. The authors argue, however, that causality is hidden in the documentation undermining discussion on the root causes and contributors to injustice. As a result, responsibility is only presented as role-responsibility and an obligation towards the future. Although an accountability approach would be useful to evaluate how responsibilities have been enacted, the largely quantitative accountability indicators easily overshadow broader obligations.

An alternative conceptualization of responsibility is present in Young's (2006) forward-looking social connection model of responsibility that emphasizes shared responsibility and collective action. Obligations of justice are considered to arise between persons by virtue of the social processes that connect them. People across the world are connected through complex structural processes and beyond political boundaries. Rather than assign responsibility to a particular agent whose actions are shown to be causally connected to the circumstances, the structural positioning of agents in Young's model recognizes the different kinds and amounts of resources and constraint in terms of power, privilege, interest and collective ability. Under this model, agents share responsibility with others who are differently situated, with whom they usually must cooperate in order to effect change rather than following pre-established roles.

In the context of our study, the role of HE in advancing global development becomes central. The role of HE in development is increasingly recognized, particularly within the current discourse on creating knowledge societies (e.g. Stein, Andreotti and Suša, 2016; Rumbley and Altbach, 2016). However, Stein, Andreotti and Suša (2016) argue that universities often position themselves within the modern/colonial global imaginary of mainstream development and are thus at risk of reproducing the colonial division of the world. Therefore, it is important to link HE with diverse perspectives about development. Critical engagement with the SDG agenda to open up critically important and reflective questions about the agenda itself could be a contribution of HE in development (Stein, Andreotti and Suša, 2016).

DE is characterized as learning based on promoting a global outlook, understanding of power and inequality, belief in social justice and commitment to reflection, dialogue and transformation (Bourn, 2014a,b). Perspectives of critical DE are important to understanding what constitutes quality education in different educational contexts (Skinner, Blum and Bourn, 2013). Drawing on this view, the University of Jyväskylä has organized annual seminars focusing on global learning and the SDG4 (quality education for all) since 2011. The seminars have provided a space for cross-cultural learning dialogue, perspective-taking and critical engagement in GE issues (Lehtomäki, Posti-Ahokas and Moate, 2015; Lehtomäki, Moate and Posti-Ahokas, 2016). In our previous research (Lehtomäki, Moate and Posti-Ahokas, 2019), we have studied how university students in education discuss and assign global responsibility in education development to 'others', 'we' and 'I'. Although our work highlights the way in which university students distinguish between key educational stakeholders, we recognize a limitation in that participation in the SDG4 seminars does not automatically mean that university students enter into the critical discussions and theorize key issues that they face as future educational professionals. The pedagogical intervention reported here is a response to this challenge and our findings point to the importance of providing a pedagogical space that fosters critical thinking around global responsibility in education.

A study of university students' online dialogues

The study focuses on the five ECTS course International Education Policies and Practices taught as part of international master's programmes in Education at the University of Jyväskylä, Finland. The annual two-day SDG4 seminar targeting a wider audience forms the core of the course. Introductory lectures, pre-seminar assignments and writing a reflective learning journal have supported students' learning on GE development. To further support HE students' critical engagement with the notion of global responsibility related to SDG4, an additional theory-based element was introduced to the course, focusing on GE development in 2017. This paper discusses how the learning dialogue initiated at the SDG4 seminar was taken forward through theory-guided online discussions.

The purpose of the exploratory dialogues on GE development was to reflect and theorize a selected topic related to SDG4 through a small-group online discussion, to practise perspective-taking and literature-based argumentation and to contribute to a shared negotiation process. To support clarification of divergent views and elucidation of arguments, a diamond ranking exercise (Education Services Australia, 2012; Clark et al., 2013) was done by the groups at the beginning and the end of the discussion. The diamond exercise aimed to provide a shared starting point for embarking on a more critical exploration of the themes and ideas that they come across in the literature related to their chosen topic. The second diamonds created at the end of the group discussion depict the way in which their understanding has developed and changed, providing a momentary resolution before moving on with critical reflections in other educational environments. A brief explanation of the learning process is given in Table 17.1.

Table 17.1 Timing, Themes and Instructions Given for the Group Dialogue

Time	Theme	Instructions given to Students
Week 1	Introduction to the process and the tools used, agreeing on groups and topics, first diamond ranking exercise to form a preliminary understanding of the selected topic.	The first diamond model exercise is done in class so you can get to know each other. Also agree on work modalities within your group. Sign and return the voluntary consent form.
Week 2	First reading and discussion: Sharon Stein, Vanessa de Oliveira Andreotti & Rene Suša (2016): 'Beyond 2015', within the modern/colonial global imaginary.	Online discussion is divided in three parts, each lasting one week. The first two weeks include a reading assignment. Read the two articles and participate in the discussion. Rather than one extensive contribution, try to carry out several dialogical cycles. Pay attention to your own positionalities/biases and to incidents where you disagree. You can also discuss these in your writing. In the end of each week, one group member can summarize the discussion (title the contribution as summary).
Week 3	Second reading and discussion: A freely selected article related to the group's topic. Each member can either choose their own article or the group can work on the same text.	
Week 4	Second diamond model exercise and group self-assessment.	During the final week, meet with the group over coffee or online (Skype, etc.) and summarize your ideas through the second diamond model exercise. During the last meeting with the group, conduct the group self-assessment.

Description of data

Two groups of students (*N*=9) who had selected global responsibility as their online discussion theme were asked for permission to use their written dialogue anonymously as material for research, without affecting course results and grading. Group A consisted of five students who sent in contributions to their online dialogue platform, from 14 to 30 November. The online dialogue of Group A comprised a total of 17 written contributions (5,180 words) submitted during this period. The four members of the second group, Group B, produced a total of 23 written contributions (3,707 words) between 11 November and 3 December. The researchers extracted and anonymized the online discussions from Moodle to start the analysis. The pictures of the two diamonds developed by each group were included in the data set.

Analysis

After the first reading of familiarization with the data, we looked at how the students' dialogues evolved, including key questions posed by the participants, the introduction of different themes and the ways in which the participants collaboratively navigate their unfolding conceptualization of global responsibility in education. The diamonds that the groups produced at the beginning and the end of the dialogues provide useful maps of participants' shared orientation and an opportunity to (temporarily) conclude their critical reflections around global responsibility in education. With regard to the analysis, the diamonds provide clear starting and end points to the learning dialogues.

An abductive approach (Patton, 2002) was used to explore how understanding of global responsibility was formed in the two group dialogues (Group A through social connections, Group B through conditions). The findings from the two different cases are outlined below. The findings are summarized through an illustration of the dimensions, attributes and qualities ascribed to responsibility through the discussions.

Findings: Dialogic positioning of global responsibility

The two learning dialogues by groups of students analysed in this chapter point to two distinct approaches to conceptualizing global responsibility from an educational perspective. The dialogue from Group A highlights the connectivity between different stakeholders, whereas the dialogue from Group B highlights the way in which wider conditions form and inform conceptualizations and practices of global responsibility. These two approaches are not exclusive, however, as both cases include connectivity and conditions. We first present the qualitative change in understanding of global responsibility in the two groups, with reference to the initial and final diamond illustrations produced by each group. We then turn to the way in which responsibility was referred to within the group discussions.

Case 1: Interconnectedness of stakeholders

The first diamond illustration (left in Figure 17.1) from Group A combines stakeholders, such as government, administration, schools, wider community and actions or requirements, including accountability, involving relevant people. In addition to naming the stakeholders, this diamond also points to the nature of actions. These two considerations are clearly present in the diamond with the lower positions occupied by the stakeholders and actions placed at the top suggesting that action is rated more highly than stakeholders. Arguably placing 'connecting policies with reality' at the centre of the diamond is an attempt to join stakeholders and actions. There is little about 'us', however, in this diamond; rather the focus is on institutional others fulfilling global responsibilities.

The online dialogue of Group A, however, suggests that reading an article on taking a critical, post-colonial stance to development theory and the global role of HE (Stein, Andreotti and Suša, 2016) was thought-provoking: 'I was left with more questions than answers.' Another group member reflected: 'The other thing I wanted to comment was this modern/colonial imaginary. I am very confused about it and I am not quite sure what to think about it. The issue is so complicated and to really give an answer to this I would have to have a lot more knowledge about the world and history.' Towards the end of the week, the group reached a conclusion related to the importance of understanding global power relations and global inequalities, emphasizing that countries should be the driving force in creating change.

During the second week, each group member selected a different article to read and to support the group discussion. Themes of responsible management education (Godemann, Haertle, Herzig and Moon, 2014), education and democratic citizenship (Nussbaum, 2006) and education for global responsibility in Finland (Kaivola and Melén-Paaso, 2007; Räsänen, 2007) were selected. Group members shared key points from the readings and connected them with the overall discussion on stakeholder roles and dimensions of global responsibility. Some members implied that they had read several of the articles and made connections between them. A discussion on (inter)cultural sensitivity provoked several questions and definitions for cultural and ethical relativism were sought from other sources. Finding a balance between universalism and respect of local contexts

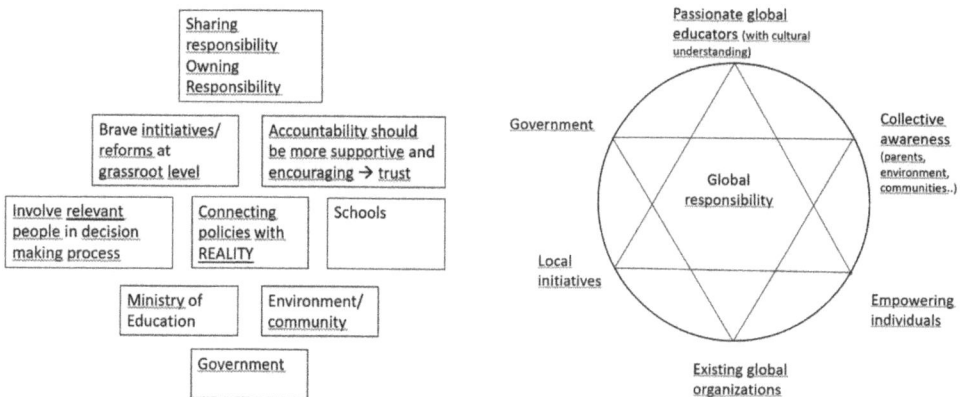

Figure 17.1 The diamonds developed by group A.

was considered a key challenge: 'The recognition of human rights as the most important must be paramount, although this process is mediated by the dominant culture, as we know, it´s a complex challenge that we are trying to reduce as responsible and equal citizens of the world.'

Moving towards a conclusion, the group members debated who is responsible for investing in GE (development). The relationship between individuals and the government was raised as a key issue: 'People are concerned about education and they want improvements, but if their concerns are not addressed by those in power, what fundamental changes can really happen?' Rather than agreeing on a single approach, the group emphasized the importance of a holistic approach assigning responsibility at different levels simultaneously.

(Figure 17.1) The final illustration from Group A (on the right) is no longer a diamond, but a star pointing out the horizontal connections between stakeholders and actions. This illustration clearly points to the connectedness between individual, local, national and global bringing in global level actors, the last missing from the first illustration. Here, individuals are present as 'passionate, global educators' as well as local initiatives. Three stakeholders are present in this illustration (from top left to bottom right) representing the three different levels of responsibility. On the right side of the figure, the group has assigned qualities to the actors, an element absent from the first illustration (left in Figure 17.1).

Above the illustration the participants include an explanation of how it should be read:

> We thought that a star model within a circle would be more appropriate, because we feel that all factors contributing to global responsibility are interconnected. Taking responsibility in education is a circular process. Collective awareness is vital for responsibility to be realised on a large scale. This includes parents, communities, schools, students, policy makers, teachers and other stakeholders. After becoming aware of the responsibility, the aim would be for the individuals to take hold of their responsibility. This could be realised on a micro-level, it could also be realised on a macro-level. For global organisations to be effective, they should work closely with local institutions and encourage the feeling of ownership among them. Although in some societies governments may be corrupt or receive less credit, they are still in a key position to enforce constructive educational reforms. (Group A conclusion)

This explanation emphasizes how global responsibility can start with passionate individuals who can support collective responsibility that results in individuals taking action at different levels, in Freirean terms, seeking to take up their place in the process of change. The mention of both micro and macro levels suggests that individual actions take place at different levels, for example, within existing global organizations. This suggests a greatly expanded understanding of 'we' not only as HE students but 'we' as part of humankind with responsibility growing from an understanding of the interconnectedness concurrently making and being made by history (Freire, 1985).

Case 2: Awareness based on understanding of underlying conditions

(Figure 17.2) Curiously the first diamond from Group B begins with the word 'equity' at the top although this receives no mention in the ensuing discussion and is absent from the final illustration. The first illustration, however, lists stakeholders other than the word 'career' placed at the centre of the diamond. The qualitative change between the first and the final illustration,

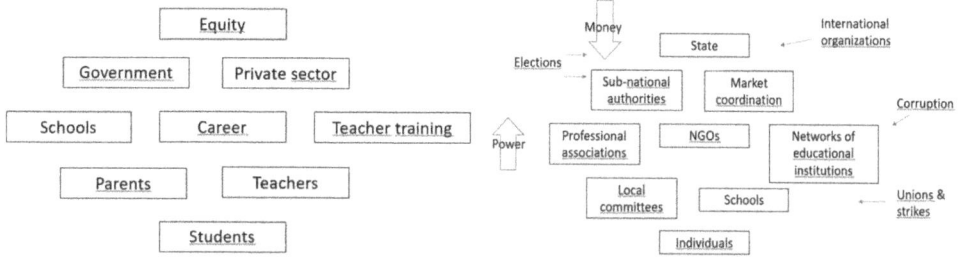

Figure 17.2 The diamonds developed by group B.

however, is striking with the second illustration including a new level of consideration, that is, the conditions which form and inform the potential realization of global responsibility.

The critical article by Stein, Andreotti and Suša (2016) encouraged Group B to discuss GE policy processes. A key argument was presented as the following: 'We do not listen to those we are making plans for,' emphasizing how global initiatives work within a global divide between objects and subjects of policy. The role of HE institutions was also discussed, criticizing universities for ignorance of global issues, competitiveness and associating knowledge solely to the West. Horizontal exchange of ideas and experiences was suggested by the group as a means to bridge the global divide in HE. In practice, this could include exchanging ideas internationally, including diverse perspectives and moving from knowledge transfer towards shared learning.

When identifying the second reading, one group member brought in several options. The article by Iris Young (2006) discussing political philosophy or responsibility and presenting a social connection model of responsibility was selected by the group after some negotiation. The text was found challenging by the group members. Apart from two initial reactions, major contributions to the discussion were given over a week after agreeing on the reading. The discussion evolved from global principles of justice and the role of political institutions to global connections and social injustice: 'As we produce injustice together, we also must solve it together. It is a "collective action".' The example of textile sweatshops presented in the article inspired a discussion on injustice in education focusing on the role of international funding agencies in influencing national education funding. The social connection model also helped the group to consider the different roles and positions of stakeholders: 'We consider that these agents have different roles defined by the different levels of responsibility they have, which, in turn, are linked to their different degrees of power, privilege and to their divergent interests.'

The final illustration for Group B includes a diamond comprising different educational stakeholders, and also places the diamond in a context.

> Our second diamond focused on how different stakeholders in the education sector are responsible for the losses or underlying issues coming in the way towards quality education. While looking at the different powers and privileges, it was necessary to understand how hierarchy decides the predisposition of the decision makers today. (Group B conclusion)

As with Group A, Group B recognize that stakeholders exist at different levels, this time including sub-national authorities, networks of educational institutions and individuals.

The group viewed responsibility from a liability perspective where rules and policy-bound regulations guide responsible action. Whereas Group A highlight the interconnectedness between the different stakeholders at different levels, Group B highlight the way in which conditions 'percolate' through different levels of stakeholders, suggesting a more complex picture of the interconnectedness of human relationships (Freire, 1985). Recognizing the conditions add another layer to understanding the notion of responsibility. Responsibility is not just given but it exists within dynamic relations and certain requirements that have to be met in order for responsibility to exist.

How is responsibility referred to within the group dialogues?

During the second round of analysis, we identified the different dimensions, attributes and qualities ascribed to responsibility by the two groups through the discussions. The aim was to analyse how the participants refer to and conceptualize the conditions that form and inform global responsibility in education. Both groups provide a number of different depictions of responsibility through the course of their online dialogues. Group A refer to responsibility as (1) a target, (2) something to be achieved or (3) enacted. They also recognize that (4) responsibility comes with power, (5) through intercultural sensitivity and that responsibility is a temporal phenomenon in that it (6) results from history. Group A also acknowledge that (7) being aware increases responsibility and that (8) responsible education is a means for future well-being including human rights, and (9) students should be prepared to be responsible.

The online dialogues of Group B also refer to responsibility in a number of different ways including (1) the political philosophy of responsibility with reference to Young (2006), (2) responsibility to act and (3) to choose, (4) responsibility for injustice and (5) responsibility for losses and underlying issues, that is recognizing obstacles, as well as (6) responsibility to remedy injustice. Group B also recognized that responsibility can be (7) collective/shared responsibility resulting in action, that different levels of responsibility exist including (8) national versus universal responsibility. The different aspects of responsibility highlighted in the online dialogues of both groups indicate the quality of their discussion, their depth of thinking and critical reflections in relation to global responsibility as a notion as well as a shared and personal responsibility.

Conclusion

The purpose of this study was to better understand how future education professionals view and negotiate the stakeholders and conditions for achieving global responsibility in education development as a way of understanding the complex notion of global responsibility in education development. The analysis of the group discussions depict how understanding of global responsibility in education was informed by readings and exchange of views between students. As the participants wrestled with new perspectives and began to acknowledge and address their assumptions, the possibility of reconceptualizing ways of being and relating began to form. Introducing students to readings that critically theorize GE agendas and processes proved to be useful, although at times challenging, as participants encountered different perspectives and terms of expression. Both groups expanded on their initial mapping of stakeholders and dimensions of responsibility and brought in a more analytical approach emphasizing interconnectedness and collective awareness of global responsibility in education. As such, these outcomes reflect Young's (2006) model of responsibility entailing shared responsibility and collective action. The students' dialogues, however, not only expanded the way in which HE students understand global responsibility but also enabled us, as researchers, to conceptualize GE from a different perspective.

As we placed the different dimensions, attributes and qualities ascribed to responsibility by the two groups side by side, the notion that global responsibility in education can be considered as both a target and a condition for GE development began to take shape. The student responses framed responsibility as a broad and fluid notion that develops and is required at all levels from individuals to global institutions, akin to the dynamism of 'revolutionary utopia' depicted by Freire (1985: 82). In order to feel responsible, we need to find a way to relate with development. Moreover, it is important for individuals to position themselves within these interconnections for a sense of responsibility to develop and, most importantly, to lead to action.

Guiding students towards critical thinking through readings and dialogue supported unveiling the notion of responsibility in terms of cause, obligation and accountability, as exemplified by Bexell and Jönsson (2017). Students discussed responsibility from the perspectives of role-responsibility and as an obligation towards the future. In addition, they brought in the (historical) causalities that, according to Bexell and Jönsson (2017), tend to remain hidden in policy documents. It was through this holistic understanding of responsibility that the students were able to perceive shared responsibility and collective action as the key features of global responsibility (see Young, 2006).

In response to the student dialogues, we asked ourselves how these different dimensions, attributes and qualities relate to one another. Initially, we sketched an arrow illustrating the ongoing dynamic of global responsibility, yet this depiction removes the conditions for global responsibility highlighted in the student dialogues. As we considered our arrow from different perspectives, we then began to reconceptualize it, using the metaphor of a tree (Figure 17.3). Figure 17.3 provides an illustrated synthesis of the dimensions, attributes and qualities ascribed to responsibility in the student dialogues as well as the conditions forming and informing global responsibility. The roots represent 'ground work' for global responsibility in education and the prerequisites for the formation of the stabilizing 'trunk' of awareness and a sense of responsibility to act. Global responsibility in education then branches out and is concretized in different forms of action, such as collective action, responsible choices, education for responsibility and responsibility through intercultural sensitivity/understanding. The targets of global responsibility for education are not part of the tree's structure, but a necessary feature of the environment enabling growth. Furthermore, this metaphor recognizes the interconnected and symbiotic relationship between global responsibility for education as a practice and an aspiration, something to do and to continually work towards.

The findings from this pedagogical intervention point to the usefulness of the notion of responsibility in supporting critical thinking and understanding of complex global structures

national vs universal responsibility, responsibility for human rights, future well-being

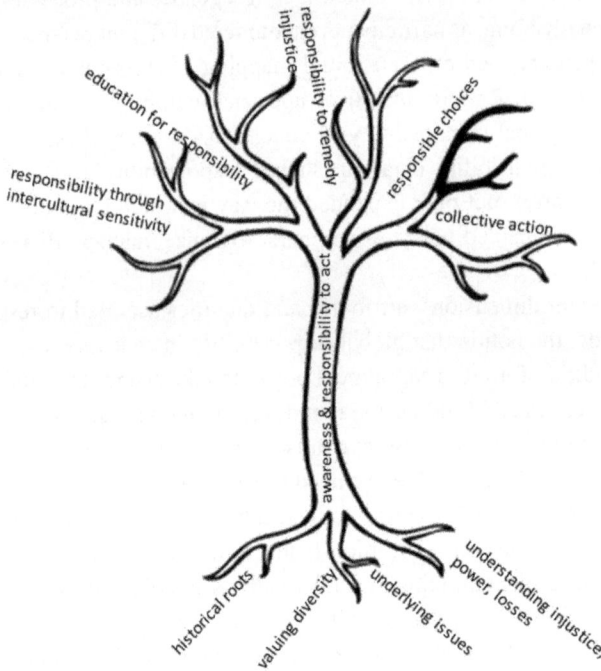

Figure 17.3 Symbiotic depiction of global responsibility in education (tree illustration from https://svgsilh.com/image/306807.html under the creative commons license).

and connections. Following Brown's (2014) notion of pedagogies for transformation in DE, the emphasis on justice and fairness in students' discussion was an indication of a growing sense of responsibility, questioning not only the place of social justice in higher education but also contributing to discourses on social justice, as Singh (2011) suggests, and furthermore, willingness to act. Our experience encourages further development of critical, dialogic, theory-informed pedagogical approaches to DE in HE contexts. Finding ways to connect GE practice (e.g. the SDG4 seminars) with critical theorizing could be a step towards implementing responsible and potentially transformative DE in HE. Moreover, this study highlights the value of bringing future educational professionals as key partners and actors into the current dialogue on global responsibility in education.

Bibliography

Bakhtin, M. (1986) *Speech Genre and Other Essays*, trans. V. W. McGee. Austin, TX: University of Texas Press.

Bexell, M. and Jönsson, K. (2017) Responsibility and the United Nations' sustainable development goals. *Forum for Development Studies*, 44(1), 13–29.

Bourn, D. (2014a) *The Theory and Practice of Development Education: A Pedagogy for Global Social Justice*. Routledge.

Bourn, D. (2014b) The Theory and Practice of Global Learning. Research Paper No.11. London: Development Education Research Centre, Institute of Education in partnership with the Global Learning Programme. Retrieved from: http://discovery.ucl.ac.uk/1492723/1/DERC_ResearchPaper 11-TheTheoryAndPracticeOfGlobalLearning%5B2%5D.pdf (accessed 19 December 2018).

Brown, E. J. (2014) Fair-minded critical thinking in development education: Reflections on pedagogies for transformation. *International Journal of Development Education and Global Learning*, 6(1), 5–25.

Bryan, A. (2008) Researching and searching for international development in the formal curriculum: Towards a postcolonial conceptual framework. *Policy and Practice: A Development Education Review*, 7(1), 68–79.

Clark, J., Laing, K., Tiplady, L. and Woolner, P. (2013) *Making Connections: Theory and Practice of Using Visual Methods to Aid Participation in Research*. Newcastle upon Tyne: Research Centre for Learning and Teaching, Newcastle University.

Education Services Australia (2012) Global Education. Teacher resources to encourage a global perspective across the curriculum. https://www.globaleducation.edu.au/verve/_resources/diamond_ ranking-1.pdf (accessed 17 December 2018).

Freire, P. (1985) *The Politics of Education: Culture, Power, and Liberation*. Westport, CT: Greenwood Publishing Group.

Freire, P. (1998) *Teachers as Cultural Workers: Letters to Those Who Dare Teach*, trans. D. Macedo, D. Koike and A. Oliveira. Boulder, CO: Westview.

Giroux, H. (1985) An introduction by Henry A. Giroux. In P. Freire, *The Politics of Education: Culture, Power, and Liberation*. Westport, CT: Greenwood Publishing Group, xi–xxvi.

Godemann, J., Haertle, J., Herzig, C. and Moon, J. (2014) United Nations supported principles for responsible management education: Purpose, progress and prospects. *Journal of Cleaner Production*, 62, 16–23.

Kaivola, T. and Melén-Paaso, M. (eds) (2007) Education for global responsibility–Finnish perspectives. *Publications of the Ministry of Education*, 31, 2007.

Lehtomäki, E., Moate, J. and Posti-Ahokas, H. (2016) Global connectedness in higher education: Student voices on the value of cross-cultural learning dialogue. *Studies in Higher Education*, 41(11), 2011–27.

Lehtomäki, E., Moate, J. and Posti-Ahokas, H. (2019) Exploring global responsibility in higher education students' cross-cultural dialogues. *European Educational Research Journal*, 18(2), 218–33.

Lehtomäki, E., Posti-Ahokas, H. and Moate, J. (2015) Meaningful internationalisation at home: Education Students' Voices on the Value of Cross-cultural Learning Dialogue. In M. Kricke, L. Kurten and B. Amrhein (eds), *Internationalisierung der LehrerInnenbildung*. Münster: Waxmann Verlag, 99–109.

Nussbaum, M. C. (2006) Education and democratic citizenship: Capabilities and quality education. *Journal of Human Development*, 7(3), 385–95.

Odora Hoppers, C. (2015) The future of development education – perspectives from the South. *International Journal of Development Education and Global Learning*, 7(2), 89–106.

Pashby, K. and Andreotti, V. de Oliveira (2016) Ethical internationalisation in higher education: interfaces with international development and sustainability. *Environmental Education Research*, 22(6), 771–87.

Patton, M. Q. (2002) *Qualitative Research & Evaluation Methods*. (3rd edn). London: Sage.

Räsänen, R. (2007) Intercultural Education as Education for Global Responsibility. In *Education for Global Responsibility–Finnish Perspectives*. Finland: Ministry of Education, Department for Education and Science, 19–30. Retrieved from: http://www.kansanopistot.fi/yhdistys/keke/educ_glob_resp.pdf #page=19 (accessed 26 August 2019).

Renshaw, P. D. (2004) Dialogic teaching, learning and instruction: Theoretical roots and analytical frameworks. In J. van den Lindenand P. Renshaw (eds), *Dialogic Learning: Shifting Perspectives to Learning, Instruction, and Teaching*. Dordrecht, The Netherlands: Springer, 1–15.

Rumbley, L. E. and Altbach, P. G. (2016) The local and the global in higher education internationalization: A crucial nexus. In E. Jones, R. Coelen, J. Beelen, et al. (eds), *Global and Local Internationalization*. Rotterdam, The Netherlands: Sense Publishers, 7–13.

Sayed, Y. and Ahmed, R. (2015) Education quality, and teaching and learning in the post-2015 education agenda. *International Journal of Educational Development 40*, 330–38.

Singh, M. (2011) The place of social justice in higher education and social change discourses. *Compare* *41*(4), 481–94.

Skinner, A., Blum, N. and Bourn, D. (2013) Development Education and Education in international Development policy: Raising Quality through critical pedagogy and global skills. *International Development Policy – Revue internationale de politique de développement, 4*, 89–103.

Stein, S., Andreotti, V. D. O. and Suša, R. (2016) 'Beyond 2015', within the modern/colonial global imaginary? Global development and higher education. *Critical Studies in Education, 60*(3), 1–21.

UNESCO (2017) Accountability in education: Meeting our commitments. Education for All Global Monitoring Report 201778. Paris, France: UNESCO. https://en.unesco.org/gem-report/report/2017/accountability-education (accessed 07 May 2018).

Young, I. M. (2006) Responsibility and global justice: A social connection model. *Social Philosophy & Policy, 23*(1), 102–30.

Chapter 18

Globality and Internationalization in Vienna: An Exploration of a Research Seminar Using Transformative Processes in Global Education

Helmuth Hartmeyer

Introduction

The chapter describes the conceptual background as well as the practical procedures of a research seminar at the Institute for International Development in Vienna (Austria) and reflects on the most relevant experiences and outcomes. Set up as an educational contribution to an interdisciplinary master's programme, 'glocality' is explored as the theoretical backbone to a seminar on Global Learning. It includes how students perceive Vienna in the context of global influences. Global Learning is suggested as a key pedagogical approach to open horizons for the students to further develop an understanding of transformative learning processes.

A key question posed in this chapter is whether studying 'International Development' has to mean that the key focus is on what is happening 'over there', that is in the Global South, which can mean the causes and consequences in our own society are tackled less frequently. Is there justification for a focus which, alternatively, suggests a starting point of 'Here' with an international, global outlook and perspective? The conceptual debate on Global Education (GE) can profit from an exploration of the tension between these two questions. By introducing 'glocalization' into practical research in the field of 'International Development', this can help to build bridges and enrich the content dimensions found on both the developmental and the educational agendas. This is the proposition on which the course discussed in this chapter is founded.

Setting of the research seminar

The Institute for International Development at Vienna University was created in response to the need for interdisciplinarity in the field of development and related fields. This interdisciplinarity focus of international development had been a key element of the debates around this field, in Europe and globally, since the 1960s. These debates included the limits of the development model, the demise of development studies and the need for broader understandings in the fields of international relations and globalization theory (Sachs 1992; Sen 1999; Tandon 2009). However, these debates also related to longer and broader debates about the nature of higher education (HE), the relationship between education ('Bildung'), learning and preparation for a globalized world (Scheunpflug and Schröck 2000; Oelkers 2001; Lang-Wojtasik and Lohrenscheit 2003; Overwien and Rathenow 2009) and the relationship between education and social change (Freire 1992; Shor 1992; Brennan 2008). Moreover, they also related to much more ancient and broader debates on how to understand complexity across disciplines (Aristotle; Leonardo da Vinci; Alexander von Humboldt).

The research seminar discussed in this chapter is offered as part of a master's programme at the Institute, which has been a fully established institute since 2010. The origins of the Institute go back to 1994. The University Board up until then thought that an explicit academic focus on international development was not needed and that this subject was sufficiently covered by courses in other faculties and studies. Students, however, protested against this and succeeded in getting the university to change its mind. Within ten years around five thousand students have registered for the course and successfully completed it.

Another argument against the establishment of an Institute of its own was that it would contribute to the increase of young academics without job prospects – an argument in line with the traditional conviction that the university is a place for training, not for education. The author of this chapter has little empirical knowledge of the professional careers of students once they have finished the programme, but it seems that those who come from other countries return to their homeland and the qualifications they have acquired become a much-needed asset back home. Those from Austria have found employment in a range of professions, business and the private sector, in international organizations or national NGOs, or for some in public administration. Few follow up with an academic career.

The master's programme offered by the Institute is open to students from all countries in Europe and beyond. The aim of the research-oriented, inter- and transdisciplinary course is to explore issues, theories and methodologies which are relevant for a critical debate with and analysis of institutions, actors, practices and concepts in the area of development and development cooperation; and to help bring students into line with a broader historical, political, economic, cultural and societal context. Theories and approaches of social, political, historical, cultural and economic transformations and inequalities and their reflection are, therefore, at the centre of teaching and research; but this is also about the critical debate of development cooperation as well as tackling questions of methodologies when dealing with the overall issue of 'development' (ID 2018). Courses on the basics of development research and on methodologies in development research are compulsory modules in the first year. In the second year, the students can choose among nine different subject areas in which they want to specialize (politics, economics, sociology, cultural studies, history, geography, gender, development cooperation or a transdisciplinary module, which could include education). They also have to attend one research seminar in the second year. It is set for two terms (credited for fifteen ECTS) and is also meant to prepare the students for their master theses. A master module concludes the course.

The current priority focus in the Institute is on 'Education and Development'. In previous years, GE was already regarded as highly relevant by a majority of colleagues, yet on the other hand, they are all very busy with their own specific subjects. The new priority has resulted in the author's research seminar, which forms the main focus of this chapter, being more central to the overall programme.

The content of the seminar

The following are some of the questions posed at the research seminar:

Vienna is a global city, a metropolis. Core questions derived from this statement are the following:

What does this mean for students of International Development?

How global and international is Vienna?

What does it mean for the concrete local context?

Which inter- and transnational developments can be detected, identified?

Which learning processes take place – within the area of research, but also on the part of the student researchers?

Examples from the seminar to illustrate answers to these questions are given in a later section.

'Glocality' as the theoretical content framework

The themes and questions posed in the research seminar lend themselves to a discussion and usage of the concept of 'glocalization'. This term seems to have originated in the specific context of discussions about globalization in Japanese business methods in the late 1980s. Regardless of its national origin and marketing background, it could be argued that it has some definite advantages in the general theorization of globalization. It facilitates a thorough discussion of various problems around the distinctions between the global and the local (Robertson 2012: 191). In other words, glocalization can be described as the simultaneous occurrence of both universalizing and particularizing tendencies in current economic, social and other systems. Thus, the notion is a challenge to simplistic conceptions of globalization processes as linear expansions of territorial scales. Glocalization emphasizes that the growing importance of global levels is occurring together with the increasing relevance of local and regional levels. Research into the local can prevent one from realizing the global dimension; on the other hand, exploring the global can lead to shying away from the local causes and consequences. Also the slogan 'think globally, act locally' may suggest a linearity which does not pay enough attention to the complexity of the interconnectedness behind it. Scheunpflug discusses what the evolution of a world society means for teaching (Scheunpflug and Hirsch, 2001). Tendencies towards homogeneity appear alongside tendencies towards heterogeneity; diversity exists in the universal. Thus, the term 'glocality' seems appropriate. Glocalization points to the interconnectedness of the global and local levels. Local spaces and local identities are created by global contexts and contacts as well as by local circumstances and events. Neither is globalization the end of geography and the end of heterogeneity, nor is the local the all-comprising answer to historical, socio-economic and cultural processes. After all, glocalization is more than the local adaptation to and interpretation of global forces and development.

The author here invites the students to find out more about the social, cultural, religious, linguistic diversity in the city; to identify the global in the local, the 'glocal'; to see where and how the local is shaped by the global, but also whether and how the opening of boundaries is strengthening the importance of location. Research should give evidence whether there is reason to believe that the many interactions on a global scale are empowering local stakeholders to win back responsibilities for political and other processes.

Glocal approaches in Vienna

Global Vienna can be viewed at a number of levels. Their order in the following section mirrors their relevance in current public debates.

At the political level Vienna is one of the few UN cities. It was established as such in 1973 as a recognition of the country's neutral role in the Cold War. Since then, Vienna has also hosted Organization of the Petroleum Exporting Countries (OPEC), The Organisation for Security and Cooperation in Europe (OSCE) and a house for the European Union. More recently, there was a fervent debate about a Saudic Centre and its role. Most of these buildings can be visited, or at least contacted, and their existence forms a proper basis for research into the direction of civic education.

At the political level, it is also worth noting the commitment and work of civil society organizations in general and of NGOs at a more specific level. In particular, there exist various global citizenship and development education (DE) initiatives, whose work and also pedagogical approaches can become interesting case studies.

Second, Vienna is an increasingly diverse city with numerous ethnic minorities living in Vienna (African, Oriental, Latin American, Chinese and others). This provides opportunities for research in terms of their background, their everyday lives and their perspectives. It also can lead to research into the very topical issues of asylum, migration and integration. Of course, all these groups do not live in isolation. People have evolved hybrid identities. Mixed cultures and identities arise. This has, however, also led to tensions and conflict. On the side of the minorities, there are those who wish to maintain ties abroad; on the side of the majority, there are those who try to defend local history and traditions. This is particularly the case with the large Turkish and ex-Yugoslavian population. Some people say the Balkans start in Vienna.

All this and research into it can become part of inter- and trans-cultural learning.

Then, there is the whole issue of religion. Almost 15 per cent of the Viennese population are Muslims, and for the first time in the history of the city, less than 50 per cent are Catholics. Not to forget there is a Jewish minority with its tragic history before and during the Second World War.[1] The students can look into the realities at kindergartens and schools and explore issues of migration, cultural diversity and the role of religion there, and thus experience and reflect on inter-religious education.

The third approach to the glocality of Vienna is to look at the city from a sociological perspective. For example, there are many tours of the city that can be made looking at specific themes: the homeless, the history of women in the city, one on African Vienna, one on critical consumption in one of the main shopping streets and many more. The research seminar always

---

[1]   The author once worked in Vienna's Berggasse, where Sigmund Freud had his praxis.

starts with a tour around the very area where the Institute is located, looking particularly at the medical history of Vienna in the area.

There are many restaurants with ethnic food, there are markets with all the exotic goods and there are international festivals in theatre (Festival Weeks), film (Viennale) and music. The annual New Year's Concert is televised all over the world. Research can be done into the globality of culture. (Inter)cultural studies can be carried out. The interconnectedness of culture and education can be explored.

Linked to this is the touristic perspective: Vienna is very popular with tourists from all over the world. For a good number of years now Vienna has been ranked first or second in the list of the cities with the highest quality of life worldwide. Vienna hosts numerous conferences, some with an attendance of more than twenty thousand. Vienna airport keeps expanding.

The positive and negative aspects of this phenomenon can be studied; the pedagogy of economics can be made an issue for research. Research can also be undertaken by looking into the names of streets and squares, into the architecture and into museums. International themes can be found everywhere.

Finally, there is the environmental dimension: the importance of the Vienna Woods, of the nature reserve along the Danube, the issue of climate change in the city, public and private traffic, litter and recycling, and many other aspects. These are very good fields for research into environmental education and Education for Sustainable Development.

In addition to these themes, the research seminar also aims to include the experiences and perspectives of the students themselves, bringing in their own social and cultural outlook on the city and encouraging critical self-reflection and peer-to-peer learning.

The pedagogical and didactical concept of the research seminar

Having reviewed the thematic focus of the seminar, the chapter now moves to the pedagogical and didactical design of the seminar.

The approach taken in the seminar is influenced by broader debates in Global Learning and GCE. These terms could be seen as umbrella terms covering themes such as education for tolerance and appreciation of diversity, conflict resolution and peace, the principles of human rights, humanitarian action, as well as civic responsibilities (Wintersteiner et al. 2014). The Maastricht Declaration of the North–South Centre of the Council of Europe defines GE as the global dimension of education for citizenship (GENE 2003).

Following on from this, the seminar core aims are to encourage the enhancement of the students' glocal experience through a critical academic exchange of political, socio-economic and cultural issues; and to encourage them to explore local and global perspectives that will enrich learning experiences in a positive way. HE should take responsibility for providing potential graduates with opportunities to become active citizens in a turbulent global society and to prepare them for their future roles in local and global environments (Patel and Lynch 2013: 225). They should be intellectually and professionally qualified, with good interpersonal skills and prepared to meet the diverse challenges in an increasingly globalized world. They should be responsive to local and global concerns along with the changing demands of global trends, with commitment to the principles of social responsibility and justice (ibid.).

The following paragraphs refer to two different but related fields: the relationship between identity and belonging, and the correlation of this process to learning about a complex and multidimensional world; and second, the pedagogical process that corresponds with time and space for biographical experience, starting where people are at, and relating to wider local and global issues.

The research seminar is based on the assumption that the construction of our identity is never complete. We are as multidimensional as the world surrounding us. This requires educational processes which attend to the field of identity. These processes give time and space to biographical experiences to all that are involved. Such learning can contribute to increasing awareness of global, local and glocal issues as well as to personal and social liberation or 'Students as global citizens' (Bourn 2010).

GE as the core conceptual approach in the seminar, according to the author, would, therefore, define itself as a principle, not as a new learning matter. The objective of this principle would be to gain insight instead of pure accumulation of knowledge, because it would be absurd to assume that learning processes, whose targets and contents are over-directed, lead to autonomy and decision-making abilities among learners. Hence, GE should not be understood as knowledge transfer about issues, but as critical reflection on interests, concerns and experiences. GE would thus not only mean theoretical learning *about* the world but it means the challenge to create space and time for concrete learning experiences *within* the world (Hartmeyer 2008: 149–58 based on for example Scheunpflug 2000; Oelkers 2001; Seitz 2002; Lang-Wojtasik and Lohrenscheit 2003; Overwien and Rathenow 2009).[2]

Through education, and especially through GE in this sense, two objectives are aimed at. It should contribute to a better orientation in our own lives. And it should enable us to develop a vision of a successful life in a humanely designed world society. Since this is an extremely ambitious undertaking, the author regards it as essential that the research seminar is experienced by the students as a chance to discover new insights, to search and explore areas relevant to them and to come up with findings that enrich their global as well as local knowledge and understanding. The interests, experiences and competencies of everyone involved in this learning process should constitute an integral part.

In GE, as understood by the author on the basis of extensive teaching experience and reflection, solutions should not be provided, but taken into consideration. Self-contained knowledge acquisition is key. Radical questions should be asked. Thinking and acting in alternatives ought to be tried out. Through practising collaboration, social virtues are required and the capability of a collaborative approach can be strengthened. The aim would be educational processes which give the students confidence, stability and self-efficacy (Hartmeyer 2008: 134–43).

The research seminar also ought to strengthen the ability to enable contact with people from other cultural contexts, to become able to communicate and to be capable of seeing the world from somebody else's viewpoint. It should be an objective to develop an opinion based on different perspectives in the light of glocal developments, as well as to act.

---

[2]   For more background references, see Hartmeyer 2008, pp. 160–77.

As our global and local experiences fuse together in the open spaces of glocalized learning, it is important to work within a framework which endorses acceptable norms of engagement: respect and dignity for all, meta-cultural sensitivity, critical self-reflection, justice, inclusivity, diversity and commitment to action for change (Patel and Lynch 2012: 227).

The methodology employed in the seminar is based on a qualitative approach to development research (Dannecker and Englert 2014; Lamnek and Krell 2016). In order to support the students, a number of excursions are undertaken, external guests are invited, the students are made familiar with methodologies of qualitative social and educational research, they are given introductory lessons on education and learning in general and on GE and global learning in particular. They write individual assignments and reflections in home-exercises, but they also work in pairs and small groups. Specific texts are offered as background and in-depth information, some are studied in common and are followed up in whole class discussions.

Finally, each student identifies one concrete approach, elaborates a research design and later writes a paper of thirty pages on the topic at the end of the academic year. Students have the choice of doing this in pairs.

With a diverse student body and a wide range of languages being spoken, the seminar is run in a combination of German and English and all papers can be submitted in either language.

Practical research

In the following section, a few examples of research undertaken by the students are summarized, with some observations on the issues they raise in terms of GE.

(Young) Spanish people in Vienna

The background of this research is that up to 7,000 Spanish people lived in Austria in 2017, approximately two-thirds of them in Vienna. There was an increase from 2,500 to 7,000 since 2008 due to the economic crisis in Spain, when mainly young people between twenty and thirty years of age left the country – some hoping to study abroad and most hoping to find a job. In Vienna, many found jobs as waiters or in other service businesses.

The student researcher, who speaks Spanish well and has a close emotional relationship with people in Latin America, interviewed a good number of Spanish people living and working in Vienna. He explored their backgrounds, their ways of life, the problems they face, their fears and hopes. Most of them want to go back as soon as possible, once they see a chance for improved circumstances in their home country.

In the GE framework of the seminar it was of special interest to explore the learning dimensions in the case study: How do the interviewees reflect on their experiences abroad? Which differences and similarities do they notice? Which lessons do they draw for their future lives? On the other hand: How did the researcher encounter his partners? Which new insights did he gain? How does he reflect on his own Austrian citizenship in the light of the research?

A diverse housing community in suburban Vienna

Research was undertaken into a communal house project, where handicapped persons, persons with LGBTIQ (Lesbian, Gay, Bisexual, Transgender, Intersexual, Queer) identification, asylum seekers and children live together. The house is situated in a working-class suburb of Vienna. The student researcher attended plenary sessions in the house, spoke to facilitators of working groups and interviewed some individuals.

From a GE perspective, it was interesting how the student, who himself is from a middle-class background, encountered a very diverse and different world from the one he is used to living in. It could open up insights into the heterogeneity in his own society, insights which he could not have gained from pure academic work in the seminar room at the university.

The special task was to reflect critically together with the fifteen inhabitants of the house on their daily challenges, their conflicts but also their potential for solidarity, their learning experiences and aspirations for the future. The student researcher explored the 'glocality' in the house, the influence of the surrounding environment on the people in the house and how they met with prejudices, discrimination and racism.

'Typical Vienna' as a space for Global Learning

Karl Kraus[3] stated: Vienna has many sights and each Viennese thinks he is one.

On the basis of the clarification of the definition of what typical means and a theoretical model of typifying, the participants in this research (i.e. fellow students) picked nine photos each, which they had been asked to bring with them; they were invited to give their thoughts and reflections about them. In an iconological three-level analysis the student researcher explored the motives behind the photos with each participant, asking first, what do you see; second, what conclusions do you draw from what you see; and third, how do you assess the societal background of what you see?

The aim was not to arrive at a conclusion as to what is typical of Vienna, but to look into the motives of the participants for their choices and their understanding of 'glocal' Viennese society. This should initiate a learning process on the part of fellow students, but also lead to a self-reflection on the part of the researcher.

Was this research a space for Global Learning? Most students were not aware of the concept, had not heard of it before, but found it interesting. As most photos reflected a touristic perspective, used in folders and leaflets for tourists in one way or another, and as global tourism plays a great role in Vienna, globality quickly became an issue in the debates between the researcher and the interviewees and thus initiated a common process of reflection.

International students in Vienna

The student researcher looked especially into the situation of students from outside Europe. They face very different legal restrictions from students from EU countries. In many cases, they never come to

---

[3] Karl Kraus, author and journalist (1874–1936): Aphorismen. Sprüche und Widersprüche. Wien 1909.

feel 'at home' in Vienna, even if they find Viennese partners or friends. Diversity overrules what they may have in common. However, when asked about their own personal development, the researcher was impressed by the very reflective answers which were very far from complaints or accusations.

The issue dealt with in this research is of special interest to the overall approach in the research seminar, as international students are the majority in the seminar group. Does studying in Vienna mean the respectful exchange of academic and cultural knowledge and ideas or is it more about the acculturation of international students into the host city culture? Is there an environment which is respectful and welcoming of difference? Which spaces for common learning exist or can be opened?

The student researcher identified unused potential for learning that would lie in a good relationship between international and Austrian students. The opportunities for the city to further develop its image as a global city could still be grasped more deliberately, and GE research can contribute to this.

International broadcasting in *Radio Orange*

Radio Orange 94.0 was the first private non-commercial radio station in Vienna, founded in 1998. It brought an enrichment to the media landscape. Its overall conceptual approach is to reach out to the listeners in the various migrant communities and to contribute to their efforts at integration.

From a GE perspective the three questions, which two researchers explored as a common initiative, were of specific relevance: Do the makers of the programmes see their broadcasts as educational programmes and if so, what do they want to achieve? Do the broadcasts promote a positive perception of foreign minorities in Vienna? What is the overall aim vis-à-vis the listeners? The grounded theory methodology served them to categorize the answers to their research issues.

Beyond these questions, the financial conditions for the radio station were investigated as a lot of work is done on a voluntary basis, and there was also an extra analysis of the languages used in the various broadcasts.

Global and local narratives in the climate movement

This research was based on the thesis that climate change is an almost ideal issue to discuss the global and the local at the same time. The research shows the fundamental connection and that climate justice is the overall issue at stake. This conviction has not fully arrived at the local level as yet.

The student researcher arrives at conclusions which are conceptually most relevant for GE: climate change forces us to think globally, but to act locally. Yet why is there not enough progress? A number of answers are given: the global issue is overwhelming and for many, still too abstract. National interests prevent effective international cooperation. Societal and cultural traditions are very strong. The capitalist system is built on growth and exploitation. Finally, there is human nature which also knows selfishness and greed.

The challenge in educational processes remains: Which 'glocal' story can, should or maybe even must be told? Research can hint at some elements for such a narrative.

Global education primary schools in Vienna

There are twenty-two so-called GE Primary Schools in Vienna.[4] They are based on the following elements:

At least one lesson a week, from Year 1 onwards, is spent learning a modern language (especially English). English is the language of instruction in the subject of Global Studies (between two and four lessons per week). A Native Speaker Teacher and the class teacher work closely together to teach the subject of Global Studies as a team. Special emphasis is placed on the use of modern information and communication technology (ICT). Finally, the schools participate in projects concerned with Global Learning (encountering both language and culture).

On the basis of the Maastricht Declaration on GE (2002)[5] and the Austrian Strategy on Global Learning (2009),[6] the student researcher explored their implementation in these schools. For the conceptual debate on GE the assertion is relevant that the core understanding in the curriculum is to prioritize the teaching of the English language and the increased use of ICT. Interviews with headmasters and staff in Vienna school administration showed that only in some schools an understanding of GE as expressed in the aforementioned documents could be met.

Historical and gender perspectives in Vienna women walks

The research looks into the historical traces of women in the fifth district of Vienna. Under the guidance of a historian and gender expert, biographies were explored of women who resisted the fascist regime before and during the Second World War.

This research contributes to a critical debate on GE. The 'women walks' lead to the conclusion that GE not only has blind spots as far as the gender issue is concerned but it tackles the whole issue of power relations too uncritically. Colonialism, neoliberalism, racism and sexism should be moved much more into the centre of the conceptual debate.

Alliances between social movements in Vienna

Social movements in Vienna whose main concern is a social-ecological transformation of society are taken as the focus of this research. Two researchers interviewed representatives of four organizations, analysed their thematic approaches and what they have in common, so that through cooperation

---

[4] https://www.eb.ssr-wien.at/index.php/en/languages/english/global-education-primary-school-geps

[5] See www.gene.eu

[6] See www.gobaleslernen.at

they can contribute to SDG 11 'to make cities and human settlements inclusive, safe, resilient and sustainable'. A close look into their internal structures was intended to help to systematize ways of actual and possible forms of cooperation and to discover collective action frames.

The student researchers conclude that the learning processes within and between organizations and social movements are decisive, if the factors which support mobilization for complex political agendas are to be taken seriously and to become a living reality in their work. Not only from a GE approach but also from a general civic education approach, the issue is raised and relevant in how far education and political mobilization go together, or do not.

Unaccompanied under-age refugees in Vienna

By looking closely into a home where unaccompanied under-age refugees live in a suburban district of Vienna, two researchers explored together concepts of fear, identity, otherness and culture. How are the young refugees perceived in and by their environment? How do they perceive the people and structures around them? But also how do they relate to each other within their refugee home?

Stuart Hall's understanding of discourse and power forms the theoretical basis of their research[7]. It helped them to identify factors which promote or prevent processes of better understanding of internal as well as external integration. From an educational perspective their research dived into the issue of interaction and change. Interaction can lead to the existence of new images and thus create room for new thinking and changed behaviour. However, it can also lead to segregation and isolation by reinforcing negative attitudes. The concept of 'the Other' is complex, on the global as well as on the local level.

To summarize: the approaches taken by the students are very different from each other. The strength of their research lies in the fact that they choose the thematic issues solely by themselves, develop the research questions and decide which methodology to apply. My task is to advise and support them. My challenge is to take care that they identify with their research, so that it leads to active learning processes and reflections. In the vast majority of their work, this is the case.

In the following section an attempt is made to reflect the summary conclusions drawn from the various pieces of research carried out by the students. Overall, they find it easier and more attractive to look closely into a concrete subject matter, but it is harder for them to explore and reflect on the learning processes taking place. Both the global as well as the pedagogical dimensions are often missing in development practice. Reflecting on the practical research, as described above, at a rather meta-level can help to understand how both dimensions are intertwined and fit into the general context of the master's course.

Reflection of the experiences

In the master's programme on International Development the global perspective is the key focus and most students come with an explicit global outlook. The author regards it, therefore, as relevant that they reconnect their perspectives with local realities, that is to identify and explore

---

[7] The students refer to Hall (1994).

the global in the local. A specifically interesting group in this context is the group of students from abroad. Rahul Choudaha calls them 'glocal' students (Choudaha 2012). They study abroad for a number of reasons such as career advancement, quality of education, special interest in the subject and the specific degree, experience of living abroad and maybe even immigration. For them to explore local realities in Vienna is at the same time another global experience. The challenge is to grasp this opportunity as transnational learning.

Overall, through the concept of 'glocalization' the thematic focus is broadened. It questions an understanding of international development as solely 'reaching out' (and maybe getting trapped in a Western hegemonial approach), but seeing it as 'crossing borders' in both directions.

The master's programme International Development is not a course in education. The students are not future teachers, although some have a bachelor degree in some form of pedagogy. However, they find it interesting and in the end relevant to look more deeply into their own learning experiences, to detect space for learning and change in their own environment, and also to do research into the learning processes of others.

The excursions are reflected as very positive by the students. They further open up Vienna as a global space to them. It is probably very important to gather experiences in other countries and cultural contexts, but it is not a necessity to, for example, go to Burma, Uganda or Mexico to find out about the globality and diversity in the world. It can also be found around the corner where you study and live. This fact allows us to make GE very concrete.

The practical side of the seminar is as relevant: for the students to develop skills in how to do proper research, how to elaborate a research design and how to experience what it means to write a longer academic paper. For some, this is the starting point into further research for their master's thesis. The final papers should be more than descriptions and more than analyses. They should identify the local as a space of globalized history, present and future. To look into Vienna as a global space allows for exploration and debate on all the political, social, environmental and cultural dimensions of International Development as the core of the master course at the Institute. Thus, this approach can be a contribution to further conceptual work at the Institute.

The seminar supports the claim that a university is a space for learning and not solely an institution for training. *Landscapes of education* instead of educational institutions would be a desirable term (Hartmeyer 2008: 155–6). They should be first and foremost environments of knowledge in which learners are accepted as subjects. These environments would not focus so much on services for knowledge acquisition, and students in this case would not be seen as objects. A teacher's competency would lie in guiding them in this sense, to challenge them, to accompany them and to reflect learning processes in a critical way. Methodologies which are conducive to learning are, therefore, strengthened. It makes positive outcomes of the learning process (a balance of knowledge, understanding, action and reflection) more likely. Thus, GE is an enrichment, and the author dares to say a requirement in any higher education.

Conclusion

In the context of the broader debate on the limits of the traditional development paradigm, the research seminar moves the discourse on DE as learning about the Global South, judging and reflecting it and arriving at an agenda for change, into a discourse on interdependencies, contingency and grasping complexity both as a political and pedagogical challenge (Treml 1996).

The seminar succeeds in opening the richness of routes and landscapes for insights and understandings of how the North and the South are globally interconnected. It may happen that all involved arrive at the understanding that occurrences in a completely different place have consequences in their own environment. Insights into the diversity of cultures and societies help to critically reflect one's own self-conception and actions – and eventually to change them. Through their focus on involvement in global developments, such learning processes can contribute to a better understanding of diverse and complex developments, to understand them and to handle them in one's personal and social responsibility.

Through a specific focus on the global in the local the seminar enriches the conceptual debate on 'Development and Education'. The annual UNESCO GE Monitoring Reports (2016, 2017/18, 2019) define it as an 'education FOR (people and the planet)' (UNESCO 2016). By retracing the necessary global outlook back into our own societies and acknowledging and reflecting our own embeddedness in globality in GE processes, such an education can develop into an 'education ABOUT and WITHIN (people and the planet)', which promotes individual and collective curiosity, independence and responsible action.

Bibliography

BMK/Austrian Development Agency (ADA) (2009) *Austrian Strategy on Global Learning*, Vienna, ADA.

Bourn, D. (2010) Students as Global Citizens. In: Jones, E. (ed.), *Internationalisation: The Student Voice*. New York, pp. 18–29.

Brennan, J. (2008) Higher Education and Social Change. In: *Higher Education*, vol. 56, Issue 3, pp. 381–93.

Choudaha, R. (2012) The Rise of 'Glocal' Students and Transnational Education. In: *The Guardian*, 21 February 2012.

Dannecker, P. and Englert, B. (eds) (2014) *Qualitative Methoden der Entwicklungsforschung*. Wien/ Vienna: Mandelbaum.

Freire, P. (1992) Pedagogy of Hope. *Reliving Pedagogy of the Oppressed*. London: Bloomsbury.

Geddes, P. (1915): *Cities in Evolution*. London: Williams and Norgate.

GENE (2003) *Global Education in Europe to 2015*, Lisbon: North-South Centre.

Hall, S. (ed.) (1994) *Rassismus und kulturelle Identität*. Hamburg: Argument Verlag, pp. 137–77.

Hartmeyer, H. (2008) *Experiencing the World*. Münster: Waxmann.

Hartmeyer, H. (2016) Globales Lernen mit Studierenden (Global Learning with Students). In: BMUK (ed.), *Magazin erwachsenenbildung.at*. Vienna, pp. 06.1–06.6.

ID: Institute for International Development: www.ie.univie.ac.at

Lamnek, S. and Krell, Claudia (eds) (2016) *Qualitative Sozialforschung*. Weinheim, Basel: Beltz.

Lang-Wojtasik, G. and Lohrenscheit, C. (eds) (2003) *Entwicklungspädagogik – Globales Lernen – Internationale Bildungsforschung*. Frankfurt/Main: IKO.

Oelkers, J. (2001) *Einführung in die Theorie der Erziehung*. Weinheim: Beltz.

Overwien, B. and Rathenow, H.-F. (eds) (2009) *Globalisierung fordert Politische Bildung*. Opladen: Budrich.

Patel, F. and Lynch, H. (2013) Glocalization as an Alternative to Internationalization in Higher Education: Embedding Positive Glocal Learning Perspectives. In: *International Journal of Teaching and Learning in Higher Education*, vol. 25, Issue 2, pp. 223–30.

Robertson, R. (2012) Globalisation or Glocalisation? In: *The Journal of International Communication,* Vol. 18, Issue 2, p. 191.

Roudemetof, V. (2015) *The Glocal and Global Studies.* Online 2 March 2015.

Sachs, W. (ed.) (1992) *The Development Dictionary.* London: Zed Books.

Scheunpflug, A. (2011) Lehren angesichts der Entwicklung zur Weltgesellschaft. In: Sander W. and Scheunpflug, A. (Hg.), *Politische Bildung in der Weltgesellschaft.* Bonn, pp. 204–15.

Scheunpflug, A. and Hirsch, K. (2001) *Globalisierung als Herausforderung.* IKO: Frankfurt/Main.

Scheunpflug, A. and Schröck, N. (2000) *Globales Lernen.* Stuttgart: Brot für die Welt.

Seitz, K. (2002) *Bildung in der Weltgesellschaft.* Frankfurt/Main: Brandes & Apsel.

Sen, A. (1999) *Development as Freedom.* Oxford: University Press.

Shor, I. (1992) *Empowering Education.* Chicago: University Press.

Tandon, Y. (2009) *Development and Globalisation.* Dakar and Oxford: Fahamu Books 2009.

Treml, A. (1996) *Die pädagogische Konstruktion der 'Dritten Welt'. Bilanz und Perspektiven der Entwicklungspädagogik.* Frankfurt/Main: Kohlhammer.

UNESCO (2014) *Global Citizenship Education.* Paris: UNESCO.

UNESCO (2016) *Education for People and Planet.* Paris: UNESCO.

UNESCO (2016, 2017/18, 2019) *Global Education Monitoring Reports.* Paris: UNESCO.

Wintersteiner, W., Grobbauer, H., Diendorfer, G. and Reitmair-Juárez, S. (2014) *Global Citizenship Education.* Vienna: UNESCO Austria.

Chapter 19

Learning with 'Generation Like' about Digital Global Citizenship: A Case Study from Spain

Eloísa Nos Aldás

Introduction

This chapter focuses on the practices and challenges faced by higher education (HE) in order to engage 'Generation Like' (Frontline 2014), the generations who have grown up with social media, in learning to be critical, cosmopolitan and global political subjects. We present here a specific case study based on experience at the *Universitat Jaume I of Castellón* (UJI), Spain, in the undergraduate degree course in advertising and public relations at the Department of Communication Sciences, Faculty of Humanities and Social Sciences, in the subject of 'Communication towards Equality' (one term, fourth year).

This pedagogical project contributes to international discourses on global education (GE) by sharing evidence from an interdisciplinary approach that combines global citizenship education (GCE) with areas of media literacy and communication for social change, to explore and design an innovative syllabus on 'transgressive communication of social change'. This aims to train future professionals in the field of communication to foreshadow in their daily practice the social and cultural effects of communicative action, considered as part of informal GE.

The adjective 'transgressive' specifies the concept and method developed, which derives from feminism and critical pedagogy (Hooks 1994; Lagarde-y-de-los-Ríos 2005) and applies ethical and political strategies for a collective and non-violent transformation of the local and global status quo. Here, it is specifically utilized to study communication for social change (CSC) (Tufte 2017). These proposals combine 'theory and practice in order to affirm and demonstrate pedagogical practices engaged in creating a new language, rupturing disciplinary boundaries, de-centring authority, and rewriting the institutional and discursive borderlands in which politics becomes a condition for reasserting the relationship between agency, power, and struggle' (Giroux and McLaren 1993 in Hooks 1994: 129). In this way, both the pedagogical foundations and the communicative perspective developed here can be transferred to the epistemology and methods of GCE as well.

In the present day, we need to link this programme to its contemporary context, which is characterized by the ambivalence between transmedia mainstream digital scenarios (Sampedro 2018) and the potentialities of techno-politics (Bennet and Segerberg 2015). Most of our students socialize on media platforms designed with business and promotional interests, which construct a segmented and homogeneous sociopolitical pseudo-reality, but they are also the generations maturing following international movements such as #MeToo and other global networking activist actions (Jenkins 2016).

Thus, this proposal is part of a broader project named 'Digital dietetics',[1] following Sampedro's metaphor of a healthy social media diet, which works towards collectively responsible media literacy actions. We address the pedagogical and political consequences of mainstream digital scenarios: how social media socialization develops into specific cultural relations and political economies resulting from the individual and collective identities they configure. The Cambridge Analytica scandal in 2018 and the sophisticated data analysis engineering of Facebook, which benefited the Trump campaign, revealed to the broader public some major questions about social media. This was already being discussed in research on media literacy and political digital communication (Livingstone 2008), mostly linked to the opaque functioning of private social media platforms and apps. Their programming and algorithms result in users relating to one another, and to information, in very determinate individualized relations trapped in an advertising rationale configured through 'liking' reactions more than dialogical interactions.

In addition, we have to take into account the background of our students, their relevant experience, social composition and global outlook. They enter our degree with a previous overall academic grade close to nine. Geographically, they do not come just from Castellón province but also from other parts of Spain, attracted by the originality and practice-oriented nature of this degree at UJI, which includes regular seminars with companies and professionals from the communication sector and the development of real campaigns for them (such as the 'Live Creativity' with McCann Group every year). Students also participate in the organization of these events. It is also worth mentioning that our university is very active in promoting student national and international exchange programmes: our students visit other universities and we receive incoming students to Castellón (from the Netherlands, Greece, France, Italy and Korea). These international students are present in higher numbers in the subject analysed here than in others (from two to ten), as it offers 30 per cent of the teaching in English (60 per cent in Spanish and just 10 per cent in Valencian, our local language). Every year, the presence of students from migrant families also increases, with several students from backgrounds such as Venezuela, Russia, Rumania or Argentina (10 per cent of the students). This also affects the composition of the group due to the fact that at least 20 per cent of the students have a part-time or full-time job simultaneously to their classes (either in the afternoons or the weekends), although only 5 per cent do not attend classes for this reason and need to be assessed with a final exam instead of the continuous evaluation presented here. It is also interesting to consider that there are always from three to five students involved in university student associations.

In this class context, how can we deal with learning aims such as living together and understanding each other, assuming a 'cognitive diversity' (Zuckerman 2014; 2013)? The following pages analyse the tensions between who our students are, how they learn (and communicate) and the challenges of a critical cosmopolitan education with regard to communicative competences, as both professionals and global citizens.

---

[1]   Further information at www.dieteticadigital.net

Theoretical and methodological framework

As mentioned above, the approach undertaken here applies a critical pedagogy which envisions alternatives. It does not focus on criticizing bad practices, but instead searches for what can be defined as successful practices to learn how to re-imagine political options through communication actions (Duncombe 2007). 'We combine an epistemological revision of how representations both subject and activate political agency along with innovative methodologies that raise students' awareness and engagement' (Gámez-Fuentes, Nos-Aldás y Farné, 2015, pp. 36–7). The main challenge is that students not only reflect on their own present role in digital scenarios (consumption or interaction) but also prepare themselves as the future designers of these scenarios. This learning model considers the class as a communication community capable of transforming reality through their learning process as citizens, and their future actions as communication professionals.

The theoretical and methodological traditions applied here define transformative communication from the tradition of communication for development and social change (CDCS) (Enghel 2013; Gumucio and Tufte 2006; Marí-Sáez 2016; Tufte 2017). This field has evolved in a continuous dialogue with development education (DE) and its latest trends as critical GCE (Torres 2017). One of the core reflections comes from the field of non-governmental organizations for Development (Bourn 2018) and their rich debate on the strategic role played by DE in their global projects and the sort of educative efficacy needed for their communication (Pinazo and Nos-Aldás 2016). This has defined the so-called CSC as communication aimed at capacities, justice and freedom, in dialogue with trends on epistemologies of the South and decolonization (Sen 1999; Da-Sousa-Santos 2012).

The epistemological lens of this model of communication is in accordance with Austin's discourse ethics (1976) on the performativity of language. This assumption on the social commitments established by language and how communicating is acting also looks at cultural studies and post-colonial proposals, and gender and queer studies to highlight discourse as a cultural representation (Hall 1997). The design of this learning programme is based on the responsibilities the students need to acquire from the belief that they are political subjects and that doing things in a different collective and rights-oriented way is possible (Martínez-Guzmán 2015; Martínez-Guzmán and Ali 2008).

The core proposal relies on the concept of an *alterative* communicative efficacy. The concept of 'alterative' is taken from the Peruvian author Roncagliolo (1988; Marí-Sáez 2017), who refers with this adjective to the belief that we are not working on an alternative proposal to hegemonic discourses, but on one which can transform them, alter them at their roots and eradicate the causes of violence, suffering and exclusion. We are, therefore, dealing with social communication as practical politics (Hopgood 2013), from a radical approach 'to assess the context, root out the problems of prevailing systems, and suggest where progressive alternatives may be found ... to advance an emancipatory project that aims at deepening and radicalizing the democratic horizon ... the conditions of possibility for radical political solutions' (Fenton 2016: 178–9). This pedagogical practice, where equal participation is a core element, explores the role of *counter-publicity* (Downey and Fenton, 2003) by looking at language, discourses, communication processes, cultural processes and social movements as the storyline of cultures, as the mediations which interweave their complexity (Martín-Barbero 1998; 2014).

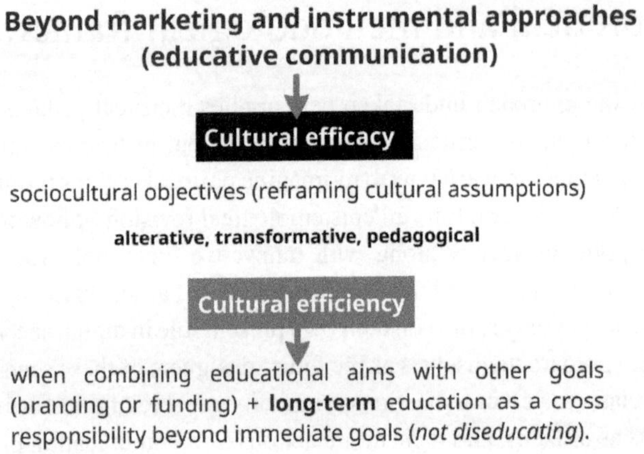

**Beyond marketing and instrumental approaches
(educative communication)**

↓

Cultural efficacy

sociocultural objectives (reframing cultural assumptions)

alterative, transformative, pedagogical

Cultural efficiency

↓

when combining educational aims with other goals
(branding or funding) + **long-term** education as a cross
responsibility beyond immediate goals (*not diseducating*).

Figure 19.1 Cultural efficacy model.
Source: Own elaboration.

From this comparative and interdisciplinary perspective, we have designed a critical methodology on how to produce and evaluate communication from a cultural perspective in order to be aware of the relations and commitments which are established by our discourses. This leads us to look at three different levels:

(1) the idea (image) of (the) reality represented (dignity or misery, for instance);
(2) the suggested type of relation with that reality (equality or superiority); and
(3) the kind of reaction sought in society (which can seek to evoke hatred or reconciliation, inclusion or exclusion, individual power or collective interests).

In general terms, our learning approach aims at the interconnection between rhetoric, values, beliefs and behaviour. Students learn how to communicate towards

- *an informed, engaged and critical civil society as the main 'engine' for social change: active(ist) global solidarity
- *societies in movement made up of political subjects triggered by 'communicative information' (illusion, hope and possibility) (Alfaro 2005).

We, therefore, position ourselves close to global and cosmopolitan media studies (Christensen and Jansson 2015) in the line of a critical cosmopolitan citizenship education framed from human rights (Starkey 2017; Osler and Starkey 2018). This adds to pedagogical methodology assumptions such as:

(1) 'Cosmopolitans recognise that there is more than one acceptable way to live in the world, and that we may have obligations to people who live in very different ways than we do' (Zuckerman 2014 on Appiah's thought).
(2) 'It's not a surprise that complex stories that require us to understand interconnection are hard to develop audiences for' (ibid.)

Challenges and practices

The specific learning process we are presenting here deals with topics and competences related to peace cultures (Martínez-Guzmán 2006) – as the effective realization of social justice and freedom – as well as a critical, social and sustainable economy (Mies and Shiva 1993; Herrero 2013) with students in the fourth year of a BA in advertising and public relations at the UJI (Spain) who are attending the compulsory subject of 'Communication towards Equality' (first term of the year, four months)[2].

Taught in HE, this subject develops innovative methodologies through the application of the latest trends in 'communication of social change', understood as those practices which civil society is successfully applying in order to achieve transformative goals towards global social justice. Educating professionals in communication of social change implies developing with them theoretical and practical wisdom for a political and radical transformation of cultural violence (Galtung 1990). This involves raising students' awareness of the relevance of symbolic violence, its effects on legitimizing and sustaining structural violence and direct violence in all different social fields (from gender violence to poverty or forced migrations) and learning strategies to transform through non-violent communicative actions the root causes and structures which maintain these situations.

This proposal is supported by the key concept of intersectionality (Crenshaw 1991), so that all different variables of exclusion/inclusion are taken into account: structural, political and representational, related to gender, race, colour, religion, geographical origin, capacities, age or class.

The first step is to train students to identify the communicative strategies that legitimize and provoke social injustices (cultural violence/symbolic violence). The second step is to use communicative creativity and potential to re-imagine oppression-free societies by re-framing representations of reality (Lakoff 2004; Darnton and Kirk 2011) through story-based strategies to re-tell hegemonic stories (Reinsborough and Canning 2017). In this learning process we work with social movements' initiatives and Third Sector campaigns, vade-mecums and other working papers elaborated by them. Moreover, students need to distinguish culturally effective proposals from those which have different intentions, such as those which commercialize social struggles or use them for corporate and private interests (Gámez-Fuentes and García-López 2015), such as the so-called *pinkwashing* or *greenwashing* trends. An underlying aim, therefore, is to challenge their own 'deep frames' (Darnton and Kirk 2011; Nos-Aldás and Pinazo 2013), as far as rewording Canning and Reinsborough's words on communication for change, 'the obstacle to learning [they say, convincing people] is often not what they don't yet know but actually what they already do know. In other words, people's existing assumptions and beliefs can act as narrative filters to prevent them from hearing social change messages' (2012).

As hinted at in the theoretical and methodological framework, the understanding of education and communication on the basis of this experience builds on the main concepts of identity (as

---

[2] More details on Spanish education and gender equality legislation can be found in Gámez-Fuentes, M.J., E. Nos-Aldás and A. Farné (2015).

individual cognitive and emotional models) and framing (the way we frame reality through representation influences our behaviour as a result of how values, emotions and beliefs play a role in such a process). Particularly, we work here on how beliefs act as filters between reality and society, and which beliefs can lead us to pro-social engaged behaviours (Nos-Aldás and Pinazo 2013). Positive pro-social values lead to 'collective action frames' (Sireau 2009 in Darnton and Kirk 2011, p. 32). Collective action frames emphasize self-determination. Self-determination refers to the individual's sense of agency to make change for the betterment of society (empowerment and self-awareness). From this perspective, we must incorporate in critical GCE values of self-transcendence, which are linked to values of personal openness to change. According to Kasser and Ryan's 'aspiration index life-goals' (1996), this approach to life has the potential to increase a feeling of agency, one connected to affiliation and community feelings instead of individualistic and consumerist interests (Kasser et al. 2004).

Thus, the starting point for this course is the learning biographies of the students, defined by the curricular and sociocultural context, namely the last year of a degree which is extensively focused on corporate and commercial communication. Moreover, a key element is to critically address the sociopolitical pseudo-reality created by the politics of consumption and sensationalism (Ouellette and Banet-Weiser 2018) and which have played an important role in Brexit, Trump's election as President of the United States, Bolsonaro's election as President of Brazil or the extreme right-wing party VOX being elected to the Andalusian Parliament in Spain. We question the influence of present-day mainstream transmedia mediated-relations (the aforementioned social media and generalized advertising rationality) on their identities, lifestyles and behaviour: whether they are 'self-centred' and 'de-politicized' identities (Chouliaraki 2018).

We consistently and slowly work on moving from their understanding of communication, from a logic of opaque individual persuasive messages to CSC based on open-source collective cooperative and participatory processes. We develop the learning process in the form of invitational (Foss and Griffin 1995) and dialogic communicative interactions (Kaplún 1998) to make them understand relations beyond reputation, branding (promotion) and business goals through an unlearning and re-learning process that searches for social and critical business models and active global citizens. This justifies the fact that we apply participatory and cooperative methodologies, a pedagogy of dialogue, in spite of working with groups of ninety students in theory classes, divided into two groups of forty-five for seminars. Nonetheless, both theory and practice lessons rely on participation and discussion.

There are two main filters which are dealt with:

First, related to their individual identities, we highlight the limits of considering themselves prosumers instead of critical and media active citizens (Jenkins 2006). We focus on the main ideas which help them realize collective identities, such as 'The personal is political' (Millet 1970) or 'What you buy is your vote' (Ballesteros 2007), so that they become familiar with the consequences of their individual choices, as well as collective political projects and the social economy.

Second, there is what Sampedro (2018: 48) defines as the chimeras of digital natives:

(1) digital natives' 'proficiency': they assume they know everything related to digital scenarios, ignoring the relevance of experience, media literacy or digital humanism.

(2) 'global (digital) village': sometimes young generations have the feeling that they are connected to the whole world through their screens, that everything is accessible for them, ignoring the technological breach or how algorithms filter their 'worlds'.

(3) 'we can be whoever we want to be' in the digital world: young generations sometimes disregard the difficulties of the real world overselling the possibilities of anonymity in digital worlds and overlooking its risks (selling your privacy).

(4) 'screens are enough', insofar as everything can be done in the digital world, ignoring the benefits of offline life.

In relation to this debate, we work on their awareness as political subjects, as citizens, and draw together the different actors who interact in multi-layered scenarios – online and offline, interpersonal and mediated – (Toret 2013) in order to conform cultures (Figure 19.2).

All in all, we could sum up the overall goal of this subject as developing their competence and agency in order to foreshadow the cultural consequences of communication and be able to effectively work on advocacy communication, which implies working on all the different interconnected areas for social change from communication, education, legislation and political decisions (Figure 19.3).

The specific syllabus, which translates the previous conceptual and methodological framework into learning practice, is structured into challenges instead of units in order to increase students' motivation and engagement. It attempts to construct a collective project in order to complete – and relate to – their previous knowledge:

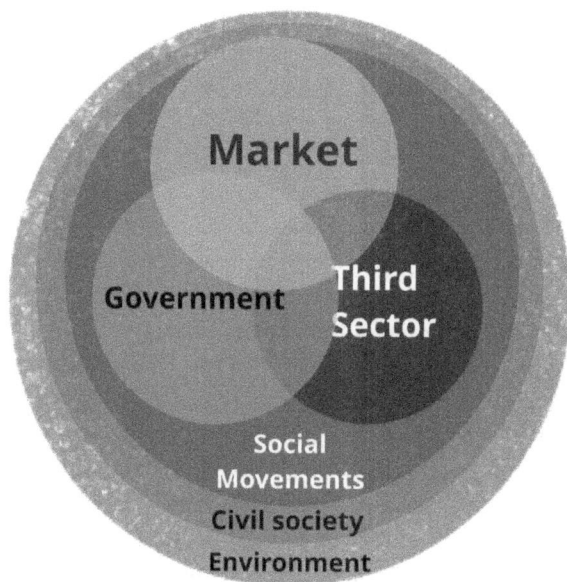

Figure 19.2 Actors on global communication scenarios.
Source: Own elaboration.

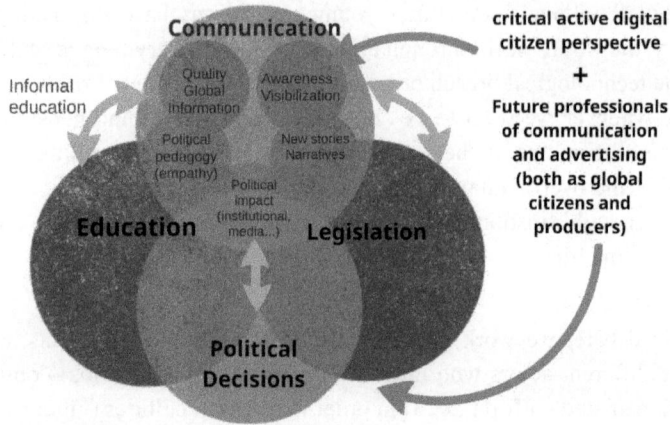

Figure 19.3 Advocacy scenarios for social change.
Source: Own elaboration.

(1) INTRODUCTION: Hacking 'Communication towards equality'

These first sessions are fundamental to start to create the group consciousness and gather information about the group's previous learning. To that end, several activities are carried out such as a sound landscape (through active listening, we sit in a circle and make the sound of rain by snapping our fingers or clapping on our legs[3]). The title itself questions students' prejudices on the subject, as they usually arrive in class limiting their expectations to gender studies applied to communication through the mere analysis of stereotyping. It also widens the focus from feminism (a root element) to intersectional social justice and peace culture. In this first section we also broaden their concept of advertising (promotional communication) to a double-sided approach which also involves publicity (public communication).

(2) CHALLENGE 1: Advertising/publicity communication, diversity, dissent and social change

We discuss the tradition regarding CSC and broaden the theories and models of communication they have previously worked with from collective, cultural and political criteria. We also approach the challenge of 'consensual dissent' (Sampedro and Lobera 2014), of being aware and communicating differences through non-violence and dialogue.

(3) CHALLENGE 2: Cultural efficacy as a new working tool

The concept and method of cultural efficacy is presented through the case study of the evolution of the communication of NGOs for development. Students critically analyse numerous communication examples and agree the main communication criteria proposed by the latest research and practical reports on this topic.

(4) CHALLENGE 3: Transgressive CSC: Applying current trends

Through the analysis of the successful practices of different social organizations (such as the Quepo Foundation for Social Communication in Barcelona[4]), students get hands-on experience of developing examples and actions of transgressive communication for change.

---

[3] An example with a big auditorium can be found at https://www.youtube.com/watch?v=yQAdfH5TtAE from minute 6:50.

[4] All their work and proposals can be found at http://www.quepo.org/

(5) CULTURAL EFFICACY FESTIVAL, conclusions and final review of the learning experience

In the final sessions, the students present their campaigns in a festival with a professional jury. Their final campaigns are assessed by participatory evaluation, both by the invited communication professionals and by their peers. The last week of the course is reserved to discuss the learning outcomes with the students: the lecturer has already corrected their different assignments during the semester, so any possible misunderstandings or weaknesses can be collectively reviewed in class.

As presented above, the first activities are related to value-based education and question the link between logics (world views) and identities. Going back to Canning and Reinsborough's reminder on how 'it is not 'the facts' that motivate people to act – it is how those facts touch their values. Our actions must communicate with values by connecting with what people already know and hold dear' (2008).

For that reason, we use a game, a values deck of cards, made by the Public Interest Research Centre (PIRC) based on Schwartz's values, in order to work on 'Finding Frames: New Ways to Engage the UK Public in Global Poverty' (Darnton and Kirk 2011). Framing theory leads us to explore their own frames and relate them to attitudes and values related to social justice:

Its translation into communicative criteria goes hand in hand with the practical proposals from international networks of CSC, such as the DevReporter (2016), whose vade-mecum insists

The attitudes we want to activate and strengthen...

Figure 19.4 Attitudes for Global Justice.
Source: Darnton and Kirk (2011: 58).

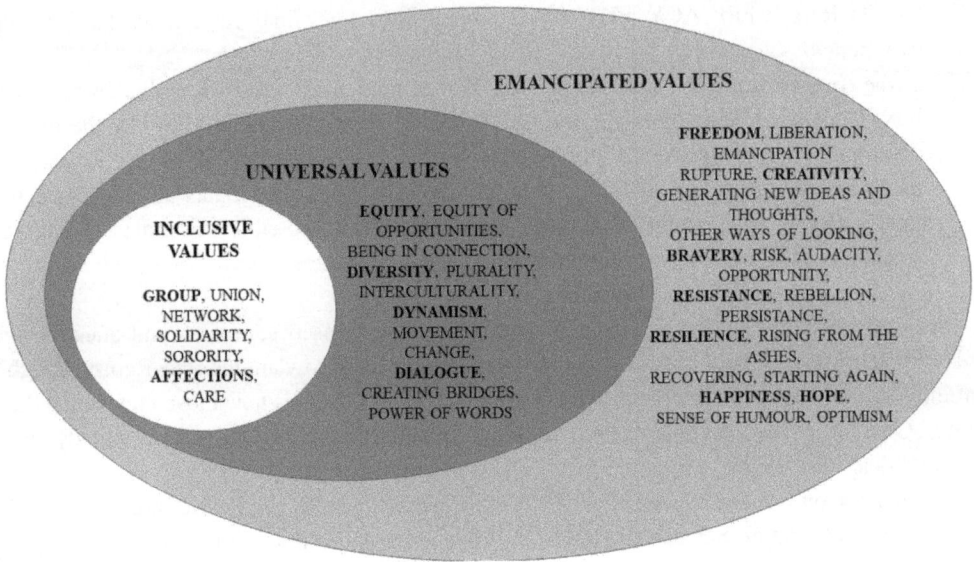

EMANCIPATED VALUES

UNIVERSAL VALUES

FREEDOM, LIBERATION, EMANCIPATION
RUPTURE, **CREATIVITY**, GENERATING NEW IDEAS AND THOUGHTS,
OTHER WAYS OF LOOKING, **BRAVERY**, RISK, AUDACITY, OPPORTUNITY,
RESISTANCE, REBELLION, PERSISTANCE,
RESILIENCE, RISING FROM THE ASHES,
RECOVERING, STARTING AGAIN, **HAPPINESS**, **HOPE**,
SENSE OF HUMOUR, OPTIMISM

EQUITY, EQUITY OF OPPORTUNITIES,
BEING IN CONNECTION, **DIVERSITY**, PLURALITY, INTERCULTURALITY,
DYNAMISM, MOVEMENT, CHANGE,
DIALOGUE, CREATING BRIDGES, POWER OF WORDS

INCLUSIVE VALUES

GROUP, UNION, NETWORK, SOLIDARITY, SORORITY, **AFFECTIONS**, CARE

Figure 19.5 Values to communicate and educate in visible and transgressive plural societies.
Source: Translated from Mesa et al. (2013: 46).

on 'viewing events in perspective, and presenting them with a global dimension to encourage understanding of present and future interdependencies'. Specifically, 'showing the relationship between causes and the impacts in the countries involved' and 'catching the interest and curiosity of the audience by presenting the common problems and the commitment of citizens in all their diversity'.

The inclusive, universal and emancipated values extracted by Mesa et al. (2013) from 1,325 pacifist women's life-stories are also transferred to transgressive communication of social change as cultural efficacy communication criteria (Figure 19.5).

International research has proved that many different lines of thought are reaching very similar proposals and criteria for critical, value-based learning. This can be seen in Sharma (2018), who analyses non-Western proposals and draws similar conclusions to those set out by recent research on social movements communication (Castells 2012; Moliner-Miravet, Francisco-Amat and Olave-García 2014; Espinar and Seguí 2016). Examples include the relevance of a sense of interdependence, a sense of climate change as planetary citizens or sustainable development, an understanding of peace and non-violence as central to the human rights agenda or a commitment to reflective or dialogic and transformative learning (ibid. 94).

To apply all these learnings continuously and at their own pace, we follow a formative assessment which is a part of the student methodology for continuous and participatory learning:

1. They carry out peer tutorials and flipped classes. Students work in groups to enliven a part of a class session, with them being the ones who are experts on the topic and deciding how to make the other students learn in a participatory and interesting way (they design the dynamics and methodologies to be used, tutored by the lecturers) (10 per cent of the final grade).

2. They prepare a final conceptual map: through creative visual thinking methodologies, they synthesize their complete learning by also applying it (20 per cent of the final grade).
3. Project oriented: they develop a final campaign, which can be a prototype or a service-learning experience (30 per cent of the final grade).
4. They write a continuous learning portfolio (40 per cent of the final grade).

In conclusion, through participatory and cooperative dynamics and group cohesion activities, students debate and discuss, constantly applying what they learn. We encourage them to innovate and produce transgressive proposals through thoughtful processes which involve going back to simple thinking strategies from philosophy for children, which guide them to approach controversial issues (OXFAM 2018) in reflective ways.

Final discussion and conclusions

The pedagogical proposal for social justice presented here is the result of twenty-one years of teaching experience in different HE levels, including master's programme on development education and communication for peace and subjects at undergraduate level such as media and peace cultures or social advertising language.

It applies action-research and innovative education approaches to the training of communication professionals as global critical citizens whose daily actions will support non-violent social transformation towards cultures of peace. However, both the theoretical and the methodological framework developed here, and the proposed criteria to address controversial issues in intersectional, non-violent and engaging ways apply to GE programmes as well.

Thus, regarding the relevance of the findings presented in this chapter for broader debates on GE, we can highlight the following:

First, the approaches to learning and the teaching dynamics presented here develop a critical perspective and eagerness to participate and be a part of the solution (testimonies of the students' final evaluation). Student satisfaction with this learning proposal is very positive. They highly appreciate being able to take part in the decision-making process of their learning, both through peer review and being responsible for the enlivenment of a class session. They value very positively having the opportunity to discuss in class with different students and get to know and understand their different contexts, opinions and perspectives.

Although the overall opinion is very satisfactory with regard to their development in terms of acquiring new knowledge and skills to communicate effectively for social change, some of them miss a clearer distinction between theoretical and practical classes due to their previous learning biographies. On the other hand, once they have experienced these new participatory and cooperative methodologies, some of them request even more responsibility and involvement in the development of the classes.

Second, every step and decision of the course is designed in accordance with the latest trends in research and practices of communication of social change and critical GCE, and applies the latest proposals, reports and guidelines debated by practitioners and international actors. The professors maintain a constant collaboration with all the different actors involved in global citizenship and social justice work (mostly NGOs, activists, international organizations, international academia, political actors, etc.), by participating in international interdisciplinary networks. These include practitioners and academia, such as #comunicambio (in English, #comm4change), mainly in Spain and Latin America or, in the broader international arena, #C4D (communication for development), and the Development Education Exchange in Europe (DEEEP) programme), the specific programme on DE of CONCORD (the European Confederation of Relief and Development NGOs) which ended in 2015. These networks gather interdisciplinary experts who combine communicative and educative perspectives and advocate for social transformation from formal and informal contexts, through the collaboration of political, educational and communicational actors.

As part of the educative actions presented, following service-learning and transformative education, this way of understanding universities' role in HE addresses real problems, collaborates on real proposals with organizations and communities, and develops real solutions though social transference. One example is the replication of the Radi-Aid Festival initiative by SAIH (the Norwegian Students' and Academics' International Assistance Fund), where they launch an annual campaign for GCE based on research on the failures and successes of NGODs communication, which they monitor[5]. This project was also developed in a university (in Norway) and inspired the Cultural Efficacy Festival presented in this chapter as a learning activity (Farné, Castillo-Mateu and Nos-Aldás 2018). Third, this design has a global scope not only in the selection of topics and competences in cosmopolitan terms but also in an interdisciplinary sense. It fosters the interconnection among formal, non-formal and informal education through a holistic approach to communication that analyses the connections between identity and social structures, using discourses as the mediation among them.

Last but not least, in keeping up with the epistemological approach to learning presented here, this is a proposal in constant change, reviewed annually and improved upon depending on contextual developments and the students' and professors' assessment of every course experience.

Bibliography

Alfaro, R. Mª. (2005), 'Sociedades en movimiento: desafíos comunicativos a la sociedad de la información', in J. Echevarría et al. (eds), *Solidaridad en red. Nuevas tecnologías, ciudadanía y cambio social*, Bilbao: Hegoa.

Austin, J. L. (1976), *How to do Things with Words*, Oxford: Oxford University Press.

Ballesteros García, C. (2007), *Tu compra es tu voto: consumo responsable, ecología y solidaridad*, Madrid: HOAC.

Bennett, W. L. and A. Segerberg (2015), 'Communication in movements', in *The Oxford Handbook of Social Movements*, 367–83, Oxford: Oxford University Press.

Bourn, D. (2018), 'Global Citizenship Education: A critical introduction to key concepts and debates', *Policy & Practice: A Development Education Review*, 27 (Autumn): 199–203.

Canning, D. and P. Reinsborough (2008), 'Changing the story: Story-based strategies for direct action design', *In the Middle of a Whirlwind*, Team Colors collective and the Journal of Aesthetics & Protest. Retrieved from http://www.racialequitytools.org/resourcefiles/canning.pdf.

---

[5] All the related information can be found at https://www.radiaid.com/

Canning, D. and P. Reinsborough (2012), 'Narrative power analysis', in A. Boyd and D. O. Mitchell (eds), *Beautiful Trouble: A Toolbox for Revolution*, New York and London: OR Books.

Castells, M. (2012), *Networks of Outrage and Hope: Social Movements in the Internet Age*, Cambridge: Polity Press.

Chouliaraki, L. (2018), 'The ethics of "lifestyle solidarity"', *ICA Pre-conference on Global Media & Human Rights*, Prague, 24 May 2018.

Christensen, M. and A. Jansson (2015), *Cosmopolitanism and the Media: Cartographies of Change*, Londres: Palgrave Macmillan.

Crenshaw, K. (1991), 'Mapping the margins: Intersectionality, identity politics, and violence against women of color', *Stanford Law Review*, 43: 1241–99.

Da-Sousa-Santos, B. (2012), 'Public Sphere and Epistemologies of the South', *Africa Development*, XXXVII (1): 43–67.

Darnton, A. and M. Kirk (2011), *Finding Frames: New Ways to Engage the UK Public in Global Poverty*, London: OXFAM-Bond for International Development.

DevReporter (2016), 'Vademecum for responsible international information', *DevReporter Network. Network of Journalists and Communicators for Development*. Retrieved from http://devreporterne twork.eu/wp-content/uploads/2016/04/vademecum_DR_ENG.pdf.

Downey, J. and N. Fenton (2003), 'New Media, Counter Publicity and the Public Sphere', *New Media & Society*, 5 (2): 185–202.

Duncombe, S. (2007), *Dream: Re-imagining Progressive Politics in an Age of Fantasy*, New York: The New Press.

Enghel, F. (2013), 'Communication, development and social change: Future alternatives', in K G. Wilkins, J. D. Straubhaar and S. Kumar (eds), *Global Communication: New Agendas in Communication*, 119–41, London and New York: Routledge.

Espinar, E. and S. Seguí-Cosme (2016), 'Comunicación y cambio social en España: el impacto del 15m, cinco años después', *OBETS. Revista de Ciencias Sociales*, 11 (1): 15–23. DOI: 10.14198/OBETS2016.11.1.01.

Farné, A., L. Castillo-Mateu and E. Nos-Aldás (2018), 'Communication towards equality for future media professionals: Implementing social awareness through a Cultural Efficacy Festival', *International Conference 'Trial and Error'*, *ECREA & CECS (Centro de Estudos de Comuniçao e Sociedade)*, Universidade do Minho, Braga (Portugal), 10–11 May 2018.

Fenton, N. (2016), *Digital, Political, Radical*, Malden: Polity Press.

Foss, S. K. and C. L. Griffin (1995), 'Beyond persuasion: A proposal for an invitational rhetoric', *Communication Monographs*, 62 (March): 2–18.

Frontline (2014), 'Generation like'. [Documentary]. New York: PBS.

Galtung, J. (1990), 'Cultural violence', *Journal of Peace Research*, XXVII (3): 291–305.

Gámez-Fuentes, M. J. and M. García-López (2015), 'Las marcas y la seducción del activismo', in E. Nos-Aldás, A. Arévalo-Salinas and A. Farné (eds), *#comunicambio: Comunicación y Sociedad Civil para el Cambio Social / #com4change: Communication and Civil Society for Social Change*, 426–37, Madrid: Fragua.

Gámez-Fuentes, M. J., E. Nos-Aldás and A. Farné (2015), 'Communication towards equality in the European higher education area: Building capacities for social change with Spanish undergraduates', *The International Journal of Learning in Higher Education*, 3 (22): 33–44.

Giroux, H. and P. Mclaren (1993), *Between Borders: Pedagogy and the Politics of Cultural Studies*, New York: Routledge.

Gumucio, D. A. and T. Tufte (2006), *Communication for Social Change Anthology: Historical and Contemporary Readings*, South Orange: Communication for Social Change Consortium.

Hall, S., ed. (1997), *Representation: Cultural Representations and Signifying Practices*, Scotland: The Open University.

Herrero, Y. (2013), 'Miradas ecofeministas para transitar a un mundo justo y sostenible', *Revista de economía crítica*, 16: 278–307.

hooks, b. (1994), *Teaching to Transgress: Education as the Practice of Freedom*, London: Routledge.

Hopgood, S. (2013), *The Endtimes of Human Rights*, New York: Cornell University Press.

Jenkins, H. (2006), *Fans, Bloggers, and Gamers: Exploring Participatory Culture*, New York: New York University Press.

Jenkins, H. (2016), 'Youth voice, media and political engagement. Introducing the core concepts', in H. Jenkins et al. (ed.), *By Any Means Necessary: The New Youth Activism*, New York: New York University Press.

Kaplún, M. (1998), *Pedagogía de la comunicación*, Madrid: La Torre.

Kasser, T. and R. M. Ryan (1996), 'Further examining the American dream: Differential correlates of intrinsic and extrinsic goals', *Journal of Personality and Social Psychology*, 22 (3): 280–7.

Kasser, T., R. M. Ryan, C. E. Couchman and K. M. Sheldon (2004), 'Materialistic values: Their causes and consequences', in T. Kasser and A. D. Kanner (eds), *Psychology and Consumer Culture: The Struggle for a Good Life in a Materialistic World*, 11–28. Washington DC: APA. DOI: http://dx.doi.org/10.1037/10658-002.

Lagarde-y-de-los-Ríos, M. (2005), 'Ética y política alternativa', *Para mis socias de la vida, Claves feministas*, 48: 304–7, Editorial horas y HORAS.

Lakoff, G. (2004), *Don't Think of an Elephant: Know Your Values and Frame the Debate*, White River Junction: Chelsea Green.

Livingstone, S. (2008), 'Taking risky opportunities in youthful content creation: Teenagers' use of social networking sites for intimacy, privacy and self-expression', *New Media & Society*, 10 (3): 393–411.

Marí-Sáez, V. M. (2016), 'Communication, development, and social change in Spain: A field between institutionalization and implosion', *International Communication Gazette*, March 11. DOI: 2016 1748048516633616.

Marí-Sáez, V. (2017), 'Towards a critical political economy of indicators: Measuring and evaluating "alteratively" communication, development and social change', *Commons. Revista De Comunicación y Ciudadanía Digital*, 6 (1). Retrieved from https://revistas.uca.es/index.php/cayp/article/view/3514. DOI: http://dx.doi.org/10.25267/COMMONS.2017.v6.i1.01.

Martín-Barbero, J. (1998), 'Heredando el futuro: pensar la educación desde la comunicación', *Cultura y Educación / Culture and Education*, 9: 17–36.

Martín-Barbero, J. (2014), 'Jesús Martin Barbero: conceptos clave en su obra. Parte 1: Mediaciones', *Pensadores*.co. Retrieved from https://www.youtube.com/watch?v=NveV5ScaZHg.

Martínez-Guzmán, V. (2006), 'Negative and positive peace', in G. Geeraerts and N. Pawvels (eds), *Dimensions of Peace and Security: A Reader*, 23–42, Brussels: Peter Lang publishers.

Martínez-Guzmán, V. (2015), 'Intersubjectivity, interculturality and politics from the philosophy for peace', *Themata-Revista de Filosofía*, 52: 147–58.

Martínez-Guzmán, V. and F. A. Ali (2008), 'Education for Human Right to Peace from a perspective of Philosophy for making peace(s)', *Cuadernos constitucionales de la Cátedra Fadrique Furió Ceriol*, 62: 197–201.

Mesa, M., L. Alonso-Cano and E. Couceiro (2013), *Visibles y transgresoras. Narrativas y propuestas visuales para la paz y la igualdad*, Madrid: CEIPAZ. Retrieved from http://www.ceipaz.org/visibles ytransgresoras/.

Mies, M. and V. Shiva (1993), *Ecofeminism*, London: Zed Books.

Millet, K. (1970), *Sexual Politics*, New York: Doubleday & Company.

Moliner-Miravet, L., A. Francisco-Amat and J. Olave-García (2014), 'El 15M como espacio de aprendizaje de una ciudadanía crítica. Indicadores para el análisis a partir de historias de vida y métodos de la antropología aplicada', *Quaderns Digitals*, 79. Retrieved from https://bit.ly/2mNh29z.

Nos-Aldás, E. and D. Pinazo-Calatayud (2013), 'Communication and engagement for social justice', *Peace Review*, 25 (3): 343–48. DOI: 10.1080/10402659.2013.816552.

Osler, A. and H. W. Starkey (2018), 'Extending the theory and practice of education for cosmopolitan citizenship', *Educational Review*, 70 (1): 31–40. DOI: 10.1080/00131911.2018.1388616.

Ouellette, L. and S. Banet-Weiser, eds (2018), 'Special issue: Media and the extreme right', *Communication, Culture and Critique*, 11 (1): 1–6. DOI: https://doi.org/10.1093/ccc/tcx021.

OXFAM (2018), *Teaching Controversial Issues: A Guide for Teachers*. Retrieved from https://www.oxfam.org.uk/education/resources/teaching-controversial-issues.

Pinazo, D. and E. Nos Aldás (2016), 'Developing moral sensitivity through protest scenarios in international NGDOs communication', *Communication Research*, 43 (1): 25–48. DOI: https://doi.org/10.1177/0093650213490721. First published online 18 June 2013.

PIRC (Public Interest Research Interest), *Values deck*. Retrieved from http://publicinterest.org.uk/.

Reinsborough, P. and D. Canning (2017), *Re:Imagining Change. How to Use Story-based Strategy to Win Campaigns, Build Movements, and Change the World*, Oakland: PM Press/SmartMeme.

Roncagliolo, R. (1988), 'Las redes de cooperación y la radio comunitaria', in M. Chaparro (ed.), *La democratización de los medios*. Sevilla, España: Diputación de Sevilla/EMA-RTV.

Sampedro, V. (2018), *Dietética Digital. Para adelgazar al Gran Hermano*, Barcelona: Icaria.

Sampedro, V. and J. Lobera (2014), 'The Spanish 15-M movement: A consensual dissent?', *Journal of Spanish Cultural Studies*, 15: 61–80. DOI: 10.1080/14636204.2014.938466.

Sen, A. (1999), *Development as Freedom*, Oxford: Oxford University Press.

Sireau, N. (2009), *Make Poverty History: Political Communication in Action*, Houndmills: Palgrave Macmillan.

Sharma, N. (2018), *Value-Creating Global Citizenship Education: Engaging Gandhi, Makiguchi, and Ikeda as Examples*, London: Palgrave Studies in Global Citizenship Education and Democracy.

Starkey, H. W. (2017), 'Globalization and education for cosmopolitan citizenship', in J. A. Banks (ed.), *Citizenship Education and Global Migration: Implications for Theory, Research, and Teaching*, Washington DC: American Educational Research Association.

Toret, J., coord. (2013), *Technopolitics: The Power of Connected Multitudes. 15m Network-system and the New Paradigm of Distributed Politics* [Working papers], Barcelona: IN3. Retrieved from http://datanalysis15m.files.wordpress.com/2013/06/technopolitics-slides.pdf.

Torres, C. A. (2017), *Theoretical and Empirical Perspectives of Critical Global Citizenship Education*, London: Routledge.

Tufte, T. (2017), *Communication and Social Change: A Citizen Perspective*, New Jersey: Wiley.

Zuckerman, E. (2013), *Rewire: Digital Cosmopolitans in the Age of Connection*, New York: WW Norton & Co.

Zuckerman, E. (2014), 'Digital Cosmopolitans: An Interview with Ethan Zuckerman (Part Two)', *CONFESSIONS OF AN ACA-FAN. The Official Weblog of Henry Jenkins*. Retrieved from http://henryjenkins.org/blog/2014/02/digital-cosmopolitans-an-interview-with-ethan-zuckerman-part-two.html.

Chapter 20

Global Citizenship Education at Home in Higher Education: Researching Values in Professional Education

Philip Bamber

Introduction

Attempts to internationalize the curriculum (Clifford and Montgomery, 2015) and promote global citizenship (Cotton et al., 2018) are pervasive across a range of countries, particularly in higher education (HE) (Horey et al., 2018), as institutions respond to educational reforms and seek to enhance both the learning experience and student employability. These interventions are now galvanized by global policy discourse: the universally applicable Sustainable Development Goals (SDGs) (UNESCO, 2015) include the expectation that global citizenship education (GCE) is mainstreamed at all levels of education in countries throughout the world. At the same time, in the UK and elsewhere, marketization of HE has encouraged transactional approaches that cultivate 'global workers' rather than 'global citizens' (Hammond and Keating, 2018). While there have been numerous investigations into educational initiatives that demand international travel to nurture global citizenship, such as study abroad (Blum, this volume) and international service-learning (SL) (Bamber, 2016), there is a paucity of evidence regarding how global citizenship can be cultivated in a domestic HE context. Developing such educational interventions with the potential for carbon neutrality must become an urgent priority (Bamber, 2019), especially when one considers the latest alarming report from the Intergovernmental Panel on Climate Change (IPCC, 2018). This chapter, therefore, presents theoretically substantiated and practically proven sustainable approaches for 'GCE at home' in HE.

The particular context for this investigation is the professional education of future teachers in England, United Kingdom, where teacher education has been subject to a concerted shift from university to school-led provision (Bamber and Moore, 2016). While international evidence suggests successful teacher education programmes make strong links between theory and practice and promote an inquiry orientation (Tatto, 2015), the policy drive in England has reduced the status of research-informed teacher education with 'the knowledge base for teaching often defined as practical, relevant and focused around contemporary, experiential knowledge of schooling' (Beauchamp et al., 2015: 159). Proponents of GCE are concerned that this approach reduces possibilities for promoting alternative perspectives that challenge the status quo in terms of practice while failing to prepare teachers for exploring complex and controversial issues (Bamber et al., 2016). Put together, this raises important questions about the interrelationship between HE, teacher education and GCE that are explored in this chapter.

This chapter is informed by a conceptualization of GCE (Bamber, Lewin and White, 2018a) that looks beyond epistemological learning processes that involve shifts in world view and habits of mind to an ontological process that accounts for changes to our being in the world. This transformative dimension of GCE is concerned more with 'how' we know rather than 'what' we know, with a particular focus on the role of values alongside tacit, aesthetic and relational ways of knowing (Bamber, 2016). Despite a groundswell of evidence of the need for 'transformative approaches' to education (UNESCO, 2015), proponents of transformative pedagogy for global citizenship (see, for example, UNESCO, 2014; Fricke and Gathercole, 2015) provide only cursory analysis of the theoretical foundations that underpin and stimulate such pedagogy, and little evidence of what transformative education looks like in practice. This chapter, therefore, explicates two innovative case studies of 'GCE at home' in UK HE with a particular focus on understanding processes of value formation in professional education to better understand the development of future educators as agents of change.

HE and global citizenship

Policy developments in the UK (DfES, 2004; Leitch, 2006; Browne, 2010) have had important consequences for the role of the university in society, eroding the ideals of a liberal education. The implementation of the Browne Review recommendations (Browne, 2010) included the introduction of tuition fees, embedding a consumerist framework that is already impacting upon fundamental aspects of HE, including the nature of the curriculum, equality of opportunity, participation, the profile of the academic and our understanding of the role and purpose of education itself. While free access to HE was seen as an entitlement to previous generations, it is now seen by some as a good investment by the individual and central to enhancing employability. Some universities are already considering awarding students of any subject extra marks for demonstrating 'corporate skills' or job experience (The Guardian, 2011). Indeed;

> It is hard to see education as a process by which students seek to understand themselves and the world they inhabit, and easier to see it as a form of learning for self-promotion and trophy hunting. (Lauder et al., 2006: 50)

Internationally, HE's role in fostering the public good is not high on the public's agenda (Saltmarsh, Hartley and Clayton, 2010: 395). Universities are more widely understood as market-driven institutions existing for the private economic benefit and upward mobility of individuals. Students are increasingly likely to go to university to secure future employment rather than to develop their civic agency. Nevertheless, the marketization of HE, in general, and metrics included in the new teaching excellence framework (TEF), in particular, have increased pressured on institutions in the UK to consider the role of pedagogical approaches such as GCE to enhance the student learning experience and improve graduate employment rates (Collini, 2010; Hammond and Keating, 2018).

It is increasingly recognized that HE not only catalyses critical thinking but contributes towards the personal development of both staff and students, nurturing relationships between individuals, groups and the wider community in multiple ways. For example, universities play a role in widening access to groups previously excluded from such opportunities; students from diverse backgrounds study together; universities assume roles both in their local community and on the world stage that demand building partnerships with diverse stakeholders; universities educate professionals such as teachers and social workers who play an ethical role as advocates of particular aspects of relationships. Walker concludes that HE should now be understood to comprise a 'three dimensional triad contributing to rich personal development and fulfilment, vocational preparation and economic opportunities, and a democratic dimension of educated citizenry' (2009: 3). Forms of GCE in practice can clearly enhance such personal, interpersonal, academic and professional outcomes for students (Cotton et al., 2018). However, GCE remains deeply contested theoretically (Bamber, Lewin and White, 2018a) with fissures existing between individual university policies and academics' understanding of the purpose of global citizenship and how to achieve it, as evidenced in an international review of empirical studies (Horey et al., 2018).

Attempts to promote GCE expose the overlapping nature of the 'internationalization' and 'internationalism' of HE (Stromquist, 2007; Kreber, 2009). While the latter emphasizes ethical notions such as 'international community, international cooperation, international community of interests, and international dimensions of the common good' (Jones, 2000: 31), the former is seen to refer to 'greater international presence by the dominant economic and political powers, usually guided by principles of marketing and competition' (Stromquist, 2007: 82). Unsurprisingly perhaps, cross-national comparison of strategies to internationalize education found the dominant approach to be primarily competitive in orientation, 'with national interest as the key driver' (Engel and Siczek, 2018: 749). GCE that teaches students to 'think for themselves and act for the common good' (MacAllister, 2016: 375) presents an opportunity to reclaim HE from such reductive, instrumental goals.

International guidance on global citizenship (UNESCO, 2014) suggests GCE prepares citizens to function in a multicultural society and a global economy through activity that seeks to support the disadvantaged. GCE, so understood, is a pedagogical approach whose motives and outcomes serve to blur the distinctions between what could be described as education for global cooperation and global competitiveness. Further research is clearly required that improves conceptual clarity regarding internationalization terminology and the use of associated notions such as global citizenship (Cotton et al., 2018). While there has been scholarly attention towards 'internationalising the home student' (Clifford, 2011: 555), research and practice on 'GCE at home', particularly in HE, remains relatively under examined and is the focus of this chapter.

Values and GCE

International efforts to improve education have recently moved beyond 'values-neutral' goals such as universal 'access to education'. The 2015 World Education Forum concluded that 'quality education' is characterized by 'the skills, values and attitudes that enable citizens to lead healthy and fulfilled lives, make informed decisions, and respond to local and global challenges' (UNESCO, 2015). Similarly, UNESCO's vision for GCE foregrounds holistic aspects of learning, acknowledging that education must move 'beyond the development of knowledge and cognitive skills to build values, soft skills and attitudes among learners that can facilitate international cooperation and promote social transformation' (UNESCO, 2014: 9). This echoes a report by UNECE (2012) that educators, across all sectors and age-phases, must learn to know (develop understanding), learn to do (develop specific abilities), learn to live together (working together with others) and also learn to be (develop personal attributes). Who the educator is as a person is also a central component of a recent European report evaluating education for global citizenship (Fricke and Gathercole, 2015). It details the values (including 'justice, curiosity, diversity, empathy and solidarity') and dispositions (including 'care for and solidarity with people over-coming injustices and inequalities') that should be embedded within the teaching and learning process.

While some object to the idea that the educator's role is to mould 'certain kinds of people' according to certain values and attitudes, education in general, and GCE in particular, is deeply value-laden. Implicitly or explicitly, values underpin practice. While educators may wish to avoid being accused of dogmatism or bias, all educators are in fact indoctrinators 'for a "doctrine" is a "teaching" and to "indoctrinate" is to lead others into that "teaching"' (Pike, 2011: 184). Interestingly, values-based themes did not emerge as important in a recent mapping of GCE research within teacher education (Yemini, Tibbitts and Goren, 2019). Concerns among educators about promoting particular value perspectives may result from a reluctance to confront controversial issues (ibid, p.87). Certainly, evidence exists that student teachers lack the required subject knowledge and confidence to teach such topics effectively (Bamber et al., 2018b).

Although identifying or evaluating values is inherently problematic both practically and ethically, values have been invoked to address challenges of social cohesion, radicalization and citizenship internationally (UNESCO, 2016), in Europe (EC, 2015) and across a range of national settings, including United States, Canada, Germany and Australia (Peterson and Bentley, 2016). Despite this interest in values education, little is known about educators' values within GCE (Scheunpflug, 2011: 37). This is particularly surprising since educators having 'the value base to be able to interpret the impact of the global society on the learner' (Bourn, 2008: 11) has been identified as an established strength of pedagogy for global social justice. It is, therefore, timely to consider what is already known about values education more broadly, in particular how this relates to professional education.

Researching values in professional education

The emergence of worldwide professional, public and political interest in 'values education' was noted almost two decades ago (Carr, 2000). Since then, values education has been implicated by researchers, policy-makers and practitioners in a growing number of initiatives that address diverse societal concerns including the breakdown of discipline, the perceived crises of multiculturalism, quality teaching, the impact of climate change and peace education more broadly. It has been suggested that values are a 'common theme', 'overriding' the 'differences' between moral, character, citizenship, civics and ethics education (Lovat and Toomey, 2009: xi).

Despite the complexity of ethical challenges facing professionals in contemporary society (Levinson and Fay, 2016), there exists limited research into the ethical dimensions of professionalism within teacher education. Commentators have debated the contrasting merits of discrete professional ethics courses and those that integrate ethics across teacher education curriculum. However, there is little empirical research evaluating the contribution of these differing approaches to professional development (Maxwell et al., 2016). It has been suggested that discussion-based case analysis around dilemmas in professional ethics (see, for example, Levison and Fay, 2016 and Warnick and Silverman, 2011) can provide the basis for stand-alone teacher education ethics provision. However, confronted with challenging situations or controversial issues in the classroom student teachers draw upon complex professional knowledge, much of which is tacit, bound up with one's own goals, beliefs and values (Elliott et al., 2011) or influenced by personal dispositions.

The approach to ethics education illustrated by the case studies here is the process of becoming a professional that requires the cultivation of inclinations, dispositions and good judgements through practice. It is concerned more with becoming a certain kind of person than following a set of rules or a particular ethical code, highlighting the integration of personal and professional development. This commitment to becoming a certain kind of person depends upon reflexivity and inter-professional dialogue about the aims and purposes of education (Carr, 2006). This 'strenuous self-cultivation' (Carr, 2001: 95) helps develop understanding of which values should be promoted and how certain values can be best expressed in a particular context equipping teachers to act as autonomous professionals. This practical approach to value formation ensures values 'can become "hidden" in educational contexts' (Carr and Landon, 1999: 24). This provides the rationale for the two case studies in this chapter that seek to better understand the cultivation of values in the context of professional education for future teachers.

While it was recently concluded that few teacher education programmes intentionally or deliberately prepare pre-service teachers for moral education (Schwartz, 2008) there is a growing literature highlighting the importance of teachers attending to the role of values in schools (Veugelers and Vedder, 2003). Teacher educators form values among student teachers who in turn nurture particular values among their pupils in schools. Recognition of this role for teacher educators is reflected in recent policy in England promoting 'fundamental British values' and movements to disrupt silences in the moral development and training of teachers (Arthur et al., 2015). This is also recognized in global policy discourse: OECD's Programme of International Student Assessment (PISA) foregrounds values in their new framework for global competency 'to stimulate a productive debate on how education can shape children's development of ethical decision-making' (OECD, 2018: 20). While values were not formally assessed in PISA 2018, the OECD has stated that 'the most urgent endeavour' is 'to experiment with and evaluate new methods to improve the measurement of the value dimensions of global competence' (OECD, 2018: 38).

Nevertheless, international research demonstrates that intense competition for space continues to obstruct enhancements to ethics content in teacher education (Maxwell et al., 2016). Radical moves towards school-based teacher education in countries such as England (Bamber and Moore, 2016) have exacerbated this pressure yet open up new opportunities for student teachers to learn in situ, developing values and virtues through practice. The two case studies presented here develop understanding of context-sensitive approaches for researching the development of this form of professional knowledge. Distinguishing between professionalism that is demanded, prescribed, deduced and enacted, Evans (2011) concludes that enacted professionalism remains the only meaningful conception of professionalism:

> The real shape of teacher professionalism will be that that teacher forge for themselves, within the confines and limitations of the context set by the government's demanded professionalism (Evans, 2011: 868).

This position renews attention upon teacher agency and the diverse influences upon professionals beyond policy pronouncements. Evans contests that understanding how teachers develop professionally must incorporate the components of professional development that are often overlooked (namely attitudinal and intellectual development). Furthermore, understanding enacted professionalism requires becoming attuned to mismatches between depictions of practice from teachers and schools and the reality of day-to-day instantiations of policy. The case studies in this chapter, therefore, explore the meanings future educators attach to education policy and locally based curriculum interventions in HE.

In researching the cultivation of values in professional education, this chapter seeks to better understand the development of future educators as agents of change. A strong discourse within GCE in particular postulates the existence of a continuum of participation from awareness of issues to action that challenges injustice (Bourn, 2015). This perspective is reinforced in the new OECD framework for measuring global competency. Particular knowledge, skills and attitudes are pre-defined as central to global competency and will be measured through young people self-reporting on their involvement in a set of particular and predetermined activities (OECD, 2018). The understanding of GCE developed here refocuses attention on the development of 'being' alongside 'agency'. The case studies, therefore, interrogate the role of HE in cultivating values and virtues, moving beyond developing awareness of issues and values transmission towards nurturing critical engagement and action.

Case study 1

This first case study reports upon the experiences of a group of tutors and students at Liverpool Hope University engaged in a curriculum development project entitled 'International Experience for Engaged Global Citizens in Education'. This project, funded by a departmental teaching grant from the Higher Education Academy, sought to develop understanding of how HE can be internationalized to develop engaged global citizens. The focus was on curriculum in the Department of Education Studies, where Eeducation students study the disciplines of education, philosophy, sociology, history and psychology. This course is not formal preparation for teaching, although many students go onto pre-service teacher education. Initial research sought to develop understanding of the role of international experience in relation to notions of global citizenship as experienced by education undergraduates. This led to the development of a 'framework for engaged global citizens in education' and the subsequent development of curriculum interventions as 'GCE at home' for all students. The broader findings and extended discussion of this initiative have been published elsewhere (Bamber, Lewin and White, 2018a).

The project brought together a group of eight academics from a range of empirical and philosophical disciplines. The group was diverse in terms of academic as well as cultural backgrounds. They were joined by eleven undergraduate students to form a steering committee to lead the project. The 'student as co-producer' metaphor has been put forward as an alternative to 'student as consumer' to help re-conceptualize the relationship between the student and university (McCulloch, 2009). This project investigated relational aspects of learning among staff and students, with a particular focus on how such partnerships to develop curricula may help explore ways to reorient HE towards a public good. Through the involvement of students as co-inquirers, it sought to go beyond simplistic notions of student voice whereby student feedback is gathered to inform tutor-led curriculum developments. The steering committee functioned as a 'community of learners' involving students as 'active learners' encouraged to lead research, negotiate with tutors and other 'more skilled partners' (Rogoff, Matusov and White, 1996: 388), as a precursor for any action for change. The aim was to conceptualize, research and practice an innovative approach to student engagement in international education (Green, 2019).

In the initial phase of the research, the project steering committee reviewed a broad range of global citizenship models. The process of constructing and reviewing conceptual frameworks for global citizenship and curriculum interventions exemplified an 'integrated, on-going, participatory process of measurement, reflection, adjustment and learning' (Storrs, 2010: 8) by a committed community of practice. In particular, the project steering committee sought to deconstruct a 'traditional' approach of encouraging global citizenship through acquisition of skills and knowledge. In problematizing curriculum development for global citizenship, the group concluded that previous frameworks in formal education have tended to homogenize, conflate the distinction between difference and otherness, be instrumental in nature and also have difficulties in establishing moral boundaries.

Particular research projects exploring international experiences for global citizenship were also undertaken as part of this first phase of the project. This included, for example, studies of study abroad, international SL and internationalization at home initiatives. A review of the data generated led to an agreement that values and attitudes must lie at the heart of the framework being developed for future curriculum developments. The values that emerged as significant in the data analysis included openness (to difference, the other, diversity), self-respect, an ease with uncertainty and a commitment to social change. It was concluded that attempts to nurture such values and dispositions require a learning process that interrupts conventional patterns and processes that seem overly staged or structured. Attempts to articulate this interruptive pedagogy invited discussion of a range of conceptual frames, such as disorienting dilemmas/ perspective transformation (Mezirow, 1991), distanciation (Ricoeur, 1973), existential homelessness (Heidegger, 1971) and liminality/threshold concepts (Meyer and Land, 2005). Taking the view that values emerge through lived experience, the project team agreed that it was only possible to fully appreciate the possibilities for developing particular values in relation to specific learning contexts.

The second phase of the project, therefore, involved the design, implementation and evaluation of structured interventions that were intended to instantiate the conceptual framework developed in the first phase of the project. Rather than adopting a prescriptive approach, the 'GCE at home' interventions aimed to create democratic spaces for learning. This included local SL, providing opportunities for participating students to reflect upon how volunteering in the local community supports them to move beyond a merely prudential understanding of their actions (and their education) towards a moral understanding of the value of inter-relatedness of persons who inhabit the same local community. A second initiative involved collaboration between UK-based students with students in Mumbai, India, as they explored ethical issues in the public sphere from domestic and foreign perspectives. In parallel, students in the two countries explored an analogous question of corruption in public life, such as MPs' expenses scandals, multinational company involvement in slum clearances and inquiries into press standards. The groups then switched perspectives: Mumbai students considered some issues around ethics in public life in the UK and vice versa, providing comments on the perspectives of the other. Technology such as Skype was used to enable deliberation. These simple and straightforward student activities were intended as an attempt to provide a space for transformative learning that interrupted habitual ways of thinking and being.

The standard approach of explicating the knowledge, skills and attributes that encapsulate learning outcomes for GCE lies in tension with the approach developed here. The reflections of the project team upon the development of an appropriate 'framework' for global citizenship are particularly insightful. Both staff and students articulated a certain ambivalence about the nature, the purpose and the use of frameworks. This ambivalence was related to a perceived 'over-determination' at work in such frameworks. The concerns raised by the project steering committee were not with frameworks per se, but with the relations and attitudes they establish and encourage. A particular conclusion was that generic frameworks intended to guide effective action appear unable to allow for the spontaneous and unanticipated – in short, the genuinely other – to interrupt the plans and schemes of teaching and learning.

Case study 2

The second case study explores processes of professional development as student teachers mediated education policy related to themes of global citizenship during pre-service teacher education within HE. It seeks to better understand how the continuities and discontinuities in official policy discourse related to GCE (Bamber et al., 2016) are experienced among those now joining the teaching profession. It focuses upon the influence of a critical GCE course, mandatory at Liverpool Hope University, titled Wider Perspectives in Education (WPE) that incorporates a university-based component and school-based projects. This provides timely and important empirical data to illuminate the possibilities for critical pedagogy within teacher education.

WPE aims to provide beginning teachers with a broader experience of professional education beyond traditional teaching practice. An introductory university-based component examines national and international education policy agendas through historical critique and critical reflection (Giroux, 2011). It introduces pedagogical approaches for teaching sensitive and controversial issues that nurture critical literacy such as philosophy for children. The project phase is facilitated by Liverpool World Centre, a non-government organization influenced by radical approaches within the lineage of development education (Mannion et al., 2011). Projects address a range of issues relating to spiritual, moral, social and cultural (SMSC) development in general (such as fair trade and climate change) and the duty in England not to undermine fundamental British values (FBV) in particular (such as refugees, rights and immigration). SMSC is enshrined in official legislation across the UK (Bamber et al., 2016) although the themes emphasized within each of the four nations have been strongly influenced by the political nuances of the respective educational regions. In England the SMSC requirement is being used as a vehicle to promote FBV as part of the UK government's approach towards tackling extremism, as will be explained further below.

To nurture mutuality and criticality (Rosenberger, 2000), student teachers are encouraged to connect theory with practice and engage with multiple stakeholders (university tutors, school teachers, school leaders, community groups and organizations, pupils and parents) to consider the wider social, moral and ethical implications of the problem being addressed and define resultant actions. Project negotiation involves teacher educators from both school and university providing a space for professional development and, wherever possible, to align broad project goals and expectations. Integrating curriculum with community engagement in this way provides a model of SL, a pedagogical approach increasingly common to citizenship education (Bamber, 2015) and also used recently within the professional education of teachers (see, for instance, Moate and Riohotie-Lyhty, 2014).

This case study focuses in particular upon the enactment of the policy to promote FBV. In England, schools must now 'promote the fundamental British values (FBV) of democracy, the rule of law, individual liberty, and mutual respect and tolerance of those with different faiths and beliefs' (OFSTED, 2016: 35), with new teachers expected not to undermine FBV in order to gain qualified teacher status (Department for Education, 2012). There is not sufficient space here to cover adequately the clearly complex and contested relationship between the promotion of such 'national' values and GCE. However, researching the influence of a critical GCE course upon the enactment of FBV by student teachers afforded the opportunity to empirically assess claims that the FBV policy creates opportunities for critical democratic engagement given that the teacher's role includes the promotion of explicit values (Bryan, 2012). Furthermore, investigating this dimension of the WPE initiative enabled the researchers to consider the relationship between university and placement school as sites for the emergence of professional dispositions.

The research exposed tensions and affordances in implementing a politically determined approach to values education and the development of future educators' critical autonomy. This suggests a more nuanced understanding of the development of criticality than existing models of critical GCE (Andreotti, 2006; Oxley and Morris, 2013). The outcome included a framework for GCE practitioners to differentiate GCE in practice and to support educators navigating contentious social policy and is reported upon fully elsewhere (Bamber et al., 2018b). In particular, the research exposed how conflict between and within particular values can be concealed in practice. For instance, it found an ambivalence among future educators regarding the meaning of tolerance, including a failure to distinguish between committed openness, deliberative engagement and a grudging or uncritical acceptance of difference. Toleration is invoked as an apparently benign uncontroversial response to cultural and religious plurality, yet remains highly contested in contemporary political philosophy (Walzer, 1997; Forst, 2013). The research found evidence of the promotion of 'uncritical tolerance' that silences difference and paralyse dialogue through failing to understand or challenge the views of others. Student teachers, teacher educators and schools were found to be complicit in the negation of alterity, entering into an implicit pact that precludes genuine critique.

The research did find evidence that the statutory requirement to promote explicit values has opened up a space for critical democratic engagement, creating possibilities for nurturing 'criticality' and 'critical being' (Bamber et al., 2018b). This could be characterized by 'positive toleration' underpinned by principled recognition of the rights of others, openness and curiosity (Walzer, 1997: 10–11). This was evidenced in constructive engagement with difference and the nurturing of empathy as student teachers, for example, simulated the experiences and feelings of a new arrival or incorporating community members from diverse backgrounds within curriculum activities. This research offers important insight into how important critical dispositions for GCE such as hospitality and humility are cultivated through encouraging mutual engagement across difference within the school and wider community. Individuals and groups were found to engage with sympathetic and transformative encounters with others' beliefs as they became 'other-wise' (Bamber, 2015).

Conclusion

The case studies expose challenges for GCE research, policy and practice with a strong values component. They suggest the imposition of values by the nation state, educational institutions, academics, teachers and parents is unlikely to inspire genuine commitment to those values. Attempts to mainstream GCE internationally in the SDGs may expose further the gap between values-driven GCE and how this is enacted by professionals in practice. For instance, in case study two, future educators and schools were found to elide differences between the language of FBV, and other professional-, personal- and faith-based values-related terminology, including that of GCE. The study found evidence that alternative values were often promoted that expand upon, diverge from and subvert policy and curriculum intentions: one school taught the rule of law by building military survival shelters to promote resilience and grit. The meaning underpinning the terminology of broad consensus values asserted within a society can easily be lost or diminished. This also demonstrates the inadequacy of success indicators for SDG4.7, such as whether particular concepts like tolerance have been mainstreamed in the curriculum (UNESCO, 2016: 287) that fail to account for how such values and related curricula are taught in practice.

Relationships between tutors, students and community partners were pivotal to both the curriculum development project detailed in case study 1 and the investigation into the enactment of policy in case study 2. Both case studies highlight the importance of GCE research focusing on both the aesthetic (understood as what is being lived through) and the efferent (understood as what is carried away or retained after the experience). Further research that moves beyond retrospective articulation and rationalization of the learning process is required. Understanding the tacit and aesthetic aspects of this learning process should not rely solely on interviews and self-reporting, but should also include methods such as observations, learning journals, blogs and videotaping. This will help capture and develop an understanding of, for example, emotive and embodied aspects of reflection that are emergent in the process.

Amid a culture of accountability, student satisfaction and measurability in HE, understanding the role of values in GCE has implications for assessment of learning that demands radical solutions. While the outcome-focused audit discourse embedded in the TEF and PISA necessitates quantification and comparison, values-infused GCE does not require students, teachers or researchers to seek correct answers. It involves a spectrum of possibility rather than a search for one particular thing. It implies finding a space for the unexpected and the tacit, aesthetic and relational aspects of learning. Practitioners and policy-makers must develop creative and innovative strategies to overcome the constraints of institutional assessment mechanisms and move beyond individual assessment. They must facilitate and assess cooperative learning and value formation that emerge through working collaboratively. Formative and informal assessments which nurture the learners' ongoing becoming should be deployed. Furthermore, professional educators should consider whether they require professional (un)development in structuring and facilitating tasks such as these with which they are unlikely to be familiar.

Bibliography

Andreotti, V. (2006), 'Soft versus critical global citizenship education: Policy and practice', *Development Education Review*, 3 (1): 40–51.

Arthur, J., Kristjánsson, K., Cooke, S., Brown, E. and Carr, D. (2015), 'The good teacher: Understanding virtues in practice'. Birmingham: Jubilee Centre for Character and Virtues. Available online: https://www.jubileecentre.ac.uk/userfiles/jubileecentre/pdf/Research%20Reports/The_Good_Teacher_Understanding_Virtues_in_Practice.pdf (accessed 28 February 2019).

Bamber, P. (2015), 'Becoming other-wise: Transforming international service-learning through nurturing cosmopolitanism', *Journal of Transformative Education*, 13 (1): 26–45.

Bamber, P. (2016), *Transformative Education through International Service-Learning: Realising an Ethical Ecology of Learning*, London: Routledge.

Bamber, P. (ed.) (2019), *Teacher Education for Sustainable Development and Global Citizenship*, New York: Routledge.

Bamber, P. and Moore, J. (eds) (2016), *Teacher Education in Challenging Times: Lessons for Professionalism, Partnership and Practice*, London: Routledge.

Bamber, P., Sullivan, A., Glover, A., King, B. and McCann, G. (2016), 'A comparative review of policy and practice for education for sustainable development/education for global citizenship in teacher education across the four nations of the UK', *Management in Education*, 30 (3): 112–20.

Bamber, P., Lewin, D. and White, M. (2018a), '(Dis-) Locating the transformative dimension of global citizenship education', *Journal of Curriculum Studies*, 50 (2): 204–30.

Bamber, P., Bullivant, A., Clark, A. and Lundie, D. (2018b), 'Educating Global Britain: Perils and possibilities promoting "national" values through critical global citizenship education', *British Journal of Educational Studies*, 66 (4): 433–53.

Beauchamp, G., Clarke, L., Hulme, M. and Murray, J. (2015), 'Teacher education in the United Kingdom post devolution: Convergences and divergences', *Oxford Review of Education*, 41 (2): 154–70.

Bourn, D. (2008), 'Introduction', in Bourn, D. (ed.), *Development Education: Debates and Dialogues*, 1–17, London: Institute of Education.

Bourn, D. (2015), *The Theory and Practice of Development Education*, London: Routledge.

Browne, J. (2010), 'Securing a sustainable future for higher education: An independent review of higher education funding and student finance'. Available online: https://www.gov.uk/government/publications/the-browne-report-higher-education-funding-and-student-finance (accessed 28 February 2019).

Bryan, H. (2012), 'Reconstructing the teacher as a post secular pedagogue: A consideration of the new Teachers' Standards', *Journal of Beliefs and Values*, 33 (2): 217–28.

Carr, D. (2000), 'Moral formation, cultural attachment or social control: What's the point of values education?', *Educational Theory*, 50 (1): 49–62.

Carr, D. (2001), 'Moral and personal identity', *International Journal of Education and Religion*, 2 (1): 79–97.

Carr, D. (2006), 'Professional and personal values and virtues in teaching', *Oxford Review of Education*, 32 (2): 171–83.

Carr, D. and Landon, J. (1999), 'Teachers and schools as agencies of values education: Reflections on teachers' perceptions. Part Two: The hidden curriculum', *Journal of Beliefs and Values*, 20 (1): 21–9.

Clifford, V. (2011), 'Internationalising the home student', *Higher Education Research and Development*, 30 (5): 555–7.

Clifford, V. and Montgomery, C. (2015), 'Transformative learning through internationalization of the curriculum in higher education', *Journal of Transformative Education*, 13 (1): 46–64.

Collini, S. (2010), 'Browne's Gamble', *London Review of Books*, 32 (21): 23–5.

Cotton, D. R. E., Morrison, D., Magne, P., Payne, S. and Heffernan, T. (2018), 'Global citizenship and cross-cultural competency: Student and expert understandings of internationalization terminology', *Journal of Studies in International Education*. DOI 10.1177/1028315318789337

Department for Education (2012), *Teachers' Standards: Guidance for School Leaders, School Staff and Governing Bodies*, London: DfE.

Department for Education and Skills (DfES) (2004), *Putting the World into World Class Education*, London: HMSO.

Elliott, J., Stemler, S., Sternberg, R., Grigorenkp, E. and Hoffman, N. (2011), 'The socially skilled teacher and the development of tacit knowledge', *British Educational Research Journal*, 37 (1): 83–103.

Engel, L. and Siczek, M. (2018), 'A cross-national comparison of international strategies: Global citizenship and the advancement of national competitiveness', *Compare: A Journal of Comparative and International Education*, 48 (5): 749–67.

European Commission (2015), *Promoting Citizenship and the Common Values of Freedom, Tolerance and Non-Discrimination through Education*, Paris: EC.

Evans, L. (2011), 'The 'shape' of teacher professionalism in England: Professional standards, performance management, professional development and the changes proposed in the 2010 White Paper', *British Educational Research Journal*, 37 (5): 851–70.

Forst, R. (2013), *Toleration in Conflict: Past and Present*, Cambridge: Cambridge University Press.

Fricke, H. J. and Gathercole, C. (2015), *Monitoring Education for Global Citizenship*, Brussels: DEEEP.

Giroux, H. (2011), *On Critical Pedagogy*, London: Continuum.

Green, W. (2019), 'Engaging students in international education: Rethinking student engagement in a globalized world', *Journal of Studies in International Education*, 23 (1): 3–9.

Hammond, C. and Keating, A. (2018), 'Global citizens of global workers? Comparing university programmes for global citizenship education in Japan and the UK', *Compare: A Journal of Comparative and International Education*, 48 (6): 915–34.

Heidegger, M. (1971), 'Building, dwelling, thinking', in Heidegger, M., *Poetry, Language, Thought*, trans. A. Hofstadter, 145–61, New York: Harper and Row.

Horey, D, Fortune, T., Nicolacopoulos, T., Kashima, E. and Mathise, B. (2018), 'Global citizenship and higher education: A scoping review of the empirical evidence', *Journal of Studies in International Education*, 22 (5): 472–92.

Intergovernmental Panel on Climate Change (2018), *Global Warming of 1.5oC*, Switzerland: IPCC. Available online: https://www.ipcc.ch/site/assets/uploads/sites/2/2018/07/SR15_SPM_High_Res.pdf (accessed 12 March 2019).

Jones, P. (2000), 'Globalization and internationalism: Democratic prospects for world education', in Stromquist, N. and Monkman, K. (eds), *Globalization and Education: Integration and Contestation across Cultures*, 27–42, Boulder: Rowmann and Littlefield.

Kreber, C. (2009), 'Different perspectives on internationalization in higher education', *New Directions for Teaching and Learning*, no. 118 (Summer 2009): 1–15.

Lauder, H., Brown, P., Dillabough, J. A. and Halsey, A. H. (eds) (2006), *Education, Globalization and Social Change*, Oxford: Open University Press.

Leitch, S. (2006), *Prosperity for All in the Global Economy – World Class Skills*, London: HMTreasury.

Levinson, M. and Fay, J. (2016), *Dilemmas of Educational Ethics*, Boston, MA: Harvard Education Press.

Lovat, T. and Toomey, R. (2009), *Values Education and Quality Teaching*, Netherlands: Springer.

MacAllister, J. (2016), 'What should educational institutions be for?' *British Journal of Educational Studies*, 64 (3): 375–91,

Mannion, G., Biesta, G., Priestley, J. and Ross, H. (2011), 'The global dimension in education and education for global citizenship: Genealogy and critique', *Globalisation, Societies and Education*, 9 (3–4): 443–56.

Maxwell, B., Tremblay-Laprise, A., Filion, M., Boon, H., Daly, C., van den Hoven, M., Heilbronn, R. and Walters, S. (2016), 'A five-country survey on ethics education in preservice teaching programs', *Journal of Teacher Education*, 67 (2): 135–51.

McCulloch, A. (2009), 'The student as co-producer: Learning from public administration about the student–university relationship', *Studies in Higher Education*, 34 (2): 171–83.

Meyer, J. and Land, R. (2005), 'Threshold concepts and troublesome knowledge (2): Epistemological considerations and a framework for teaching and learning', *Higher Education*, 49 (3): 373–88.

Mezirow, J. (1991), *Transformative Dimensions of Adult Learning*, San Francisco: Jossey-Bass.

Moate, J. and Ruohotie-Lyhty, M. (2014), 'Identity, agency and community: Reconsidering the pedagogic responsibilities of teacher education', *British Journal of Educational Studies*, 62 (3): 249–64.

OECD (2018), *Preparing Our Youth for an Inclusive and Sustainable World: The OECD Global Competence Framework*, Paris: OECD.

OFSTED (2016), *School Inspection Handbook*, London: HMSO.

Oxley, L. and Morris, P. (2013), 'Global citizenship: A typology for distinguishing its multiple conceptions', *British Journal of Educational Studies*, 61 (3): 301–25.

Peterson, A. and Bentley, B. (2016), 'Securitisation and/ or Westernisation: Dominant discourses of Australian values and the implications for teacher education', *Journal of Education for Teaching*, 42 (2): 239–51.

Pike, M. A. (2011), 'Ethics and citizenship education', in J. Arthur (ed.), *Debates in Citizenship Education*, 181–93, London: Routledge.

Ricoeur, P. (1973), 'The hemeneutical function of distanciation', *Philosophy Today*, 17 (2): 129–41.

Rogoff, B., Matusov, E. and White, C. (1996), 'Models of teaching and learning: Participation in a community of learners', in Olsen, D. and Torrance, R. (eds), *The Handbook of Education and Human Development*, 388–414, Oxford: Blackwell.

Rosenberger, C. (2000), 'Beyond empathy: Developing critical consciousness through service-learning', in O'Grady, C. (ed.), *Integrating Service-Learning and Multicultural Education in Colleges and Universities*, 23–44, New Jersey: Lawrence Erlbaum.

Saltmarsh, J., Hartley, M. and Clayton, P. (2010), 'Is the civic engagement movement changing higher education?', *British Journal of Educational Studies*, 58 (4): 391–406.

Scheunpflug, A. (2011), 'Global education and cross-cultural learning: A challenge for a research-based approach to international teacher education', *International Journal of Development Education and Global Learning*, 3 (3): 29–44.

Schwartz, M. (2008), 'Teacher preparation for character development', in Nucci, L. (ed.), *Handbook of Moral and Character Education*, 583–600, Mahwah, NJ: Erlbaum.

Storrs, G (2010), 'Evaluation in development education: Crossing borders', *Policy & Practice: A Development Education Review*, 11 (Autumn 2010): 7–21.

Stromquist, N. P. (2007), 'Internationalization as a response to globalization: Radical shifts in university environments', *Higher Education*, 53 (1): 61–105.

Tatto, M. T. (2015), 'The role of research in the policy and practice of quality teacher education: An international review', *Oxford Review of Education*, 41 (2): 171–201.

The Guardian (2011), 'Students could boost marks by showing 'corporate skills'', 2 January 2011. Available online: http://www.guardian.co.uk/education/2011/jan/02/universities-corporate-workplace-skills-accreditation (accessed 28 February 2019).

UNECE (2012), *Learning for the Future – Competencies in Education for Sustainable Development*, Geneva: UNECE.

UNESCO (2014), *Global Citizenship Education: Preparing Learners for the Challenges of the 21st century*, Paris: UNESCO.

UNESCO (2015), *Incheon Declaration*, Paris: UNESCO. Available online: https://en.unesco.org/world-education-forum-2015/incheon-declaration (accessed 4 April 2017).

UNESCO (2016), *A Teacher's Guide on the Prevention of Violent Extremism*, Paris: UNESCO.

Veugelers, W. and Vedder, P. (2003), 'Values in teaching', *Teachers and Teaching: Theory and Practice*, 9 (4): 377–89.

Walker, M. (2009), 'Critical capability pedagogies and university education', *Educational Philosophy and Theory*, 42 (8): 898–917.

Walzer, M. (1997), *On Toleration*, New Haven and London: Yale University Press.

Warnick, B. and Silverman, S. (2011), 'A framework for professional ethics courses in teacher education', *Journal of Teacher Education*, 62 (3): 273–85.

Yemini, M., Tibbitts, F. and Goren, H. (2019), 'Trends and caveats: Review of literature on global citizenship education in teacher training', *Teaching and Teacher Education*, 77 (2019): 77–89.

Part V

Global Education and Learning within Schools

Chapter 21

Development Education or Global Learning? Evidence from Spanish Schools

Adelina Calvo

General framework: The situation of development education in Spain

The field of study which I refer to as development education (DE) in this chapter is known in other countries as global learning, global education or global citizenship education, albeit with different nuances. This diversity of terminology is a result of cultural and linguistic differences in each country or region and the historical evolution of the field of DE itself. This conceptual diversity also responds to the fact that since the 1990s there has been a fall in the use of the term 'DE' in favour of other terms, such as those mentioned above, which focus less on development and more on globalization (Bourn, 2012).

As I highlighted in a previous study (Calvo, 2017), significant progress has been made in Spain over the last few decades, both in terms of legislation and research and educational practice. DE in Spain falls within the 'standard model' of DE in a European context, which consists of a ministry responsible for development cooperation. This ministry finances DE activities as a part of official development aid (ODA) and NGDOs play an important role in implementing DE. There is also an official national DE strategy or policy involving the ministries of education and the formal education sector. Finally, local and regional governments also play an important role in DE (Krause, 2010).

However, these advances should be seen as unstable or not definitive as demonstrated by the impact of the economic crisis on this field. The economic crisis and its management had a very negative impact on the Development Agenda and DE. Although the budget for the Spanish Agency for International Development Cooperation (AECID: *Agencia Española para la Cooperación Internacional al Desarrollo*) increased progressively from 2007 to 2011, from 2012 onwards it has nevertheless suffered significant cuts. As a result, major cuts have been applied to the field of DE in Spain (Hartmeyer and Wegimont, 2015), a trend that, as is known, can be identified at international levels (McAuley, 2018; McCloskey, 2015).

This instability is seen not only in the withdrawal of public funding but also in the lack of support from some institutions which, like the Ministry of Education, should play a central role in supporting DE. This lack of support prevents the school curriculum focusing on the construction of an active critical global citizenship, through a greater presence of DE dimensions and subjects in the curriculum at all levels of education. Current law governing education in Spain (LOMCE,

2013: Law for the Improvement of Educational Quality) has not favoured this curricular change, viewing education in terms of employability and economic competition, giving priority to improving the situation of Spanish education with regard to international standardized tests and relegating the contents of citizenship to an optional subject (non-compulsory) in secondary education: ethical values (Digón, Méndez, DePalma and Longueira, 2017).

On the other hand, in Spain there is a decentralized policy of international cooperation for development, which explains the existence of DE initiatives in schools supported by public funding from various regional or local governments. Although this clearly demonstrates that DE is alive and that it is a current concern for these administrations, this decentralized policy also involves some risks such as the dispersion and lack of coordination of these different initiatives. It is important to highlight that the maturity of DE should become evident through a progressive independence of ODA and its developmental, economistic and colonial perspectives in relation to the concept of development. Scholars and practitioners agree that development cooperation strategies have not achieved the objective of improving the societies receiving this aid, hence talk of the existence of a crisis in development cooperation, at both political and academic levels (Barrenechea, 2012; Marren, 2015; Unceta, 2013).

The growth of DE initiatives has been aided by decentralization and the commitment of the NGDOs which, although not specifically dedicated to DE, often have a group specializing in DE with a perspective on DE as well as funded projects, educational material and guides for its implementation at different levels of education. Among the most important examples and most widely recognized throughout the country are the Network of Educators for Global Citizenship (Red de Educadores y Educadoras para la Ciudadanía Global) supported by Oxfam-Intermon and the Andalusian Agency for International Development Cooperation; the Movement for Transformative Education and Global Citizenship (Movimiento por la Educación Transformadora y la Ciudadanía Global) promoted by four of the most influential NGDOs in the field of DE in Spain (InteRed, Entreculturas, Oxfam-Intermon and Alboan) or the Teachers for Development Programme promoted within the framework of the Spanish Cooperation Strategy on DE and the 4th Master Plan for Spanish Cooperation. The following section will analyse the educational practices that are being carried out within this framework.

Last but not least, it should be noted that in order to fully understand this analysis it is important to recognize that academic debate in this field (affecting educational practice) has taken place based on the theory of DE generations (Barrenechea, 2012; Calvo, 2017; Lozano, 2009; Mesa, 2000 y 2011; Ortega, 2007). The generations are theoretical constructions representing different concepts of DE. Although the specialized literature presents these generations in evolutionary or historic terms, it is also certain that the complexity of this field does not require them to be viewed in a linear way and there should be an understanding that these coexist in time. Due to the limits of this study, I will summarize the six DE generations in Table 21.1 showing their main characteristics and the dates in which each generation appeared. Those interested in more in-depth information with regard to these should look at the references cited in this section.

In line with the debates that are developing at an international level on the definition of global citizenship education (GCE), its current situation and importance (UNESCO, 2015; Sant et al., 2018), there is a positive consensus on the Spanish Cooperation Strategy on DE in the specialized

Table 21.1 Conceptual Evolution of DE in Spain. Theory of Generations

Generations	Dates	Main concepts
First	1940–50	• Charitable point of view. • Focus on awareness-raising.
Second	1960–70	• Providing information about the situation of the South. • Economic concept of development. Eurocentric.
Third	1970	• Analysis of the structural causes of poverty and underdevelopment. Solidarity. • Opening the school curriculum to problems with a global/international dimension.
Fourth	1990	• Human development and sustainability. • Gender, HR, immigration and so on (multidimensional agenda).
Fifth	2000	• DE for a global citizenship. • To address the challenges posed by globalization.
Sixth	2010	• Post-development Education ('Educación al Postdesarrollo'). • Is development education a form of domination, an attempt to universalize the norms and Western way of life?

Spanish literature, and it is assumed, from a theoretical point of view, that this supports a DE for global citizenship, in Spain called the fifth-generation DE.

At the same time, the main criticisms that post-colonial thinking and Southern epistemologies DE are making of the epistemologies of the North are becoming increasingly visible, questioning the idea that any subject, in any place or space, is considered a member of the community which we call 'global citizenship'. In other words, is citizenship a right, a duty, a condition which is recognized by all human beings all over the world? On the other hand, can we talk about Education for Global Citizenship? What characteristics should this Education for Global Citizenship have in order not to risk becoming a new form of domination, an attempt to universalize Western life? This perspective is known as Post-development Education or sixth-generation DE (Lozano, 2009) and connects with other international debates in the field, based on post-colonial theory (Andreotti, 2010; Andreotti and Souza, 2008; Odora Hoppers, 2015). The presence of this perspective in educational practice is still scarce, but its discussion at a theoretical level points towards a promising future for its progress, viability and visibility in schools in the near future.

Internal analysis: DE in Spanish schools

Taking into account this general framework, in this section, I will analyse the educational practices developed in Spanish schools which have been recognized by the Spanish Agency for International Development Cooperation (AECID) as good DE practices through the award of the 'Vicente Ferrer' National Education Prize for Development. After receiving this prize, the teachers linked to the award-winning schools have the opportunity to join the network: Teachers for Development Programme.[1]

In 2009, the AECID implemented an initiative called Teachers for Development Programme within the framework of the Spanish Cooperation Strategy, targeted at schools all over Spain. Its aim was to generate networks and spaces for exchanging experiences, contributing to the construction of a citizenship committed to the eradication of poverty and the promotion of human development. Currently around 150 teachers participate in the Network, working in classrooms from a perspective of global citizenship. The programme includes two different actions:

(1) The National Award for Development Education. In the year 2018, the National Education Award celebrated its tenth year. Every year, fifteen DE practices from different levels are given awards and a publication is produced.
(2) The National Meeting of Teachers. The winning teachers and schools meet at a national seminar for exchanging experiences and good practices. This is held outside Spain, in countries where development cooperation projects exist.

I have analysed all of the experiences that have been awarded. My analysis is based on publications produced by the Agency each year, which include the experiences of the winning schools. Unfortunately, as a result of cuts in DE funding, since 2016 (eighth edition of the prize) an annual publication of the winning experiences has not been produced.

The award began in 2009; therefore, to date, there have been ten editions (this year's is still in progress). In theory, this makes a total of 150 educational experiences (15 per year), although in reality I have only been able to analyse 105 experiences corresponding to the period 2009–15. As pointed out earlier, and as a result of the cuts in the budget for DE from 2016 to the present, the publication of the experiences is several years behind schedule.

The analysis is based on matters such as the type of experiences awarded, the methodology and activities used, the aims pursued and the generation of DE in which these experiences can be placed. In order to illustrate this I will give some specific examples.

What kinds of experiences are given awards?

According to the instructions in the call for the award (AECID, 2009–18), experiences are those which

(1) involve the entire educational community of the school, that is, they are not classroom experiences or those which involve a single teacher;
(2) promote learning about the realities and causes that explain and provoke poverty and inequality;

---

[1] See the website: https://docentesparaeldesarrollo.blogspot.com

(3) facilitate the critical understanding of the economic, political, social and cultural interrelations between the North and the South; and

(4) promote values and attitudes in our students related to solidarity, social justice, achieving human development and reinforcing critical thinking in order to progress towards a global citizenship.

Likewise, the call specifies that to be eligible, they must be experiences with a clearly innovative dimension, which promote an approach to development from a gender and human rights perspective, as well as being experiences that have the potential to be replicated at other levels of education and in other schools.

For example, in 2015, at the level of nursery and primary education, an award was given to an experience entitled 'The Solidarity Suitcases' which was developed in the Castilla-León region in a Rural School Group. Through five suitcases which travelled around the five schools which make up the Rural School Group, work was carried out on the Millennium Development Goals (MDGs) throughout the academic year. The suitcases were thematic (poverty, gender equality, the environment, education for all and fair trade and responsible consumption) and contained a wide variety of educational material developed by several NGOs. Each suitcase had a similar structure and the activities consisted of viewing videos, cooperative work dynamics, reading material and reflection activities. A web space was created which provides access to several of the dynamics developed in the project.[2]

A second example which illustrates the type of projects that have been awarded is the 2013 prize given to a project entitled 'Schools without Racism, Schools for Peace and Development' carried out by a secondary school in Galicia. The project revolved around a television workshop on education and communication for development. The development of the workshop involved linking the objectives of DE with the students' daily activities. The students were given the task of choosing what type of problems they wanted to investigate and how they were going to do this in order to then be able to communicate their findings using television. Work was carried out on questions such as racism and migration, human rights, the social participation of people with reduced mobility and fair trade, etc.[3] Various subjects of the curriculum and different educational skills were also addressed during the workshop.

Where in the country do experiences receive more and less awards? What are the educational levels of the winning experiences?

According to my analysis the schools which receive the most awards are situated in the centre of the country (Madrid, Castilla-La Mancha and Castilla-León) and Navarra, and the least awarded are found in other communities such as Murcia, Extremadura or The Basque Country. However, this does not necessarily represent the level of activity of schools and teachers in the field of DE all over the country. For example, the Basque Country is very active in DE and development

---

[2] http://maletassolidarias.blogspot.com
[3] http://www.agareso.org/es/escuelas-sin-racismo/

cooperation, but there is little participation in state calls, with a preference for those from its own community. A similar situation can also be observed in Catalonia.

There are winning experiences at all educational levels, from nursery to adult education, but more awards have been given at the level of secondary education (compulsory and non-compulsory) and fewer in the field of adult education. The figures are the following:

1. Nursery education: 10.67 per cent
2. Primary education: 30.09 per cent
3. Secondary education: (a) compulsory: 38.83 per cent; (b) non-compulsory: baccalaureate 7.76 per cent
4. Professional training: 11.65 per cent
5. Adult education (in a prison): 0.97 per cent (one experience)

What objectives are pursued in the awarded experiences?

The experiences awarded pursue a wide range of objectives, which means they represent various DE generations, including the charitable and solidarity approach or the global citizenship approach.

For example, in some of the experiences vocabulary such as 'developing countries', 'underdeveloped countries', 'third world countries', 'poverty and lack of development' or 'collection of donations' is still used. Current research in the field of DE has now overcome this type of terminology, which belongs to first- or second-generation DE (Argibay and Celorio, 2005; Mesa, 2000; Ortega, 2007).

Another of the terms most used in the definition of the objectives is 'solidarity', which brings these experiences closer to second-generation DE (NGO Coordinator for Development-Spain, 2005; Padial, 2011). In fact, in some autonomous communities (Navarra, Cantabria or the Canary Islands) there is a programme called The Network of Solidarity Schools. Although the experiences within it and in each autonomous community are very diverse, it is also true that the existence of this Network, whose schools have been awarded a number of times by the AECID, denotes the importance that the term 'solidarity' still has in the field of DE, in a moment in which it would need to be adjectival (critical solidarity) in order to be able to move away from its more compassionate vision linked to charity.

There are also a great number of experiences, which are still very focused 'on the problems and situations of the countries of the South'. These have aims such as 'raising awareness about the socio-economic situation of impoverished countries, creating solidarity consciousness or creating a community of solidarity with the less fortunate'. In this regard, we can see a DE clearly influenced by the idea of 'repairing' or 'helping to repair' the situation of the countries of the South, without complicating the relationships that are formed between areas and countries situated in different parts of the planet and without analysing the inequalities and injustices that occur in countries of the North.

Meanwhile the increasing number of experiences that cite the creation of a global citizenship among their goals, or even clearly place themselves within fifth-generation DE, should be welcomed. In the definition of objectives, terms such as 'social justice', 'critical thinking', 'links between the local and the global', 'human development', etc. can be found. An example of this would be: 'analysing the keys which explain the world, the classroom as a place for raising awareness about world reality, awareness about situations of social injustice at both local and global levels, eliminating stereotypes and discriminatory attitudes, reinforcing respect for individualities'.

What type of educational methodologies and activities are used?

In general terms, the winning educational experiences use a wide range of methodologies. Some of the most cited methodologies are group work, cooperative learning, discovery learning, service-learning, project work and problem-based learning. These methodologies require a high degree of student participation and aim to generate a collaborative school culture and a commitment to the local community. The words most used to describe them are active, motivating, supportive, inclusive, ludic, participatory, linked to real life, globalizing and socio-affective approach.

In many of them, the description of the methodology (active, participatory, critical, etc.) does not correspond with the activities, objectives, etc. of the experience or it is not visible enough in the description of the rest of the experience (e.g. when it is said that 'the school is a laboratory of democracy that enhances critical thinking, respect for human rights and the active participation of society'). Thus, in many of the good practices described above, there is a lack of coherence between the objectives pursued and the activities and methodologies used.

With regard to the activities, which we will analyse in further detail in the following section, on the one hand, we can identify more specific works that take place in parallel to the curriculum without an apparent profound change in school culture and, on the other hand, more complex activities that are clearly related to different subjects in the curriculum and that would change school culture. In this second case, there is a greater level of coherence between all the elements of the curriculum and DE is visible in the school not only in the contents but also in the activities, methodologies and types of evaluation.

These are some specific examples of the first type of activities:

(1) Exhibitions: craft work on the MDGs done by an African school with which a twinning has been organized, photographs of countries considered to be 'developing', photographs of the educational experience exchange programme entitled 'Education without Borders', photographs relating to human rights or the rights of children organized by various NGOs, etc;
(2) Solidarity activities for raising money: races, collecting food and didactic material, the sale of solidarity sandwiches, etc.;
(3) The celebration of 'The Day of...' (peace, volunteering, women, etc.);
(4) School Twinning projects;
(5) Competitions involving stories, photos, short videos, etc.;
(6) Workshops for making products based on local cuisine;
(7) A school allotment; and
(8) Visits and talks with specialists.

Written, visual or audio-visual research projects on social issues, continents, etc. in different languages are examples of the second more complex types of activities which run over the long term and which are more closely linked to the curriculum. Generally, out of the total number of practices analysed, specific activities are the most frequent.

Ethnographic research is clearly required in order to learn more about the type of methodology and activities used in these experiences. Research projects based on qualitative methodologies and participatory research aimed at describing and analysing the educational reality of these experiences in depth would help to clarify the pedagogic models in use. They would also contribute to improving them and thus encourage a move towards more appropriate pedagogic models (Blackmore, 2016; Pino et al., 2000). In line with the general objectives of this field of work, they should be guided by a critical pedagogy and a pedagogy for global social justice in which the voices of the Global South are not silenced (Bourn, 2014).

What about the curriculum?

Taking into account the four dimensions that make up DE – awareness-raising, training in DE, DE research and social action (Ortega, 2007) – my analysis reveals that the dimensions most used in these experiences are awareness-raising and training in DE. The least used dimensions are DE research and social action, as indicated by other authors who have carried out an analysis of the situation of DE in the Spanish formal education system both at national and regional levels (Ruiz-Varona, 2012; Ruiz-Varona y Celorio, 2012). Likewise, training in DE is an important dimension in these experiences if we take into account that the teacher participants in the practices that have received the award have the opportunity of participating in a seminar for the exchange of experiences in a country where Spain has development cooperation projects. The collaboration of many NGDOs in the development of these projects in schools has also helped to improve this dimension of DE.

With regard to the DE agenda, my analysis demonstrates that the most common topics are the culture of peace and restorative conflict resolution, and economic, social and environmental sustainability, while the least common are governance and human rights, and interculturality and gender. These results partially support the results of an earlier study which analysed the presence of DE in the field of practices and Spanish educational research, analysing the scientific productions of four Spanish journals in the field of educational sciences over the last three years. This work found a lack of development of the gender perspective in relation to the rest of DE topics (Rodríguez-Hoyos, Calvo y Fernández-Díaz, 2012).

There is a clear difference between the experiences that have a direct link with the curriculum and those that run parallel to it without modifying it. Generally, all those activities, closer to the charitable and solidarity approach (races, solidarity markets, donations, talks, workshops, etc.), usually run parallel to the curriculum on which DE culture has little impact. These are activities that have a soft link to the curriculum.

On the other hand, there is another set of activities such as research projects, recording short videos or documentaries that achieve a degree of transversality with regard to DE in the curriculum, for example, when statistics, graphs and functions, algebra, etc. are taught in the subject of maths through research into the level of racism in the world or access to education globally. Another example is learning how to use different technologies by making a documentary and researching social issues in different countries. A further example could be when a workshop on fair trade and responsible consumption is held during tutorials. These are activities that have a strong link with the curriculum.

Finally, in most of these experiences schools collaborate with all types of NGDOs (local, international, etc.) as well as with local government institutions and those belonging to the autonomous community. Furthermore, many of the award-winning schools belong to a wider network such as 'Schools without racism', 'Schools in favour of a living rural world' or 'The Eco-schools Network'.

What approach do the experiences adopt?

Following the analysis of all the experiences and taking into account the previous sections I can confirm that in each of the experiences one of the following approaches is dominant:

(1) The charitable and solidarity approaches. These are the most numerous experiences to date and are usually focused on helping the most needy countries and communities through money-raising activities. Activities for learning about these realities are also implemented, although these imply a somewhat superficial approach to these issues and are primarily focused on 'what the country needs' and 'what it does not have'. An example of this is when a school organizes an activity so that children understand what it means to go to school in a poor country: they have to walk 2 km to get to school, they have classes without desks or educational material, and they receive water and bread as food.

(2) When the curriculum is organized to study the reality of a country or a specific area. These are experiences that revolve around the knowledge of a specific problem in one country where twinning activities have usually been established. These practices are common with respect to Latin American countries, the Sahara, Africa or India.

(3) Harmony with international agendas. These are experiences that focus on elevating, internally and externally (in the local community), the goals promoted in international agendas such as MDGs, Sustainable Development Goals or campaigns (led by different NGDOs) aimed at promoting schooling for all children, combating poverty, etc.

(4) Transversalising DE. To date this is the minority approach, but there are some very interesting experiences. They require effort on the part of the whole educational community because the objectives of DE and its topics are present in all subjects and activities included in the school's curriculum. This approach requires ongoing teacher training processes.

Understanding and critically analysing the presence of these DE curricular approaches is important, since it has been demonstrated that long-term, sustainable actions and a cross-curricular perspective are among the factors that promote successful GCE (UNESCO, 2015).

What DE generations are present in experiences?

My analysis demonstrates that educational practices in Spanish schools are based on several DE generations. This can be deduced from the objectives, activities and methodologies used, given that there are few experiences that explain which DE generation they belong to. In fact, only the ones that identify with the fifth generation do so.

The emphasis on collecting economic and material resources for making donations, focusing on the problems of the South, and the emphasis on solidarity as a principal value to be promoted lead us to the second- and third-generation DE. These are the majority of the experiences.

Meanwhile, the emphasis on global and local aspects, the definition of a global citizenship approach or the declaration of social justice as the aim of practices leads us closer to the fifth-generation DE. These practices, although still in a minority, play a very significant role in the country and are becoming more and more visible. Finally, a sixth-generation DE appears to exist, albeit at a theoretical level rather than a practical one.

Conclusion

Although this is necessarily a partial analysis which has left out many other initiatives that are currently taking place in Spanish schools, supported by various NGDOs and national, regional and local organizations, it has nevertheless identified some significant trends in DE in Spain which coincide with what is reflected in other studies, at both national and international levels.

The educational experiences that take place under the umbrella of DE are very diverse and within these there are very different objectives which involve different ways of understanding what development, North–South relations and globalization mean. In this regard a study by the NGO coordinator for development-Spain, which focused on analysing the 'master plans for cooperation' between the different autonomous communities, pointed out that the majority approach in these was close to the third- and second-DE generations, and found that plans close to the fourth and fifth generations, based on values such as respect, tolerance, attention to diversity, respect for the environment and global citizenship, were still scarce (Padial, 2011). From this same field of NGDOs, practitioners have highlighted that on many occasions DE is still very dependent on the field of development cooperation, it is subsidiary, something which represents a barrier for progress towards more complex, just and politically committed visions of DE (NGO Coordinator for Development-Spain, 2005).

In the field of formal education, both in the English and Spanish secondary education curricula, a setback has been perceived with regard to the presence of DE, which, on the one hand, relates to the consideration of citizenship education as a second-class subject in schools, and, on the other hand, is linked to the centrality that European values and contents still have in these curricula, in the face of more global, intercultural and diverse perspectives that do not silence the perspectives of the Global South. More specifically, it has been highlighted that 'both Spanish/Galician and English curricula seem to lose sight of the global dimension of education and society. Instrumental competencies, disciplinary content and local issues predominate in both cases, demonstrating the continuing trend to exclude DE from mainstream curricula' (Digón et al., 2017: 104).

Currently, in Spain, there is an effective theoretical discussion about DE generations. This theoretical discussion is countered by educational practices in which the presence of various generations of DE which coexist at the same time can be seen. Thus, the charity-welfare perspective still has a lot of influence, which is probably maintained due to the fact that a significant number of the award-winning schools receive both state and private funding (that is, these are schools that receive some state funding but are privately owned by the Catholic church). Meanwhile, the more critical and politically committed perspective of Education for Global Citizenship is paving the way in Spanish schools, at a time when, both at theoretical and practical levels, it is affirmed that DE should broaden its horizons and look beyond education focused on issues on the international cooperation agenda and move towards a Global Learning perspective.

This characteristic of DE in the Spanish education system, where different generations of DE coexist and in which the first DE generations still carry a lot of weight (those which analyse social problems in a less complex way, avoid confronting power relations, focus on the countries of the South and are less political) should make us think at an international level about the importance of the commitment of state-funded education and public administrations to a DE for global citizenship which overcomes the charitable, less political approach and instead commits to a definition of DE that addresses present-day challenges. It should also involve a dimension of social action. The task today is more urgent than ever if we consider the international political panorama where there has been a surge in populism, far-right political movements, a crisis in liberal democracy and the emergence of what has been called post-truth, characterized by a distortion of reality in which objective facts are displaced by personal beliefs and appeals to our emotions. The question we need to ask ourselves is which DE is required in this new scenario where global citizenship needs to be reinvented towards something more inclusive, and which allows us to view reality from both a critical and a political perspective.

We must not forget that Education for global citizenship is an educational approach which gains meaning in each teaching practice and requires reflection on how to achieve a greater level of activity, compromise and critical perspective. The metaphor of global citizenship as a journey can serve as a tool for understanding its performative meaning and the need to recognize the starting point for each group, class or age with whom we work, as well as understanding that as teachers, we are also involved in this process of questioning our beliefs and our practices (Temple and Laycock, 2009).

In general terms, the results of this analysis of good practices coincide with the trends highlighted in the recent evaluation by the AECID of the Spanish Cooperation Strategy on Development Education in which it is affirmed that since the publication of this strategy in 2007

there have been important changes in carrying out DE resulting in broadening the view of DE: from raising awareness on the problems of the countries of the South to their understanding as global problems; from more isolated actions to processes in general and educational processes in particular, which involve longer terms, and the transition from extensive actions in terms of target population to more intensive ones, in which the support role of channelling entities becomes paramount. However, according to the available sources this evaluation has verified that these changes are present more at conceptual and discursive levels than in actions observed. This should be put into context, since there are important differences in the ways of carrying out DE, in the practices and in the importance awarded to each area or dimension. (General Secretariat for International Development Cooperation, 2016: 22–3)

As stated in other studies, analysing the discourse of teachers and practitioners in the field of DE is important in order to understand what visions they have of their work and of how their professional identity is shaped. It is equally important to analyse and understand their practices, in a way in which we can advance research in this field and identify whether the changes that are perceived in the field, towards more global, critical visions based on social justice, exist only at the level of discourse or, on the contrary, are translated into significant changes in practices (Coelho, Caramelo and Menezes, 2018).

Bibliography

AECID (2010–2018), *I-VII Premio nacional de educación para el desarrollo 'Vicente Ferrer'*. Madrid: AECID. Available online: http://www.aecid.es/ES/Paginas/La%20AECID/Educación%20y%20sensibilización%20para%20el%20Desarrollo/Publicaciones-de-Educación-para-el-Desarrollo.aspx (accessed 23 October 2018).

Andreotti, V. (2010), 'Global education in the '21st century: Two different perspectives on the 'post-' of postmodernism', *International Journal of Development Education and Global Learning*, 2 (2): 5–22.

Andreotti, V. and de Souza, L. M. (2008), 'Translating theory into practice and walking minefields: Lessons from the project "Through Other Eyes"', *International Journal of Development Education and Global Learning*, 1 (1): 23–36.

Argibay, M. and Celorio, G. (2005), *La Educación para el Desarrollo*. Vitoria-Gasteiz: Servicio Central de Publicaciones del Gobierno Vasco.

Barrenechea, A. (2012), *Hacia una agenda alternativa de Educación para el Desarrollo desde una perspectiva ecofeminista*. Master en Desarrollo y Cooperacion Internacional, Hegoa. Available online: http://biblioteca.hegoa.ehu.eus/registros/author/16897 (accessed 5 April 2018).

Blackmore, C. (2016), 'Towards a pedagogical framework for global citizenship education', *International Journal of Development Education and Global Learning*, 8 (1): 39–56.

Bourn, D. (2012), 'Development education', in J. Arthur and A. Peterson (eds), *The Routledge Companion to Education*, 254–62, Oxon: Routledge.

Bourn, D. (2014), 'What is meant by development education?' *Sinergias: Diálogos educativos para a transformação social*, 1: 7–23.

Calvo, A. (2017), 'The state of development education in Spain: Initiatives, trends and challenges', *International Journal of Development and Global Learning*, 9 (1): 18–32.

Coelho, D. P., Caramelo, J. and Menezes, I. (2018), 'Why words matter: Deconstructing the discourses of development education practitioners in development NGOs in Portugal', *International Journal of Development and Global Learning*, 10 (1): 39–58.

Digón, P., Méndez, R. M., DePalma, R. and Longueira, S. (2017), 'A place for development education in the current Spanish and English curricula: Finding possibilities for practices', *International Journal of Development and Global Learning*, 9 (2): 97–114.

General Secretariat for International Development Cooperation (2016), *Evaluation of the Education for Development Strategy of Spanish Cooperation (2007–2014): Synthesis Report*. Available online: http://www.cooperacionespanola.es/sites/default/files/evaluacion_eed_sintetico_en.pdf (accessed 8 September 2018).

Hartmeyer, H. and Wegimont, L., eds (2015), *The State of Global Education in Europe 2015: A GENE Report. Dublin: Global Education Network Europe*. Available online: http://gene.eu/wp-content/uploads/State-of-GE-2015-with-covers.pdf (accessed 11 June 2018).

Krause, J. (ed.) (2010), *European Development Education Monitoring Report: 'DE Watch'*. European Multi-Stakeholder Steering Group on Development Education. Bruxelles: DEEEP.

Law 8/2013, of 9 December, for the Improvement of Educational Quality (LOMCE). (BOE 295, 10 December 2013).

Lozano, J. (2009), *¿Qué educación para qué desarrollo? Pistas de reflexión para la sexta generación de Educación para el Desarrollo. Master en Educación para el Desarrollo*, Universidad Pablo de Olavide. Available online: http://pdf2.hegoa.efaber.net/entry/content/1126/Memoria_Julian_Lozano. pdf (accessed 10 February 2018).

Marren, P. (2015), 'Overseas development aid: Is it working?', in G. McCann and S. McCloskey (eds), *From the Local to the Global: Key Issues in Development Studies*, 59–77, London: PlutoPress.

McAuley, J. (ed.) (2018), *The State of Global Education in Europe 2018*. GENE Report. Dublin: Global Education Network Europe.

McCloskey, S. (2015), 'Development education as an agent of social change', in G. McCann and S. McCloskey (eds), *From the Local to the Global: Key Issues in Development Studies*, 302–20, London: PlutoPress.

Mesa, M. (2000), 'La educación para el desarrollo: Entre la caridad y la ciudadanía global', *Papeles*, 70: 11–26.

Mesa, M. (2011), 'Reflections on the five-generation model of development education', *International Journal for Global and Development Education Research*, 0: 161–7.

NGO Coordinator for Development-Spain (2005), *Educación para el Desarrollo: Una estrategia de cooperación imprescindible*. Available online: http://guiarecursosepd.coordinadoraongd.org/uploads/ documentos/que_es_la_educacion_para_el_desarrollo.pdf (accessed 6 May 2017).

Odora Hoppers, C. (2015), 'Think piece: Cognitive justice and integration without duress. The future of development education-perspectives from the South', *International Journal of Development and Global Learning*, 9 (2): 89–106.

Ortega, M. L. (2007), 'Educación para el Desarrollo: Evolución', in G. Celorio and A. López de Munain (eds), *Diccionario de Educación para el Desarrollo*, 130–2, Bilbao: Hegoa.

Padial, E. (2011), *La educación para el desarrollo en las coordinadoras autonómicas de ONGD*. Madrid: Publicaciones Coordinadora.

Pino, E., De la Fuente, C., Ferrándiz, J. L. and Gago, A. (2000), *Una mirada hacia el futuro: Panorama actual y desafíos de la Educación para el Desarrollo en las ONGD de la Coordinadora* (Temas de Cooperación 12). Madrid: Coordinadora de ONG para el Desarrollo-España.

Rodríguez-Hoyos, C., Calvo, A. y Fernández-Díaz, E. (2012), 'La Educación para el Desarrollo en España. Una revision de las prácticas docentes e investigadoras en los tres últimos años', *Revista Electrónica Interuniversitaria de Formación del Profesorado*, 15 (2): 111–21.

Ruiz-Varona, J. M. (2012), *Educación para el desarrollo en las escuelas de Cantabria: Diagnóstico, propuestas y recursos*. Available online: http://historicosweb.unican.es/perfilcontratante/RuizVarona_ EDEscuelasCantabria2012.pdf (accessed 9 April 2018).

Ruiz-Varona, J. M. and Celorio, G. (2012), 'Una mirada sobre las miradas: Los estudios de diagnostic en Educación para el Desarrollo', *Revista Electrónica Interuniversitaria de Formación del Profesorado*, 15 (2): 79–88.

Sant, E.; Daves, I., Pashby K. and Shultz, L. (2018), *Global Citizenship Education: A Critical Introduction to Key Concepts and Debates*. London: Bloomsbury.

Temple, G. and Laycock, A. L. (2009), 'Education for global citizenship: Towards a clearer agenda for change', in D. Bourn (ed.), *Development Education: Debates and Dialogues*, 99–109, London: IOE.

Unceta, K. (2013), 'Cooperación para el desarrollo: Anatomía de una crisis', *Íconos: Revista de Ciencias Sociales*, 47: 15–29.

UNESCO (2015), *Global Citizenship Education: Topics and Learning objectives*. France: UNESCO.

Chapter 22

Global South–North School Linking

Alison Morrison

Introduction, context and aims

As the third decade of the twenty-first century is upon us, the interconnectedness of our lives is clear. Promoting the UN's Sustainable Development Goals (SDGs), including addressing different forms of poverty, climate change and social justice concerns, is the prominent agenda across the globe but controversy persists. Global learning and development education (DE) can be a vehicle in schools to spearhead young people's knowledge in these areas. In the Global North and the Global South, young people's awareness and knowledge about these may partly originate from taking part in the school linking process (Disney 2008).

My interest in school linking began before the Millennium, as a geography teacher of ten- to eleven-year-old students in a nascent Ghana/UK link; I knew nothing of DE or the writing of Paolo Freire (1970). Concerned I might inadvertently compromise students' learning, I researched how UK schools engaged in the linking process (Leonard, 2005). Through that early research I discovered (i) the significance of geography, (ii) the existence of a supportive DE community, (iii) that little was known about the effects that the linking process brought in the Global South.

For a decade, since 2006, my qualitative research sought to address that knowledge gap, enabling unheard voices from the Global South to be voiced (Leonard, 2008, 2010, 2012, 2014a,b and 2015). It has shown real-world examples of how teachers, students and local communities in Ghana, Uganda and Tanzania have benefited. It has also grappled with uneasy tensions in links: of unequal power relationships, appropriateness of projects undertaken, transparency in decision-making and social justice issues.

Andreotti's work (including 2006; 2011) has highly influenced both my personal participation in school linking and my research. She introduced me to the canons of post-colonialist and intercultural literature (including Said 1978; Spivak 1988 and Gundara 2000). Through face-to-face training, she also demonstrated pedagogical skills enabling controversial classroom discussions in a 'safe space' (Andreotti and Warwick 2008; Bourn and Leonard 2009).

My chapter shows how global learning and DE are manifest in the Global South–North school linking process, referred to here as 'School Linking', creating and enabling personalized 'real-world' entrées that assist more adults to self-identify as critical global citizens – questioning issues with resultant tensions, such as the appropriateness of transferring aid from North to South (Quist-Adade and van Wyk 2007), the domination of the English language (Dobson 2006; MacCallum 2012; Sharp 2009; Vellai 2011), and North–South power relations (Disney 2008;

Martin, 2012; Martin and Griffiths 2010). I build on my earlier research and also report new rich, qualitative research on two contrasting Tanzanian/UK school links.

After an outline of the methodology for that new research, the chapter is organized into four aspects of the linking process. Inevitably some overlaps occur:

(1) Professional learning – because adults participating in the linking process are key to the quality and depth of global learning enjoyed by young people in their charge. Adults' learning and confidence in their pedagogical skills is key to teachers' and students' global learning (Alcock and Ramirez Barker 2016).

(2) How links are sustained – because valuable practical lessons can be learnt when successful linkers share their advice. It is particularly important that aspirations are realistic.

(3) How links contribute to quality global learning, critical global citizenship and mutual learning – the chapter gives up-to-date examples. Much of my research drew instead on case studies I carried out between 2005 and 2010 (Leonard: including 2010, 2012, 2014a,b and 2015). Mutuality is defined as 'the sharing of a feeling, action, or relationship between two or more parties'. This definition of critical global citizenship is used: it 'tries to promote change without telling learners what they should think or do, by creating spaces where they are safe to analyse and experiment with other forms of seeing/thinking and being/relating to one another' (Andreotti 2006: 45). This approach avoids the dangers of over-simplistic, 'soft' Citizenship (Andreotti 2006: 45; Burr 2008; Andreotti and Warwick 2008).

(4) How aspirations of friendship, equality, mutuality, cooperation and critical global citizenship are shared – a school link can promote these across the global economic divide. External funding agencies may not.

Finally, the chapter outlines implications and recommendations for the future of the school linking process. I hope this will stimulate further debate and discussion in schools, non-governmental organizations (NGOs), higher education (HE) institutions and among policy-makers on what is a contested process.

Outline of new research methodology

There are four secondary schools involved in the new 'rich' qualitative research reported – School A [unnamed] in Tanzania linked with School B [who also wished to remain unnamed] in the UK are both in urban areas. The second link features Queen Elizabeth High School (QEHS), Gainsborough, UK, linked with DCT Mvumi Secondary School, a remote rural school in the Dodoma region of Tanzania. School B has linked with Tanzanian schools since 2003. QEHS's link is less than five years old. Interviews conducted with four Mvumi teachers who had visited their UK linking partners in 2015 or 2017 also inform my analysis.

My personal relationship with Mvumi, where some of this research took place, is through an NGO for whom I worked as their in-country coordinator, based at the Mvumi school.

Bryan and Bracken (2011) would apply the term 'immersion scheme', to the first link, since it involves young people from School B in UK 'immersing' themselves in the life of School A and its local Tanzanian community.

Both links involve reciprocal staff visits and students from UK visiting Tanzania.

Professional Learning

Teachers' confidence in their skills and knowledge is central to their students' global learning (Alcock and Ramirez Barker 2016). A Professional learning course, for practising teachers and school leaders and offered free by the British Council[1] through its Connecting Classrooms programme[2], places an emphasis on professional learning or continuing professional development (CPD), aimed at 'Quality Education for all'. Connecting Classrooms in its fourth iteration as 'Connecting Classrooms through Global Learning' (CCGL) provides free CPD to linked schools registered through its 'Schools Online' portal. Qualifying schools can obtain grants for reciprocal staff visits if certain criteria are met, contingent upon linked schools' participation in British Council–approved CPD and students working on a collaborative project related to the UN's SDGs. UK schools must link with overseas partners from 'eligible' countries in the Global South (see Table 22.1).

Teachers at both ends of the Mvumi/QEHS link have participated in the 'Connecting Classrooms Professional Learning' programme. UK teachers completed online CPD. In 2016, Mvumi acted as a global learning hub, or 'lead school' for a network of other schools (Egan 2010), disseminating the link's benefits widely in Chamwino district. Three consecutive days of seminars, led by British Council Connecting Classrooms three trainers, allowed more than thirty Mvumi staff, visiting head teachers and staff from five local schools to be introduced to the British Council's 'Global Learning Core Skills' programme.[3] Such concentrated externally provided CPD was unusual and welcomed; over fifty people attended. For later accreditation by the British Council, teachers were required to implement the core skills into their teaching practice across the curriculum, in particular 'critical thinking' and 'problem solving', facilitating their students' personal global learning.

Table 22.1 'Southern' Countries Eligible for British Council's Connecting Classrooms through Global Learning' (CCGL) Reciprocal Visit Grants

Region	Country
Sub-Saharan Africa	Ethiopia, Ghana, Kenya, Lesotho, Malawi, Mozambique, Nigeria, Rwanda, Sierra Leone, South Attica, South Sudan, Sudan, Tanzania, Uganda, Zambia, Zimbabwe
South Asia	Afghanistan, Bangladesh, Nepal, Pakistan
MENA	Egypt, Iraq, Jordan, Lebanon, Morocco, Occupied Palestinian Territories, Tunisia, Yemen
East Asia	Burma

Source: British Council (2018)

---

[1] The United Kingdom's international organization for cultural relations and educational opportunities (British Council (2019), https://www.britishcouncil.org (accessed 9 March 2019)).

[2] https://connecting-classrooms.britishcouncil.org (accessed 8 March 2019).

[3] This third iteration of the Connecting Classrooms programme ended in July 2018.

School B's link with its partners at School A has not involved any external agency. Teachers from School B deliver bespoke demand-led CPD in Tanzania; an example included 'time-tabling and rooming classes'. Subsequently School A attributed its much-improved academic performance in national examinations to its complete reorganization of its teaching timetable.

During more recent biennial month-long visits to School A, professional learning featuring critical thinking has taken place. This led to mutual observation and cooperation:

> One of my colleagues was asked to run a CPD session … on a Saturday morning for the English teachers in the school. It was about very specific things, but we turned it into various activities you know, about how to get students thinking. And that was a huge success, because it enabled them to talk about how to do things and to share things.
>
> In the two weeks following a lot of the teachers … were trying out these things in the classroom … and were asking us to give feedback and were watching each other deliver the lessons. (LCB)

In both links professional learning is taking place. Reflective practice on global learning is evident among staff and students.

LCB believes that the personal global learning of UK colleagues and students who have visited link schools in Tanzania has improved. She is keenly aware of the aspiration of Andreotti's critical global citizenship approach, to allow 'space' for her students' 'other forms of seeing':

> I never tell them you are going to see this, you are going to see that, you are going to see the other, because if I put that idea into their head then they have already formed that thought, haven't they? (LCB)

Both my links have created space for global learning and personal reflection. How young people respond to differing cultural norms of mental health, body-image, gender equality and empowerment of women, sexual orientation or cultural attitudes to disability and diversity, family planning, religion, 'glass ceilings', social exclusion and immigration beyond their schools (Leonard, 2014b, 2017) or behaviour management in classrooms and challenging authority figures in school (Leonard, 2019), are all examples of 'other forms of seeing/thinking and being/relating to one another' that can arise within a school link. All fall within the gamut of global learning. In UK secondary schools similar themes can be captured within schools' personal, social, health, economics (PSHE) education or citizenship, geography, history, psychology, sociology and religious studies curricula.

It is vital to celebrate activities taking place in a school link, raising awareness with the public of developments. I suggest school-level self-assessments of global learning (Hunt and King 2015) and reporting on school linking and global learning to parents, school governors and the wider public would raise the profile of global learning. School newsletters to parents, for example, can celebrate linking activities; school websites can feature classroom global learning displays; celebratory evenings can be arranged during a reciprocal visit with local press invited too. If students visit their link partners collaborative student performances might feature (Leonard 2014a).

The British Council's International School Award (ISA) celebrates global learning in schools' curricula and its dissemination to other schools. School links may be central to accreditation. The Geography Quality Mark,[4] awarded by the Geographical Association, is also sought by UK schools; again the school linking process can be instrumental.

Without similar incentives there is perhaps a risk that a school link's importance will be diminished over time, the recruitment of suitable individuals to staff visits becomes problematic, staff and students lose interest in the process of school linking and even a long-standing relationship flounders (Leonard 2014a; Unwin 2018).

Section 1 has showcased examples of professional learning in the school linking process, contrasting external and 'in-house' CPD provision; it has identified a need for space to reflect on global learning and recommended that linked schools self-assess their global learning and are incentivized to persist in their links.

The following themes and questions emerge from this section:

- How can mutual observation and cooperation between teachers become routine practice, forming part of continuous rather than CPD?
- How can global learning and school linking awareness-raising measures be incentivized?

How links are sustained?

A sustained link, maintained for a period of several years, may be extremely significant, especially to those in the Global South (Leonard, 2014a). Other links may fail to develop or thrive, due to poor communication, lack of funding and competing and shifting demands on teachers' time (Leonard, 2008).

David Allsop, QEHS's head teacher, suggests funding for visits, made available to UK schools under the British Council's Connecting Classrooms 3 programme, was essential in the facilitation of his school's relatively youthful link, 'because we wouldn't have been able to afford to do it otherwise', corroborating Sizmur et al. (2011). Reflecting on his students' 2017 visit to Tanzania he added, 'The school cannot afford to put funding in, other than we will support the teacher, by paying for the supply teachers if they are needed when the teacher is away'. To embed this link and establish its importance he considered it vital to meet his counterpart in Mvumi:

> I think the direct Head to Head link is very important. A Headteacher to me is, *you are the school*. A direct link between two Heads is very powerful. … There were practical reasons as well. … And also, getting to see the rest of the staff, the face of the staff demonstrates how important we see this link. You know, the Headteacher giving up the time to go over is effectively saying that we see this link as very important.

Interviewed shortly after her return from 2018's student visit to Tanzania, LCB, a mathematician (Pendry 2018) and her school's head of year for twelve- to thirteen-year-olds explained that she too highly values the opportunity for her head teacher to visit School A in Tanzania:

---

[4]   https://www.geography.org.uk/quality-marks (accessed 8 March 2019)

She visited in 2014, only for four days, but to me that was really important because that meant that she actually saw what it was and saw what the school was and experienced it: met the people and got a little bit more of an understanding of what it is actually that we do over there. And I think that through that, that has meant that we have been able to carry on this visit … and she saw the value of it.

Particularly during continuing constraints on UK education budgets (Coghlan 2018; George 2018) facilitating reciprocal staff visits should be encouraged. Reciprocal visits are important not just at the outset but also in sustaining even long-standing links, as shown here.

School B and School A have undergone changes of head during this link's existence. I suggest that their link's endurance and sustainability have been secure since, as the UK coordinator stated, 'there has not been a change of personnel altogether'. My doctoral studies (Leonard 2014a) similarly established that links survive changes of head, if other staff are sufficiently passionate and committed to these relationships. Bourn (2014b: 38), reviewing experiences of seven UK schools with links in the Global South, also emphasized the importance of committed enthusiasts and 'face-to-face encounters between key people in both schools'.

Directly reaching the bulk of teachers in a school through global learning is important too in sustaining a school link. Adult participation in the Mvumi/QEHS link involves 'at least half the staff, if not more, from both schools' including teachers and administrative staff at QEHS. At School B, employing approximately 110 adults, LCB estimated that since 2003, 'about 40 staff at the school have been involved; either through going as an accompanying adult on the visit, or our Geography Department used to use it as a case study'.

Another factor contributing to sustaining links in the Global South is their importance in terms of the English language – the dominant language of the globalized world (Dobson 2006). Secondary schools delivering a curriculum taught in English, to non-first-language speakers, report benefits to staff and pupils alike from taking part in school links (Leonard, 2014b). This advantage may be central to the Southern end's desire to sustain their links.

Taught in English, sixteen- to nineteen-year-old Tanzanian advanced-level science students' learning typically face language barriers, as explained by Mvumi's deputy head:

One of the problems I am facing with my students is that every time I tell something about, for example about a certain topic, when you give them the questions, they don't produce the answers as I expected from them.

If you ask them, they say, 'Sorry teacher; I didn't understand the question'. Some, they may say, 'I understood the questions, but I didn't, I was unable to write the correct answers you required'. If you ask them why, they say, 'Maybe our English is a problem'. And it is true; if you ask them to explain for example the same concept in Kiswahili, they do it correctly. They do it correctly; but if you say, 'Why didn't you [*sic*] put it now?' 'I am not used to speak[ing] English; that is why perhaps I didn't get it correct.'

School linking has been shown to promote improved standards of spoken and written English in Southern schools (Bourn and Cara 2012; Edge et al. 2009; Leonard 2014a). A link can enhance students' proficiency in English. Students gain increased exposure to a range of written and spoken English, their teachers' spoken English benefits and their vocabulary improves; students' confidence improves when visitors from English first-language link schools engage in close working relationships, collaborative projects and visits (Bourn and Cara 2012; Leonard, 2014a). Other teachers, with little exposure to such links, lacking fluency and/or confidence in their oracy may restrict their use of English in the classroom to that needed to use school text books, likely to be published in English.

Improved standards of English emanating from the linking process may also be important in instigating and sustaining links for Northern schools. Research by Alcock and Ramirez Barker (2016) shows that the quality of UK primary school pupils' written English has improved through their school's engagement in the linking process. They assessed how global learning and DE methodologies affect the quality of pupils' written work in the primary phase (teaching four- to eleven-year-olds). Cross-curricular extended writing emerging from a linking collaborative project might be such an activity. Their case study, an English primary school, has a link with a rural Kenyan school. They noted, 'As part of this process the school began to use both local and regional Development Education Centres as well as access training available through the British Council's GSP programme'[5] (Alcock and Ramirez Barker 2016: 7). English primary schools, required to regularly report on how students' written English compares to national averages, would find improved standards in written English an attractive motivator. Governing bodies too might encourage linking with such a potential advantage in mind. Raising attainment in written English in the primary phase is also central to students' successful transition to the secondary phase – in Kenya, Tanzania, Uganda and Ghana, or Wales and England in the UK.

A curriculum requiring young children to engage in dialogue and debate around global issues and challenges affecting the lives of young people is likely to enrich their vocabulary and exercise students' high-order thinking skills and critical thinking (Andreotti 2013; Lewis 2016; Scoffham 2007).

Face-to-face encounters between head teachers, linking coordinators and other adults in schools, accompanied by up-to-date global learning resources relevant to school curricula, contribute to the sustainability of school links (Bourn 2014b) and a commitment to create curricula which address social justice concerns and global issues.

If senior management in schools withdraw support for any international partnership, no matter how long it has existed, it is likely that such links would cease, threatening delivery of effective DE and global learning. The long-standing relationship featured in my in-depth case study of a South–North school link between schools (and their local communities) in urban Sheffield, UK, and a remote Tanzanian rural community in Zanzibar (Leonard 2012) has ceased (Unwin 2018). Its demise results partly from the changed status of the UK lead secondary school, following its 'Academisation', partly from large-scale changes in school personnel and also the new Academy's senior management's reduced enthusiasm for the school linking process and global learning.

A national curriculum, specifying content – including 'knowledge' – which teachers must deliver, can promote or restrict students' global learning opportunities (Lambert and Morgan 2011; Scoffham 2018). School linking may be affected as a result. When teachers feel pressurized to cover content-heavy curricula the linking process might be regarded as a luxury add-on. National-scale curricular changes, in response to governments' priorities, can act as stimuli for global learning and the school linking process (Digón Regueiro et al. 2017).

---

[5]   This was the UK's Department for International Development (DfID) Global Schools Partnerships (DGSP) programme; the British Council was one among several supporting organizations.

But why should schools in the Global North care about a curriculum examining human rights, social justice issues or sustainable development to 'address topics which are high on the agenda for governments around the world'? (British Council CCGL 2019b) Competing pressures persist in schools worldwide for constant school improvement. I maintain that if teachers are to deliver effective global learning to young people the curriculum must facilitate schools' inclusion of content relevant to their lives, also obliging students to study this content through the application of critical thinking and problem-solving skills.

Section 2 shows how reciprocal staff visits are central to sustaining links, how exposure to global learning should ideally reach the bulk of adults in linked schools, how improvements in the quality of students' English are important and how guaranteed support from a school's senior management is key. I have also argued that national curricula should mandate teachers' global learning/DE content.

The following questions emerge from this section:

- How can pressure be exerted to ensure that global learning forms a required content in national curricula?
- What obstacles at national level may constrain committed, creative teachers from integrating more global learning and DE methodologies in their daily practice?

How links contribute to quality global learning, critical global citizenship and mutual learning

If global learning is integral to a school link it is important that students' and teachers' learning is of a good quality to avoid the occurrence of superficial or 'soft' global citizenship, with its unchallenged unreliable stereotypes – moving linkers instead from a charity to a social justice mentality and critical global citizenship (Andreotti 2006; Disney 2008; Pickering 2008; Simpson 2016).

Andreotti promotes five 'shifts' for how North–South relationships are perceived (2011); her five shifts of understanding are summarized in Table 22.2. I suggest that considerable effort, time, reflection and much skill are required to move linking participants towards the five 'mindsets' on the left-hand side. Adults may need CPD to assist them to grapple first with the complex nature

Table 22.2 Shifts of Learners' Understanding

Shifted understanding, towards	Away from
Conceptualization of knowledge as located in culture and social/historical contexts.	Ethnocentrism
Analyses of power relations.	Depoliticization
Awareness of the situatedness of selves, relationships and events.	Ahistoricism
Openness in ethical solidarity.	Paternalism
Difference as an ethical relationship towards the other.	The deficit theorization of difference

of her ideas, before their students can be guided to make similar 'shifts of understanding'. Adults and young people could then move away from 'soft' global citizenship too.

In a school link Andreotti's shifts affect how participants respond to their partners, including how 'othering' occurs, between North and South (Said, 1978).

In row 1, Andreotti's 'openness' to different perspectives in a school link, requiring much sensitivity, displaces ethnocentric behaviour (judging those at the 'other' end relative to preconceptions of one's own culture).

In row 2, depoliticization is replaced by overt analysis of power relations, something possibly alien to some adults working in schools. A link may need to consider its internal power relations, particularly when selecting staff for a reciprocal visit or setting a budget and accounting for funds in a joint project. Science students contrasting rubbish found around their schools, as Ghanaian and UK students did in a link which I took part in, required equipment for accurate weighing of items found and protective clothing (Bourn and Leonard 2009; Leonard 2014b). While equipment costs were not incurred for the Northern School the Southern partners' costs were not inconsiderable.

In row 3, acknowledgement of historical domination in colonial relationships and its modern incarnation of neocolonialism replace ahistoricism (a lack of concern for history, historical development or tradition). So how do young people acquire such understanding? Where does this feature in their curriculum? Adults and students in a link may 'know' little of even their own traditions and history. Yet a link would need to grapple with such concerns, particularly when students visit their link partners. In that same Ghanaian/UK link, a student visit to a UNESCO fort and a sacred final bathing place for enslaved Ghanaians 'exported' from the Gulf of Guinea required skilful, adroit discussion and debate on the Atlantic Slave Trade 'to negotiate the historical baggage of colonialism' (Scoffham 2018: 143) and modern-day global economic divides.

In row 4, moving to a position of 'ethical solidarity' avoids vestiges of paternalism (or a possible 'charitable mentality') and is integral to Andreotti's 'shifts'. In a South–North link this may confound people's expectations, that the Global North is superior, and knows best educationally (Leonard 2014a); or that Northern schools will resource Southern partners, fundraising mimicking International Aid, flowing North to South (Bryan and Bracken 2011; Simpson 2016). This shift may be unpopular and risk disappointing people's expectations and result in tensions (Holliday 2010; Leonard, 2014a; McNicoll 2012; Martin and Griffiths 2010).

Finally, in row 5, differences between the Global South and the Global North, the South in deficit, 'lacking' and expecting Northern 'help', are replaced by an ethical relationship between the parties (Andreotti, 2006; Hunt 2012; Quist-Adade and van Wyk 2007). Active critical global citizenship addresses shared social justice issues.

I maintain that a stance, shifting understanding towards the left-hand side in each row of Table 22.2, is required at both ends of a South–North link, for critical global citizenship (Leonard, 2014a), as is high-quality global learning.

Writing in the context of Irish school linking with the Global South, Bryan and Bracken (2011) argued forcefully against paternalism and depoliticization. Many Irish links' origins lay in religious foundations. Charitable giving to Roman Catholic schools' local communities in the Global South had been an expectation in the past, with the South stereotypically viewed negatively as 'needy' and inferior:

> School links initiated for charitable reasons are counterproductive to the aims of global education and global citizenship and reinforce stereo-typical thinking which, in turn, can lead to feelings of intellectual and moral superiority. (Bryan and Bracken 2011: 28)

Yet there is a tension: global learning and school links may owe their origins to charitable reasons (Bourn 2014b; Hunt and King 2015; O'Keeffe 2006). At School B a teacher's personal connections with Farm Africa were used to add the Tanzanian link into the whole school curriculum. School B's website places an emphasis on 'help' brought in the Tanzanian community at A through the linking process. A science teacher's family connections with another charity led to the Mvumi/QEHS link. Neither link is based on a donor–recipient relationship or 'helping model'. Both seek to avoid those in the Global South being viewed as needy and aid-dependent.

> From this focus on equality and not helping … I think that will enable friendships to form and lifelong friendships to form, and unless you focus on what everyone has, rather than the have nots, I don't think that is going to be possible. (FSB)

A former student at School B (FSB), a master's student and geography graduate, she still participates in the process linking School A with School B, which she had first taken part in as a fifteen-year-old student. She expressed a keen desire to avoid 'reinforcing negative stereotypes, cultivating paternalistic or neo-colonialist attitudes and promoting pity instead of empathy' (Bryan and Bracken 2011: 236) in this link:

> If the focus was on this thing about tackling poverty I think achieving a friendship, which I would define as like a relationship of equality, mutuality and reciprocity, it would make it really difficult to achieve, because you are then thinking, 'I can help' … but I would say that trying to move away from that is the best, and trying to move towards an equal and a reciprocal relationship is the better focus.

Making time during a reciprocal visit is important to debate culturally uncomfortable topics between students or teachers and other school staff; facilitating a benefit of critical global citizenship, 'independent/critical thinking and more informed, responsible and ethical action' (Andreotti 2006: 9) can address them. Enabling difficult, often culturally controversial ideas (Badshah 2019; Mitchell 2013) to be voiced if the facilitator has sufficient skills in negotiating and guidance, resultant discussions and critical thinking in a 'safe space', can lead to deep learning (Andreotti 2011; Bourn 2014a; Bryan and Bracken 2011; DeSouza 2008; Leonard 2014a; Martin 2012), even discovery of one's 'authentic cultural voice'. Adichie's influential TED talk (2009) recounts her warning that hearing only a single story about another person or country risks a critical misunderstanding that discussion in a school link can avoid. FSB's reflections on why differing cultural attitudes to diversity and sexual orientation between Tanzanian and British young people occur highlight this:

> Things like LGBT rights. There are very, very different opinions. That conversation was still very important, even if people were aware of different opinions. … Why do you have this opinion? And it is asking that, 'Why?' I think it is something that you can't get in other

situations …? You can't just impose, saying, 'This is just the right thing to do' … there are so many structural and like cultural things that are going to affect that.

While my earlier research (Leonard 2012; 2014a; 2015) examined how school linking addressed the UN's Millennium Development Goals (MDGs), this chapter now considers their replacements, the Goals of the 2030 Agenda for Sustainable Development (SDGs). Importantly the SDGs approach goals from the perspective of mutuality, whereas the MDGs had not done this. The CCGL programme provides SDG-focused teaching resources on its website, trialled with teachers and students; their quality is 'assured' by the British Council.

Lessons can be downloaded from the CCGL website (including embedded video clips), for several SDGs, saving teachers a considerable amount of precious preparation time. Students in linked schools might follow up their learning by swapping their findings, perhaps through the creation of presentations or short videos filmed in their local settings. Completion of a task together is significant in developing relationships (Amin 2002: Robinson-Miles 2017). Modern low-cost technology can allow creative teachers and students to do this, facilitating students' 'quality' mutual learning. Video conferencing could be carried out using Skype, if schools have internet access (Leonard 2015). The cost, expertise and considerable time required to edit video footage must, however, be borne in mind.

Adapting pre-prepared lesson plans can greatly assist busy teachers. Accessing the internet, possible for some teachers in the Global South, is still costly (Leonard 2014a). Accessing digital resources in many Tanzanian schools remains highly problematic. Alternative provision of global learning materials, such as providing them on a flash or pen drive, could allow Southern teachers owning laptops to download and then share the British Council's 'quality-assured' global learning resources with other schools and teachers.

FSB argues, 'Global Learning should be about how you portray your culture and how you think about somebody else's'. She questions the appropriateness of global learning emphasizing SDGs, particularly SDG 1, to 'end poverty in all its forms everywhere':

I think that having your focus on the SDGs can potentially create this unequal power dynamic, because there is a lot more focus on the 'have-nots' and the 'lacks'. Rather than, 'Oh well, they do have this' and 'They can offer this.' And in a way I think it almost assumes that (school B) here are in a superior position because they can help tackle poverty.

Her concerns should be heeded; she is airing tensions of paternalism and a deficit theorization of difference (Bryan and Bracken 2011; Lawson 2018; Martin 2012). FSB's understanding has shifted considerably over the time in which she has taken part in this link; I would argue that she has moved towards the left-hand side of all five rows in Table 22.2 based on Andreotti's work (2011).

In contrast to FSB, David Allsop celebrated sixteen- to nineteen-year-old students' and teachers' collaborative mutual learning, undertaken at QEHS and Mvumi, both schools focusing on another SDG, number 12, to 'ensure sustainable consumption and production patterns'. During his week-long visit to Mvumi in May 2018, funded by the British Council, ninety students, studying Tanzanian science 'A levels', took part in a collaborative project focused on pollution.

David collaborated with Mvumi's head of science, Baraka Mwiyoha. They agreed a project theme of plastic waste in both schools' local environments. QEHS students worked on three sessions first. In Tanzania David 'did exactly the same sessions with a group of students in Tanzania … I brought the responses from the Tanzanian students back.' The follow-up was a letter exchange and ongoing dialogue – about taking positive action to solve the problem.

This example demonstrates how high-quality mutual global learning emerges when teachers within a link make time to plan together, in the light of the relevant curricula in their nations. Additionally students were asked to take effective action for change in their personal lives; Standish (2009; 2012) views similar commitments as potentially burdensome for young people, since they feel powerless to act. I demur from that judgement. The following quotation from David Allsop indicates that young people do not lack agency to address environmental concerns about plastic waste:

> You know, the students that I have been working with here are changing their practices. They are using less plastic; they are trying to use alternative materials, and all of the students in Tanzania I asked to write down an action that they are going to take.

Costs of postage (and time between communications) must be considered to achieve effective student letter exchanges (Leonard 2012; Weale and Adams 2019). While adults' communications might be using email, Skype and phone (for SMS and WhatsApp messages), pupils' physical artefacts are often still swapped. The involvement of local communities at both ends of the link, upon completion of such collaborative projects, could permit quality global learning to extend into the lives of students' families, community leaders (Leonard 2014a, b.) or even local government officials, contributing to SDG 4, the 'promotion of lifelong learning opportunities for all'. Physical letter exchanges and other paper artefacts are still 'swapped' between pupils in schools.

My analysis of interviews with seven adults engaged in these two Tanzanian/UK school links shows that, with appropriate skills, high-quality global learning, deep critical global citizenship and mutual learning can be achieved. Global learning CPD provided by the British Council is central to this, and has benefited UK and Tanzanian teachers in the Mvumi/QEHS link. Mvumi continues to serve as a CPD (and IT) hub to local schools. Pedagogical skills needed to stimulate young people's critical thinking have spread beyond Mvumi. It is likely that benefits to many students will extend beyond global learning. An emphasis, for example, on critical thinking, debating skills and 'digging deeper' should filter through to promote students' scholarship across their curricula. As David Allsop implied, some at both ends of this link may also take positive action for change, students and adults.

Section 3 introduces Andreotti's five 'shifts of understanding' in the context of critical global citizenship within a school link while being aware of inherent difficulties in making such 'shifts'. My new research considers tensions and dissonance if global learning focuses on the UN's SDGs. Section 3 also shows how, with appropriate skills, quality global learning and mutual learning take place in a link. Throughout, Section 3 confronts practical challenges faced in the school linking process.

The following questions emerge from these points:

- How can other linking participants be encouraged to replicate FSB's shifts in learners' understanding?
- How can initial enthusiasm for the implementation of critical-thinking learning approaches be consolidated and extended?

How are aspirations of friendship, equality, mutuality, cooperation and critical global citizenship shared?

In a school link it is possible that those taking part are not just cooperating as part of an educational agendum; they become friends.

Friendship is defined in this section as 'a relationship of equality, mutuality and reciprocity' (Bunnell et al. 2011); all three traits are qualities sought in WorldWise, Ireland's school linking programme (Bryan and Bracken 2011). Friends support and help one another; they actively share advice; they often exchange gifts. Robinson-Miles (2017, p2) found that 'the lens of friendship is ignored in existing literature' concerning school partnerships. She studied a link between schools in Tanzania and UK through the lens of 'friendship in a post-colonial context'. She found evidence for equality, mutuality and reciprocity, despite an absence of reciprocal student exchanges. Significantly, she also recognized the importance of 'link partners having the time and agency to shape their own informal encounters' (p48).

> We have made friends and the friends, some of it I think it will be a life-long [*sic*] friendship. Yes, we have made friends and we have met friends and through which we are still active in communication. That is a good thing. We are still sharing; yes. We are exchanging emails and things like that … We have a saying, that if you have a friend in need he is like your relative. So we have, not just as friends, but we have extended our families. (Baraka Mwiyoha)

Baraka Mwiyoha, David Allsop's collaborator in May 2018, is Mvumi's head of science and the link's coordinator: he reflects above on his 2015 visit to UK, and friendship. We have gone on, as friends and fellow professionals, to co-author a book chapter about inclusion of visually impaired learners in science lessons (Mwiyoha and Leonard, 2019).

Figure 22.1 shows linking characteristics italicized; 'friendship' is absent, but its traits often feature in a linking process (Leonard 2008), as shown by Robinson-Miles (2017). The linking process can accommodate many guises, from two schools' completion of a one-off project to a complex long-lasting relationship, encompassing a network of schools and others (Leonard 2015). Friendships vary too, and, as Bunnel et al (2011: 49) noted, 'can be extremely short-lived or very long-lasting'. Asked about School B's relationship with School A, LCB, the UK coordinator, constantly speaks of a 'link', acknowledging inequalities in the power dynamics within her school's relationship with Tanzanian schools. Like FSB, I suggest she has shifted towards the left-hand side of Andreotti's 'learners' understandings' in Table 22.2 (see page 299). School A is not seen as aid-dependent:

> When it first started, there was a different thing, of building of classrooms, of building of computer rooms and so on, but I've tried to move the link away from that, because I feel like the Tanzanian government can do that.

FSB remarked in terms of this link:

> This is a relationship of equality, and I think that that is so important to emphasise; that contributions from this link come from two ways; nobody is superior and we can learn so much from each other. Not that we are going to tell them what to do, or we are not going to help them.

South/North Educational Linking Process

School link ⟶ **School partnership**

Time scale/sustainability

Short term or long term | Long term

School personnel

Limited | Integrated across teaching staff, School Management and wider School community

Pupils' or students' involvement

Limited awareness of Link | Universally aware

Nature of activities

Project
Data sharing
Subject specific
Resource donation | Integrated across School curriculum
School Visitor Exchanges
Joint resource creation

Reciprocity

Reciprocity and equality of decision-making may be aspired to | Reciprocity and equality of decision-making aspired to.
Junior and senior partners

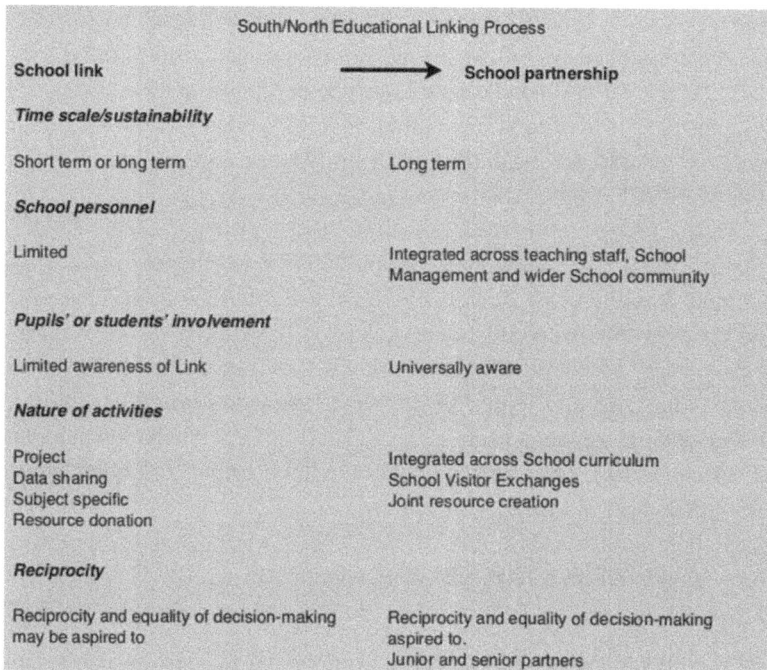

Figure 22.1 A linking/partnership continuum.
Source: A. Leonard (School Linking: Southern Perspectives on the South/North Educational Linking Process: from Ghana, Uganda and Tanzania).

In 2018 a UK-fundraising initiative aimed to support or gift a 'hand-up', to School A's aspirations to build up their library's collection of books in English, in response to Tanzanian teachers' ideas about promoting their students' reading for pleasure:

> The students raised about £3000 before we went, and we've used that, and are going to continue to use that to purchase reading books, so that the Tanzanian students can have something to read for pleasure and to improve their language skills. ... Because I have found that that is one of the biggest barriers to their learning, is that it is all in English. (LCB)

Rowan Williams, former Archbishop of Canterbury, chose to identify similar projects as a 'hand-up', in contrast to the 'hand outs' or donor–recipient relationships that had typified charitable interventions of the past and colonial relationships (Quist-Adade and van Wyk 2011). I borrow his terminology here; the parties in a link often exchange gifts (including time, 'hand-ups' and expertise) in the same manner that friends (or family members) seek advice, ideas, support or encouragement. Within educational hubs, labelled as 'Partnerships', or sometimes as 'Educational Trusts' in the UK, similar cooperation is evident. When government funds are lacking, schools will seek alternative support (Leonard 2014a). Rowan Williams's terminology may disappoint post-colonial theorists, but I adopt it deliberately because such gestures of mutuality are made between friends, as equals. The alternative, to await the library's acquisition of English language materials funded by Tanzania's education ministry, could deprive School A of resources in English which will boost academic attainment, possibly for generations of young people. The use of English language is also necessary to establishing the friendships found in Tanzania/UK links; yet from a post-colonialist theoretical stance the use of English in Tanzanian schools rather than Kiswahili may be opposed (Thiong'o 1986). That debate cannot be developed in this chapter.

Additionally, 'gifting' is a cultural expectation in Tanzania; gifts from visitors to hosts are required to promote respect and establish friendship (Martin and Pirbhai-Illich 2016; Mauss 2011; Robinson-Miles 2017).

Teachers' effectiveness benefits from reflection (Biddulph et al. 2015; Brookfield 1995; Capel et al. 2013; Kolb 1984; Marsh 2008; Moon 2004) it is a central pillar of professional learning (Atkins and Murphy 1994; Boud, 1995; Jesson, 2010; Race 2006; Tennant et al. 2010). Reciprocal visits present experienced teachers, such as LCB, with cause to re-examine their daily practice: 'We have taken on board I think little things that they do within Tanzania. ... Every time I come back I think, actually, it jogs me back into, "How do I teach?"' Friendship, equality, mutuality and cooperation are fundamental in her school's links with Tanzanian partners.

Despite LCB's commitment and enthusiasm for the linking process it is evident that the link now has a lower profile than was the case at its inception: UK student applicants to visit Tanzania, for example, have fallen considerably.

David Allsop regards QEHS's relatively short relationship with Mvumi as a key means of raising global awareness:

> In terms of the Global Awareness: students from rural Lincolnshire don't get that much opportunity, especially students who don't get to go on foreign holidays, to have any awareness of Global Issues. So, the teachers from Tanzania did assemblies here. Which means that they have now heard about the life of people in rural Tanzania. So all the students have heard that; they have all been impacted, they have had their awareness raised of the people in rural Tanzania.

Knowles and Ridley (2005) advise that linked schools must work hard to include activities in which perceptions of other places, held by students and adults, can be discussed and regularly revisited. FSB and LCB both reflected at length upon the importance of such discussions, particularly during immersive visits to Tanzania. Their acute awareness of inequalities that could emanate from fundraising activities for their Tanzanian link perhaps originates from cognizance that this could turn their link into a financial relationship; it could also reinforce negative stereotypes, endangering the link's principles of critical global citizenship.

I suggest that support for School A's 'reading for pleasure' project, to benefit students' greater fluency in English, does not compromise the link's commitment to equality and mutuality.

David Allsop will send other student groups from QEHS to Tanzania and, if practical, host reciprocal visits from teachers and students from Mvumi. Mvumi's deputy head endorses this link's aspiration for future reciprocal student exchanges; he said:

> I think if there is a chance for others to learn, especially students, they can see their fellow students, what is happening there; it can be a good lesson to them. But also it can help me a lot actually also to explain some of the issues which are taking place there.

Mvumi's director of studies too sought such ethical solidarity developments. Baraka Mwiyoha also spoke of the profound impact that his week-long study visit to the UK in 2015 has brought to his pedagogy and motivation as a science teacher:

To be in the UK actually has helped me to change my way of thinking as a teacher … through that week, and through the places that we visited, particularly the Academic Institutions, actually it has ringed me [*sic*] in my brain, that whatever, a 'Good teacher': if you want to be a good teacher, you must plan first to be a good learner.

Alcock and Ramirez Barker (2016: 74) concur: 'Good professional development and conditions for learning for teachers may lead to a high-quality learning experience for pupils, creating a positive feedback loop', replicating a finding from Sarason (cited in Aubusson et al. 2009).

FSB described mutuality and equality when students from School B visit School A in Tanzania:

They do absolutely everything as a [School A] student would do; whether that is like helping to clean the school or helping them build something. And that means it is equal. And that really does emphasise the equality; they are not kind of like going in there as, you know, superior visitors.

School B currently visits its Tanzanian 'link' every two years. In terms of School Visitor Exchanges, LCB and FCB are against reciprocal student exchanges; both fear that exposing Tanzanian young people to extreme contrasts in wealth that would be encountered in a large UK conurbation could result in the deficits between the two lifestyles being stressed and the 'have-nots' taking centre stage. Risks from such 'exposure' might include dissatisfaction, feelings of helplessness; lack of self-esteem; depression or possibly even – 'Why bother to work hard, when I can never have any of this at home?' The 'reciprocal' of this could be that UK students return from Tanzania feeling, 'Can't wait to get home', or even pity, rather than Andreotti's 'openness in ethical solidarity'. Such neocolonial interpretations are equally problematic.

Lack of reciprocity in student exchanges is a deliberate choice in this link. Although post-colonial theory might assume that this inequality establishes an unequal power-dynamic I suggest that it is rather an example of cooperation and mutuality: teachers acting 'in loco parentis' for Tanzanian students. A shared common 'duty of care' towards young people in education is requisite for teachers throughout the world.

Friendships between linking participants, whether enduring or short-term (Bunnel et al. 2011; Leonard 2014b), may be demonstrated by adoption of a protective stance towards friends (or 'family'). A student-created publication, crafted through sharing traditional stories from the two cultures, represented the culmination of the hours linking partners spent each afternoon during the 2018 visit, telling one another their respective traditional stories:

Stories have been used to dispossess and to malign, but stories can also be used to empower and to humanise. Stories can break the dignity of a people, but stories can also repair that broken dignity. (Adichie 2009)

Significantly students selected the book's title *Urafiki*, Kiswahili for friendship. Friendships evident between some staff and some students at Schools A and B are arguably characteristics of partnership; yet the restricted student and staff numbers engaged at both ends in this relationship are features of a link in my linking/partnership continuum (See (Figure 22.1), page. 305).

In other school linking research I have recognized that teachers' aspirations for their students' academic achievement, adults' aspirations for young people (and those of their local communities' representatives) as well as teachers' pedagogy are often very similar in the Global South and the

Global North (Leonard 2014b). Baraka Mwiyoha spoke in the context of disaffected Mvumi students, apparently disengaged from learning in their science lessons:

> The role of the teacher is to make these students study or learn to their best. And yes, as teachers, we face challenges which are more than [*sic*] likely the same. (Mwiyoha and Leonard, 2019)

Another Mvumi science teacher identified similarities in teachers' practice across the Global South and the Global North; he had spent two weeks in the UK in 2017:

> One, which I can remember is about lesson preparation. It is almost the same [as] the way that we prepare our lessons here … I have noted that the way especially in the Science subjects, the way they do practicals, it is almost the same. There is not much difference between what we are doing and what they are doing.

Differences are invariably found between school linking participants, particularly in terms of material wealth, educational resources and digital access (Leonard 2014a, 2017). It can be too easy to focus on deficits (Andreotti 2011; Martin and Griffiths 2010). UK linking and DE practitioners, including Robinson-Miles (2017) and Burr (2008), warn forcefully against such an emphasis. Martin (2012) advocates that North–South comparisons start from a premise of commonalities. In a school link, professionals, confident in their own knowledge and skills, can guide the global learning of students (and possibly colleagues) to grapple with a range of intellectually complex and sometimes controversial ideas, encountered through the linking process.

Section 4 shows examples of how friendship, equality, mutuality, cooperation and critical global citizenship are aspired to and shared in school links. Friendship is considered at length. My new research elaborates upon the practice of gifting; contrasting attitudes towards reciprocal student exchanges are also explored. I indicate how teachers engaged in the linking process, given sufficient 'space' to reflect, can re-motivate themselves as classroom teachers, re-energize their practice and even rediscover how to engage learners.

Implications and recommendations for the future of Global South–North school linking

Internationally, funding streams for DE and global learning have faced severe financial constraints since 2006; expertise was lost. Several large-scale school linking programmes shut as a result. The UN's MDGs, with their implied emphasis on difference as deficits, have been replaced with SDGs, characterized by global mutuality. Processes of change in the wider world have changed; and often school curricula have lagged behind.

Global citizenship should be the required content in school curricula so that children and young people are adequately equipped with relevant knowledge and skills to act as adult critical global citizens; Global South–North school links can provide an entrée for this. In future, whether global citizenship is lacking in the curriculum, or in retreat, creative, skilled, committed global learning teachers in links should lobby for its inclusion.

In 2006 Martin commented, 'When thought through, based on mutuality and equality, and incorporated in a global citizenship curriculum, school linking can be challenging in an exciting and enjoyable way for all involved' (2006: 8).

The two Tanzanian/UK links featured at length in this chapter meet the majority of Martin's requirements for successful school linking. For teachers, other participating adults, and students affected by the linking process, the examples I cited can represent only a 'snap-shot' of the mutuality enjoyed.

Section 1 showcased examples of professional learning in the school linking process, contrasting external and 'in-house' CPD provision. It identified a need for space to reflect on global learning and recommended that linked schools self-assess their global learning and are incentivized to persist in their links.

Section 2 established how links can be sustained. Links cannot rely on external funding. I showed how reciprocal staff visits are central to sustaining links, how exposure to global learning should ideally reach the bulk of adults in linked schools, how improvements in the quality of students' English are important and how guaranteed support from a school's Senior Management are key. I also argued that national curricula should mandate teachers' global learning/DE content.

Section 3 demonstrated examples of how Andreotti's five 'shifts of understanding' occur in the context of school linking. I considered possible tensions if global learning focuses on the UN's SDGs. Throughout Section 3 I outlined the encountered dissonance and practical challenges faced in the school linking process.

Section 4 showed examples of how friendship, equality, mutuality, cooperation and critical global citizenship are aspired to and shared in school links. Friendship is considered at length. The practice of gifting and contrasting attitudes towards student exchanges were also explored. I indicated how teachers engaged in the linking process can re-motivate themselves, re-energize their practice and even rediscover how to engage learners.

Recommendations

For the future I recommend an agreed focus for international educational relationships, a link, a partnership or an immersive scheme, and regular evaluation and reporting of global learning and other educational developments. The focus must be adaptable, in the light of participating schools' shifting educational priorities and the needs of their respective students, communities and stakeholders. Additionally,

- Accountability to a link's stakeholders should ensure that funds are managed transparently and effectively; resultant educational benefits should be disseminated to others.
- In the Global South the benefits of linking should be cascaded as widely as possible. Linking should reduce, not widen, gaps in educational provision.
- Caution should inform any plans for student exchanges.
- Difference should always be theorized as an ethical relationship between the parties engaged in the linking process, not as a deficit.

Bourn recommends that learning about the Global South moves 'to an approach that challenges stereotypes and perceptions and locates learning within a broader understanding of inequality and processes of change in the world' (Bourn 2014b: 38). The school linking process should surely facilitate such moves.

Bibliography

Adichie, C. N. (2009), *The Dangers of a Single Story*, Available Online: https://www.ted.com/talks/chim amanda_adichie_the_danger_of_a_single_story (accessed 30 January 2019).

Alcock, H. L. and Ramirez Barker, L. (2016), *Can Global Learning Raise Standards Within Pupils' Writing in the Primary Phase?* DERC Research Paper no. 16 for the GLP, London: UCL Institute of Education. Available online: https://www.ucl.ac.uk/ioe/sites/ioe/files/DERC-Research-paper_16-pweb.pdf (accessed 3 January 2019).

Amin, A. (2002), 'Ethnicity and the multicultural city: Living with diversity', *Environment and Planning A*, 34, 959–80.

Andreotti, V. (2006), 'Soft versus critical global citizenship education', *Policy & Practice: A Development Education Review*, 3(Autumn), 40–51. Available online: https://www.developmenteducationreview.com/issue/issue-3/soft-versus-critical-global-citizenship-education (accessed 28 September 2018).

Andreotti, V. (2011), *Actionable Postcolonial Theory in Education*, New York: Palgrave Macmillan.

Andreotti, V. (2013) 'Taking minds to other places', *Primary Geography*, 80, 12–13, Sheffield: Geographical Association (GA).

Andreotti, V. and Warwick, P. (2008), 'Engaging students with controversial issues through a dialogue based approach', *International Journal of Citizenship and Teacher Education*, citizED. Available online: http://www.citized.info/pdf/commarticles/Post16%20Paul%20Warwick.doc (accessed 31 January 2019).

Atkins, S. and Murphy, K. (1994), 'Reflective practice', *Nursing Standard* 8(39), 49–56.

Aubusson, P., Ewing, R. and Hoban, G. (2009), *Action Learning in Schools: Reframing Teachers' Professional Learning and Development*, London: Routledge.

Badshah, N. (2019), '"White saviour row": David Lammy denies snubbing Comic Relief', *The Guardian*, 28 February.

Biddulph, M., Lambert, D. and Balderstone, D. (eds) (2015), *Learning to Teach Geography in the Secondary School*, 3rd edn, London: Routledge.

Boud, D. (1995), *Enhancing Learning through Self Assessment*. London: Kogan Page.

Bourn, D. (2014a), *Theory and Practice of Global Learning*, DERC Research Paper no. 11, London: UCL Institute of Education.

Bourn, D. (2014b), *School Linking and Global Learning – Teachers' Reflections*, GLP Research Paper no. 12, London: IOE.

Bourn, D. and Cara, O. (2012), *Evaluating Partners in Development: Contribution of International School Partnerships to Education and Development*, Development Education Research Centre Research Paper No. 5. London: Development Education Research Centre, Institute of Education, University of London in partnership with Link Community Development.

Bourn, D. and Leonard, A. (2009), 'Living in the wider world - the global dimension', in D. Mitchell (ed.), *Living Geography*, London: Optima Publishing.

British Council CCGL (2018) https://connecting-classrooms.britishcouncil.org/apply-for-funding/how-funding-works (accessed 23 September 2018).

British Council (2019a), https://www.britishcouncil.org (accessed 9 March 2019).

British Council CCGL (2019b), 'Decent work and economic growth', https://connecting-classrooms.britishcouncil.org/classroom-resources/collaborative-template/decent-work-economic-growth (accessed 2 January 2019).

Brookfield, S. (1995), *Becoming a Critically Reflective Teacher*. San Francisco: Jossey-Bass.

Bryan, A. and Bracken, M. (2011), *Learning to Read the World? Teaching and Learning about Global Citizenship and International Development in Post Primary Schools*, Dublin: Irish Aid.

Bunnell, T., Yea, S., Peake, L., Skelton, T. and Smith, M. (2011), Geographies of Friendships, Progress in Human Geography, *Sage Journals*, 36(4), 490–507.

Burr, M. (2008) 'Thinking about Linking?' *DEA Thinkpiece*. Available at: www.think-global.org.uk/resources/item/910

Capel, S., Leask, M. and Turner, T. (2013), 'Introduction', in S. Capel, M. Leask and Turner (eds), *Learning to Teach in the Secondary School. A Companion to School Experience*', 6th edn, London: Routledge.

Coghlan, S. (2018), *DFE School Funding Claims Face Watchdog Investigation*, BBC, Family and Education, October 4th, https://www.bbc.co.uk/news/education-45746062 (accessed 7 March 2019).

De Souza, L. M. T. M. (2008), *A Pedagogy of Dissensus*. Keynote address at 'Shifting Margins, Shifting Centres: Negotiating Difference in Education in the 21st century' Conference. Institute of Education, University of London. 17 September 2008.

Digón Regueiro, P., Méndez García, R. M., DePalma, R. and Longueira Matos, S. (2017), 'A place for development education in the current Spanish and English curricula: Finding possibilities for practice', *International Journal of Development Education and Global Learning*, 9(2): 97–114. Available online: https://doi.org/10.18546/IJDEGL.09.2.04 (accessed 28 September 2018).

Disney, A. (2008), 'The contribution of school linking projects to global education: Some geographical perspectives', *GTIP-GeogEd E-Journal*, 2, 2, Article 2. Autumn 2008.

Dobson, A. (2006), 'Thick cosmopolitanism', *Political Studies*, 54(1), 165–84.

Edge, K., Frayman, K., and Lawrie, J. (2009), *The Influence of North-South School Partnerships: Examining the Evidence from Schools in the UK, Africa and Asia*, London: Institute of Education.

Egan, A. (2010), *One World, One People: Global School Partnerships and Development Education*, unpublished North South Educational Partnerships (NSEP) assignment, MA in Development Education. Institute of Education, London.

Friere, P. (1970) [1996], *Pedagogy of the Oppressed*, London: Penguin.

George, M., (2018), 'Exclusive: Anger as 30% schools drop into the red, School governors call for action, warning cuts will harm education', *TES*, 17 September. Available online: https://www.tes.com/news/exclusive-anger-30-schools-drop-red (accessed 30 September 2018).

Gundara, J. (2000), 'Interculturalism in Europe', *Interculturalism, Education and Inclusion*, 105–27, London: Sage.

Holliday, A. R. (2010), 'Submission, emergence and personal knowledge. New takes and principles for validity in decentred qualitative research', in F. Shamim and R. Qureshi (eds), *Perils, Pitfalls and Reflexivity in Qualitative Research in Education*, 10–31, Oxford: Oxford University Press.

Hunt, F. (2012), *Global Learning in Primary Schools: Practices and Impacts*, DERC Research Paper no. 9, London: IOE.

Hunt, F. and King, R. P. (2015), *Supporting Whole School Approaches to Global Learning: Focusing Learning and Mapping Impact*, Research Paper No. 13 for the Global Learning Programme, London: Development Education Research Centre.

Jesson, J. (2010), 'University teaching: Unpicking some issues', in J. Jesson, V. M. Carpenter, M. McLean and M. Stephenson (eds), *University Teaching Reconsidered: Justice, Practice, Inquiry*, 15–24, Wellington, New Zealand: Dunmore Publishing.

Knowles, E. and Ridley, W. (2005), *Another Spanner in the Works: Challenging Prejudice and Racism in Mainly White Schools*, Stoke-on-Trent: Trentham Books.

Kolb, D. (1984), *Experiential Learning: Experience at the Source of Learning and Development*. London, England: Kogan Page.

Lambert, D. and Morgan, J. (2011), *Geography and Development: Development Education in Schools and the Part Played by Geography Teachers*. Development Education Research Centre Research Paper No.3, London: Development Education Research Centre.

Lawson, H. (2018), 'Primary pupils' attitudes towards and understandings of poverty'. Available online: http://discovery.ucl.ac.uk/10047519 (accessed 3 January 2019).

Leonard, A. (2008), 'Global school relationships: School linking and modern challenges', in D. Bourn (ed.), *Development Education: Debates and Dialogue*, 64–98, London: Institute of Education.

Leonard, A. (2010), 'The South/North Educational Linking process (S/NELP): Learning from linking', Paper presented at: Education and Citizenship in a Globalising World conference at Institute of Education (co-hosted with Beijing Normal University). November.

Leonard, A. (2012), '*The "Aston-Makunduchi Partnership"*: South-North School Link – *In-depth* Case Study', Development Education Research Centre Research Paper No. 8, London: Development Education Research Centre. Available online: http://discovery.ucl.ac.uk/1503405/1/DERC08_Aston-Makunduchi.pdf (accessed 3 January 2019).

Leonard, A. (2014a), 'School Linking: Southern Perspectives on the South/ North Educational Linking process: From Ghana, Uganda and Tanzania', Doctoral thesis. Available online: British Library: http://ethos.bl.uk/OrderDetails.do?uin=uk.bl.ethos.643018 http://www.leonardmorrison.org and UCL http://discovery.ucl.ac.uk/10021648/

Leonard, A. (2014b), 'The South/North Educational Linking process: Young people's perspectives from the Global South', in M. Thomas (ed.), *A Child's World– Contemporary Issues in Education*, 288–314, Cardiff, Centre for Educational Studies: University of Wales.

Leonard, A. (2015), 'SOUTH NORTH SCHOOL LINKING: How are those in the Global South affected when they form relationships with UK schools?' *Sinergias*, Numéro 2, Setembro 2015, 79–95. Available online: www.sinergiased.org/index.php/revista/item/74-south-north-schools (accessed 3 January 2019).

Leonard, A. (2017), 'The role of Assistive Technologies in the Learning of Visually Impaired Young People at a Rural Tanzanian Secondary School', Paper and conference presentation at Beijing Normal University/ UCL, Institute of Education Mobilities conference, 12 May, Beijing.

Leonard, A. (2019), 'How can we learn about teaching in another country?' in S. Hammond and M. Sangster (eds), *Perspectives on Educational Practices Around the World*, 93–100, London: Bloomsbury.

Leonard, F. (2005), 'Lessons from UK Secondary Schools: School linking and teaching and learning in Global Citizenship and Geography', *Development Education Journal*, 11(2), Stoke-on-Trent, Trentham Books/DE.

Lewis, M. (2016), *A Study of a Focused, Critical Approach to Pupils' Images and Perceptions of Africa*, GLP Innovation Fund Research Paper no. 3, London: UCL Institute of Education.

MacCallum, C. (2012), personal communication, 21 August.

McNicoll, K. (2012), 'Do students benefit from North/South School Partnerships?' Thesis submitted for Master of Arts Degree in Development and Emergency Practice, Oxford Brookes University, Centre for Development and Emergency Practice (CENDEP) School of Built Environment.

Marsh, C. (2008), *Becoming a Teacher: Knowledge, Skills and Issues*, 4th edn, Frenchs Forest, NSW: Pearson.

Martin, F. (2006), 'School Linking: A controversial issue'. Available online: http://www.academia.edu/1221100/School_linking_A_controversial_issue (accessed 3 January 2019).

Martin, F. (2012), 'The geographies of difference', *Geography*, 97(3), 116–22.

Martin, F. and Griffiths, H. (2010), 'Global Partnerships for Mutual Learning: Exploring issues of power and representation in researching teacher development through North-South study visits', Paper presented at Education and Citizenship in a Globalising World conference, Institute of Education (co-hosted with Beijing Normal University). November.

Martin, F. and Pirbhai-Illich, F. (2016), 'Towards decolonising teacher education: Criticality, relationality and intercultural understanding', *Journal of Intercultural Studies*, 37(4), 352–72.

Mauss, M. (2011), reprint of 1954 edition. *The Gift: Forms and Functions of Exchange in Archaic Societies*, Routledge Publications.

Mayblin, L., Valentine, G. and Andersson, J. (2016), 'In the contact zone: Engineering meaningful encounters across difference through an interfaith project', *The Geographical Journal*, 182(2), 213–22.

Mitchell, D. (2013), 'How do we deal with controversial issues?' in D. Lambert and M. Jones (eds), *Debates in Geography Education*, London: Routledge.

Moon, J. (2004), *A Handbook of Reflective and Experiential Learning: Theory and Practice*, London: Routledge Falmer.

Mwiyoha, B. and Leonard, A. (2019), 'How Can Visually Impaired Children Be Supported?' in S. Hammond and M. Sangster (eds), *Perspectives on Educational Practice Around the World*, 101–6, London: Bloomsbury.

O' Keeffe, C. (2006), *Linking between Ireland and the South: A Review and Guidelines for Good Practice*, Dublin: Irish Aid, Suas Education Development.

Pendry, V. (2018), 'Using global data in primary mathematics', Development Education Research Centre Research Paper No. 20, London: UCL Institute of Education.

Pickering, S. (2008), 'What do children really learn? A discussion to investigate the effect that school partnerships have on children's understanding, sense of values and perceptions of a distant place', *GeogEd*, 2: 1 [online]. Available online: https://www.geography.org.uk/download/ga%20geogedvol2i1 a3.pdf (Accessed 28 January 2019).

Quist-Adade, C. and van Wyk, A. (2007), 'The Role of NGOs in Canada and the USA in the Transformation of the Socio-Cultural Structures in Africa', *Africa Development*, XXXII(2), Council for the Development of Social Science Research in Africa, 66–96.

Race, P. (2006), *Evidencing Reflection: Putting the 'w' into Reflection.* http://escalate.ac.uk/resources/ref lection/02.html (accessed 8 March 2019).

Robinson-Miles, M. (2017), 'The KEFW-Bagara Link: Friendship in a postcolonial context?' BA diss., submitted University of Sheffield, Sheffield.

Said, E. (1978), *Orientalism*, Harmondsworth: Penguin.

Scoffham, S. (2007), 'Please Miss, Why are they so Poor?' *Primary Geographer*, Spring 2007, 5–7, Sheffield: Geographical Association (GA).

Scoffham, S. (2018), 'Global learning: A catalyst for curriculum change', *International Journal of Development Education and Global Learning*, 10(2): 135–46.

Sharp, J. (2009), 'Can the subaltern speak?' *Geographies of Postcolonialism*, 109–30, London: Sage.

Simpson, J. (2016), 'A study to investigate, explore and identify successful "interventions" to support teachers in a transformative move from a charity mentality to a social justice mentality', GLP Innovation Fund Research Paper no. 2, London: UCL Institute of Education.

Sizmur, J., Brzyska, B., Cooper, L., Morrison, J., Wilkinson, K. and Kerr, D. (2011), *Global School Partnerships Programme Impact Evaluation Report*, London: National Foundation for Educational Research (NFER).

Spivak, G. (1988), 'Can the subaltern speak?' in C. Nelson and L. Grossberg (eds), *Marxism and the Interpretation of Culture*, 271–313, Chicago: University of Illinois Press.

Standish, A. (2009), *Global Perspectives in the Geography Curriculum: Reviewing the Moral Case for Geography*, London: Routledge.

Standish, A. (2012), *The False Promise of Global Learning: Why Education Needs Boundaries*, London: Continuum.

Tennant, M., McMullen, C., and Kaczynski, D. (2010), *Teaching, Learning and Research in Higher Education*, New York: Routledge.

Thiong'O, N. (1986), *Decolonising the Mind: The Politics of Language in African Literature*, East African Education Publishers.

United Nations (2015), 'Transforming our world. The 2030 Agenda for Sustainable Development. A/ Res/70/1 United Nations'. Available online: https://sustainabledevelopment.un.org/content/documents /21252030%20Agenda%20for%20Sustainable%20Development%20web.pdf (accessed 3 January 2019).

Unwin, R. (2018), Personal communication, 27 September.

Vellai, L. (2011), Unpublished North South Educational Partnerships MA activity, (NSEP), Activity 5, MA in Development Education, London: Institute of Education.

Weale, S. and Adams, R. (2019), '"It's dangerous": Full chaos of funding cuts in England's schools revealed', *The Guardian*, 8 March. https://www.theguardian.com/education/2019/mar/08/its-danger ous-full-chaos-of-funding-cuts-in-englands-schools-revealed (accessed 8 March 2019).

Chapter 23

Critical Global Citizenship Education in the Era of SDG 4.7: Discussing HEADSUP with Secondary Teachers in England, Finland and Sweden

Karen Pashby and Louise Sund

In 2015, member states of the United Nations (UN) adopted the 2030 agenda for sustainable development by setting seventeen Sustainable Development Goals (SDGs). Goal Four focuses on quality education, and target 4.7 includes education for sustainable development and global citizenship, two areas given separate focus in UNESCO work and tending to run parallel to one another. While the Millennium Development Goals (MDGs) that preceded the SDGs focused on action in so-called 'developing' countries, a significant change in the SDGs is required action within all signatory nations. Currently, work is being mobilized to action SDG 4.7 in Global North contexts. This raises important questions around to what extent pedagogies and approaches in support of SDG 4.7 in European contexts can account for critiques of education for sustainable development (ESD) and global citizenship education (GCE), particularly the call for more critical approaches. As two researchers and educators who have been active in the fields of critical global citizenship and environmental and sustainability education (ESE), respectively, we argue for a bridging of critical scholarship in the two fields and an engagement of the substantive theoretical work in these areas with the lived practices of secondary school teachers. This chapter draws on a small-scale research project funded by the British Academy that engaged secondary and upper secondary teachers with a framework for ethical global issues pedagogy.

According to scholarship in the field of ESE, UNESCO support for the decade for the United Nations Decade for Sustainable Development (UNDSD) (2005–14) tended, despite good intentions, to rely on universalizing approaches (e.g. Wals 2009; Sund and Öhman 2014) and to promote behaviour modification rather than systemic change (e.g. Jickling and Wals 2008; Van Poeck and Vandenabeele, 2012). Matthews (2011) pointed to a tendency in environmental education to perpetuate Western epistemologies and correspondingly has raised the importance of connecting globalization, post-colonialism and environmental matters. Similarly, scholars of critical GCE have warned against a tendency in formal and non-formal education towards superficial approaches to global learning that ignore and/or step over complex ethical issues, thereby contributing to the unconscious reproduction of colonial systems of power (e.g. Andreotti 2011; Martin 2011; Pashby 2012, 2015). Huckle and Wals (2015) argue for a critical and transformative ESD anchored in appropriate social theory, and suggest combining sustainability and ecopedagogy with what they call global education for sustainability citizenship. Building from this rationale for bridging critical approaches to ESE and GCE, we argue for an explicit focus on the contribution of theoretical resources that highlight post-colonial engagements in each field (e.g. Sund 2016; Pashby 2012).

Framework

In our respective research and practice, we have used Andreotti's (2006, 2011) work on actioning post-colonial theory in education. Drawing on Leela Gandhi (1998), Andreotti (2011) argues that post-colonial studies can contribute to social and educational theory by opening up possibilities to theorize non-coercive relationships with those Global 'Others' who are the production and subject of Western humanitarianism. Her work contributes ways in which such theory can be 'actioned' through educational analysis and pedagogy. In her seminal piece, Andreotti (2006) contributed an analytical tool to help distinguish between soft and critical approaches to GCE. Whereas a *soft* approach assumes a universal view of the world and focuses on a notion of global citizens as those who help people who suffer from lack of development, a *critical* approach applies a post-colonial critique of modernity by acknowledging a complicity on the part of 'the West' and 'the Global North' in global issues. By moving from soft to more critical approaches, educators and learners can work towards establishing more equal terms for understanding and responding to issues. The article is widely used, with over 500 citations, and is drawn on across recent GCE literature (e.g. Bamber and Hankin 2011; Bourn 2009; Edge and Khamsi 2012).

Andreotti (2012) contributed a further tool in response to the Kony 2012 video created by NGO Imaginary Children which was shared and viewed over 100 million times in 10 days (Engelhardt and Jansz 2014). The video aimed to make warlord Joseph Kony a household name and to stop exploitation of child soldiers but was criticized for presenting a simplistic view, and the NGO itself was critiqued over its use of the funds raised (Gregory 2012). In response to these critiques, Andreotti (2012) wrote an editorial for the journal *Critical Literacy: Theories and Practices* in which she argued that the Kony 2012 phenomenon demonstrated a need for stronger critical literacy in development education and global learning. She proposed the HEADSUP tool to enable critical interventions in the contexts of educational initiatives aiming to address global justice and enact social change (Andreotti 2012). It helps learners and educators to identify seven problematic patterns of representations and engagements commonly found in narratives presented in educational approaches to global issues, particularly North–South engagements with local populations who are structurally marginalized (Andreotti et al., 2018: 15).

- hegemonic practices (reinforcing and justifying the status quo),
- ethnocentric projections (presenting one view as universal and superior),
- ahistorical thinking (forgetting the role of historical legacies and complicities in shaping current problems),
- depoliticized orientations (disregarding the impacts of power inequalities and delegitimizing dissent),

- self-serving motivations (invested in self-congratulatory heroism),
- uncomplicated solutions (offering 'feel-good' quick fixes that do not address root causes of problems) and
- paternalistic investments (seeking a 'thank you' from those who have been 'helped').

As the HEADSUP framework was something we had both used in our research and teaching on GCE and ESD respectfully (Pashby and Andreotti, 2015; Sund, 2016), and due to its explicit actioning of post-colonial engagements, we chose it as a central framework for our study. We argue that this tool can be engaged with as a way to attend to the critiques raised of the extent to which both GCE and ESD approaches can, unintentionally, reproduce colonial systems of power in creating an 'us' in the Global North who solve the problems and a 'them' who have the problems. Specifically, we argue such engagement is essential amid the mobilization of SDG 4.7 in European contexts (Sund and Pashby, 2018).

Andreotti's (2006) soft versus critical tool has been applied to analyse work in schools. For example, Niens and Reilly's (2012) research on critical GCE approaches in Northern Ireland found that when teachers fully committed to teaching global citizenship from multiple perspectives, students aged eight to nine and twelve to thirteen were able to deeply understand different living conditions of people living in other parts of the world and were empathetic to issues facing immigrants in their own communities. However, teachers were often constrained by a lack of critical perspectives on the relationships between local issues and Global North–South relationships. Truong-White and McLean (2015) also took a critical GCE approach to studying a programme that connects middle and secondary school classrooms in India and the United States through digital storytelling. They found that students did engage with non-mainstream perspectives and critical self-reflection; however, similarly to Niens and Reilly's (2012) study, a lack of emphasis on systemic causes and impacts of global problems in their findings led them to call for more attention to critical pedagogical practices.

Research applying the HEADSUP tool has tended to focus on non-formal education. For example, Grain and Lund (2016) propose it as a catalyst for important reflection and dialogue in in-service learning, and Kuleta-Hullboj (2016) adapted HEADSUP as a tool to analyse interviews with employees of a Polish NGO to examine their views of global citizenship. In a formal education setting, Sund (2016) modified and developed Andreotti's tool to facilitate an analysis of how upper secondary teachers in Sweden articulated different ways of utilizing the curriculum and enacting pedagogies relating to colonialism and complex global issues. Teachers in her study problematized a tendency to focus on a Western perspective, prioritized offering students historical aspects so that they could contextualize global sustainability issues and invited students to see themselves as active participants. The findings also indicated that a range of factors influence how and why these teachers teach global issues and that teachers could use more resourcing support to promote a critical approach. In Sund's (2016) study, HEADSUP was applied by the researcher, as an analytical tool for analysis of the classroom and interview data, and not by the teachers themselves. Therefore, working together from the two fields of ESE and GCE, we decided it was important to engage the tool directly with teachers to support a critical approach.

This chapter shares selected findings from research with secondary and upper secondary teachers in England, Finland and Sweden who participated in a workshop about HEADSUP. We were interested in the extent to which the tool was useful for reflection and application, and what the teacher comments demonstrate about possibilities and challenges for ethical global issues pedagogy.

Methodology

In the winter and spring of 2018, as part of a one-year project funded by the British Academy, we ran a set of workshops on bridging ESD and GCE through critical GCE approaches centred on the HEADSUP tool. Through social media and professional networks as well as global education networks, we invited secondary and upper secondary teachers (of students ranging in ages from fourteen to eighteen) in England, Finland and Sweden who teach about global issues to participate. Based on the most obvious curriculum links, we targeted geography teachers in England and social studies and natural science teachers in Sweden and Finland. Other subjects were represented, including religious education and foreign language education.

We hosted three workshops in England (Manchester, Birmingham and London), one in Stockholm and one in Helsinki. Participation ranged from three teachers to ten teachers per workshop with a total of twenty-six participants, and locations were based on access to networks who could help recruit participants within the short project timeline and with good transportation links. Teachers travelled from within a day's return journey to the workshops, and we had a range of areas represented including urban, suburban and rural. Nine males and seventeen females participated, reflecting the over-representation of females in the profession. Participants ranged from very new teachers to those with decades of experience including school subject leads. Most were born and raised in their respective national contexts; however, two participants had immigrated and one participant's family had immigrated. Many had experience of travelling abroad, some had lived abroad and some had very little experience abroad. The participants also ranged in level of experience in teaching global issues, from those who work in global issues–focused schools to those who were very new to the concepts; but all identified the SDGs as a priority, and all indicated they taught about global issues in their practice and/or participated in school-wide activities related to global learning.

At each workshop we relayed key concerns from the research in critical GCE and ESE and discussed SDG 4.7. We facilitated activities using critical GCE tools (i.e. Andreotti, 2006), considered rationales for a complex and critical approach by linking to the International Youth White Paper on Global Citizenship (IYWPGC, 2017) and reviewed the Kony 2012 video and uptake in pop culture and social media before reviewing Andreotti's (2012) HEADSUP. We applied HEADSUP through different activities, including a teacher reflection (see Figure 23.1). Teachers then worked together or on their own to consider ways HEADSUP could be applied in their practice before engaging in a full group discussion. Three teachers in England and two teachers in Sweden volunteered to invite one of the researchers to a class where they applied key ideas from the workshop. Two to three months after the workshops, we hosted a full-day focus group of teachers from across the England workshops to begin co-developing a resource based on what they had applied from the workshop in practice. At the time of writing, the resource was being piloted.

Identify awareness of and challenge the patterns – educational practices	Notes/ideas/ connections to my practice	What might I continue/start/stop in my practice?
In my teaching, how can I raise inherited and taken -for-granted power relations? Do I identify mainstream discourses and marginalized perspectives/norms and trends? (H)		
In my teaching can classes address that there are other logical ways of looking at the same issue framed by different understandings of reality/ experiences of the world? (E)		
In my teaching, how can I avoid treating an issue out of context as if it just happened now? How are today's issues tied to on going local and global trends/patterns/narratives? (A)		
In my teaching, how can I ensure I don't treat issues as if they are politically neutral? Who is framing the issue and who is responsible for addressing it? Who are the agents of change and what mechanisms for change are available? (D)		
How can I take up good intentions to want to help others through generosity and altruism without reinforcing an us/them, saviour/victim relationship? (S)		
How can I address people's tendency to want a quick fix? How can I grapple with the complexities, root causes and lack of easy solutions? (U)		
How can I put aside our egos and self-interest? Are I open to being wrong, to not being the ones who know best? (P)		

Figure 23.1 Application of HEADSUP for teacher reflection used in workshops.

In this chapter, we will draw on transcriptions of the workshop discussions and pictures of written work produced by teachers at the workshop to relay key themes that emerged regarding to what extent they found the HEADSUP framework useful to their practice. These themes are by no means generalizable nor are they representative of all teachers in England, Finland and Sweden; however, this project mobilized important conversations that indicate the possibilities for and constraints to a critical approach.

Findings

Teachers found critical GCE very relevant to discussions of teaching global issues and as a way to voice some possibilities and challenges. While some teachers felt HEADSUP and critical approaches to GCE mapped onto existing pedagogical approaches, for some these raised new questions, and all participants applied the workshop ideas to reflecting critically on their own practice.

A key theme across the workshops was the importance of taking a more critical and complex approach to teaching about global issues in general. Teachers found the HEADSUP tool very useful for directing their own critically reflective practice. Teachers spoke about the need to be aware of mainstream approaches to development and aid. As a teacher from the Manchester workshop explains,

> I'm taking away from this basically having an opportunity to question and think and give students that opportunity or maybe encourage that, more so than I definitely do at the moment. [… Development aid may be] required, but why should the people in India or Syria or wherever want to be like us, are we perfect? Because that's it, that's what aid and development in general is always trying to say the world should be like...

Similarly, a participant from Helsinki reflected on the question of salvationist approaches, recognizing that many approaches she has seen 'promote saviour/victim relationality' by appealing to emotions. She reflected on paternalism, suggesting she needs to encourage students to 'be aware that you should not just give and be the 'know all', but you could yourself learn in the process'. Connecting HEADSUP to her practice, she questioned whether the Tanzania project in her school presents an easy solution that relies on a 'feel good factor'. She also connected her work directly with ethnocentrism, writing that she intends to start taking 'a more in-depth look in the current teaching material. They usually present the problems through Western/Northern Europe mindset'. This was echoed by a participant in London who also found that the HEADSUP reflective tool provoked critical reflection and questioning of priorities:

> I think [HEADSUP] opens your eyes to just, like how much the curriculum does need to be revisited, you know, [...] because I'm so busy looking at my [curriculum] spec and making sure that my spec matches [the lesson] so that the kids can do well in the exam, you know, we're missing a beat there.

While many teachers were new to the concepts presented in the HEADSUP tool, others felt these ideas were not new. An experienced teacher at the Helsinki workshop, reflecting on work he did with Oxfam in Belgium in the late 1980s, suggested that he did not 'see anything new in [HEADSUP]'. The project he participated in previously had raised awareness to key issues like bananas and coffee beans in schools and connecting social, political and economic issues. However, reflecting back, he laments that

> somehow you get a feeling that you haven't gone very far ... You're still going around and around in circles, despite the fact that technology has really got rid of this awareness-raising issue. But we're still stuck with [simplistic messages in] media and videos.

Later in the discussion, this participant argued there was a need to reassert a critical framework today, particularly as global citizenship takes an increasingly prevalent place in formal education:

'More and more teachers want this [critical approach], really. I think so.' The tool is thus useful for teachers to reflect on the key debates they see today and to consider to what extent such an approach is similar or different from activities in the past. It also opens up opportunities to challenge soft approaches to GCE and to critically engage in the concept of global citizenship more broadly.

Similarly to the participant in Helsinki, a teacher at the Stockholm workshop also shared that she already thinks quite deeply about these issues. She reacted to the HEADSUP reflection activity by expressing the challenge of taking up politically charged issues in a classroom and trying to manage her own political positioning. She expressed that she 'struggles with dismantling the hegemony' because she worries too many of her students think she represents a very 'PC left institution' where issues of feminism and racism are often being raised. This is a particularly salient issue given the pushback against what is perceived as anti-political correctness associated with the prevalence of the far right across Europe (as elsewhere).

Others at the Stockholm workshop also felt a need for a critical approach to engaging in local and global relations. Reinforcing Niens and Reilly's (2012) findings, and as this teacher expresses, they speak to a tendency to step over local issues and social inequalities and differences within the local community when studying global issues:

> What I thought about [when thinking through HEADSUP] is that we have so much here in Sweden so it's very easy to talk about African, Asian, climate change, internationally, when it's so much to be done here, so, you know, it's easier to talk about racism and slavery, Africa and America, but we don't talk about what's here.

Similarly, a teacher at the Birmingham workshop used HEADSUP as a jumping-off point for discussing how the demographic make-up of a particular school or classroom mediates her approach to global issues pedagogy. She described how often 'students refer to Africa as one place and [make] just sweeping generalisations'. In seeking to combat these hegemonic discourses, she draws on the diverse demographic of her classroom. In her previous school which lacked racial diversity, she felt in a position of having to 'fight in that corner alone', and being White British born, she felt she lacked 'clout'. In her current school she is 'in a much more fortunate position' because she has 'students that can actually fight back':

> So if a student makes a sweeping statement, you've then got a student who's perhaps from that location who can actually turn around, and [students are] all much more careful in what language they're using because they know they've got students from different countries whether they're first generation or things like that.

Thus, the classrooms themselves, and the interactions among students and their teacher are deeply embedded in the politicized global issues they are discussing.

Teachers at all the workshops discussed the way they either do already or should explicitly address colonialism in historicizing global issues and examining the extent to which we reproduce colonial relations through soft approaches to GCE. A teacher at the London workshop expressed the need to complexify the treatment of international development and specifically to make connections to colonialism. Similarly to the teacher in Stockholm quoted above, she finds that her students generally think that colonialism is about Africa and America and do not recognize colonialism as deeply connected to local issues in England.

Because we've got this one [view] which has got, Africa, the continent, and it's got a massive hole in it and a big pile of stuff which is on top of North America. And it takes them ages to get that it's the colonialism idea of all their resources have been taken by somebody else so they haven't got anything to use to develop with. But it takes them ages to get it because they just haven't got that concept in their head because this is before we do anything about colonialism.

This participant engaged in an interesting discussion with another participant in London about their approaches to connecting colonialism with case studies of 'developing' countries. Discussion between these two geography teachers demonstrates the various strategic ways teachers take up colonialism and attempt to avoid ahistorical approaches in response to assumptions they make about how their students will react. The same participant who lamented the lack of knowledge of and attention to colonialism called herself 'quite anti-colonial' and suggested she needs to 'rein in [her] bias slightly'. She noted that she teaches about colonialism explicitly when looking at reasons for the so-called development gap, a key curriculum content topic. She talks to students about how materials have been taken away from developing countries,

and [the students] go, 'Well, we weren't very nice to them, were we?' And it's like, that's the point. And we talk about, especially with Nigeria and the fact that it stabilised quite quickly after becoming independent compared to a lot of other countries, but it still had a lot of issues and why did it have those issues?

A second participant offered that she too points to colonialism in her treatment of 'hindrances to development', but she uses a different tactic whereby she focuses on Belgium's colonial history in the Democratic Republic of the Congo: 'So I can sit there going on about all these Belgians colonising DRC, and I will say, obviously the UK colonised a lot of places just like Belgium'. She explained, 'It kind of like disarms them a little bit, and they're less on the defensive'. The first participant then responded by offering, 'I don't think mine get defensive at all. Once you explain it, they're actually very like, yeah, we shouldn't have done that, [...] once you go into it, [the students are] quite open to it.' The HEADSUP tool provoked discussions that enabled these teachers to share and seek feedback on approaches to bringing up colonialism in discussing development issues. In both cases, the teachers have a strong rationale for their approach. The discussions among supportive peers and a sense of being among a critical mass was a significant outcome of the workshops.

Participants offered critiques of the framework as well, and discussions of HEADSUP provoked opportunities for teachers to air their concerns about teaching global issues more broadly. For example, participants raised a concern about too much focus on analysis and not enough on action although the tool is intended to contribute to analysis. A discussion in Stockholm suggested that critical GCE affords a more critically reflective approach but that bridging it with sustainable development requires a more behaviour-based action-taking stance. This concern might be influenced by a more than twenty-year-old Nordic tradition and a goal of environmental education to let students grow into responsible and action-minded citizens (Jensen and Schnack, 1997) and focusing on individuals engaging in behavioural actions to ameliorate environmental problems and contribute to social change. This came out strongly in a response from one of the most experienced teachers at the workshop who has leadership responsibilities in regards to global issues teaching:

I was thinking about sustainable development and thinking of solutions and the future, is it there [in HEADSUP]? [...] something with being active, and yeah, change agents, or something that is more pushing or that the, act, I don't know what word it would be, but something not only. ... Yes, that is what I, to me I would not be able to use this alone. I would like to add something.

Perhaps also related to the strength of an action discourse in the Nordic context, the issue around action was also raised in Helsinki, particularly in discussions about connecting GCE with education for sustainable development and environmental education. Another very experienced lead teacher at that workshop agreed on the importance of engaging with critical approaches as an absolute must, and while firmly endorsing a critical approach, pushed the discussion towards consideration of the role of action:

But the thing is also that if we just keep them on deconstructing stories and just keep them on kind of discussion, then there is no application in real life. And that's why for special environmental and ecological issues, we need to put also the hands on, so that there is also a kind of promotion of how you can do things differently.

At the Birmingham workshop, a similar point was made when discussing how students could be inspired to take action and identify a 'next step'; however, the participants suggested a future-oriented approach as action in itself. A participant suggested, 'There could be a question that forces them to think about uncertainty, so what maybe are the future uncertainties ... and gets them to look at all the evidence to actually think about a next step, so they know that the conversation's continuing.' Another participant agreed that an emphasis on change is very important when looking at sustainable development 'because it's not just linear, it's not just static'.

Related to this discussion of action, across the contexts, a key theme was the need to critique a charity approach which appears to remain prevalent, particularly in school-wide activities. In Helsinki, participants reflected on a recent UNICEF walk fundraising initiative where students are sponsored by family and friends who pay per kilometre walked. One suggested, 'The problem is that I don't know whether the children actually know what the cause is.' She goes on to report that her thirteen-year-old niece reported to her that she had done ten rounds: 'And that was the only thing she talked about, about the UNICEF-walk. And I'm sure if her teacher had told her a bit of context, of why they're doing it, she would have been more sort of aware of the reason why they're walking.' This response points to an important tension between what happens in school-wide projects and in specific subject-based classroom lessons where teachers can play an important role in raising critical conversations to contribute towards more complex understandings.

Conversely, participants at the Manchester workshop were quite concerned that students should remain positive about participating in school-wide charity appeals and that critical approaches to GCE might make them feel bad. They worked together to try to make the HEADSUP checklist more 'positive'. Interestingly, one of the participants who worked on changing HEADSUP into positive words came to the resource development meeting a few months later and, having tried that with his students had decided that it was important to engage in critique without adding a positive spin. He contributed some important critical questioning series to the resource which is currently being piloted.

It appears that classroom discussions related to curricula remain an important place for critical reflection on dominant narratives, but also that many teachers are concerned about coming across as negative. Yet, as the participant at the Manchester workshop came to understand, other teachers saw this as an area of possibility. In response to the reflection question regarding paternalism and the extent to which 'we are open to being the ones who know best' (Figure 23.1), a Helsinki participant replied, 'by knowing ourselves, feeling ok to feel sometimes nervous or unhelpful, understanding our own boundaries (even if not fully possible)'. Thus, in line with what Niens and Reilly (2012) found, it is important for teachers to have spaces to discuss these tensions and come to their own position on how they want to take up politicized issues.

Discussion

We have shared a selection of responses from teachers who attended workshops as part of our small project. The HEADSUP tool provoked reflections about the possibilities, challenges and deep complexities of teaching about global issues in today's classrooms. Teachers expressed possibilities for deepening the treatment of development and development aid more broadly, including more context and history of colonialism in the treatment of global issues, and critically reflecting on their own pedagogical approaches and selection of materials. They also spoke of the importance and challenges of taking a strong political stance, and this related deeply to the demographics in their classrooms. A central theme was how the identities, views and positionalities of students in their classrooms are very much connected to the topics and approaches to teaching about global issue, and, relatedly, the importance and challenges of connecting global issues to local inequalities.

To varying extents teachers were comfortable challenging charity-based school-wide initiatives or talking directly about colonialism in their classes. Some were doing this in confident and strategic ways, a small but significant number had not thought about it before and conflated a critical approach with being negative, and others were deeply inspired to critique their own approaches and enact HEADSUP in their practice. The sense among a segment of the participants of needing to present a positive perspective connects to Taylor's (2012) warning, based on research engaging pre-service teachers in Quebec with critical approaches to GCE, of 'the crisis in learning initiated when children are exposed to knowledge of global inequity is closed down when pedagogy offers *consolation* rather than critical and ethical tools to respond to this crisis'. (p. 181). It appears, however, that for many participants, HEADSUP offered an opportunity to reflect critically on soft approaches, particularly when given time to consider it in practice and come back to discuss and apply further.

A particularly interesting finding for us is the way teachers who already identified as critically-oriented engaged with the tool. We are interested in the concern on the part of a teacher in Sweden that students read her as being too 'politically correct' which we see as related to the participant in London's comment that she needs to 'reign in her bias' towards discussing post-colonial issues. We also note the teacher in Birmingham who actively politicizes her classrooms in relation to their demographic make-up. The positionality of the teacher politically seems to permeate school practice and teachers' daily practice; however, the political correctness discourse may defeat substantive aims, that is, a reflective teaching that address 'root' narratives of unprecedented global challenges (Cf. Andreotti, 2014).

We suggest this could be an effect of the 'uncomplicated solutions' part of the HEADSUP being taken out of its related context, as integrated with other historical patterns in the list such as salvationism and paternalism. When this occurs, 'uncomplicated solutions' is applied as a challenge against a critical stance where teachers, including the one who raised concerns about being too 'PC' worry that students think they are presenting the fact that colonialism continues to reinforce inequities today as a 'simple solution'. This surprised us, as we consider that a colonial narrative opens up complexity. This is an important area for further research and connects strongly to the work of Sharon Stein in deconstructing various significations of global education.

While her work focuses on higher education, we find her description of the anti-oppressive position salient to our findings. She argues that this position challenges Eurocentric notions of cosmopolitanism and identifies 'how colonial, racialised, and gendered flows of power and knowledge operate to the advantage of the Global North' (247). A limitation of this position, Stein (2015) argues, is an inadvertent assertion of innocence associated with a lack of recognition of one's complicity in the systems being critiqued. Also, change can be seen to be engineered through rational policy and a sense of moral agency; thereby, despite seeming to critique universalism, the anti-oppressive position can 'overlook the possibility that it, too, maintains some Eurocentric assumptions' (247). Applying this to our findings, some teachers are able to articulate an anti-oppressive stance but appear to lack resources to mediate questions of complicity. Without exploring complicity through unpacking salvationism and paternalism alongside a colonial analysis, and with the addition of a strong sense of a need to encourage students to 'take action', this may translate into a solutions-focused approach that reinforces a hegemonic approach to development aid.

Building from this critique, Stein (2015) presents the incommensurable position 'in which existing scripts for thought and action are not outright rejected, but their limitations are illuminated through encounters with and across difference' (247). Stein (2015) notes that the incommensurable position is similar to the anti-oppressive position in recognizing the oppressive nature of the enactment of symbolic and material violence on the part of the Universalism ascribed to by 'the West'. However, it presents a possibility of engaging differently with existing ordering of the world. Citing scholars engaged in de- and post-colonial analyses (e.g. Povelinni, Nayar, Mignolo, Santos), Stein (2015) posits that 'many of these thinkers explicitly draw on possibilities offered by relationships across difference that do not need to be reconciled through consensus or synthesis' (247).

An important question emerging from our findings is to what extent the HEADUP tool was effectively taken up as an anti-oppressive approach by some teachers, particularly when they already identified as enacting critical approaches. Do they take from HEADSUP a critique of ethnocentrism but remain, perhaps understandably, rooted in universalist scripts? Does an anti-oppressive position tend to focus on certain concepts in the tool, such as uncomplicated solutions, in isolation from the other historical patterns? This is certainly understandable as Stein (2015) points out that a limitation of an incommensurable position is a lack of intelligibility from within mainstream institutions, particularly educational institutions with defined and progressive outcomes defining student learning. Thus, we wonder to what extent HEADSUP encouraged some teachers to start a process of criticality but for others, reinforced an already existing anti-oppressive position? And, we wonder to what extent HEADSUP served to open up further pedagogical possibilities informed by post-colonial and decolonial theory as described by Stein (2015), and/or what further resources would support such an approach? We also realize the importance of promoting the interaction among the seven historical patterns which will inform future work with the tool. While the HEADSUP tool demonstrated great possibilities for critical reflection, community building and application, it also demonstrated constraints and challenges. We hope the discussion in this chapter has evoked the question of what may be possible, but also what may seem impossible, as such 'questions enable new, and previously unimaginable, possibilities to emerge' (Stein, 2015: 249).

Bibliography

Andreotti, V. (2006). Soft vs. critical global citizenship education. *Policy and Practice: A Development Education Review*, 3, 40–51.

Andreotti, V. (2011). *Actionable Postcolonial Theory in Education*. New York: Palgrave Macmillan.

Andreotti, V. (2012). Editor's preface: HEADS UP. *Critical Literacy: Theories and Practices*, 6(1), 1–3.

Andreotti, V. (2014). Critical and Transnational Literacies in International Development and Global Citizenship Education. *Sisyphus Journal of Education*, 2, 32–50.

Andreotti, V., Stein, S., Sutherland, A., Pashby, K., Suša, R. and Amsler, S. (2018). Mobilising different conversations about global justice in education: Toward alternative futures in uncertain times. *Policy and Practice: A Development Education Review*, 26, 9–41.

Bamber, P. and Hankin, L. (2011). Transformative learning through service-learning: No passport required. *Education+ Training*, 53(2/3), 190–206.

Bourn, D. (2009). Students as global citizens. In E. Jones (ed.), *Internationalisation: The Student Voice* (pp. 18–29). London: Routledge.

Edge, K. and Khamsi, K. (2012). International school partnership as a vehicle for global education: Student perspectives. *Asia Pacific Journal of Education*, 32(4), 455–72.

Gandhi, L. (1998). *Postcolonial Theory: A Critical Introduction*. New York: Columbia University Press.

Grain, K. M. and Lund, D. E. (2016). The social justice turn: Cultivating 'critical hope' in an age of despair. *Michigan Journal of Community Service Learning*, 23(1), 45–60.

Gregory, S. (2012). Kony 2012 through a prism of video advocacy practices and trends. *Journal of Human Rights Practice*, 4(3), 463–8.

Huckle, J. and Wals, A. E. J. (2015). The UN Decade of Education for Sustainable Development: Business as usual in the end. *Environmental Education Research*, 21(3), 491–505.

(IYWPGC) International Youth White Paper on Global Citizenship (2017). *Centre for Global Education/ Taking It Global*. http://www.epageflip.net/i/796911-international-youth-white-paper-on-global-citizenship

Jensen, B. and Schnack, K. (1997). The action competence approach in environmental education. *Environmental Education Research*, 3(2), 163–78.

Jickling, B. and Wals, A. E. J. (2008). Globalization and environmental education: Looking beyond sustainable development. *Journal of Curriculum Studies*, 40(1), 1–21.

Kuleta-Hulboj, M. (2016). The global citizen as an agent of change: Ideals of the global citizen in the narratives of Polish NGO employees. *Journal for Critical Education Policy Studies (JCEPS)*, 14(3), 22–250.

Martin, F. (2011). Global ethics, sustainability and partnership. In G. Butt (ed.), *Geography, Education and the Future* (pp. 206–24). London: Continuum.

Matthews, J. (2011). Hybrid pedagogies for sustainability education. *Review of Education, Pedagogy, and Cultural Studies*, *33*(3), 260–77.

McKenzie, M. (2012). Education for y'all: Global neoliberalism and the case for a politics of scale in sustainability education policy. *Policy Futures in Education*, *10*(2), 165–77.

Niens, U. and Reilly, J. (2012). Education for global citizenship in a divided society? Young people's views and experiences. *Comparative Education*, *48*, 103–18.

Pashby, K. (2012). Questions for global citizenship education in the context of the 'new imperialism'. In V. de Oliveira Andreotti and L. M. T. M. de Souza (eds), *Postcolonial Perspectives on Global Citizenship Education* (pp. 9–26). New York: Routledge.

Pashby, K. (2015). Conflations, possibilities, and foreclosures: Global citizenship education in a multicultural context. *Curriculum Inquiry*, *45*(4), 345–66.

Pashby, K. and Andreotti, V. (2015). Critical global citizenship in theory and practice: Rationales and approaches for an emerging agenda. In J. Harshman, T. Augustine and M. Merryfield (eds) *Research on Global Citizenship Education* (pp. 9–23). Charlotte, NC: Information Age Publishing, Research in Social Education Series.

Stein, S. (2015). Mapping global citizenship. *Journal of College and Character*, *16*(4), 242–52.

Sund, L. (2016). Facing global sustainability issues: Teachers' experiences of their own practices in environmental and sustainability education. *Environmental Education Research*, *22*(6), 788–805.

Sund, L. and Öhman, J. (2014). On the need to repoliticise environmental and sustainability education: Rethinking the postpolitical consensus. *Environmental Education Research*, *20*(5): 639–59.

Sund, L. and Pashby, K. (2018). 'Is it that we do not want them to have washing machines?': Ethical global issues pedagogy in Swedish Classrooms. *Sustainability*, *10*(10), 35–52.

Taylor, L. K. (2012). Beyond paternalism: Global education with Preservice Teachers as a Practice of Implication. In V. Andreotti and L. Souza (eds), *Postcolonial Perspectives on Global Citizenship Education* (pp. 177–99). Routledge: New York.

Truong-White, H. and McLean, L. (2015). Digital storytelling for transformative global citizenship education. *Canadian Journal of Education*, *38*, 1–28.

Van Poeck, K. and Vandenabeele, J. (2012). Learning from sustainable development: Education in the light of public issues. *Environmental Education Research*, *18*(4): 541–52.

Von Engelhardt, J. and Jansz, J. (2014). Challenging humanitarian communication: An empirical exploration of Kony 2012. *International Communication Gazette*, *76*(6), 464–84.

Wals, A. (2009). *United Nations Decade of Education for Sustainable Development (DESD, 2005–2014)– Review of Contexts and Structures for Education for Sustainable Development 2009*. Paris: UNESCO.

Chapter 24

Is Global Citizenship Education Relevant in Sub-Saharan African School Curricula? Options and Challenges for Teaching Global Citizenship through a Social Studies Curriculum in Ghana

Simon Eten Angyagre

Introduction

A key differentiation of the United Nations Sustainable Development Goal (SDG) 4 from the erstwhile education-related Millennium Development Goals (MDGs) is the inclusion of a learning target on global citizenship, around which students' knowledge, attitudes and skills are expected to be developed towards empowering them to contribute to sustainable development around the world (UNESCO, 2016). The inclusion of global citizenship as an SDG 4 target places the development of students' non-cognitive skills high on the international education policy agenda, which hitherto had a relatively low profile (Skinner et al., 2013). Furthermore, the SDG framework presents all seventeen SDGs as relevant to countries in both the Global North and South, presupposing that the principles and values that undergird their formulation, to a large extent, are all-embracing of the diverse economic, political and sociocultural aspirations of countries in most parts of the world.

However, critical education theorists in particular have expressed the view that the normative values and principles that underpin mainstream conceptions of global citizenship as promoted by international organizations such as UNESCO and OXFAM are drawn mainly from the Western liberal intellectual tradition and aim at promoting a Western hegemonic agenda (Bowden, 2003; Andreotti, 2006; Abdi, 2015). Bowden (2003: 350), for example, has noted that global citizenship can be associated with the Western world's 'history of engaging in overzealous civilising-cum-universalising missions in non-Western world'. As a result of the Western-centric origins of mainstream conceptions of global citizenship, there is a certain ambivalence within critical education scholarship in engaging with and promoting what is thought of as a hegemonic and homogenizing understanding of global citizenship.

Beyond the conceptual relevance of global citizenship in non-Western settings, there are contextual factors for the focus of this chapter that might constrain efforts to integrate global citizenship into Sub-Saharan African school curricula. A significant contextual issue in this respect relates to the view that GCE may not be a practical educational need in resource-poor and conflict-prone countries. This perspective views global citizenship as an educational luxury and not a necessity in education systems that are still battling with issues around access and participation, and lack basic infrastructure and measurable educational inputs such as textbooks (UNESCO, 2018). Torres (2017) has also noted a number of challenges that might apply to teaching global citizenship in African education systems, including the lingering impacts of colonialism on education systems in Sub-Saharan African countries; the need to develop autonomous education systems in the light of neoliberal forces; and the increasing influence of China on Sub-Saharan African countries, a phenomenon that is likely to impact on education systems in the near future. There are also challenges that pertain to differences in educational and political systems across Sub-Saharan African countries, as well as the heterogeneous character of African societies, that might pose difficulty in aligning educational goals, school practices and cultural values around which global citizenship could be appropriated for African schools.

These conceptual and contextual challenges notwithstanding, drawing on post-colonial and critical theory perspectives in education can centre African ontologies and epistemologies in global citizenship discourses to make the concept relevant in African schools. African ontologies that border on conceptions of being, humanity and social relations, as well as epistemologies that relate to the practical and community-driven orientations of African indigenous education, can be drawn upon to 'Africanize' global citizenship for African schools (Andreotti, 2006; de Oliveira Andreotti and De Souza, 2012; Dei, 2014; Abdi, 2015). Within African sociocultural frames, the usefulness of GCE in education systems could go beyond ridding school curricula of colonial influences and dealing with some of the neoliberal influences on education, to playing a more instrumental role in the promotion of pan-Africanism, around which peace-building and social cohesion within and across African states can be pursued.

Based on broad theoretical debates on GCE and findings from an exploratory study, this chapter discusses the conceptual, contextual and pedagogical possibilities of integrating themes and pedagogies of global citizenship into Ghana's social studies curriculum. This introduction is followed by a description of Ghana's secondary education policy context, highlighting its current state and limitations, around which the need for a global dimension to social studies education is articulated. After a brief elucidation of what the concept GCE means in its different expressions and forms, there is a discussion of the study findings, situated within broader theoretical debates on the relevance and appropriation of GCE for Ghana's social studies curriculum, using a framework of a critical global pedagogy.

Ghana's secondary education policy in an era of globalization

Ghana as a developing lower middle-income country is gaining visibility in the international scene and its educational goals and strategies, for higher education, in particular, are increasingly being framed around producing graduates who can participate in the global economy (Manuh, Gariba and Budu, 2007; Kuyini, 2013). The global context within which Ghana has to pursue its development agenda and the need to position itself strategically in the global knowledge economy makes it imperative for the country's educational goals to aim, among other things, at developing a globally competent citizenry. Secondary education has a significant role to play in this respect, particularly for Ghana, where returns on secondary education are said to be higher and curricula goals focus not only on preparing students for entry into the tertiary level but for entry into the world of work with appropriate apprenticeship experience (Akyeampong, 2010).

In seeking to develop school curricula fit for the purpose of developing globally competent citizenry, Ghana's secondary education curricula need to look beyond the neoliberal focus on market-driven, job-specific technical skills and to prioritize curriculum content and pedagogy that develop a versatility in the attitudes, behaviours and skills of students and imbue in them values that prepare them to navigate the exigencies of globalization. In developing Ghana's long-term development plan, the National Development Planning Commission (NDPC) cites civic and cultural literacy, critical-thinking skills, problem-solving skills, among others, as essential for Ghanaian students and workers (NDPC, 2016). The development of these skills, however, need to be situated in a global context to enhance the ability of Ghanaian students and workers to participate in the global economy. The relevance of the set of skills that encapsulate both social/civic skills and employability skills lies in its potential to develop Ghanaian youth into active social citizens who can take up active roles in development processes. This set of skills also constitutes relevant skills for employability, particularly for professions that are rapidly globalizing (Bourn, 2018). In preparing youth for a globalizing world, school curricula need to address the fallouts of globalization that pertain to the diversity and difference that have become part of contemporary society, owing to the high incidence of intercultural contacts. For the Sub-Saharan African context, traditional sociocultural norms and values, and communal forms of living that were once the defining elements of African societies, are significantly being impacted by globalization, and understandings of 'community' and 'identity' are increasingly been altered by global forces (Dei, 2004). This calls for innovation in exploring curricula options and devising educational strategies that prepare students to participate in the processes of globalization while developing a capacity to maintain their cultural composure as African youth in a world that is constantly globalizing. Such curricula innovations should not be limited to pedagogical approaches that raise students' awareness on globalization and its processes, but should also enhance an understanding of how globalization impacts on society, and foster in students the civic courage to become critical agents of development at local, regional and global levels. Drawing on the significance of this global perspective to secondary education, this chapter calls for integrating global themes and pedagogies into Ghana's social studies curriculum, an educational innovation that is all the more relevant within the framework of the United Nations SDG 4 which calls for the promotion of Education for Sustainable Development (ESD) and global citizenship. In order to appreciate the significance of a global perspective to social studies education in Ghana's education system, an understanding of Ghana's secondary education policy as it relates to citizenship development will suffice.

The policy challenges facing Ghana's secondary education system are multifaceted, but the scope of this chapter will focus on how the country's secondary education policy is increasingly being cast in a neoliberal framework, while losing sight of its critical social function in developing transformative citizenship (Del Mar, 2012). The content and pedagogy of Ghana's secondary education curriculum is said to emphasize the development of attitudes of uniformity and conformity rather than fostering independent and critical thinking (Del Mar, 2012; Eten, 2015), a phenomenon that is symptomatic of a general lack of critical elements in content and pedagogies in education systems across Sub-Saharan Africa, where citizenship education programmes have predominantly served the purpose of social control (Siganke, 2011). Del Mar (2012) has further observed that Ghana's Senior High School social studies curriculum tends to denigrate the country's traditions and indigenous practices while glorifying its colonial past, a phenomenon that is at odds with the conscientization project that the country's intellectual class in academic institutions have been preoccupied with over the years, towards lessening the negative impacts of colonialism on Ghana's national psyche. Consequently, the curricular goals that guide teaching and learning activities, in social studies as an example, are defined narrowly around inculcating in students attitudes of respect for authority, obedience, honesty, fairness, efficiency and self-control, among others. With a narrow focus on developing this set of attitudes and values, school curricula have contributed to developing a sense of civic apathy among educated youth. There is also a general lack of interest among the youth in the country's cultural heritage, and by extension Africa's culture and colonial past. In connection with this, Hartman (2007:71) has noted that Ghanaians have 'too many pressing concerns in everyday life to ruminate about the past'. There is rather a preoccupation with meeting daily needs under economic and political conditions that the political elite foster and under a neoliberal national narrative of economic prosperity and progress (Del Mar, 2012). School subjects such as civics and social studies as well as civic education programmes run by Ghana's National Commission for Civic Education, a statutory institution, tend to focus more on promoting citizens' responsibility in payment of taxes and voting, while glossing over citizens' roles in holding public officials accountable through civic engagement.

Educational reforms in much of Ghana's post-colonial history have not addressed the political and civic apathy noted as pervasive among Ghanaian youth. Such reforms are dictated rather by neoliberal agendas, the result of which is the merger or complete removal of school subjects that focus on the moral and civic development of students – thought to be less relevant in contemporary society (Danso, 2018). In light of this problematic, this chapter is aimed at highlighting the significance of a critical global pedagogy in addressing the absence of transformative content and pedagogy in Ghana's social studies curriculum.

What is GCE?

GCE, also referred to as global education (GE) or global learning among other terminologies, is citizenship education cast within a transnational framework and driven by social justice and sustainable development imperatives. Bourn (2014) traces the historical development of GE from the term 'development education' (DE) and its original association with NGO campaign and awareness-raising activities. He notes that at the turn of the twenty-first century, terms like GE and GCE began to gain popularity and to replace DE, as part of the recognition of the impacts that globalization began to have on international development processes. Given the different themes around which GE is usually conceptualized, and the different thematic focus of each terminology, it is easier to identify defining themes in GCE rather than give an all-encompassing definition. The constitutive themes in GCE are reflected in the different thematic foci on international education, citizenship education, multicultural education, peace education, human rights education, and ESD (Oxfam, 2006; Rapoport, 2009; Davies, Evans and Reid, 2005; Banks, 2004; Smith and Fairman, 2005; Gaudelli and Fernekes, 2004). The discursive topics in these different frameworks accordingly relate to diversity, multiculturalism, interculturalism; global systems and structures; human rights, equality, social justice and conflict resolution; among others (Reynolds, 2015).

In contemporary usage, however, GCE, GE and learning are much in vogue in research, academic and international development policy circles. A significant difference between GCE, and GE and learning is that the former centres social justice imperatives in citizenship discourses that relate to human rights, citizenship obligations and responsibilities, whereas GE and learning focus more on fostering international awareness with the aim of developing well-rounded individuals who can navigate the processes of globalization (Davies. Reid and Evans, 2005; Davies, 2006).

An overarching consideration that makes imperative a global citizenship perspective to social studies education in Sub-Saharan African schools draws on the international policy significance global citizenship has assumed within the framework of the 2030 SDGs, and the increasing uptake of global citizenship in education systems in Europe and North America. This, no doubt, has implications for education systems in Sub-Saharan Africa and highlights the need for Sub-Saharan African countries to begin to prepare their education systems for appropriating GCE relevant for their educational contexts.

Findings from study

An exploratory qualitative study was conducted across five senior high schools in the Tamale Metropolis of the Northern Region of Ghana to assess the social studies curriculum in respect of teachers' and students' views, classroom teaching methodologies, syllabus and textbook provisions, using a critical GCE framework (Andreotti, 2006; Blackmore, 2016). The study mainly employed individual and group interviews, lesson observation and document analysis, with twenty teachers and fifty students constituting study participants. In the following sections, I discuss the findings of the study pertaining to the relevance of GCE, the presence of topics on Africa's culture and history, and the extent to which dimensions of critical pedagogy as a teaching methodology are employed in Ghana social studies curriculum.

Views on global citizenship and Ghana's social studies curriculum

From interviews and focus groups, most teachers and students demonstrated a limited familiarity with the concept of global citizenship but were able to relate to the concept's constitutive terms of globalization and citizenship. Teachers, in particular, were of the view that integrating themes on global citizenship into the social studies curriculum was important for addressing issues around globalization and its impacts. A teacher reiterated this by noting that 'we are now living in a global village'. The consensus on the significance of global citizenship in social studies education notwithstanding, teachers pointed out a number of factors that might constrain efforts to introduce themes on global citizenship into their lessons. This is evident in a statement by one of the teachers:

> The first time I heard about global citizenship was when a friend of mine (who is the Regional Director of the National Commission for Civic Education in the Northern Region of Ghana) asked me what social studies teachers were doing to introduce to our students the concept of global citizenship. My reply to him was that, as social studies teachers, we were only responsible for teaching what was in the social studies syllabus and if the policy makers (Ministry of Education) decide that we should teach about global citizenship, we will teach it, if it is added to the syllabus.
>
> (Teacher 1)

This statement highlights the significance of curriculum provision and teacher training in broadening Ghana's school curriculum with themes and pedagogies on global citizenship. Most teachers indicated that global citizenship was not part of the initial teacher education courses they undertook in their training – the main reason they were unable to introduce the concept into their lessons – coupled with the absence of the concept in the social studies teaching syllabus.

With regard to topics in the teaching syllabus that discuss globalization and global issues, teachers noted there were just a few topics connected to globalization, global systems and structures, and generally on Ghana's relationship with other countries. These topics were named as:

- National Independence and Self-reliance
- Ghana and the International Community
- Constitution, Democracy and Nation-Building

In highlighting the limited scope of the social studies curriculum on global issues, Teacher 1 in an interview explained,

> The Senior High School Social Studies syllabus is structured to discuss national issues with only a few topics that focus on Ghana's relationship with the international community … even in those cases where the international community is discussed, such discussions are limited to descriptions and not the impact of such relations.

For students, many of the lessons in social studies were not directly linked to global issues. However, a few topics were cited as directly linked to Ghana's bilateral and multilateral relations. In naming these few topics, students confirmed the topics listed by teachers.

On a related question of whether there was the need for a review of the social studies teaching syllabus to address issues around globalization, the head of Department for social studies in one of the study schools noted that the need for reviewing the social studies syllabus was discussed in a meeting convened by the Ghana Association of Teachers of Social Studies (GATESS) – a subject association. He, however, pointed out that discussions on the need for the review were mainly centred on introducing financial literacy into the social studies curriculum. Though financial literacy constitutes an important skill and knowledge dimension for the youth, one wonders if social studies is the appropriate subject area for teaching this knowledge area, an attestation of the view that Ghana's education system and school curricula are being heavily influenced by neoliberal agendas.

Beyond curriculum provisions, initial teacher education and continuous professional development, the experiences and personal attributes of teachers have been found to directly or indirectly influence teachers' abilities and readiness to incorporate themes and pedagogies on GCE into lessons (Reynolds, 2015). Some of the experiential factors that might apply in this respect include exposure to diversity, international travel, minority status, experience of professional service and familial relations (Reynolds, 2015). It is, however, important to note that, for many teachers in a developing country like Ghana, there is little such opportunity of exposure to these experiences. Moreover, most teachers in schools in developing contexts usually feel bound by a subject's teaching syllabus in what they teach and how they teach it, since the teaching syllabus largely dictates the planning and delivery of lessons.

To put into wider context and perspective the views teachers articulated on the need for global citizenship in Ghana's social studies curriculum, it is worth situating these views within the broader theoretical debates on the potential significance GCE might have in education systems in Sub-Saharan Africa.

The impacts of neoliberalism on African societies, including their education systems, makes it imperative for education policy-makers to begin to envision ways school curricula can prepare students to respond to the fallouts of globalization. The increasing neoliberal grip on government education policy in Sub-Saharan African states is evident in the policy tendency to exclude from school curricula subjects that are deemed 'irrelevant', based on a neoliberal logic. Alongside a neoliberal definition of 'relevant' education, there is a growing fixation on improving students' test scores through controlled and regimented school and curricula practices, manifest in classroom activities that quantify, fragmentize and categorize students for assessment purposes. These activities, though sometimes well-intended, reduce the creative spaces within which students can learn collaboratively to foster both cognitive and non-cognitive skills, in the form of critical-thinking skills, empathy, respect, self-control, intercultural/inter-ethnic awareness and mutual tolerance. GCE offers a framing paradigm around which the aforementioned values and attitudes can be developed in students through curricular activities.

Global citizenship themes and pedagogies in social studies education can contribute to tackling some of the sociocultural ills that manifest in inter-ethnic and religious conflicts and violence, prejudice and stereotypes that minority groups within African states contend with. Sub-Saharan African states can boast of some of the most diverse societies around the world, and yet the differences that come with this diversity are sometimes a source of strife and conflict within and between communities. Some key themes in GCE are directly linked to, and are useful for promoting, nation-building and social cohesion through which positive values and attitudes for fostering peace, solidarity and social harmony in young people can be pursued (UNESCO, 2014). A critical global pedagogy informed by post-colonial and critical theory is centred on teaching approaches with the potential to empower students to see beyond their narrow ethnocentric and racial identities, appreciate diversity and difference and challenge stereotypes and prejudice often associated with the 'other' (Said, 1989). Moreover, through a conscientization of youth on the positioning of Africa in contemporary and historical global development processes, GCE can promote active citizenship by empowering youth to find their voice in both local and global development discourses (Edge and Khamsi, 2012; Eten, 2015; Quaynor, 2015).

Furthermore, the appropriation of global citizenship can contribute to strengthening ongoing efforts by regional bodies such as the African Union (AU) in promoting regional integration among African states, and further serve as an intermediate platform for integrating African countries into the global economy. The difficulty in achieving meaningful integration among Sub-Saharan African nation-states partly stems from the politics of nationalism and ethnocentrism that characterize relations between these countries. Attitudes that reflect national parochialism continue to manifest across the continent, seen, for example, in the xenophobic attitudes prevalent among some Africans towards Africans of different nationalities.

Curriculum provision on themes on Africa's culture and history

Central to critical discourses on global citizenship are themes related to identity, culture, power and history (Andreotti, 2006; Dei, 2014; Abdi, 2015). As such, for the purpose of the study, an appreciation of Africa's culture and history and how this impacts on its sociocultural development was considered instrumental in understanding the sociocultural formations of African youth. Shiza (2013), for example, has noted that Africa's colonial encounter has contributed to the development of education systems that are decontextualized, and produce youth who are culturally alienated (Quist, 2001).

Most teachers in the study were of the view that the social studies syllabus did not contain adequate provision on themes that discuss Africa's culture and history, reflected, for example, in the absence of topics that discuss Africa's colonial experience. In this regard, Teacher 6 expressed the concern that

> the social studies syllabus does not provide for discussing colonialism because there are no topics that directly talk about colonialism ... and also because of the lack of time. Even if a teacher is competent enough to introduce and discuss colonialism in his or her lessons with students, the limited time he or she has will not make that possible.

In responding to the same question, Teacher 2 noted,

> No, because colonialism is rarely discussed and only discussed if teacher decides to link it up to other topics, but there is no stand-alone topic on colonialism.

A different dimension of the limited provision in the social studies curriculum on themes on Africa's culture and colonial past came to the fore when Teacher 8 observed that

> social studies does not adequately address issues of colonialism because the few topics which relate to colonialism (such as National Independence and Self-Reliance) only focus on the processes that led to independence, and not on the impact of colonialism on the Ghanaian society.

These quotes from teachers reveal a lack in the social studies curriculum of themes that discuss Africa's culture and colonial past. In the few cases where these themes are captured in topics and discussed in lessons, they are addressed rather superficially, a possible explanation for why the subject does not develop in students an interest in Africa's culture and history. This could further explain the cultural disinterest which Del Mar (2012) noted is endemic among Ghanaians.

Within the framework of critical and post-colonial perspectives in education, global citizenship can centre Africa's culture and history in social studies education. In the following, I discuss some of Africa's sociocultural norms around which global citizenship can be contextualized in African schools.

As a libertarian construct, global citizenship derives mainly from a Western liberal understanding of citizenship which centres on the rule of law, individual liberty, human rights and responsibilities and the concomitant roles of governments to guarantee and protect these rights. African indigenous understandings of citizenship, however, are aligned more to communitarian and civic republican approaches to citizenship, with a focus on social rights, group identity and citizen participation in public life (Jochum, Pratten and Wilding, 2005; Andani and Naidoo, 2013). I draw on such African indigenous communitarian understandings of citizenship to suggest that, in order to contextualize global citizenship for African education systems, Ubuntu as an African ontological conception around which communitarian citizenship is lived out in African communities can provide a narrative for contextualization.

Ubuntu originates from an isiXhosa statement which is *umuntu ngumuntu ngabantu*, translated to mean 'a person is a person through their relationships to others' (Swanson, 2007: 55). According to this philosophy of living, dignity and identity are achieved through mutualism, empathy, generosity and community building. With these virtues, the strength of communal living made possible by Ubuntu is rooted in the community support it provides the individual, especially the vulnerable. In doing this, Ubuntu emphasizes responsibility and obligation towards the collective well-being of a community (Swanson, 2015). If transposed to a transnational level, Ubuntu as a philosophy of care in the community shows how international understanding and cooperation can be harnessed to build a more peaceful and sustainable world towards the care of the world's vulnerable and destitute, as is implicit in GCE discourse. This way of promoting international understanding and development reduces strife in relations between countries that come in the form of unbridled competition, international conflict and terrorism.

As an ontological proposition as to how humans should relate in community for support, care, solidarity and consensus building, Ubuntu is centred on an African communitarian value system and aligns well with the goals of GCE in respect of the normative values, attitudes and skills, and in that sense can serve as a reference point for appropriating global citizenship for African schools. Ubuntu strengthens the case of global citizenship by underscoring the significance of values and ideals that go beyond a neoliberal understanding of education centred on market-defined skills (Nkondo, 2007). Ubuntu, therefore, has significance in enabling a global citizenship discourse that goes beyond a neoliberal understanding of education to a human-centred approach that fosters sensibilities such as compassion, care and empathy around which students' commitment to the good of society can be harnessed.

Suffice it to note, however, that appropriating global citizenship for African schools should not end with drawing parallels in the normative values of global citizenship and Ubuntu, as this may only serve to patronize Ubuntu for entrenching hegemonic conceptions of global citizenship.

The goal of such appropriation should be to mainstream and centre African ontologies and epistemologies into global citizenship discourses around which an African rendition of global citizenship can be articulated for African schools. In order to achieve this, post-colonial theory and critical pedagogy can serve the purpose of deconstructing Western hegemonic conceptions of global citizenship and create the conceptual space within which African cultural values and ideals can be forged into the international discourse on global citizenship.

The significance of teaching GCE from such a pan-African perspective is in drawing from the sociocultural realities and the common historical experiences of African peoples, around which an African citizen identity can be constructed to engage with the global world. Such an approach comes with a contextualization power that centres global citizenship themes and pedagogies in the ecological, sociocultural and historical formations of African peoples. Ndoye (2009) has noted that African history can provide a unifying curriculum discourse in African schools around which pan-Africanism can be inculcated into African youth, employing a pedagogical approach that exposes students to the common past encounters, exchanges, reciprocal influences and acts of solidarity that have characterized relations between African peoples through times good and bad.

It is, however, worth cautioning that such a pan-Africanist approach to promoting GCE may slip into an exercise of essentializing and romanticizing African peoples and their cultures, and end up 'demonising' other racial groups, and detract from the 'global' in global citizenship. To avoid such a possibility, the ideal approach to centring African history and culture in global citizenship discourse within African schools is to avoid using Africa's historical experiences and culture for the purposes of manipulation and propaganda through which hatred, mistrust, discord, intolerance, racism, xenophobia and violence are propagated (Ndoye, 2009).

Dimensions of critical pedagogy in Ghana's social studies curriculum

A significant dimension of critical GCE is a Freirean approach to teaching (which is centred on the dialogic method of teaching, as expounded in Paulo Freire's *'pedagogy of the oppressed'* (1970). Pedagogies of active and collaborative learning are particularly well-suited in social studies lessons because of their inherent potential to develop students' civic competencies and skills (Plantan, 2004).

The majority of teachers indicated that they employed the discussion method of teaching as opposed to the lecture method. This was confirmed by the views of students on the methodologies their teachers employed in lessons. Relating the responses of both teachers and students, the following were named as the teaching strategies mostly employed in social studies lessons:

- putting students in groups and giving them projects to accomplish,
- asking and distributing questions equitably across class,
- using the discussion method of teaching and
- putting students in groups to brainstorm given topics and report back to class.

Closely linked to the dialogic approach to teaching is democratic teaching practices in the classroom, which instil in students values such as tolerance, respect for diversity, inclusion and solidarity for active global citizenship (Fricke, Gathercole and Skinner, 2015). One of the teaching strategies teachers can use to foster these democratic values is encouraging students to express their views during lessons and creating space for students to critique and assess their (teachers') views and the overall delivery of lessons. Though the majority of teachers indicated they were tolerant of students' views, a few teachers noted they disallowed this practice in their lessons for 'good' reasons. One of these reasons was related by Teacher 1:

> We have over the years noticed how significant it is for students to critique and assess how we teach them, but there is actually no time to do that. If you take your lesson that far, you are not going to be able to cover your syllabus.

This quote highlights syllabus overload as one of the likely practical challenges that might constrain teaching global citizenship through the social studies curriculum, coupled with the limited time mostly allotted to social studies lessons. Some of the teaching strategies and practices recommended by Freirean critical pedagogy, such as students' active participation in classroom lessons, group work and democratic classroom processes, require ample time to implement.

The study further reviewed a number of social studies topics in an attempt to investigate the criticality embedded in them, with 'criticality' defined in terms of content that fosters attitudes and skills for promoting civic engagement. A suitable topic from the syllabus for the review is leadership and followership, given the significance of agency and autonomy in discussions on critical global citizenship (Andreotti, 2006). In the teaching syllabus, the problem statement for this topic is framed around the poor conception of leadership and followership among Ghanaians. Poor conception of leadership is linked to leaders focusing on the acquisition of wealth through leadership positions, while poor understanding of followership among Ghanaians is expressed in attitudes of sycophancy and boot licking. This problem statement in the syllabus highlights very well some of the root causes of corruption and resource mismanagement in Ghana.

The syllabus further recommends a set of qualities for ideal leadership and followership, but a close examination of the recommended qualities of a follower shows that these qualities do not fall within qualities that promote critical followership. Blackmore (2016) notes in her conceptualization of a framework of critical GCE that any teaching and learning process based on critical pedagogy should develop in students competencies and readiness to engage and dialogue with the 'other' over difference. In the spheres of governance and politics, dialogue and engagement over difference could be expressed in the form of civic engagement with political leaders, to demand accountability and good governance. However, not many of the recommended qualities for a follower captured in the social studies syllabus resonate with civic competencies for engaging with difference. Most of the qualities (humility, loyalty, cooperation, dedication and sense of team work) outlined in the syllabus in some sense relate more to promoting 'sycophancy' and 'boot-licking' than to promoting civic engagement. Critical citizenship education that aims at promoting responsible followership among Ghanaians should rather focus on promoting 'civic courage and civic empowerment' (Kickbusch, 1987).

Findings from the study point to a number of enabling factors needed for the integration of a global citizenship perspective into Ghana's social studies curriculum. Key among these is a curriculum review to include themes and pedagogies on global citizenship in the social studies syllabus. A potential key challenge is an overloaded social studies syllabus, which calls for a minimalist approach to introducing global citizenship into the social studies curriculum. UNESCO (2015) has put forward four ways GCE could be introduced into school curricula, which include the school-wide approach, the cross-curricular approach, the subject-integration approach and the stand-alone subject approach. Towards addressing the challenge of curriculum overload, the subject-integration approach presents itself as an ideal approach to introducing global citizenship into Ghana's social studies curriculum.

Conclusion

Drawing from both empirical and theoretical arguments, this chapter has sought to demonstrate how GCE might be relevant in African schools. The discussions have highlighted a number of conceptual-, contextual- and curriculum-related challenges that might constrain the introduction of global citizenship into African school curricula. For Ghana's secondary education, the challenges that apply include, among others, the increasing neoliberal focus of school curricula, overloaded school curricula, inadequate educational inputs and quality issues in basic education. However, beyond these specific challenges, there is a more systemic challenge embedded in Ghana's education system and across many Sub-Saharan African countries that derives from broader sociocultural, political and historical factors. This pertains to the phenomenon of resistance to change and transformation, a phenomenon that is evident in the continuous use of outdated pedagogies in schools in some Sub-Saharan African countries, though new pedagogies and approaches to education delivery have been found to be more effective. The phenomenon of resistance to change is likely to inhibit efforts to introduce global citizenship into social studies education in African schools. To address this challenge, political will from Sub-Saharan African governments, and policy autonomy from neoliberal agendas, would constitute significant enabling factors in introducing global citizenship into school curricula. Policy autonomy, in particular, is significant in ensuring that the type of GCE that is introduced into African schools is relevant to the sociocultural, economic and political aspirations of these countries, and is also fit for preparing the youth for a rapidly globalizing world.

Bibliography

Abdi, A. A. (2015), 'Decolonizing global citizenship education', in A. A. Abdi, L. Shultz and T. Pillay (eds), *Decolonizing Global Citizenship Education*, 11–26, Rotterdam: Sense Publishers.

Akyeampong, K. (2010), '50 years of educational progress and challenge in Ghana'. Available at http://www.createrpc.org/pdf_documents/50%20Years%20of%20Educational_Progress_%20in_Ghana.pdf (accessed 15 February 2019).

Andani, A., and Naidu, R. (2013), From subject to citizen: Building active citizenship through community dialogues and radio stations. In Good Governance Learning Network [GGLN]. Active citizenship matters: Perspectives from civil society on local governance in South Africa. Kenilworth, South Africa: Isandla Institute, 79–89.

Andreotti, V. (2006), 'Soft versus critical global citizenship education', *Policy and Practice: A Development Education Review*, 3, 40–51.

Banks, J. A. (2004), 'Teaching for social justice, diversity, and citizenship in a global world', *The Educational Forum* 68(4), 296–305.

Blackmore, C. (2016), 'Towards a pedagogical framework for global citizenship education', *International Journal of Development Education and Global Learning*, 8(1), 39–56.

Bourn, D. (2014), 'The theory and practice of global learning', *Development Education Research Centre*, Research Paper No. 11.

Bourn, D. (2018). *Understanding Global Skills for 21st Century Professions*, Switzerland: Palgrave Macmillan.

Bowden, B. (2003), 'The Perils of Global Citizenship', *Citizenship Studies*, 7(3), 349–62.

Charania, G. (2011), 'Grounding the global: A call for more situated practices of pedagogical and political engagement', *ACME: An International Journal for Critical Geographies*, 10(3), 351–71.

Danso, S. A. (2018), 'Moral education and the curriculum: The Ghanaian Experience', *International Journal of Scientific Research and Management*, 6(01), 34–42.

Davies, I., Evans, M. and Reid, A. (2005), 'Globalizing citizenship education? A critique of "global education" and "citizenship education"', *British Journal of Educational Studies*, 51 (1), 66–89.

Davies, L. (2006), 'Global citizenship: Abstraction or framework for action?', *Educational Review*, 58(1), 5–25.

de Oliveira Andreotti, V. and de Souza, L. M. T. M. (eds) (2012), *Postcolonial Perspectives on Global Citizenship Education*, New York: Routledge.

Dei, G. J. S. (2004), *Schooling and Education in Africa: The Case of Ghana*, Trenton: Africa World Press.

Dei, G. (2014), 'Global education from an "Indigenist" Anti-colonial Perspective', *Journal of Contemporary Issues in Education*, 9(2), 4–23.

Del Mar, D. P. (2012), 'A pragmatic tradition: The past in Ghanaian education', *Africa Today*, 59(2), 23–38.

Edge, K. and Khamsi, K. (2012), 'International school partnerships as a vehicle for global education: Student perspectives', *Asia Pacific Journal of Education*, 32(4), 455–72.

Eten, S. (2015), 'The prospects of development education in African Countries: Building a critical mass of citizenry for civic engagement', *Policy & Practice: A Development Education Review*, 20(Spring), 136–51.

Fellner, G. (2011), *Reflections on Joe Kincheloe's Schools Where Ronnie and Brandon would have Excelled*, in K Hayes, S. R. Steinberg and K. Tobin (eds), *Key Works in Critical Pedagogy*, Rotterdam, The Netherlands: Sense Publishers.

Fricke, H. J., Gathercole, C. and Skinner, A. (2015), Monitoring education for global citizenship: A contribution to debate. DEEEP-CONCORD DARE Forum. Available at http://deeep.org/wp-content/up loads/2015/01/DEEEP4_QualityImpact_Report_2014_web2.pdf (accessed 15 October 2018).

Freire, P. (1970), *Pedagogy of the Oppressed*, New York: Continuum.

Gaudelli, W. and Fernekes, W. (2004), 'Teaching about global huma rights for global citizenship', *The Social Studies*, 95(1), 16–26.

Hartman, S. (2007), *Lose Your Mother: A Journey Along the Atlantic Slave Route*, New York: Farrar, Straus and Giroux.

Jochum, V., Pratten, B. and Wilding, K. (2005), *Civil Renewal and Active Citizenship*, London: NCVO.

Kickbusch, K. W. (1987), 'Civic education and preservice educators: Extending the boundaries of discourse', *Theory & Research in Social Education*, 15(3), 173–88.

Kuyini, A. B. (2013). 'Ghana's education reform 2007: A realistic proposition or a crisis of vision?', *International Review of Education*, 59(2), 157–76.

Manuh, T., Gariba, S. and Budu, J. (2007), 'Change and transformation in Ghana's publicly funded universities', in *Partnership for Higher Education in Africa*, Oxford: James Currey and Accra, Ghana: Woeli Publishing Services.

National Development Planning Commission (NDPC) (n.d.), 21st Century Skills and Values for Ghanaian Students and workers, NDPC website (accessed 15 February 2019).

Ndoye, M. (2009), 'Pedagogical use of the General History of Africa: Conceptual framework', UNESCO. Available at http://www.unesco.org/new/fileadmin/MULTIMEDIA/HQ/CLT/CLT/pdf/General_Histo ry_of_Africa/Conceptual%20Framework%20for%20the%20PU-GHA%20(Full)%20(2).pdf (accessed 20 March 2019).

Nkondo, G. M. (2007), 'Ubuntu as public policy in South Africa: A conceptual framework', *International Journal of African Renaissance Studies*, 2(1), 88–100.

Oxfam (2006), Education for global citizenship: A guide for schools, Oxfam development education programme UK. Available at http://www.oxfam.org.uk/~/media/Files/Education/Global%20Citizens hip/education_for_global_citizenship_a_guide_for_schools.ashx (accessed 5 November 2018).

Oxley, L. and Morris, P. (2013), 'Global citizenship: A typology for distinguishing its multiple conceptions', *British Journal of Educational Studies*, 61(3), 301–25.

Plantan, F. (2004), 'The university as site of citizenship', in S. Bergan (ed.), *The university as res publica*. Strasbourg: Council of Europe Publishing, 83–128.

Rapoport, A. (2009), 'A forgotten concept: Global citizenship education and state social studies standards', *Journal of Social Studies Research*, 33(1), 91–112.

Reynolds, R. (2015), 'One size fits all? Global education for different educational audiences', in R. Reynolds, D. Bradbery, J. Brown, K. Carroll, D. Donnelly, K. Ferguson-Patrick and S. Macqueen (eds), *Contesting and Constructing International Perspectives in Global Education*, Rotterdam: Sense Publishers, 27–41.

Reynolds, R., Bradbey, D., Brown, J., Carroll, K., Donnelly, D., Ferguson, P. and Macqueen, S. (2015), *Introduction: Contesting and Constructing International Perspectives in Global Education*, Rotterdam: Sense Publishers.

Said, E. W. (1989), 'Representing the colonized: Anthropology's interlocutors', *Critical Enquiry*, 15(2), Winter, 205–25.

Shizha, E. (2013), 'Reclaiming our indigenous voices: The problem with postcolonial Sub-Saharan African School Curriculum', *Journal of Indigenous Social Development*, 2(1), 1–18.

Siganke, A. T. (2011), 'Citizenship and citizenship education: A critical discourse analysis of the Zimbabwe Presidential Commission Report', *Education, Citizenship and Social Justice*, 6(1), 69–86.

Skinner, A., Blum, N. and Bourn, D. (2013), 'Development education and education in international development policy: Raising quality through critical pedagogy and global skills', *International Development Policy*, 5(2), 89–103.

Smith, S. N. and Fairman, D. (2005), 'The integration of conflict resolution into the high school curriculum: The example of workable peace', in N. Noddings (ed.), *Educating Citizens for Global Awareness*, New York: Teachers College Press, 40–56.

Swanson, D. M. (2007), 'Ubuntu: An African contribution to (re) search for/with a "humble togetherness"'. *Journal of Contemporary Issues in Education*, 2(2), 53–67.

Swanson, D. M. (2015), 'Ubuntu, Indigeneity and an Ethic for Decolonising Global Citizenship', in Ali A. Abdi, L. Shultz and T. Pillay (eds), *Decolonising Global Citizenship Education*, Rotterdam: Sense Publishers, 27–38.

Torres, C. A. (2017), *Theoretical and Empirical Foundations of Critical Global Citizenship Education*, New York and London: Routledge.

UNESCO (United Nations Educational, Scientific and Cultural Organization) (2014), *Global Citizenship Education: Preparing Learners for the Challenges of the 21st Century*, Paris: UNESCO. Available at http://www.eunec.eu/sites/www.eunec.eu/files/attachment/files/global_citizenship_education_report.. pdf (accessed 10 June 2018).

UNESCO (United Nations Educational, Scientific and Cultural Organization) (2015), *Global Citizenship Education: Topics and Learning Objectives*, Paris: UNESCO. Available at http://www.skoly-unesco. cz/wp-content/uploads/Global-Citizenship-Education-Topics-and-Learning-Objectives.pdf (accessed 11 July 2018).

UNESCO (United Nations Educational, Scientific and Cultural Organization) (2016), Unpacking Sustainable Development Goal 4, UNESCO. Available at https://www.right-to-education.org/sites/ right-to-education.org/files/resource-attachments/Unesco_Guide_to_unpacking_SDG4_2015_En.pdf (accessed 20 May 2018).

UNESCO (United Nations Educational, Scientific and Cultural Organization) (2018), Global Citizenship and the Rise of Nationalist Perspectives, United Nations Educational Scientific and Cultural Organisation. Available at www.unesdoc.unesco.org/images/0026/002654/265414e.pdf (accessed 17 September 2018).

Woolman, D. C. (2003), 'Education for social integration and civic stability in Sub-Saharan Africa: A foundation for national progress in the global economy?', *World Studies in Education*, 4(2), 29–51.

Quaynor, L. (2015), '"I do not have the means to speak": Educating youth for citizenship in post-conflict Liberia', *Journal of Peace Education*, 12(1), 15–36.

Quist, H. O. (2001), 'Cultural Issues in Secondary Education Development in West Africa: Away from colonial survivals, towards neo-colonial influences?', *Comparative Education*, 37(3), 297–314.

Chapter 25

Characteristics of a Global Learning School

Frances Hunt

Introduction

The purpose of this chapter is to examine what is meant by a 'global learning school' and to identify key characteristics that might help to define it. The term 'global learning school' has been used for some time within global learning circles as a useful shortcut to describe a school that has adopted global learning as a core focus, where global learning is encouraged and embedded throughout the school and where it becomes part of the school identity. But little evidence-based research exists as to whether there is such thing as a global learning school and what one might look like in practice. Bourn (2014a: 33) alludes to a school that has taken their global learning activities to another stage:

> It is where the school has moved to the next level and looked at its engagement in global learning in a more strategic way that one can start to talk about a 'global learning school'.

While other literature provides more of a checklist of attributes that might make up aspects of a global learning school – global curriculum, leadership, planning, teaching about diversity, teamwork, criticality, communication, attitudes and knowledge (Edge, Khamsi and Bourn, 2009; Cotton, 2018; Blackmore, 2014).

It is my aim in this chapter to bring evidence from the Global Learning Programme (GLP) in England to help define what a global learning school might look like, and to identify the common features and key characteristics that emerge from the data collected from a sample of schools at the forefront of global learning delivery in England. The GLP was a five-year national programme running from 2013 to 2018 and had one-third of schools (almost 8,000) in England participating. A key feature of the programme was its focus on peer-led global learning support, with 336 Expert Centres (ECs) being established to provide training and assistance in global learning to networks of local schools. It is these EC schools that provide the evidence-base for this chapter, based on the assumption that a GLP EC could act as a proxy for a 'global learning school'. The research identifies the common factors that identify these ECs as global learning schools and indicates those aspects that set them apart from other schools where global learning is less prevalent. While previous research has looked at global learning in individual and/or small numbers of schools, this is the first time a larger data set has been used to support such analysis.

The chapter draws on evidence from schools in England, so relates to its particular educational context. Global learning does not currently have a strong role in the national curriculum or educational policy in England, although there are a few key policy areas where global themes can be explored (Bourn et al., 2016). Rather, global learning tends to be driven by schools: keen teachers and head teachers who choose to include a global learning agenda within the teaching and learning of their schools in order to enhance the learning experiences of their pupils. In this context schools are often guided and supported by external initiatives, such as those offered by the GLP. The GLP was exceptional in that it was a national programme of support to schools funded by the British government, which offered global learning a legitimacy in schools and resulting in a greater number of schools being recruited than previous initiatives. With the ending of the GLP, the Connecting Classrooms through Global Learning Programme looks to take the success of the GLP forward as the British government's follow-up programme for schools[1].

In this chapter I initially provide further information about the GLP and the data on which this chapter is based. Then using a focus on literature and evidence from the GLP, I identify eight attributes that characterize a global learning school. I finish with discussion on points raised and suggestions for further research.

GLP and methods of data collection

The aim of the GLP was to support teachers to deliver effective teaching and learning about development and global issues at Key Stages 2 and 3 (pupils aged seven to fourteen). The premise being that teachers who are more confident and able in global learning would adapt teaching and encourage whole school change. As a result much of the focus of the GLP was on developing the knowledge, skills and confidence of teachers to support global learning in their schools.

A network model was adopted as it provided local support to teachers from peers with experience and/or expertise in this area – and provided ECs with the opportunity to take their learning further into the community. Through the network model ECs acted as hubs to recruit and support teachers in local GLP 'Partner Schools'. Each EC was expected to recruit between fifteen and twenty-three local partner schools, though smaller and larger networks also exist. The Lead Coordinator attended a two-day EC training session and they were expected to deliver eight training sessions to their partner schools over a period of eighteen months. ECs were supported by GLP Local Advisors and had access to external continuing professional development (CPD) and could take part in the GLP Lead Practitioner training programme.

This chapter draws on findings from three main sources from the GLP:

- The GLP Whole School Audit is an online survey tool which maps against the progression framework of the GLP Whole School Framework (Hunt and King, 2013; King, Hunt and Hopkin, 2013; Hunt and King, 2015). The focus of analysis is on data from ECs, in particular where their responses differ from those of partner schools as this data, I suggest, is indicative of that of a 'global learning school'. (For further analysis and actual data, see (Hunt and Cara, 2018b; Hunt and Cara, 2018a).)

---

[1] https://connecting-classrooms.britishcouncil.org

- Baseline and impact interviews took place in eight GLP ECs with school leaders, teachers and pupils.
- The GLP Innovation Fund, which supported teacher-led research, produced a number of useful findings which I draw on (Simpson, 2018; Simpson, 2016; Cotton, 2018; Alcock and Ramirez Barker, 2016; Lewis, 2016; Heuberger, 2014; Yates, 2018; Pendry, 2018).

The characteristics presented are evidence-based, but do not suggest a rigid and prescriptive account of a global learning school. Schools differ in their contexts, experiences and relationships, meaning each global learning school will have its own story (ies), of which this chapter attempts to draw some of these together. While there are other factors associated with increased global learning in schools (e.g. higher school inspection ratings and schools serving more affluent communities (Hunt and Cara, 2018b)), as these are not in necessary characteristics of a global learning school, they have not been included. So, on this basis, drawing on evidence from GLP ECs, the chapter responds to the question:

- What are the key characteristics of a global learning school?

Characteristics of the global learning school

Supportive leadership and vision

School leaders' educational values, strategic intelligence and leadership strategies shape the school and classroom processes and practices (Day et al., 2009), which suggests that a global learning school needs a leader who is able to champion global learning: someone with personal values to support a global ethos and the strategic drive and skill to see this put into action.

Research indicates that school leadership that provides a school vision and supports a global ethos is critical for the success of global learning on any scale (Coe, 2007; Bourn et al., 2016; Hunt, 2012). In a global learning school, leaders understand the value in global learning and the benefits this brings to pupils' ability to navigate complex global issues and can use effective planning to embed a school vision, preparing pupils for a global world. Supportive leadership are important not only in terms of setting the tone for global learning in the school but for ensuring continuity of global learning champion(s) (Bourn et al., 2016). Leaders can determine the extent to which the school engages with external global learning providers and supports the professional development of teachers.

Evidence from the GLP supports the importance of leadership for the global school (Cotton, 2018; Hunt, 2018; Alcock and Ramirez Barker, 2016). This sees global learning in many GLP schools embedded within the school vision and translated into school development plans and pupil learning outcomes. It also sees supportive heads ensuring a range of staff attend training on global learning, which means expertise is not only concentrated in one or two champions. Also heads in leading global learning schools allocate time to key staff to drive engagement within the school and time for curriculum mapping to pull in. Indeed, school leaders in global learning schools are able to identify global learning as a priority and set in place measures to realize this.

One school leader describes aspects of this process:

> Global Schools is written into the development plan ... we've literally mapped out the whole year of what's happening ... we've put in dedicated staff meetings for ... global schools so that we can develop some more, what I want to be seeing as more sustainable ways of bringing Global Schools into the curriculum. (head teacher, Expert Centre (EC) primary school)

Alcock and Ramirez Barker (2016) in particular provide an example of a school leader in a GLP EC using global learning as a mechanism to raise standards in writing within the school after a 'requires improvement' Ofsted[2] inspection. Here:

> The head teacher was keen to find ways to identify that global learning could be used and seen to contribute towards raising standards within a core curriculum area as well as develop the breadth and balance of the curriculum and support the school's ethos. ... It was decided that [using Development Education (DE) methodologies to support improvement in writing] would be a priority within the school by senior leadership. (2016: 7)

It was the drive and vision of the head teacher who ensured all staff were trained in global learning methodologies and this was infused into the writing curriculum across the school. She had the foresight to see that resulting changes to pedagogy could lead to enhanced pupil progress. Alcock and Ramirez Barker (2016: 78) state:

> Senior leadership and vision are essential to ensure progress with this type of intervention, where global learning falls outside of the current conceived agenda for raising standards.

In another GLP Innovation Fund report, Cotton (2018) notes the importance of school leaders in ensuring the sustainability of global learning in schools, with strong leadership as well as support from the governing body, seen as key. In global learning schools, not only do school leaders drive global learning but they also foster it across the whole school, meaning the global momentum can remain, even if key staff leave:

> [The head teacher has] told me ... that if I left tomorrow (global learning) wouldn't go with me now, because it's now part of the school and it's part of children's lives. (lead coordinator, EC primary school)

Global learning champion

All global learning schools have a global learning champion or champions, whether it is a school leader, a trusted member of teaching staff or a group of global enthusiasts. We know from previous research that global learning champions tend to have been educators for a period of time, often have a subject specialism in geography, history, personal/social or religious education and many have personal experience travelling or living abroad for periods of time (Hunt, 2012). Bourn et al. (2016) state that

---

[2]   Ofsted is the Office for Standards in Education, Children's Services and Skills. They inspect services providing education and skills for learners of all ages and give each school a rating.

support for global learning and sustainability has … relied heavily for its successful implementation and influence in schools on individual champions, teachers who are passionate, committed and enthusiastic about these issues.

Individual champions can be particularly important where there is a lack of policy support for global learning, such as the case in England. However, the emphasis on individual champions can lead to a lack of engagement from the school as a whole and if an enthusiastic teacher moves on, the involvement in global and sustainability themes within the school can disappear.

Evidence from the GLP supports the importance of global learning champions to the drive and success of global learning schools (Hunt, 2018; Cotton, 2018). Each EC had a member of staff leading global learning within the school, driving the engagement of staff and helping to embed global learning within the curriculum. In some instances that staff member becomes a symbol for or reminder of global learning, by their mere presence.

Everything started with me driving it and me being kind of the face of global learning. (lead coordinator, EC primary school)

When we see her …, (we know she's) coming in to support (global learning activities), which is brilliant. (head teacher, EC primary school)

Similarly, the global learning champion can fulfil the wishes of school leadership and also serve as a reminder to them, who may be busy with a range of priorities, to back global learning:

If you've got a (global learning) zealot they're always making it a priority you know. (head teacher, EC secondary school)

Whole school approach

Evidence suggests a global learning school operates (or is working towards) a whole school approach to global learning (Hunt and King, 2015; Edge, Khamsi and Bourn, 2009). The aim being that global learning is part of a school vision, a strategic approach to teaching and learning that maps across the whole school, and not a series of isolated or piecemeal interventions. A whole school approach suits global learning, in that it can be

delivered across a variety of both formal and informal learning spaces, and involve a range of stakeholders across the school and its community. Global learning also supports the development of wider values and skills, which can connect to key aspects of a school's ethos and the wider purpose or vision of a school. (Hunt and King, 2015: 3)

In engaging with whole school approaches a global learning school might nurture global learning as a lived, active experience (Shallcross and Robinson, 2007), where it is integrated into all aspects of the school,[3] rather than something that is solely taught within lessons. Indeed, global

---

[3] For example, outside of the classroom, these learning spaces might include school assemblies, the school councils, school displays and speakers brought in to talk to pupils.

learning has been most effective where it has become part of the broader curriculum and ethos of the school (Hunt, 2012).

The GLP advocated a whole school approach to global learning as imagined through its Whole School Framework (King, Hunt and Hopkin, 2013), where twelve categories for global learning were identified, including

- pupils' knowledge and awareness of global issues;
- teachers knowledge and confidence to teach global learning;
- how school leadership and vision supported global learning;
- how the school supported values such as fairness, empathy and tolerance;
- the extent to which the school supported staff CPD on global issues and
- global learning within the curriculum.

Evidence from the GLP shows the importance of whole school approaches to global learning schools. GLP ECs have higher levels of global learning across all whole school categories, meaning in these leading schools global learning is more embedded across the whole school. For many global learning schools this means global learning is embedded within the school ethos, values and purpose of the school, something that binds the school together and provides the focus. One head teacher explains this:

> It is just a thread that's continual throughout all the children's learning. So we don't say, we're going to do some global learning now. It's sort of ... it's just there all the time with links to it. (head teacher, EC primary)

Global learning in teaching and learning

Incorporating global learning within the formal and informal curriculum is an important part of the global learning school (Hunt, 2012; Bourn et al., 2016; Cotton, 2018; Edge, Khamsi and Bourn, 2009). In order to do this global aspects can be mapped and planned into the curriculum or global learning subject guides can be used to support inclusion and the GLP provided support to schools to embed global learning into the formal curriculum through subject guides.

Evidence from the GLP shows the importance of embedding global learning in the curriculum for global learning schools. It shows ECs integrating global learning into a range of subject or topic areas. While schools embarking on a global learning journey might focus their activities in geography, this focus often expands to history, religious education and some sort of personal social learning as they embed further. While schools tend to identify fewer curriculum links with core subjects, such as mathematics, reading and writing (Hunt and Cara, 2018b; Hunt and Cara, 2015), research from two EC leads challenges this assumption. Alcock and Ramirez Barker (2016) provide an account where the focus of global learning is on improving writing in a primary school. Pendry (2018) advocates for the inclusion of global data in mathematics as a way of engaging and inspiring teachers and pupils, as well as raising levels of participation from more reluctant mathematicians.

There is evidence that some global learning schools take global learning curriculum mapping very seriously. Various accounts focus on school staff taking time to identify where best to include global aspects, often in time for the new school year. Indeed, Hallam (2017), a former head teacher and EC lead, produced a written account of how primary and secondary schools can embed the UN Sustainable Development Goals within the curriculum. Another head teacher talks about the need for a sustainable global learning curriculum drawn together by a 'golden thread' which pulls the curriculum together, focuses school activities and shapes the ethos:

> If we just keep doing projects in their own right – which is lovely and great – we won't get that ... (head teacher, EC primary school)

In other schools, global learning is the driver that shapes what pupils learn across subject areas and learning spaces:

> We have fully embraced global learning across our curriculum with global learning sessions every day as well as links in whole school and assembly themes. It has vastly increased the children's awareness of the world around them and given them a much more nuanced view of people and places around the world away from the usual stereotypes. (lead coordinator, EC primary school)

A key focus of teaching and learning in global learning schools is supporting pupils to see links between the local and the global (and vice versa), and how communities across the world are interconnected, to not only have an understanding of the wider world but to identify themselves within the context of that world and being to explore the part they can and might play within it.

> We use it across the curriculum to bring real life examples and to give children a global perspective. It helps the children see that they are connected with people across the world, that our actions affect other people. (lead coordinator, primary school)

> Global learning enables our children to look beyond their streets and gives them a better understanding of the world beyond and their role in making it better. (lead coordinator, primary school)

Moving towards a pedagogical framework for global learning

Various research notes the importance of appropriate pedagogic approaches to support global learning (Simpson, 2018; Bourn, 2014b; Bourn, 2014d; Miller et al., 2012; Bourn et al., 2016; Blackmore, 2016; Yates, 2018), but what this means in practice varies. For example, Bourn provides a number of accounts on the importance of pedagogy (e.g. Bourn et al., 2016; Bourn, 2011; Bourn, 2014b; Bourn, 2014d) in global learning. He recognizes the role of power, inequalities, identity and the opportunity for learning to support a process of transformation. Bourn et al. (2016: 19) describe the need for many teachers to shift their pedagogical thinking:

> Whilst recognising increasing children's knowledge is important, it is how this knowledge is presented to, as well as understood and received by learners that makes a distinctive area of learning. Above all it means recognising that the learners' own experience, outlook and socio-cultural background need to be recognised and responded to as part of the pedagogical process

They describe initiatives that make the global relevant to the lives of pupils, recognizing different perspectives, voices and views of the world. They also recognize the growing importance of approaches such as Philosophy for Children (P4C)[4] in supporting active participation and discussion of pupils (Bourn et al., 2016).

In other literature, Blackmore (2016) develops a pedagogical framework for global citizenship education which includes aspects of critical thinking, dialogue, reflection and responsible being/action (transformation). Through examples based on classroom observations, she shows how classroom activities can encourage pupils' to question, discuss, think, explain, work out a response and identify potential action. Simpson (2018), for example, describes a participatory pedagogy framework which shifts more traditional classroom hierarchies, whereby equality, equity and co-agency are promoted within relationships.

So, while the actual approach taken may differ, a key characteristic of a global learning school is that educators have adopted pedagogical approaches that support global learning. This means offering opportunities for pupil voice, critical engagement and self-reflection and giving pupils space to grapple with different ideas, where there may not be just one answer and enabling them to engage with complexity.

Evidence from the GLP shows the importance of pedagogy to the global learning school, with staff in ECs more likely to adopt pedagogic approaches (e.g. critical thinking, ethical enquiry or developing multiple perspectives) which support global learning. In many instances staff in global learning schools describe using approaches which support pupil voice and critical engagement in particular. So, for example, there is focus in their accounts on group work, discussions and debates.

In global learning schools there is a particular emphasis on teachers' supporting the critical engagement of pupils and opening them up to different perspectives or viewpoints. Staff indicate the usefulness of approaches such as school linking and P4C to challenge pupils' perceptions, open them up to new alternatives and get them to see things from different perspectives (Yates, 2018; Lewis, 2016). Indeed, there is evidence that approaches such as P4C have had considerable influence on teaching and learning in global learning schools, with P4C the most attended training course on the GLP (Bentall, 2019). This is partly because of the shared approaches and commonalities between the two approaches which seem to add depth to both. In her description of P4C, EC lead Yates (2018) suggests an emphasis on

> the community critically and creatively examining ... their ideas and opinions, with a helpful focus on agreement and disagreement ... (with) children (learning) to think for themselves through thinking with others.

She also describes clear links between global learning and P4C, where for example, schools are able to use global learning materials as a stimulus for P4C; the participatory methodology of P4C aligns with that of global learning and with regular practice there is a transformational dimension to P4C, that can lead to a change in thinking and actions, similar to global learning.

---

[4] Philosophy for Children is an enquiry-based approach to unlock children's learning through the exploration of ideas. A stimulus is shared with a group of children who with the help of a trainer engage with philosophical questions about the stimulus. P4C aims to help children's thinking, communication skills and boosts their self-esteem.

The importance of P4C to global learning is evidenced in a number of ways, for example:

> When we first introduced these debates some of the children could be almost ... aggressive towards each other. Some of the younger children say things like, well my mum thinks this so I'm going to say this ... quite closed opinions and almost trying to put each other down. ... And so (P4C) has completely changed their attitudes towards each other when you're talking about these issues. (teacher, primary school)

Engaging with external providers and award programmes

To support a whole school approach global learning schools are often involved in global learning initiatives where support is given to the school by external providers[5] (Edge, Khamsi and Bourn, 2009). This might involve external providers working directly with children, training teachers or working with the school to enhance whole school approaches to global learning.

Research from the GLP shows the important role external providers can play in the global learning school, with ECs tending to engage with a range of external providers. Indeed, analysis shows schools working with one or more global learning external providers have higher levels of global learning across the whole school. Staff in these schools acknowledge the important role external providers can offer them on their journey (Cotton, 2018; Alcock and Ramirez Barker, 2016) and how they can provide the building blocks for further global engagement. One teacher describes how taking part in a rights-based awards programme has enhanced their global awareness:

> I think that's given us a really good foundation. ... I think staff are tuned into global issues and becoming a global citizen and what that means. I think they're a bit more tuned in than maybe some other schools. (lead coordinator, EC primary school)

In another example, Alcock and Ramirez Barker (2016) suggest that an external provider was able to provide specific expertise to enhance training on their curriculum project, which included a wide knowledge of DE frameworks, resources and methodologies.

Staff development and confidence

Evidence suggests the importance of staff training to embed global learning in schools (Bentall and Hunt, 2018; Bourn et al., 2016; Bourn, Hunt and Bamber, 2017). Not only does training support the development of knowledge and skills, it helps develop teachers' confidence to engage in global issues, engage with strategies to incorporate these into teaching. Specifically within global learning there is a focus on teachers having the space to explore their values and attitudes towards global issues and to critically self-reflect and examine their own beliefs. Where global learning training might be transformative, a critical assessment of teachers' existing beliefs and frames of reference may be required (Bentall, 2019; Mezirow, 2009).

---

[5] This might include NGOs, local global learning providers and/or involvement in global learning awards programmes or school partnerships.

Evidence from the GLP shows the importance of staff training and development to the global learning school. Evidence indicates that EC staff are more likely to be trained in an aspect of global learning, either through internal staff training or external CPD. They are more confident in their ability to teach global issues and train other teachers to do so. Evidence shows EC teachers involved in the GLP have built their confidence and ability to lead other teachers to support global learning and to develop an enriched global focus within their own school. Moreover, analysis shows us that external CPD training and peer-led network training has positively influenced the quality and quantity of global learning in schools.

There is a focus in global schools to ensure that a range of staff are trained in aspects of global learning, so not just relying on one champion or leader to run everything. For example, on the GLP there was a drive in many ECs to use the network training sessions developed for staff in other local schools, to train in-house staff.

> We thought by the end of the course we'll be able to get probably every teacher and every teacher assistant (TA) involved in our training. (head teacher, EC primary school)

There is also evidence that suggests that staff in global learning schools, often the global learning champions, have through training reflected on their own ideas and practices and gained confidence to critically engage pupils to think more deeply about global issues:

> [Expert Centre training included] engaging in discussions with other colleagues and being presented with … different materials, different perspectives. [It] was also really useful because it questions your practices, improves your practice, it changes your methods and the resources that you use. And I feel that was really, really useful. (lead coordinator, EC primary school)

> I've been on so many global learning workshops, or similar types of events now, it kind of … I feel really confident in doing things like that. Whereas other teachers obviously haven't had that experience, so they might come to a point where they think, well that's it now; we've covered it. When this is kind of where you really want to get into it and have those discussions and challenge [pupils] and what do you think about this? Go a bit deeper. (lead coordinator, EC primary school)

Moving from charity to social justice

Adopting a critical social justice approach to action is important to global learning schools and one of the core goals of the GLP was to support schools to move from charity to social justice. Many schools start their global learning engagement by introducing fundraising for overseas causes, but this has been critiqued (Tallon et al., 2016; Bourn, 2014c), as it has the

> potential to distort people's perceptions of other countries or peoples, particularly of those in the 'South'. (Simpson, 2016: 2)

In her research for the GLP Simpson (2016) describes an action research project she carried out in a school to support teachers to make the move away from a charitable perspective. Here she describes what this might mean:

> If we consider a social justice mentality in relation to a charity mentality, the main difference is that we remove the smokescreen of 'sanctioned ignorance'. By engaging in critical reflections

on local and global injustices, especially from the perspectives of others, we begin to disrupt those 'myths' about our relationship with the global 'South'. (Simpson, 2016: 2)

A social justice approach requires teachers (and pupils) to be critically engaged, committed to asking questions about power and justice and inequality. It can be uncomfortable, challenging and transformational. It can also produce a range of positive outcomes such as challenging stereotypes, promoting equality on a personal level or affecting changes within society on a social level (Simpson, 2016). A social justice approach requires time and effort, over and above that of most fundraising initiatives.

As (Simpson, 2016) indicates, the path towards a social justice approach in global learning schools can be challenging, particularly as it requires shifting the practices and mindsets of teachers (and pupils). Many teachers, particularly those with younger pupils, shy away from critical and controversial engagements (Hunt, 2012). However, there is evidence from global learning schools of the desire and shift towards a social justice approach, regardless of how difficult this is to achieve:

> I don't think we're quite there yet. I mean I'm very aware of it and that is definitely one of the great aims, to get there. But I don't think we're there yet ... but we are on our way to move to social justice. (lead coordinator, EC primary school)

> And we are moving away from charity work, which we do a lot of as a Catholic school, but trying to do more campaigning, so being proactive with things like writing to the prime-minister, our local Member of Parliament. (lead coordinator, EC primary school)

Discussion and conclusion

This chapter has focused on identifying characteristics that make up a global learning school by using GLP data to imagine a global learning school, combined with an awareness of existing literature. It shows how global learning schools are able to embrace a range of approaches and attributes in order to deliver a global experience, no matter where the school is located. For many global learning schools, 'being global' is a driving force of the school's identity.

Table 25.1 provides a summary of the features identified in this chapter as characteristics of a global learning school.

How this works in practice and the interplay between the different elements differs between schools. Case study examples of good practice from the GLP[6] show a variety of approaches and drivers, such as the global goals, values and rights-based education and critical approaches to engagement (for other examples of this, see Bourn et al., 2016) and the characteristics identified in a global school are able to work with these approaches.

Schools are fluid and moving spaces, each comprising of unique experiences, contexts and relationships. With this in mind I aim not to offer a fixed and prescriptive account of what a

---

[6]   https://files.globaldimension.org.uk/wp-content/uploads/2019/02/12154601/Case-studies-and-films
      -from-schools.pdf

Table 25.1 Global Learning School Characteristics

Global learning school characteristics	Examples in practice
Supportive leadership and vision	• School leader's personal values embody global learning. • School leader prioritizes global learning in strategic planning of school, for example, curriculum, staff training and workload allocations. • School governors supportive of global learning. • School vision includes global learning and plans are in place to achieve this vision on a sustainable basis.
Global learning champion(s)	• One or more global learning champions drive global learning engagement within the school. • Global learning champions feel confident to train others in this approach. They are given support and time to drive engagement.
Whole school approach	• School adopts a whole school approach to global learning, whereby global learning is present regularly across the school rather than piecemeal and isolated interventions. • Whole school approach supports global learning as a lived experience.
Global learning in teaching and learning	• Global learning included in a range of subject and topic areas. • Schools move away from concentrating all global learning in geography, to include other subject areas. • Pupils learn about interdependence and how they play a part in global world.
Pedagogical framework for global learning	• Teachers adopt pedagogical approaches that support global learning: offering opportunities for pupil voice, critical engagement and self-reflection. • Pupils have safe spaces to engage with different ideas and engage with complexity. • Pupils have a voice within the school.
Engaging with external providers	• Global learning support provided to school by external providers such as non-governmental organizations (NGOs). • External providers work directly with pupils, train teachers or work to enhance whole school approaches to global learning.
Staff development and confidence	• Most or all staff have participated in activities to develop their confidence using global activities and/or pedagogical approaches. • Teachers have space to explore their values and attitudes towards global issues and to critically self-reflect and examine their own beliefs. • Teachers confident to introduce global aspects into teaching and learning.
Moving from charity to social justice	• Forms of action draw on social justice approaches, with teachers and pupils critically engage with issues, asking questions about power, justice and inequality.

global learning school might look like, rather I suggest a range of attributes and approaches that analysis indicates might be present in a school that has chosen to embrace global learning. This might serve as a guide to schools who are possibly looking to enhance their own global learning. Many schools talk about global learning as a journey (Cotton, 2018; Hunt and Cara, 2020 forthcoming); if their aim is to move towards embedding global learning, then I hope this account might support schools looking to do so.

From a research perspective, while this account locates a global learning school clearly in an English context, it would be interesting to understand how the notion of a global learning school translates into other contexts. Are there similarities between how schools approach global learning in schools in England and elsewhere, or is the global learning school more context-specific? Ultimately, is it possible to refine these understandings of what a global learning school might look like, based on evidence from elsewhere?

This account has taken on Bourn's (2014a) use of the term 'global learning school' and explored what a school that has moved to the 'next level' and approached global learning strategically might look like. The development of global learning schools on such a scale in England has been made possible because motivated educators have found support in initiatives such as the GLP, where whole school approaches, staff development and critical engagement were key drivers. It is crucial that funding of this type continues to reach schools in order to sustain engagement and inspire the next generation of global learning schools.

Bibliography

Alcock, H. L. and Ramirez Barker, L. (2016) Can global learning raise standards within pupils' writing in the primary phase? DERC Research Paper no. 16. London: UCL Institute of Education.

Bentall, C. (2019) Continuing professional development of teachers in global learning: What works? In Bourn, D. (ed.), *Bloomsbury Handbook on Global Education and Learning*. London: Bloomsbury.

Bentall, C. and Hunt, F. (2018) Teachers and the GLP in England: Engagement and impact. In *DERC Seminar Series Presentation*, 20 November 2018. London: UCL Institute of Education.

Blackmore, C. (2014) *The Opportunities and Challenges for a Critical Global Citizenship Education in One English Secondary School*. Bath: University of Bath.

Blackmore, C. (2016) Towards a pedagogical framework for global citizenship education. *International Journal of Development Education and Global Learning* 8: 39–56.

Bourn, D. (2011) Discourses and practices around development education: From learning about development to critical global pedagogy. *Policy & Practice-A Development Education Review* 13: 11–29.

Bourn, D. (2014a) School linking and global learning – teacher reflections. DERC Research Papers no. 12. London: IOE.

Bourn, D. (2014b) *The Theory and Practice of Development Education: A Pedagogy for Global Social Justice*. Abingdon: Routledge.

Bourn, D. (2014c) The Theory and Practice of Global Learning: A think-piece for the Global Learning Programme. DERC Research Paper no. 11. London: Institute of Education.

Bourn, D. (2014d) Typologies of development education: From learning about development to critical global pedagogy, in McCloskey S. (ed.), *Development Education in Policy and Practice*, London: Palgrave, 47–64.

Bourn, D., Hunt, F. and Bamber, P. (2017) A review of education for sustainable development and global citizenship education in teacher education. *GEM Background Paper*. Paris: UNESCO.

Bourn, D., Hunt, F., Blum, N., et al. (2016) *Primary Education for Global Learning and Sustainability*. Cambridge: Cambridge Primary Review Trust.

Coe, J. (2007) Oxfam-funded project: 'Aiming High through Education for Global Citizenship'. Oxfam and CDEC.

Cotton, C. (2018) A study exploring the sustainability of global learning in schools. *GLP Innovation Fund no. 7*. London: GLP.

Day, C., Sammons, P., Hopkins, D., et al. (2009) *The Impact of School Leadership on Pupil Outcomes Final Report*. Nottingham: University of Nottingham.

Edge, K., Khamsi, K. and Bourn, D. (2009) *Exploring the Global Dimension in Secondary Schools*. London: IOE.

Hallam, J. (2017) Possible and practical ways to ensure that the Sustainable Development Goals (SDGs) are embedded in the school curriculum and seen as relevant. Unpublished.

Heuberger, M. (2014) 'Worldmindedness' and Development Education: A Teacher Voice. GLP Innovation Fund Report no. 1. London: GLP.

Hunt, F. (2012) Global Learning in Primary Schools in England: Practices and Impacts. DERC Research Paper no. 9. London: Institute of Education.

Hunt, F. (2018) Global learning programme: Emerging research findings. *National Network*. London: GLP.

Hunt, F. and Cara, O. (2015) *Global Learning in England: Baseline Analysis of the Global Learning Programme Whole School Audit 2013–14*. London: GLP.

Hunt, F. and Cara, O. (2018a) Global Learning Programme in England 2013–8: Whole School Audit initial impact analysis. Unpublished research findings. London: GLP.

Hunt, F. and Cara, O. (2018b) Global Learning Programme Whole School Audit 2013–18: Initial baseline analysis. Unpublished research findings. London: GLP.

Hunt, F. and Cara, O. (2020 forthcoming) *Global Learning in England: Baseline Evidence from the Global Learning Programme 2013–2018*. London: UCL Institute of Education.

Hunt, F. and King, R. P. (2013) *Global Learning Programme England: Whole School Audit*. London: GLP-E.

Hunt, F. and King, R. P. (2015) Supporting whole school approaches to global learning: Focusing learning and mapping impact. DERC Research Paper no. 13. London: DERC, IOE.

King, R. P., Hunt, F. and Hopkin, J. (2013) *GLP Whole School Framework*. London: GLP.

Lewis, M. (2016) A study of a focused, critical approach to pupils' images and perceptions of Africa. GLP Innovation Fund Research Paper no. 3. London: GLP.

Mezirow, J. (2009) An overview of transformative learning. In Illeris, K. (ed.), *Contemporary Theories of Learning*. London: Routledge, 90–105.

Miller, G., Bowes, E., Bourn, D., et al. (2012) Learning about development at A-Level: A study of the impact of the world development A-level on young people's understanding of international development. DERC Research Paper no. 7. London: IOE.

Pendry, V. (2018) *Using Global Data in Primary Mathematics*. London: UCL Institute of Education.

Shallcross, T. and Robinson, J. (2007) Sustainability education, whole school approaches, and communities of action. In Reid, A., Jensen, B. B., Nikel, J., et al. (eds), *Participation and Learning*. Dordrecht: Springer, 299–320.

Simpson J. (2016) *A Study to Investigate, Explore and Identify Successful 'Interventions' to Support Teachers in a Transformative Move from a Charity Mentality to a Social Justice Mentality*. London: UCL Institute of Education.

Simpson, J. (2018) Participatory pedagogy in practice: Using effective participatory pedagogy in classroom practice to enhance pupil voice and educational engagement. *GLP Innovation Fund no. 5*. London: GLP.

Tallon, R., Milligan, A. and Wood, B. (2016) Moving beyond fundraising and into ... What? Youth transitions into higher education and citizenship identity formation. *Policy and Practice: A Development Education Review* 22: 96–109.

Yates, J. (2018) How can the Philosopher's Backpack enrich critical global thinking? GLP Innovation Fund Report no. 6. London: GLP.Notes

Chapter 26

Continuing Professional Development of Teachers in Global Learning: What Works?

Clare Bentall

Introduction

Since the 1960s, non-governmental organizations (NGOs) have been involved in the implementation of development education (DE) and global learning within schools: providing resources, delivering lessons and activities for pupils and in providing continuing professional development (CPD) for teachers (Mundy and Manion 2008; Tallon and Milligan 2018; Tarozzi and Inguaggiato 2018). Where there is varying political support for global education (GE), and little coverage in pre-service teaching training, such CPD remains crucial in supporting teachers. However, there have been concerns about the levels of provision and quality of CPD for global learning in formal education (DEF and DEEEP 2009). There are also concerns about the distinction between advocacy and education with externally provided CPD (Bourn et al. 2016). There is also evidence, however, that it can be effective. Simpson's (2017) and Cusack and Rush's (2010) analyses of certain interventions illustrate that teachers do develop when provided with the opportunity. McCarthy and Gannon's (2016) evaluation of an Irish DE programme also demonstrates that CPD needs to be included in support for schools. There are also articles on pre-service teacher training (e.g. Dariji and Lang-Wojtasik 2014; Kirkwood-Tucker, Morris and Lieberman 2011; Scoffham 2014), on the competencies teachers and educators need, which have implications for all teacher development (Büker and Schell-Straub 2017; Scheunpflug 2011). This literature all points to the potential for CPD for global learning, though detailed evidence of what makes it effective is limited.

In this chapter, I contribute to addressing this gap this by analysing the experience of teachers and schools engaging with externally provided CPD as part of the Global Learning Programme (2013–18) in England (GLP-E). First, I identify key characteristics of effective CPD for global learning. 'Global learning' is the current term used to refer to GE in the UK, and I define it briefly in the literature discussion. Then I outline the approaches to CPD within GLP-E, and to the data collection and analysis. In discussing the findings, I argue that CPD for global learning can inspire teachers to a renewed commitment to teaching through the impact on pupils' learning. With the support of external expertise, it can meet teachers' needs to explore and develop pedagogical approaches, and through collaborative models and suitable follow-up, it can support more sustained engagement with global learning. But this is also contingent on support being available for schools and CPD providers to develop relevant courses that respond to teacher and pupil needs.

Effective CPD for global learning

CPD is linked to improved teaching and student learning (see Timperley et al. 2007; Hanushek and Rivkin 2012); therefore, it is reasonable to anticipate that CPD for global learning can have similar outcomes. However, this requires understanding what makes such CPD effective. Before examining the evidence in the literature, CPD and global learning need defining.

Day's (1999:4) definition of CPD sets out the full scope and purpose of CPD:

> Professional development consists of all natural learning experiences and those conscious and planned activities which are intended to be of direct benefit to the individual, group or school and which contribute, through these, to the quality of education in the classroom. It is the process by which, alone and with others, teachers review, renew and extend their commitment as change agents to the moral purposes of teaching; and by which they acquire and develop critically the knowledge, skills and emotional intelligence essential to good professional thinking, planning and practice with children, young people and colleagues through each phase of their teaching lives.

This definition prioritizes teachers' and pupils' learning (see Avalos 2011; Beijaard et al. 2007, Murphy and De Paor 2017, Postholm 2012, Vescio et al. 2008) and rejects teacher-as-technician delivery models (Dadds 2014) and deficit approaches (Hardy and Rönnerman 2011).

Global learning has many definitions (see Bourn 2012). In this chapter I understand it to be learning that prepares people for life in a globalized world, that challenges them engage in and understand their personal responsibility for global social justice (Scheunpflug 2008). Content and approaches vary. However, there is usually a focus on global issues, learners' experiences of these in relation to their local contexts and critical exploration of development, poverty and power relationships globally (Foghani-Arani and Hartmeyer 2010). This is accompanied by the development of associated skills and attitudes, such as critical thinking, and a pedagogical approach that prioritizes multiple perspectives and participatory activities. Global learning demands a move from awareness of issues to action for a better world (Andreotti 2010; Asbrand 2008). The theory underpinning the GLP's approach also emphasized a focus on social justice, reflection and dialogue, understanding power globally and developing a 'global outlook' (Bourn 2014: 5).

Clearly an important starting point for any CPD, but particularly CPD for global learning – an area which cuts across subject disciplines and rarely is the basis for teachers' initial qualifications – is the teachers' subject knowledge (see Cordingley et al. 2015). If teachers are to support pupils' learning about global issues, they need to enhance their own knowledge, and explore their values and attitudes towards those global issues (Scheunpflug 2011). This knowledge can come from external sources, such as CPD providers, research evidence or teachers' reflection on practice and collaboration with peers (Cochran-Smith and Lytle 1999).

Global learning has a strong values base, a focus on social justice, and requires critical self-examination on attitudes, values and beliefs. For teachers to help pupils develop a global mindset and characteristics of citizens willing to act for social justice, they need to experience a similar transformation (Andreotti in Bourn 2015; Dariji and Lang-Wojtasik 2014; Scheunpflug 2011). Creating a sense of disjuncture between existing and new understandings is important (Mezirow

2000), so that teachers learn new things that are not congruent with existing understandings, as well as ones that are (Timperley et al 2007). This requires an attitude of inquiry and reflection (Capps et al. 2012; McArdle and Coutts 2010).

CPD should challenge teachers' beliefs (Cordingley et al. 2015). These beliefs are informed by practice, particularly by teachers' experience of changes in their pupils' learning (Guskey 2002), which presents a challenge if teachers have limited experience of global learning. Their beliefs are, therefore, more amenable to change in-service, for example, through CPD (Ofper, Pedder and Lavicza 2011), but they need some experience to reflect on. Time and ongoing support are, therefore, important. Teachers need to be able to learn new approaches, implement, reflect and refine them (Capps et al. 2012), meaning one-off CPD events are likely to be less effective (El-Deghaidy, Mansour and Alshamrani 2015; Opfer and Pedder 2011b).

Teachers also need to develop subject-specific pedagogical knowledge (Cordingley et al. 2015; Shulman 1986). Global learning has a 'commitment to interactive and participatory pedagogies' (Scoffham 2014: 29) with multiple perspectives offered and all voices heard (Bennell 2015). If CPD is most effective when it 'requires teachers to learn in ways that reflect how they should teach pupils' (Opfer and Pedder 2011a: 385), CPD for global learning needs to prioritize the same interaction and participatory approaches with teachers.

An extension of this interaction and participation is the creation of opportunities for genuine collaboration, within or between schools. With collaboration, 'a learning community emerges, the participating teachers are more likely to discuss problems, strategies, and solutions. Change in teaching behaviour then becomes an ongoing, collective responsibility rather than an individual one' (Opfer and Pedder 2011a: 385). Ultimately, CPD for global learning asks teachers to consider what type of world they want for their pupils, and how to help them prepare for it. Collective opportunities to discuss their 'aspirations for their pupils' and develop a shared sense of purpose are therefore crucial (Cordingley et al. 2015:5).

CPD for global learning, with its focus on real-world issues that concern pupils, has the potential to tap into teachers' motivations, in ways other mandated CPD may not. Motivation for CPD is affected by teachers' personal desire to grow, school policy, whether CPD is part of school culture (McMillan et al. 2016) and teachers' orientation towards subject or learner (see de Vries, van de Geift and Jansen 2013). It is also influenced by teachers' agency in the design and implementation of CPD (Mansour et al. 2014). Effective CPD for global learning, therefore, requires collaboration between teachers, schools and external providers as to its form and approach.

To deliver CPD as described above, external providers need a commitment to the principles and approaches to global learning. They need to help teachers make sense of difficult and often controversial topics, present and model appropriate pedagogy. They need to understand teachers' starting points, build relationships with them, understand their school contexts, yet also challenge their existing understandings and beliefs (see Cordingley et al. 2015: 6-7). The use of external expertise is, however, no guarantee of teachers' learning. Facilitators of CPD for global learning need suitable training and the development of relevant competencies (Büker, and Schell-Straub 2017). As Timperley et al. (2007: xxix) conclude, 'Experts need more than knowledge of the content of changes in teaching practice that might make a difference to students; they also need to know how to make the content meaningful to teachers and manageable within the context of teaching practice' and such 'provider pedagogical content knowledge' comes through training and experience.

GLP-E and the UK global learning context

CPD for global learning in the UK started in the 1960s, when international NGOs, such as Oxfam, were working to educate the public on aid and development issues (Harrison 2008). In 1975, the first development education centre (DEC) was set up at Selly Oak college, with the support of the city council and Oxfam. A network of DECs then grew.[1] By 1993, when the Development Education Association was established, there were 230 organizations, campaigning and working in DE and then global learning nationally.[2] Those facilitating CPD for global learning come from a variety of backgrounds, with different levels of training (Büker and Schell-Straub 2017). As in other contexts, UK government funding for global learning in schools comes from the ministry for overseas development (Surian 2001; Tarozzi and Inguaggiato 2018). In 2012, the ministry decided to fund a national global learning programme.

The GLP-E (2013–18) had a focus on pupils aged seven to ten and ten to fourteen (end of primary and beginning of secondary). Its aims were to

- help teachers to encourage children and young people to understand their role in a globally interdependent world and to explore strategies by which they can make it more just and sustainable;
- provide strategies to familiarize pupils with the concepts of interdependence, development, globalization and sustainability;
- enable teachers to move pupils from a charity mentality to a social justice mentality;
- provide strategies for teachers to stimulate critical thinking about global issues both at whole school and at pupil level;
- help schools to promote greater awareness of poverty and sustainability;
- enable schools to explore alternative models of development and sustainability in the classroom.

Schools joined in different cohorts (Waves) for five terms. For each Wave, expert centre (EC) schools (those with more experience of global learning) recruited partner schools (PSs), forming local networks. The ECs, supported by sixteen local and four national advisors, ran CPD sessions for their networks, covering some compulsory and optional topics. In addition, GLP-E offered each school £500 to spend on externally provided CPD, on condition of completing an initial audit of their school's work in global learning (Whole-school audit, WSA1). This involved a self-assessment of their work on global learning using an online tool. This externally provided CPD is the focus of this chapter.

Externally provided CPD

One hundred and nine organizations registered as CPD providers and had courses approved, of which seventy-one had courses booked. The organizations included the network of development

---

[1] see CODEC: http://www.codec.org.uk/
[2] https://www.eldis.org/organisation/A1564

education centres (CODEC), international NGOs, smaller organizations and individual consultants. The approval process involved checking whether courses met GLP-E aims, used appropriate training methods and were run by experienced trainers. Courses, on a wide range of topics, included whole school courses; courses related to awards; full-day, half-day, after school (twilight) courses; and conference packages. The cost, set by the providers, ranged from £45 to £500, meaning schools could book more than one course.

Overall, 2,552 out of 7,843 schools (32.5 per cent) registered on GLP-E booked externally provided CPD, with 11,977 teacher attendances. This was 61.8 per cent of the sub-total of 4,125 schools eligible to receive the £500 funding for CPD, having completed WSA1. The biggest challenge to schools was finding time to decide what CPD would best suit their schools' priorities and then scheduling it. The data discussed below is from those schools that were able to attend CPD.

Methods

GLP-E recruited a record number of schools to date on a single government-funded global learning programme in England, so there is a wealth of data generated. My role in overseeing the externally provided CPD, including assuring the quality of provision, gave me access to this data. I draw on a selection in this chapter:

- booking and attendance statistics,
- observations of twenty-three courses,
- teacher course evaluations,
- provider feedback and
- eight interviews with lead teachers.

In the discussion below, I quote from statistics, observations and interviews, and use the provider and evaluation data as context. The interviews were undertaken with eight (from forty-eight) schools that booked additional CPD. (68 per cent of eligible schools only booked one course.) The interviews provided interesting perspectives on the impact of longer-term engagement with CPD. I chose semi-structured phone interviews to provide answers to specific questions and to allow teachers to describe their experience in depth (Lechuga 2012). These were recorded with the teachers' permission. They were sent a transcript and a draft of the final programme report to check. Ethics approval was granted by UCL IOE ethics review committee. The data was analysed using a standard content analysis with coding and a search for themes (Cohen et al. 2011). The quotations from teachers are pseudonymized (A–H).

Effective externally provided CPD for global learning

The most interesting findings to emerge in relation to how teachers responded to CPD, what they found most helpful and effective, are about teachers regaining a sense of purpose, the importance of pedagogy, the value of collaboration and longer-term engagement with CPD.

Regaining a sense of purpose

I start with the effect of CPD for global learning on teachers and pupils as it needs to motivate teachers to further engage with global learning, if it is to have lasting impact.

Much has been written on problems with different forms of CPD (Done et al. 2011), so it was particularly heartening that teachers found the CPD for global learning 'professionally leavening' (Sugrue and Mertkan 2017: 172). It increased their confidence and enthusiasm for teaching, a finding supported by other GLP-E evaluation data[3]. For example, Teacher G said 'that last year was probably the best year of my entire teaching career and a big part of it was because I was involved in a lot of CPD. And I just felt that I had really developed as a teacher and … I have learnt a lot of new things.' CPD for global learning is particularly inspiring when linked to individuals' motivations and sense of their identity as teachers, in contexts where this can easily get lost.

Teachers identified that global learning CPD offered them a new direction. For example, Teacher B said, it 'ignites something in terms of a passion for teaching and a desire to do things a bit differently'. The response from pupils was key. As Vescio et al. (2008) point out, CPD must link to pupils' learning. Teacher Y explained, 'It has been the children who have responded positively. They've learnt things from it, they've started questioning things more. And I just thought, this is fantastic – and it's just sort of grown. Had the children not responded so, then I wouldn't have pursued it.'

Clearly, it is not possible to claim a universal effect from a small interview sample. But the overwhelmingly positive evidence from course evaluations confirms that the focus on teaching pupils to engage with global issues and consider their place in a globalized world relates directly to teachers' intrinsic motivation for teaching – their 'moral purpose' (Day 1999).

Knowledge and pedagogy

Having established that CPD for global learning can motivate teachers to re-engage with their professional practice, it is important to understand how it achieves that. The literature clearly lists many characteristics of effective CPD which are potentially important features of CPD for global learning (see Cordingley et al. 2015, DFES 2016). This includes focus on subject knowledge and subject-specific pedagogy. The responses of teachers to these aspects of CPD were particularly interesting.

Given that GLP-E had a clear emphasis on developing pupils' knowledge, particularly of development and poverty, and that many teachers would not have covered knowledge of global issues in pre-service training, one might expect they would choose opportunities to improve their own knowledge. However, the CPD courses on specific global issues were less popular than generic global learning courses, or bespoke courses designed in consultation with schools. For example, courses with development and poverty as the main theme accounted for only 49 out of

---

[3] See chapter in this volume by Hunt.

11,977 teacher attendances (0.4 per cent) and only 742 attended courses on sustainability and environmental courses.

There are various possible explanations, including potentially some mismatch between programme and school priorities; the challenge for teachers of subjects other than geography, history or economics to see the relevance for their learners; or a need for more introductory courses. As many as 58 per cent of schools starting on GLP-E self-assessed as having no experience of global learning, so this choice is logical. However, the data suggests that an additional key explanation is a preference for learning content through pedagogy (Timperley et al. 2007).

This can be illustrated with the example of philosophy for children (P4C) courses, which had 2,574 (21 per cent) teacher attendances, and the popularity of courses focusing on linking global learning to the curriculum. P4C is an approach that helps children learn to communicate more effectively and think critically[4] and can be used with all ages. It teaches pupils to listen to alternative viewpoints, make their case, come to their own conclusions, in a 'community of enquiry'. The teacher, using stimuli such as stories or pictures, facilitates a process where children generate philosophical questions to discuss. The children chose a question and the teacher facilitates a group discussion, in which there are clear rules on turn-taking, listening, presenting views, etc. It is particularly well-suited to global learning; as the stimuli can be about global issues, the method is participatory and it emphasizes using critical thinking (Bourn et al. 2016).

What the P4C and other courses on the programme had in common was an experiential, inquiry-based, participatory approach, which modelled teaching, used activities relevant for the content and thereby connected to classroom experience (Capps et al. 2012). Teachers experienced activities that served multiple purposes simultaneously, and that reflected approaches to pupils' learning (Cordingley et al. 2015). Teachers therefore gained an understanding of a pedagogical approach that they could apply across subjects and topics. Teacher E's response was illustrative: 'Actually, it's the methodology that I realised is part of the key of it: not just the content, but ways to engage children and make them better learners.' This was also illustrated in the action points set by one group I observed: 'Teach how we can impact the future, joined up view of the world, encourage children to look further than the local environment, talk more about the world, use critical thinking.' Teachers also need concrete ideas of how to implement a new approach, and practical suggestions on incorporating global learning and guidance on using resources were the two most cited benefits in the interviews and were frequently mentioned in course evaluations. But it seemed that it was the combination of theory and practice that matters (Timperley et al. 2007). The contextualizing of pupil activities and interesting resources within an overall approach helped teachers see how to improve their pupils' learning.

Collaboration

Another key feature that teachers valued was the opportunity to collaborate, share and discuss approaches with peers, within and between schools. Collaboration is recommended in the

---

[4] https://www.sapere.org.uk/about-us.aspx

literature, generally (see Kennedy 2011), but it is particularly relevant for global learning. It reflects global learning principles and gives less experienced teachers opportunities to learn from others. In contexts with no or limited curriculum guidance, embedding global learning within a school is also only possible if teachers share their understandings.

Whole-school and 'cluster' CPD were the two main collaborative models on GLP-E. Whole-school CPD was popular with schools that had timetable space and with small schools, where all staff could participate. This reflects a common teacher preference for in-house CPD, where collaboration is in 'an authentic context' (Mansour et al. 2014: 968). There are many benefits of whole-school CPD. It can link to school development plans. For example, I observed a whole-school CPD in a primary school in the North West, where the head teacher had prioritized implementing P4C for the coming school year. Whole-school CPD ensured all staff developed shared understandings of P4C and agreed implementation strategies. In another example, Teacher C found whole-school CPD 'was an opportunity of looking at our curriculum and seeing where we could really embed it'.

Cluster CPD was CPD for a group of schools. Where existing EC networks chose this approach, they could continue to work with each other as an extension to the network CPD, with more opportunities to reflect on implementation (McArdle and Coutts 2010). Some were able to plan their external CPD to fit the timetable of the EC twilight sessions so developing a logical, coherent thread of learning (Cordingley et al. 2015). These networks developed into informal communities of practice, providing opportunities for exploring new understandings and applications to teaching, and reflecting on the impact on pupils' learning (Timperley et al. 2007).

One of the main benefits of collaborative approaches is in ensuring sustainability of global learning, by developing a sense of collective responsibility (Ofper and Pedder 2011a). Teacher D said, 'Everybody is doing the same thing at the same time. And the conversations that come out of that as well, out of those sessions, can be quite good. Learn and take the subject … take you further.' Teacher B found sharing 'a very motivating thing and, as I say, there aren't loads of opportunities for that anymore'. As some of the providers pointed out, the challenge is in creating the thinking space for teachers and school to engage with global learning.

The social aspect of the learning also matters, as teachers prefer to develop professional knowledge with others (Mansour et al. 2014). 'It is through addressing the challenge of this creative tension between the individual and the social that professionals, through negotiation of ideas and actions for change with others, can be assisted to make sense of their own practice and attempts at professional renewal' (McArdle and Coutts 2010: 213).

Follow-up and consolidation

Judging the effectiveness of CPD requires considering its longer-term impact. Guskey (2002) argues that teachers' beliefs about their practice change after implementation and seeing the improvement in pupils' learning. One-off CPD events, though useful and inspiring, are unlikely to be best for sustained change. Ongoing support is important (De Paor 2016). One of the less successful aspects of the GLP-E CPD was that most schools booked relatively late (in term 4 or 5) for very understandable practical reasons. But this meant only forty-eight schools booked more than one course, despite many schools not having spent their full £500. The experience of teachers from schools that were able to consolidate their learning in various ways is therefore particularly valuable.

Some providers offered bespoke courses which were designed in two parts to maximize opportunities for teachers to learn together and implement in their own classrooms and schools, with follow-up to reflect and share. Teacher A liked this format: 'That was the idea, that you went away and tried things and came back and discussed and reflected on what you'd done.' In other examples, schools chose different types of CPD to build their learning. Teacher F was inspired by one course, which opened her eyes to the lack of experience of diversity in her rural school. So, she then chose a course linking to a school in London, enabling her 'to access something that I don't think we would have done otherwise'. Others consolidated by re-running the CPD for different parts of the school community. Teacher G took a course, then booked a whole-school version. Attending as an individual increased her confidence to advise colleagues, and helped her assess what they would find useful, while booking a provider for the follow-up gave others the opportunity to benefit from external expertise. Teacher D booked a course on values for parents, pupils and the wider school, having initially booked one for teaching staff. She saw this as part of a two- to three-year process to embed the learning in the school, as she said effort was needed not to 'revert to what you know and are comfortable with'. Finding ways to deliver CPD and support teachers over the longer term is important for sustainability. Otherwise global learning becomes something interesting that maybe a small number of teachers, or just an individual, experiences and then the realities of school life erode their commitment and possibilities to influence practice more widely.

Discussion and implications

This chapter has focused on how teachers on one programme responded to CPD for global learning, what they found most effective, what they prioritized in terms of the focus of that CPD. Clearly this was a specific context, one of the first national programmes for schools in this area and a new initiative within the UK. However, the findings are more widely relevant and have implications for sustainability of global learning within schools.

As stated at the outset, there are few places globally that have a coordinated national strategy for global learning that involves government, schools, teacher training institutions and NGOs (Tarozzi and Inguaggiato 2018). Global learning is not routinely included in pre-service teacher education, and therefore CPD, delivered mainly by external organizations, remains the core of teacher support. There are few signs, in the UK at least, that this is likely to change, though there is continued focus on school to school support through networks. With increasing pressures on schools and teachers, with greater focus on managerial approaches and accountability for school performance, and issues with funding, global learning is not an education priority. However, the global context sees increased focus on the SDGs, including education for global citizenship, and young people becoming increasingly vocal about their concerns for the future. As I write, pupils globally are engaged in a series of strikes to protest at adults' inadequate responses to climate change. In a sense, there has not been a greater need for quality education that prepares young people for a more uncertain, globalized world. This in turn requires motivated, committed and appropriately trained teachers. In this context, CPD for global learning, provided by external organizations, remains a key mechanism for achieving this.

However, that CPD also needs to be effective. Again, it is worth stressing that unlike some other CPD provision which essentially updates already well-qualified teachers, CPD for global learning can be teachers' first exposure. Any programme of support needs to factor in the time for schools to decide their priorities, choose relevant CPD, fit it in the timetable, implement the learning, assess the impact and response from pupils, reflect and identify further needs. This requires more than one-off CPD events, however, inspiring. External providers and schools need to be supported to provide opportunities to challenge teachers' beliefs, encourage and support them in trying out different pedagogical approaches, give them confidence to tackle difficult issues in the classroom and undergo a process of change in relation to their practice, and possibly their identity as teachers. As it takes courage to undertake such a process of transformation (Kennedy 2005), this is unlikely to be achievable without ongoing support.

This is also best achieved collaboratively, within or between schools and schools need to retain their agency in deciding what CPD is relevant. Although CPD for individual teachers' development is important (Postholm 2012) and individual champions within schools can do amazing work in inspiring and training colleagues, relying on their motivation, energy and enthusiasm is not sustainable. Unless global learning becomes a mandated part of national curricula, prioritizing it will remain at the discretion of schools' senior management. External experts can take pressure of expertise away from senior staff, allowing those staff to participate more fully in the CPD, thereby fostering sense of collective responsibility (Opfer and Pedder 2011a).

Finally, it is worth considering the wider benefits of CPD for global learning for the education profession. Where education systems like the English system face increasing levels of teacher turnover and burnout (Worth et al. 2017), CPD for global learning could be part of the solution. CPD which has the potential to re-ignite teachers' passion for teaching, reinforces their intrinsic motivation, and which reflects 'their aspirations for their pupils' (Cordingley et al 2015), offers a way of supporting teachers to do more than survive. But this will only work with a flourishing third-party sector, appropriately equipped and funded to support schools. This includes opportunities for newer providers to develop their 'pedagogical content knowledge' (Timperley et al. 2007: xxix), if the quality of that CPD is to be maintained.

Bibliography

Andreotti, V. (2010), 'Global education in the "21st Century": two different perspectives on the "post-" of postmodernism', *International Journal of Development Education and Global Learning*, 2(2): 522.

Asbrand, B. (2008), 'How adolescents learn about globalisation and development'. In D. Bourn (ed.), *Development Education Debates and Dialogues*, 28–44, London: Institute of Education, University of London.

Avalos, B. (2011), 'Review: Teacher professional development in Teaching and Teacher Education over ten years', *Teaching and Teacher Education*, 27: 10–20.

Beijaard, D., F. Korthagen and N. Verloop (2007), 'Understanding how teachers learn as a prerequisite for promoting teacher learning', *Teachers and Teaching*, 13(2): 105–8.

Bennell, S. J. (2015), 'Education for sustainable development and global citizenship; leadership, collaboration and networking in primary schools', *International Journal of Development Education and Global Learning*, 7(1): 5–32.

Bourn, D. (2012), 'Development education'. In J. Arthur and A. Peterson (eds), *The Routledge Companion to Education*, London: Routledge.

Bourn, D. (2014), *The Theory and Practice of Global Learning*, Research paper 11 for the Global Learning Programme, London: Development Education Research Centre, Institute of Education

Bourn, D. (2015), 'Teachers as agents of social change', *International Journal of Development Education and Global Learning*, 7(3): 63–77.

Bourn, D., F. Hunt, N. Blum and H. Lawson (2016), *Primary Education for Global Learning and Sustainability*, York: Cambridge Primary Review Trust.

Büker, G. and S. Schell-Straub (2017), 'Global how? – Linking practice to theory: A competency model for training global learning facilitators', *International Journal of Development Education and Global Learning*, 9(2): 71–83.

Capps, D. K., B. A. Crawford and M. A. Constas (2012), 'A review of empirical literature on inquiry professional development: Alignment with best practices and a critique of the findings', *Journal of Science Teacher Education*, 23: 291–318.

Cochran-Smith, M. and S. L. Lytle (1999), 'Relationships of knowledge and practice: Teacher learning in communities'. In A. Iran-Nejar and P. D. Pearson (eds), *Review of Research in Education*, 249–305, Washington DC: AERA.

Cohen L., L. Manion and K. Morrison (2011), *Research Methods in Education*, 7th edn, London and New York: Routledge.

Cordingley, P., S. Higgins, T. Greany, N. Buckler, D. Coles-Jordan, B. Crisp, L. Saunders and R. Coe (2015), *Developing Great Teaching: Lessons from the International Reviews into Effective Professional Development*, Teacher Development Trust.

Cusack, M. and A. Rush (2010), '"The authority of a lived experience": An investigation of study visits as a professional development opportunity for post-primary development educators', *Policy and Practice: A Development Education Review*, 10: 9–24.

Dadds, M. (2014), 'Continuing Professional Development: Nurturing the expert within', *Professional Development in Education*, 40(1): 9–16.

Dariji, B. B. and G. Lang-Wojtasik (2014), 'Preparing globally competent teachers: Indo-German perspectives on teacher training', *International Journal of Development Education and Global Learning*, 6(3): 49–62.

Day, C. (1999), *Developing Teachers: The Challenges of Lifelong Learning*, London: Falmer.

De Paor, C. (2016), 'The impact of school-based continuing professional development: Views of teachers and support professionals', *Irish Educational Studies*, 35(3): 289–306.

Development Education Forum (DEF) and Development Education Exchange in Europe Project (DEEEP) (2009), *Development Education and the School Curriculum in the European Union: A Report on the Status and Impact of Development Education in the Formal Education Sector and School Curriculum in Member States of the European Union*, Brussels: DEEEP.

De Vries, S., W. J. C. M. van de Grift and E. P. W. A. Jansen (2013), 'Teachers' beliefs and continuing professional development', *Journal of Educational Administration*, 51(2): 213–31.

DFES (2016), *Standard for Teachers' Professional Development Implementation Guidance for School Leaders, Teachers, and Organisations that Offer Professional Development for Teachers*, London: Department for Education.

Done, E., H. Knowler, T. Rea and K. Gale (2011), '(Re)writing CPD: Creative analytical practices and the "continuing professional development of teachers"', *Reflective Practice*, 12(3): 389–99.

El-Deghaidy, H., M. Mansour and S. Alshamrani (2015), 'Science teachers' typology of CPD activities: A socio-constructivist perspective', *International Journal of Science and Mathematics Education*, 13(6): 1539–66.

Foghani-Arani, N. and H. Hartmeyer (2010), 'Global learning in Austria: Towards a national strategy and beyond', *International Journal of Development Education and Global Learning*, 2(3): 45–58.

Guskey, T. (2002), 'Professional development and teacher change', *Teachers and Teaching: Theory and Practice*, 8(3/4): 381–91.

Guskey, T. R. (2003) 'What makes professional development effective?' *Phi Delta Kappan*, 84(10): 748–50.

Hanushek, E. and S. Rivkin (2012), 'The distribution of teacher quality and implications for policy', *Annual Review of Economics*, 4: 131–57.

Hardy, I. and K. Rönnerman (2011), 'The value and valuing of continuing professional development: current dilemmas, future directions and the case for action research', *Cambridge Journal of Education*, 41(4): 461–72.

Harrison, D. G. (2008), 'Oxfam and the rise of development education in England from 1959 to 1979', Unpublished PhD thesis, Institute of Education, London.

Hunt, F. (2012), *Global Learning in Primary Schools in England: Practices and Impacts*, DERC Research Paper no. 9, London: Institute of Education.

Kennedy, A. (2005), 'Models of continuing professional development: A framework for analysis', *Journal of In-service Education*, 31(2): 235–50.

Kennedy, A. (2011), 'Collaborative continuing professional development (CPD) for teachers in Scotland: Aspirations, opportunities and barriers', *European Journal of Teacher Education*, 34(1): 25–41.

Kirkwood-Tucker, T. F., J. D. Morris and M. G. Lieberman (2011), 'What kind of teachers will teach our children? The worldmindedness of undergraduate elementary and secondary Social Studies teacher candidates at five Florida public universities', *International Journal of Development Education and Global Learning*, 3(3): 5–28.

Lechuga, V. M. (2012), 'Exploring culture from a distance: The utility of telephone interviews in qualitative research', *International Journal of Qualitative Studies in Education*, 25(3): 251–68.

Mansour, N., H. EL-Deghaidy, S. Alshamrani and A. Aldahmash (2014), 'Rethinking the theory and practice of continuing professional development: Science teachers' perspectives', *Research in Science Education* 44: 949–73.

McArdle, K. and N. Coutts (2010), 'Taking teachers' continuous professional development (CPD) beyond reflection: Adding shared sense-making and collaborative engagement for professional renewal', *Studies in Continuing Education*, 32(3): 201–15.

McCarthy, M. and M. Gannon (2016), 'Embedding development education in post-primary teaching and learning: Lessons from Worldwise Global Schools', *Policy and Practice: A Development Education Review*, 23: 102–23.

McMillan, D. J., B. McConnell and H. O'Sullivan (2016), 'Continuing professional development – why bother? Perceptions and motivations of teachers in Ireland', *Professional Development in Education*, 42(1): 150–67.

Mezirow, J. (2000), 'Learning to think like an adult: Core concepts of transformation theory'. In J. Mezirow and Associates (eds), *Learning as Transformation: Critical Perspectives on a Theory in Progress*, San Francisco: Jossey-Bass, 3–33.

Mundy, K. and C. Manion (2008), 'Global education in Canadian Elementary Schools: An exploratory study', *Canadian Journal of Education*, 31(4): 941–74.

Murphy, T. R. N. and C. De Paor (2017), 'Teachers' CPD and sectoral interests: Opportunities for convergence and divergence', *Teaching and Teacher Education*, 66: 242–9.

Opfer, V. D. and D. Pedder (2011a), 'Conceptualising professional learning', *Review of Educational Research*, 81(3): 376–407.

Opfer, V. D. and D. Pedder (2011b), 'The lost promise of teacher professional development in England', *European Journal of Teacher Education*, 34(1): 3–24.

Opfer, V. D., D. Pedder and Z. Lavicza (2011), 'The role of teachers' orientation to learning in professional development and change: A national study of teachers in England', *Teaching and Teacher Education*, 27: 443–53.

Postholm, M. B. (2012) 'Teachers' professional development: A theoretical review', *Educational Research*, 54(4): 405–29.

Sachs, J. (2007), *Learning to Improve or Improving Learning: The Dilemma of Teacher Continuing Professional Development*, Proceedings of the 20st Annual World ICSEI Congress 3–6 January 2007, Convention Center Bernardin Portorož, Slovenia.

Scheunfplug, A. (2008), 'Why global learning and global education? An educational approach influenced by the perspectives of Immanuel Kant'. In D. Bourn (ed.), *Development Education Debates and Dialogues*, 18–27, London: Institute of Education, University of London.

Scheunpflug, A. (2011), 'Global education and cross-cultural learning: A challenge for a research-based approach to international teacher education', *International Journal of Development Education and Global Learning*, 3(3): 2–44.

Scoffham, S. (2014), '"Do we really need to know this?" The challenge of developing a global learning module for trainee teachers', *International Journal of Development Education and Global Learning*, 5(3): 28–45.

Shulman, L. S. (1986), 'Those who understand: Knowledge growth in teaching', *Educational Researcher*, 15(2): 4–14.

Simpson, J. (2017), 'Learning to unlearn the charity mentality within schools', *Policy and Practice: A Development Education Review*, 25: 88–108.

Sugrue, C. and S. Mertkan (2017), 'Professional responsibility, accountability and performativity among teachers: The leavening influence of CPD?' *Teachers and Teaching*, 23(2): 171–90.

Surian, A. (2001), 'A comparative look at European policies on development education', *The Development Education Journal*, 7(2): 4–7.

Tallon, R. and A. Milligan (2018), 'The changing field of development and global education resource provision in New Zealand', *International Journal of Development Education and Global Learning*, 10(1): 59–71.

Tarozzi, M. and C. Inguaggiato (2018), 'Implementing global citizenship education in EU primary schools: The role of government ministries', *International Journal for Development Education and Global Learning*, 10(1): 21–38.

Timperley, H., A. Wilson, H. Barrar and I. Fung (2007), *Teacher Professional Learning and Development Best Evidence Synthesis Iteration [BES]*, Ministry of Education, Box 1666, Wellington, New Zealand.

Vescio, V., D. Ross and Adams, A. (2008), 'A review of research on the impact of professional learning communities on teaching practice and student learning', *Teaching and Teacher Education*, 24: 80–91.

Worth, J., G. De Lazzari and J. Hillary (2017), *Teacher Retention and Turnover Research: Interim Report*, Slough: NFER.

Chapter 27

Research and Innovation in Education: A Case for Inclusion of Global Perspectives for Effective Learning in Formal Education in Ondo, Nigeria, in the Twenty-first Century

Opeyemi Aderonke Oyekan, Roy Tokunbo Olowu and Olutosin Awolalu

Introduction

In Nigeria innovations in the curriculum were adopted in the 2007 National Policy on Education (NPE) specifically to meet the 2015 Millennium Development Goals (MDGs), but these targets were not achieved. The educational opportunities of both educators and learners in Nigeria have become vulnerable to the country's sociopolitical dysfunctions. The inability to manage the diversity of ethnic, cultural and religious communities designates Nigeria as a country to focus on in terms of quality education, social justice, human rights, religious tolerance and the protection of indigenous communities, all equating to the seventeen objectives of the United Nations 2030 Sustainable Development Goals (SDGs).

Nigeria's national educational goal is clearly captured in the NPE, Section 1, subsections 1.4, 1.5 and 1.6 state that 'education is an instrument for national development', that it 'fosters the worth and development of the individual … into a sound and effective citizen', that 'every Nigerian child shall have a right to equal educational opportunities irrespective of any real or imagined disabilities…, and for the 'philosophy (of education) to be in harmony with the nation's goals, it has to be geared towards self realisation, better human relationship, individual and national efficiency, effective citizenship, national consciousness, national unity, as well as towards social, cultural, economic, political, scientific and technological progress'.

A key focus of Nigeria's NPE is about leveraging technology to transform teacher training and the quality of learning. In other words, there must be a significant level of affordability and accessibility of education in sufficient quantity and quality, if the trend of underdevelopment is to be arrested. Appropriate adoption of global perspectives in teacher training should transform teachers from their current status of knowledge experts into facilitators of new paradigms of learning. This will demand an increase in capacity for teaching training systems but also opportunities to enhance the articulation between theory and practice, and support for teachers in becoming reflective practitioners. Teacher training in Nigeria needs to adopt a method of learning that integrates an appreciation of global issues of social justice and equality, value and respect for diversity, and needs to create an environment for sustainable development in the teacher training system. The totality of the experience will be an enrichment of teacher training and the quality of learning culminating in the development of the 'global teacher' – a global learner trained to relate cultural differences and understand socio-economic and educational disparities.

This study investigates the knowledge and awareness of global learning perspectives as an inclusive research and innovation tool for effective and efficient education delivery by head teachers of Ondo West Local Government Education Authority. It analyses the extent of head teachers' knowledge and awareness of global learning, its effectiveness and the need for its application in the classroom.

Nigeria's national policies on education and teachers

In recognition of the role of teachers in national development, the NPE document (2004) states that 'Teacher education will continue to be given a major emphasis in all our educational planning because no educational system can rise above the quality of its teachers' (NPE, 2004: 53). Objectives in the NPE document specific to this study are the following:

- 'To provide teachers with the intellectual and professional background adequate for their assignments.
- To make the Nigerian Teacher adaptable to any changing situation not only in the life of their country but in the wider world.
- The encouragement of the spirit of enquiry and creativity in teachers and providing them with the intellectual and professional background that will be adequate for their assignments and also make them adaptable to changing situations' (FME, NPE, 2004).

Teacher education programmes have a responsibility to prepare teachers to be skilled and competent professionals. This is normally achieved by developing each teacher's knowledge of teaching, improving their knowledge of subject content and their skills as educators. The classroom context that teachers find themselves in can be quite vulnerable to changing demographics and sometimes infrastructural shortfalls and challenges, which have been significant over the years. One major influence, however, that has had a very profound impact on the teaching profession is the phenomenon of increased global interconnectedness. In a world where people and information travel the globe at a speed not experienced in previous generations, there is a clear motivation for education to support students in their development of knowledge, skills and attitudes necessary for effective participation in an increasingly interconnected world characterized by cultural pluralism (Merryfield, 1994). Zhao (2010) notes that globalization is one of the most powerful forces that will shape the future, and that is a critical consideration in the future-oriented business of teacher education. To successfully address the global influence on local education, teacher education needs to be considered in a global context (Bates, 2008).

Globalization in context

Contributing to the debate about the impact of globalization on teaching practice in Nigeria, Fakoya (2009) says, 'increasing globalisation and the emergence of the knowledge-based economy are calling into question traditional perspectives on the transformational capacity of education systems and the conceptions of teaching as a profession, and the roles of teachers' (Fakoya, 2009). 'There is a necessity for schools and learning institutions in Nigeria to become vital instruments of human capital development and the creation of a knowledge-based community equipped to play significant roles in the global economy' (Akani, 2012). There needs to be a method of customizing globalization to fit and support the ideals of progressive educational systems. Increasing the number of teachers in Nigeria has not and will not solve problems pertaining to teacher training. There needs to be an awareness and advocacy to implement ways of improving how teachers teach. Sanyal (2013) states that 'it has not been possible to supply qualified teachers to cope with the increase of primary and secondary school students in sub-Saharan Africa which projects a requirement of 4 million teachers in 2015, with 44 per cent required in Nigeria' (Sanyal, 2013). Improving the quality of instruction is dependent on the pedagogical support and training given to the teacher during and prior to service.

The main problem Nigeria is facing is the failure to provide quality teachers to the educational system due to the ever-increasing rate of enrolment into primary and secondary schools. 'Of the thousands of teachers recruited each year, they largely have inadequate subject knowledge and little, if any, pedagogic training' (Leach, 2008). Traditional methods of learning by rote still permeate Nigeria's educational system, especially in teacher training. In his contribution Ajibola opines that 'this form of instruction and learning hampers creativity and does little to foster innate abilities for problem-solving and decision-making … the focus is not so much on how much is remembered but how much is understood and if this can be applied appropriately in real life situations'. This, he says, 'is the measure of an effective educational system' (Ajibola, 2008). 'Teacher training institutions in Nigeria have been critiqued for their inability to produce teachers who are properly grounded in pedagogy and content as well as having the ability to collaborate professionally in a working environment. The Nigerian teacher training curriculum does not currently adopt the new age constructivist learning, learner-centred instructions and integrating technology into the processes of teaching and learning' Adeosun (2006).

Teacher training methods in Nigeria

In Nigeria professional teacher education programmes have developed within the framework of

- initial training (pre-service) for inexperienced teachers, often immediately after they leave primary or secondary school.
- in service for experienced but unqualified teachers, often done as part of their practice.
- continuing lifelong education for continuous growth after initial training.

Fareo (2013) states that unlike other countries, the retraining of teachers has not received the desired attention from the local, state and federal government in Nigeria. There has not been any systematic attention to regularly update the knowledge and skills of teachers in the light of the curriculum and the wider society. This neglect has in turn affected the quality of teaching in schools (Fareo, 2013: 66). The current strategy to develop, update and upgrade teachers is the Teachers Training Programme (TTP). In TTP pre-service training includes the orientation of participants to the school and community and working as a teaching assistant using the mentoring approach.

Teacher training in Nigeria also adopts the workplace training approach otherwise known as on the job training. This opportunity is open to those who have the desire to upgrade their professional skills and for those who after the induction training have started to practise on a full-time basis. Off-the-job training exists where learning involves attending workshops, presentations and seminars. Teachers are given the opportunity to attend block release or sandwich courses.

The other type of teacher training approach is referred to as conversion training. This approach is designed to train teachers in dealing with a new range of unfamiliar subject areas). One of the objectives for teacher training in the Nigerian NPE (2004) is 'the encouragement of the spirit of enquiry and creativity in teachers and providing them with the intellectual and professional background that will be adequate for their assignments and also make them adaptable to changing situations' (FME, NPE, 2004). In the drive to achieve this objective, the National Certificate of Education has become the minimum level of qualification to teach in Nigeria and replaces the Grade 2 certificate of the past. Secondary school teachers are expected to have a university degree to teach at that level. The conversion training approach provides a conducive environment where global learning for global citizenship can be embedded in the training of teachers in Nigeria.

The need for global learning

The changing educational landscape places critical demands on teachers to be culturally and pedagogically competent in addressing issues of globalization, racism, diversity and social justice, and in creating an equitable and inclusive learning environment for all students (Guo, 2013; Pike, 2008). Today's students are graduating into a world that is interconnected as never before. As citizens in the twenty-first century, they are required to be responsible and responsive to the myriad complex problems and issues of global and local concern, whether in health, environment, peace or economic security. This shifting global context demands that students today develop the knowledge, skills, attributes and commitment to global citizenship through the educational process.

With ethnic, cultural and linguistic backgrounds of students becoming increasingly diverse, teachers in Nigeria need to have the skills and understanding to address diversity and have a firm understanding of the cultural identities of their students, as well as of themselves. Teachers must also be prepared for the demands imposed by globalization so that they are competent to guide their students to explore issues of global and local importance within and beyond the curriculum, and to prepare students for global citizenship and their role in an interconnected and interdependent world. There are few teacher training programmes that explicitly address the goal of preparing teachers to be global educators and many teachers enter the profession with insufficient experience or training to enable them to bring a global perspective to their teaching (Reimers, 2009). The need for a global perspective in education is not predicated on the need to discard the traditional local context, but for education to take notice that the rest of the world matters (Britzman, 2000).This need seeks an effective way to address global awareness through creative and insightful teacher education programmes that do not simply perpetuate the norms of the past, and has been addressed through a collaboration between Soft Contents UK, the Publishing Open Institute, Nigeria and Ondo West Local Government Education Authority, Ondo State, Nigeria, in a workshop on 'Learning in a Global dimension for Headteachers'. Global dimension in context refers to a learning environment that 'has as its central focus the promotion of learning in an interdependent world, addressing the similarities of peoples around the world and a belief in working towards a fairer and more sustainable world' (Bourn, 2014). The objective of the workshop was to ascertain the head teachers' perception and appreciation of global learning and to out find out if the head teachers saw themselves as part of the community of global educators. This training and its structure provided conducive learning space dedicated to the concept of global education and enabled dialogic and participative learning.

The Learning in a Global Dimension workshop took place in Ondo West Local Government Education Authority (LGEA), one of the eighteen LGEAs in Ondo State, Nigeria. Ondo State is one of the most educationally advantaged of the thirty-six states that make up Nigeria. The Ondo West LGEA administers 104 primary schools, the largest number in any LGEA in Ondo state. When the global learning proposal submitted by Soft Contents UK was approved, the executive board of LGEA chose thirty-five head teachers from urban and rural schools in the area as participants and provided the venue and logistics required for the one-day Learning in a Global Dimension training session.

We recognized how their wealth of professional experience positioned them for school leadership, staff and learning resource management, and evaluating and reporting as required by the LGEA. Head teachers and the LGEA work together to ensure educational activities are in alignment with the objectives of the NPE and Sustainable Development Goals No. 4 (accessibility to and affordability of quality education). It was agreed that the current working relationship between the Ondo West LGEA and its head teachers provides opportunities for rolling out teacher training initiatives such as Learning in a Global Dimension.

Purpose of the study

The purpose of this study is to assess head teachers' knowledge and attitudes towards global learning, by participating in a teacher training programme under the theme of Learning in a Global Dimension.

The decision to choose head teachers emerged from the recognition of the key roles they play working with the LGEA in the planning and execution of educational objectives of the Federal Ministry of Education (FME). In the first section of the training, participants were made aware of the importance of understanding what global learning was about, for it to be practised effectively; they were told that global learning could be used to create awareness of perspectives from other parts of the world and by doing so create opportunities to look at topics and issues from a wider perspective. Participants were made to understand how globalization calls for updating conventional approaches to learning by enabling new methods of learning that complement subject-based knowledge with real-time global perspectives. The concept of Learning in a Global Dimension on which the project was themed was defined as when the teacher or facilitator enables subject disciplines to be approached using local and global perspectives. This was explained as 'a pedagogy of making connections between the individual and personal, from the local to the global, and which by its very nature is transformative' (Bourn, 2012: 9). The final part of the workshop involved participants in groups giving micro-teaching sessions on global issues they could adapt to their subject disciplines. The groups were asked to consider the research questions that follow below, while planning their presentations.

The Learning in a Global Dimension workshop in 2016 was a one-day tester event which saw the coming together of head teachers in great anticipation, even though the professional experience in the group averaged twenty-five years. In closing the workshop, a communique was issued by Ondo West LGEA in which they expressed appreciation for the training of their head teachers, making the following statements:

- Global learning is a unique method of improving the quality of teaching.
- Global learning enriches subject-based learning and makes learning favourable.
- Global learning provides a significant contribution to the pedagogy of a subject.
- Global learning programmes should be extended to every teacher.
- The workshop encourages teachers to improve professional practice.

Research questions

In October 2017, Soft Contents UK issued a questionnaire to evaluate the impact of the Learning in a Global Dimension workshop held in 2016 in Ondo West, LGEA, Nigeria. In 2018, the feedback was collated and analysed with the National Institute of Educational Planning and Administration and the Publishing Open Institute, Ibadan, Nigeria.

The following research questions guided this study:

(1) To what extent do head teachers have the required knowledge of global learning?
(2) How does the Learning in a Global Dimension make it possible for head teachers to develop global competency?
(3) To what extent do head teachers possess the required skills for global learning?

Methodology

Introduction

This chapter explains in detail the methods that were used to carry out the research under the following headings: Research Design, Sample and Sampling Technique, Research Instrument, Validity of Instrument, Reliability of Instrument, Method of Data Collection and Method of Data Processing and Data Analysis.

Research design

The descriptive survey research design was adopted for the study. This involves gathering data that describe events and then organizes, tabulates, depicts and describes the data collection. This type of survey design allows for a brief interview or discussion with the respondents on how to complete the research instrument and often uses visual aids such as graphs and charts to aid the reader in understanding the data distribution. As the survey design depicts, this study ensured that questions were structured both in multiple choice and in open-ended forms where participants were at liberty to choose any of the options and express their thoughts, respectively.

Sample and sampling technique

The sample size was drawn from the total population of 104 head teachers selected for impact assessment in Ondo West Local Government. The total population of 104 (one hundred and four respondents) was used for the study to eliminate any potential bias, out of which 51 were males and 53 were females with professional experience being 25 years and above.

Research

The research instrument entitled 'Research and Innovation in Education: A Case for the Inclusion of Global Perspectives for Effective Learning in the 21st Century' was carefully designed with the items structured to suit the objectives of the study. The design and construction of the questionnaire items were carried out by Soft Contents UK and the Publishing Open Institute, Ibadan, Nigeria.

The questionnaire was made up of five major sections. Section A presented the preliminary information of the respondents, section B elicited information on the knowledge of head teacher on global learning and section C looked at the application of global learning in the workplace.

Validity of instrument

The items on the questionnaire were subjected to scrutiny by experts in educational measurement and evaluation/testing. Results were incorporated in the final copy of the questionnaire and pilot tested.

Reliability of instrument

The test-retest method was used in ascertaining its criterion and to construct the validity of the instruments. The results of correlation yielded a coefficient of 0.93 at 0.05 alpha levels. This was considered high enough to make the instrument reliable.

Method of data collection

A team of four researchers, constituted from the technical working group of the project, were trained on modalities for the data collection and deployed to the field. Respondents were drawn from participants of the 'Learning in Global Dimension' training programme held on 23 November 2016 at Ondo West Local Government Secretariat.

Method of data processing and data analysis

The National Institute for Educational Planning and Administration (NIEPA)'s Research Department processed and analysed the data retrieved. Data analysis was carried out using Microsoft Excel and Statistical Package for Social Science (SPSS) applications. Frequency, simple percentage and relative importance index (RII) was used to answer the research questions.

Presentation of findings

The findings

(Figures 27.1, 27.2 and 27.3) Chart 1 shows that gender participation was almost equal. Out of 104 sampled respondents 49.04 per cent were male while 50.96 per cent female. Chart 2 shows that in terms of qualification 48.08 per cent of the respondents were BA/BSc/B.Ed. graduates and 51.92 per cent MSc/ MTech. Chart 3 shows all the head teachers having at least twenty-five years of professional experience. This was seen to be beneficial to the aims and objectives of the project, and to capture participants' understanding of the concept of global learning and its impact in the classroom.

Gender

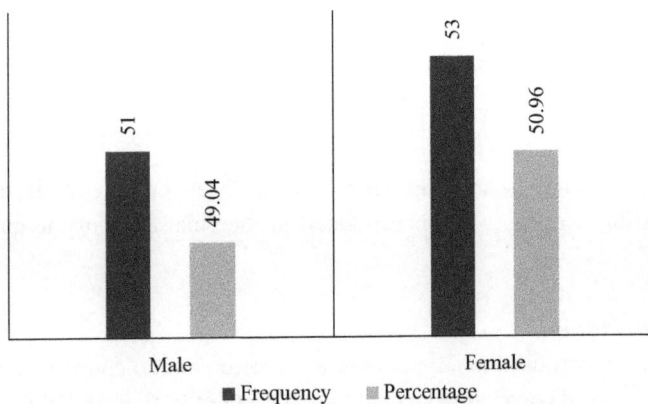

Figure 27.1 Learning in a global dimension for head teachers (*Source:* Soft Contents UK 2016).

Qualifications

■ Frequency ▓ Percentage

M.Ed	54	51.92
BA/BSc/B.Ed	50	48.08
Ed Diploma		
National Cert in Ed		
TCII		

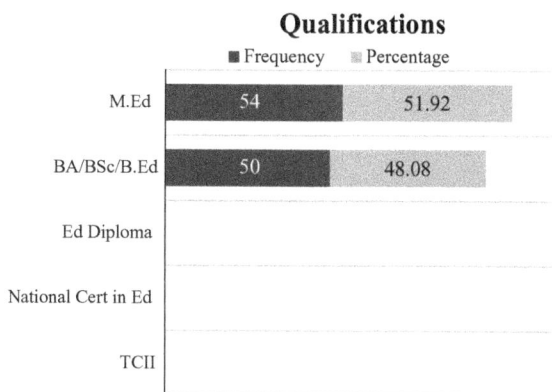

Figure 27.2 Learning in a global dimension for head teachers (*Source:* Soft Contents UK 2016).

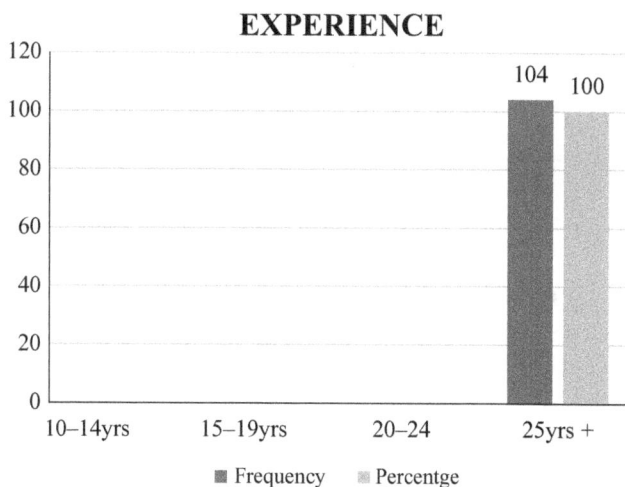

EXPERIENCE

(bar chart: 25yrs + — Frequency 104, Percentge 100)

Categories: 10–14yrs, 15–19yrs, 20–24, 25yrs +

■ Frequency ▓ Percentge

Figure 27.3 Learning in a global dimension for head teachers (*Source:* Soft Contents UK 2016).

Knowledge of school heads on global learning

The head teachers and teachers in the selected schools (104 in number) were asked to rate their knowledge on a four-point Likert scale: Strongly Agree (SA), Agree (A), Disagree (D) and Strongly Disagree (SD). This aspect of the questionnaire intends to examine and ascertain how much knowledge was gained during the training, any imbibed attitudinal change and sharpened skills of the respondents. Their responses were analysed and summarized in Table 27.1 with their RII values.

Table 27.1 shows the frequency and RII for each item under investigation. The criterion RII score is fifty and above. Using this criterion measure, the results show that the head teachers had the required knowledge of global learning with an overall RII of 69 per cent. The table further revealed that 90 per cent of the school heads affirmed that we live in a fast-changing

Table 27.1 Knowledge by School Heads of Global Learning

Knowledge	Responses				Descriptive	
	1	2	3	4	Rank	RII (%)
We live in a fast, changing and globalized world so knowledge of the use of internet is essential for any teacher to be effective.	0	0	42	62	1	90
Global learning should be a subject on its own and introduced into the curriculum.	0	0	62	42	2	85
Critical thinking is a skill. Learning should take place in a dialogic environment more than in a didactic/instructional one.	0	0	62	42	3	85
Global citizenship is the outcome of global learning. Critical thinking is a skill and a key element of global citizenship.	0	21	62	21	4	75
One of the elements of global citizenship is knowledge and understanding of global perspectives.	0	0	104	0	5	75
A global citizen is a person well connected to the internet. Every teacher connected to the internet is a global citizen.	0	42	41	21	6	70
Global learning is specifically about human development and nothing else.	42	0	21	41	7	65
A major responsibility of teachers is to prepare students to work in a global economy. Local economies are no longer relevant.	21	42	0	41	8	65
Values and attitudes form a key element of global citizenship, and climate change falls under this category.	0	62	42	0	9	60
Exceptional mastery of a subject discipline is enough for the teacher to provide the tools for learning in a global dimension.	0	62	21	21	10	50
It is not possible to address social justice, human rights and conflict in all subject disciplines.	42	62	0	0	11	40
Pooled						69

and globalized world; so knowledge of the use of the internet is essential for any teacher to be effective. Eighty-five per cent believed that global learning should be a subject on its own and introduced into the curriculum as well. Learning should take place in a dialogic environment more than in a didactic/instructional one, while the head teachers did not agree with the assertion that it is not possible to address social justice, human rights and conflict in all subject disciplines with an RII of 40 per cent.

Table 27.2 Friedman Test on Knowledge of School Heads on Global Learning

N	8
Chi-Square	32.865
Df	10
Asymp. Sig.	.000

Table 27.2 shows the chi-square value of 32.865 with ten degrees of freedom and asymptotic significant probability of 0.000 less than alpha value of 0.05. This analysis implies that the knowledge acquired during the training had significant effects on respondents' attitudes in relation to the need for more knowledge about global skills and competency.

Effectiveness of school heads in applying twenty-first-century skills in global learning

The responses of head teachers on their effectiveness in applying twenty-first-century skills in global learning are summarized in Table 27.3.

Table 27.3 shows a high-level awareness among the respondents in applying global perspectives, and willingness to play an active role in society at local, national and international level had an RII of 84 per cent; while three out of five items on effectiveness of the school head namely ability to communicate with a range of cultural backgrounds; openness to a range of

Table 27.3 Effectiveness of School Heads in Applying Twenty-first-century Skills in Global Learning

Knowledge	Responses					Descriptive	
	1	2	3	4	5	Rank	RII (%)
Willingness to play an active role in society at local, national and international level.	0	0	0	83	21	1	84.0
Ability to communicate with a range of cultural backgrounds.	0	21	21	21	41	2	76.0
Openness to a range of perspectives from around the world.	0	0	21	83	0	3	76.0
Willingness to resolve problems and seek solutions.	21	0	0	41	42	4	76.0
Ability to work within teams of diverse backgrounds	21	21	0	62	0	5	60.00
Pooled							**74.4**

perspectives from around the world, authentic sources of information, requirement for effective school administration; and willingness to resolve problems and seek solutions had common RII value of 76 per cent, respectively.

It could be deduced from these findings that the majority of respondents are quite effective in applying twenty-first-century skills in global learning because of the training acquired.

Conclusion

As the world is increasingly becoming interconnected, with a corresponding effect on the cultural, ethnic, language and religious diversity in the Nigeria education system, the teachers' education programme in the country is challenged with the task of developing the delivery of effective and efficient teaching and learning for the twenty-first century. In promoting a successful education system, education managers and administrators must be in touch with the constant change in teaching and learning skills and methods. This is especially so given the inherent challenges in current national reform efforts to achieve high academic standards, earn social promotion and foster globally rewarding learning return on every possible human investment.

The teacher education paradigm is shifting from the simple training of teachers towards the education of globally competent teachers. The efficacy of teacher training programmes is dependent on the pedagogy used to facilitate it. One of the teacher training objectives stated in the Nigerian NPE (2004) is 'the encouragement of the spirit of enquiry and creativity in teachers … providing them with the intellectual and professional background that will be adequate for their assignments and also make them adaptable to changing situations' (FME, NPE, 2004). If there is going to be an improvement in the skilling of teachers in this context it must start with those who will be responsible for the facilitation of such skills. A major objective of global learning is to develop teachers and educators as global citizens, policy-makers and practitioners, skilled and competent in the use of best practices that enable positive change and collaborative innovation in education.

Learning in a Global Dimension has been introduced to the Ondo West LGEA as a new paradigm that can be rolled out in schools to complement mainstream learning all over the Ondo State. This report recommends modalities of partnerships and collaboration be put in place to develop this project. It recommends the creation of a committed network of teachers who are skilled and competent in educating within the context of human rights and sustainable development, to meet the target for the provision of quality education in every primary school in Nigeria.

Bibliography

Adeosun, O. (2006). *Teacher Education Programmes and the Acquisition of 21st Century Skills: Issues and Challenges in Nigeria University of Lagos Nigeria*. Nigeria: University of Lagos.

Adesina, S. (1977). *Planning and Educational Development in Nigeria*. Lagos: Educational Industries Nigeria

Ajibola, M. A. (2008). Innovations and curriculum implementation for basic education in Nigeria: Policy priorities and Challenges of practices and implementation. *Research Journal of international studies*, Issue 8, 51–8.

Akani, O. (2012). Resources for Effective Implementation of UBE in Nigeria: Challenges and Remedies. Paper presented at the 53rd Conference of Science Teachers Association of Nigeria, Akure, Nigeria.

Bates, R. (2008). Teacher education in a global context: Towards a defensible theory of teacher education. *Journal of Education for Teaching: International Research and Pedagogy*, 34(4), 277–93.

Bourn, D. (2012). *Global learning and Subject Knowledge Development Education Research Centre.* Institute of Education, University of London, Research Paper No. 4.

Bourn, D. (2014). The theory and practice of global learning. *Development Education Research Centre, Research Paper 11*, 18.

Britzman, D. P. (2000). Teacher education in the confusion of our times. *Journal of Teacher Education*, 51(3), 200–5.

Fakoya, O. (2009). Teaching profession and factors affecting teaching profession in Nigeria A TEE report 403 University of Ibadan, Nigeria.

Fareo, D. O. (2013). Professional development of teachers in Africa: A case study of Nigeria. *The African Symposium, African Educational Research Network*, 13(1), 63.

Federal Republic of Nigeria (2004). National Policy on Education. *Nigerian Educational Research and Development Council. NERDC. Press Lagos Nigeria.*

Guo, L. (2013). Translating global citizenship education into pedagogic actions in classroom settings. *Ottawa Education Review*, 3(4), 8–9.

Gyoh, S. (2009). Structural constraints to global South actor involvement in development education in Ireland. *Policy & Practice: A Development Education Review, 8* (Springer 2009), 41–8. Available: http://www.developmenteducationreview.com/issue8-perspectives3

Leach, J. (2008). Do new information and communications technologies have a role to play in the achievement of education for all? *British Educational Research Journal*, 34(6), 783–805.

Merryfield, M. (1988). Pedagogy for Global Perspectives in Education: Studies in Teachers Thinking and Practice. *Theory and Research in Social Education*, 26(3), 342–79.

Merryfield, M. (1994, October). Teacher education in global & international education. *Viewpoints 120*, 2–9.

Obanya, P. (2002). *Revitalizing Education in Africa.* Ibadan: Stirling-Horden Publishers Nigeria Ltd.

Okonjo, C. (2000). *The Quiet Revolution – On Creating an Information–Age Education System for Nigeria.* Spectrum Books.

Pike, G. (2008). Reconstructing the legend: Educating for global citizenship. In A. Abdi and L. Shultz (eds), *Educating for Human Rights and Global Citizenship.* Albany: State University of New York Press, pp. 223–38.

Reimers, F. M. (2009). Global competency: Educating the world. *Harvard International Review*, Winter 2009, 24–7.

Sanyal, C. (2013). *Quality Assurance of Teacher Education in Africa Addis Ababa.* UNESCO: International Institute for Capacity Building in Africa.

Walters, L. M., Garii, B. and Walters, T. (2009). Learning globally, teaching locally: Incorporating international exchange and intercultural learning into pre-service teacher training. *Intercultural Education*, 20, 151–8.

Zhao, Y. (2010). Preparing globally competent teachers: A new imperative for teacher education. *Journal of Teacher Education*, 61(5), 422–31.

Part VI

Learning and Experience and Being Global Citizens

Chapter 28

Gesturing towards New Horizons of North–South Community-Engaged Learning

Ali Sutherland, Rene Suša and Vanessa Andreotti

Introduction

Theoretical debates about the potential for community-engaged learning in cross-cultural, international contexts have added much nuance to assumptions around the possibilities and limitations of developing global justice literacies in contexts of educational North–South engagements. According to Stein, '[t]here are multiple theories of global justice, which are in turn premised on different ideas and imaginaries of social change. ... [I]n any effort to intervene within global contexts of education, it is important to develop critical literacy around different visions of justice – to trace where they come from, what investments they rest on, and where they (potentially) lead' (2017: 222). Teaching for global justice literacies involves the use of pedagogical methods or theoretical concepts that 'prepare people to engage the complexity, uncertainty, and plurality of the world' (Stein, 2017: 222). Given the rise of community-engaged learning (Botchwey and Umemoto, 2018; Hatcher and Erasmus, 2008; Crabtree, 2008; Bringle and Hatcher, 2002) and the persistence of North–South learning experiences (Bringle, Hatcher and Jones, 2011; Tiessen and Grantham, 2017), it is important to consider what kind of pedagogies can help participants in programmes of North–South community-engaged learning develop more genuine and ethical relationships that extend beyond the usual transactional frameworks? By transactional frameworks we refer to the kind of North–South engagements that prioritize the learners' desires for self-realization and self-fulfilment that get actualized through commodification and consumption of relationships and experiences, including the consumption of the other's difference. This prioritization of learners' desires over more complex and troubling engagements that challenge normalized assumptions, privileges and projections severely restricts the possibilities for developing deeper and more responsible relationships.

In a time where critiques of the (white) saviour complex and the risks associated with educational programmes that send students from the Global North to the Global South are no longer confined to academia (see: barbiesavior.com; Irwar, 2014; Cole, 2012; Gharib, 2017), the questions of whether and how to reorient these kinds of programmes in ways that leverage their potential to be disruptive, generative and transformative are beginning to take hold among wider audiences. Despite the mounting critiques of these types of educational programmes, they persist.

There is a need to experiment pedagogically with new horizons of community-engaged learning, especially in a North–South context. The possibilities for developing global justice literacies through North–South community-engaged learning lie in the potential for these programmes and experiences to provoke a shift in how participants relate to themselves, to others and to knowledge.

This chapter draws on a case study of a community-engaged learning programme in Fortaleza, Brazil, that is attempting to expand the possibilities of developing more nuanced, ethical and genuine relationships between (and among) students from the North and communities in the South that are mindful of existing power relations and that attempt to make visible the complicities of learners in the reproduction of systemic harm. This programme created both a formal and an informal curriculum that supported learners in facing the contradictions of North–South community-engaged learning, and this chapter discusses the lessons learned from this experiment for the field of community-engaged learning and other associated fields (Sutherland, 2018).

One persistent limitation of mainstream community-engaged learning practices in North–South contexts is that students 'often pay little attention to understanding how their privilege and the historical relations of power reproduce global inequalities' (Karim-Haji, Roy and Gough, 2016: 7). A pedagogy that aims to develop global justice literacies prepares learners to consider layers of any global justice issue with attention to

> the past, to develop a critical historical memory, and learn the sources and root causes of novel developments; the present to identify recurrent patterns of inequality, in order to interrupt them and stop repeating the same mistakes; and the future, to pluralize what is possible by recognizing the limits of dominant narratives and knowledges, maintaining a global-mindedness to other narratives and knowledges without co-opting them, and possibly creating new ones. (Stein, 2017: 222)

In order to undertake this approach, learners must be encouraged to engage in self-reflexivity about how their actions and intentions are informed by their personal experiences and history, their collective referents and shared social meanings or roles, and institutional patterns and practices (Stein, 2017: 222). It is important to make the distinction that

> where self-reflection may be defined as individuals thinking about their personal experiences and assumptions, self-reflexivity is defined as connecting our individual assumptions to collective socially, culturally and historically situated 'stories' and assumptions that define what is real, ideal (right), and knowable (Andreotti et al., 2015). When we are self-reflexive, we challenge our own thinking, what we take for granted, and truly seek to learn through the perspective of another cultural perspective. (Karim-Haji, Roy and Gough, 2016: 13)

The chapter begins by tracing some of the recent debates in the literature regarding community-engaged learning in North–South mobility contexts by presenting a selective synthesis of relevant critiques and offers arguments for a need to develop approaches to community-engaged learning that are not only critical but that seek to explore also other, non-cognitive dimensions of ethical global justice–based learning engagements. To illustrate this point, the chapter offers the example of the EarthCARE global justice pedagogical framework that seeks to integrate five different and interrelated approaches to global justice and that might widen the possibilities of these types of educational experiences. In the second part, the chapter presents the findings from a case study of a community-engaged learning programme that attempted to do just that. The selected case promoted the practice of self-reflexivity while exploring the root causes of the issues of systemic poverty and structural inequality the learners observed. It also emphasized learning through physical (i.e. Capoeira, dance, etc.) academic exercises and activities, and attention to diverse forms of spirituality that encouraged learners to confront and unravel some of the contradictions inherent in North–South community-engaged learning. The programme framed its community development project component of the course (which involved each student being placed to work with one community or organization) as one where the learners were tasked with learning about the organization or community they were placed with and taking action as directed by the partners rather than the students; this encouraged students to operate from dispositions of humility, rather than superiority or mastery. The programme spent significant time working to reduce assumptions that the students had brought with them by engaging global justice literacy tools and integrating discussions that guided self-reflexivity practices for students to explore their preconceptions (and the roots of those preconceptions). This example offers insight into how applying such pedagogical frameworks can help open up new horizons for different kinds of education in North–South learning programmes, as well as some of the challenges and difficulties in trying to open up these horizons.

This chapter engages with the following questions: How might community-engaged learning in North–South contexts (as heavily critiqued and rife with layers of power, privilege and neocolonial tendencies as it is) be leveraged to establish more ethical relationships? In what ways might this widen the possibilities for these types of educational engagements to disrupt and transform dominant narratives? How do we learn from current practices and foster a pedagogy that addresses ongoing and historical global inequities while also opening up new possibilities for the future that do not reinscribe the same patterns? With these questions in mind, this chapter briefly outlines the current debates in community-engaged learning in North–South contexts.

Recent debates in the literature

Community-engaged learning, often referred to as 'service learning', is experiential

> learning that enhances the education of students and advances the aims of a community or organization. ... Community engaged pedagogy is designed to meet critical learning objectives for students while addressing the needs of a community. ... [Students] are placed in guided situations where they may question their own assumptions, hear others' voices, and see the world and its possibilities within the context of larger social processes from critical standpoints. (Botchwey and Umemoto, 2018: 1)

While this definition describes programmes and pedagogy across various institutions, faculties and geographic locations, the scope of this chapter is focused on community-engaged learning in North–South contexts and its propensity to provoke and instil global justice literacies. North to South mobility experiences are processes and programmes in which North American 'students travel to countries in the "Global South" for educational purposes including studying, doing practicum placements (co-op, volunteer, experiential learning) or combining study and practicum work' (Tiessen and Grantham, 2017: 3).

Proponents of community-engaged learning in North–South contexts often speak of their potential to solve or smooth over cross-cultural misunderstandings, prejudiced assumptions and respond to an ignorance of other cultures. However, many scholars (Zemach-Bersin, 2007; Jefferess, 2008; Bryan, 2013; Heron, 2007) demonstrate that these kinds of educational programmes have a deep history of and ongoing linkage to colonial and imperialist desires as well as a cultivation of benevolence and moral superiority. In fact, recently, there has been growing critique for their tendencies to reflect 'legacies of imperialism, geo-political interests, [and] historical biases' in ways that leave unquestioned international power relations imbued in narratives of development, progress, universality and innocence (Biles and Lindsey, 2009: 151). Additionally, there has been increasing academic discussion concerning the risks of North to South mobility experiences in contributing to neocolonial projects (Wright, 2015). As Wright (2015) describes, North to South mobility experiences are 'fundamentally linked to questions of power, privilege and the operation of "global coloniality" today ... yet, many of the inequalities present within the field are so stark, that they often go unnoticed' (p. 18). Jorgenson elaborates, recognizing 'the lack of mutuality in these exchanges in terms of people and knowledge, a call to problematize the notion that international programmes have the right to enter and intervene (predominantly on the Northerner's terms) in Southern contexts has begun' (2014: 43). Zemach-Bersin (2007), for example, highlights how despite an association with improving global awareness and lessening cross-cultural misunderstandings or prejudice, scholars often overlook how the current discourse 'is nationalistic, imperialist, and political in nature'. Pluim and Jorgenson (2012) continue to explore how North–South programmes are a reproduction of colonial relations through their tendency to reinforce dominant values and 'a superiority-inferiority binary'. They consider if it is possible 'that the harm incurred by these programmes might outweigh the good? And if this is the case, what do we, as [...] participants, practitioners and policy-makers, do about it?' (Pluim and Jorgenson, 2012: 25). As well, Stein, Andreotti, Suša and Bruce summarize that (from a critical or 'anti-oppression' standpoint) North–South educational experiences 'are critiqued for [being] potentially exploitive or disruptive for host communities (Jefferess, 2012); promoting an elitist and exclusionary cosmopolitanism (Rizvi, 2008); and perpetuating Western students' feelings of universal entitlement (Zemach-Bersin, 2007)' and 'for forestalling students' interrogation of how their own positions within the highly uneven and racialized global political economy contribute to the very harm they have supposedly travelled abroad to address (Andreotti, 2011; Bryan, 2013; Heron, 2007; Jefferess, 2012)' (Stein et al., 2016: 8). Pluim and Jorgenson (2012) highlight how a thorough post-colonial critique does seem to suggest that the appropriate response in light of the neocolonial tendencies would be to halt such programmes, a suggestion that other post-colonial analyses have touched on as well (Angod, 2015; Zemach-Bersin, 2007). However, Pluim and Jorgenson (2012) continue to state that 'not only unlikely, this solution ultimately throws the proverbial baby out with the bathwater' as community-engaged learning in North–South contexts does have the potential for new approaches to intercultural and interdependent relationships (p.32). In order for these kinds of educational programmes to disrupt hierarchical narratives and relationships in the pursuit of new pedagogical horizons, we need to document where the potential for provoking an educational experience that is disruptive, generative and transformative might lie. Epprecht (2004) illustrates how North–South community-engaged learning programmes are 'so obviously a powerful and attractive method of teaching about the complexities and challenges of development that it is tempting to assume that the benefits automatically outweigh the risks' (p.704). While Epprecht outlines some of the ethical and neocolonial risks of study abroad programmes, no matter how well thought out or well intentioned, he admits that 'on the other hand, to acknowledge the risks is to invite doubt' and that 'the task, therefore, is to find a balance between presumption (of intrinsic good) and pre-occupation (with risks)' (p.704). We tend to agree and it is within this paradox that this chapter situates itself. While aware of the rigorous post-colonial (and other) critiques of community-engaged learning in North–South contexts, this chapter seeks to explore the limits and possibilities of this type of education and its potential for global justice literacy.

The intended outcomes and benefits of community-engaged learning in North–South contexts for participants of these educational programmes often includes 'the development of "global awareness and knowledge", "intercultural competencies" and "global citizenship", as a means to improve students' employability and prepare them for the demands placed on today's global workforce' (Wright, 2015: 16), or how such programmes provide access to experiential learning and the development of intercultural skills necessary for global education (Golay, 2006; Clarke et al., 2009). The rationale for community-engaged learning revolves around the student who stands to benefit through the attainment of intercultural, language and communication skills and a (at times implicit, at others explicit) link between the development of these competencies and the education for global citizenship (Bringle, Hatcher and Jones, 2011; Lutterman-Aguilar and Gingerich, 2002). The impetus for community-engaged learning in North–South contexts is often traced back to an assumption that it will instil a sense of interconnectedness, global awareness and understanding that might generate non-exploitative relationships between people from different places and cultures (Lutterman-Aguilar and Gingerich, 2002). The unarticulated assumption here, to be clear, is that by becoming more aware of global conditions, systems and learners' complicity in them, those learners who are exposed to this new (and now visibly made real) knowledge will be compelled to change. The authors of this chapter take issue with this assertion that implicitly underlies much justification and pedagogy in community-engaged learning in North–South contexts. While we too articulate non-exploitative relationships that acknowledge interdependency and incommensurability as a desired outcome of North–South community-engaged learning, we find that it is not the provision of more information or acquisition of more knowledge that might enable, foster or encourage this. Thus, it is necessary to explore what else could be generative of those types of relationships within North–South community-engaged learning; what type of pedagogy might facilitate a transformation that shifts learners' relationships to self, others and knowledge in ways that might disrupt and reorient the investments that currently limit the types of global social change that is possible for learners to imagine? In light of the recent critique of the notion that simply participating in community-engaged learning in North–South contexts equips learners with the knowledge, perspective and skills important for living and working in a global society (Vande Berg, Paige and Lou, 2012; Bringle, Hatcher and Jones, 2011; Lutterman-Aguilar and Gingerich, 2015), the authors of this chapter seek to consider what pedagogical frameworks and approaches might best encourage students to engage with uncertainty and unpredictable outcomes in the learning experience, while remaining attentive and accountable to historical and ongoing global inequities?

Engaging with the EarthCARE framework

One such pedagogical framework that might be taken up in a North–South community-engaged learning context is the EarthCARE framework (see Andreotti et al., 2018). EarthCARE is a continuously evolving pedagogical framework that emerged through collaboration of educational practitioners from very diverse contexts, both in the geographical sense and in terms of the struggles and challenges they were facing. The framework was developed in the context of overlapping conversations happening in two networks: a cluster of indigenous and racialized communities in Latin America involved in the research project 'Social Innovation for Decolonial Futures', and the 'Ecoversities' network.

The EarthCARE global justice framework combines five complementary approaches to justice (earth justice, cognitive justice, affective justice, relational justice and economic justice) that encourage 'alternative approaches to engagement with alternatives' (Santos, 2007), moving beyond the search for universal models and problem-solving approaches towards preparing people to work together with and through the complexities, uncertainties, paradoxes and complicities that characterize efforts to address unprecedented global challenges collaboratively today. The key concept of earth justice reframes the 'environment' as a set of human and other-than-human relations and interdependencies, rather than a set of resources to be extracted/exploited by humans. By paying attention to multiple dimensions and possible understandings of global justice that often remain unacknowledged, the framework requires that learners engage in (self)reflexive practices that complexify their required level of engagement, especially when they begin to explore the cognitive, affective and relational aspects of global justice – that is, the multiple ways in which our thought processes, desires and relational possibilities have been restricted by the monoculture of thought premised on a singular narrative of human progress, development and evolution. The framework thus explores how economic and ecological problems and their proposed (political and/or technological) solutions remain overwhelmingly conditioned by the wider cognitive, affective and relational investments that circulate in society within the global modern/colonial imaginary. Pedagogically, the framework invites learners to explore the contributions, paradoxes and limits of their current problem-posing and problem-solving paradigms; engage experientially with alternative practices that challenge the limits of their thinking and capabilities; and contribute to the emergence of new paradigms of social change that open up not-yet-imaginable possibilities for coexistence in the future.

How might an engagement with the EarthCARE framework in North–South community-engaged learning contexts foster the ability to embrace new modes of relating (to self, others and knowledge)? In the following section of this chapter, the authors will trace the findings of a case study of a programme in its initial attempts to do so. However, before delving into the case study, it is important that the author articulates more fully some of the key concepts that the EarthCARE framework integrates, specifically the understanding and the use of the concepts of affective, relational and cognitive justice. As both theory (Santos, 2007, 2014; Jorgenson, 2014; Andreotti, 2015, Andreotti et al., 2018) and our findings from the case study presented below suggest that cognitive justice may be considered an indispensable (but also insufficient) precondition for development of affective and relational justice, this text engages primarily with the concept of cognitive justice, discussing only tangentially the possibilities of developing affective and relational justice as something that may (or not) emerge from dis-investments in narratives that affirm superiority of certain (dominant) kinds of knowledge. Cognitive justice 'asserts the diversity of knowledge and equality of knowers (Visvanathan, 2007), [and] also provides a lens for looking at the inequities being created and reproduced through some discourses and practices of internationalization and global citizenship' (Jorgenson, 2014: 60). Essentially, it affirms the rights of multiple knowledges (one of which is modern science) to exist simultaneously in plurality (Sousa Santos, 2007). The struggle to achieve global cognitive justice requires the development and practice of an ecology of knowledges (Sousa Santos, 2007). The recognition of the dominance of one way of thinking is the prerequisite to begin to think and/or act differently (Sousa Santos, 2007). Cognitive justice would embrace the pursuit of inter-knowledge which entails 'learning other knowledges without forgetting one's own' (Sousa Santos, 2007). To work towards global cognitive justice (or other forms of justice) can be difficult and uncomfortable, but this does not mean it should, therefore, be avoided. The EarthCARE collective has outlined the possibilities that pursuing cognitive justice might generate and these include identifying and interrupting harmful effects of a monoculture of thought premised on a single narrative of human progress and development, recognizing the contextual possibilities and limitations of all knowledge systems and creating interfaces between different knowledge systems (Andreotti et al. 2018). These possibilities are essential in reorienting community-engaged learning in a way that might disrupt the investments that currently constrain even those built on deeper engagement with complicity and self-reflexivity through a social justice approach.

The ability to engage with cognitive justice and thus allow for the recognition and existence of different knowledge systems simultaneously is required if there is to be a shift in affective investments. While some community-engaged learning programmes are able to articulate the existence of a plurality of knowledge systems and the gifts and limitations of these in ways that are intelligible to learners, it is rare that they go deeper and engage with the affective investments that produce the narratives which reinscribe monocultures of thought, narratives of progress, development, superiority. Although the social justice turn (Grain and Lund, 2017) might mean that students are encouraged to face knowledge that provokes discomfort, this acknowledgement of complicity can still be accompanied by learners' ensuing desire for mastery of their complicity and virtue signalling when such mastery is achieved, or a desire to absolve the discomfort associated with realizations of complicity and thus the pursuit of quick fixes and tangible solutions that move towards absolution and a reassertion of innocence (underwritten by the desire to feel good; an affective investment in which community-engaged learning in North–South contexts is deeply embedded in). To engage with affective justice in this context is to disrupt the narratives of progress, development, universality, mastery, superiority and innocence which inform students' attachments to their self-image and subsequent scope and understanding of their role in social change in ways that somehow straddle the balance between prompting inertia/paralysis and escaping back into the desire to feel good. Zembylas's (2015) theorizing on difficult knowledge adds nuance to its links to affective justice and how it can pedagogically result in 'having to tolerate the loss of certainty in the very effort to know' (Farley, 2009: 543). He outlines how difficult knowledge often involves uncertainty and disruption, and that those are, in fact, necessary in the pursuit of affective justice. Pedagogies that embrace difficult knowledge must also respond to 'the inadequacies and uncertainties of learners' responses as well as the loss of mastery and hope' (2015: 396). Much of the scholarship on affect thus deals with notions of loss – of sense of self, of historical narratives, etc. Thus, in reorienting desires towards new and different identities and aspirations, a pedagogy that works towards affective justice must not remain in disruption, loss and pain but mobilize it for the development of other dispositions. It is in these ways that we might gesture towards new horizons of pedagogy in this educational context and field. Affect is, therefore, understood as 'a category that encompasses affect, emotion, and feeling and "includes impulses, desires, and feelings that get historically constructed in a range of ways" (Cvetkovich, 2012: 4)'(Zembylas, 2015). This distinguishes affect from individual emotional processes and draws the link to wider social practices and norms. In pursuing affective justice, 'good pedagogy' would incorporate difficult knowledge with the aims of provoking and inviting learners to engage with the 'consequences of difficult knowledge' (Zembylas, 2015); the purpose is not mere disruption, but disruption that allows for new relations and desires to emerge.

Finally, it is pedagogy that works to create the conditions for this shift in desire that might provoke a relational justice. Andreotti (2017) details how this requires 'dismantling divisions caused by inherited social, cultural, economic and epistemological hierarchies that hinder symmetrical relationships'. Gaztambide-Fernandez reiterates the importance of considering pedagogically 'how to enter into ethical relationships that don't simply ignore the 'inherited social categories that shape the conditions of our lives" (2011: 323). If North–South community-engaged learning is to explore the possibilities of developing and sustaining encounters and relationships not based on superiority, helping or righteousness, those relationships will need to be guided by something else. Rather than learning about hierarchies that have historically characterized North–South relationships, there is a need to 'move beyond curriculum (as either knowledge or experience) to a focus on relationship, which might be better understood as a form of pedagogy' (Gaztambide-Fernandez, 2011: 326). This move towards emphasizing the relationships rather than the outcomes of North–South mobility experiences is growing in the literature, and is accompanied by a call for a consideration of the ontological dimension in these very experiences. McMillan and Stanton (2014) demonstrate that 'learning in complex unfamiliar contexts … [like those in which community engaged learning and study abroad take place] … is not just about knowledge and action – or knowledge and doing. It is crucially about being as well' (p.66). A consideration of an ontological project is required in order for the learning about and through relationships between self, other and knowledge to go beyond a mere intellectual engagement with what North–South educational experiences have to offer. The findings from the case study detailed below trace the need for, and the possibilities and limitations of, integrating attention to cognitive, affective and relational justice in North–South community-engaged learning.

Findings from a case study of a community-engaged learning programme in Fortaleza, Brazil

This section draws on a case study centred around participants of a programme based in Fortaleza, Ceará, in Brazil that brings students from various American universities to participate in community-engaged learning, specifically in a programme that is oriented by a commitment to social innovation and community development (Sutherland, 2018). This study grew out of an identified lack of well-documented alternatives to the dominant approaches to North–South community-engaged learning and attempted to respond to the need to develop 'more theoretically informed practical tools, frameworks, and resources for prompting and fostering ethical local and global engagements among practitioners and students alike' (Stein, 2017: 221) by exploring a case that attempts to do just that. This particular case, a US accredited study abroad programme centred around social innovation and community development, was selected because it used and engaged with global justice literacy tools such as social cartographies and metaphors to trace different visions of global justice through the context of Fortaleza, Brazil. As Stein states, 'Developing literacy for global justice might entail familiarizing students with the following processes: tracing and denaturalizing uneven distributions of wealth, power and resources; attending to the politics of knowledge production and epistemic authority/certainty, including asking what/ who is absent from a context or conversation, and why' (2017: 222). The social innovation and community development programme in Brazil attended to the politics of knowledge production and epistemic authority/certainty explicitly in the texts, resources, materials and discussions introduced within the classroom, but more significantly, the programme also spent significant time working to challenge who learners expected to hold or produce knowledge. By visiting with communities who had a long-standing relationship with the programme and engaging with them on their terms, the case challenged notions of expertise, authority, and respect as most of the people who represented communities, organizations and issues did not hold formal educational degrees, or privilege only the intellect as a way of knowing. During these visits, the students employed global justice literacy tools that they had co-constructed at the initial stages of the programme. One such tool was a matrix that encouraged students to locate the community or organization's approach to global justice and how it conceptualized wealth and power. They also engaged with a set of questions oriented towards tracing the vision of global justice employed by those they met with. These questions were formulated in an early open discussion and then woven through (and often adapted) for the different contexts in which the learners engaged.

Over the course of the programme, the participants visited diverse communities and organizations in Manaus, Rio de Janeiro, Paraty and Salvador who are practising community action, de-colonial grass roots movement building and innovative community-based models of development. After these short visits, the students individually partnered with one of the communities or organizations to work collaboratively on a multi-week community action and development project. The case itself was attempting to approach the educational encounter in a way that not only contests these trends but works to facilitate something that gestures to other and different possibilities. The study treated the selected case as a living example of the tensions and paradoxes inherent in North–South contexts of community-engaged learning and aimed to tease out the possibilities for community-engaged learning in North–South contexts to provoke different possibilities of relating to self, others and knowledge. The study involved participant observation and in-depth semi-structured interviews with five of the participants of the 2017 cohort of the semester long programme. Ultimately, the case study showed that implementing a pedagogical approach to North–South community-engaged learning that pursues cognitive, affective and relational justice faces two major challenges (that of articulation and of design) that must be engaged in any consideration of the implications for practice that these theoretical insights might contribute.

Learners' expectations for community-engaged learning and the transformation they hope for or anticipate are often structured by ideas associated with either the attainment of personal development and cross-cultural competencies or the acquisition of concrete tools for action to enact social change in light of the problems they encountered. Learners' expectations and understandings of transformation are framed by the vocabulary that is available and familiar to them. The diversity of personal and educational histories of the learners has an enormous influence on how they articulate their experience. How learners understand and conceptualize transformation then conditions what they are open to experiencing. Their expectations were framed in narratives of intercultural exposure, of developing an increased awareness about the world, and the development of individual qualities and mindsets to foster social change and avoid reproducing unjust structures that are often found in mainstream rationales for global citizenship education.

Thus, articulating an approach that seeks to expand the ways in which learners imagine global social change is a difficult task for both educators and learners alike. Part of the challenge of articulating an approach to North–South community-engaged learning that is attempting to foster a shift in cognitive, affective and relational investments is determining if we, as educators and practitioners, are asking the right questions.

The case study notes how a visit to a favela in Rio de Janeiro led by one of its residents brought up tensions among the students in the reflection discussion that ensued around the questions of whether one needs 'to go to know' and what happens as a result of 'knowing'? What does knowing more about the lived experiences of the communities mean? What does 'knowing about the other' do and what is the point if it does not aim to change the situation? These questions were articulated from a social justice approach. If these questions were articulated from an approach that gestures towards widened possibilities for global social change, the questions would focus on systemic complicity in harm and on corresponding affective investments. Examples of such questions could be: What is the encounter teaching you about your complicity? How do your affective investments influence the relationship between yourself and the visited community? Articulating these questions in ways that are intelligible to learners is very difficult and requires significant pedagogical work and support.

There is also a need to explicitly frame the intentions and expectations of an approach that is oriented towards global justice literacies. This is essential in communicating to students why they meet with various communities and how to frame their expectations of the encounter. In an informal meeting with indigenous students at university in Manaus, the students from the North engaged in a discussion of what their expectations and preconceptions of Amazonian communities had been prior to their arrival. The opportunity to talk about these expectations, to confront them and to modify them is one of the strengths that these community-engaged learning encounters offer as an educational space. In that example, the case study draws attention to the shift in conversation where narratives of personal benevolence and community-action-based approaches were replaced by those of systemic critique that offered no simple solutions. This shift occurred, because the indigenous students considered capitalism as an important part of the cause of the suffering felt by Amazonian communities and wanted to discuss its relationship to the destruction of their lands and displacement of their peoples. The students from the Global North were familiar with this critique, but were hesitant to engage without a proposal of an alternative system. The students from the North wanted the young people from the South to tell them an alternative to the system that was harming them and they could not imagine working towards a change that they could not guarantee. Part of the immense difficulty of articulating an approach that takes into account cognitive, affective and relational investments is that it requires that the learners suspend their desires to propose alternatives to (quickly) fix the complex problems they encounter and their tendencies to invoke epistemic certainty and privilege in formulating such solutions. In order to work towards an approach that aims to widen the spectrum of possibilities for global change, it is essential that educators face the challenge of articulating problematic assumptions and desires that will likely be met with considerable cognitive and affective resistance from the learners. In such attempts the educators need to clearly emphasize a shift from relating to knowledge in a way that values, rewards and promotes description and (then) prescription towards educating for an ability to identify and cope with the paradoxes, contradictions and complexity inherent in these engagements.

Each of the learners in the case study, in different ways, alluded to interpersonal relationships as the most important component of the programme, but also, for some, it was an area that they felt was hindered by a variety of logistical constraints (e.g. time, language ability and cultural differences). They showed a desire for meaningful relationships and a frustration in their inability to fully realize these in their interactions with people they met through the programme. Despite this desire for 'meaningful and authentic relationships' (which is fraught with a tendency to instrumentalize the 'Other' for their own learning), almost all of the participants mentioned fellow students or staff of the programme as the people with whom they developed the most significant relationships during their time in Brazil. This highlights a need for restructuring the programmes of North–South community-engaged learning in ways that allow for maximum contact between groups in a de-centred, horizontal manner. Such a restructuring could help develop new and different (deeper) relationships between participants from the North and the South.

Although the research suggests a need for development of more reciprocal models of community-engaged learning, it is important to unpack this desire for meaningful relationships in the context of the educational approach. In fact, just as the learners' expectations of self-growth/self-actualization and searches for appropriate action to change the world were evidently framed by dominant narratives structured into the programmes, their pursuit of 'meaningful relationships' also remained based on the same ontological parameters that characterize these narratives. The instrumentalization of others to meet self-actualization places learners in a position of entitlement in relation to others. It is, therefore, essential for educators in this context to consider how the experiential component of North–South mobility encounters has a generative potential in 'making real' the realities of their interdependency but must be extremely cautious of instrumentalizing other bodies for the purpose of learning. Learners' desire for relationality is important and can be problematic or generative depending on the intentions and frames of reference that inform this desire. While the development of relationships both informs and emerges from North–South experiences, significant attention to the ethics of relations must be considered and explicitly incorporated into such programmes; however, the types of relations that participants desire must be pedagogically addressed. Therefore, while learners articulate this desire for meaningful relationships or relationships, their desires are less different from dominant and pervasive narratives framing the motivations, expectations and outcomes of community-engaged learning programmes in a North–South context than they may appear. Learners' desire to learn about people first hand demonstrates a return to the search for the same affective and intellectual economies that structure the dominant approach to North–South community-engaged learning, rather than an approach that generates new and different ways of relating to oneself, knowledge and others. While it is important to note the desire emerging from learners for North–South experiences that are structured differently, their notion of 'different' falls within the realm of they can imagine (due in part to the lack of vocabulary to articulate what it would look/be like otherwise).

In the case study, one of the learners stated that she was initially looking for a programme that might allow for the development of reciprocal relationships. To an extent, this indicates a growing demand for North–South education that does not continue to contribute to neocolonial tendencies (likely given to the way in which critique of these types of learning contexts have become accessible through mainstream media). This demand for alternative programmes, although voiced in the case study, was also contradicted by the very same learners who described how they 'wouldn't be here if I didn't want to feel a certain way'. It is this underlying desire to be made to feel a certain way (which can be read as an expression of a deeper desire to 'feel good') that heightens the risk for relationship building as a move towards reciprocity/ethical engagement to potentially lead to the instrumentalization of these very relationships for self-actualization. As Gaztambide-Fernandez and Howard (2013) demonstrate, 'Part of what motivates privileged adolescents to engage in benevolent acts, especially community service activities, is the ability to present themselves to others as caring, engaged, and generous' (p.2). What learners see as an alternative or different future model seems to be more of the same, and so a big part of the challenge facing educators who wish to leverage the disruptive, generative and transformative potential of community-engaged learning is in designing a programme that attempts to prevent the learners from falling back into the same desires and investments framed by the vocabulary and economies they are most familiar with.

Beyond complicating the desire for 'more meaningful' relationships, the case study demonstrated a need for the development of a pedagogical 'unloading process' for learners to begin to engage differently with dominant discourses about social, political, economic and technological development. The case study points to an example of where this might be necessary that comes from the intercultural gathering of youth that happened at a school organized by residents of a Movimento dos Trabalhadores Sem Terra (MST; Landless Workers' Movement) settlement in the state of Ceará. This gathering served to bring together diverse youth to discuss and share the pressing issues of their time, across cultures and contexts. The youth engaged in facilitated and unfacilitated activities together, and heard from different speakers who provided context on the incidences of violence among youth in Ceará, and the gendered dynamics of the issues facing young people in north-eastern Brazil. As part of a wider, facilitated discussion, the youth from vastly different backgrounds (a landless movement settlement, a nearby Quilombo, a local university, Tremembe youth, the American students, and students living and working in a favela community of Bom Jardim) were asked whether they considered life in Canada to be better than life in Brazil.

Although coming from very different social backgrounds, all the young people in the gathering agreed that life in Canada was better than in Brazil, without questioning what 'life' was supposed to mean and whose life was being compared. This situation may be considered indicative of very real, persistent and pervasive narratives of superiority and inferiority that are the foundation for ideas and commitments to 'development in the name of progress' in people from various backgrounds. There is an urgent need for activities that allow people to engage with superiority, inferiority, development and progress – all narratives that persisted strongly among the various groups present and that have been well documented in (global citizenship) education literature (see Andreotti 2015; Willinsky 1998; Heron 2007; Shultz 2007 as examples). The notion of a single story of progress and development that has divided humanity 'between those who are perceived to be leading progress, development and human evolution; and those who are perceived to be lagging behind' is best traced to a 'dominant modern/colonial global imaginary ... that ascribes differentiated value to cultures/countries that are perceived to be 'behind' in history and time and cultures/countries perceived to be 'ahead'' (Alaasutari and Andreotti, 2015: 64). This imaginary has the power to capture and frame 'our collective imagination' and desires in ways that are so normalized and invisibilized that they are hard to point out or challenge (Alaasutari and Andreotti, 2015: 71). The hands raised by both Americans and Brazilians of various backgrounds to indicate that the majority of attendees of the gathering believed that quality of life was better in Canada than in Brazil demonstrates the normalization of this single story which evidently poses a challenge to practices that seek to engender global justice literacies. There is a need for activities in these educational settings that go beyond the sharing of peoples' personal experiences and relations to manifestations of violence that could connect these 'separate' experiences to the larger narratives that we buy into on a daily basis and that shape our interactions and realities. This work of allowing people to feel that they are connected to the same stories and desires requires an unloading process that encourages learners to identify their desires and to examine how they shape their relationships to themselves, others and knowledge.

Conclusions

Designing a programme that embraces discomfort as a source of learning that is disruptive but generative requires significant educational and pedagogical work on the behalf of the educator. It is difficult to create curriculum and pedagogy that provokes discomfort in ways that do not produce inertia or paralysis, and at the same time do not push learners to re-invest in the desire for immediate action required to re-establish the means for 'feeling good'. In many of the learners' narratives emerging in the case study, they were able to speak to the value of being uncomfortable and how this had been a generative part of their learning process. However, as Andreotti (2016) writes, 'we may even say we want to learn from discomfort, but when it actually happens, when we lose epistemic privilege, we feel wronged and fight to regain that privilege again'. This process of reasserting epistemic privilege was evident in the learners' narratives in the case study. It is one of the key challenges of designing an approach that widens the possibilities for global social change and gives weight to the question of how pedagogy can be implemented in a way that does not shortcut the possibilities for different relationships to self, others and knowledge in the name of coping with discomfort.

A final challenge in designing community-engaged learning that encourages learners to move from describing and then prescribing (i.e. becoming aware of problems and then seeking out appropriate actions to solve it), and instead emphasizes holding the complexity and uncertainty that they encounter in the learning experience is resisting the temptation to 'fix'. This is a complicated endeavour as it requires balancing the need for certainty of knowing past and present global inequities with a sense of accountability and responsibility, with the need for uncertainty in terms of what ways of knowing and being might generate new possibilities for the systems we currently have. Part of holding the tensions and complexities that the learners encounter is important not only to design against the impulse that often characterizes how they position themselves in relation to these uncertainties (and leads to a reification of those in the Global North as unquestioned changemakers), but also as a demonstration of willingness to listen to the partners with whom the programme liaises and works with. This was made visible especially in the encounters where community partners did not necessarily (or at all) expect a direct action from the students, but were rather more interested in their stories being carried back to students home circles or were interested in exploring how to develop and sustain deeper relationships or collaboration.

As Osberg (2017) mentions, 'it is generally accepted that education is at least partly responsible for the kinds of futures that emerge' (p.13). The relationship, however, between education, action and what kind of future emerges must be seriously considered. This calls for learners to act in ways that are responsible without a guarantee of feedback or immediate reward, progress, change or impact. The desire of wanting to fix, to (ab)solve, to change or make better that emerged through the participant narratives in the case study is not unique to the individuals who voiced it, but rather is indicative of socialization and investments in narratives of 'correcting' and 'solving' the present for an imagined future on the behalf of a universal humanity. If education is tied morally and politically to the possible futures, it is imperative that work be done to allow learners to engage differently with the ways of knowing and the ways of being that we have inherited, been socialized into and accepted as the norm. The ability to imagine outside of these is an enormous task for education, and this chapter has highlighted one case study of an attempt to explore the contexts in which such an imagining might be provoked and/or possible.

Both examples from existing literature and the lessons learned from the presented case study demonstrate a need for students to learn how to face complexity and uncertainty, especially in North–South educational encounters. In developing more ethical, responsible and deeper relationships between partners in these encounters it is important to consider that the ability to face uncertainty and complexity presents the cognitive component of what allows for a pursuit of affective justice that enables possibilities of healing historical and intergenerational trauma. Only in learning how the kinds of knowledge that we have been socialized into are foreclosing on the possibilities of seeing the world from someone else's eyes, in acknowledging the epistemic and ontological erasures (Santos, 2007, 2014), can we break with some of the harmful exploitative and hegemonic patterns of behaviour that more often than not dominate the North–South encounters. By relating to knowledge, to others and to the self differently, we can begin to shift our desires from structures and systems that reassert and reaffirm our mastery and innocence in global social change and impact. The terms of engagement widen once we reorient the desire 'to be made to feel a certain way' and thus open the possibilities for educational engagements that foster global justice literacies and engage with communities in ways that do not repeat the same processes that have historically structured these processes.

Bibliography

Alaasutari, H. and Andreotti, V. (2015). Framing and Contesting the Dominant Global Imaginary of North-South Relations: Identifying and Challenging the Dominant Global Imaginary of North-South Relations: Identifying and Challenging Socio-Cultural Hierarchies. *Policy & Practice: A Development Education Review*, 20: 64–92.

Andreotti, V. (2017). *Decolonizing Teacher Education*. Presentation, University of Regina, Regina, Saskatchewan.

Andreotti, V. (2011). *Actionable Postcolonial Theory in Education*. New York: Palgrave Macmillan [introduction].

Andreotti, V. (2015). Global Citizenship Education Otherwise: Pedagogical and Theoretical Insights. In A. Abdi, L. Shultz and T. Pillay (eds), *Decolonizing Global Citizenship Education*. Rotterdam, The Netherlands: SensePublishers.

Andreotti, V. (2016). Multi-layered Selves: Colonialism, Decolonization and Counter-Intuitive Learning Spaces. http://artseverywhere.ca/2016/10/12/multi-layered-selves/

Andreotti, V., Stein, S., Sutherland, A., Pashby, K., Suša, R., Amsler, S. and the Gesturing Towards Decolonial Futures Collective (2018). Mobilising Different Conversations about Global Justice in Education: Toward Alternative Futures in Uncertain Times. *Policy and Practice: A Development Education Review*, 26(Spring): 9–41.

Angod, L. (2015). Behind and Beyond the Ivy: How Schools Produce Elites through the Bodies of Racial Others. Doctoral Thesis, University of Toronto.

Biles, J. J. and Lindley, T. (2009). Globalization, Geography, and the Liberation of Overseas Study. *Journal of Geography*, 108(3): 148–54.

Botchwey, N. and Umemoto, K. (2018). A Guide to Designing Engaged Learning Courses in Community Planning. *Journal of Planning Education and Research*, 1–13. https://doi.org/10.1177/0739456X18772075.

Bringle, R. and Hatcher, J. (2002). Campus-Community Partnerships: The Terms of Engagement. *Partnerships/ Community*, 23. https://digitalcommons.unomaha.edu/slcepartnerships/23

Bringle, R., Hatcher, J. and Jones, S. (2011). *International Service Learning: Conceptual Frameworks and Research*. Stylus Publishing.

Bryan, A. (2013). 'The Impulse to Help'. (Post)humanitarianism in an era of the 'new' development advocacy. *International Journal of Development Education and Global Learning*, 5(2): 5–29.

Clarke, I., Flaherty, T., Wright, N. and McMillen, R. (2009). Student intercultural proficiency from study abroad programs. *Journal of Marketing Education*, 31(2): 173–81.

Cole, T. (2012). The White Savior Industrial Complex. *The Atlantic*. https://www.theatlantic.com/international/archive/2012/03/the-white-savior-industrial-complex/254843/

Crabtree, R. (2008). Theoretical Foundations for International Service Learning. *Michigan Journal of Community Service Learning*, 15(1): 18–36.

Cvetkovich, A. (2012). *Depression: A Public Feeling*. Durham, NC: Duke University Press.

Epprecht, M. (2004). Work-Study Abroad Courses in International Development Studies: Some Ethical and Pedagogical Issues. *Canadian Journal of Development Studies / Revue canadienne d'études du développement*, 25(4): 687–706.

Farley, L. (2009). Radical Hope: Or, the Problem of Uncertainty in History Education. *Curriculum Inquiry*, 39(4): 537–54.

Gaztambide-Fernandez, R. (2011). Possible Impossibles: Four Pedagogies for the Present and Pressing Moment. *Curriculum Inquiry*, 41: 3.

Gaztambide-Fernandez, R. and Howard, A. (2013). Social Justice, Deferred Complicity, and the Moral Plight of the Wealthy. A Response to "With Great Power Comes Great Responsibility': Privileged Students' Conceptions of Justice-Oriented Citizenship'. *Democracy and Education*, 21(1): 1–4.

Gharib, M. (2017). Volunteering Abroad? Read This Before You Post That Selfie. *National Public Radio*. https://www.npr.org/sections/goatsandsoda/2017/11/26/565694874/volunteering-abroad-read-this-before-you-post-that-selfie

Golay, P. (2006). The Effects of Study Abroad on the Development of Global Mindedness Among Students Enrolled in International programs at Florida State University. Unpublished doctoral thesis.

Grain, K. and Lund, D. (2017). The Social Justice Turn: Cultivating 'Critical Hope' in an Age of Despair. *Michigan Journal of Community Service Learning*, 45–59.

Hatcher, J. and Erasmus, M. (2008). Service-Learning in the United States and South Africa: A Comparative Analysis Informed by John Dewey and Julius Nyerere. *Michigan Journal of Community Service Learning*, 15(1): 49–61.

Heron, B. (2007). *Desire for Development: Whiteness, Gender, and the Helping Imperative*. Wilfrid Laurier University Press.

Irwar, S. (2014). We Day to Me Day: The Damaging Effect of Voluntourism. *The Huffington Post*. https://www.huffingtonpost.co.uk/iram-sarwar/voluntourism-travelling_b_4931814.html?guccounter=1&guc e_referrer_us=aHR0cHM6Ly93d3cuZ29vZ2xlLmNvLnRoLw&guce_referrer_cs=C5zPKbkCX_jCrt fy4pyUug

Jefferess, D. (2008). Global Citizenship and the Cultural Politics of Benevolence. *Critical Literacy: Theories and Practices*, 2(1): 27–36.

Jefferess, D. (2012). The 'Me to We' Social Enterprise: Global Education as Lifestyle Brand. *Critical Literacy: Theories and Practices*, 6(1): 18–30.

Jorgenson, S. (2014). (De)colonizing Global Citizenship: A Case Study of North American Study Abroad Programs in Ghana. Doctoral Thesis. University of Alberta.

Karim-Haji, F., Roy, P. and Gough, R. (2016). Building Ethical Global Engagement with Host Communities: North-South Collaborations for Mutual Learning and Benefit. Resource Guide presented at the 10th Annual Global Internship Conference 15–17 June 2016, Boston, MA, USA.

Lutterman-Aguilar, A. and Gingerich, O. (2002). Experiential Pedagogy for Study Abroad: Educating for Global Citizenship. *Frontiers: The Interdisciplinary Journal of Study Abroad*, 8: 41–82.

McMillan, J. and Stanton, T. (2014). 'Learning Service' in International Contexts: Partnership-based Service Learning. *Michigan Journal of Community Service Learning*, 21(1): 64–78.

Osberg, D. (2017). Education and the Future: Rethinking the Role of Anticipation and Responsibility in Multicultural and Technological Societies. In R. Poli (ed.), *Handbook of Anticipation*. Springer, 1–20.

Pluim., G. W. J. and Jorgenson, S. R. (2012). A Reflection on the Broader, Systemic Impacts of Youth Volunteer Abroad Programmes: A Canadian Perspective. *Intercultural Education*, 23(1): 25–38.

Rizvi, F. (2008). Epistemic Virtues and Cosmopolitan Learning. *The Australian Educational Researcher*, 35(1): 17–35.

Shultz, L. (2007). Educating for Global Citizenship: Conflicting Agendas and Understandings. *The Alberta Journal of Educational Research*, 53(3): 248–58.

de Sousa Santos, B. (2007). Beyond Abyssal Thinking: From Global Lines to Ecologies of Knowledge. *Review*, XXX(1): 45–89.

de Sousa Santos, B. (2014). *Epistemologies of the South: Justice against Epistemicide*. Boulder, CO: Paradigm Press, 212–35.

Stein, S. (2017). Contested Imaginaries of Global Justice in the Internationalization of Higher Education. Doctoral Thesis. The University of British Columbia.

Stein, S., Andreotti, V., Bruce, J. and Suša, R. (2016) Towards Different Conversations About the Internationalization of Higher Education. *Comparative and International Education / Education Comparée et Internationale*, 45(1): 1–18.

Sutherland, A. (2018). Exploring the Possibilities of a Post-critical Approach to Student North-South Mobility Experiences: A Case Study of the Social Innovation and Community Development Program in Fortaleza, Brazil. Master's Thesis. The University of British Columbia.

Tiessen, R. and Grantham, K. (2017). *Overview: North-South Student Mobility in Canada's Universities*. Issue briefs on North-South student mobility. Universities Canada: The Voice of Canada's Universities.

Vande Berg, M., Paige, R. and Lou, K. (2012). *Student Learning Abroad: What Our Students Are Learning, What They're Not, And What We Can Do About It*. Virginia: Stylus Publishing.

Visvanathan, S. (2007). Knowledge, Justice and Democracy. In Melissa L., Ian S. and Brian W. (eds), *Science and Citizens*. London, Zed Books, 83–94.

Wade, R. C. (2000). From a Distance: Service-learning and Social Justice. In C. R. O'Grady (ed.), *Integrating Service Learning and Multicultural Education in Colleges and Universities*. Mahwah, NJ: Lawrence Erlbaum Associates, 93–111.

Willinsky, J. (1998). *Learning to Divide the World: Education at Empire's End*. Minneapolis, MN: University of Minnesota Press.

Wright, E. (2015). North to South Mobility: Study Abroad in Ecuador, Towards an Understanding of Decolonial Education. Master's Thesis.

Zemach-Bersin, T. (2007). Global Citizenship and Study Abroad: It's all about US. *Critical Literacy: Theories and Practices*, 1(2): 16–28.

Zembylas, M. (2015). Theorizing 'Difficult Knowledge' in the Aftermath of the 'Affective Turn': Implications for Curriculum and Pedagogy in Handling Traumatic Representations. *Curriculum Inquiry*, 44(3): 390–412.

Chapter 29

The Role of Informal Spaces in Global Citizenship Education

Madeleine Le Bourdon

Introduction

Global learning has been part of pedagogical initiatives within the UK since the 1970s (Humble 2013; Bourn 2014), yet the term 'global citizenship education' (GCE) has only gained increasing traction over the past decade. GCE has become part of formal curricula from primary to tertiary level (Le Bourdon 2018), is often a significant feature of educational initiatives by global civil society organizations (e.g. Oxfam) and cited as an additional outcome of volunteer programmes (see Griffith 2016). Scholarly discourse has often centred around the conceptualization of global citizenship (see Oxley and Morris 2013) and best practices for teaching and learning (see Percy Smith 2012; Van Peski 2012). The majority of research has focused upon purposeful and structured learning spaces delivering GCE through formal institutions such as schools and universities (see Hicks and Holden 2007; Nussbaum 2010), with some research acknowledging GCE as part of the experience of international volunteering (Baraldi, Malleti and Manicardi 2014; Griffith 2016).

However, GCE has been widely understood as a lifelong learning journey rather than a specific skill or knowledge to acquire (Golmohamad 2004; Schattle 2008), suggesting that learning continues to take place even beyond structured activities. Despite this, there remains little understanding of the role of informal spaces within an individual's day-to-day life as places for GCE (Le Bourdon 2018)

This chapter seeks to address this by examining these informal spaces between set learning and the lived experience of GCE. Building on previous research highlighting these spaces as fruitful sites for global citizenship learning (see Le Bourdon 2018) the chapter looks more closely at what makes the informal so impactful. To do this it uses findings from qualitative research into a case study organization providing non-formal GCE within a multicultural environment. Through examining the lived experience of participants, rich insight was gained into the micro-level actions and interactions shaping these spaces. Analysis highlights the importance of informal interactions as a way of creating moments of affective learning while at the same time fostering strong bonds and feelings of belonging.

The chapter will begin by outlining current discourse around GCE which has focused upon its conceptualization and best practices for teaching and learning. In doing so, it will show how research has concentrated on formal education (Le Bourdon 2018) and global civil society organizations providing GCE. The latter has been referred to by scholars as both 'informal' and 'non-formal' (see Jeffs and Smith 2005); here 'non-formal' will be used to distinguish from traditional pedagogical settings but also to provide a clear distinction from the informal spaces this chapter discusses. In outlining previous research, gaps in knowledge will be highlighted around the spaces between structured learning and their role on an individual's GCE journey.

The methodological approach to research will then be outlined, which centred on capturing the lived experience of participants as a way of understanding the micro-level process shaping GCE. Lastly, the chapter will discuss three key findings from analysis: that informal spaces provide an opportunity for further, independent learning; that unlike in structured learning, earnest interactions take place creating strong bonds between individuals; and that what makes these informal spaces so impactful is the sharing of and shared emotional experience within them. Thus, the chapter will conclude that informal spaces are not only important for GCE as places for further learning and practice but also in enabling organic, strong bonds to foster feelings of belonging through shared experience and emotions.

Locating GCE and research

GCE has become increasingly promoted and practised within formal educational institutions and by global civil society actors. Its conceptualization remains open to interpretation, often interchanged with development, human rights or sustainable development education despite nuances in their framings (Humble and Smith 2007). GCE, as argued by Wintersteiner et al. (2015), combines these pedagogies and encapsulates their key components. However, the use of 'citizenship' adds an extra layer to this expression of global learning, implying a sense of responsibility and loyalty to shared global issues and wider humanity. Tarozzi and Inguaggiato claim GCE thus goes beyond promoting international awareness which scholars warn can be seen as covert colonialism, to instead provide:

a special focus emphasizing global themes such as peace, a sustainable future, human rights, addressing poverty ... reading them through the meaningful lenses of citizenships as the key educational. (2018: 4)

Thus, tackling global issues through the angle of citizenship allows learners to locate and consider their own positionality and role in relation to the topic, consequently stimulating self-reflexivity and critical thinking. For Baillie Smith this is key in GCE to

foster more critical and reflexive understandings ... in the belief that these will produce more active global citizens and better informed engagement with the causes rather than effects of global poverty and justice. (2014: 486)

At the same time, scholars such as Schattle (2008) and Golmohamad (2004, 2009) see GCE as essential for fostering feelings of belonging and global solidarity. Thus, for this chapter GCE can be understood as a pedagogical approach in which knowledge and skills are gained helping learners to critically analyse our increasingly interconnected world and our positionality within it. At the same time it recognizes the important role of both the local and the global in addressing global challenges, and thus the need to build feelings of belonging to multiple communities for the betterment of the whole of humanity.

Beyond its conceptualization scholars have widely discussed pedagogical approaches to GCE, helping to build a framework of best practices (see Dower 2003,;Baillie Smith 2004; Davies 2006; Bourn 2008; Van Peski 2012; Tarozzi and Torres 2016). Particular attention has been given to the environment, structure and content of teaching and learning which Bourn claims directly shapes the 'orientation and knowledge of learners' (2008: 31). Experiential learning practices or 'learning by doing' have been championed, allowing learners the space to explore complex topics more freely (see Van Peski 2012; Percy Smith 2012). Through providing non-judgemental safe spaces, learners can independently consider multiple angles, ask questions, push boundaries, make mistakes and come to their own judgements on topics. Such an approach decreases the likelihood of simplistic understandings which research has shown direct learning risks providing (Hicks and Holden 2007), and which risks leading to understandings centring on dependency or subordination of the Global South (Dobson 2006; Andreotti 2011). Instead through considering multiple perspectives and examining traditional knowledge sources, learners are able to develop critical-thinking skills and form their own informed understanding and response.

This requires not only the teaching environment but also the teaching methods to be open, pragmatic and fluid. Thus, rather than only providing information through direct teaching, teachers instead take a facilitating role allowing room for discussion and debate (Conway and Heynen 2002; Andreotti 2006; Khoo 2006, Asbrand 2008). This reflects Paulo Freire's theory of the pedagogical process of 'action-reflective-transformative action' which the scholars sees as essential for fostering individuals who can 'deal critically and creatively with reality and discover how to participate in the transformation of their world' (1970: 15). In other words, providing space and time to engage with topics develops critical-thinking skills through practice and encourages learners to become agents for change. Interestingly, interactive learning has been credited in discussions around best practices for traditional citizenship education as essential to cultivate 'active citizenship' and positive participation within society (Warming 2012). By actively engaging with topics and issues, learners not only reflect on their role but also gain a sense of agency, realizing the power in their actions. Therefore, rather than *changing* learners, experiential learning within GCE instead seeks to create a *change in* learners (Temple and Laycock 2008).

This raises questions around the ability of formal education to provide effective, critical GCE. Within the UK, schools and universities face increasing pressure to meet targets and obtain funding (Body, Holman and Hogg 2017), thus global learning has been neglected in favour of fostering work-ready, target-driven individuals (Baillie Smith 2004). Research has also shown that when GCE is delivered, teachers own knowledge and confidence in teaching on such complex or controversial topics within GCE is lacking. This risks the oversimplification or even avoidance of topics completely (Holden and Hicks 2007).

Outside of formal education, global civil society organization's providing affective, critical GCE (such as Oxfam 2018; Tide Global Learning 2018) has been seen as a way of addressing these restrictions in time, knowledge and structure found in schools and universities (Holden and Hicks 2007). These organizations often provide resources or deliver workshops around global learning topics (such as Oxfam International and Tide Global Learning). However, they too face similar obstacles in delivering best practices outlined in the literature. Studies have identified a trend in the professionalization of development spaces including areas of education (Bondi and Laurie

2005). Organizations are forced to conform to formal education's strict schedule and budgets, meaning programmes provided by are often episodic. These ad hoc, short bursts of learning could also lead to complex or controversial topics not being given enough time to analyse and unpack sufficiently. Thus, GCE actors working both inside and beyond the classroom setting are forced to negotiate between the informal and formalized neoliberalized structures (Baillie Smith 2014).

Yet, scholars also emphasize the importance of independent learning with GCE seen not as the fostering of a set of skills and practices one acquires but as personal lifelong learning process (Schattle 2008; Temple and Laycock 2008). This understanding sees individuals developing and practising global citizenship throughout their lifetime through participation and experience. It is, therefore, imperative to look beyond structured learning environments to the spaces between them. These informal spaces have the potential to provide the time and space lacking in structured learning environment, as well as the opportunity for peer and independent learning. In order to understand the role of these informal spaces, attention must be turned to the micro-level actions and interactions within these spaces. To do this the research methodology centres on capturing the lived experiences of individuals as they journey through GCE.

Methodology

Methodology for this research took a qualitative approach designed to capture the lived experience of individuals through GCE. To do this, a case study was used of an international non-formal educational camp provided by a global civil society organization, Children's International Summer Villages (CISV) International, which aims to build 'active global citizens'.

A volunteer programme founded in the United States, CISV International is now present in 69 countries around the world, with over 200 local, often city-based, 'Chapters'. The organization runs several different international programmes designed for children ranging from aged eleven to eighteen years. The local Chapters act as federal branches of the organization financed through national and local fundraising initiatives. With minimal permanent staff within CISV International, the development of educational content and logistical running of Chapters and camps is predominately reliant on local volunteers. CISV International flagship programme, the 'Village' camp, brings several delegations made up of two boys and two girls aged eleven years and an adult 'Leader' from multiple cultural backgrounds and countries together to live and learn with each other for a month as a community. Educational activities are designed and delivered, using experiential learning practices, by the leaders of the camp, based around themes such as sustainable development and human rights. It is important to note here that to attend as a child participant there is both a membership and a participation fee. This fee varies across Chapters depending on the local organizations' funding streams, with some able to offer schemes and bursaries for lower income families. The lack of diversity, and thus exclusive nature of CISV International, brings into question the organization's ability to deliver best practices for GCE. However, for the purpose of this chapter, CISV International's camps offer a fruitful setting for capturing the role of informal space within GCE.

This research used CISV International 'Village' camp as a case study offering an insightful 'window' into micro-level practices on the ground and in doing so, a richer understanding of the 'broader picture' of GCE (O'Neill et al. 2002: 78). To understand where global citizenship learning took place research methods were designed to capture the whole journey of participants through the camp. Thus, two sets of semi-structured interviews with the adult leaders took place, two weeks prior to the camp and four weeks post camp, both through Skype. This was complemented by observations on the camp taking an ethnographic approach with the researcher taking a 'Staff' role, helping with the logistics of the day-to-day running of the camp. Taken together, interviews and observations enabled the full journey of participants' experience to be explored exposing the subtle and distinct informal spaces along it. Analysis took a thematic approach using the online software NVivo, helping to draw out key themes from the rich data. Findings revealed the importance of informal spaces not only for further learning but for creating bonds and feelings of belonging among participants through earnest interactions and shared emotional experiences.

The role of informal spaces: learning, interaction and emotion

Previous research has shown how informal spaces provide a space for further learning through cultural experiences, habitual living practices and play (Le Bourdon 2018). Building on this, analysis went further, providing original insight into the micro-level processes that make these experiences so impactful. Three key linked findings were identified: (1) informal spaces provided the opportunity for learners to reflect and practise what they had learnt but also to reflect on further independent learning; (2) away from structured learning participants interacted more earnestly, reflecting and learning together, consequently fostering bonds through shared experience; and (3) the experience of learning and interacting in these spaces was intense for participants due to the strong emotions felt and expressed within them.

Using examples from the data this section will unpack each finding giving a deeper understanding of the role of informal spaces for GCE through this micro-level lens. It will argue that informal spaces are important places for further learning on global topics, providing learners with the freedom to practise what they have learnt as well as to help create feelings of solidarity with others through interactions and shared emotions.

Spaces for reflexivity, learning and practice

Analysis of the data revealed how these informal spaces allowed time and space for participants to digest and reflect on what they had learnt from structured learning activities provided by the organization. In the down time, participants were able to contemplate or to discuss with others what they had experienced and learnt within the sessions. At first these discussions would occur simply within their country delegation often reflecting on applying what they had learnt to their home context. However, as time went on these conversations were more frequently shared with participants from multiple delegations. Here, debates or points which had been explored within the activities would often be further discussed, with more time and space for topics to be explored. This enabled learners to formulate and express their own ideas while also listening to others. This can be seen through observations following an activity exploring ideas of trust:

> In the free time discussions around trust in their community continue. Children start to consider how they felt and give examples of them not trusting certain people they don't identify with and how problematic that may be. (Field notes)

Such reflection, linking learning to wider issues, has been seen as critical in GCE. Golmohamad (2004) states that reflective thinking is essential for assessing one's own positionality in the world and to evaluate how our actions impact on society. Andreotti sees its role as wider reaching, arguing self-reflexivity rather than self-reflection can help to identify and critically analyse the root of 'collective socially, culturally and historically' assumptions and narratives (2014: 17). Therefore, spaces in between structured learning grant learners the opportunity to exercise self-reflexivity and critical thinking. In doing so, they can consider their own positionality more deeply while also analysing wider power structures through the freedom of contemplation and relaxed discussion. Percy Smith (2012) states that practising these skills within such informal settings is seen as essential in order for individuals to practise them within their everyday life, which in turn can been considered positive active participation in society. Therefore, informal spaces between set GCE can be understood as playing an important role in ensuring what is learnt is applied in the learner's day-to-day life.

Sharing the rhythm of everyday life also opened up informal spaces for further learning and interaction. Differences or similarities in customs or practices highlighted in the day-to-day life of the camp often led to enquiry and conversations between participants from different cultural backgrounds. Thus the multicultural environment of the camp meant participants were being directly exposed to different customs, understandings and opinions from around the world. This not only allowed for direct intercultural learning through engagement with their peers but also provided a richer, more personal educational experience. This can be seen through the case that Magnus from Norway recalls below, after the children from his delegation ask why the Japanese delegations are wearing face masks:

> They see something for the first time is weird for them about another culture and then I explained to them but I also asked Dan [Japanese leader] because I'm not sure and I really get the right answer and I give it to the kids and they are like 'ahhh ok, it makes sense now'. And all of those small things when it comes to cultural differences is helping the kids not only cope with being around other cultures but understanding it as well.

Magnus goes on to describe how his delegates discussed the logic in preventing germs through wearing of the facemasks and how some started to adopt the practice. This example shows how through experiencing and directly engaging with different cultures and customs intercultural learning was not only richer but made learners reflect on their personal beliefs and practices. Reflecting on this in the post-camp interviews the adult leaders emphasized the benefit in making learning personal for a more affective experience:

> I think being exposed to something … experiencing it is far more educational then hearing about it or seeing about it … in a classroom. (Bernie, USA)

Personal engagement not only made for a richer intercultural experience but also made learning topics more tangible too. Habitual practices stimulated debates and reflection around global issues too, most starkly seen through meal times. The sharing of this human necessity seemed to relax participants, creating a natural and familiar environment. Consequently, this seemed to break down sociocultural barriers between participants, cutting across generations and delegations and opening up additional informal channels of interaction. Unsurprisingly, conversation was often stimulated by questions around different foods and mealtime customs, which in turn often led to discussions around food security or sustainable development. Yet, data also demonstrates that these shared habitual practices not only went beyond just conversations but also led to some participants actively changing their habits. In his post-camp interview Gabriel from Brazil described how his relationship with food had transformed as a result of these informal moments on the camp:

> I used to eat loads more food … now I just take a little and see what I need … I'm eating a lot less red meat too. It's because, I think, of how I see other cultures respect for food and talking about food … food insecurity … I think it's made the kids think it's unfair others have so little.

For Gabriel the experience of sharing meal times had made him critically analyse his own and others' eating habits and the wider consequences of their actions. This had consequently stimulated a *change in* his actions which were taken beyond the immediate learning environment into his everyday life. This provides original insight into how the self-reflexivity and further learning occurring in informal spaces shaped not only their actions within the camp but also created subtle transformations in the way they engage with the world around. This section thus highlights the importance of informal spaces as places for GCE and the need for further insight into the affective interactions within these.

Earnest interactions and shared experience

While experiential learning practices within structured GCE activities saw participants constantly interacting, the time between sessions allowed learners to engage with each other freely and organically. These earnest interactions saw participants not only learning from each other but alongside each other too. This happened most commonly through play.

While play has been recognized as a key part of learning more widely (see Göncü and Gaskins 2007) there has been little attention paid to informal moments of play in GCE. Games and play bring experiential learning into the 'real world', creating safe spaces for learners to apply skills and knowledge while allowing learners' imagination to flourish. Through learning games, hearing new stories and creating imaginary worlds, child participants exchange ideas, are exposed to different viewpoints and are free to express themselves. Such experiences in turn form and/or reshape individuals' own understandings, opinions and actions. This is reflected in the data where play saw learners exercise their curiosity, ask questions and learn. Role-play games were commonly played on the camp by child participants in their free time which interestingly often touched upon topics that stimulated discussion. This is especially apparent in the data when one child participant was given the role of 'maid' when playing 'families'. Coming from a country where having a maid is not common practice the participant questioned her role. This, consequently, stimulated discussion among adults and participants alike about rights and roles of domestic workers. These informal spaces allowed adult and child participants from different cultural backgrounds to discover and deepen their knowledge together through natural enquiry. What is important to note here is that this example does not simply show one participant learning from another, but participants learning together, side by side through the everyday. Thus participants became connected through the shared experience of naturally exploring and learning together.

The experience shared within these informal moments created strong bonds among participants. The everyday rhythm of the camp saw participants interacting beyond the learning activities with habitual living practices – cleaning, eating and relaxing together – bringing the unfamiliar into the familiar. These moments opened up pockets of opportunity for more informal interactions more naturally. Free time between activities was often commented on as child participants' favourite time on the camp, where they could 'just be with friends … my best friends'. Reflecting upon this in post-camp interviews one leader suggested why these times were so crucial to participants' experience:

> Our free time, like, because that is how we decided, because it is a wonderful moment, it is a moment where the kids can interact in earnestly, we can interact with the leaders earnestly, if we want to, and we can interact with the kids. (Gabriel, Brazil)

Participants would ask others to play, create friendship bands for each other or simply listen to music together. Having the freedom to choose to spend time and engage with each other in a relaxed environment helped to create feelings of appreciation. In the absence of a common language, intimate exchanges were used within these spaces cutting across sociocultural and linguistic barriers, as Shail from India describes:

> Actually, it (interaction) nurtures the belief of trust. If you (are) cuddling, touching, hugging each other that develops the bond of trusting each other, more than words. If I say 'Oh Maddy I love you!' and you say it back to me, I think if I hug you when I say it, I think it makes more sense and you will trust me more than just words.

These expressions of fondness appeared within these informal spaces throughout the camp, but got more frequent and expressive as time went on. At first, this was communicated through high fives as they played games, greeting each other with enthusiasm at breakfast time, turning into hand-holding as they travelled through camps or spontaneous hugging before bed. Such expressions did too occur within activities; however, their appearance within informal spaces is significant. It tells us that these were not simply expressions of how participants felt in the moment in reaction to something but are expressions of how they felt towards each other more widely. These informal interactions created a warmth on the camp which can only be described as a feeling of togetherness. Discussing these moments in between structured learning, Magnus from Norway states:

> They (the child participants) trusted, bonded with each other making friendships … they are like building bridges between each other, building their own bridge together.

Magnus here sees the trust and bonds felt between child participants coming together to create wider feelings of community. This is something which scholars have discussed within the literature, with positive recognition deemed crucial for mutual trust which in turn creates feelings of a collective and can stimulate active participation within society (Luhmann 2000; Delanty 2003; Hart 2009; Warming 2012). Warming states that the establishment of mutual trust is *essential for shared horizons (2012: 45)* while Appiah emphasizes fostering connections with others as a key condition for creating communities built on moral concerns and obligations (2009: 29). GCE provides the opportunity for such shared horizons and communities of moral concerns to be found. However, drawing on innovative data from this research, it is arguable that informal spaces between learning allows trust and bonds between individuals to be strengthened through shared experience and earnest interaction. Thus, this process of trust and bonding can be seen as playing a key role in not only creating feelings of solidarity and belonging but also in developing active agents of change (Schattle n.d; Golmohamad 2009). What made these moments so impactful, however, were the strong emotions which were both expressed and shared by individuals.

The expression and sharing of emotion

Emotions, here understood as personal feelings of intensity (Paterson 2007: 164), have become widely recognized as part of citizenship learning (Osler and Starkey 2005; Wood 2013) and active participation (Ho 2009; Jupp 2008; Warming 2012), creating positive relationships between citizens and wider society. Considering traditional citizenship Wood states,

> A focus on the informal and everyday social interchanges which inform every aspect of our lives, and the emotions which are imbued in such interactions, presents an opportunity to consider how different forms of political deliberation, including 'bodily and affective' are manifested within public participation processes. (2013: 52)

Though reflecting on traditional forms of citizenship, Wood here identifies the significant role of emotions within informal spaces. Here, the scholar states that emotions affect how we frame and engage with the world around us. It is, therefore, unsurprising that analysis revealed that emotions arising within these informal spaces had a significant impact on participants' learning journey through the camp.

As explored earlier, informal spaces provide an additional space for reflection, practice and further learning. Discussions which occurred here were emotive, with participants meditating on how it made them feel about themselves, others and wider society. We have seen how scholars have emphasized the need for learners to contemplate their own positionality through reflexivity and that informal spaces provide the time and freedom to do so. However, analysis of the lived experience of individuals helps us to understand what is happening in these moments of reflexivity and that a key part of this is the sharing of emotion. Participants in this case study would voice how they felt about activities with each other or how they felt about issues which activities touched upon. With time to digest and reflect, these informal spaces provide learners with the opportunity to digest what they have learnt, to connect to it and make it personal. Furthermore, emotions which inevitably occur within activities can be identified, reflected on and questioned in the spaces beyond activities: 'Why did I feel like that?' 'How do I feel now?' 'How do others feel?' Despite there being discussions at the end of each activity, it was in the informal discussions later in the day which adult participants stated the *deep and meaningful* discussions took place. What this shows is that what makes informal spaces so important for further global citizenship learning is the time and room for learners to contemplate, express and share their feelings.

Emotions shared with others were not only in reaction to what they had learnt but a key part of how they communicated to one another. In earnest interaction, participants often expressed the emotional attachments they felt towards others, expressed through the feeling of being part of a newly formed community. Adults and children frequently demonstrated feelings of attachment towards each other on the camp with rhetoric often describing one another as family:

> There are lots of expression of it feeling like a family, that they love one another that they feel so close and they don't want to leave. (Field notes)

> US leader at dinner and at the end emphasises the need for us to 'be lucky enough to eat a warm meal as a family' and 'take down our flag like a family'. (Field notes)

Living so closely side by side and sharing the day-to-day rhythms of life helped to emulate the environment of a family household. Interestingly, these expressions did not occur within activities but in the moments around structured learning when participants were interacting organically. Describing the group as a family demonstrates the level of bonds, which participants felt between each other, and the type of feelings too. It seemed that participants' interpretation of family here was used to describe not only the feelings of warmth and safety but also the strength and unity fostered through adversity. Adult participants reflected upon how challenges they faced in the camp and the rollercoaster of emotions which came with it helped to unify the group:

> We worked hard but I think in that everyone gets frustrated but we bonded over frustration which is rare, instead of like coming apart … (we could) be vulnerable to each other like 'look I need some help' and people jumped over that. Like I said I needed help with one of my boys and within two hours I felt I had 15 people trying to do my job which was amazing. (Bernie, USA)

Travelling to a different country, learning about different cultures and tackling complex issues created a journey full of emotion. Yet, although the obstacles rendered individuals vulnerable, in these moments of informal interaction these vulnerabilities broke down sociocultural barriers. Participants were forced to reach out, to help and to accept help and work together. These emotive moments were for many participants where they located significant points on their own global citizenship journey. For Myra from India these shared emotional interactions:

> Give us that moment of realisation, that 'Yes, we belong to each other and we have our gods connected', it's just you have to realise that. 'Yes, we are connected'

Here these informal moments of shared emotion are understood as creating not only bonds with others but also feelings of belonging. Thus, the emotions occurring within these informal spaces can be seen as playing a key role in cultivating feelings of a global collective and solidarity.

This does not mean that all global learning requires adversity in the same way as on this camp, but that the sharing of emotional burdens can lead to feelings of unity. This could be through global learning topics themselves which can be intense and require individuals to dig deep to explore and challenge their own beliefs. In unpacking and discussing this in a more informal setting, learners can ruminate and express how they really feel, share in their insecurities and empower one another.

Indeed the feelings of inclusivity are what scholars such as Honneth claim is crucial for active participation. The scholar cites emotional recognition as an essential element for inclusive and empowering citizen identity (Honneth in Warming 2012: 37). Emotional recognition acknowledges intimate relationships cultivated as part of the citizenship learning process. It can be seen through

> mutual care and emotional attachment, i.e. the providing and receiving of emotional support, a mutually dependent relationship which produces a sense of being something special for someone else'. (38)

Interestingly, following these moments of intense emotional expression, participants did seem to not only see themselves as part of a global collective but also as more motivated to act as one. Instead of simply recalling their own experiences in discussions, narratives instead saw participants looking to how they could move forward as a collective. These emotional moments of connection seemed to create not only a shift beyond feelings of just belonging, but also ignite an energy in participants. Adult participants often referred to these as 'moments of realisation' where what they had learnt and experienced came together causing an internal transformation in participants:

> What these moments do, it is not just simple interaction or bringing the people of different countries together, but with that mind-set or with that motive… to help bring about change. (Shail, India)

Thus, building of trust, establishment of bonds and the feelings of belonging established through the interactions within these informal moments could be seen as the fostering of globally aware individuals. As well as forming strong bonds between participants, these intense emotional moments and exchanges shift participants' framing of their positionality and the world around them. What this shows is that these interactions did not just influence the way participants encountered each other but also resulted in a shift to feeling part of a global collective. This supports narratives such as Gerard Delanty (2009) who describes this process towards imaginaries of a global community as 'cosmopolitan transformation'. The scholar here sees these transformations occurring both for the group in question and for the individual. However, findings from this research provide original insight into the where and how of what Delanty describes through analysis of the lived experience. Informal spaces open up room for important work to be done on a very personal and an emotive level for learners on their transformative journey. The interactions which occur and importantly the strong emotions felt make the experience help to make what is learnt within structured learning and the spaces in between them so impactful. This demonstrates the very personal process of learning in GCE even beyond structured learning and the need to engage individuals on an emotional level in order to build active global citizens. Informal spaces between structured learning provide important sites for this, and thus for GCE.

Conclusion

This chapter provides original insight into the role of informal spaces within GCE, arguing that these spaces between structured learning offer fruitful sites for learning on an individual's lifelong pedagogical journey. It began by exploring current trends in GCE research which have focused upon best practices in, and limitations of, formal and non-formal education. It revealed that the spaces in between structured learning have been under-researched, despite the emphasis on global citizenship learning being a lifelong journey requiring independent learning. Using data collected through innovative research and using a global civil society organization providing GCE, the chapter examined the role of informal spaces. Analysis uncovered three key original findings. First, that informal spaces offer room for further learning and time for participants to exercise self-reflexivity which has been widely championed for fostering critical-thinking global citizens. Second, these spaces allow individuals to interact freely and earnestly, allowing for trust, strong bonds and feelings of being part of a global collective among participants to be cultivated organically through shared experience. Third, at the heart of these findings were the strong emotions which occurred within these interactions, making them profoundly impactful on individuals and how they positioned themselves in the world. Further research is needed into the role of informal spaces in GCE as learners continue in their everyday lives outside this unique setting. However, for GCE practitioners, these findings provide three key recommendations for best practice: the need to recognize informal spaces as places of further learning and development; the importance of providing learners with the time and space to interact freely; and crucially, the need to honour emotions felt, expressed and shared in these spaces.

Thus, this chapter argues that informal spaces allow individuals to interact more earnestly with each other, creating a more intense learning experience through stronger personal, emotional connections with others and with global learning topics.

Bibliography

Andreotti, V. (2006) 'Soft versus critical GCE', *Policy & Practice: A Development Education Review* 3, Autumn: 40–51.

Andreotti, V. (2011) *Actionable Postcolonial Theory in Education*, New York: Palgrave Macmillan.

Andreotti, V. (2014) 'Critical literacy: Theories and practices in development education', *Policy and Practice: A Development Education Review* 19, Autumn: 12–32.

Asbrand, B. (2008) 'How adolescents learn about globalisation and development', in D. Bourn (ed.), *Development Education: Debates and Dialogue*, London: Institute of Education, pp. 18–27.

Baillie Smith, M. (2014) 'Development education, global citizenship and international volunteering', in D. Vandana and P. Robert (eds), *The Companion to Development Studies*, London: Routledge, pp. 485–90.

Baillie Smith, M. and Humble, D. (2007) 'What counts as development research?' in M. Bailie Smith (ed.), *Negotiating Boundaries and Borders: Qualitative Methodology and Development Research*, Elsevier: Oxford, pp. 13–34.

Baraldi, C., Malleti, M. and Manicardi, E. (2014) *Research Report: Understanding the Effects of Interpreting in CISV Villages*. Retrieved November 2018 from https://cisv.org/resources/educational-content-research/research/.

Body, A., Holman, K. and Hogg, E. (2017) 'To bridge the gap? Voluntary action in primary schools', *Voluntary Sector Review* 8, 3: 251–71.

Bondi, L. and Laurie, N. (2005) 'Working the spaces of Neoliberalism: Activism, professionalism and incorporations. Introduction', *Antipode* 37, 3: 393–401.

Bourn, D. (2008) *Development Education Debates and Dialogue*, London: Institution of Education.

Bourn, D. (2014) 'The theory and practice of global learning', DERC Research Paper No. 11 for the GLP, London: Institute of Education.

Conway, D. and Heynen, N. (2002) *Globalization's Contradictions: Geographies of Discipline, Destruction and Transformation*, Oxon: Routledge Ltd.

Davies, L. (2006) 'Global citizenship: Abstraction or framework for action?' *Education Review* 58, 1: 5–25.

Delanty, G. (2003) 'Citizenship as a learning process: Disciplinary citizenship versus cultural citizenship', *International Journal of Lifelong Education* 22, 6: 597–605.

Delanty, G. (2009) *The Cosmopolitan Imaginary: The Renewal of Critical Social Theory*, Cambridge: Cambridge University Press.

Dobson, A. (2006) 'Thick cosmopolitanism', *Political Studies* 54: 165–84.

Dower, N. (2003) *An Introduction to Global Citizenship*, Edinburgh: Edinburgh University Press.

Freire, P. (1970) *Pedagogy of the Oppressed*, New York: Herder and Herder.

Golmohamad, M. (2004) 'World citizenship, identity and the notion of an integrated self', *Studies in Philosophy and Education* 23: 131–48.

Golmohamad, M. (2009) 'Education for world citizenship: Beyond national allegiance', *Educational Philosophy and Theory* 41, 4: 466–86.

Göncü, A. and Gaskins, S. (2007) *Play and Development: Evolutionary, Sociocultural, and Functional Perspectives*, New Jersey: Taylor and Francis Group.

Griffiths, M. (2016) 'Writing the body, writing others: A story of transcendence and potential in volunteering for development', *The Geographical Journal* 184, 2: 109–216.

Hart, S. (2009) 'The "Problem" with Youth: Young People, Citizenship and the Community', *Citizenship Studies* 13, 6: 641–57.

Hicks, D. and Holden, C. (2007) *Teaching the Global Dimension: Key Principles and Effective Practice*, Oxon: Routledge.

Ho, E. L. (2009) 'Constituting citizenship through the emotions: Singaporean transmigrants in London', *Annals of the Association of American Geographers* 99, 4: 788–804.

Humble, D. (2013) 'An ethnography of development education: From development politics to global learning', PhD diss., University of Northumbria at Newcastle: Newcastle-Upon-Tyne.

Jeffs, T. and Smith, M. (2005) *Informal Education: Conversation, Democracy and Learning*, Nottingham: Education Heretics Press.

Jupp, E. (2008) 'The feeling of participation: Everyday spaces and urban change', *Geoforum* 39, 1: 331–343).

Khoo, S. (2006) 'Development education, citizenship and civic engagement at third level and beyond in the Republic of Ireland', *Policy & Practice-A Development Education Review* 3, Autumn: 26–39.

Le Bourdon, M. (2018) 'Informal spaces in GCE', *Policy & Practice: A Development Education Review* 26, Spring: 105–21.

Luhmann, N. (2000) 'Familiarity, confidence, trust: Problems and alternatives', in D. Gambetta (ed.), *Trust: Making and Breaking Cooperative Relations*, Oxford: University of Oxford, pp. 94–107.

Nussbaum, M. (2010) *Not for Profit: Why Education Needs the Humanities*, Princeton and Oxford: Princeton University Press.

O'Neill, M., Giddens, Breatnach, P., Bagley, C., Bourne, D. and Judge, T. (2002) 'Renewed methodologies for social research: Ethno-mimesis as performative praxis', *The Sociological Review* 50, 1: 69–88.

Osler, A. and Starkey, H. (2005) *Changing Citizenship: Democracy and Inclusion in Education*, Maidenhead: Open University.

Oxfam Education (2018) *What Is Global Citizenship?* Retrieved November 2018 from https://www.oxfam.org.uk/education/who-we-are/what-is-global-citizenship.

Oxley, L. and Morris, P. (2013) 'Global citizenship: A typology for distinguishing its multiple concepts', *British Journal of Educational Studies* 61, 3: 301–25.

Paterson, M. (2007) *The Senses of Touch: Haptics, Affects and Technologies Senses and Sensibilities*, Oxford: Berg.

Percy Smith, B. (2012) 'Participation as mediation and social learning: Empowering children as actors in social contexts', in C. Baraldi and V. Ieverse (eds), *Participation, Facilitation and Mediation*, New York: Routledge, pp. 12–29.

Schattle, H. (2008) *The Practices of Global Citizenship*, Plymouth: Rowman and Littlefield Publishers Inc.

Schattle, H. (n.d.) 'Reviewing global citizenship', in M. Faul, A. Prandle and A. Short (eds), *Education for an Age of Interdependence: A Series of Provocation Papers*, Oxford: Oxfam GB, pp. 1–6.

Smith, M. (2004) 'Mediating the world: Development, education and global citizenship', *Globalisation Societies Education* 2, 1: 67–82.

Tarozzi, M. and Inguaggiato, C. (2018) 'Implementing GCE in EU primary schools: The role of government ministries', *International Journal of Development Education and Global Learning* 10, 1: 21–38.

Tarozzi, M. and Torres, C. (2016) *Global Citizenship Education and the Crises of Multiculturalism: Comparative Perspectives*, London: Bloomsbury Academic.

Temple, G. and Laycock, A. L. (2008) 'Education for global citizenship: Towards a clearer agenda for change', in D. Bourn (ed.), *Development Education: Debates and Dialogue*, London: Institution of Education, pp. 99–109.

Tide Global Learning. *About*. Retrieved November 2018 from https://www.tidegloballearning.net/.

Van Peski, C. (2012) 'International education and global citizenship', in C. Baraldi and V. Ieverse (eds), *Participation Facilitation and Mediation*, New York: Routledge, pp. 219–39.

Warming, H. (2012) 'Theorizing adult's facilitation of children's participation and citizenship', in C. Baraldi and V. Iervese (eds), P*articipation, Facilitation, and Mediation*: *Children and Young People in Their Social Contexts*, New York: Routledge, pp. 30–48.

Wintersteiner, W., Grobbauer, H., Diendorfer, G. and Reitmair-Juárez, S. (2015) *Global Citizenship Education Citizenship Education for Globalizing Societies*, Klagenfurt, Salzburg, Vienna: Austrian Commission for UNESCO.

Wood, B. E. (2013) 'Young people's emotional geographies of citizenship participation: Spatial and relational insights', *Emotion, Space and Society* 9: 50–8.

Chapter 30

Apprenticeship of Reflexivity: Immersive Learning from International Volunteering as Teacher Professional Development

Mags Liddy

Introduction

Overseas volunteering is viewed as one way to enhance teacher knowledge of global issues as well as developing values of empathy towards different communities and possibly leading to greater engagement with development education. The experience of spending time living and working with communities in developing countries provides an opportunity for immersive learning where the volunteers are surrounded by a different culture and environment. This chapter examines learning arising from the short-term volunteering experience of Irish teachers working in India as teacher educators, using practice theory (Bourdieu 1977; 2000) as a lens of interpretation. Their volunteering work gives them the opportunity to constitute meaning and knowledge from the volunteering experience and to translate this into their classroom teaching and professional practices (Hoban 2002). This translation of learning from their experience is termed an apprenticeship of reflexivity and can be seen in both the volunteer-teachers' professional learning and in their learning about global development concerns. A clear successful translation of learning from experience can be seen in their professional context; however, other factors within their habitus can act to limit the translation of learning with regard to global development. Liminality is suggested as a transitional stage in this apprenticeship where learners need to be supported to learn, particularly in understanding the complexities of global development.

Theoretical context of the research

Overseas volunteering has become an increasingly visible and attractive option for young people; for example, the UK Gap Year phenomenon has grown with many commercial volunteering enterprises (Simpson 2004). Butcher and Smith (2010) suggest that the phenomenon is beyond an impulse to travel; rather it reflects 'life political' forms of agency and the desire to make a difference in a postmodern era where grand narratives have declined. In Ireland, overseas volunteering is a growing sector, from just 11 volunteer sending agencies before the 1970s to 40 organizations in 2012, which received almost 3,800 applications from predominately professional people (Comhlámh 2013).

Some research suggests international volunteering can broaden and deepen understanding of aid and global development issues. Machin (2008) noted that it can facilitate a stronger sense of global citizenship and solidarity, and contribute to greater awareness and understanding of development issues, poverty and diversity. On the other hand, there is some evidence that not all volunteers experience 'transformative' changes and some return home disillusioned. Sin concludes that overseas volunteering could 'easily fail to achieve its purported intentions of being "pro-poor" or addressing social inequalities' (2009, p. 497) while Georgeou and Engel ask if development volunteering should be viewed as citizenship without politics (2011, p. 308). With regard to teaching global development issues and development education, O'Neill warns not to

> assume that returned volunteers automatically have the skills and knowledge needed to act as development education multipliers. It is vital for returnees to have access to appropriate training to support an understanding of a development education approach and tools to effectively engage with people locally (2012, p. 1).

Furthermore, Machin (2008) argues that returned volunteers can encounter resistance or indifference which negates their desire and commitment to address global development. Research has shown that some volunteers experienced corruption and inefficiency and as a result have a weakened commitment to international development on return (DFID 2011).

This chapter examines the potential of volunteering for being a transformative experience, with the potential to interrupt volunteers' taken-for-granted practices and understandings (Bourdieu 1977) arising from the physical movement from Ireland to India. Lizardo (2012) claims that a dramatic change and disorientation is required in habitus to disrupt taken-for-granted practices, thus for learning and change to happen. The volunteer setting examined here has this dramatic difference. In contrast to their usual professional setting in Ireland, the Irish volunteers work as teacher educators rather than teachers and are outside their familiar professional role. On a wider level, the social and cultural circumstances of their volunteering exchange and location in the isolated communities of North East India are different. The Irish teachers witness specific global development challenges facing the region and are immersed in a society where teachers have different social roles and expectations (Chambers 1987; Cushner and Mahon 2002). However, the setting of the Irish teacher-volunteers' work also has many familiar features: namely the professional setting of schools, familiar daily routines and familiar religious orders as school management.

This mix of familiar and different sets up a deliberate reflection process for the research participants, which I term an apprenticeship of reflexivity (Liddy, 2016). The translation process of learning from volunteering is where the volunteers negotiate meaning from their experiences and attempt to integrate it into their professional practices and habitus (Bourdieu 1977). When applied to a professional context, reflection is a systematic process for making sense of experience, and it increases professional knowledge and capacity (Schön 1983). Reflective practice occurs when teachers critically consider their work practice and reframe complex professional questions, which may lead them to modify their professional behaviours and actions as a result. It centres on the belief that in modern society human beings are reflexive and have agency to reflect on their actions and identities in relation to the social world (Giddens 1990). Bourdieu described reflexivity as the need to examine your 'social origins and coordinates'

(Bourdieu and Wacquant 1992, p. 39). This approach shares some parallels with actionable post-colonial education of learning and unlearning (Andreotti 2011), as the Irish teachers learn about global development during their overseas experience and attempt to integrate this knowledge into their lives and worldviews. Their learning process is embodied through the physical experience of this developing region with particular challenges. Experience and questioning is central to the learning process of reflexivity, but learning may also be limited or hindered. Taken from post-colonial theory, the concept of liminality (Bhabha 1994) is utilized to describe a stage in their apprenticeship of learning. I suggest that reflective practice is affected by the wider habitus of the volunteer: where habitus is understood as the 'systems of durable transposable dispositions … as generation and structuring of practices' (Bourdieu 1977, p. 72). This determines what practices, behaviours and beliefs are appropriate and possible; as we will see later a number of factors can limit both the possibility of change and the extent of the volunteer learning. Liminality is what I term this phase of the apprenticeship of reflexivity when answers are not readily found to the questions arising from reflections.

Methodology

The overall research project examined the learning of twenty-eight volunteers from Ireland, working as short-term overseas volunteers in North East India. The work was subject to full ethical review by the relevant university process. Two groups of volunteers were accompanied to India and on their return to Ireland, data was gathered through interviews (28) and reflection sheets (7). These were transcribed and analysed using inductive analysis and constant comparison to identify emerging themes (Boeije 2010). The volunteer-teachers were all given pseudonyms used here in this chapter. In particular this chapter uses quotes from volunteers Davinia, Isabel and Joy, all of whom are primary teachers; Laura, Barbara and Nicole, all post-primary teachers; and Natalie, who works in an adult education setting. All are experienced teachers selected for volunteering through an application form and interview process.

Changes in practice: Learning about teaching

The focus of my research is on the impact of overseas volunteering on the participating Irish teachers working as teacher educators. They volunteer to work as teacher educators in a peer-to-peer environment to share their experience and professional knowledge of teaching and learning with practising members of their profession in India. Below Davinia sums up her learning from India:

> I have rediscovered what education is all about, it is important about education, what it is all about. Why is it that I am teaching? What did I value in teaching? … Looking at the Indian education system has given me the foil to look at those questions, to look back at the system here – I think coming out of my context helped me look back at the context here. (Davinia interview extract, October 2012)

Laura highlighted the familiarity between schools in Ireland and India saying:

> It was like watching a mirror of it. There were good schools, there were bad schools. And the learning was that no matter where you go, the people are the same. The same sense of insecurity about their own skills. The same sense of being put upon by the parish priest. The same sense of not being paid enough, classes too big or too small, it's the same. (Laura, interview 1 October 2011)

These quotes illustrate that the familiarity of the immersive setting can enable learning and aid professional development.

The process of the volunteering programme centres on small teams working together which enables reflection and learning about their teaching practices arising from this immersive experience. Lynch and Lodge (2002) refer to Irish teachers as relatively autonomous in their classrooms, while Hargreaves (1994) critiques the Balkanization of teaching subjects from each other. Natalie identified the sense of being part of a team as a valuable learning for her, in contrast with her individualized work context in Ireland:

> We were very much a team before, and during the whole six months. You were looking at the skills that the other person had and what you could add, how you could, what areas you could contribute maybe more strongly in. But here [in Ireland] … we don't see ourselves as a team. We actually see ourselves, in certain [ways as] individual. (Natalie, adult education teacher, interview November 2011).

As the volunteering setting is similar to the professional habitus of the Irish teacher-volunteers, reflection on and experimentation with professional practices is a straightforward process with a clear relationship to their work in Ireland. The professional setting of schools and teaching work shares much commonality in their professional habitus: the religious management and ethos of the schools; the familiarity of schedules; design and classroom layout; and the similarities of challenges in working with young people. In contrast to Lizardo, I suggest that the sense of familiarity of habitus encourages social learning on teachers' professional knowledge and role, and this familiarity enables the integration of learning from one setting to another. Within a familiar professional habitus, the teacher-volunteers engage in a deliberate process of reflection on their work: 'travel with intention', as Davinia describes it. There is a clear, purposeful value to the knowledge they gain from their volunteering experience and this is supported by opportunities for integration into their everyday professional work on their return to Ireland.

This process of professional learning is the mirror that Laura referred to earlier and can be seen clearly in the use of observations, which form a key element of the volunteer-teacher programme.

Observations of teaching as learning

Observation of teachers was identified as one specific way the Irish teacher-volunteers learned and developed their professional practice. There is a cumulative effect of teaching observations across all of these levels of interaction, where peer learning occurs between Irish primary and secondary teachers, as well as between Irish and Indian teachers. While engaging in the programme, the Irish teachers observe each other teaching the Indian teachers, set up deliberate observations of teaching to demonstrate techniques or teaching dilemmas, and act as mentors to the Indian teachers in their classrooms. There was a real sense that they valued the opportunity to watch colleagues at work. The inclusion of observations in the volunteering programme is significant because of the contrast to dominant forms of teacher professional development in Ireland. Research shows that the most common form of professional development for teachers in Ireland was attendance at courses and workshops (Shiel, Perkins and Gilleece 2009). Fewer teachers in Ireland participate in mentoring, peer observations or observation visits to schools than their OECD colleagues (ibid.). Natalie said:

> The majority of us don't watch other people teaching ... when you see other people teaching it makes you think about yourself ... this could be fairly different or this could be organised differently. (Natalie, adult education teacher, interview 1 November 2011)

The benefits of both observations and reflection on their learning can be viewed as guiding rethinking and learning on teaching and teaching behaviour. Laura felt affirmed in her teaching skill and ability by observing the other approaches adopted by her team colleagues:

> I felt really affirmed by talking to other colleagues and seeing the characteristics each of them had and they brought to their own schools. (Laura, post-primary teacher, interview October 2011)

To Barbara the diversity of methods and approaches employed by the different team members provided a good learning opportunity for the Indian teacher-students as:

> Our teaching methods probably are all very different. I suppose it allowed Indian teachers to see okay – you don't have to have just one method to get a class interested. ... They have a wide spectrum to choose from. (Barbara, post-primary teacher, interview, November 2011)

The teaching observations are different as there is a conscious effort being made to model good practice for colleagues and to provide constructive feedback to Indian colleagues, and as the teaching observation is a grading requirement for programme completion. This conscious observational work acts as a disruption to dispositions and taken-for-granted beliefs (Bourdieu 1977) about teaching. The translation process of experience, questioning, reflection and professional change can be seen in the data. Thus a successful apprenticeship of reflexivity does not require dramatic disruption; rather the familiarity of habitus enabled learning to be achieved.

Changes in practice: Learning about global development

The following section focuses on my participants' learning about global development, arising from their first-hand experiences of North East India. In contrast to the earlier focus on similarity as aiding professional development, here the focus is on difference as an opportunity for reflection, questioning and learning. The physical move from Ireland to India entails learning from the dispositional challenges wrought by the changes to the teacher-volunteers' sociocultural habitus (Bourdieu 1977). This is reminiscent of Lizardo's (2012) claim that dramatic changes to habitus are required for dispositional reconsideration. Their voluntary role as teacher educators differs from their everyday role as teachers. Furthermore, their wider social and cultural setting is different. This difference can be seen in the everyday interactions at market-places, different religious practices, thoughtful encounters with political and historical aspects of India, or visiting people's homes and witnessing distinctive dancing traditions and clothing. Engagement with these differences provides an opportunity for learning and insight into other ways of being and doing; namely challenging their dispositions.

The change of setting offers the opportunity to make links between the volunteer lifeworlds and others, or the opportunity to transgress representational boundaries and to gain a view into the Other as Andreotti (2011) describes it. This can be seen in how research participants demonstrate their understanding of inequalities between Ireland and India. Below, Isabel describes her understanding of development inequalities, challenging simplistic dichotomies by not thinking of Ireland as rich and India as poor, but rather seeing the commonalities across the two, particularly in expressed values of social justice and understanding of why poverty exists:

> They [the Indian teachers] thought they were – they had airs and graces. ... Their houses – much bigger than my house ... there was a class thing going on ... when they talked about the poor people, it was the same as how Western people would talk about poor people. And I was surprised about that – I don't think they realised they were being offensive. (Isabel, primary teacher, interview October 2012)

Isabel's recognition of class issues was insightful, highlighting her awareness of social divisions and the impact of class and socio-economic factors. She also displays a complex view of poverty and social justice in contrast to the use of binary divisions between them and us, rich and poor, or white and black, which can be based on a hierarchical conception of one as better (Jefferess 2008).

Nicole questions the impact of increased and improved education for the villagers she worked with. Ultimately, she is questioning the modernization as development premise of the volunteering programme, as it aims to develop teaching quality:

> When we did the small bit of travel, and you saw how horrific some of the larger urban areas are and you're thinking the first generation of children that are educated, this is what they're going to be coming to. ... Because they will leave [name of village she worked in], I think they will leave all the good things of a close community behind. (Nicole, post-primary teacher. Interview November 2012).

Nicole has been reflecting considerably on her role as a volunteer working to improve education and thus further the life chances of the people in communities where she worked. This community was quite isolated and rural, with an agriculture-based economy and limited access to electricity and to health services. However, the people have strong connections to each other and retain a tribal right to land ownership. She is questioning the overall purpose of education, recognizing the changes it will bring to the lives and welfare of people there as she sees education as linked to migration to cities for employment opportunities. Nicole is asking questions about modernization processes of urbanization, employment and progress – the big questions of global development. She is negotiating the ambivalent nature of the issues, where no easy solutions exist and there can be an ambiguity in the outcomes. This learning space can be termed the liminality of learning or a third space (Bhabha 1994), the questioning stage in the apprenticeship of reflexivity.

Liminality highlights difficulties in the translation dynamic from experience into changed beliefs or practices where learners can struggle to integrate new knowledges into existing ways of reading the world. The Irish volunteer-teachers are confronted by the unfamiliar lifeworld of North East India and witness diverse social and cultural ways. This global setting raises the issue of wider socio-economic conditions and exposes the material and resource differentials between Ireland and India, and between Irish and Indian schools.

Their learning about global development may be hampered by their lack of prior knowledge and thus the context to integrate their new experiences. Participants' lack of knowledge of global development topics may not be the result of individual error or lack of learning, but the result of social processes that define our understanding of reality (Ball 1998). Global development is a complex topic with much debate on solutions and the value of development programmes (Sachs 1992). Promotion of a particular path of social progress, particularly an economic path, is open to critique and charges of cultural imperialism. The development debate in Ireland is viewed as limited, lacking critiques of dominant development discourses (Kirby 2012) and with widespread public support for neoliberal policies (O'Callaghan, Boyle and Kitchin 2014). Liminality and the questioning stage could be compounded by the uncertainty and the strength of these forms of taken-for-granted beliefs on human development. There are factors which challenge the transformative potential of volunteering by demonstrating the complexity of learning outcomes and highlighting that the apprenticeship of reflexivity is not a straightforward process.

Affective moments of learning

One suggested way through liminality centres on the affective learning moments or 'constitutive embodied moments of the volunteer-host encounter' (Griffiths 2014, p. 2) with their potential for enhancing global citizenship, and with the emotional responses to global development as powerful learning moments (Bailie-Smith and Jenkins 2012). Possibly these affective moments of learning contain potential for addressing this liminality and finding a way out by prodding the uncomfortable (Andreotti 2011). Affective and emotional responses can be valuable learning moments; Nicole spoke of her uncomfortableness with poverty in Kolkata while Karen describes herself as 'feeling icky' with the notion of saviour which arose in her fundraising activities. She is sensitive to the portrayal of her as a do-gooder and works hard to overcome this in her choice of words and descriptions of Indian communities.

Research into overseas learning refer to the challenges of questioning Western privilege as a difficult and uneasy process: Brock et al. (2006) refer to the uncomfortableness of the displacement space that intercultural encounters can engender. Andreotti describes actionable post-colonial education as hard and painful work involving the provoking of crises and the realization of complicities (2011, p. 176). Bryan (2013) speaks of the need for a pedagogy of discomfort to awaken Western learners into reassessing their privilege and place in the world. Possibly these affective moments of learning contain potential for addressing this liminality and finding a way out by prodding the uncomfortable (Andreotti 2011). However, this approach to learning has been questioned – for example, Loughran and Berry's (2005) research work in

Australian teacher education programmes questions the use and benefit of emotional challenges as part of a formal learning programme, as they may be potentially harmful and learners may need support and careful management of their emotional outcomes.

Joy describes what she witnessed during her visit to Kolkata, and her emotional reaction came through very powerfully. She was still quite upset by some of the things she experienced and she was struggling not to cry when describing what she saw:

> It's under a flyover, there's a slum and there's a school down there, there's children there ... and to get to it you have to go past a shantytown ... I was thinking there is no way I am going down there. No way. I wouldn't go in there. ... And the teacher came from there, she established a school. ... They have a restaurant there, we were brought there and ate there – but it's run by children, street children. ... [The Hope Foundation] go out at night and find children and [pause – waver in her voice] its harrowing actually, very neglected – they are abandoned. They came in from the countryside and they are stolen. ... But they pick them up from streets, bring them to the school and feed them. (Joy, primary teacher, interview October 2012)

Her reactions and strong emotional engagement with what she witnessed in Kolkata has remained with her. Her words highlight the emotional element to learning where Joy is shocked and upset by the street children's lifestories. Since her return to Ireland, she has struggled with how to relate these experiences to her life and work. She spoke of the migrant children in her classroom in Ireland as one way to reconcile them, as her overseas experiences has given her understanding and empathy of the impact migration can have on children and families.

Liminality as learning space

I use the term liminality as meaning a reflexively conscious and questioning learning space. In this learning space volunteer-teachers can question the purpose and role of education in global development, learn about causes of global poverty and gain knowledge of alternative development paradigms. But remaining in the liminal works to undermine any positive impact of overseas experience as new knowledges or ways of seeing are not integrated into practices. Volunteers can remain sited in the liminal and transitional phase, with ambivalence and epistemological uncertainty, requiring support and interventions to move beyond this stage. Designing a pedagogical intervention based on the identified objective factors is straightforward, as these topics lie within development studies and political economy; however, addressing the subjective factors in teacher learning on global development is more complex. It is necessary to increase knowledge of development topics and objective structures of political economy, but also this learning process must address the personal and subjective factors which mediate learning, the affective domain including motivations, efficacy and emotions. These form the basis of a decolonization of the mind and of our world knowledge (Mignolo 2004), and the unlearning colonial patterns of relating to the 'Other' (Andreotti 2007). Liminality is used here as a reflexively conscious and questioning learning space; thus it is a stage in the apprenticeship of reflexivity in working through subjective reactions and reconciling them with objective knowledge of global development.

Conclusion

This chapter described learning arising from international volunteering as an apprenticeship of reflexivity (Liddy 2016). The volunteer-teacher educators' learning with regard to their professional context is contrasted with their learning on global development. They are away from their everyday context, yet remain working in the familiar field of schools and their profession. The familiarity of setting facilitates a successful apprenticeship of reflexivity where volunteers' learning can be purposeful and integrated into their professional habitus and everyday practices of teaching. Additionally, the Irish volunteer-teacher educators are confronted by the unfamiliar lifeworld of North East India, and witness diverse social and cultural ways, and the inequalities of human development. This global setting for reflection and learning raises the issue of wider socio-economic conditions and the material differentials between Ireland and India. As a distinct field of social relations, global development is complex and there is a lack of easy solutions. Emotional responses also play a role in this apprenticeship of reflexivity. Furthermore, the wider habitus of Irish public opinion and debate on human development can be read as oriented towards a particular economic model. A diverse range of interpretations of this difference in learning can be seen, with some volunteers demonstrating complex understanding of global concerns, while others are questioning and unsure.

In this liminal space, some volunteers can be seen as struggling for resolution; this highlights the difficulties of translating experience into changed beliefs. Viewing liminality as a transitional phase of volunteers' apprenticeship of reflexivity allows volunteers the opportunity to question the purpose of education in global development, and to understand how what they experience fits within the broader global picture. Liminality has good potential for learning, but without further intervention and support, it may not be a useful place to be, in terms of a change in understanding of global development or encouraging teaching on global development. The apprenticeship of reflexivity requires support and structure for the translation of learning from immersive experience into fuller understanding, learning and transformation.

Bibliography

Andreotti, V. (2007) An ethical engagement with the other: Spivak's ideas on education, *Critical Literacy: Theories and Practices*, 1(1), pp. 69–70.

Andreotti, V. (2011) *Actionable Postcolonial Theory in Education*, London: Palgrave Macmillan.

Baillie Smith, M. and Jenkins, K. (2011) Disconnections and exclusions: Professionalization, cosmopolitanism and (global?) civil society, *Global Networks*, 11(2), pp. 160–79.

Baillie Smith, M. and Jenkins, K. (2012) Emotional methodologies- The emotional spaces of international development, *Emotion, Space and Society*, 5(2) pp. 75–7.

Ball, S. J. (1998) Big Policies/Small World: An introduction to international perspectives in education policy, *Comparative Education*, 34(2), pp. 119–30.

Bhabha, H. (1994) *The Location of Culture*, London: Routledge.

Boeije, H. (2010) *Analysis in Qualitative Research*, London: Sage.

Bourdieu, P. (1977) *Outline of a Theory of Practice*, Cambridge: Cambridge University Press.

Bourdieu, P. (2000) *Pascalian Meditations*, translated by Richard Nice, California: Stanford University Press.

Bourdieu, P. and Wacquant, L. J. (1992) *An Invitation to Reflexive Sociology*, Cambridge: Polity Press.

Brock, C., Wallace, J., Herschbach, M., Johnson, C., Raikes, B., Warren, K., Nikoli, M. and Poulsen, H. (2006) Negotiating displacement spaces: Exploring teachers' stories about learning and diversity, *Curriculum Inquiry*, 36(1), pp. 35–62.

Bryan, A. (2013) Using international development themed film to promote a pedagogy of discomfort, in Liddy, M. and Parker-Jenkins, M. (eds), *Education that Matters: Critical Pedagogy and Development Education at Local and Global Levels*, Oxford: Peter Lang, 75–101.

Butcher, J. and Smith, P. (2010) 'Making a difference': Volunteer tourism and development, *Tourism Recreation Research*, 35(1), pp. 27–36.

Chambers, R. (1987) *Whose Reality Counts?: Putting the First Last*, London: Intermediate Technology Publications.

Comhlámh (2013) *New Evidence on Overseas Volunteering from Ireland and Its Socio-Economic Impact in Ireland*, PMCA Economic Consulting, Dublin: Comhlámh.

Cushner, K. and Mahon, J. (2002) Overseas student teaching: Affecting personal, professional and global competencies in an age of globalization, *Journal of Studies in International Education* 6, pp. 44–58.

Department for International Development (2011). Mid Term Review: Evaluation of DFID's International Citizen Service (ICS) Pilot Stage, UK DFID 2011, available online at https://assets.publishing.serv ice.gov.uk/government/uploads/system/uploads/attachment_data/file/67460/eval-int-citz-serv-ics-pilot -stg.pdf

Georgeou, N. and Engel, S. (2011) The impact of neoliberalism and new managerialism on development volunteering: An Australian case study, *Australian Journal of Political Science*, 46(2), pp. 297–311.

Giddens, A. (1990) *The Consequences of Modernity*, Cambridge: Polity.

Griffiths, M. (2014) I've got goose bumps just talking about it!: Affective life in neoliberalised volunteering programs, *Tourist Studies*, 14(4), pp. 1–17.

Hargreaves, A. (1994) *Changing Teachers, Changing Times: Teachers' Work and Culture in the Postmodern Age*, London: Cassell.

Hoban, G. (2002) *Teacher Learning for Educational Change: A Systems Thinking Approach*. Open University Press.

Jefferess, D. (2008) Global citizenship and the cultural politics of benevolence, *Critical Literacy: Theories and Practices*, 2(1), pp. 27–36.

Kirby, P. (2012) Educating for paradigm change, *Policy & Practice: A Development Education Review*, 14, Spring, pp. 19–32.

Liddy, M. (2016) Teachers as overseas volunteer teacher educators: A case study of global schoolroom as a professional encounter, unpublished Phd thesis, University of Limerick.

Lizardo, O. (2012) Habitus, in Kaldis (ed.), *Encyclopaedia of Philosophy and the Social Sciences*. London: Sage Publications, [online] http://www3.nd.edu/~olizardo/papers/habitus-entry.pdf (accessed September 2012).

Loughran, J. and Berry, A. (2005) Modelling by teacher educators, *Teaching and Teacher Education*, 21(2), 193–203.

Lynch, K. and Lodge, A. (2002) *Equality and Power in Schools: Redistribution, Recognition*, London: Routledge Falmer.

Machin, J. (2008) *The Impact of Returned International Volunteers on the UK: A Scoping Review*, London: Institute for Volunteering Research.

Martin, F. (2012) Study visits as sites for transformative learning: Education for development or development education? *Presentation at Development and Development Education Conference at the Institute of Education*, 23 January 2012.

Mignolo, W. (2004) *The Idea of Latin America*, Oxford: Blackwell, 2004.

O'Callaghan, C., Boyle, B. and Kitchin, R. (2014) Post-politics, crisis, and Ireland's 'ghost estates', *Political Geography*, 42, pp. 121–33.

O'Neill, G. (2012) Back to the future: Engaging returned volunteers in development education, *Policy & Practice: A Development Education Review*, 15, Autumn, pp. 65–73.

O'Reilly, C. C. (2006) From drifter to gap year tourist: Mainstreaming backpacker travel, *Annals of Tourism Research*, 33(4) pp. 998–1017.

Sachs, W. (1992) *The Development Reader, A Guide to Knowledge and Power*, London: Zed Books.

Schön, D. (1983) *The Reflective Practitioner- How Professionals Think in Practice*, New York: Basic Books.

Shiel, G., Perkins, R. and Gilleece, L. (2009) *OECD Teaching and Learning International Study (TALIS): Summary Report for Ireland*, Dublin: Educational Research Centre, [online] http://www.erc.ie/do cuments/talis_summary_report2009.pdf (accessed September 2014).

Simpson, K. (2004) Doing development: The Gap Year, volunteer-tourists and a popular practice of development, *Journal of International Development*, 16, pp. 681–92.

Sin, H. L. (2009) Volunteer tourism- 'involve me and I will learn', *Annals of Tourism Research*, 36(3), pp. 480–501.

Chapter 31

Study Abroad as a Route to Global Citizenship? Undergraduate Student Perspectives in the UK

Nicole Blum

Introduction

The opportunity to study abroad is widely hailed as a key route for young people to develop a wide range of knowledge and skills, including intercultural understanding, interpersonal skills, language learning, among many others. Universities around the world have invested significant resources in developing a variety of study abroad programmes, ranging from short term to long term and from guided to independent study. These programmes may have a number of aims, including to promote individual student learning and development and to enhance student mobility and employability, particularly in the context of a rapid and changeable global employment market. The terms 'global citizen', 'global graduate', 'global skills' and 'global mindset' have all taken on increased significance within this context, along with accompanying debates about the relative merits of these as aims for higher education. Key questions remain, however, about the central meaning of terms such as 'global citizenship', and especially whether this is – or should be – more strongly linked to economic concerns (e.g. employment and mobility) or social ones (e.g. the development of skills such as critical thinking and a sense of social justice) (Hammond and Keating, 2017; Bourn, 2018).

At the root of these queries is the issue of what types of learning can or do take place during study abroad experiences as well as the ways in which these can support students to develop particular knowledge, skills and understandings. A vast body of research over the last thirty years has explored a range of both short- and long-term impacts which study abroad programmes can have on the personal and the professional development of participants (Lutterman-Aguilar and Gingerich, 2002; Paige et al., 2009; Tarrant, 2010). However, there are still significant questions about how and when this learning and change takes place. Braskamp et al. (2009), for instance, argue that study abroad can encourage development in three major domains: cognitive (epistemological, awareness and knowledge), intrapersonal (identity, attitudes and emotion) and interpersonal (behavioural, skills and social responsibility), although this will vary at the individual level. However, they also insert a note of caution about assuming which types of learning and development may actually occur:

> We often hear that students enjoy being abroad and that they learned so much, but the instruction still may be focused on what they learned rather than on how they think. Knowing

that differences exist may not have been internalized enough so that it impacts the way students regard knowledge. Thinking critically may not be stressed in comparison to knowledge acquisition. (2009, p. 110)

So, while it is clear that a number of different kinds of learning *can* take place during study abroad – including gaining new knowledge about particular topics, issues and academic subjects, experiences of particular places or exposure to new ideas and ways of life – it is also clear that the impacts of these learning experiences may not always be straightforward. In relation to global citizenship, in particular, a number of authors suggest that international travel and study enables students to develop the capacity to engage in transformative experiences with cultural 'others' (Williams, 2005; Schattle, 2007; Killick, 2012). Others, however, have argued that there is not yet sufficient knowledge or understanding of how intercultural competence, growth and transformation occur as a result of mobility, and there is a need for more critical analysis of the relationships between mobility and global citizenship (Caruana, 2014) as well as the ways in which young people see themselves as located in complex webs of relationships (Reddy, 2018). As Lilley, Barker and Harris (2015, p. 229) note: 'The literature suggests that university and stakeholder groups identify the global citizen as an ethical and critical thinking disposition. Yet, despite the available evidence, there is limited knowledge of what the process of global citizen learning entails.' The study which is explored in this chapter, therefore, sets out to explore how one group of undergraduate students understand their experiences of study abroad and the ways in which their learning informs their ideas about both global issues and global citizenship.

Study abroad, mobility and global citizenship

It is perhaps useful to begin by setting out the key concepts and themes which are relevant to this research – study abroad, mobility and global citizenship – and the relationships between them. The literature on these areas is vast, so it is not possible to provide a comprehensive review here, but rather to highlight a few key points of discussion and debate.

Research has explored the range of drivers for young people's individual choices to study abroad as well as the wider factors which can both promote and inhibit mobility (Findlay et al., 2006; Caruso and De Wit, 2013; Van Bouwel and Veugelers, 2013). On the individual level, this can include both economic and social drivers such as the desire for increased employability (see Boden and Nedeva, 2010 for a useful critique of this concept), to have an 'international experience' or to develop particular skills (e.g. language, intercultural communication).

Within higher education, an increasing emphasis on mobility through study abroad can be seen as part of a wider response to the demands of globalization and internationalization, with students in a growing number of disciplines now being provided with opportunities for overseas study. At the university level, such initiatives may also be complemented by efforts to 'internationalise at home' and to 'internationalise the curriculum' (de Wit 2002 cited in Dvir and Yemini, 2017). Recent research has noted that opportunities to study abroad are increasingly valued as a kind of 'passport to new professional, social, cultural and above all personal experiences' (Pedro and Franco, 2016, p. 1630).

Similarly, the demands of globalization and internationalization have forged strong links between mobility, study abroad and the idea of global citizenship. While the term global citizenship is increasingly prominent in discourses of higher education, there continues to be substantial debate about its core meaning and aims. Scholars such as Caruana (2014), for instance, suggest a split between initiatives which tend to emphasize a more cosmopolitan or 'soft' approach to global citizenship (e.g. learning *about* global issues) and those that encourage development of more critical perspectives on global issues and concerns, with the first tending to be more common in practice. Although a few useful typologies have been proposed as a way of interrogating the concept more deeply (see Andreotti, 2006; Oxley and Morris, 2013), these have tended to be based on educational practice in schools and/or informal education, with global citizenship continuing to be under-theorized within higher education.

One helpful exception to this is the recent work by Stein (2015) which identifies three positions on global citizenship within contemporary higher education – entrepreneurial, liberal humanist and anti-oppressive. While the entrepreneurial position focuses on the economic imperatives of preparing graduates with the skills needed to successfully engage in the global labour market, the liberal humanist position emphasizes the need for young people to cultivate greater understanding and appreciation of difference, sometimes as a complement to entrepreneurialism. The anti-oppressive position critiques both of these as located solely within Western world views which are not sufficiently critical, politicized or historicized, and advocates instead 'for more equitable distribution of resources, cognitive justice, and more horizontal forms of governance, and aspires to radical transformation of existing structures, up to and including their dismantling' (Stein, 2015, p. 246).

UCL's own definition of global citizenship suggests an approach which incorporates elements of all three existing approaches in Stein's typology, although perhaps to varying degrees (see Box 1). This variation is also evident in practice within the university, with diverse initiatives and programmes adapting the concept to particular disciplines and student groups (Bentall, 2018).

Box 1: What is global citizenship? UCL's definition

Our world is now more connected than ever before. But it also faces challenges. Big ones. Like infectious diseases, rapid urbanization and sustainability. To solve these global challenges, we need global citizens. We need people who

- understand the complexity of our interconnected world;
- understand our biggest challenges;
- know their social, ethical and political responsibilities;
- display leadership and teamwork;
- solve problems through innovation and entrepreneurship;[1]

---

[1] https://www.ucl.ac.uk/global-citizenship-programme/what-is-global-citizenship

This attention to both economic and social concerns, as well as a sense of responsibility, can be seen as a strength of the UCL approach to global citizenship, in that it provides opportunities for a range of areas of exploration. However, its breadth may also be a source of confusion for students, who may need greater clarity and opportunities to discuss the concept, as will be clear from the discussion to follow.

UCL BASc Arts and Sciences programme

The BASc Arts and Sciences programme was launched in 2012 with the aim of providing students with an opportunity for interdisciplinary undergraduate study.[2] Students are required to choose a major in one of four pathways which make up 50 per cent of their studies: Cultures, Health and Environment, Sciences and Engineering or Societies. In order to ensure a mix of arts and sciences courses across the degree, those who major in Cultures or Societies must take a minor in Health and Environment or Sciences and Engineering, and vice versa. The other 50 per cent of courses is composed of compulsory interdisciplinary core modules and study of a modern language.

The programme runs over four years, with students required to study abroad during their third year. Students have a number of options for study abroad location, and may either choose to study in a context linked to their language studies (e.g. students studying French at UCL may choose a university in France or in Montreal) or in a new language context (e.g. a student studying German at UCL may choose to study abroad in Japan, but will be required to keep up their study of German while abroad). A clear rationale is provided for the role of study abroad within the programme:

> In addition to enhancing employability, studying abroad enables you to expand your world view, become a true global citizen, improve your confidence, immerse yourself in a different culture, meet new friends and create international networks.[3]

In parallel with their experiences abroad, for the last several years, students have also been required to complete a Study Abroad dissertation (5,000 words) on the themes of globalization and global citizenship.[4] The author of this chapter has been a lead tutor on the dissertation for the last several years, and the tutoring team has noted that study abroad often has a profound impact on students in terms of the knowledge and skills they have developed, their world outlook and their sense of social and political engagement. This study was, therefore, designed to investigate these themes further, and to gather further evidence from the students themselves in order to better understand their perspectives on the learning they gained as a result of their experiences abroad.

---

[2] See https://www.ucl.ac.uk/basc/

[3] https://www.ucl.ac.uk/basc/sites/basc/files/10_reasons_to_choose_the_basc.pdf

[4] The dissertation was unfortunately removed from the BASc programme requirements starting from 2018 to 2019 due to changes in UCL regulations about the work that students can be required to complete for UCL during their time overseas. The BASc team is now exploring alternative ways of embedding discussion of global citizenship within the programme.

Research strategy

Given the discussions above, key questions for this study, therefore, were the following:

- What are students' perspectives on how the study abroad experience had an impact on their world outlook and their views of global citizenship?
- To what extent do students see their study abroad experience as enabling them to develop new knowledge and/ or skills?
- How and in what ways do students perceive that studying abroad has influenced their plans for the future?

In order to do this, the research was framed around four key methods: a literature review, a questionnaire and interviews with study abroad students, and analysis of student dissertations. The initial literature review explored the themes of study abroad, student mobility and global citizenship, the key messages from which are presented above. Both the literature and the author's previous experience of research on related issues informed the creation of an anonymous online questionnaire, which was distributed by email to all BASc students who studied abroad between 2015 and 2017 (n=77). At the end of the questionnaire, participants were also asked for permission to analyse their study abroad dissertations and if they would be willing to take part in a follow-up interview.

In line with the exploratory and qualitative nature of the study, the data from the survey and interviews, as well as the text of participants' study abroad dissertations, were interrogated using coding (open and analytical) and content analysis in order to identify themes for discussion (Silverman, 2006; Cohen, Manion and Morrison, 2011). A number of key themes emerged from this process – a discussion of which is provided below.

The participants

Perhaps due to the heavy workload commitments of the students, participation in the study was limited, with eleven students completing the anonymous online questionnaire and three completing a follow-up interview.[5] Nevertheless, both methods revealed a range of interesting perspectives and narratives of study abroad, learning, mobility and global citizenship which are worth exploring.

Of the students who participated in the study, ten had studied abroad for a full academic year in one country and one split the year between two locations, so all had spent substantial time at a university overseas. The locations where they studied included Canada (3), China (1), Australia (1), France (1), Hong Kong (1), the Netherlands (1), United States (2) and Russia (1). All were aged between twenty and twenty-four, and the majority were female (9). Students self-identified as UK (7), EU (3) or international (1) in terms of their student status at UCL.

---

[5] Ethical approval for the project was granted by the UCL Research Ethics Committee prior to any data collection.

Student reflections on study abroad and learning

In line with the existing literature, students taking the questionnaire identified three key motivations for studying abroad, including personal development, international experience or learning a new language or area of study. Perhaps unsurprisingly, when this was further explored in the interviews, students often identified a mixture of these motivations as relevant to their experiences, often seeing them as complementary to one another:

> I definitely wanted to be studying in French, and so that left UDM or Paris. I thought, well Paris I can go to any time, and also, I know that Paris is a lot more like London in the way it's a sort of fast paced, cosmopolitan city. So … and I've never left Europe before actually, so I was like 'I want to go as far away as possible'. (laughs) (S3)

> I wanted to reinvent myself, I wanted to achieve academically … I wanted to play sports, do debating … (S2)

A similarly complex view emerged when students were asked in the questionnaire to reflect on the things they felt they had *actually gained* from the experience (see Table 31.1):

While most of the students identified learning around specific academic areas/subjects (e.g. knowledge of a new subject/discipline or a new language), quite a few also noted an increasing awareness of broader global issues such as an understanding of a new culture or of global issues and concerns. Perhaps most interestingly, all of the students responding to the questionnaire noted that they had a 'greater understanding of myself and how I learn' as a result of studying abroad. This suggests that the students were able to actively reflect on their experiences and its impacts on them.

Similarly, all of the interviewees also reflected that they had undergone significant personal changes through their experiences abroad:

> I'm actually probably more open now to going and working in other countries or studying in other countries, and it doesn't feel impossible, it doesn't feel like this huge ordeal, like you know, this huge challenge because 'Oh I've done it now.' (S3)

> Unfortunately, bad things usually come from places with good intentions – that was me years ago … because I want to save the world, I see myself as the saviour, right? Now thankfully

Table 31.1 What Do You Feel You Gained from Studying Abroad?

Greater understanding of myself and how I learn	11
Understanding of a new/diverse culture	10
International experience	9
Greater understanding of global issues/concerns	8
Knowledge of a new subject/discipline	8
Knowledge of a new language	6
New relationships and connections	1

since I'm in university and [have] resources to read about these things critically and see what other people say and how they conceptualise it, I've come to understand how possibly harmful these kinds of perceptions about myself are. (S2)

This student further noted that on reflection his expectations for the experience had been far too ambitious:

I came to McGill thinking I'm going to reinvent myself as a person, which was an expectation that from inside sounds very bold. It means that in a course or just changing the environment I'm going to change how I behaved for 22 years, Having strongly felt that it was kind of okay, to go into something completely different – I'm going to go to parties, and party and be outgoing and just like talk to people ... and that didn't happen because I didn't feel comfortable in doing that. And I just actually realised that that radical change of personality doesn't come easy. (S2)

Despite such thoughtful reflections from a number of the individual student participants, several also expressed a strong desire for more opportunities to reflect on their learning after returning from study abroad. While all students are offered support for the transition by the BASc team, and many had taken this up, they also expressed a strong desire for more opportunities to reflect on their learning with their peers:

I do think there should be some more structure for meeting with other people and sharing experiences. Because you know we haven't seen each other for a year and we've all gone off and had like really different experiences, and we sort of want to talk about that. ... It would be really nice to hear other people's experiences. Because I think that would help you solidify and keep hold of some of what you've learnt out of it. (S3)

Finally, in contrast to much of the discourse around study abroad as an opportunity for career development, relatively few of the student participants noted that they expected these personal changes to result in any changes to their career plans. Only two individuals outlined any concrete changes in this respect:

The experience of studying abroad had a significant impact on my BASc dissertation in final year, as well as on choice of further studies (a MSc in Law & Anthropology, where questions related global citizenship are often discussed and challenged). (Questionnaire respondent)

I really thought I was just going to learn French, but actually I got a lot out of it academically. I did new subjects, so I did sociology, and actually my dissertation I'm now doing on Environmental Sociology which I'd never encountered till I'd been there. So that's pretty cool. But then also I took quite a lot of creative ... studies in sort of creative art, so like I say video games and the cinema and comic books. And there's a huge industry, there's a huge games industry out there but also the arts is quite strong in Montreal. And it sort of convinced me that that was a legitimate career choice. I think before then I'd sort of seen that as ... you know creative industries is kind of a pipe dream, or like you know it's something you do if you get lucky. But actually, out there [in Canada] there are people writing scripts for video games or films or ... and the fact that I could study it as an academic discipline made me realise like this is a legit thing ... it's not just like this fanciful dream. So actually, I'm now hoping to go into radio. (S3)

Reflections on global citizenship and study abroad

Both the questionnaire and interviews indicated that participants were often thinking deeply about the world and their place in it, and saw clear relationships between their study abroad experiences and the idea of global citizenship. All of the group were familiar with the term through their studies at UCL (most often the study abroad dissertation), while three also noted that they had participated in the UCL Global Citizenship Programme, and two others that they had some previous experience of international volunteering:

> I really do think my sort of sense of history has changed and sense of international politics has changed, and also a sense of what an English person is had changed. (S3)

> Studying abroad was the first time I felt like I could call myself a global citizen. Before this, I had some awareness and interest in international issues, but had never left Europe and only travelled for brief periods of time. On returning, I found I had a reverse culture shock, and could relate better to international students studying in the UK. (Questionnaire respondent)

> I think for me it's a concept that resonates personally with my study abroad experience because like I'm kind of myself from a mixed cultural background. I was able to explore just how my personal identity worked in that kind of conception because I think that a lot of people who are in my position who come from a mixed background – and I think there are a lot of BASc students who are like that – we do see ourselves a lot as people who are global citizens. We do see ourselves as part of like different areas in the world. (S1)

> Learning about colonialism and racism in the Netherlands taught me to reflect more on my own country's issues and ugly history. Thus, making me think more globally about the lives of individuals who have suffered as a result of colonialism. (Questionnaire respondent)

> Studying abroad gives you the opportunity to understand a different culture and way of life. In this way, it is one of the most effective ways to cultivate global citizenship. An understanding of other people's way of life is crucial to developing global citizenship, and this can only be done by spending a considerable amount of time in a foreign location. (Questionnaire respondent)

There was, however, also some strong critique of the idea of the concept of global citizenship:

> There might be some obvious connections – such as exposure to new cultures/societies that can help one be more empathetic to 'global' issues that influence some societies but not one's own. On the other hand, I do feel that any links between global citizenship and study abroad should be pointed out as they are not self-evident. This is especially the case if one travels to a culture similar to one's own, or if one travels to high-income countries which might have the same blind spots as the UK when it comes to 'global' citizenship. (Questionnaire respondent)

There was also some critical commentary about UCL's approach to global citizenship, although it is not clear whether this related to the term as it is formally outlined in UCL's overarching definition or more generally in discourse around the university:

> [I have gained] a better idea of the diversity of cultures around the world, but also of the very limited scope of 'global citizenship', as a very 'UCL' idea. I have never heard of it anywhere

except UCL and struggled to write my year abroad dissertation about it because I felt it had no relevance to my study abroad. In my experience, it is not a concern in France, where being a good citizen is being a good citizen of France. I struggle with the idea that being a 'global citizen' is the 'right' way to be, because this is a concept, as far as I am aware, that was made up at UCL. (Questionnaire respondent)

Such discussion suggests that students would welcome more opportunities to explore the concept of global citizenship through their studies abroad as well as during their time at UCL.

Conclusions: Study abroad as a route to global citizenship?

While this study reports on the perspectives of a relatively small group of students, it nevertheless raises a number of issues which are echoed in the broader research on study abroad, mobility and global citizenship. It also further highlights the need for consideration of these issues in the design of study abroad programmes which aim to promote particular types of global citizenship.

First, it is clear that the students in this study are very aware of the learning dimensions of study abroad and also able to actively reflect on their experiences. This is despite the fact that their initial motivations ranged from the largely practical (e.g. to learn a language) to the more existential (e.g. personal development or even self-transformation). Both the data from this study and the existing literature highlight a range of push and pull factors which influence young people's initial decisions to study abroad, as well as a wide range of ways in which the experience encourages (or does not) reflection on global issues and on students' sense of themselves in the world. Some recent attempts in the literature to understand how different groups of young people are situated within the study abroad 'industry' (e.g. Choudaha, Orosz and Chang, 2012 discussion of students as 'strivers, strugglers, explorers and highfliers'; Caruso and De Wit, 2013) may provide a useful way forward in further exploring students' initial motivations and the kinds of learning they expect to gain through study abroad.

The students' perspectives also highlight the need for greater support for returning students to reflect on and integrate their learning, as this is a significant factor in encouraging long-term impacts (Rowan-Kenyon and Niehaus, 2011). This finding builds on the work of key theorists of transformative and experiential learning, such as Mezirow (1991) and Dewey (1997), who insist that deep learning and changes in perspective require reflection. This needs to be taken into account within study abroad programmes, particularly if they aim to help students develop a critical sense of global issues and of their own identities. As Lutterman-Aguilar and Gingerich note:

While all study abroad programs hold the potential for experiential education, there is a continuum within study abroad from programs that simply transfer academic credits from one traditional discipline-based institution to another without intentionally utilizing the international experience as the basis for learning, to those that try to incorporate some aspects of experiential education such as the use of learning contracts to programs whose design is thoroughly grounded in the principles of experiential education. (Lutterman-Aguilar and Gingerich, 2002, p. 43)

Attention to the learning aims of study abroad programmes and the connections (or disconnections) to ideas of global citizenship is perhaps particularly important in light of the highly diverse nature of contemporary student groups, and the complex ways in which they may be connected to local, national and international networks. As noted by several participants in this study, it is clear that students need more support to understand, and even critique, their experiences and learning both during and after studying abroad.

Acknowledgements

This study was made possible through funding from University College London's Global Engagement Office. The author would also like to thank Douglas Bourn and Karen Edge for their support with the research outlined in this chapter as well as Carl Gombrich and the rest of the BASc team for their help in communicating with the student participants.

Bibliography

Andreotti, V. (2006) 'Soft versus critical global citizenship education', *Policy & Practice – A Development Education Review*, 3, pp. 40–51.

Bentall, C. (2018) 'Competing or complementary priorities? Global citizenship education in UK higher education'. *Paper for the British Association for International and Comparative Education Conference*, 12–14 September 2018, University of York.

Boden, R. and Nedeva, M. (2010) 'Employing discourse: Universities and graduate "employability"', *Journal of Education Policy*, 25(1), pp. 37–54. Doi: 10.1080/02680930903349489.

Bourn, D. (2018) *Understanding Global Skills for 21st Century Professions*. London: Palgrave.

Van Bouwel, L. and Veugelers, R. (2013) 'The determinants of student mobility in Europe: The quality dimension', *European Journal of Higher Education*, 3(2), pp. 172–90. Doi: 10.1080/21568235.2013.772345.

Braskamp, L. A., Braskamp, D. C., Merrill, K., Braskamp, L., Braskamp, D. and Merrill, K. (2009) 'Assessing progress in global learning and development of students with education abroad experiences', *The Interdisciplinary Journal of Study Abroad*, 18, pp. 101–18.

Caruana, V. (2014) 'Re-thinking global citizenship in higher education: From cosmopolitanism and international mobility to cosmopolitanisation, resilience and resilient thinking', *Higher Education Quarterly*, 68(1), pp. 85–104. Doi: 10.1111/hequ.12030.

Caruso, R. and De Wit, H. (2013) *Determinants of Mobility of Students in Europe: A Preliminary Quantitative Study*. Munich.

Choudaha, R., Orosz, K. and Chang, L. (2012) 'Not all international students are the same: Understanding segments, mapping behavior', *World Education News and Reviews*, 25(7), pp. 1–5.

Cohen, L., Manion, L. and Morrison, K. (2011) *Research Methods in Education*. 7th edn. Abingdon: Routledge.

Dewey, J. (1997) *Experience and Education*. Touchstone. New York: Simon and Schuster.

Dvir, Y. and Yemini, M. (2017) 'Mobility as a continuum: European commission mobility policies for schools and higher education', *Journal of Education Policy*, 32(2), pp. 198–210. Doi: 10.1080/02680939.2016.1243259.

Findlay, A., King, R., Stam, A. and Ruiz-Gelices, E. (2006) 'Ever reluctant Europeans: The changing geographies of UK students studying and working abroad', *European Urban and Regional Studies*, 13(4), pp. 291–318. Doi: 10.1177/0969776406065429.

Hammond, C. D. and Keating, A. (2017) 'Global citizens or global workers? Comparing university programmes for global citizenship education in Japan and the UK', *Compare*, 7925(November), pp. 1–20. Doi: 10.1080/03057925.2017.1369393.

Killick, D. (2012) 'Seeing ourselves-in-the-world: Developing global citizenship through international mobility and campus community', *Journal of Studies in International Education*, 16(4), pp. 372–89.

Lilley, K., Barker, M. and Harris, N. (2015) 'Exploring the process of global citizen learning and the student mind-set', *Journal of Studies in International Education*, 19(3), pp. 225–45. Doi: 10.1177/1028315314547822.

Lutterman-Aguilar, A. and Gingerich, O. (2002) 'Experiential pedagogy for study abroad: Educating for global citizenship', *Frontiers: The Interdisciplinary Journal of Study Abroad*, 8, pp. 41–82.

Mezirow, J. (1991) *Transformative Dimensions of Adult Learning*. San Francisco, CA: Jossey-Bass.

Oxley, L. and Morris, P. (2013) 'Global citizenship: A typology for distinguishing its multiple conceptions', *British Journal of Educational Studies*, 61(3), pp. 301–25. Doi: 10.1080/00071005.2013.798393.

Paige, R. M., Fry, G. W., Stallman, E. M., Josić, J. and Jon, J. (2009) 'Study abroad for global engagement: The long-term impact of mobility experiences', *Intercultural Education*, 20(sup1), pp. S29–44. Doi: 10.1080/14675980903370847.

Pedro, E. and Franco, M. (2016) 'The importance of networks in the transnational mobility of higher education students: Attraction and satisfaction of foreign mobility students at a public university', *Studies in Higher Education*, 41(9), pp. 1627–55. Doi: 10.1080/03075079.2014.999321.

Reddy, S. (2018) 'Going global: Internationally mobile young people as caring citizens in higher education', *Area* (September), pp. 1–9. Doi: 10.1111/area.12503.

Rowan-Kenyon, H. T. and Niehaus, E. K. (2011) 'One year later: The influence of short-term study abroad experiences on students', *Journal of Student Affairs Research and Practice*, 48(2), pp. 213–28. Doi: 10.2202/1949-6605.6213.

Schattle, H. (2007) *The Practices of Global Citizenship*. Lanham, MD: Rowman and Littlefield.

Silverman, D. (2006) *Interpreting Qualitative Data: Methods for Analyzing Talk, Text and Interaction*. 3rd edn. London: Sage Publications.

Stein, S. (2015) 'Mapping global citizenship', *Journal of College and Character*, 16(4), pp. 242–52. Doi: 10.1080/2194587X.2015.1091361.

Tarrant, M. A. (2010) 'A conceptual framework for exploring the role of studies abroad in nurturing global citizenship', *Journal of Studies in International Education*, 14(5), pp. 433–51. Doi: 10.1177/1028315309348737.

Williams, T. R. (2005) 'Exploring the impact of study abroad on students' intercultural communication skills: Adaptability and sensitivity', *Journal of Studies in International Education*, 9(4), pp. 356–71. Doi: 10.1177/1028315305277681.

Chapter 32

Am I a Global Citizen? Reflections of Young People in Tobago

Yvette Allen

Introduction

Over the past few years, the concept of global citizenship has gained popularity (particularly among European countries) with its association with the United Nations (UN) Sustainable Development Goals (SDGs). This has maintained and even stimulated greater discussions about global citizenship and how this concept can become integrated within formal/informal educational curriculum. The main aim of this chapter is to present the views of global citizenship from young people in Tobago. It was felt to be important to discuss global citizenship with young people, who may feel socially or geographically marginalized. These young people share their perception, personal identification and relation to global citizenship. At a time when national identity is regularly called into question, this chapter sought to explore a wider sense of belonging.

As a rapidly, ongoing and highly interactive process, globalization has surpassed the boundaries of economics and actively challenges all aspects of life, including education; therefore, schools are required to address the repercussions of globalization. As international interconnectedness has intensified, schools have been commissioned to prepare pupils to live and work within a 'global village'. Education or the 'knowledge economy' has become an essential aspect of the globalization debate, with responsibility to address global issues, promote intercultural awareness and develop global competences. Currently, education is shaped by demands to prepare a labour force fit to participate in a global economy and for citizens to engage in the polity (Torres, 2009: 114). Over the past three decades, schools have been increasingly encouraged to incorporate global education (GE) within its curricula and to support pupils to gain a global awareness. Global school partnerships/links provided strategic support for developing a global outlook, as part on an overall preparation for life in the twenty-first century. The global rhetoric within schools gained momentum and attracted both political and economic support. Consequently, global school links became part of national and international development priorities (Bourn and Brown, 2011; Taylor, 2007; DfID, 2010). The promotion of global citizenship has since evolved. The importance of the global dimension has become embedded within UN initiatives and developmental goals.

In 2012, the UN Global Education First Initiative set three priorities: (1) a reiteration of *Education for All* (universal primary education by 2015), (2) improving the quality of learning and (3) fostering global citizenship education (GCE) to not only prepare pupils to secure employment on a global market but also strive for a better world and sustainable future, with the promotion of respect and responsibility across cultures, countries and regions (Tarozzi and Torres, 2016). Currently, international development is promoting global citizenship as an essential part of the UN's SDGs:

> By 2030, ensure that all learners acquire the knowledge and skills needed to promote sustainable development, including, among others, through education for sustainable development and sustainable lifestyles, human rights, gender equality, promotion of a culture of peace and non-violence, global citizenship and appreciation of cultural diversity and of culture's contribution to sustainable development. (Sustainable Development Goal 4, Target 4.7 (2015))[1]

The main aim of this research study was to examine Caribbean pupils' understanding of global citizenship and if the perception of being a global citizen could enhance their lives through possible opportunities to increase social/cultural capital and economic mobility/development. This chapter is part of a larger study, a doctoral thesis which wished to 'document the voices of those who were previously silenced' or had rare opportunities to be heard. The research questions from the main study were the following:

(1) From the UK/Tobago school link, what are the impacts on pupils' global outlook?
(2) To what extent does the UK/Tobago school link develop a sense of global citizenship among pupils within linked schools?
(3) How do pupils of Caribbean heritage in Tobago and the UK perceive the concept of global citizenship and its relevance to their lives? (Allen, 2014)

For the thesis, pupils of Caribbean heritage in the UK were also interviewed. However, this chapter focuses solely on the views of young people in Tobago. It has been suggested global citizenship is an elitist ideology (Pike, 2008; Gilbourn, 2008), which can further perpetuate inequity and only the privileged assume this identity. Hence, this study also wanted to explore if certain groups felt eliminated and excluded from the concept, which is supposed to be inclusive.

It could be argued that there is a lack of theoretical foundation for the concept of global citizenship. For the purposes of my doctoral research, globalization and post-colonial theories were used as the theoretical construction of global citizenship. These theories are popular within critical educational studies and are dialectically related as they provide a critical way to engage with politics of the empire (Apple, 2009) and the legacy of colonialism. Globalization theory as the primary theoretical framework provides a wider world view and acknowledges the globalization phenomenon of increased interconnectedness. However, post-colonial theory provided a vital, critical secondary lens, as it was important to recognize power and inequality and to interpret the relationship between Tobago and the UK and deconstruct underlying layers, structures and forms that exist within the colonial past. The entry point to access the respondents was through the Tobago/UK school links and global citizenship was being discussed with pupils, whose island (a developing country and former colonized island) had been previously been connected to the UK (the colonizer); therefore, colonialism and imperialism was relevant to the overall study.

---

[1] www.un.org/sustainabledevelopment/education

Global citizenship

Before discussing the young people's perceptions of global citizenship, this section provides a summary of academic interpretations of global citizenship. These interpretations offered a theoretical grounding for data analysis and in locating the study more generally.

There is a melee of definitions of global citizenship. Oxley and Morris (2013) describe eight typologies under two main types: cosmopolitan (political, moral, economic and cultural) and advocacy (social, critical, environmental and spiritual). These typologies provide a powerful device to analyse policies and proposals on global citizenship. Dill (2013) also discusses global citizenship within two main strands: global consciousness – developing an understanding of oneself and the world and global competencies – skills and knowledge for prosperity within the competitive global marketplace. Dower (2003) highlights the ethic of extensive benevolence and the responsibility of helping at a distance, while working to produce a better world and Tarozzi and Torres (2016) perceive global citizenship as having an understanding of global ties and connections and with a commitment to collective good, where principles of human rights and respect for diversity is important. However, critics of global citizenship describe a 'utopian dream of a global ethical state in perpetual peace' (Tarozzi and Torres, 2016) or its ability to reflect, reinforce, reproduce inequalities, power imbalances and global injustices (Andreotti, 2006; Schattle, 2008)). There is further tension as some literature on global citizenship present a pluralistic view, with a sense of care/interest for others; however, the economic aspect of global citizenship can be individualistic and linked to self-interest and competition (Oxley and Morris, 2013). Dill's (2013) description of global competency also focuses on the personal aspect of human capital development.

Other perspectives suggest that since the late 1990s, the concept of global citizenship signifies one's identity and ethical responsibility; thus, providing a 'conceptual framework for transcending barriers of ethnicity, religious or racial difference' (Jefferess, 2012: 29). It could also be argued that along with a sense of identity, global citizenship encourages behavioural change, where one should act responsibly at local, national and global levels. However, there is literature, which suggest global citizenship can avoid the 'harsh material realities in which marginalized citizens shape their imagination of citizenship in ways that often contradict with the ideals of the global citizen' (Balarin, 2014: 48). Eurocentrism and triumphalism within global citizenship exists 'when people think they live in the centre of the world and they have the responsibility to help the rest, especially people from other parts of the world, who are not fully global' (Andreotti, 2006: 5).

The global citizenship debate has included discussions on the role of education (Zagda, Biraimah and Gaudelli, 2008). Some commentators believe schools have a moral obligation to prepare pupils for their role as global citizens (Dill, 2013: 21). UNESCO elaborated on the importance of developing global competency skills and urged for the strengthening of links between education and economic development, where the 'curricula responds to the demands of the global market and knowledge economy, providing skills such as communication, critical-thinking … and learning how to go on learning' (UNESCO-IBE, 2008: 6). The UN's focus on GCE appears to be less 'market-driven', as the goal is for children and young people's eyes and minds to become open to the realities of our globalized world.

Globalization theory is suggested here as an important theoretical lens with which to explore global citizenship, within a wider world view. It provides an explanation to the globalization phenomenon, which continues to have consequences on people's lives worldwide. Globalization theory provides an understanding and explanation for the increase in international relations (at both personal/social and national levels), technological processes, international economic transactions and greater interdependence. Globalization has encouraged greater interconnectedness and the necessity for understanding of differences.

The Tobago context

The island of Tobago is part of the Republic of Trinidad and Tobago. Tobago is largely monocultural (African heritage), differing from the more multicultural and cosmopolitan sister-isle of Trinidad. It is a small (population 60,874 – 2011 census), quiet, laid-back island, which remains largely unspoiled and unexploited by large multinational corporations; however, while for some this is a feature of its beauty; for others, it indicates a lack of progressiveness. The Republic of Trinidad and Tobago is a member of Caribbean Community (CARICOM), an organization similar to the European Union, but with a focus on trade and economic relations; however, CARICOM lacks status in comparison to more 'powerful' international conglomerates. Although the Caribbean is part of the Commonwealth, this region rarely features internationally.

Historically, the Republic of Trinidad and Tobago inherited its education system, with its focus on public examination performance, from British colonial rule. Over the years, Tobago has become increasingly concerned with the implications and impact of an ever-expanding globalized economy on this relatively small island (Ministry of Education, 2004). As Tobago's main revenue is tourism, the local community are accustomed to the movement of people inwards; however, a lack of global competency skills (communication, technology, innovation and critical thinking) poses challenges, particularly within rural communities. The Trinidad and Tobago Ministry of Education duly noted the importance of twenty-first-century skills, when stating:

> The Republic of Trinidad and Tobago has not escaped nor can hope to escape the political, social, cultural and economic impact of constant, rapid and vertiginous change. … Our very survival as a people and as a nation depends on … knowledge … driven, particularly by the information and communication technologies. (Ministry of Education, 2002: 3)

Since 2010, the Government of the Republic of Trinidad and Tobago (GORTT) has placed a revised emphasis on higher education, with particular focus on science, technology, entrepreneurship and critical thinking. There is recognition that 'in order to survive in a world of rapid innovation and borderless trade, countries have to become competitive and innovative' (Thomas, 2014: 399). The focus on pupils' developing 'global' skills and competencies has been much in line with the government's plans for sustaining economic growth; therefore, Tobago has been amenable to become involved in programmes, which expose its young people to the 'global'. However, currently, GE and GCE is not a feature of the educational curriculum. Within the Caribbean Social Studies for Caribbean Secondary Education Certificate (CSEC, 2012) programme of study, the section on globalization briefly comments on how economies around the world have become interconnected, with the removal of barriers of trade. The text book also notes that some Caribbean producers are losing out to international markets, with more efficient foreign companies and cheaper goods. There is mention of migration, which focuses on travel between Caribbean islands and 'push and pull' factors of employment and educational opportunities. The issue of 'brain drain' is also highlighted, where skilled workers are migrating internationally. Regarding wider GE and themes, the social studies programme briefly looks at sustainable development, through encouraging sustainable consumption as a way of achieving higher standards of living for Caribbean citizens. Pupils are encouraged to support local and regional businesses, local investment and to develop cultural industries. From this review of the national Social Studies text book, the globalization section appears to be quite localized (nationally and within the Caribbean region) and does not expose pupils to wider GE or development issues (global warming, global poverty or environmental issues, etc.). This may not be unique to Tobago, but may in fact reflect educational provision in other similar middle-income islands, which has adopted an inward-looking approach in an attempt to preserve its culture; however, there is also value of exposing pupils to a wider world view.

Tobago/UK school links

When the British Council (UK) approached the education department within the Tobago House of Assembly (THA), Education Officers believed Global school links could be an effective strategy for developing a global outlook and raising awareness of global citizenship. The DFID Global School Partnerships (GSP)[2] programme focused on establishing mutually beneficial partnerships between UK schools and schools in Africa, Asia, the Caribbean and Latin America. This programme encouraged a global dimension within the curriculum and promoted an understanding of global development issues. The four UK nations were linked to schools in sixty-eight Southern countries, including the Caribbean (Jamaica and Trinidad and Tobago). The programme promoted values of active global citizenship, social justice, human rights, sustainable development, conflict resolution, diversity and equality and interdependence.

> DFID Global School Partnerships is an exciting and innovative way to teach and learn about global development. Teachers and students from UK and Southern schools are being inspired to understand our mutual interdependence and to help each other become active global citizens. (Taylor, 2007: 3)

The British Council–led consortium managers of the GSP programme suggested global learning should become an everyday feature of schools' curriculum in an endeavour to 'bridge cultural and economic divides':

> As the gap between rich and poor widens within and between countries, it is also starkly apparent that learners from poor backgrounds achieve less through education. Developing

---

[2] The Global School Partnerships programme evolved from a Millennium initiative called 'On the Line'. This initiative partnered schools on the Greenwich Median with similar schools in Ghana.

global citizenship through mutually beneficial school partnerships, we believe, is one way of bridging the divide and looking forward in the 21st century. (Foreword in Edge, Frayman and Lawrie, 2009)

From 2009 to 2012, twenty-one pre-schools, primary and secondary schools in Tobago were partnered/linked to similar institutions in the UK. These educational partnerships were initiated through British Council programmes (engagement varied from registered but did not get off the ground to actively engaging with exchanged visits). Other international events like the Olympic Games (2012) and the Commonwealth Games (2014) used the international platform to promote global school links and global citizenship. In 2012, the British Council launched the 'International Inspiration' programme (Olympic focused), which linked schools in the UK with schools in Trinidad and Tobago. This programme used sports to tackle social, health, economic and development issues and counteract a lack of safe spaces for young people, poor sports infrastructure and a rise in young gangs. The British Council worked with the governments of Trinidad and Tobago to establish a sporting legacy for at least one out of ten children/young people over three years. Along with the practical aspects of sports, the programme also included leadership skills development, conflict resolution and working as a team.

These school links provided a vital opportunity for pupils, who live on a small, quite insular island like Tobago to be exposed to other cultures, in a meaningful way. Intercultural dialogue developed with peers, who lived thousands of miles away. According to two senior officers at the THA, they viewed Tobago's participation in the GSP programme as a strategic approach to develop an existing and growing interest in infusing the global dimension within the schools' curriculum and to encourage a sense of global citizenship among its pupils. Globalization and the information age have placed significant demands on education. Pupils in Tobago are required to foster competencies, which encourage greater propensity to survive and thrive within the global marketplace; therefore, human capital development is a priority. The education department in Tobago is aware of a lack of employment opportunities on the island and that it may be difficult for every educated child in Tobago to find a job on the island; therefore, schools in Tobago should prepare pupils to become 'global citizens' and think 'outside of the box and outside of Tobago'. Pupils in Tobago should be prepared for travelling to other parts of the world to gain qualifications or employment. In 2012, just as the 'veil was being lifted', funding from the British Council ceased and the global dimension within schools in Tobago diminished. Although there is still a need to expose pupils to GE, it is no longer a national priority.

The thesis study, upon which this chapter is based, utilized post-colonial theory as an important secondary lens to explore the historical link between the UK/Tobago and the more recent global school link relationship. However, this chapter only highlights global school links and does not discuss in any detail the related issues of post-colonialism. Global school links was the vehicle to access the young people's perceptions of global citizenship, which is the primary focus of this chapter.

Methodology and theoretical framework

A social constructivist approach was espoused and underpinned in this study, as the perception and discussion of global citizenship was socially constructed. Interpretivist paradigm encouraged a subjective relationship between the researcher and the participants and supported the use of qualitative data collection. The pupils' phenomenological accounts were obtained primarily through interviews (a most widely used methodology for conducting systematic social enquiry), which engendered knowledge and looked empirically at specific forms of knowledge.

For the data collection, an initial questionnaire was circulated to UK/Tobago linked schools to gather contextual information and useful baseline data. The British Council assisted with circulating questionnaires in the UK and the THA assisted with circulation in Tobago. Twelve questionnaires were completed, which accounted for 57 per cent participation of linked schools. Following the questionnaire, focus group interviews were conducted at three secondary schools (two urban and one rural) and individual semi-structured interviews of two senior education officers. Nineteen pupils (aged between sixteen and eighteen) participated in the focus group interviews. These young people answered questions, which covered

- an awareness of the UK/Tobago school link;
- personal involvement in the UK/Tobago school link;
- importance (and reason) for a UK/Tobago school link;
- impact on global outlook;
- awareness of global citizenship and personal application;
- the pros and cons of global citizenship and
- general opinion of Caribbean young people's identification as a global citizen.

All interviews were recorded and transcribed, and open-coded thematic analysis was used to analyse the data.

Findings

This research study utilized the UK/Tobago school link platform to explore the concept of global citizenship and what this meant to pupils of Caribbean heritage. The UK/Tobago school links, although brief, showed promising signs not only of broadening pupils' horizons but also for curriculum and professional development, as the responses from the initial questionnaire highlighted a unique relationship between Tobago and the UK, with no signs of a charitable relationship. Currently, GE and global citizenship within the Caribbean region is an under-researched area; however, it is important to highlight Caribbean views on the debate of global citizenship; therefore, this chapter specifically discusses the views of young people in Tobago. All respondents attended a school that had been involved in a UK/Tobago school link; however, most pupils (84 per cent) were not aware of their schools' involvement, and only one pupil had been actively involved with school link activities.

Global citizenship has become a central theme of North–South educational partnerships, particularly with the rise in significance with the UN's 2030 Agenda for Sustainable Development.[3] Traditionally, global citizenship involves being concerned about global issues and wanting to make a difference within the global community; however, this study specifically wanted to explore if Caribbean pupils' engagement with global citizenship could broaden horizons, encourage greater aspirations, enhance social and economic mobility and increase human capital. Dill's (2013) view on global citizenship highlights a consciousness and empathy for humankind and the environment, but it also concurs with literature which debates the role of education in preparing pupils for the global workplace; therefore, pupils need global competency skills. This aspect of Dill's work was pertinent and relevant to this study, as the data revealed that these young people did not possess traditional views of global citizenship and its concern for others, rather their perceptions were more personalized about their own development.

The young peoples' perception of global citizenship correlated with the economic, cultural and social aspects of global citizenship (Oxley and Morris, 2013) and Dill's (2013) global competences. The pupils described a global citizen as someone who was 'educated about what is happening around the world'; therefore, they had an awareness of what was going on beyond national boundaries. These young people were very aware of interconnectedness and whatever happened in one country could have an impact on countries near and far. They felt intercultural exchange had increased due to global interconnectedness and believed a global citizen was familiar with other cultures and countries. These young people were keen to learn about others, but they also wanted others to learn about their indigenous culture and national heritage. They had touched on what Dill (2013: 53) suggests, 'The ideals of tolerance and understanding differences [should be] coupled with the rhetoric of human capital and economic purposes; we need to understand each other, so we can do business with each other.' Therefore, intercultural competency skills could enhance human and economic capital.

These young people identified migration as an important feature of global citizenship and believed a global citizen is not constrained to one country, but can travel and live anywhere in the world or perhaps be 'transferred like exchange students to international institutions'. Their perceptions of global citizenship included increased prospects and the possibility of a 'better life', arising from the opportunity to travel abroad to pursue undergraduate/graduate studies. They also felt that as a well-travelled global citizen, one's identity would be affected and become merged with the location one had moved to. Although most pupils expressed positive views on migration, a few had concerns that the limited career opportunities on the island was causing a 'brain drain' effect, as many young people travelled abroad to study, with a number choosing not to return. The concept of global citizenship is largely collective; however, these young people's perceptions represented individualistic personal achievement, promoted by opportunities to travel abroad for study or work. Their views were firmly located within the social and economic aspects of global citizenship and what Tarrozzi and Torres (2016) suggested as economic citizenship forms part of GCE. Their constructed reflections also concurred with Dill's (2013) definition of global competency, particularly when they discussed issues of identity and travel for study or work.

---

[3] For more information visit: https://suatainabledevelopment.un.org/post2015/transformingourworld

Along with the specific feature of travel, these young people believed a global citizen belonged to a 'world group'. Globalization has escalated cosmopolitanism and 'increases the reality and awareness of human interconnectedness across borders, it simultaneously enhances the capacity for individuals to imagine themselves as members of a global community' (Croucher, 2004: 190). Generally, they viewed belonging to a global community as something positive; however, there were a few pupils who were apprehensive about negative influences from other countries and that young people in the Caribbean were quick to 'adopt other people's culture'. In Tobago, there appears to be some resistance to rapid modernization, brought about by globalization and endeavours have been made to maintain, preserve and celebrate its traditionally African culture. This is manifested in annual celebrations, like the Harvest and Heritage Festivals. These pupils highlighted the complexity of national versus global identity and the shifts in identity, which has been escalated through the free movement of people. This poses that as a global citizen, one can develop a two-tier identity (national then global), with a range of rights (right to vote, right to wok, etc.) and responsibilities. Pashby (2008: 76) suggests that 'a global citizen is one who responsibly interacts with and understands others, whilst being self-critical of his/her position and who keeps open a dialogical and complex understanding rather than a closed and static notion of identities'. Globalization has created additional and alternative membership and forms of belonging, altered people's perceptions of how they identify themselves and has caused an erosion of traditional boundaries and blurred national sovereignty.

However, the concept of being part of a 'world group' appeared abstract and remote from these young people's realities. They reflected on their insularity and felt that most pupils in Tobago did not engage with the rest of the world. They gave examples of a lack of travel and not being familiar with different cultures, lifestyles and ways of living (apart from what is seen on the television). One young person commented on the lack of travel even between the sister isles of Trinidad and Tobago, much less the rest of the world.

All nineteen young people perceived global citizenship as something positive and valued opportunities to engage with the 'global' and develop intercultural awareness, both formal (school activities) and informal (media). They believed it is important to be socially aware of happenings around the world and to gain the necessary skills to help themselves and then others; however, there was no personal link to how they could contribute to or shape world events. They associated global citizenship with having the ability to expand their horizons and increase prospects and opportunities in the future. Their constructed view of global citizenship reflected a transformative power, which conveyed messages of hope; however, most pupils were preoccupied with their current existence. Global citizenship has the potential to not only create hope but transfer this hope into reality; however, the respondents indicated they had not been supported to embrace global citizenship and its potentially life-enhancing capital and their limited engagement appeared to be superficial with no sustainable development. The concept of global citizenship appeared to be elusive and beyond their grasp, confirming how some literature describes global citizenship as not always inclusive (Langmann, 2014: 93).

Interestingly, these young people's responses did not correspond with popular views of global citizenship and its 'concern for the planet'; however, their perceptions were firmly located within Oxley and Morris's cosmopolitan typology (Economic) and Dill's global competences. Despite lacking popular understanding of global citizenship, they had begun to consider the important skills and features of global citizenship. They had reflected on their knowledge, considered the relationship they had with others in other parts of the world and recognized that much of the resources they considered to be progressive were in Western countries (United States and United Kingdom) and may require leaving Tobago in order to access these resources. They believed global citizenship could enhance social and economic mobility/development and acquiring skills to increase employment opportunities was important to them.

In Tobago, both the education department and schools recognize the need for pupils to be equipped with twenty-first-century skills. During the research study, I had visited three schools, that proudly displayed Mission/Vision statements, stating something like the following: '(Name of School) will be a premier institution, which provides learning experiences conducive to the holistic development of literate, critical thinkers, problem-solvers and lifelong learners, who are able to contribute effectively and competently in a changing global environment.' The sentiment embodied within this statement is not exclusive to Tobago, as many institutions around the world have adopted a mandate to prepare students for the global community. This transmits the values of a G8 document (2006) entitled 'Education for Innovative Societies in the 21st Century', which states:

> Education is at the heart of human progress. Economic and social prosperity in the 21st century depend on the ability of nations to educate all members of their societies to be prepared to thrive in a rapidly changing world.

One of the senior officers discussed Tobago's brief involvement with the British Council's global school linking programme and described that 'the veil had just started to be lifted' and lamented that the pupils had only began to gain a global view. This image of a veil reflects the North–South Centre of the Council of Europe's (2003) description of GCE as 'education that opens people's eyes and minds to the realities of the globalized world'. However, some pupils believed Tobagonians are not 'being taken seriously', which resonated with the lack of consultation about Trinidad and Tobago being excluded from the British Council's decision to close the global school linking programme with the UK. There was no sustainability; therefore, the 'veil' had not been sufficiently removed.

The THA had welcomed my research study and the possibility it could stimulate discussion and policy proposals, with a particular reference to rural schools and if all pupils are being equipped with twenty-first-century skills. However, the importance of global citizenship education has not yet been translated into classroom practice. The data revealed the vision of incorporating a global outlook/dimension and preparing pupils for a global environment is not embedded within the schools' curriculum/ethos in Tobago, reflecting a deficient engagement with the UN's SDGs for education (Goal 4) and in particular section (4.7). The pupil's inadequate exposure to the concept of global citizenship is largely due to a lack of commitment from national government.

Analysis and recommendations

Despite the pupils' positive perceptions of global citizenship, for most of them this concept was elusive and remote, with little or no real connection to their lives. Even their limited perception of global citizenship and possible increased opportunities appeared to be accessible by only a few, who may have the right connections. Although global citizenship is about being part of a world community, which is inclusive, tolerant and embracing, these young people did not feel included within an inclusive concept; rather their views indicated exclusion and marginality. Their constructed perceptions expressed omission from a global movement. Pike (2008: 48) warns:

> The elitism that can easily suffuse the rhetoric of global citizenship education: for the countless millions of people worldwide who daily struggle for survival and satisfaction of basic human rights, or for recognition of their cultural identity, global citizenship is not even on the agenda.

Global citizenship should promote belongingness and inclusivity to diverse groups (Gundara, 2011). Tarozzi and Torres (2016) highlight global citizenship could provide an alternative to communities, which have experienced national marginalization and alienation. Pashby (2012: 12) also notes global citizenship should be inclusive and ties a notion to a global community, but the history of imperialism and, more recently, the neoliberal aspects of global citizenship perpetuates injustice and determines who does and does not belong. There is a lack of challenge, particularly in relation to the associated privilege of the West. From a post-colonial perspective, one could question if global citizenship is the domain of white and/or middle-class sections of society, reserving the benefits of global citizenship to the privileged. Dill (2013: 6) suggests the universal rhetoric of global citizenship is rooted within Western liberal individualism, eluding cultural and group differences; therefore, global citizenship is embedded within Western assumptions. Critical race theory suggests that for certain groups engaging with global citizenship is eliminated and there is a tendency for inequities to be reinforced (Gillborn, 2008); therefore, only the privileged can assume this identity and benefit from increased capital. Langmann (2014: 93) also highlight global citizenship has the capacity of 'whether or how to include or exclude those who are not the same as us':

> It rarely recognises that this presumed empirical reality is entrenched within a liberal democratic framework that assumes all citizens have the same rights, opportunities and responsibilities, when some marginalized communities and individuals in the world experience a very different lived reality. (Langmann, 2014: 107)

Global citizenship involves young people being prepared to play a positive, active and responsible role locally, nationally and globally. They should be empowered with knowledge, skills and values, including a respect for diversity and human rights. Increasingly, young people are encouraged to gain an awareness of the global relevance of their experiences to prepare them for future challenges within our global society. Dill (2013: 3) reminds us that 'schooling is fundamentally about inculcating the rising generation … [to gain] an understanding of themselves and their place in the world'. Irrespective of personal values, as educators, we are part of a larger global community; therefore, our responsibility should be to support the development of pupils' knowledge and skills for the twenty-first century.

Dill (2013) highlights that in the current climate of an ever-present and all-powerful global economy, schools have a moral obligation to prepare pupils for life within a global community, with an awareness of cultural diversity and skilled for economic prosperity. Education should enhance the values of one's own culture and focus on the development of personal potential and employment opportunities (Mayer, 2003). This study affirmed the important role education plays in exposing young people to knowledge of the world and their potential role within it.

GCE can enhance the development of skills and competences to equip young people to fulfil this role, as well as supporting social, cultural and economic capital development. However, the evidence confirmed education in Tobago is neglecting to support pupils to gain the knowledge, skills and values to assist them to become responsible citizens of the world (Walker, 2006: 7). The national focus appears to be on the former colonial values of passing examinations and not on holistic development. It has been highlighted that sometimes teachers are unable to engage pupils with the global, as they are preoccupied with their local environment (Veugelers, 2014: 171). Nevertheless, all young people should be supported to develop global competency skills to compete for employment wherever these opportunities may be. This study indicates some groups within society are being kept disadvantaged, through being denied the tools for improvement and self-sufficiency.

Further frank discussions should ensue about the inclusivity of global citizenship and if all pupils are being adequately prepared for our globalized world in the twenty-first century. It is hoped that the findings from my research will prompt the Ministry of Education in Trinidad and Tobago to review the curriculum provision to ensure policy and practice addresses opportunities and challenges both locally and globally. There is an awareness of the need to prepare young people for a sustainable future; therefore, the challenge is to ensure that the curriculum adequately supports this vital preparation. From general observation, there appears to be a resistance to anything that may disrupt the culture and traditions of the local community; therefore, the challenge is how can pupils gain an education that exposes them to a global dimension, while gaining twenty-first-century knowledge and skills, which enhances the young person's life and that of their family and community? Also, can young people in Tobago embrace global citizenship when they are so preoccupied with local issues?

Bibliography

Allen, Y. (2014). *Global School Partnerships: When Is a Developing Country too Developed?* (Institute Focused Study - unpublished). London: Institute of Education.

Andreotti, V. (2006). Soft versus critical global citizenship education. *Policy and Practice: A Development Education Review*, 3: 40–51.

Andreotti, V. and de Souza, L. M. T. M. (eds) (2012a). *Postcolonial Perspectives on Global Citizenship.* New York and London: Routledge.

Apple, M. W. (2009). Foreword in Torres, C. Globalisations and education: Collected essays on class, race, gender and the state. *British Journal of Sociology of Education*, 30(3): 379–87.

Balarin, M. (2014). Global citizenship and marginalisation: Contributions towards a political economy of global citizenship, in V. de Oliveira Andreotti (ed.), *The Political Economy of Global Citizenship Education*. London: Routledge, 48–60.

Bourn, D. and Brown, K. (2011). *Young People and International Development: Engagement and Learning*. DERC Research Paper No. 2. London: Think Global/IOE.

Caribbean Social Studies for CSEC Textbook (2012). Oxford, London: Oxford University Press.

Croucher, S. (2004). *Globalisation and Belonging: The Politics of Identity in a Changing World*. Oxford: Rowman and Littlefield Publishers.

Davies, I. (2006). Global citizenship: Abstraction or framework for action? *Educational Review*, 58(1): 5–25.

Department for International Development (2010). *Public Attitudes towards Development*. London: DfID.

Dill, J. (2013). *The Longings and Limits of Global Citizenship Education: The Moral Pedagogy of Schooling in a Cosmopolitan Age*. New York: Routledge.

Dower, N. (2003). *An Introduction to Global Citizenship*. Edinburgh: Edinburgh University Press.

Dower, N. (2008). Are we all global citizens or are only some of us global citizens? in A. Abedi and L. Shultz (eds), *Educating for Human Rights and Global Citizenship*. New York: State University of New York Press, 39–54.

Edge, K., Frayman, K. and Lawrie, J. (2009b). *The Influence of North South School Partnerships. Examining the Evidence from Schools in the UK, Africa and Asia* - Final Report. London: Institute of Education, University of London.

Gilborn, D. (2008). *Racism and Education: Coincidence or Conspiracy?* Abingdon: Routledge.

Gundara, J. (2011). Citizenship and intercultural education, in C. Grant and A. Portera (eds), *Intercultural and Multicultural Education: Enhancing Global Interconnectedness*. New York: Routledge, 97–111.

Jefferess, D. (2012). Unsettling cosmopolitanism: Global citizenship and the cultural politics of Benevolence, in V. Andreotti and L. de Souza (eds), *Postcolonial Perspectives on Global Citizenship Education*. New York: Routledge, 42–59.

Langmann, E. (2014). Representational and territorial economies in global citizenship education: Welcoming the other at the limit of cosmopolitan hospitality, in V. Andreotti (ed.), *The Political Economy of Global Citizenship Education*. New York: Routledge, 91–101.

Martin, F. (2006). North-South school-linking as a controversial issue. *Prospero*, 14(4): 16–24.

Mason, A. (2012). Personal communication.

Mayer, S. (2003). *What is a 'Disadvantaged Group?'* – unpublished paper. www.RainbowResearch.org (last accessed December 2004).

Ministry of Education (2002). *Strategic Plan 2002–2006*. Government of the Republic of Trinidad and Tobago, Ministry of Education.

Ministry of Education (2004). *National Report on the Development of Education in Trinidad and Tobago 2004, Quality Education for All Young People: Challenges, Trends, Priorities*. Republic of Trinidad and Tobago, Ministry of Education.

North South Centre of the Council of Europe (2003). The Maastricht Declaration, in Forghani-Arani, N., Hartmeyer, H., O'Loughlin, E. and Wegimont, L. (eds), *Global Education in Europe to the Year 2015. Strategies, Policies and Perspectives*. Lisbon.

Oxley, L. and Morris, P. (2013). Global citizenship: A typology for distinguishing its multiple conceptions. *British Journal of Educational Studies*, 61(3): 301–25.

Pashby, J. (2008). Demands on and of citizenship and schooling: 'belonging' and 'diversity' n the global imperative, in O'Sullivan, O. and Pashby, K. (eds), *Citizenship Education in the Era of Globalisation: Canadian Perspectives*. Rotterdam: Sense Publishers B.V., 9–26.

Pashby, K. (2012). Questions for global citizenship education in the context of the 'new imperialism': For whom, by whom? in V. Andreotti and L. deSouza (eds), *Postcolonial Perspectives on Global Citizenship Education*. New York: Routledge, 56–69.

Pike, G. (2008). Citizenship education in global context. *Brock Education*, 17: 38–49.

Schattle, H. (2008). Education for global citizenship: Illustrations of ideological pluralism and adaption. *Journal of Political Ideologies*, 13(1): 73–94.

Tarozzi, M. and Torres, C. (2016). *Global Citizenship Education and the Crises of Multiculturalism: Comparative Perspectives*. London: Bloomsbury Publishing Plc.

Taylor, D. (2007). *Learning Together about Global Development: A Three-Year Review of DFID Global School Partnerships 2003–2006*. London: British Council.

Thomas, E. (ed.) (2014). *Education in the Commonwealth Caribbean and Netherland Antilles*. London: Bloomsbury Academic.

Torres, C. (2009b). *Globalisations and Education*. New York: Teachers' College Press.

Trinidad and Tobago Ministry of Education (2008). *Forty-Eighth Session of the International Conference on Education (ICE): National Report on the Development of Education in Trinidad and Tobago*. Port of Spain: Government Printery.

UNESCO - IBE (2008). *IBE Strategy 2008–2013*. Geneva, Switzerland.

UNICEF (2014). www.unicef.org/easterncaribbean/ECAO_TNT_Strategic_Actions_for Children.pdf (last accessed October 2015).

Veugelers, W. (2014). The moral and the political in global citizenship: Appreciating differences in education, in V. de Oliveira Andreotti, *The Political Economy of Global Citizenship Education*. Abingdon: Routledge, 163–76.

Walker, G. (2006). *Educating the Global Citizen*. Woodbridge: John Catt Educational Ltd.

Zagda, J., Biraimah, K. and Gaudelli, W. (eds). (2008). *Education and Social Inequality in the Global Culture*. New York: Springer Publishing Company.

Chapter 33
Conclusion

Douglas Bourn

This handbook has been aimed to introduce academics, researchers, students, policy-makers and educational practitioners to the field of global education (GE). It has shown through a wide range of chapters from different regions of the world that there is a distinctive educational field that not only promotes learning about global issues but does so in a form that recognizes the importance of social justice, a range of pedagogical approaches and theoretical influences. Above all what can be identified from many of the chapters is an emerging body of evidence about how GE is put into practice and the impact this is having.

Chapters in this volume have covered countries as diverse as Austria, Brazil, Canada, Finland, Germany, Ghana, Ireland, Italy, Japan, Nigeria, Poland, Spain, Tobago, Taiwan, South Africa, United States, UK and Zanzibar. What this shows is that GE themes have relevance throughout the world. The increased interest and engagement in these themes by international bodies such as the UN, UNESCO and OECD have clearly helped and as a consequence terms such as global citizenship, global competencies and skills to engage in a global world are becoming part of the everyday vocabulary of many educational policies.

A number of themes can be identified from the chapters. The first is the influence of critical pedagogy and post-colonial and post-structural thinking. The work of the Brazilian educationalist and social theorist Paulo Freire and his ideas on pedagogy, dialogue and social action is mentioned by several authors. Another Brazilian educationalist Vanessa Andreotti and her thinking in these areas can be seen also in several chapters as well as from the co-authored chapter she has written.

A second theme and one that comes from the influence of a range of social theorists is the construction of knowledge, the relationship between knowledge and power and in identifying the importance of listening to a range of voices and perspectives. The reference in more than one chapter to the African concept of Ubuntu is one manifestation of this.

A third theme is that of interdisciplinarity and the value of looking at issues from differing disciplines and as a consequence breaking down the silos that can often result from subject-based approaches to learning. GE and learning have all too often been seen as only relevant in subjects such as geography. This volume has shown through a number of contributions that this area of learning has relevance across all subjects and disciplines.

A fourth theme is that of relating learning to real-world experiences. Some of this could mean some form of international experience or it could just mean bringing in examples from everyday life into the learning process. While, as some of the chapters identify, there are dangers of international experiences reproducing paternalistic relationships, they can also result in learners having to rethink their own assumptions about communities and places around the world.

A fifth and final theme is that much of the thinking and practices around GE is the desire to challenge dominant orthodoxies about how global issues are perceived, to recognize the continued influence of colonial thinking, to challenge the social and economic injustices that still exist in the world and to strive for a more equitable world. This is why the term GE has become a part of the vocabulary of GE in the past twenty years or so. There is a sense from many of the authors in this volume that just understanding about global issues is not enough, it is what you do with this knowledge that is today becoming so important.

It is for these reasons that this volume has consciously included examples of research and reviews of practice that demonstrate how educators have taken forward the learning they have gained into their own communities. For example, several chapters make reference to the value of professional development for educators, to review the impact of this learning and what learners do as a consequence of being exposed to ideas and perspectives they may well have challenged their own assumptions. The examples include courses for practising teachers as well as degree courses for students and forms of international experience including partnership programmes.

While this volume has shown some excellent examples of research, the importance of building bodies of evidence remains an important challenge for GE. Scheunpflug in her chapter outlines a strong rationale as to why this is important and gives some indication of priorities. But what she also states is the need for this research to be rigorous and of high quality.

All too often, because GE practices have been heavily influenced by policy agendas including funding, research has often been subsumed within evaluation and as a consequence has lost its independent rigour and analysis.

One of the ways of ensuring good quality independent research is to encourage and support doctoral students to produce theses on GE. The consequences of the value of such work can be seen in this volume through the chapters by MacCallum, Pieniazek, Allen, Le Bourdon, Morrison, Liddy and Bosio. But compared to similar fields such as environmental education, there are still a relatively small number of PhDs completed every year covering GE.

GE as suggested throughout the chapters in this volume can mean a number of different things but what has brought them together here has been a common thread of seeking global social justice, of challenging dominant new-liberal orthodoxies and offering different solutions and ways of working.

It is anticipated that this Handbook will lead to a range of publications on GE that move the debates forward even more, that encourage differing voices and outline the outcomes of empirical research from all regions of the world.

Index